THE Java™ Tutorial

Object-Oriented Programming for the Internet

The Java™ Series

Lisa Friendly, Series Editor
Bill Joy, Technical Advisor

The Java™ Programming Language
Ken Arnold and James Gosling

The Java™ Application Programming Interface, Volume 1
Core Packages
James Gosling, Frank Yellin, and the Java Team

The Java™ Application Programming Interface, Volume 2
Window Toolkit and Applets
James Gosling, Frank Yellin, and the Java Team

The Java™ Language Specification
James Gosling, Bill Joy, and Guy Steele

The Java™ Virtual Machine Specification
Tim Lindholm and Frank Yellin

The Java™ Tutorial
Object-Oriented Programming for the Internet
Mary Campione and Kathy Walrath

The Java™ Class Libraries
An Annotated Reference
Patrick Chan and Rosanna Lee

The Java™ FAQ
Frequently Asked Questions
Jonni Kanerva

THE Java™ Tutorial

Object-Oriented Programming for the Internet

Mary Campione
and
Kathy Walrath

ADDISON-WESLEY

An imprint of Addison Wesley Longman, Inc.

Reading, Massachusetts • Harlow, England • Menlo Park, California
Berkeley, California • Don Mills, Ontario • Sydney
Bonn • Amsterdam • Tokyo • Mexico City

Library of Congress Cataloging-in-Publication Data

Campione, Mary.
    The Java tutorial : object-oriented programming for the Internet /
Mary Campione, Kathy Walrath.
       p.   cm. -- (The Java series)
    Includes bibliographical references and index.
    ISBN 0-201-63454-6 (alk. paper)
    1. Object-oriented programming (Computer science) 2. Java
(Computer program language) 3. Internet (Computer network)
I. Walrath, Kathy. II. Title. III. Series.
QA76.64.C35   1996
005.13'3--dc20   96-9348
                                            CIP

The publisher offers discounts on this book when ordered in quantity for special sales.
For more information, please contact:
        Corporate & Professional Publishing Group
        Addison-Wesley Publishing Company
        One Jacob Way
        Reading, Massachusetts 01867

Index by Henry McGilton at Trilithon Software
Text design by Wilson Graphics & Design (Kenneth J. Wilson)
Text printed on recycled and acid-free paper

ISBN 0-201-63454-6
1 2 3 4 5 6 7 8 9-MA-99989796
First Printing, August 1996

To Richard Campione
—*Mary*

To Nathan, Laine, and the mystery baby
—*Kathy*

Contents

Writing Applets 145

Using the Core Java Classes 209

Creating a User Interface 357

Custom Networking and Security 483

Integrating Native Methods into Java Programs 541

Appendixes 579

Colophon 803
Example Index 807
Index. 811

Preface

MANY excellent and varied histories of the Java language have been written. We will not attempt to record that history here, or even rewrite the history itself. Just let it be said "and unto James Gosling Java was born." From this birth came the need for the Java team to spread the word about this technology and teach people how to use it. And from that came the opportunity for us to write this tutorial.

From the beginning our intention has been to create an easy-to-read, fun, task-oriented tutorial with lots of practical examples that help people learn how to program in Java.

The first draft of the tutorial was made available on-line at our Web site, `http://java.sun.com/`, in May 1995. This draft contained a few basic lessons on writing applets, the fundamentals of the language itself, and some key classes. Since then, the tutorial has grown to contain 7 trails containing 27 lessons covering topics ranging from applet communication to writing native methods.

We wanted to give customers early access to this material so that they could learn Java before any books were on the market. In the year after the tutorial first appeared on our Web site, we released several drafts of the tutorial to the Web site. Internet readers benefited from this early access, and so did we—Internet readers helped us a great deal and improved the quality and usability of this tutorial by sending us feedback on our prose, examples, and style.

What Is Java?

The Java language and companion class libraries provide a portable, interpreted, high-performance, simple, object-oriented, development environment. The Java environment is suitable for programming tasks ranging in scope from dressing up your Web page to writing full-fledged, production-quality applications. *The Java Language Environment: A White Paper,*[1] written by James Gosling and Henry McGilton, provides a thorough overview of the Java language and the Java development environment.

Who Should Read This Book?

This tutorial assumes that you have some programming experience, whether it be traditional procedural programming or object-oriented programming, and are familiar with programming tenets, terminology, and at least one high-level programming language.

Internet programmers, novice and experienced alike, will benefit from this book. The book begins by presenting you with two Java programs—one application and one applet—and shows you how to compile and run these programs. This first section also describes how these programs work.

From this hands-on beginning, you can follow your own course of learning. New programmers will want to read the book from beginning to end, including the beginning material on object-oriented concepts, the standard features of the Java language, and the object-oriented features of the Java language. Programmers experienced with procedural languages such as C may wish to skip the section that describes the standard features of Java and start with the material on object-oriented concepts and the object-oriented features of Java. Experienced object programmers may want to jump feet first into the trail on applets. No matter what type of programmer you are, you will find a path through this book that fits your learning requirements.

What You Need

As of press time, to compile and run the examples in this book you will need one of the following systems:
- Solaris 2.3, 2.4, or 2.5 running on SPARC
- Microsoft Windows NT/95 running on Intel (or compatible) x86
- Macintosh System 7.5 on PowerPC or Motorola 68030 (or better)

You also need Java development tools, such as those provided in the Java Developers Kit (JDK). You can download the JDK from our Web site,[2] or you can use the 1.0.2 version of the JDK that's on the CD-ROM accompanying this book.

---

[1] To find the white paper, go to the Web page for this book: http://java.sun.com/Series/Tutorial/book.html

[2] To find out the current version of the JDK and how to get it, visit the JDK Web page:
http://java.sun.com/products/JDK/CurrentRelease/

If you are developing applets, you will need a Java-compatible browser, such as HotJava or Netscape 2.0, or an applet viewer such as the one that's included with the JDK. For information about the browsers and other applet viewers that are currently available, see the Web page for this book:

```
http://java.sun.com/Series/Tutorial/book.html
```

Finally, you need an editor that can save files in ASCII format with a `.java` extension. On Solaris, this means you can use your favorite editor: `vi`, `emacs`, `textedit`, or some other editor. On Windows NT/95 use NotePad or a similar editor. On a Macintosh use an editor such as BBEdit or SimpleText.

Acknowledgments

Of course, the Java team made everything possible by creating Java in the first place. But many individuals contributed to getting this book out the door.

A million thanks go to the Java team members who answered questions, reviewed material, and in some cases contributed examples—all of this in the face of tight deadlines: Thomas Ball, Brenda Bowden, David Brown, Patrick Chan, Tom Chavez, David Connelly, Pavani Diwanji, Amy Fowler, Jim Graham, Herb Jellinek, Jonni Kanerva, Doug Kramer, Eugene Kuerner, Tim Lindholm, Ron Mandel, Henry McGilton, Marianne Mueller, Scott Rautmann, Benjamin Renaud, Hassan Schroeder, Richard Scorer, Sami Shaio, Arthur van Hoff, Frank Yellin, and Steve Zellers.

Painful though it may have been, our reviewers provided us with invaluable feedback on the manuscript: Mike Ballantyne, Richard Campione, Lee Collins, Greg Crisp, Matt Fahrner, Murali Ghanta, Bill Harts, Eileen Head, Murali Murugan, Roberto Quijalvo, Philip Resnik, Roger Riggs, Roman Rorat, Neil Sundaresan, Michael Weiss, the ones who preferred to remain anonymous, and all of the Internet readers who were kind enough to take the time to send us e-mail and let us know of problem areas.

Chris Warth spent several weeks writing scripts and filters to convert our complex web of HTML pages into MIF format and was most patient with us in spite of our demands and changes. Marsh Chamberlain designed and created our trail icons, and Jan Kärrman provided us with the `html2ps` script, which we used to create PostScript files from HTML and print our first review copy of the manuscript. Nathan Walrath created the figure in the Trail Map section. When we both went on maternity leave after giving the book to Addison-Wesley, Randy Nelson served as our backup, taking care of the CD-ROM and the Web site for the tutorial.

The staff at Addison-Wesley—Mike Hendrickson, Katie Duffy, Pamela Yee, and Marty Rabinowitz—were professional, competent and courteous throughout the development of this book and provided us with guidance, encouragement, and instruction. They also managed the practical things like copyediting, page design, graphics, and reviewers so all we had to do was worry about content.

And finally, Lisa Friendly, the Java Series editor, our manager, and our friend, made this book possible by suggesting that we turn the online tutorial into a book. She kept us calm, reassured us often, and managed everything from our relationship with Addison-Wesley to consistency with other books in the series. Without her encouragement and hard work, this tutorial would not exist.

About the Dedication

Mary: This book is dedicated to Richard Campione for being my greatest friend and husband. He encourages, cajoles, counsels, prods, loves and believes in me, and makes me get out of bed in the morning.

Kathy: This book is dedicated to my husband, Nathan Walrath, who played Mr. Mom during the months when I couldn't help out much at home. He even helped with the content, drawing the trail map figure and providing insight into the animation section. This book is also dedicated to our daughter Laine and to the baby who's pushing up against my ribs as I write this. They both help me remember that there's more to life than work.

And now that we've delivered this book, we're taking some time off to deliver our other babies . . .

Trail Map

WELCOME to *The Java Tutorial*! This book is adapted from the online Java tutorial, drafts of which have been available on the JavaSoft Web site since May 1995. We're dedicated to keeping this book up-to-date with the most current information. To learn what's new since this book went to press, use any Web browser to visit the following URL:

```
http://java.sun.com/Series/Tutorial/book.html
```

How to Use this Book

True to its hypertext roots, this book is designed so that you can either read it straight through or skip around from topic to topic. Whenever a topic is discussed in another place, you'll see a link to that place in the tutorial. Links are underlined and are followed by page numbers, like this: **The "Hello World" Applet** (page 13).

Where to Start

We recommend that you start with the **Getting Started** trail (page 1). This trail lets you dive in quickly—writing, compiling, and running a simple application and a simple applet.

Terminology Note: *Applications* are stand-alone Java programs, such as the Hot-Java browser. *Applets* are similar to applications, but they don't run standalone. Instead, applets adhere to a set of conventions that lets them run within a Java-compatible browser.

What Next?

The table and figure that follow might help you decide where to go after you've finished **Getting Started**.

Trail	Program Types	Notes
Getting Started (page 1) **The "Hello World" Application** (page 3) **The "Hello World" Applet** (page 13)	All	Quick, easy introduction to writing Java programs. Goes on to discuss the anatomy of an application and of an applet. Introduces some basic Java concepts along the way.
Writing Java Programs (page 27) **Object-Oriented Programming Concepts: A Primer** (page 31) **The Nuts and Bolts of the Java Language** (page 43) **Objects, Classes, and Interfaces** (page 77)	All	Introduces object-oriented concepts and Java's implementation of them. Experienced object-oriented programmers might be able to skip this trail, especially **Object-Oriented Programming Concepts: A Primer**.
Writing Applets (page 145) **Overview of Applets** (page 149) **Creating an Applet User Interface** (page 169) **Communicating with Other Programs** (page 185) **Understanding Applet Capabilities and Restrictions** (page 197) **Finishing an Applet** (page 201)	Applets only	Has (or points to) everything you need to know to write applets.
Using the Core Java Classes (page 209) **The String and StringBuffer Classes** (page 215) **Setting Program Attributes** (page 227) **Using System Resources** (page 237) **Handling Errors Using Exceptions** (page 253) **Threads of Control** (page 285) **Input and Output Streams** (page 325)	All	Background information needed for most nontrivial programs. In the online version of the tutorial, the lessons in this trail are actually in the **Writing Java Programs** trail.
Creating a User Interface (page 357) **Overview of the Java UI** (page 361) **Using Components, the GUI Building Blocks** (page 379) **Laying Out Components Within a Container** (page 415) **Working with Graphics** (page 437)	All	Lists all programs' UI options, and then gives in-depth descriptions of how to construct a graphical UI using the AWT (Abstract Window Toolkit).
Custom Networking and Security (page 483) **Overview of Networking** (page 487) **Working with URLs** (page 493) **All About Sockets** (page 509) **All About Datagrams** (page 521) **Providing Your Own Security Manager** (page 529)	All	Tells you how to use the standard Java networking and security classes.
Integrating Native Methods into Java Programs (page 541) **Step By Step** (page 545) **Implementing Native Methods** (page 555)	Applications and other trusted programs only	Tells you how to add non-Java libraries to Java applications.

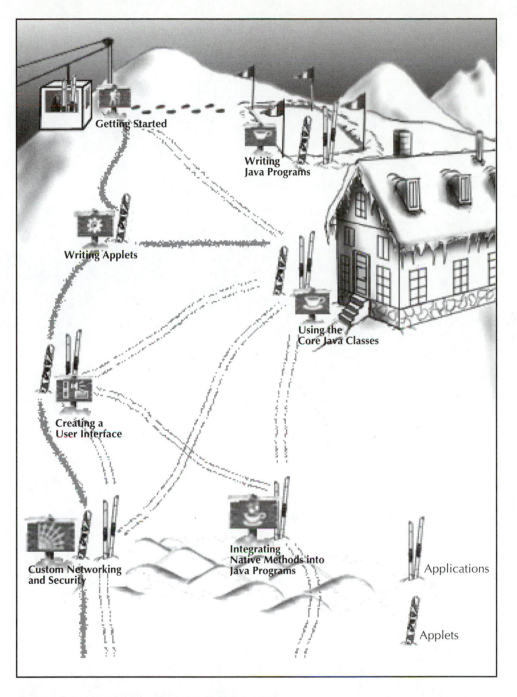

Getting Started

Writing
Java Programs

Writing Applets

Using the
Core Java Classes

Creating a
User Interface

Custom Networking
and Security

Integrating
Native Methods into
Java Programs

Applications

Applets

Some Possible Paths Through the Tutorial

Getting Started

THE lessons in this trail show you the simplest possible Java programs and tell you how to compile and run them. They then go on to explain the programs, giving you the background knowledge you need to understand how they work.

Before you can compile a program, you need to have a Java compiler. The Java Developers Kit (JDK) provides a compiler you can use. The JDK also provides an interpreter you can use to run Java applications. To run Java applets, you can use the JDK Applet Viewer or any Java-compatible Web browser, such as the HotJava browser. The 1.0.2 JDK is included on the CD that accompanies this book. You can also download the latest version of the JDK from our Web site. See this book's Web page for information about the JDK and other development environments:

```
http://java.sun.com/Series/Tutorial/book.html
```

The "Hello World" Application lesson (page 3) is where you should start if you're interested in writing a stand-alone application—a Java program that executes independently of any browser. This lesson also introduces some concepts that will help you understand any Java program: how to define a Java class and how to use supporting classes and objects.

The "Hello World" Applet lesson (page 13) is the place to start if you want to write an applet—a Java program to be included in HTML pages and executed in Java-compatible browsers.

If you have trouble compiling a Java program or running a Java application, see **<u>Common Compiler and Interpreter Problems (and Their Solutions)</u>** (page 21).

The "Hello World" Application

BY following the steps on this page, you can create and use a stand-alone Java application.

Create a Java Source File

Using a text editor, create a file named <u>HelloWorldApp.java</u> (page 583) with the following Java code:

```
/**
 * The HelloWorldApp class implements an application that
 * simply displays "Hello World!" to the standard output.
 */
class HelloWorldApp {
    public static void main(String[] args) {
        System.out.println("Hello World!"); //Display the string.
    }
}
```

Compile the Source File

Compile the source file using the Java compiler.

Platform-Specific Details: Compiling a Java Source File Using the JDK

UNIX:
```
javac HelloWorldApp.java
```

DOS shell (Windows 95/NT):
```
javac HelloWorldApp.java
```

MacOS:
Drag the `HelloWorldApp.java` file icon onto the Java Compiler icon.

If the compilation succeeds, the compiler creates a file named `Hello-WorldApp.class` in the same directory (folder) as the Java source file (`Hello-WorldApp.java`). This class file contains Java *bytecodes*, which are platform-independent codes interpreted by the Java runtime system.

If the compilation fails, make sure you typed in and named the program exactly as shown above, using the capitalization shown. If you can't find the problem, Compiler Problems (page 21) might be able to help you.

Run the Application

Run the program using the Java interpreter.

Platform-Specific Details: Interpreting a Java Application Using the JDK

UNIX:
```
java HelloWorldApp
```

DOS shell (Windows 95/NT):
```
java HelloWorldApp
```

Note: For the UNIX and Windows 95/NT JDK, the argument to the Java interpreter is the name of the class to run, not the name of a file. Be sure to capitalize the class name exactly as shown above.

MacOS:
Double-click the `HelloWorldApp.class` file icon.

You should see "Hello World!" displayed. If you have any trouble running the "Hello World" application, see Interpreter Problems (page 23).

What Next?

Now you can:
- Continue on in this lesson to learn more about the anatomy of applications, how the "Hello World" application works, and how the Java language implements object-oriented concepts.
- Go to the next lesson, **The "Hello World" Applet** (page 13), which steps you through writing and running an applet, and introduces you to a few more Java features.
- Learn more about the Java language by going to the **Writing Java Programs** trail (page 27).

The Anatomy of a Java Application

Now that you've seen a Java application, and perhaps even compiled and run it, you might be wondering how it works and how similar it is to other Java applications. Remember that a *Java application* is a stand-alone Java program—a program written in the Java language that runs independently of any browser.

Note: If you couldn't care less about Java applications, you're already familiar with object-oriented concepts, and you understand the Java code you've seen so far, feel free to skip ahead to **The "Hello World" Applet** (page 13).

This section dissects the "Hello World" application you've already seen. Here, again, is its code:

```
/**
 * The HelloWorldApp class implements an application that
 * simply displays "Hello World!" to the standard output.
 */
class HelloWorldApp {
    public static void main(String[] args) {
        System.out.println("Hello World!"); //Display the string.
    }
}
```

The "Hello World" application has two blocks of comments. The first block, at the top of the program, uses /** and */ delimiters. Later, a line of code is explained with a comment marked by // characters. The Java language supports

a third kind of comment—the familiar C-style comment, which is delimited with /* and */. Comments in Java Code (page 6) further explains the three forms of comments that the Java language supports.

In the Java language, each method (function) and variable exists within a *class* or an *object* (an instance of a class). The Java language does not support global functions or variables. Thus, the skeleton of any Java program is a *class definition*. Defining a Class (page 7) gives you more information.

The entry point of every Java application is its main method. When you run an application with the Java interpreter, you specify the name of the class that you want to run. The interpreter invokes the main method defined within that class. The main method controls the flow of the program, allocates whatever resources are needed, and runs any other methods that provide the functionality for the application. The main Method (page 8) tells you more.

The other components of a Java application are the supporting objects, classes, methods, and Java language statements that you write to implement the application. Using Classes and Objects (page 10) introduces you to these components.

Comments in Java Code

The bold characters in the following listing are comments.

```
/**
 * The HelloWorldApp class implements an application that
 * simply displays "Hello World!" to the standard output.
 */
class HelloWorldApp {
    public static void main(String[] args) {
        System.out.println("Hello World!"); //Display the string.
    }
}
```

The Java language supports three kinds of comments:

/* *text* */

The compiler ignores everything from /* to */.

/** *documentation* */

This indicates a documentation comment (*doc comment*, for short). The compiler ignores this kind of comment, just like it ignores comments that use /* and */. The JDK javadoc tool uses doc comments when preparing automatically generated

documentation. For more information on `javadoc`, see the <u>Java tool documentation</u>.[1]

`// text`   The compiler ignores everything from `//` to the end of the line.

Defining a Class

The first bold line in the following listing begins a *class definition block*.

```java
/**
 * The HelloWorldApp class implements an application that
 * simply displays "Hello World!" to the standard output.
 */
class HelloWorldApp {
    public static void main(String[] args) {
        System.out.println("Hello World!"); //Display the string.
    }
}
```

A *class*—the basic building block of an object-oriented language such as Java—is a template that describes the data and behavior associated with *instances* of that class. When you *instantiate* a class you create an *object* that looks and feels like other instances of the same class. The data associated with a class or object is stored in *member variables*; the behavior associated with a class or object is implemented with *methods*. Methods are similar to the functions or procedures in procedural languages such as C.

Julia Child's recipe for rack of lamb is a real-world example of a class. Her rendition of the rack of lamb is one instance of the recipe, and mine is quite another. While both racks of lamb may "look and feel" the same, I imagine that they "smell and taste" different.

A more traditional example from the world of programming is a class that represents a rectangle. The class contains variables for the origin of the rectangle, its width, and its height. The class might also contain a method that calculates the area of the rectangle. An instance of the rectangle class contains the information for a specific rectangle, such as the dimensions of the floor of your office, or the dimensions of this page.

In the Java language, the simplest form of a class definition is as follows:

```java
class name {
    . . .
}
```

---

1. http://java.sun.com/Series/Tutorial/book.html

The keyword class begins the class definition for a class named *name*. The variables and methods of the class are embraced by the curly brackets that begin and end the class definition block. The "Hello World" application has no variables and has a single method named main.

For more information about object-oriented concepts, see **Object-Oriented Programming Concepts: A Primer** (page 31). To learn how to implement object-oriented concepts in the Java language, see **Objects, Classes, and Interfaces** (page 77).

The main Method

The first bold line in the following listing begins the definition of a main method.

```
/**
 * The HelloWorldApp class implements an application that
 * simply displays "Hello World!" to the standard output.
 */
class HelloWorldApp {
    public static void main(String[] args) {
        System.out.println("Hello World!"); //Display the string.
    }
}
```

Every Java application must contain a main method that starts like this:

```
public static void main(String[] args)
```

The main method declaration starts with three modifiers:
- public indicates that the main method can be called by any object. <u>Controlling Access to Members of a Class</u> (page 105) covers the ins and outs of the access modifiers supported by the Java language.
- static indicates that the main method is a class method. <u>Instance and Class Members</u> (page 111) talks about class methods and variables.
- void indicates that the main method does not return any value.

How the main Method Gets Called

The main method in the Java language is similar to the main function in C and C++. When the Java interpreter executes an application (by being invoked upon the application's controlling class), it starts by calling the class's main method. The main method then calls all the other methods required to run your application.

If you try to invoke the Java interpreter on a class that does not have a `main` method, the interpreter refuses to compile your program and displays an error message similar to this:

```
In class NoMain: void main(String argv[]) is not defined
```

Arguments to the `main` Method

As you can see from the following code snippet, the `main` method accepts a single argument: an array of elements of type `String`.

```
public static void main(String[] args)
```

This array is the mechanism through which the runtime system passes information to your application. Each `String` in the array is called a *command-line argument*. Command-line arguments let users affect the operation of the application without recompiling it. For example, a sorting program might allow the user to specify that the data be sorted in descending order with this command-line argument:

```
-descending
```

Note to MacOS JDK Programmers ONLY:

An application that does not need to accept command-line arguments can declare its `main` method without any arguments, like this:
```
public static void main() {

    . . .

}
```

An application with such a `main` method will *not* prompt the user for command-line arguments.

The "Hello World" application ignores its command-line arguments, so there isn't much more to discuss here. However, you can get more information about command-line arguments, including the framework for a command-line parser that you can modify for your specific needs, in the Command-Line Arguments section (page 230).

Note to C and C++ Programmers: The number and type of arguments passed to the `main` method in the Java runtime environment differ from the number and type of arguments passed to the C and C++ `main` function. For further information refer to Command-Line Arguments (page 230).

Using Classes and Objects

This section explains how the "Hello World" application uses classes and objects. If you aren't familiar with object-oriented concepts, then you might find this section confusing. If so, feel free to skip ahead to the lesson **Object-Oriented Programming Concepts: A Primer** (page 31).

The "Hello World" application is about the simplest Java program you can write that actually does something. Because it is such a simple program, it doesn't need to define any classes except for `HelloWorldApp`. However, most programs that you write will be more complex and require you to write other classes and supporting Java code.

The "Hello World" application does *use* another class—the `System` class—that is part of the *API* (application programming interface) provided with the Java environment. The `System` class provides system-independent access to system-dependent functionality. For information about the `System` class, see the **Using System Resources** lesson (page 237).

The bold code in the following listing illustrates the use of a *class variable* of the `System` class, and the use of an *instance method*.

```
/**
 * The HelloWorldApp class implements an application that
 * simply displays "Hello World!" to the standard output.
 */
class HelloWorldApp {
    public static void main(String[] args) {
        System.out.println("Hello World!"); //Display the string.
    }
}
```

Using a Class Method or Variable

Let's take a look at the first segment of the statement:

```
System.out.println("Hello World!");
```

The construct `System.out` is the full name of the `out` variable in the `System` class. Note that the application never instantiates the `System` class and that `out` is referred to directly from the class name. This is because `out` is a class variable—a variable associated with the class rather than with an instance of the class. You can also associate methods with a class—*class methods*.

To refer to class variables and methods, you join the class name and the name of the class method or class variable together with a period (" .").

Using an Instance Method or Variable

Methods and member variables that are not class methods or class variables are called *instance methods* and *instance variables*. To refer to instance methods and instance variables, you must reference the methods and variables from an object.

While `System`'s `out` variable *is* a class variable, it *refers* to an instance of the `PrintStream` class (a class provided with the Java environment) that implements the standard output stream.

When the `System` class is loaded into the application, it instantiates `PrintStream` and assigns the new `PrintStream` object to the `out` class variable. Now that you have an instance of a class, you can call one of its instance methods:

```
System.out.println("Hello World!");
```

As you can see, you refer to instance methods and variables similarly to the way you refer to class methods and variables. You join an object reference (`out`) and the name of the instance method or variable (`println`) together with a period ("`.`").

The Java compiler allows you to cascade references to class and instance methods and variables together, resulting in constructs like the one that appears in the sample program:

```
System.out.println("Hello World!");
```

This line of code displays "Hello World!" to the application's standard output stream.

Summary

A class method or class variable is associated with a particular class. The Java runtime system allocates a class variable once per class, no matter how many instances exist of that class. You access class variables and methods through the class.

An instance method or instance variable is associated with a particular object (an instance of a class). Every time you create an object, the new object gets a copy of every instance variable defined in its class. You access instance variables and methods through objects.

The "Hello World" Applet

BY following the steps on this page, you can create and use an applet. If you aren't interested in applets, you might want to skip ahead to the **Writing Java Programs** trail (page 27).

Create a Java Source File

Using a text editor, create a file named <u>HelloWorld</u> (page 584) with the Java code shown here:

```java
import java.applet.Applet;
import java.awt.Graphics;

public class HelloWorld extends Applet {
    public void paint(Graphics g) {
        g.drawString("Hello world!", 50, 25);
    }
}
```

Compile the Source File

Compile the source file using the Java compiler.

Platform-Specific Details: Compiling a Java Source File Using the JDK

UNIX:
```
javac HelloWorld.java
```

DOS shell (Windows 95/NT):
```
javac HelloWorld.java
```

MacOS:
Drag the `HelloWorld.java` file icon onto the Java Compiler icon.

If the compilation succeeds, the compiler creates a file named `Hello-World.class` in the same directory (folder) as the Java source file (`Hello-World.java`). This class file contains Java bytecodes.

If the compilation fails, make sure you typed in and named the program exactly as shown above. If you can't find the problem, **Common Compiler and Interpreter Problems (and Their Solutions)** (page 21) might be able to help you.

Create an HTML File
That Includes the Applet

Using a text editor, create a file named <u>Hello.html</u> (page 584) in the same directory that contains `HelloWorld.class`. Your HTML file should contain the following text:

```
<HTML>
<HEAD>
<TITLE> A Simple Program </TITLE>
</HEAD>
<BODY>

Here is the output of my program:
<APPLET CODE="HelloWorld.class" WIDTH=150 HEIGHT=25>
</APPLET>
</BODY>
</HTML>
```

Run the Applet

To run the applet, you need to load the HTML file into an application that can run Java applets. This application might be a Java-compatible browser or another

Java applet viewing program, such as the Applet Viewer provided in the JDK. To load the HTML file, you usually need to tell the application the URL of the HTML file you created. For example, you might enter something like the following into a browser's URL or Location field:

```
file:/home/kwalrath/java/Hello.html
```

Platform-Specific Details: Viewing an Applet Using the JDK

> UNIX:
> ```
> appletviewer file:/home/kwalrath/java/Hello.html
> ```
>
> DOS shell (Windows 95/NT):
> ```
> appletviewer file:/home/kwalrath/java/Hello.html
> ```
>
> MacOS:
> Start up the Applet Viewer. From the File menu, choose Open URL and enter the URL of the HTML file you created (for example, `file:/home/kwalrath/java/Hello.html`).

Once you've successfully completed these steps, you should see something like this in the browser window:

> Here is the output of my program: Hello world!

What Next?

Now you can:
- Continue in this lesson to learn about the anatomy of applets and about importing classes.
- Go back to The Anatomy of a Java Application (page 5), if you haven't already read it and you're interested in a quick introduction to key Java concepts.
- Learn more about writing applets by going to the **Writing Applets** trail (page 145).
- Return to the Trail Map (page xv) to get an overview of the trails you can follow.

The Anatomy of a Java Applet

Now that you've seen a Java applet, you're probably wondering how it works. Remember that a *Java applet* is a program that adheres to a set of conventions that allows it to run within a Java-compatible browser.

Here again is the code for the "Hello World" applet:

```
import java.applet.Applet;
import java.awt.Graphics;

public class HelloWorld extends Applet {
    public void paint(Graphics g) {
        g.drawString("Hello world!", 50, 25);
    }
}
```

The code above starts off with two `import` statements. By importing classes or packages, a class can more easily refer to classes in other packages. In the Java language, *packages* are used to group classes, similar to the way libraries are used to group C functions. Importing Classes and Packages (page 17) gives you more information about packages and the `import` statement.

Every applet must define a subclass of the `Applet` class. In the "Hello World" applet, this subclass is called `HelloWorld`. Applets inherit a great deal of functionality from the `Applet` class, ranging from communication with the browser to the ability to present a graphical user interface (GUI). Defining an Applet Subclass (page 18) tells you more.

The "Hello World" applet implements just one method, the `paint` method. Every applet must implement at least one of the following methods: `init`, `start`, or `paint`. Unlike Java applications, applets do *not* need to implement a `main` method. Implementing Applet Methods (page 19) talks about the `paint` method, how the "Hello World" applet implements it, and the other methods applets commonly implement.

Applets are meant to be included in HTML pages. Using the `<APPLET>` HTML tag, you specify (at a minimum) the location of the `Applet` subclass and the dimensions of the applet's on-screen display area. When a Java-compatible browser encounters an `<APPLET>` tag, it reserves on-screen space for the applet, loads the `Applet` subclass onto the computer the browser is executing on, and creates an instance of the `Applet` subclass. Running an Applet (page 19) gives more details.

Importing Classes and Packages

The first two lines of the following listing import two classes used in the applet: Applet and Graphics.

```
import java.applet.Applet;
import java.awt.Graphics;


public class HelloWorld extends Applet {
    public void paint(Graphics g) {
        g.drawString("Hello world!", 50, 25);
    }
}
```

If you removed the first two lines, the applet could still compile and run, but only if you changed the rest of the code like this:

```
public class HelloWorld extends java.applet.Applet {
    public void paint(java.awt.Graphics g) {
        g.drawString("Hello world!", 50, 25);
    }
}
```

As you can see, importing the Applet and Graphics classes lets the program refer to them later without any prefixes. The java.applet. and java.awt. prefixes tell the compiler which packages it should search for the Applet and Graphics classes. The java.applet package contains classes that are essential to Java applets. The java.awt package contains the most frequently used classes in the Abstract Window Toolkit (AWT), which provides the Java graphical user interface (GUI).

You might have noticed that **The "Hello World" Application** (page 3) uses the System class with any prefix, and yet does not import the System class. The reason is that the System class is part of the java.lang package, and everything in the java.lang package is automatically imported into every Java program.

Besides importing individual classes, you can also import entire packages. Here's an example:

```
import java.applet.*;
import java.awt.*;

public class HelloWorld extends Applet {
```

```
    public void paint(Graphics g) {
        g.drawString("Hello world!", 50, 25);
    }
}
```

In the Java language, every class is in a package. If the source code for a class doesn't have a `package` statement at the top declaring the package the class is in, then the class is in the *default package*. Almost all of the example classes in this tutorial are in the default package. See <u>Creating and Using Packages</u> (page 135) for information on using the `package` statement.

Within a package, all classes can refer to each other without prefixes. For example, the `java.awt` `Component` class refers to the `java.awt` `Graphics` class without any prefixes and without importing the `Graphics` class.

Defining an Applet Subclass

The first bold line of the following listing begins a block that defines the `HelloWorld` class.

```
import java.applet.Applet;
import java.awt.Graphics;

public class HelloWorld extends Applet {
    public void paint(Graphics g) {
        g.drawString("Hello world!", 50, 25);
    }
}
```

The `extends` keyword indicates that `HelloWorld` is a subclass of the class whose name follows: `Applet`. If the term *subclass* means nothing to you, you'll learn about it soon in the lesson **Object-Oriented Programming Concepts: A Primer** (page 31).

From the `Applet` class, applets inherit a great deal of functionality. Perhaps most important is the ability to respond to browser requests. For example, when a Java-compatible browser loads a page containing an applet, the browser sends a request to the applet, telling the applet to initialize itself and start executing. You'll learn more about what the `Applet` class provides in the **Overview of Applets** (page 149).

An applet is not restricted to defining just one class. Besides the necessary `Applet` subclass, an applet can define additional custom classes. When the applet attempts to use a class, the application that is executing the applet first

looks on the local host for the class. If the class is not available locally, it is loaded from the location that the `Applet` subclass originated from.

Implementing `Applet` Methods

The bold lines of the following listing implement the `paint` method.

```
import java.applet.Applet;
import java.awt.Graphics;


public class HelloWorld extends Applet {
    public void paint(Graphics g) {
        g.drawString("Hello world!", 50, 25);
    }
}
```

Every applet must implement one or more of the `init`, `start`, and `paint` methods. You'll learn about these methods in the **Overview of Applets** (page 149).

Besides the `init`, `start`, and `paint` methods, applets can implement two more methods that the browser calls when a major event occurs, such as leaving the applet's page: `stop` and `destroy`. Applets can implement any number of other methods, as well.

Returning to the above code snippet, the `Graphics` object passed into the `paint` method represents the applet's onscreen drawing context. The first argument to the `Graphics drawString` method is the string to draw on screen. The second and third arguments are the (x,y) position of the lower left corner of the text onscreen. This applet draws the string "Hello world!" starting at location (50,25). The applet's coordinate system starts at (0,0), which is at the upper left corner of the applet's display area. You'll learn all about drawing to the screen in the **Creating a User Interface** trail (page 357).

Running an Applet

The bold lines of the following listing comprise the <APPLET> tag that includes the "Hello World" applet in an HTML page.

```
<HTML>
<HEAD>
<TITLE> A Simple Program </TITLE>
</HEAD>
<BODY>
```

```
Here is the output of my program:
<APPLET CODE="HelloWorld.class" WIDTH=150 HEIGHT=25>
</APPLET>
</BODY>
</HTML>
```

The above <APPLET> tag specifies that the browser should load the class whose compiled code (bytecodes) are in the file named `HelloWorld.class`. The browser looks for this file in the same directory as the HTML document that contains the tag.

When the browser finds the class file, it loads it over the network, if necessary, onto the computer the browser is running on. The browser then creates an instance of the class. If you include an applet twice in one page, the browser loads the class file once and creates two instances of the class.

The `WIDTH` and `HEIGHT` attributes are like the same attributes in an <IMG> tag: They specify the size in pixels of the applet's display area. Most browsers do not let the applet resize itself to be larger or smaller than this display area. For example, every bit of drawing that the "Hello World" applet does in its `paint` method occurs within the 150x25-pixel display area that the above <APPLET> tag reserves for it.

For more information on the <APPLET> tag, see <u>Adding an Applet to an HTML Page</u> (page 163).

Common Compiler
and Interpreter Problems
(and Their Solutions)

IF you're having trouble compiling your Java source code or running your application, this section might be able to help you. If nothing in this section helps, please refer to the documentation for the compiler or interpreter you're using.

Compiler Problems

Can't Locate the Compiler

On UNIX systems, you may see the following error message if your path isn't set properly.

```
javac: Command not found
```

Use setenv or a similar command to modify your PATH environment variable so that it includes the directory where the Java compiler lives.

Syntax Errors

If you mistype part of a program, the compiler may issue a *syntax* error. The message usually displays the type of the error, the line number where the error was detected, the code on that line, and the position of the error within the code. Here's an error caused by omitting a semicolon (;) at the end of a statement:

```
testing.java:14: ';' expected.
System.out.println("Input has " + count + " chars.")
                                                     ^
1 error
```

Sometimes the compiler can't guess your intent and prints a confusing error message or multiple error messages if the error cascades over several lines. For example, the following code snippet omits a semicolon (;) from the bold line.

```
while (System.in.read() != -1)
    count++
System.out.println("Input has " + count + " chars.");
```

When processing this code, the compiler issues two error messages:

```
testing.java:13: Invalid type expression.
        count++
              ^
testing.java:14: Invalid declaration.
    System.out.println("Input has " + count + "chars.");
                          ^
2 errors
```

The compiler issues two error messages because after it processes count++, the compiler's state indicates that it's in the middle of an expression. Without the semicolon, the compiler has no way of knowing that the statement is complete.

If you see any compiler errors, then your program did not successfully compile, and the compiler did not create a .class file. Carefully verify the program, fix any errors that you detect, and try again.

Semantic Errors

In addition to verifying that your program is syntactically correct, the compiler checks for other basic correctness. For example, the compiler warns you *each time* you use a variable that has not been initialized:

```
testing.java:13: Variable count may not have been initialized.
        count++
```

```
^
testing.java:14: Variable count may not have been initialized.

System.out.println("Input has " + count + " chars.");
                                     ^
2 errors
```

Again, your program did not successfully compile, and the compiler did not create a `.class` file. Fix the error and try again.

Interpreter Problems

Can't Find Class

A common error of beginner Java programmers using the UNIX or Windows 95/NT JDK is to try to interpret the `.class` file created by the compiler. For example, if you try to interpret the file `HelloWorldApp.class` rather than the class `HelloWorldApp`, the interpreter displays this error message:

```
Can't find class HelloWorldApp.class
```

The argument to the Java interpreter is the *name of the class* that you want to use, *not* the filename.

The `main` Method Is Not Defined

The Java interpreter requires that the class you execute with it have a method named `main`, because the interpreter must have somewhere to begin execution of your Java application. The main Method (page 8) discusses the `main` method in detail.

If you try to run a class with the Java interpreter that does not have a `main` method, the interpreter prints the following error message:

```
In class classname: void main(String argv[]) is not defined
```

In the above message, `classname` is the name of the class that you tried to run.

Changes to My Program Didn't Take Effect

Sometimes when you are in the edit/debug/run cycle, it appears that your changes to an application didn't take effect, a print statement isn't printing, for

example. This is common when running Java applications on MacOS using Java Runner. If you recompile a `.class` file, you must quit Java Runner and bring it up again, since Java Runner does not reload classes.

Applet Problems

See **Common Applet Problems (and Their Solutions)** (page 205) if you have trouble getting your applet to run.

End of Trail

YOU'VE reached the end of the **Getting Started** trail. Take a break—have a cup of steaming hot java.

What Next?

Once you've caught your breath, you have several choices of where to go next. You can go back to the **Trail Map** (page xv) to see all of your choices, or you can go directly to one of the following popular trails:

Writing Java Programs (page 27): This trail is a gentle introduction to object-oriented concepts and how the Java language implements them.

Writing Applets (page 145): This is the starting point for learning everything about writing applets.

Using the Core Java Classes (page 209): This trail discusses strings, exceptions, threads, and other Java features that are used in all kinds of Java programs.

Writing Java Programs

THIS trail covers the fundamentals of programming in the Java language.

Object-Oriented Programming Concepts: A Primer (page 31) cuts through the hype surrounding object-oriented technology and teaches you its core concepts: objects, messages, classes, and inheritance. It is important to understand these key concepts before studying the specifics of the Java language. This lesson also contains a bibliography for further reading on the subject. Feel free to skip this lesson if you are already familiar with object-oriented programming.

The Nuts and Bolts of the Java Language (page 43) introduces you to several components of the Java language by explaining a simple Java application line by line. You will learn about the syntax and semantics of the Java language, and you will learn about several features of the Java programming environment.

Because Java's syntax is similar to that of other programming languages, particularly C and C++, much of this material will be familiar to seasoned programmers. You may wish to skim this lesson for its main points and use it as a reference source.

Objects, Classes, and Interfaces (page 77) takes the concepts you learned in the first lesson of this trail and shows you how to make use of those concepts in the Java language. You will learn how to create, use, and destroy objects, how to write your own classes, and how to create and use interfaces. And finally, this lesson will show you how to manage your classes and interfaces within packages. This lesson is a complete do-it-yourself "Object-Oriented Programming in Java" lesson.

27

Again programmers experienced in other object-oriented languages may wish to skim this lesson and use it later as a reference source.

Object-Oriented Programming Concepts: A Primer

YOU'VE heard it a lot in the past several years. Everybody is saying it.

What is all the fuss about objects and object-oriented technology? Is it real? Or is it hype? Well, the truth is—it's a little bit of both. Object-oriented technology, does, in fact, provide many benefits to software developers and their products. However, historically a lot of hype has surrounded this technology, causing confusion in both managers and programmers alike. Many companies fell victim to this hardship (or took advantage of it) and claimed that their software products

were object-oriented when, in fact, they weren't. These false claims confused consumers, causing widespread misinformation and mistrust of object-oriented technology.

However, in spite of the overuse and misuse of the term object-oriented, the computer industry is now beginning to overcome the hype. People's understanding is growing about object-oriented technology and its benefits.

This lesson slashes through the hype and explains the four key concepts behind object-oriented programming, design, and development by answering these four questions:

- <u>What Is an Object?</u> (page 32)
- <u>What Are Messages?</u> (page 35)
- <u>What Are Classes?</u> (page 36)
- <u>What Is Inheritance?</u> (page 39)
  (Or what does my grandmother's money have to do with all of this?)

If you already know the answers to these questions, consider skipping this lesson and moving on to the next lesson—**The Nuts and Bolts of the Java Language** (page 43).

What Is an Object?

As the term *object-oriented* implies, *objects* are key to understanding object-oriented technology. You can look around you now and see many examples of real-world objects: your dog, your desk, your television set, your bicycle.

These real-world objects share two characteristics: they all have *state* and they all have *behavior*. For example, dogs have state (name, color, breed, hungry) and dogs have behavior (barking, fetching, slobbering on your newly cleaned slacks). Bicycles have state (current gear, current pedal cadence, two wheels, number of gears) and behavior (braking, accelerating, slowing down, changing gears).

Software objects are modeled after real-world objects in that they, too, have state and behavior. A software object maintains its state in *variables* and implements its behavior with *methods*.

Definition: An object is a software bundle of variables and related methods.

You can represent real-world objects using software objects. You might want to represent dogs as software objects in an animation program or a bicycle as a software object within an electronic exercise bike. However, you can also use software objects to model abstract concepts. For example, an event is a common

object used in GUI window systems to represent the action of a user pressing a mouse button or a key on the keyboard.

The following illustration is a common visual representation of a software object:

An Object

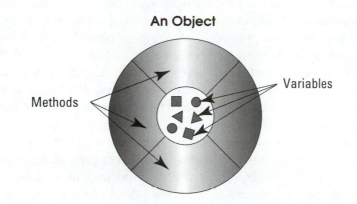

Everything that the software object knows (state) and can do (behavior) is expressed by the variables and methods within that object. A software object that models your bicycle has variables that indicate the bicycle's current state: its speed is 10 mph, its pedal cadence is 90 rpm, and its current gear is fifth gear. These variables and methods are formally known as *instance variables* and *instance methods* to distinguish them from class variables and class methods (described later in <u>What Are Classes?</u> (page 36)). The following figure illustrates a bicycle modeled as a software object.

Your Bicycle

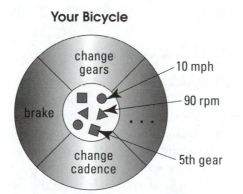

The software bicycle also has methods to brake, change the pedal cadence, and change gears. (The bike does not have a method for changing the speed of the bicycle, as the bike's speed is really just a side effect of what gear it's in, how fast the rider is pedaling, whether the brakes are on, and how steep the hill is.)

Anything that an object does not know or cannot do is excluded from the object. For example, your bicycle (probably) doesn't have a name, and it can't run, bark, or fetch. Thus, there are no variables or methods for those states and behaviors in the bicycle class.

As you can see from the previous figures, the object's variables make up the center or nucleus of the object. Methods surround and hide the object's nucleus from other objects in the program. Packaging an object's variables within the protective custody of its methods is called *encapsulation*. Typically, encapsulation is used to hide unimportant implementation details from other objects. When you want to change gears on your bicycle, you don't need to know how the gear mechanism works, you just need to know which lever to move. Similarly in software programs, you don't need to know how a class is implemented, you just need to know which methods to invoke. Thus, the implementation details can change at any time without effecting other parts of the program.

This conceptual picture of an object—a nucleus of variables packaged within a protective membrane of methods—is an ideal representation of an object and is the ideal that designers of object-oriented systems strive for. However, it's not the whole story. Often, for implementation or efficiency reasons, an object may wish to expose some of its variables or hide some of its methods.

In many languages, including Java, an object can choose to expose its variables to other objects allowing those other objects to inspect and even modify the variables. Also, an object can choose to hide methods from other objects, forbidding those objects from invoking the methods. An object has complete control over whether other objects can access its variables and methods and in fact, can specify which other objects have access. Variable and method access in Java is covered in <u>Controlling Access to Members of a Class</u> (page 105).

The Benefits of Encapsulation

Encapsulating related variables and methods into a neat software bundle is a simple yet powerful idea that provides two major benefits to software developers:

- Modularity—The source code for an object can be written and maintained independently of the source code for other objects. Also, an object can be easily passed around in the system. You can give your bicycle to someone else and it will still work.
- Information hiding—An object has a public interface that other objects can use to communicate with it. However, the object can maintain private information and methods that can be changed at any time without affecting the other objects that depend on it. You don't need to understand the gear mechanism on your bike in order to use it.

What Are Messages?

A single object alone is generally not very useful and usually appears as a component of a larger program or application that contains many other objects. Through the interaction of these objects, programmers achieve higher order functionality and more complex behavior. Your bicycle hanging from a hook in the garage is just a bunch of titanium alloy and rubber; by itself, the bicycle is incapable of any activity. The bicycle is useful only when when another object (you) interacts with it (starts pedaling).

Software objects interact and communicate with each other by sending *messages* to each other. When object A wants object B to perform one of B's methods, object A sends a message to object B.

Messaging

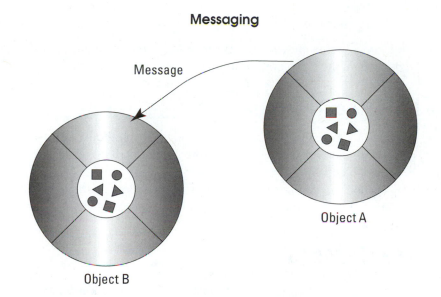

Message

Object A

Object B

Sometimes the receiving object needs more information so that it knows exactly what to do. For example, when you want to change gears on your bicycle, you have to indicate which gear you want. This information is passed along with the message as *parameters*.

Three components comprise a message:
1. The object to whom the message is addressed (Your Bicycle)
2. The name of the method to perform (`changeGears`)
3. Any parameters needed by the method (lower gear)

A Message with Parameters

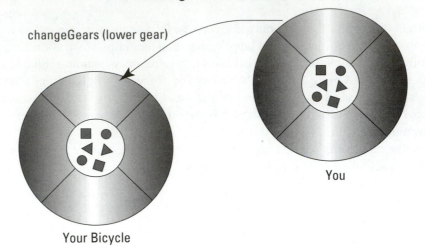

changeGears (lower gear)

You

Your Bicycle

These three components are enough information for the receiving object to perform the desired method. No other information or context is required.

The Benefits of Messages

- An object's behavior is expressed through its methods, so, aside from
  direct variable access, message passing supports all possible interactions
  between objects.
- Objects don't need to be in the same process or even on the same machine
  to send and receive messages back and forth to each other.

What Are Classes?

In the real world, you often have many objects of the same kind. For example,
your bicycle is just one of many bicycles in the world. Using object-oriented terminology, we say that your bicycle object is an *instance* of the class of objects
known as bicycles. Bicycles have some state (current gear, current cadence, two
wheels) and behavior (change gears, brake) in common. However, each bicycle's
state is independent of and can be different from other bicycles.

When building bicycles, manufacturers take advantage of the fact that bicycles share characteristics by building many bicycles from the same blueprint—it
would be very inefficient to produce a new blueprint for every individual bicycle
they manufactured.

In object-oriented software, it's also possible to have many objects of the
same kind that share characteristics: rectangles, employee records, video clips,

and so on. Like the bicycle manufacturers, you can take advantage of the fact that objects of the same kind are similar and you can create a blueprint for those objects. Software blueprints for objects are called *classes*.

A Class

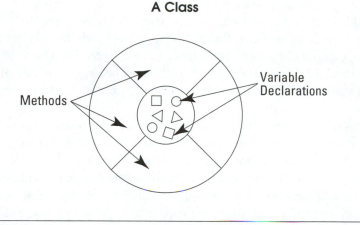

Definition: A class is a blueprint or prototype that defines the variables and methods common to all objects of a certain kind.

For example, you can create a bicycle class that declares several instance variables to contain the current gear, the current cadence, and other characteristics, for each bicycle object. This class also declares and provides implementations for the instance methods that allow the rider to change gears, brake, and change the pedaling cadence.

The Bicycle Class

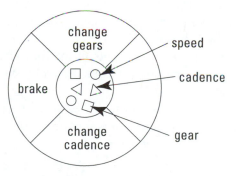

The values for instance variables are provided by each instance of the class. So, after you've created the bicycle class, you must *instantiate* it (create an instance of it) before you can use it. When you create an instance of a class, you create an object of that type and the system allocates memory for the instance variables declared by the class. Then you can invoke the object's instance methods to make it do something. Instances of the same class share the same instance method implementations which reside in the class itself. (Method implementations are not duplicated on a per object basis.)

In addition to instance variables and methods, classes can also define *class variables* and *class methods*. You can access class variables and methods from an instance of the class or directly from a class—you don't have to instantiate a class to use its class variables and methods. Class methods can operate only on class variables—they do not have access to instance variables or instance methods.

The system creates a single copy of all class variables for a class the first time it encounters the class in a program; all instances of that class share its class variables. For example, suppose that all bicycles have the same number of gears. In this case, defining an instance variable for number of gears is inefficient. Each instance would have its own copy of the variable, but the value would be the same for every instance. In situations such as this, you can define a class variable that contains the number of gears. All instances share this variable. If one object changes the variable, it changes for all other objects of that type.

Instance and Class Members (page 111) discusses instance variables and methods and class variables and methods in detail.

Objects vs. Classes

You probably noticed that the illustrations of objects and classes look very similar to one another. And indeed, the difference between classes and objects is often the source of some confusion. In the real world it's obvious that classes are not themselves the objects that they describe—a blueprint of a bicycle is not a bicycle. However, it's a little more difficult to differentiate classes and objects in software. This is partly because software objects are merely electronic models of real-world objects or abstract concepts in the first place. But it's also because many people use the term "object" inconsistently and use it to refer to both classes and instances.

In the figures, the class is not shaded because it represents a blueprint of an object rather than an object itself. In comparison, an object is shaded indicating that the object actually exists and you can use it.

The Benefit of Classes

Objects provide the benefit of modularity and information hiding. Classes provide the benefit of reusability. Bicycle manufacturers reuse the same blueprint over and over again to build many bicycles. Software programmers use the same class and thus the same code, over and over again to create many objects.

What Is Inheritance?

Generally speaking, objects are defined in terms of classes. You know a lot about an object by knowing its class. Even if you don't know what a penny-farthing is, if I told you it was a bicycle, you would know that it had two wheels, handle bars, and pedals.

Object-oriented systems take this a step further and allow classes to be defined in terms of other classes. For example, mountain bikes, racing bikes, and tandems are all different kinds of bicycles. In object-oriented terminology, mountain bikes, racing bikes, and tandems are all *subclasses* of the bicycle class. Similarly, the bicycle class is the *superclass* of mountain bikes, racing bikes, and tandems.

Hierarchy of Classes

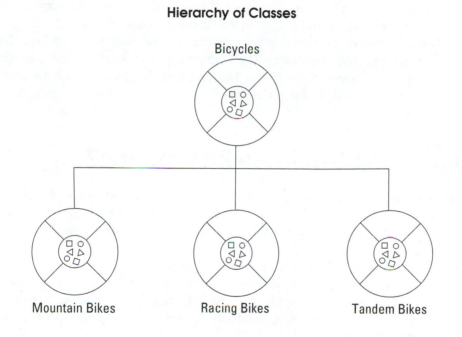

Each subclass *inherits* state (in the form of variable declarations) from the superclass. Mountain bikes, racing bikes, and tandems share some states: cadence, speed, and the like. Also, each subclass inherits methods from the superclass. Mountain bikes, racing bikes, and tandems share some behaviors: braking and changing pedaling speed, for example.

However, subclasses are not limited to the state and behaviors provided to them by their superclass. What would be the point in that? Subclasses can add variables and methods to the ones they inherit from the superclass. Tandem bicycles have two seats and two sets of handle bars; some mountain bikes have an extra set of gears with a lower gear ratio.

Subclasses can also *override* inherited methods and provide specialized implementations for those methods. For example, if you have a mountain bike with an extra set of gears, you can override the changeGears method so that the rider can use those new gears.

You are not limited to just one layer of inheritance. The inheritance tree, or *class hierarchy*, can be as deep as needed. Methods and variables are inherited down through the levels. In general, the further down in the hierarchy a class appears, the more specialized its behavior.

The Benefits of Inheritance

- Subclasses provide specialized behaviors from the basis of common elements provided by the superclass. Through the use of inheritance, programmers can reuse the code in the superclass many times.
- Programmers can implement superclasses called *abstract classes* that define "generic" behaviors. The abstract superclass defines and may partially implement the behavior but much of the class is undefined and unimplemented. Other programmers fill in the details with specialized subclasses.

Where Can I Get More Information?

This lesson gave you a glimpse into the world of object-oriented design and development and may have whet your appetite for more. Check out the following fine object-oriented titles to get more information about this exciting technology!

An Introduction to Object-Oriented Programming

An introduction to the topic of object-oriented programming, as well as a comparison of C++, Objective C, Smalltalk, and Object Pascal. Written by Timothy Budd. Published by Addison-Wesley Publishing Company, Reading, Massachusetts, 1991.

Object-Oriented Technology: A Manager's Guide

An excellent discussion of object-oriented technology for the nontechnical reader. Includes an assessment of the advantages and disadvantages of this technology. Written by David A. Taylor, Ph.D. Published by Servio Corporation, Alameda, California, 1990.

NEXTSTEP Object-Oriented Programming and the Objective C Language

The book on Objective C. A good introduction to object-oriented programming concepts. Published by Addison-Wesley Publishing Company, Reading, Massachusetts, 1993.

This lesson gave you a basis for understanding key object-oriented terminology and concepts. Understanding these new terms and concepts is just the beginning. As you begin to design and program in the Java language, a truly object-oriented language, the power of objects and classes will become apparent.

The Nuts and Bolts
of the Java Language

THE following application reads and counts characters from the standard input and then displays the number of characters read. Even a small program such as this uses many of the traditional language features provided by Java and several classes in the libraries shipped with the Java environment.

```
class Count {
    public static void main(String[] args)
        throws java.io.IOException
    {
        int count = 0;

        while (System.in.read() != -1)
            count++;
        System.out.println("Input has " + count + " chars.");
    }
}
```

To <u>Run the Character-Counting Application</u> (page 45), you must enter characters at the keyboard.

Through a line-by-line investigation of this simple Java application, this lesson will describe Java's traditional language features such as variables and data types, operators, expressions, control flow statements, and so on. You will also be introduced to some of Java's other features: the main method, exceptions, and standard input and output.

The following paragraphs introduce variables and data types, operators, expressions, and control flow statements. Each of these topics is covered in detail in this lesson.

<u>Variables and Data Types</u> (page 46): Like other programming languages, Java allows you to declare variables in your programs. You use variables to contain data that can change during the execution of the program. All variables in Java have a type, a name, and scope. The example program at the beginning of this lesson declares two variables:

- `int count = 0;`
- `String[] args`

<u>Operators</u> (page 50): The Java language provides a set of operators which perform a function on one or two variables. The character-counting program uses several operators, including the ones shown here in bold:

- `int count = 0;`
- `System.in.read() != -1`
- `count ++;`
- `"Input has " + count + " chars."`

<u>Expressions</u> (page 58): Operators, variables, and method calls can be combined into sequences known as *expressions*. The real work of a Java program, including the character-counting example, is achieved through expressions.

<u>Control Flow Statements</u> (page 60): The `while` statement in the character-counting program is one of a group of statements known as a *control flow statements*. As the name implies, control flow statements control the flow of the program. Control flow statements govern the sequence in which a program's statements are executed.

<u>Arrays and Strings</u> (page 68): Two important data types in any programming language are *arrays* and *strings*. In Java, both arrays and strings are full-blown objects. Other languages force programmers to manage data in arrays and strings at the memory level using direct pointer manipulation. The character-counting program defines an array of strings:

<u>Other Features of the Character-Counting Application</u> (page 71): In addition to the traditional programming language features highlighted in the paragraphs above, the character-counting program introduces several other features with which you will become familiar over the course of this lesson: the `main` method, exceptions, and standard input and output.

But before getting into the nitty-gritty of each of these features of the character-counting application, let's see the program in action.

Run the Character-Counting Application

The output of the character-counting program depends on the input you enter for it. When an application reads from the standard input stream, like the character-counting application does, the application blocks and waits for you to type something in. The application continues to wait for input until you give it some indication that the input is complete. For any program that reads from the standard input stream, you must type the end-of-input character at the beginning of a new line to indicate that you have finished entering characters. When the character-counting program receives an end-of-input character, it prints out the number of characters you typed.

Platform-Specific Details: Running the Character-Counting Application Using the JDK

UNIX:
```
% java Count
This is a test.
^D
Input has 16 chars.
```

Use the control-D character (type D while holding down the control key) to indicate to a program reading from the standard input stream that you have finished entering input. The control-D character is often written as ^D.

DOS shell (Windows 95/NT):
```
C:\> java Count
This is a test.
^Z
Input has 17 chars.
```

Use the control-Z character (type Z while holding down the control key) to indicate to a program reading from the standard input stream that you have finished entering input. Alternatively, you can press the F6 key. The control-Z character is often written as ^Z.

MacOS:
First, the character-counting application brings up a window prompting you for command-line arguments. Just press the Return key to indicate that there aren't any. Next, the character-counting application brings up a window prompting you to type characters into standard input. When you've typed in an entire line, press the Return key and continue typing. To indicate that you are finished typing,

press the Return key twice in succession. The program displays its results in a window: `Input has 15 chars.`

In the sample below, the user enters "This is a test." followed by the appropriate end-of-input character. In response, the application displays `Input has 16 chars.`

```
This is a test.
Input has 16 chars.
```

At first glance it may appear that the output is incorrect, since "This is a test." has only 15 characters. But the user entered a new line as the 16th character.

Note: The program gives different results for different platforms. On UNIX when you press the Return key, you get a single character: \n. However, in Windows 95/NT when you press the Return key, you get two characters: \r\n.

Now that you've seen the character-counting program in action, let's look at the various components that make up the program and see how they fit into the Java language.

Variables and Data Types

Variables are the nouns of a programming language: they are the entities (values and data) that act or are acted upon. The character-counting program uses two variables—count and args. The program increments count each time it reads a character from the input source and ignores args. The declarations for both variables appear in bold in the following listing:

```
class Count {
    public static void main(String[] args)
        throws java.io.IOException
    {
        int count = 0;

        while (System.in.read() != -1)
            count++;
        System.out.println("Input has " + count + " chars.");
    }
}
```

A variable declaration always contains two components: the type of the variable and its name. The location of the variable declaration, that is, where the declaration appears in relation to other code elements, determines the scope of the variable.

Variable Types

All variables in the Java language must have a data type. A variable's type determines the values that the variable can have and the operations that can be performed on it. For example, the declaration `int count` declares that `count` is an integer (`int`). Integers can have only whole number values (both positive and negative) and you can use the standard arithmetic operators (+, -, *, /) on integers to perform the standard arithmetic operations (addition, subtraction, multiplication, and division).

There are two major categories of data types in the Java language: *primitive types* and *reference types*. Primitive data types contain a single value and include types such as integer, floating point, character, and boolean. The following table lists, by keyword, all of the primitive data types supported by Java, their size and format, and a brief description of each.

Type	Size/Format	Description
(*whole numbers*)		
byte	8-bit two's complement	Byte-length integer
short	16-bit two's complement	Short integer
int	32-bit two's complement	Integer
long	64-bit two's complement	Long integer
(*real numbers*)		
float	32-bit IEEE 754	Single-precision floating point
double	64-bit IEEE 754	Double-precision floating point
(*other types*)		
char	16-bit Unicode character	A single character
boolean	`true` or `false`	A boolean value (`true` or `false`)

Reference types are called such because the value of a reference variable is a reference (a pointer in other terminology) to the actual value or set of values represented by the variable. For example, the character-counting program declares but never uses one variable of reference type, `args`, which is declared to be an array of `String` objects. When used in a statement or expression, the name `args` evaluates to the address of the memory location where the array lives. Compare that to the name of a primitive variable, the `count` variable, which evaluates to the variable's actual value.

Besides arrays, classes and interfaces are also reference types. When you create a class or interface you are in essence defining a new data type. See **Objects, Classes, and Interfaces** (page 77) for information about defining your own classes and interfaces.

Note to C and C++ Programmers:

There are three C data types not supported by the Java language. They are pointers, structures, and unions. These data types are not necessary in Java; you use classes and interfaces instead.

Pointers

Some data types in Java, such as objects and arrays, are reference data types. The value of a variable whose data type is a reference type is a reference (or a pointer in other terminology) to the actual data. However, Java does not have an explicit pointer type. You cannot construct a reference to anonymous memory. In addition to making programming easier, this prevents common errors due to pointer mismanagement.

Structures and Unions

The Java language does not support either structures or unions. Instead you use classes or interfaces to build composite types. Classes and interfaces are a much more powerful mechanism than structures or unions, as they allow you to bundle together data and methods, and to control who has access to those class members.

Variable Names

A program refers to a variable's value by its name. For example, when the character-counting program wants to refer to the value of the `count` variable, it simply uses the name `count`. By convention, variable names begin with a lowercase letter and class names begin with an uppercase letter.

In Java, a variable name

1. must be a legal Java identifier comprised of a series of Unicode characters. Unicode is a character-coding system designed to support text written in diverse human languages. Unicode allows for the codification of up to 34,168 characters. This allows you to use characters in your Java programs from various alphabets such as Japanese, Greek, Russian, Hebrew, and so on. This is important so that programmers can write code that is meaningful in their native languages.
2. must not be the same as a keyword (page 799) or a boolean literal (`true` or `false`).
3. must not have the same name as another variable whose declaration appears in the same scope.

Rule #3 implies that variables may have the same name as another variable whose declaration appears in a different scope. This is true. In addition, in some situations, a variable may share names with another variable which is declared in a nested scope.

By convention, variable names begin with a lowercase letter. If a variable name is comprised of more than one word, such as `isVisible`, the words are joined together and each word after the first begins with an uppercase letter.

Scope

A variable's scope is the block of code within which the variable is accessible. A variable's scope determines when the variable is created and destroyed. You establish the scope of a variable when you declare it. Scope places a variable into one of these four categories:

- member variable
- local variable
- method parameter
- exception handler parameter

A member variable is a member of a class or an object and is declared within a class, but not within any of the class's methods. The character-counting program declares no member variables. For information about declaring member variables and their scope, refer to Declaring Member Variables (page 91) in Lesson 5, **Objects, Classes, and Interfaces** (page 77).

Local variables are declared within a method or within a block of code in a method. In the character-counting program, `count` is a local variable. The scope of `count`, that is, the code that can access `count`, extends from the declaration of `count` to the end of the `main` method (indicated by the first right curly bracket (}) that appears in the sample code). In general, a local variable is accessible from its declaration to the end of the code block in which it was declared.

Method parameters are formal arguments to methods and constructors and are used to pass values into methods and constructors. The discussion about writing methods in the Implementing Methods (page 94) section of Lesson 5 talks about passing values into methods and constructors through method parameters. In the character-counting program, `args` is a method parameter to the `main` method. The scope of a method parameter is the entire method or constructor for which it is a parameter. So, in the character-counting program, the scope of `args` is the entire `main` method.

Exception handler parameters are similar to method parameters but are arguments to an exception handler rather than to a method or a constructor. The character-counting program does not have any exception handlers, so it doesn't have any exception handler parameters. **Handling Errors Using Exceptions** (page 253) talks about using Java exceptions to handle errors and shows you how to write an exception handler with a parameter.

Variable Initialization

Local variables and member variables can be initialized when they are declared. The character-counting program provides an initial value for count when declaring it:

```
int count = 0;
```

The type of the value assigned to the variable must match the type of the variable. Method parameters and exception handler parameters cannot be initialized in this way. The value for a parameter is set by the caller.

Operators

The character-counting program uses several operators, including =, !=, ++, and +, which appear in bold in this listing:

```
class Count {
    public static void main(String[] args)
        throws java.io.IOException
    {
        int count = 0;

        while (System.in.read() != -1)
            count++;
        System.out.println("Input has " + count + " chars.");
    }
}
```

Operators perform some function on either one or two operands. Operators that require one operand are called *unary operators*. ++ is a unary operator that increments the value of its operand by one. Operators that require two operands are *binary operators*. The = operator is a binary operator that assigns the value from its right-hand operand to its left-hand operand.

Java's unary operators can use either prefix or postfix notation. Prefix notation means that the operator appears *before* its operand:

```
operator op
```

Postfix notation means that the operator appears *after* its operand:

```
op operator
```

All of Java's binary operators use infix notation which means that the operator appears *between* its operands:

```
op1 operator op2
```

In addition to performing the operation, an operator also returns a value. The value and its type depend on the operator and the type of its operands. For example, the arithmetic operators, which perform basic arithmetic operations such as addition and subtraction, return numbers—typically the result of the arithmetic operation. The data type returned by the arithmetic operators depends on the type of its operands: if you add two integers, you get an integer back. An operation is said to *evaluate to* its result.

It's useful to divide Java's operators into these categories: arithmetic, relational and conditional, bitwise and logical, and assignment.

Arithmetic Operators

The Java language supports various arithmetic operators—including + (addition), – (subtraction), * (multiplication), / (division), and % (modulo)—on all floating-point and integer numbers. For example, you can use the following Java code to add two numbers:

```
addThis + toThis
```

Or you can use the following Java code to compute the remainder that results from dividing divideThis by byThis:

```
divideThis % byThis
```

This table summarizes Java's binary arithmetic operations:

Operator	Use	Description
+	op1 + op2	Adds op1 and op2
–	op1 – op2	Subtracts op2 from op1
*	op1 * op2	Multiplies op1 and op2
/	op1 / op2	Divides op1 by op2
%	op1 % op2	Computes the remainder of dividing op1 by op2

Note: The Java language extends the definition of the operator + to include string concatenation. The character-counting program uses + to concatenate `"Input has "`, the value of `count`, and `" chars."` Note that this operation automatically coerces the value `count` to a String.

```
System.out.println("Input has " + count + " chars.");
```

You'll see more about this in <u>Arrays and Strings</u> (page 68).

The + and – operators have unary versions which set the sign of the operand:

Operator	Use	Description
+	+ op	Indicates a positive value
–	– op	Arithmetically negates op

In addition, there are two shortcut arithmetic operators: ++ which increments its operand by one, and -- which decrements its operand by one. The character-counting program uses ++ to increment the `count` variable each time it reads a character from the input source with the following Java statement:

```
count++;
```

Note that the ++ operator appears after its operand in this example. This is the postfix version of the operator. ++ also has a prefix version in which ++ appears before its operand. Both the prefix and postfix versions of this operator increment the operand by one. So why are there two different versions? Because each version evaluates a different value: op++ evaluates to the value of the operand *before* the increment operation and ++op evaluates the value of the operand *after* the increment operation.

In the character-counting program suppose that `count` is 5 before the following statement is executed:

```
count++;
```

After the statement is executed, the value of `count` is 6. No surprises there. However, the statement `count++` evaluates to 5. In the same scenario, the prefix version of ++ also sets `count` to 6. However, the statement ++count does not evaluate to 5 like the postfix version of ++, but 6:

```
++count;
```

This difference is unimportant in the character-counting program but is critical in situations where the value of the statement is used for a computation, for flow control, or for something else. For example, the following loop will execute one less time if you change `count++` to `++count`:

```
do {
    . . .
} while (count++  < 6);
```

You'll learn more about flow control in <u>Control Flow Statements</u> (page 60).

Similarly, `--` also has prefix and postfix versions which function in the same way as `++`.

Operator	Use	Description
++	op ++	Increments op by 1; evaluates to value before incrementing
++	++ op	Increments op by 1; evaluates to value after incrementing
--	op --	Decrements op by 1; evaluates to value before decrementing
--	-- op	Decrements op by 1; evaluates to value after decrementing

Relational and Conditional Operators

Relational operators compare two values and determine the relationship between them. For example, `!=` returns `true` if the two operands are unequal. The character-counting program uses `!=` to determine whether the value returned by `System.in.read` is not equal to -1.

The following table summarizes Java's relational operators:

Operator	Use	Returns true if
>	op1 > op2	op1 is greater than op2
>=	op1 >= op2	op1 is greater than or equal to op2
<	op1 < op2	op1 is less than to op2
<=	op1 <= op2	op1 is less than or equal to op2
==	op1 == op2	op1 and op2 are equal
!=	op1 != op2	op1 and op2 are not equal

Often the relational operators are used with the conditional operators to construct more complex decision-making expressions. One such operator is `&&` which performs the *boolean and* operation. For example, you can use two different relational operators along with && to determine if both relationships are true. The following line of code uses this technique to determine if an array index is between two boundaries; it determines if the index is both greater than 0 and less than NUM_ENTRIES (which is a previously defined constant value):

```
0 < index && index < NUM_ENTRIES
```

Note that in some instances, the second operand to a conditional operator may not be evaluated. Consider this statement:

```
((count > NUM_ENTRIES) && (System.in.read() != -1))
```

If count is less than NUM_ENTRIES, the left-hand operand for && evaluates to false. The && operator returns true only if *both* operands are true. So in this situation, the return value of && can be determined without evaluating the right-hand operand. In a case such as this, Java does not evaluate the right-hand operand. Thus, System.in.read *won't get called and a character will not be read from standard input.*

There are three conditional operators:

Operator	Use	Returns true if
&&	op1 && op2	op1 and op2 are both true
||	op1 || op2	either op1 or op2 is true
!	! op	op is false

The operator & can be used as a synonym for && if both of its operands are boolean. Similarly, | is a synonym for || if both of its operands are boolean.

Bitwise Operators

The bitwise operators allow you to perform bit manipulation on data. The following table summarizes the bitwise and logical operators available in the Java language:

Operator	Use	Operation
>>	op1 >> op2	shift bits of op1 right by distance op2
<<	op1 << op2	shift bits of op1 left by distance op2
>>>	op1 >>> op2	shift bits of op1 right by distance op2 (unsigned)

continued

Operator	Use	Operation
&	op1 & op2	bitwise and
|	op1 | op2	bitwise or
^	op1 ^ op2	bitwise xor
~	~ op	bitwise complement

The three shift operators simply shift the bits of the left-hand operand over by the number of positions indicated by the right-hand operand. The shift occurs in the direction indicated by the operator itself. For example, the following statement shifts the bits of the integer 13 to the right by one position.

```
13 >> 1;
```

The binary representation of the number 13 is 1101. The result of the shift operation is 1101 shifted to the right by one position—110 or 6 in decimal. Note that the bit farthest to the right falls off the end into the bit bucket. A right shift of one bit is equivalent to, but more efficient than, dividing the left-hand operand by two. A left shift of one bit is equivalent to multiplying by two.

The bitwise and operation performs the "and" function on each parallel pair of bits in each operand. The "and" function sets the resulting bit to one if both operands are 1.

op1	op2	result
0	0	0
0	1	0
1	0	0
1	1	1

Suppose you were to "and" the values 12 and 13 as in the following statement:

```
12 & 13
```

The result of this operation is 12. Why? Well, the binary representation of 12 is 1100, and the binary representation of 13 is 1101. The "and" function sets the resulting bit to 1 if both operand bits are 1; otherwise, the resulting bit is 0. So, if you line up the two operands and perform the "and" function, you can see that

the two high-order bits (the two bits farthest to the left of each number) of each operand are 1. Thus, the resulting bit in the result is also 1. The low-order bits evaluate to 0 because either one or both bits in the operands are 0:

```
    1101
  & 1100
  ------
    1100
```

The | operator performs the inclusive or operation and ∧ performs the exclusive or operation. Inclusive or means that if either of the two bits are 1 then the result is 1. The following table shows the results of your inclusive or operations:

op1	op2	result
0	0	0
0	1	1
1	0	1
1	1	1

Exclusive or means that if the two operand bits are different the result is 1, otherwise the result is 0. The following table shows the results of your exclusive or oeprations.

op1	op2	result
0	0	0
0	1	1
1	0	1
1	1	0

And finally, the complement operator inverts the value of each bit of the operand: if the operand bit is 1, the result is 0. If the operand bit is 0, the result is 1.

Among other things, bitwise manipulations are useful for managing sets of boolean flags. Suppose for example, that you have several boolean flags in your program that indicate the state of various components in your program: is it visible, is it draggable, and so on. Rather than defining a separate boolean variable to hold each flag, you can define a single variable, flags, for all of them. Each bit

within `flags` represents the current state of one of the flags. You then use bit manipulations to set and get each flag.

First, set up constants that indicate the various flags for your program. These flags should each be a different power of two to ensure that the "on" bit doesn't overlap with another flag. Define a variable, `flags`, whose bits are set according to the current state of each flag. The following code sample initializes `flags` to 0 indicating that all flags are false (none of the bits are set):

```java
final int VISIBLE = 1;
final int DRAGGABLE = 2;
final int SELECTABLE = 4;
final int EDITABLE = 8;

int flags = 0;
```

To set the visible flag when something became visible, use this statement:

```java
flags = flags | VISIBLE;
```

To test for visibility, you then write:

```java
flags & VISIBLE
```

Assignment Operators

You use the assignment operator, =, to assign one value to another. The character-counting program uses = to initialize `count` with this statement:

```java
int count = 0;
```

In addition to the basic assignment operator, Java provides several shortcut assignment operators that allow you to perform an arithmetic, logical, or bitwise operation and an assignment operation, all with one operator. Specifically, suppose you want to add a number to a variable and assign the result back into the variable, like this:

```java
i = i + 2;
```

You can shorten this statement using the shortcut operator +=.

```java
i += 2;
```

The two previous lines of code are equivalent.

The following table lists the short cut assignment operators and their lengthy equivalents:

Operator	Use	Equivalent to
+=	op1 += op2	op1 = op1 + op2
-=	op1 -= op2	op1 = op1 - op2
*=	op1 *= op2	op1 = op1 * op2
/=	op1 /= op2	op1 = op1 / op2
%=	op1 %= op2	op1 = op1 % op2
&=	op1 &= op2	op1 = op1 & op2
|=	op1 |= op2	op1 = op1 | op2
^=	op1 ^= op2	op1 = op1 ^ op2
<<=	op1 <<= op2	op1 = op1 << op2
>>=	op1 >>= op2	op1 = op1 >> op2
>>>=	op1 >>>= op2	op1 = op1 >>> op2

Expressions

Expressions perform the work of a Java program. Among other things, expressions are used to compute and assign values to variables and to help control the execution flow of a program. The job of an expression is two-fold: perform the computation indicated by the elements of the expression and return some value which is the result of the computation.

Definition: An expression is a series of variables, operators, and method calls (constructed according to the syntax of the language) that evaluates to a single value.

As you learned in the previous section, operators return a value, so the use of an operator is an expression. For example, the statement from the character-counting program is an expression:

```
count++;
```

This particular expression evaluates to the value of `count` before the operation occurs.

The data type of the value returned by an expression depends on the elements used in the expression. The expression `count++` returns an integer because `++` returns a value of the same data type as its operand and `count` is an integer. Other expressions return boolean values, strings, and so on.

Besides the `count++` expression, the character-counting program contains a few other expressions including:

```
System.in.read() != -1
```

This expression is interesting because it's actually comprised of two expressions. The first expression is a method call:

```
System.in.read()
```

A method call expression evaluates to the return value of the method. Therefore, the data type of a method call expression is the same as the data type of the return value of that method. The `System.in.read` method is declared to return an integer, so the expression `System.in.read()` evaluates to an integer.

The second expression contained in the statement `System.in.read() !=` `-1` is the use of the `!=` operator. Recall that `!=` compares its two operands for inequality. In the statement in question, the operands are `System.in.read()` and `-1`. `System.in.read()` is a valid operand for `!=` because `System.in.read()` is an expression and evaluates to an integer. So `System.in.read() != -1` compares two integers, the value returned by `System.in.read()` and `-1`. The value returned by `!=` is either `true` or `false` depending on the outcome of the comparison.

As you can see, Java allows you to construct compound expressions and statements from various smaller expressions as long as the data types required by one part of the expression match the data types of the other. Also, as you may have concluded from the previous example, the order in which a compound expression is evaluated matters!

Take for example this compound expression:

```
x * y * z
```

In this particular example, the order in which the expression is evaluated is unimportant because the results of the multiplication operations are independent of order—the outcome is always the same regardless of the order in which you apply the multiplications. However, this is not true of all expressions. For

example, the following expression gives different results depending on whether you perform the addition or the division operation first:

```
x + y / 100
```

You can direct the Java compiler to evaluate an expression in a specified order with balanced parentheses (and). For example, to make the previous statement unambiguous, you could write (x + y)/ 100.

If you don't explicitly tell the compiler the order in which you want operations to be performed, it decides based on the *precedence* assigned to the operators and other elements in use within the expression. Operators with a higher precedence get evaluated first. For example, the division operator has a higher precedence than the addition operator. Therefore, in the compound expression shown previously, x + y / 100, the compiler evaluates y / 100 first. Thus

```
x + y / 100
```

is equivalent to

```
x + (y / 100)
```

To make your code easier to read and maintain you should be explicit and indicate with parentheses which operators should be evaluated first.

The table, <u>Operator Precedence in Java</u> (page 800), shows the precedence assigned to Java's operators. The operators in this table are listed in precedence order: the higher in the table an operator appears, the higher its precedence. Operators with higher precedence are evaluated before operators with a lower precedence. Operators on the same line have equal precedence.

Control Flow Statements

The character-counting program uses a `while` statement to loop through all the characters of the input source and count them.

```
class Count {
    public static void main(String[] args)
        throws java.io.IOException
    {
        int count = 0;

        while (System.in.read() != -1)
```

```
        count++;
    System.out.println("Input has " + count + " chars.");
    }
}
```

Generally speaking, a `while` statement performs some action *while* a certain condition remains true. The general syntax of the `while` statement is:

```
while (expression)
    statement
```

That is, while *expression* is true, do *statement*. In the character-counting application, while the `read` method returns a value that is *not* -1, the program increments `count`.

statement can be one statement as shown in the character-counting example, or it can be a statement block. A statement block is a series of legal Java statements contained within curly brackets ({ and }). For example, suppose that in addition to incrementing `count` within the `while` loop, you also wanted to print the count each time a character was read. You could write the following `while` loop instead:

```
while (System.in.read() != -1) {
    count++;
    System.out.println("Read a character. Count = " + count);
}
```

By convention, the opening curly bracket is at the end of the same line as the `while` statement and the closing curly bracket begins a new line aligned with the `while` as shown.

Statements such as the `while` statement are control flow statements which determine the order in which other statements are executed. Besides `while`, the Java language supports several other control flow statements, including:

Statement	Keyword
decision making	`if-else, switch-case`
loop	`for, while, do-while`
exception	`try-catch-finally, throw`
miscellaneous	`break, continue, label:, return`

> **Note:** Although `goto` is a reserved word, currently the Java language does not support the `goto` statement. Use <u>Branching Statements</u> (page 67) instead.

The `if-else` Statement

Java's `if-else` statement provides your programs with the ability to selectively execute other statements based on some criteria. For example, suppose that your program prints debugging information based on the value of some boolean variable named DEBUG. If DEBUG is set to `true`, then your program prints debugging information such as the value of a variable x. Otherwise, your program proceeds normally. A segment of code to implement this might look like this:

```
if (DEBUG)
    System.out.println("DEBUG: x = " + x);
```

This is the simplest version of the `if` statement: the statement governed by the `if` statement is executed if some condition is true. Generally, the simple form of `if` can be written like this:

```
if (expression)
    statement
```

So, what if you want to execute a different set of statements if *expression* is false? Well, you can use the `else` statement for that. Consider another example. Suppose that your program needs to perform different actions depending on whether the user clicks on the OK button or the Cancel button in an alert window. Your program could do this using an `if` statement:

```
// response is either OK or CANCEL depending
// on the button that the user pressed

if (response == OK) {

// code to perform OK action

} else {

// code to perform Cancel action

}
```

This particular use of the else statement is the catch-all form. The else block is executed if the if part is false. There is another form of the else statement, else if, which executes a statement based on another expression. For example, suppose that you write a program that assigns grades based on the value of a test score: an A for a score of 90% or above, a B for a score of 80% or above, and so on. You can use an if statement with a series of companion else if statements, and an else to write this code:

```java
int testscore;
char grade;

if (testscore >= 90) {
    grade = 'A';
} else if (testscore >= 80) {
    grade = 'B';
} else if (testscore >= 70) {
    grade = 'C';
} else if (testscore >= 60) {
    grade = 'D';
} else {
    grade = 'F';
}
```

An if statement can have any number of companion else if statements, but only one else. You may have noticed that some values of testscore could satisfy more than one of the expressions in the compound if statement. For example, a score of 76 evaluates to true for two of the expressions in the if statement: testscore >= 70 and testscore >= 60. However, as the runtime system processes a compound if statement such as this one, once one of the conditions is satisfied (76 >= 70), the appropriate statements are executed (grade = 'C';), and control passes out of the if statement without evaluating the remaining conditions.

The switch Statement

Use the switch statement to conditionally perform statements based on some expression. For example, suppose that your program contains an integer named month whose value indicates the month in some date. Suppose also that you want to display the name of the month based on its integer equivalent. Use Java's switch statement to perform this feat:

```java
int month;
. . .
switch (month) {
```

```
case 1:  System.out.println("January"); break;
case 2:  System.out.println("February"); break;
case 3:  System.out.println("March"); break;
case 4:  System.out.println("April"); break;
case 5:  System.out.println("May"); break;
case 6:  System.out.println("June"); break;
case 7:  System.out.println("July"); break;
case 8:  System.out.println("August"); break;
case 9:  System.out.println("September"); break;
case 10: System.out.println("October"); break;
case 11: System.out.println("November"); break;
case 12: System.out.println("December"); break;
}
```

The `switch` statement evaluates its expression, in this case, the value of `month`, and executes the appropriate `case` statement. Of course, you could implement this as an `if` statement:

```
int month;
. . .
if (month == 1) {
    System.out.println("January");
} else if (month == 2) {
    System.out.println("February");
. . .
// you get the idea
. . .
```

Deciding whether to use an `if` statement or a `switch` statement is a judgment call. You can decide which to use based on readability and other factors. Each `case` statement must be unique and the value provided to each `case` statement must be of the same data type as the data type returned by the expression provided to the `switch` statement.

Another point of interest in the `switch` statement are the `break` statements after each `case`. The `break` statements cause control to break out of the `switch` and continue with the first statement following the `switch` statement. The `break` statements are necessary because `case` statements fall through. That is, without an explicit `break` statement, control will flow sequentially through subsequent `case` statements. In the previous example, you don't want control to flow from one `case` to the next, so you have to put in `break` statements. However, there are certain scenarios when you do want control to proceed sequentially through `case` statements. Like in the following Java code that computes the number of days in a month according to the old rhyme that starts "Thirty days hath September...":

```
int month;
int numDays;
. . .
switch (month) {
  case 1:
  case 3:
  case 5:
  case 7:
  case 8:
  case 10:
  case 12:
    numDays = 31;
    break;
  case 4:
  case 6:
  case 9:
  case 11:
    numDays = 30;
    break;
  case 2:
    if ( ((year % 4 == 0) && (year % 100 != 0)) ||
                          (year % 400 == 0) )
        numDays = 29;
    else
        numDays = 28;
    break;
}
```

You can use a default statement at the end of the switch to handle all values
that aren't explicitly handled by one of the case statements.

```
int month;
. . .
switch (month) {
  case 1:  System.out.println("January"); break;
  case 2:  System.out.println("February"); break;
  case 3:  System.out.println("March"); break;
  case 4:  System.out.println("April"); break;
  case 5:  System.out.println("May"); break;
  case 6:  System.out.println("June"); break;
  case 7:  System.out.println("July"); break;
  case 8:  System.out.println("August"); break;
  case 9:  System.out.println("September"); break;
  case 10: System.out.println("October"); break;
  case 11: System.out.println("November"); break;
  case 12: System.out.println("December"); break;
  default: System.out.println("Hey, that's not a valid month!");
    break;
}
```

Loop Statements

You were introduced to Java's <u>while</u> statement previously (page 60). Java has two other looping constructs that you can use in your programs: the for loop and the do-while loop.

Use the for loop when you know the constraints of the loop: its initialization instruction, termination criteria, and increment instruction. For example, for loops are often used to iterate over the elements in an array, or the characters in a String.

```
// a is an array of some kind
. . .
int i;
int length = a.length;
for (i = 0; i < length; i++) {
    . . .
    // do something to the ith element of a
    . . .
}
```

You know when writing the program that you want to start at the beginning of the array, stop at the end, and hit every element. Thus the for statement is a good choice. The general form of the for statement can be expressed like this:

```
for (initialization; termination; increment)
    statements
```

initialization is a statement that initializes the loop—it is executed once at the beginning of the loop. *termination* is an expression that determines when to terminate the loop. This expression is evaluated at the top of each iteration of the loop. When the expression evaluates to false, the for loop terminates. Finally, *increment* is an expression that gets invoked for each iteration through the loop. Any (or all) of these components can be empty statements. An empty statement is represented by a single semicolon by itself.

Java provides another loop, the do-while loop, which is similar to the while loop you met earlier except that the expression is evaluated at the bottom of the loop:

```
do {
    statements
} while (booleanExpression);
```

The do-while statement is a less common loop construct in programming but does have its uses. The do-while loop is convenient to use when the statements within the loop must be executed at least once. For example, when reading information from a file, you always have to read at least one character:

```
int c;
InputStream in;
. . .
do {
    c = in.read();
    . . .
} while (c != -1);
```

Exception Handling Statements

When an error occurs within a Java method, the method can use the `throw` statement to throw an exception indicating to its caller that an error occurred and the type of error that occurred. The calling method can use the `try`, `catch`, and `finally` statements to catch and handle the exception. See <u>Handling Errors Using Exceptions</u> (page 253) for information about throwing and handling exceptions.

Branching Statements

You saw the `break` statement used in the `switch` statement earlier. As noted there, `break` causes the flow of control to jump to the statement immediately following the current statement.

Another form of the `break` statement causes flow of control to jump to a labeled statement. You label a statement by placing a legal Java identifier (the label) followed by a colon (:) before the statement:

```
breakToHere: someJavaStatement
```

To jump to the statement labeled `breakToHere`, use the following form of the `break` statement:

```
break breakToHere;
```

Labeled breaks are an alternative to the `goto` statement, which is not supported by the Java language.

Use the `continue` statement within loops to jump from the current statement back to the top of the loop or to a labeled statement. Consider this implementation of the `String` class's `indexOf` method, which uses the form of `continue` that continues to a labeled statement:

```
public int indexOf(String str, int fromIndex) {
    char[] v1 = value;
    char[] v2 = str.value;
    int max = offset + (count - str.count);
  test:
    for (int i = offset + ((fromIndex < 0) ? 0 : fromIndex);
                        i <= max ; i++) {
```

```
int n = str.count;
        int j = i;
        int k = str.offset;
        while (n-- != 0) {
            if (v1[j++] != v2[k++]) {
                continue test;
            }
        }
        return i - offset;
    }
    return -1;
}
```

Note: The `continue` statement can be called only from within a loop.

The last of Java's branching statements is the `return` statement. Use `return` to exit from the current method and jump back to the statement within the calling method that follows the original method call. There are two forms of `return`: one that returns a value and one that doesn't. To return a value, simply put the value, or an expression that calculates the value, after the `return` keyword:

```
return ++count;
```

The value returned by the `return` statement must match the type of method's declared return value.

When a method is declared `void`, use the form of `return` that doesn't return a value:

```
return;
```

Arrays and Strings

Like other programming languages, Java allows you to collect and manage multiple values through an array object. You manage data comprised of multiple characters through a `String` object.

Arrays

The character-counting program declares an array as a parameter to the `main` method but never uses it. This section will show you what you need to know to create and use arrays in your Java programs.

As for other variables, before you can use an array you must first declare it. Again, as for other variables, a declaration of an array has two primary components: the array type and the array name. The array type includes the data type of the elements contained within the array. For example, the data type for an array that contains all integer elements is array of integers. You cannot have a generic array—the data type of its elements must be identified when the array is declared. Here's a declaration for an array of integers:

```
int[] arrayOfInts;
```

The `int[]` part of the declaration indicates that `arrayOfInts` is an array of integers. The declaration does not allocate any memory to contain the array elements.

If your program attempts to assign or access any values to any elements of `arrayOfInts` before memory for it has been allocated, the compiler prints an error similar to the following error message and refuses to compile your program:

```
testing.java:64: Variable arrayOfInts may not have been
initialized.
```

To allocate memory for the elements of the array, you must instantiate the array. Do this using Java's `new` operator. Actually, the steps you take to create an array are similar to the steps you take to create an object from a class: declaration, instantiation, and initialization. You can learn more about creating objects in the **Objects, Classes, and Interfaces** (page 77) lesson. In particular, look at the Creating Objects (page 78) section.

The following statement allocates enough memory for `arrayOfInts` to contain ten integer elements.

```
int[] arrayOfInts = new int[10]
```

In general, when creating an array, use the `new` operator, the data type of the array elements, and the number of elements desired enclosed within square brackets [and].

```
elementType[] arrayName = new elementType[arraySize]
```

Now that some memory has been allocated for your array, you can assign values to its elements and retrieve those values:

```
for (int j = 0; j < arrayOfInts.length; j++) {
    arrayOfInts[j] = j;
```

```
    System.out.println("[j] = " + arrayOfInts[j]);
}
```

As you can see from this example, to reference an array element, append square brackets to the array name. Between the square brackets indicate (either with a variable or some other expression) the index of the element you want to access. Note that in Java, array indices begin at 0 and end at the array length minus one.

There's another interesting element (so to speak) in the small code sample above. The `for` loop iterates through each element of `arrayOfInts`, assigning values to its elements and printing out those values. Note the use of `array-OfInts.length` to retrieve the current length of the array. `length` is a property provided for all Java arrays.

Arrays can contain any legal Java data type including reference types such as objects or other arrays. For example, the following declares an array of ten `String` objects.

```
String[] arrayOfStrings = new String[10];
```

The elements in this array are reference types, that is, each element contains a reference to a `String` object. At this point, enough memory has been allocated to contain the `String` references, but no memory has been allocated for the `String` objects themselves. If you attempt to access one of the `arrayOfStrings` elements at this point, you will get a `NullPointerException` because the array is empty and contains no `String` objects. This is often a source of some confusion for programmers new to the Java language. You have to allocate the actual `String` objects separately:

```
for (int i = 0; i < arrayOfStrings.length; i++) {
    arrayOfStrings[i] = new String("Hello " + i);
}
```

Strings

A sequence of character data is called a string and is implemented in the Java environment by the <u>String</u>[1] class (a member of the `java.lang` package). The character-counting program uses Strings in two different places. The first is in the definition of the `main` method:

```
String[] args
```

---

[1] http://java.sun.com/products/JDK/CurrentRelease/api/java.lang.String.html

This statement explicitly declares an array named `args` that contains `String` objects. The empty brackets indicate that the length of the array is unknown at compilation time because the array is passed in at run time.

The second use of `String` objects in the example program are these two uses of *literal strings* (series of characters between double quotation marks):

```
"Input has "
    . . .
" chars."
```

The program implicitly allocates two `String` objects, one for each of the two literal strings shown previously.

String objects are immutable—they cannot be changed once they've been created. The `java.lang` package provides a different class, `StringBuffer`, which you can use to create and manipulate character data on the fly. The String and StringBuffer Classes (page 215) is a complete lesson on the use of both the `String` and `StringBuffer` classes.

String Concatenation

Java lets you concatenate strings together easily using the + operator. The example program uses this feature of the Java language to print its output. The following code snippet concatenates three strings together to produce its output:

```
"Input has " + count + " chars."
```

Two of the strings concatenated together are literal strings: `"Input has "` and `" chars."` The third string—the one in the middle—is actually an integer that first gets converted to a string and then is concatenated to the others.

Other Features of the Character-Counting Application

Here, to remind you, is the character-counting program in its entirety:

```
class Count {
    public static void main(String[] args)
        throws java.io.IOException
    {
```

```
        int count = 0;

        while (System.in.read() != -1)
            count++;
        System.out.println("Input has " + count + " chars.");
    }
}
```

The parts shown in bold are features of the Java language or the Java environment that have not yet been explained in this lesson. See the following sections for a brief introduction to the concepts highlighted in the code sample. Each section will direct you to the appropriate lesson within the tutorial that discusses each topic in more detail.

The `main` Method

As you learned in The `main` Method (page 8) in The "Hello World" Application (page 3), the runtime system executes a Java program by calling the application's `main` method. The `main` method then calls all the other methods required to run your application.

The `main` method in the character-counting example initializes the `count` variable, then stops at `System.in.read` and waits for the user to enter characters. When the user finishes typing, the program displays the number of characters typed.

Accepting a Filename on the Command Line

Let's modify the program to accept a command-line argument and have it count the characters in the file specified on the command line. Compare this version (page 585) of the character-counting program with the original version (page 585) listed above.

```
import java.io.*;

class CountFile {
    public static void main(String[] args)
        throws java.io.IOException,
        java.io.FileNotFoundException
    {
        int count = 0;
        InputStream is;
        String filename;

        if (args.length >= 1) {
            is = new FileInputStream(args[0]);
```

```
            filename = args[0];
    } else {
        is = System.in;
        filename = "Input";
    }

    while (is.read() != -1)
        count++;

    System.out.println(filename + " has " + count +
                            " chars.");
    }
}
```

In this implementation of the character-counting program, if the user specifies a name on the command line, then the application counts the characters in the specified file. Otherwise, the application acts as it did before and reads from the standard input stream. Now, run the new version of the program on a text file and specify the filename on the command line. The following platform-specific instructions run the CountFile application on a text file named `testing` (page 586) that contains this text:

```
Now is the time for all good men to come to the aid of their
country.
```

Platform-Specific Details: Running a Java Application with Command-Line Arguments Using the JDK

UNIX:
> `% java CountFile testing`
> testing has 70 chars.

DOS shell (Windows 95/NT):
> `C:\> java CountFile testing`
> testing has 71 chars.

MacOS:
> Double click the `CountFile.class` file or drop it on the Java Runner application.. The program displays a window prompting you for command-line arguments. Type in the name of the file, `testing`, and click the OK button.

For information about command-line arguments, refer to the **Setting Program Attributes** (page 227) lesson.

Introducing Exceptions

The declaration for the `main` method in the character-counting program has an interesting clause shown here in bold:

```
public static void main(String[] args)
    throws java.io.IOException
```

This clause specifies that the `main` method can throw an exception called `java.io.IOException`. So, what's an exception? An *exception* is an event that occurs during the execution of a program that prevents the continuation of the normal flow of instructions. For example, the following code sample is invalid because it tries to divide 7 by 0, which is an undefined operation.

```
int x = 0;
int y = 7;
System.out.println("answer = " + y/x);
```

The divide by zero operation is an exception because it prevents the code from continuing. Different computer systems handle exceptions in different ways, some more elegantly than others. In Java, when an error occurs, such as the divide by zero above, the program throws an exception. You can catch exceptions and try to handle them within a special code segment known as an *exception handler*.

In Java, a method must specify the checked (non-runtime) exceptions, if any, it can throw. This rule applies to the `main` method in our example, thus the `throws` clause in the method's signature.

You may have noticed that the `main` method does not throw any exceptions directly. But it can throw a `java.io.IOException` indirectly through its call to `System.in.read`.

This has been a brief introduction to exceptions in Java. For a complete explanation about throwing, catching, and specifying exceptions refer to **Handling Errors Using Exceptions** (page 253).

The Standard Input and Output Streams

The character-counting program uses the following statement to read characters from its input source:

```
System.in.read()
```

The <u>System</u> class[1] is a member of the `java.lang` package and provides access to system functionality such as standard input and output, copying arrays, get-

---

[1] http://java.sun.com/products/JDK/CurrentRelease/api/java.lang.System.html

ting the current date and time, and properties. The `while` loop uses the `System` class's standard input stream to read characters typed in by the user at the keyboard.

In addition, the character-counting program uses the `System` class's standard output stream to display its output:

```
System.out.println(. . .);
```

`System.in` is a class variable that is a reference to an object implementing the *standard input stream*. Similarly, `System.out` is a class variable that is a reference to an object implementing the *standard output stream*. In addition to `System.in` and `System.out`, the `System` class provides a third stream, referred to by `System.err`, that implements the standard error stream.

The standard I/O streams are a C library concept that has been assimilated into the Java language. Simply put, a stream is a flowing sequence of characters. The standard input stream is a stream that reads characters from the keyboard. The standard input stream is a convenient place for an old-fashioned text-based application to get input from the user.

The standard output stream is a stream that writes its contents to the display. The standard output stream is a convenient place for an old-fashioned text-based application to display its output. And finally, a Java program uses the standard error stream to display error messages to the user.

Reading from the Standard Input Stream

The `System.in.read` method reads a single character and returns either the character that was read or, if there are no more characters to be read, it returns -1. As mentioned before, when a program reads from the standard input stream, the program blocks and waits for you to type something in. The program continues to wait for input until you give it some indication that the input is complete. To indicate to any program that reads from the standard input stream that you have finished entering characters, type the end-of-input character appropriate for your system at the beginning of a new line. When the character-counting program receives an end-of-input character, the loop terminates and the program displays the number of characters you typed.

Writing to Standard Output

`System.out.println` displays its `String` argument followed by a new line. `println` has a companion method `print` that displays its argument with no trailing new line. This section introduced you to the standard input and output

streams provided by the System class. The System class is described in more detail in **Using System Resources** (page 237). In addition, you can find general information about input and output streams in **Input and Output Streams** (page 325).

5

Objects, Classes, and Interfaces

IN the lesson titled **Object-Oriented Programming Concepts: A Primer** (page 31) you learned the concepts behind object-oriented programming. Now that you have a conceptual understanding of object-oriented programming, it's time to get to work and put those concepts to practical use in Java. This lesson shows you how to use the object-oriented paradigms of the Java language.

This lesson will show you how to create and destroy objects, how to create and subclass classes, how to write methods, how to create and use interfaces, and how to create and use packages. This lesson covers everything from how to protect the innards of an object from other objects, to writing abstract classes and methods, to the use of the root of the Java object hierarchy—the Object class.

As you learned in Object-Oriented Programming Concepts: A Primer (page 31), an object is a software module that has state and behavior. An object's state is contained in its member variables and its behavior is implemented through its methods.

Typically, Java programs that you write will create many objects from prototypes known as classes. These objects interact with one another by sending each other messages. The result of a message is a method invocation which performs some action or modifies the state of the receiving object. Through these object interactions, your Java program can implement a graphical user interface, run an animation, or send and receive information over the network. Once an object has completed the work for which it was created, it is garbage collected and its resources recycled for the use of other objects.

The first three sections in this lesson are listed below. They describe the typical life cycle of an object: 1) creation, 2) use, and 3) destruction.

A Java object is an *instance of a class*. Frequently, we say that an object's class is the object's *type*. The Java environment comes with many classes that you can use in your programs. Or you can write your own. The section titled Creating Classes (page 85) shows you how to write your own classes, including how to declare member variables and write methods.

In Java you can define one class as a subclass of another. This ability to sub-class one class from another and inherit its state and behavior is one of object-oriented programming's most powerful paradigms. Inheritance provides a powerful and natural mechanism for organizing and structuring software programs. The most general classes appear higher in the class hierarchy and the most specific classes appear lower in the class hierarchy. In addition, because classes inherit state and behavior from their superclasses, you don't have to write that code again—inheritance allows you to reuse code over and over again in each subclass you create. Subclasses, Superclasses, and Inheritance (page 119) shows you how to create, design, and implement subclasses.

An *interface* is a collection of method definitions (without implementations) and constant values. Use interfaces to define a protocol of behavior that can be implemented by any class anywhere in the class hierarchy. Creating and Using Interfaces (page 130) describes interfaces in Java.

Once you've created your classes and interfaces, you can group them together into a *package*, which is simply a collection of related classes and interfaces. The Java development environment provides several packages of classes that you can use in your Java programs. You can also create your own. Creating and Using Packages (page 135) describes how to create a package and manage your classes and interfaces using packages. In addition, this section provides a tour of the packages that ship with the Java development environment. You can use the package tour (page 140) as a launching point into subsequent lessons within this tutorial that cover the classes in each package.

Creating Objects

In Java, you create an object by creating an *instance of a class* or, in other words, *instantiating a class*. You will learn how to create a class in Creating Classes (page 85). Until then, the examples contained herein create objects from classes that already exist in the Java environment.

Often, you will see a Java object created with a statement like this one:

```
Date today = new Date();
```

This statement creates a new `Date` object (`Date` is a class in the `java.util` package). This single statement actually performs three actions: declaration, instantiation, and initialization. `Date today` is a variable declaration which simply declares to the compiler that the name `today` will be used to refer to an object whose type is `Date`. The `new` operator instantiates the `Date` class (thereby creating a new `Date` object) and `Date()` initializes the object.

Declaring an Object

While the declaration of an object is not a necessary part of object creation, object declarations often appear on the same line as the creation of an object. Like other variable declarations, object declarations can appear alone like this:

```
Date today;
```

Either way, declaring a variable to hold an object is just like declaring a variable to hold a value of primitive type:

```
type name
```

where *type* is the data type of the object and *name* is the name to be used for the object. In Java, classes and interfaces are just like a data type. So *type* can be the name of a class such as the `Date` class or the name of an interface. Variables and Data Types (page 46) in the previous lesson discussed variable declarations in detail.

Declarations notify the compiler that you will be using *name* to refer to a variable whose type is *type*. *Declarations do not create new objects.* `Date today` does not create a new `Date` object, just a variable named `today` to hold a `Date` object. To instantiate the `Date` class or any other class, use the `new` operator.

Instantiating an Object

The `new` operator instantiates a class by allocating memory for a new object of that type. `new` requires a single argument: a call to a constructor method. Constructor methods are special methods provided by each Java class that are responsible for initializing new objects of that type. The `new` operator creates the object, and the constructor initializes it.

Here's an example of using the `new` operator to create a `Rectangle` object (`Rectangle` is a class in the `java.awt` package):

```
new Rectangle(0, 0, 100, 200);
```

In the example, `Rectangle(0, 0, 100, 200)` is a call to a constructor for the `Rectangle` class.

The `new` operator returns a reference to the newly created object. This reference can be assigned to a variable of the appropriate type as in the following Java statement.

```
Rectangle rect = new Rectangle(0, 0, 100, 200);
```

(Recall from <u>Variables and Data Types</u> (page 46) that a class essentially defines a new reference data type. So, `Rectangle` can be used as a data type in your Java programs. The value of any variable whose data type is a reference type, such as `rect`, is a reference (a pointer in other terminology) to the actual value or set of values represented by the variable. In this tutorial, a reference may also be called an object reference or an array reference depending on the data that the reference is referring to.)

Initializing an Object

As mentioned previously, classes provide constructor methods to initialize a new object of that type. A class may provide multiple constructors to perform different kinds of initialization on new objects. When looking at the implementation for a class, you can recognize the constructors because they have the same name as the class and have no return type. Recall the creation of the `Date` object used at the beginning of this section. The `Date` constructor used there doesn't take any arguments:

```
Date()
```

A constructor that takes no arguments, such as the one shown, is known as the *default constructor*. Like `Date`, most classes have at least one constructor, the default constructor.

If a class has multiple constructors, they all have the same name but a different number or type of arguments. Each constructor initializes the new object in a different way. Besides the default constructor used to initialize a new `Date` object earlier, the `Date` class provides another constructor that initializes the new `Date` with a year, month, and day:

```
Date myBirthday = new Date(1963, 8, 30);
```

The compiler can differentiate the constructors through the type and number of the arguments.

This section talked about how to use a constructor. <u>Constructors</u> (page 115) later in this lesson explains how to write constructor methods for your classes.

Using Objects

Once you've created an object, you will probably want to use it for something. Suppose, for example, that after creating a new `Rectangle` object, you want to move it to a different location. Say, the rectangle is an object in a drawing program and the user just clicked the mouse over the rectangle and dragged it to a new location.

The `Rectangle` class provides two equivalent ways to move the rectangle:

1. Manipulate the object's x, y variables directly.
2. Call the move method.

Option 2 is often considered "more object-oriented" and safer because you manipulate the object's variables indirectly through its protective layer of methods rather than twiddling directly with them. Manipulating an object's variables directly is often considered error-prone; you could potentially put the object into an inconsistent state. However, a class would not (and should not) make its variables available for direct manipulation by other objects if it were possible for those manipulations to put the object in an inconsistent state. Java provides a mechanism whereby classes can restrict or allow access to its variables and methods by objects of another type. This section discusses calling methods and manipulating variables that have been made accessible to other classes. To learn more about controlling access to members, refer to <u>Controlling Access to Members of a Class</u> (page 105).

`Rectangle`'s x and y variables are accessible to other classes so we can assume that manipulating a `Rectangle`'s x and y variables directly is safe.

Referencing an Object's Variables

First, let's focus on how to inspect and modify the `Rectangle`'s position by modifying its x and y variables directly. The next section will show you how to move the rectangle by calling the move method.

To access an object's variables, simply append the variable name to an object reference with an intervening period (.).

```
objectReference.variable
```

Suppose you have a rectangle named `rect` in your program. You can access its x and y variables with `rect.x` and `rect.y`, respectively. Now that you have a name for `rect`'s variables, you can use those names in Java statements and expressions as though they were the names of regular variables. To move the rectangle a new location you would write:

```
rect.x = 15;        // change x position
rect.y = 37;        // change y position
```

The Rectangle class has two other variables—width and height—that are accessible to objects outside the Rectangle. You can use the same notation to access them: rect.width and rect.height. So you could calculate the rectangle's area using this statement:

```
area = rect.height * rect.width;
```

When you access a variable through an object, you are referencing that particular object's variables. If bob is also a rectangle with a different height and width than rect, then the following instruction, which calculates the area of the rectangle named bob, will give a different result than the previous instruction, which calculates the area of the rectangle named rect:

```
area = bob.height * bob.width;
```

Note that the first part of the name of an object's variables (the *objectReference* in *objectReference.variable*) must be a reference to an object. While you can use a variable name here, you can also use any expression that returns an object reference. Recall that the new operator returns a reference to an object. So you could use the value returned from new to access a new object's variables:

```
height = new Rectangle().height;
```

Calling an Object's Methods

Calling an object's method is similar to getting an object's variable. To call an object's method, simply append the method name to an object reference with an intervening period (.), and provide any arguments to the method within enclosing parentheses. If the method does not require any arguments, just use empty parentheses.

```
objectReference.methodName(argumentList);
    or
objectReference.methodName();
```

Let's see what this means in terms of moving the rectangle. To move rect to a new location using its move method, write the following Java statement:

```
rect.move(15, 37);
```

This Java statement calls `rect`'s move method with two integer parameters, 15 and 37. This statement has the effect of moving the `rect` object by modifying its x and y variables and is equivalent to the assignment statements used previously:

```
rect.x = 15;
rect.y = 37;
```

If you want to move a different rectangle, the one named bob, to a new location you write:

```
bob.move(244, 47);
```

As you see from these examples, method calls are directed at a specific object; the object specified in the method call is the object that responds to the instruction. Method calls are also known as *messages*. Like real-world messages, object messages must be addressed to a particular recipient. You get different results depending on which object is the recipient of the message. In the example above, when you send the object named `rect` a move message, `rect` moves to the new location. When you send the object named bob a move message, bob moves. Very different results. To understand messages more fully, please see What Are Messages? (page 35)

A method call is an expression (see Expressions (page 58) for more information) and evaluates to some value. The value of a method call is its return value, if it has one. You will often wish to assign the return value of a method to a variable or use the method call within the scope of another expression or statement. The move method doesn't return a value (it's declared `void`). However, Rectangle's `inside` method does. The `inside` method takes an x, y coordinate and returns `true` if that point lies within the rectangle. So you can use the `inside` method to do something special if some point, say the current mouse location, were inside the rectangle:

```
if (rect.inside(mouse.x, mouse.y)) {
    . . .
        // mouse is in the rectangle
    . . .
} else {
    . . .
        // mouse is outside of the rectangle
    . . .
}
```

Remember that the method call is a message to the named object. In this case, the object named is the `Rectangle` named `rect`. Asking `rect` if the mouse cursor

location represented by `mouse.x` and `mouse.y` is in it is a message to `rect`—the named object:

```
rect.inside(mouse.x, mouse.y)
```

You will likely get a different response if you send the same message to bob.

As stated before, the *objectReference* in the method call *objectReference.method()* must be an object reference. While you can use a variable name here, you can also use any expression that returns an object reference. Recall that the new operator returns a reference to an object. You can use the value returned from new to call a new object's methods:

```
new Rectangle(0, 0, 100, 50).equals(anotherRect)
```

The expression new `Rectangle(0, 0, 100, 50)` evaluates to an object reference that refers to a `Rectangle` object. As you can see, you can use the dot notation to call the new rectangle's `equals` method to determine if the new rectangle is equal to the one specified in `equals`'s argument list.

Cleaning Up Unused Objects

Many other object-oriented languages require that you keep track of all the objects you create and that you destroy them when they are no longer needed. Writing code to manage memory in this way is tedious and often error-prone. Java allows you to create as many objects as you want (limited of course to whatever your system can handle), but you never have to destroy them. The Java runtime environment deletes objects when it determines that they are no longer being used. This process is known as *garbage collection*.

An object is eligible for garbage collection when there are no more references to that object. References that are held in a variable are naturally dropped when the variable goes out of scope. Or you can explicitly drop an object reference by setting the value of a variable whose data type is a reference type to `null`.

The Garbage Collector

The Java runtime environment has a garbage collector that periodically frees the memory used by objects that are no longer needed. The Java garbage collector is a *mark-sweep* garbage collector that scans Java's dynamic memory areas for objects, marking those that are referenced. After all possible paths to objects are investigated, those objects that are not marked (that is, not referenced) are known to be garbage and are collected. (A more complete description of Java's garbage collection algorithm might be "a compacting, mark-sweep collector with some conservative scanning.")

The garbage collector runs in a low-priority thread and runs both synchronously and asynchronously depending on the situation and the system on which Java is running.

The garbage collector runs *synchronously* when the system runs out of memory or in response to a request from a Java program. Your Java program can ask the garbage collector to run at any time by calling `System.gc`. <u>Forcing Finalization and Garbage Collection</u> (page 246) has more details.

Note: Asking the garbage collection to run does not guarantee that your objects will be garbage collected.

On systems that allow the Java runtime environment to note when a thread has begun and to interrupt another thread such as Windows 95/NT, the Java garbage collector runs *asynchronously* when the system is idle. As soon as another thread becomes active, the garbage collector is asked to get to a consistent state and then terminate.

Finalization

Before an object gets garbage collected, the garbage collector gives the object an opportunity to clean up after itself through a call to the object's `finalize` method. This process is known as *finalization.*

During finalization an object may wish to free system resources such as files and sockets or drop references to other objects so that they in turn become eligible for garbage collection.

The `finalize` method is a member of the `Object` class. A class must override the `finalize` method to perform any finalization necessary for objects of that type. <u>Writing a `finalize` Method</u> (page 118) later in this lesson shows you how to write a `finalize` method for your classes.

Creating Classes

Now that you know how to create, use, and destroy objects, it's time to learn how to write the classes from which objects can be created.

A class is a blueprint or prototype that you can use to create many objects. The implementation of a class is comprised of two components: the class declaration and the class body.

```
classDeclaration {
    classBody
}
```

The class declaration component declares the name of the class along with other attributes such as the class's superclass and whether the class is public, final, or abstract.

The class body follows the class declaration and is embedded within curly brackets { and }. The class body contains declarations for all instance variables and class variables (known collectively as member variables) for the class. In addition, the class body contains declarations and implementations for all instance methods and class methods (known collectively as methods) for the class.

A class's state is represented by its member variables. You declare a class's member variables in the body of the class. Typically, you declare a class's variables before you declare its methods, although this is not required.

```
classDeclaration {
    member variable declarations
    method declarations
}
```

Note: To declare variables that are members of a class, the declarations must be within the class body, but *not* within the body of a method. Variables declared within the body of a method are local to that method.

As you know, objects have behavior that is implemented by its methods. Other objects can ask an object to do something by invoking its methods. This section tells you everything you need to know about writing methods for your Java classes. For information about calling methods see Using Objects (page 81).

In Java, you define a class's methods in the body of the class for which the method implements some behavior. Typically, you declare a class's methods after its variables in the class body, although this is not required.

Member variables and methods are known collectively as *members*. When you declare a member of a Java class, you can allow or disallow other objects of other types access to that member through the use of *access specifiers*. Controlling Access to Members of a Class (page 105) shows you how.

A Java class can contain two different types of members: instance members and class members. Instance and Class Members (page 111) shows you how to declare both types of members and how to use them.

The Class Declaration

At minimum, a class declaration must contain the `class` keyword and the name of the class that you are defining. The simplest class declaration that you can write looks like this:

```
class NameOfClass {
    . . .
}
```

For example, the following code declares a new class named `ImaginaryNumber`:

```
class ImaginaryNumber {
    . . .
}
```

Class names must be a legal Java identifier and, by convention, begin with a capital letter. Often, a minimal class declaration such as this one is all you'll need. However, the class declaration can say more about the class. More specifically, within the class declaration you can:
- Declare what the class's superclass is.
- List the interfaces implemented by the class.
- Declare whether the class is public, abstract, or final.

Declaring a Class's Superclass

In Java, every class has a superclass. If you do not specify a superclass for your class, it is assumed to be the `Object` class (declared in `java.lang`). In the previous code example, the superclass of `ImaginaryNumber` is `Object` because the declaration did not explicitly declare it to be something else. For more information about the `Object` class, see The Object Class (page 128).

To specify an object's superclass explicitly, put the keyword `extends` plus the name of the superclass between the name of the class that you are declaring and the curly bracket that opens the class body, like this:

```
class NameOfClass extends SuperClassName {
    . . .
}
```

For example, suppose that you want the superclass of `ImaginaryNumber` to be the `Number` class rather than the `Object` class. You write the following statement:

```
class ImaginaryNumber extends Number {
    . . .
}
```

This explicitly declares that the `Number` class is the superclass of `ImaginaryNumber`. (The `Number` class is part of the `java.lang` package and is the base class for the `Integer`, `Float` and other subclasses.)

Declaring that `Number` is the superclass of `ImaginaryNumber` implicitly declares that `ImaginaryNumber` is the subclass of `Number`. A subclass inherits variables and methods from its superclass. Creating a subclass can be as simple as including the `extends` clause in your class declaration. However, you usually have to make other provisions in your code when subclassing a class, such as overriding methods. For more information about creating subclasses, see <u>Subclasses, Superclasses, and Inheritance</u> (page 119).

Listing the Interfaces Implemented by a Class

When declaring a class, you can specify which, if any, *interfaces* are implemented by the class. So, what's an interface? An interface declares a set of methods and constants without specifying the implementation for any of the methods. When a class claims to implement an interface, it's claiming to provide implementations for all of the methods declared in the interface.

To declare that your class implements one or more interfaces, use the keyword `implements` followed by a comma-delimited list of the interfaces implemented by your class. For example, imagine an interface named `Arithmetic` that defines methods named `add`, `subtract`, and so on. The `ImaginaryNumber` class can declare that it implements the `Arithmetic` interface like this:

```
class ImaginaryNumber extends Number implements Arithmetic {
    . . .
}
```

This guarantees that the `ImaginaryNumber` class provides implementations for `add`, `subtract` and other methods declared by the `Arithmetic` interface. If any implementations for methods defined in `Arithmetic` are missing from `ImaginaryNumber`, the compiler prints an error message and refuses to compile your program:

```
nothing.java:5: class ImaginaryNumber must be declared
abstract.
    It does not define java.lang.Number
    add(java.lang.Number, java.lang.Number) from
    interface Arithmetic.
class ImaginaryNumber extends Number implements Arithmetic {
    ^
```

By convention, the `implements` clause follows the `extends` clause if there is one.

Note that the method signatures of the methods declared in the `Arithmetic` interface must match the method signatures of the methods implemented in the

ImaginaryNumber class. This and other information about how to create and use interfaces is in Creating and Using Interfaces (page 130).

Public, Abstract, and Final Classes

You can use one of three modifiers in your class declarations to declare that your class is public, abstract, or final. The modifiers go before the class keyword and are optional.

The public modifier declares that the class can be used by objects outside the current package. By default, a class can only be used by other classes in the same package in which it is declared. You'd probably like other classes and objects to be able to use ImaginaryNumber, so it should be declared public:

```
public class ImaginaryNumber extends Number implements
    Arithmetic {
    . . .
}
```

By convention, when you use the public keyword in a class declaration, make it the very first item in the declaration.

The abstract modifier declares that your class is an abstract class. An abstract class may contain abstract methods (methods with no implementation). Abstract classes are intended to be subclassed and cannot be instantiated. For a discussion about when abstract classes are appropriate and how to write them, see Writing Abstract Classes and Methods (page 125).

When you use the final modifier, you declare that your class is final; that your class cannot be subclassed. There are (at least) two reasons why you might want to do this: security reasons and design reasons. For further discussion of final classes, see Writing Final Classes and Methods (page 124).

Note that it doesn't make sense for a class to be both final and abstract. In other words, a class that contains unimplemented methods cannot be final. Attempting to declare a class as both final and abstract results in a compile-time error.

Summary of a Class Declaration

In summary, a class declaration looks like this:

```
[ modifiers ] class ClassName [ extends SuperClassName ]
                [ implements InterfaceNames ] {
    . . .
}
```

The items between the square brackets, [and], are optional. A class declaration defines the following aspects of the class:

- *modifiers* declare whether the class is public, abstract, or final

- *ClassName* sets the name of the class you are declaring
- *SuperClassName* is the name of *ClassName*'s superclass
- *InterfaceNames* is a comma-delimited list of the interfaces implemented by *ClassName*

Only the class keyword and the class name are required in a class declaration. The other items are optional. If you do not make an explicit declaration for the optional items, the Java compiler assumes certain defaults: a non-final, non-public, non-abstract, subclass of Object that implements no interfaces.

The Class Body

Earlier you saw the general outline of a class implementation:

```
classDeclaration {
    classBody
}
```

The previous section, The Class Declaration (page 87), described all of the components of the class declaration. This section describes the general structure and organization of the class body.

The class body can contain two different sections: variable declarations and methods. A class's member variables represent a class's state and its methods implement the class's behavior. Within the class body you define *all* the member variables and methods supported by your class.

Typically, you declare a class's member variables first and then you provide the method declarations and implementations, although this is not required.

```
classDeclaration {
    memberVariableDeclarations
    methodDeclarations
}
```

Here's a small class that declares three member variables and a method:

```
class TicketOuttaHere {
    Float price;
    String destination;
    Date departureDate;
    void signMeUp(Float forPrice, String forDest,
                  Date forDate) {
        price = forPrice;
        destination = forDest;
        departureDate = forDate;
    }
}
```

For more information about how to declare member variables, see <u>Declaring Member Variables</u> (page 91). For more information about how to implement methods, see <u>Implementing Methods</u> (page 94).

In addition to the member variables and methods you explicitly declare within the class body, your class may also inherit some variables and methods from its superclass. For example, every class in the Java environment is a descendent (direct or indirect) of the `Object` class; that is, every class in Java inherits variables and methods from `Object`. The `Object` class defines the basic state and behavior that all objects must have such as the ability to compare oneself to another object, to convert to a string, to wait on a condition variable, to notify other objects that a condition variable has changed, and so on. Thus, as descendents of this class, *all* objects in the Java environment inherit this behavior from the `Object` class.

<u>Subclasses, Superclasses, and Inheritance</u> (page 119) contains more information about inheritance. <u>The `Object` Class</u> (page 128) talks about the features of the `Object` class.

Declaring Member Variables

At minimum, a member variable declaration has two components: the data type of the variable and its name.

```
type variableName;          // minimal member variable declaration
```

A minimal variable declaration is like the declarations that you write for variables used in other areas of your Java programs such as local variables or method parameters. The following code snippet declares an integer member variable named `anInteger` within the class `IntegerClass`.

```
class IntegerClass {
    int anInteger;
    . . .
    // define methods here
    . . .
}
```

Note that the member variable declaration appears within the body of the class implementation but not within a method. This positioning within the class body identifies that variable as a member variable.

Like other variables in Java, member variables must have a type. A variable's type determines the values that can be assigned to the variable and the operations that can be performed on it. You should already be familiar with data types in Java through your reading of <u>Variables and Data Types</u> (page 46) in the previous lesson.

A member variable's name can be any legal Java identifier and by convention, begins with a lowercase letter. (Class names typically begin with uppercase letters.) You cannot declare more than one member variable with the same name in the same class. However, a member variable and a method can have the same name. For example, the following code is legal:

```
class IntegerClass {
    int anInteger;
    int anInteger() {
    // a method with the same name as a member variable
        . . .
    }
}
```

Besides type and name, you can specify several other attributes for the member variable when you declare it, including whether other objects can access the variable, whether the variable is a class or instance variable, and whether the variable is a constant.

In short, a member variable declaration looks like this:

```
[accessSpecifier] [static] [final] [transient]
                        [volatile] type variableName
```

The items between the square brackets, [and], are optional. Italic items are to be replaced by keywords or names.

A member variable declaration defines the following aspects of the variable:

- *accessSpecifier* defines which other classes have access to the variable. You control access to methods using the same specifiers, so <u>Controlling Access to Members of a Class</u> (page 105) covers how you can control access to both member variables and methods.
- `static` indicates that the variable is a class member variable as opposed to an instance member variable. You also use `static` to declare class methods. <u>Instance and Class Members</u> (page 111) talks about declaring instance and class variables and writing instance and class methods.
- `final` indicates that the variable is a constant.
- `transient` variables are not part of the object's persistent state.
- `volatile` means that the variable is modified asynchronously.

Discussions about final, transient, and volatile variables follow.

Declaring Constants

To create a constant member variable in Java, use the keyword `final` in your variable declaration. The following variable declaration defines a constant

named AVOGADRO whose value is Avogadro's number (6.023×10^{23}) and cannot be changed:

```
class Avo {
    final double AVOGADRO = 6.023e23;
}
```

By convention, the names of constant values are spelled in uppercase letters. If your program ever tries to change a constant, the compiler displays an error message similar to the following, and refuses to compile your program.

```
AvogadroTest.java:5: Can't assign a value to a final variable:
AVOGADRO
```

Declaring Transient Variables

By default, member variables are part of the persistent state of the object. Member variables that are part of the persistent state of an object must be saved when the object is archived. You use the `transient` keyword to indicate to the Java virtual machine that the indicated variable is *not* part of the persistent state of the object.

The JDK 1.0 version of the Java runtime system ignores the `transient` keyword. Future releases of the Java system will use the `transient` keyword to implement various object archiving functions.

Like other variable modifiers in the Java system, use `transient` in a class or instance variable declaration like this:

```
class TransientExample {
    transient int hobo;
    . . .
}
```

This example declares an integer variable named `hobo` that is not part of the persistent state of the `TransientExample` class.

Declaring Volatile Variables

If your class contains a member variable that is modified asynchronously by concurrently running threads, use Java's `volatile` keyword to notify the Java runtime system of this.

The JDK 1.0 version of the Java runtime system ignores the `volatile` marker. However, future releases of the Java runtime system will use this information to ensure that the volatile variable is loaded from memory before each use, and stored to memory after each use, thereby ensuring that the value of the variable is consistent and coherent within each thread.

The following variable declaration is an example of how to declare that a variable can be modified asynchronously by concurrent threads:

```
class VolatileExample {
    volatile int counter;
    . . .
}
```

Implementing Methods

Similar to a class implementation, a method implementation consists of two parts: the method declaration and the method body.

```
methodDeclaration {
    methodBody
}
```

At minimum, a method declaration has a name and a return type indicating the data type of the value returned by the method:

```
returnType methodName() {
    . . .
}
```

This method declaration is very basic. Methods have many other attributes such as arguments, access control, and so on. This section will cover these topics as well as expand upon the features illustrated in the previous method declaration.

Perhaps the most commonly used optional components of a method declaration are *method parameters*. Similarly to functions in other programming languages, Java methods accept input from the caller through its parameters. Parameters provide information to a method from outside the scope of the method.

The method body is where all of the action of a method takes place; the method body contains all of the legal Java instructions that implement the method.

The Method Declaration

A method's declaration provides a lot of information about the method to the compiler, the runtime system, and to other classes and objects. Besides the name of the method, the method declaration carries information such as the return type of the method, the number and type of the arguments required by the method, and what other classes and objects can call the method.

While this may sound like writing a novel rather than simply declaring a method for a class, most method attributes can be declared implicitly. The only two required elements of a method declaration are the method name and the data type returned by the method. For example, the following code declares a method named isEmpty in the Stack class that returns a boolean value (true or false):

```
class Stack {
    . . .
    boolean isEmpty() {
        . . .
    }
}
```

Returning a Value from a Method. Java requires that a method declare the data type of the value that it returns. If a method does not return a value, it must be declared to return void.

Methods can return either values of primitive data types or values of reference data types. The isEmpty method in the Stack class returns a primitive data type, a boolean value:

```
class Stack {
    static final int STACK_EMPTY = -1;
    Object[] stackelements;
    int topelement = STACK_EMPTY;
    . . .
    boolean isEmpty() {
        if (topelement == STACK_EMPTY)
            return true;
        else
            return false;
    }
}
```

However, the pop method in the Stack class returns a reference data type: an object.

```
class Stack {
    static final int STACK_EMPTY = -1;
    Object[] stackelements;
    int topelement = STACK_EMPTY;
    . . .
    Object pop() {
        if (topelement == STACK_EMPTY)
            return null;
        else {
```

```
            return stackelements[topelement--];
        }
    }
}
```

Methods use the `return` operator to return a value. Any method that is *not* declared `void` must contain a `return` statement.

The data type of the value returned by the `return` statement must match the data type that the method claims to return; you can't return an `Object` type from a method declared to return an integer. When returning an object, the returned object's data type must be either a subclass of or the exact class indicated. When returning an interface type, the object returned must implement the specified interface.

A Method's Name.   A method name can be any legal Java identifier. There are three special cases to consider in regards to Java method names:

1. Java supports method name overloading so that multiple methods can share the same name. For example, suppose you were writing a class that can render various types of data (strings, integers, and so on) to its drawing area. You need to write a method that knows how to render each data type. In other languages, you have to think of a new name for each method: `drawString`, `drawInteger`, `drawFloat`, and so on. In Java, you can use the same name for all of the drawing methods but pass a different type of parameter to each method. So, in your data rendering class, you can declare three methods named `draw`, each of which takes a different type parameter:

```
class DataRenderer {
    void draw(String s) {
        . . .
    }
    void draw(int i) {
        . . .
    }
    void draw(float f) {
        . . .
    }
}
```

Note: The information within the parentheses in the method declaration are arguments to the method. Arguments are covered in the next section: Passing Information into a Method (page 98).

---

2. The methods are differentiated by the compiler by the number and type of the arguments passed into the method. Thus, draw(String s) and draw(int i) are distinct and unique methods. You cannot declare more than one method with the same signature: draw(String s) and draw(String t) are identical and will result in a compiler error. You should note that overloaded methods must return the same data type; so void draw(String s) and int draw(String t) declared in the same class produces a compile-time error.

3. Any method whose name is the same as its class is a *constructor* and has a special duty to perform. Constructors are used to initialize a new object of the class type. Constructors can be called only with Java's new operator. You learned how to create an object in Creating Objects (page 78). To learn how to write a constructor, see Constructors (page 115).

4. A class may override a method in its superclass. The overriding method must have the same name, return type, and parameter list as the method it overrides. Overriding Methods (page 122) will show you how to override the methods in your class's superclass.

Advanced Method Declaration Features. Besides the two required elements of a method declaration, a method declaration may contain other elements as well. These elements declare the arguments accepted by the method, whether the method is a class method, and so on.

All told, a method declaration looks like this:

```
[accessSpecifier] [static] [abstract] [final] [native]
        [synchronized] returnType methodName ([paramlist])
        [throws exceptionsList]
```

Each of these elements of a method declaration is covered somewhere in this tutorial. The first four bullet items in the following list are covered in this lesson.

The last three items in this list cover topics that either warrant their own lesson, or are already included in another lesson in a different part of this tutorial. If you check out some of that information, be sure to come back!

- You pass information into a method through its arguments. See the next section, Passing Information into a Method (page 98).
- Like variable declarations, a method declaration can use *access specifiers* to control whether other objects and classes in your program can call your method. See Controlling Access to Members of a Class (page 105).
- You can also specify whether the method is an instance method or a class method. Click here for Instance and Class Members (page 111).

- Your method may have to provide information about itself to subclasses, such as whether the method can be overridden or whether your class even provides an implementation for the method. See <u>Subclasses, Superclasses, and Inheritance</u> (page 119) for information about how subclassing your class can affect your method declarations.
- If your method throws any exceptions, your method declaration must indicate which exceptions it can throw. See **Handling Errors Using Exceptions** (page 253) for information. In particular, refer to the section <u>Specifying the Exceptions Thrown by a Method</u> (page 276)
- If you have a significant library of functions written in another language such as C, you may wish to preserve that investment and use those functions from Java. Methods implemented in a language other than Java are called *native methods* and must be declared as such within the method declaration. To learn how to integrate Java code with code written in other languages, see the **Integrating Native Methods into Java Programs** trail (page 541).
- Concurrently running threads often invoke methods that operate on the same data. These methods must be synchronized to ensure that the data remains in a consistent state throughout the life of the program. You can declare that a method must be synchronized with the synchronized keyword. Synchronizing method calls is covered in the **Threads of Control** (page 285) lesson. Take particular note of the section titled <u>Synchronizing Threads</u> (page 311).

Passing Information into a Method

When you write your method, you declare the number and type of the arguments required by that method. You must declare the type and name for each argument in the method signature. For example, the following code is a method that computes the monthly payments for a home loan based on the amount of the loan, the interest rate, the length of the loan (the number of periods), and the future value of the loan (presumably the future value of the loan is zero because at the end of the loan, you've paid it off):

```
double computePayment(double loanAmt, double rate,
                      double futureValue, int numPeriods) {
    double I, partial1, denominator, answer;

    I = rate / 100.0;
    partial1 = Math.pow((1 + I), (0.0 - numPeriods));
    denominator = (1 - partial1) / I;
    answer = ((-1 * loanAmt) / denominator) - ((futureValue *
            partial1) / denominator);
    return answer;
}
```

This method takes four arguments: the loan amount, the interest rate, the future value, and the number of periods. The first three are double-precision floating-point numbers, and the fourth is an integer.

As with this method, the set of arguments to any method is a comma-delimited list of variable declarations where each variable declaration is a type/name pair:

```
type name
```

As you can see from the body of the computePayment method, you simply use the argument name to refer to the argument's value.

Argument Types. In Java, you can pass an argument of any valid Java data type into a method. This includes primitive data types such as double, float, and integer as you saw in the computePayment method, and reference data types such as classes and arrays. Here's an example of a constructor that accepts an array as an argument. In this example, the constructor initializes a new Polygon object from a list of Points. (Point is a class that represents an x, y coordinate):

```
Polygon polygonFrom(Point[] listOfPoints) {
    . . .
}
```

Unlike in some other languages, you cannot pass methods into Java methods. But you can pass an object into a method and then invoke the object's methods.

Argument Names. When you declare an argument to a Java method, you provide a name for that argument. This name is used within the method body to refer to the item.

A method argument can have the same name as one of the class's member variables. If this is the case, then the argument is said to *hide* the member variable. Arguments that hide member variables are often used in constructors to initialize a class. For example, take the following Circle class and its constructor:

```
class Circle {
    int x, y, radius;
    public Circle(int x, int y, int radius) {
        . . .
    }
}
```

The Circle class has three member variables: x, y, and radius. In addition, the constructor for the Circle class accepts three arguments, each of which shares

its name with the member variable for which the argument provides an initial value.

The argument names hide the member variables. So using x, y, or radius within the body of the constructor refers to the argument, *not* to the member variable. To access the member variable, you must reference it through this, the current object:

```
class Circle {
    int x, y, radius;
    public Circle(int x, int y, int radius) {
        this.x = x;
        this.y = y;
        this.radius = radius;
    }
}
```

Names of method arguments cannot be the same as another argument name for the same method, the name of any variable local to the method, or the name of any parameter to a catch clause within the same method.

Pass-by-Value.

In Java methods, arguments of methods are *passed by value*. When invoked, the method receives the value of the variable passed in. When the argument is a primitive type, pass-by-value means that the method cannot change its value. When the argument is a reference type, pass-by-value means that the method cannot change the object reference, but the method can invoke the object's methods and modify the accessible variables within the object.

This is often the source of confusion—a programmer writes a method that attempts to modify the value of one of its arguments and the method doesn't work as expected. Let's look at such method and then investigate how to change it so that it does what the programmer originally intended.

Consider this series of Java statements which attempts to retrieve the current color of a Pen object in a graphics application:

```
. . .
int r = -1, g = -1, b = -1;
pen.getRGBColor(r, g, b);
System.out.println("red = " + r + ", green = " + g +
                   ", blue = " + b);
. . .
```

When the getRGBColor method is called, the variables r, g, and b all have the value -1. The caller is expecting the getRGBColor method to pass back the red, green, and blue values of the current color in the r, g, and b variables.

However, the Java runtime system passes the variables' values (-1) into the getRGBColor method; *not* a reference to the r, g, and b variables. Visualize the call to getRGBColor like this: getRGBColor(-1, -1, -1).

When control passes into the getRGBColor method, the arguments come into scope (get allocated) and are initialized to the value passed into the method:

```java
class Pen {
    int redValue, greenValue, blueValue;
    void getRGBColor(int red, int green, int blue) {
        // red, green, and blue have been created and
        // their values are -1
        . . .
    }
}
```

So getRGBColor gets access to the values of r, g, and b in the caller through its arguments red, green, and blue, respectively. The method gets its own copy of the values to use within the scope of the method. Any changes made to these local copies are not reflected in the original variables from the caller.

Now, look at the implementation of getRGBColor within the Pen class that the method signature above implies:

```java
class Pen {
    int redValue, greenValue, blueValue;
    . . .
        // this method does not work as intended
    void getRGBColor(int red, int green, int blue) {
        red = redValue;
        green = greenValue;
        blue = blueValue;
    }
}
```

This method will not work as intended. When control gets to the println statement in the following code, which was shown previously, getRGBColor's arguments, red, green, and blue, no longer exist. Therefore, the assignments made to them within the method had no effect; r, g, and b are all still equal to -1.

```java
    . . .
    int r = -1, g = -1, b = -1;
    pen.getRGBColor(r, g, b);
    System.out.println("red = " + r + ", green = " + g +
                       ", blue = " + b);
    . . .
```

Passing variables by value affords the programmer some safety: Methods cannot unintentionally modify a variable that is outside of its scope. However, you often want a method to be able to modify one or more of its arguments. The `getRGB-Color` method is a case in point. The caller wants the method to return three values through its arguments. However, the method cannot modify its arguments, and, furthermore, a method can only return one value through its return value. So how can a method return more than one value, or modify some value outside of its scope?

For a method to modify an argument, it must be of a reference type such as a class or an array. Objects and arrays are also passed by value, but the value of an object is a reference. The effect is that arguments of reference types are passed in by reference. Hence the name. A reference to an object is the address of the object in memory. Now, the argument in the method is referring to the same memory location as the caller.

Let's rewrite the `getRGBColor` method so that it actually does what you want. First, introduce a new object, `RGBColor`, that can hold the `red`, `green`, and `blue` values of a color in RGB space:

```java
class RGBColor {
    public int red, green, blue;
}
```

Now, rewrite `getRGBColor` so that it accepts an `RGBColor` object as an argument. The `getRGBColor` method returns the current color of the pen by setting the `red`, `green`, and `blue` member variables of its `RGBColor` argument:

```java
class Pen {
    int redValue, greenValue, blueValue;
    void getRGBColor(RGBColor aColor) {
        aColor.red = redValue;
        aColor.green = greenValue;
        aColor.blue = blueValue;
    }
}
```

And finally, rewrite the calling sequence:

```java
. . .
RGBColor penColor = new RGBColor();
pen.getRGBColor(penColor);
System.out.println("red = " + penColor.red + ", green = " +
                    penColor.green + ", blue = " + penColor.blue);
. . .
```

The modifications made to the RGBColor object within the getRGBColor method affect the object created in the calling sequence because the names penColor (in the calling sequence) and aColor (in the getRGBColor method) refer to the same object.

The Method Body

In the code sample that follows, the method bodies for the isEmpty and pop methods are shown in bold:

```
class Stack {
    static final int STACK_EMPTY = -1;
    Object[] stackelements;
    int topelement = STACK_EMPTY;
    . . .
    boolean isEmpty() {
        if (topelement == STACK_EMPTY)
            return true;
        else
            return false;
    }
    Object pop() {
        if (topelement == STACK_EMPTY)
            return null;
        else {
            return stackelements[topelement--];
        }
    }
}
```

Besides regular Java language elements, you can use this in the method body to refer to members in the *current object*. The current object is the object whose method is being called. You can also use super to refer to members in the super-class that the current object has hidden or overridden. Also, a method body may contain declarations for variables that are local to that method.

this. Typically, within an object's method body you can just refer directly to the object's member variables. However, sometimes you need to disambiguate the member variable name if one of the arguments to the method has the same name.

For example, the following constructor for the HSBColor class initializes some of an object's member variables according to the arguments passed into the constructor. Each argument to the constructor has the same name as the object's member variable whose initial value the argument contains.

```
class HSBColor {
    int hue, saturation, brightness;
    HSBColor (int hue, int saturation, int brightness) {
        this.hue = hue;
        this.saturation = saturation;
        this.brightness = brightness;
    }
```

You must use this in this constructor because you have to disambiguate the argument hue from the member variable hue (and so on with the other arguments). The Java statement hue = hue; makes no sense. Argument names take precedence and hide member variables with the same name. To refer to the member variable, you must do so through the current object—this—explicitly.

Some programmers prefer always to use this when referring to a member variable of the object in whose method the reference appears. Doing so makes the intent of the code explicit and reduces errors based on name sharing.

You can also use this to call one of the current object's methods. Again this is necessary only if there is some ambiguity in the method name and is often used to make the intent of the code clearer.

super. If your method hides one of its superclass's member variables, your method can refer to the hidden variable through the use of super. Similarly, if your method overrides one of its superclass's methods, your method can invoke the overridden method throught the use of super.

Consider this class:

```
class ASillyClass {
    boolean aVariable;
    void aMethod() {
        aVariable = true;
    }
}
```

and its subclass which hides aVariable and overrides aMethod():

```
class ASillierClass extends ASillyClass {
    boolean aVariable;
    void aMethod() {
        aVariable = false;
        super.aMethod();
        System.out.println(aVariable);
        System.out.println(super.aVariable);
    }
}
```

First aMethod sets aVariable (the one declared in ASillierClass that hides the one declared in ASillyClass) to false. Next aMethod invoked its overridden method with this statement:

```
super.aMethod();
```

This sets the hidden version of aVariable (the one declared in ASillyClass) to true. Then aMethod displays both versions of aVariable which have different values:

```
false
true
```

Local Variables. Within the body of the method you can declare more variables for use within that method. These variables are called *local variables* and live only while control remains within the method. This method declares a local variable i that it uses to iterate over the elements of its array argument.

```
Object findObjectInArray(Object o, Object[] arrayOfObjects) {
    int i;        // local variable
    for (i = 0; i < arrayOfObjects.length; i++) {
        if (arrayOfObjects[i] == o)
            return o;
    }
    return null;
}
```

After this method returns, i no longer exists.

Controlling Access to Members of a Class

One of the benefits of classes is that classes can protect their member variables and methods from access by other objects. Why is this important? Well, consider this. You're writing a class that represents a query on a database that contains all kinds of secret information, say employee records or income statements for your startup company.

Certain information and queries contained in the class, the ones supported by the publicly accessible methods and variables in your query object, can be accessed by any other object in the system. Other queries contained in the class are there simply for the personal use of the class. They support the operation of the class but should not be used by objects of another type—you've got secret information to protect. You'd like to be able to protect these personal variables and methods at the language level and disallow access by objects of another type.

In Java, you can use access specifiers to protect both a class's variables and its methods when you declare them. The Java language supports four distinct access levels for member variables and methods: private, protected, public, and, if left unspecified, package.

Note: The 1.0 release of the Java language supported five access levels: the four listed above plus `private protected`. The `private protected` access level is not supported in versions of Java higher than 1.0; you should no longer be using it in your Java programs.

The following table shows the access level permitted by each specifier.

Specifier	class	subclass	package	world
private	✔			
protected	✔	✔*	✔	
public	✔	✔	✔	✔
package	✔	✔		

The first column indicates whether the class itself has access to the member defined by the access specifier. As you can see, a class always has access to its own members. The second column indicates whether subclasses of the class (regardless of which package they are in) have access to the member. The third column indicates whether classes in the same package as the class, regardless of their parentage, have access to the member. The fourth column indicates whether all classes have access to the member.

Note that the protected/subclass intersection has an '*'. This particular access case has a special caveat discussed in detail on page 109.

Let's look at each access level in more detail.

Private

The most restrictive access level is private. A private member is accessible only to the class in which it is defined. Use this access to declare members that should be used only by the class. This includes variables that contain information that, if accessed by an outsider, could put the object in an inconsistent state, or methods that, if invoked by an outsider, could jeopardize the state of the object or the program in which running. Private members are like secrets you never tell anybody.

To declare a private member, use the `private` keyword in its declaration. The following class contains one private member variable and one private method:

```
class Alpha {
    private int iamprivate;
    private void privateMethod() {
        System.out.println("privateMethod");
    }
}
```

Objects of type `Alpha` can inspect or modify the `iamprivate` variable and can invoke `privateMethod`, but objects of other types cannot. For example, the Beta class defined in the following code cannot access the `iamprivate` variable or invoke `privateMethod` on an object of type `Alpha` because `Beta` is not of type `Alpha`:

```
class Beta {
    void accessMethod() {
        Alpha a = new Alpha();
        a.iamprivate = 10;      // illegal
        a.privateMethod();      // illegal
    }
}
```

When one of your classes is attempting to access a member variable to which it does not have access, the compiler prints an error message similar to the following and refuses to compile your program:

```
Beta.java:9: Variable iamprivate in class Alpha not accessible
from class Beta.
        a.iamprivate = 10;      // illegal
          ^
1 error
```

Also, if your program is attempting to access a method to which it does not have access, you will see a compiler error like this:

```
Beta.java:12: No method matching privateMethod() found in class
Alpha.
        a.privateMethod();          // illegal
1 error
```

New Java programmers might ask if one `Alpha` object can access the private members of another `Alpha` object. This is illustrated by the following example. Suppose the `Alpha` class contained an instance method that compared the current `Alpha` object (`this`) to another object based on their `iamprivate` variables:

```
class Alpha {
    private int iamprivate;
    boolean isEqualTo(Alpha anotherAlpha) {


        if (this.iamprivate == anotherAlpha.iamprivate)
            return true;
        else
            return false;
    }
}
```

This is perfectly legal. Objects of the same type have access to one another's private members. This is because access restrictions apply at the class or type level (all instances of a class) rather than at the object level (this particular instance of a class).

Note: `this` is a Java language keyword that refers to the current object. For more information about how to use `this` see The Method Body (page 103).

Protected

The next access level specifier is protected which allows the class itself, subclasses (with the caveat that we referred to earlier), and all classes in the same package to access the members. Use the protected access level when it is appropriate for a class's subclasses to have access to the member, but not to unrelated classes. Protected members are like family secrets—you don't mind if the whole family knows and even a few trusted friends, but you don't want any outsiders to know.

To declare a protected member, use the keyword `protected`. First, let's look at how the protected specifier affects access for classes in the same package. Consider the following version of the `Alpha` class. It is declared to be within a package named `Greek`, and it has one protected member variable and one protected method declared in it:

```
package Greek;

class Alpha {
    protected int iamprotected;
```

```
        protected void protectedMethod() {
            System.out.println("protectedMethod");
        }
    }
```

Now, suppose that the class Gamma is also declared to be a member of the Greek package (and is not a subclass of Alpha). The Gamma class can legally access an Alpha object's iamprotected member variable and can legally invoke its protectedMethod:

```
    package Greek;

    class Gamma {
        void accessMethod() {
            Alpha a = new Alpha();
            a.iamprotected = 10;    // legal
            a.protectedMethod();    // legal
        }
    }
```

That's pretty straightforward. Now, let's investigate how the protected specifier affects access for subclasses of Alpha.

Let's introduce a new class, Delta, that derives from Alpha but lives in a different package—Latin. The Delta class can access both iamprotected and protectedMethod, but only on objects of type Delta or its subclasses. The Delta class cannot access iamprotected or protectedMethod on objects of type Alpha. accessMethod in the following code sample attempts to access the iamprotected member variable on an object of type Alpha, which is illegal, and on an object of type Delta, which is legal. Similarly, accessMethod attempts to invoke an Alpha object's protectedMethod which is also illegal:

```
    package Latin;

    import Greek.*;

    class Delta extends Alpha {
        void accessMethod(Alpha a, Delta d) {
            a.iamprotected = 10;    // illegal
            d.iamprotected = 10;    // legal
            a.protectedMethod();    // illegal
            d.protectedMethod();    // legal
        }
    }
```

If a class is both a subclass of and in the same package as the class with the protected member, then the class has access to the protected member.

Public

The easiest access specifier is public. Any class in any package has access to a class's public members. Declare members to be public only if such access cannot produce undesirable results if an outsider uses them. There are no personal or family secrets here; this is for stuff you don't mind anybody else knowing.

To declare a public member, use the keyword `public`. For example,

```
package Greek;

class Alpha {
    public int iampublic;
    public void publicMethod() {
        System.out.println("publicMethod");
    }
}
```

Let's rewrite our `Beta` class one more time, put it in a different package than `Alpha`, and make sure that it is completely unrelated to (not a subclass of) `Alpha`:

```
package Roman;

import Greek.*;

class Beta {
    void accessMethod() {
        Alpha a = new Alpha();
        a.iampublic = 10;       // legal
        a.publicMethod();       // legal
    }
}
```

As you can see from the above code snippet, `Beta` can legally inspect and modify the `iampublic` variable in the `Alpha` class and can legally invoke `public-Method`.

Package

The package access level is what you get if you don't explicitly set a member's access to one of the other levels. This access level allows classes in the same package as your class to access the members. This level of access assumes that classes in the same package are trusted friends. This level of trust is like that which you extend to your closest friends but wouldn't trust even to your family.

For example, the following version of the `Alpha` class declares a single member variable and a single method, both with default (package) access. `Alpha` lives in the Greek package:

```
package Greek;

class Alpha {
    int iampackage;
    void packageMethod() {
        System.out.println("packageMethod");
    }
}
```

The Alpha class has access both to iampackage and packageMethod. In addition, all the classes declared within the same package as Alpha also have access to iampackage and packageMethod. Suppose that both Alpha and Beta are declared as part of the Greek package:

```
package Greek;

class Beta {
    void accessMethod() {
        Alpha a = new Alpha();
        a.iampackage = 10;      // legal
        a.packageMethod();      // legal
    }
}
```

Beta can legally access iampackage and packageMethod as shown.

Instance and Class Members

When you declare a member variable such as aFloat in MyClass, you declare an *instance variable*:

```
class MyClass {
    float aFloat;
}
```

Every time you create an instance of a class, the runtime system creates one copy of each of the class's instance variables. You can access an object's instance variables from an object as described in <u>Using Objects</u> (page 81).

Instance variables are in constrast to *class variables,* (which you declare using the static modifier. The runtime system allocates class variables once per class regardless of the number of instances created of that class. The system allocates memory for class variables the first time it encounters the class. All instances share the same copy of the class's class variables. You can access class variables through an instance or through the class itself.

Methods are similar: Your classes can have instance methods and class methods. Instance methods operate on the current object's instance variables but also have access to the class variables. Class methods, on the other hand, cannot access the instance variables declared within the class unless they create a new object and accesses the instance variables through that object. Also, class methods can be invoked on the class; you don't need an instance to call a class method.

By default, unless otherwise specified, a member declared within a class is an instance member. The class defined below has one instance variable, an integer named x, and two instance methods, x and setX, that let other objects set and query the value of x:

```
class AnIntegerNamedX {
    int x;
    public int x() {
        return x;
    }
    public void setX(int newX) {
        x = newX;
    }
}
```

Every time you instantiate a new object from a class, you get a new copy of each of the class's instance variables. These copies are associated with the new object. Every time you instantiate a new AnIntegerNamedX object from the class, you get a new copy of x that is associated with the new AnIntegerNamedX object.

All instances of a class share the same implementation of an instance method; all instances of AnIntegerNamedX share the same implementation of the x and setX. Note that both methods, x and setX, refer to the object's instance variable x by name. "But", you ask, "if all instances of AnIntegerNamedX share the same implementation of x and setX isn't this ambiguous?" The answer is "no." Within an instance method, the name of an instance variable refers to the current object's instance variable, assuming that the instance variable isn't hidden by a method parameter. So, within x and setX, x is equivalent to this.x.

Objects outside of AnIntegerNamedX that wish to access x must do so through a particular instance of AnIntegerNamedX. Suppose that this code snippet is in another object's method. It creates two different objects of type AnIntegerNamedX, sets their x values to different values, then displays them:

```
. . .
AnIntegerNamedX myX = new AnIntegerNamedX();
AnIntegerNamedX anotherX = new AnIntegerNamedX();
myX.setX(1);
anotherX.x = 2;
System.out.println("myX.x = " + myX.x());
System.out.println("anotherX.x = " + anotherX.x());
. . .
```

Note that the code uses `setX` to set the x value for `myX` but just assigns a value to `anotherX.x` directly. Either way, the code is manipulating two different copies of x: the one contained in the `myX` object and the one contained in the `anotherX` object. The output produced by this code snippet is:

```
myX.x = 1
anotherX.x = 2
```

This shows that each instance of the class `AnIntegerNamedX` has its own copy of the instance variable x and each x has a different value.

When declaring a member variable, you can specify that the variable is a class variable rather than an instance variable. Similarly, you can specify that a method is a class method rather than an instance method. The system creates a single copy of a class variable the first time it encounters the class in which the variable is defined. All instances of that class share the same copy of the class variable. Class methods can operate only on class variables—they cannot access the instance variables defined in the class.

To specify that a member variable is a class variable, use the `static` keyword. For example, let's change the `AnIntegerNamedX` class such that its x variable is now a class variable:

```
class AnIntegerNamedX {
    static int x;
    public int x() {
        return x;
    }
    public void setX(int newX) {
        x = newX;
    }
}
```

Now the exact same code snippet shown previously on page 112 that creates two instances of `AnIntegerNamedX`, sets their x values, and then displays them produces this, different, output.

```
myX.x = 2
anotherX.x = 2
```

The output is different because x is now a class variable so there is only one copy of that variable and it is shared by all instances of `AnIntegerNamedX`, including `myX` and `anotherX`. When you invoke `setX` on either instance, you change the value of x for all instances of `AnIntegerNamedX`.

You use class variables for items that you need only one copy of and which must be accessible by all objects inheriting from the class in which the variable is declared. For example, class variables are often used with `final` to define constants; this is more memory efficient than final instance variables because constants can't change so you really only need one copy.

Similarly, when declaring a method, you can specify that method to be a class method rather than an instance method. Class methods can operate only on class variables and cannot access the instance variables defined in the class.

To specify that a method is a class method, use the `static` keyword in the method declaration. Let's change the `AnIntegerNamedX` class such that its member variable x is once again an instance variable, and its two methods are now class methods:

```
class AnIntegerNamedX {
    private int x;
    static public int x() {
        return x; //won't work
    }
    static public void setX(int newX) {
        x = newX; //won't work
    }
}
```

When you try to compile this version of `AnIntegerNamedX`, you will get the following compiler errors:

```
AnIntegerNamedX.java:4: Can't make a static reference to
nonstatic
            variable x in class AnIntegerNamedX.
        return x;
             ^
AnIntegerNamedX.java:7: Can't make a static reference to
nonstatic
        variable x in class AnIntegerNamedX.
        x = newX;
        ^
2 errors
```

The errors occur because class methods cannot access instance variables unless the method created an instance of `AnIntegerNamedX` first and accessed the variable through it.

Let's fix `AnIntegerNamedX` by making its x variable a class variable:

```
class AnIntegerNamedX {
    static private int x;
    static public int x() {
        return x;
    }
```

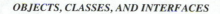

```
static public void setX(int newX) {
    x = newX;
}
}
```

Now the class will compile and the same code snippet from before (shown on page 112) that creates two instances of `AnIntegerNamedX`, sets their x values, and then prints the x values produces this output:

```
myX.x = 2
anotherX.x = 2
```

Again, changing x through `myX` also changes it for other instances of `AnIntegerNamedX`.

Another difference between instance members and class members is that class members are accessible from the class itself. You don't need to instantiate a class to access its class members. Let's rewrite the code so that it accesses x and `setX` directly from the `AnIntegerNamedX` class:

```
. . .
AnIntegerNamedX.setX(1);
System.out.println("AnIntegerNamedX.x = " +
    AnIntegerNamedX.x());
. . .
```

Note that you no longer have to create `myX` and `anotherX`. You can set and retrieve x directly using the `AnIntegerNamedX` class. You cannot do this with instance members; you can invoke instance methods only using an object and can access instance variables only using an object. You can access class variables and methods either using an instance of the class or using the class itself.

Constructors

All Java classes have special methods called constructors that are used to initialize a new object of that type. Constructors have the same name as the class—the name of the `Rectangle` class's constructor is `Rectangle`, the name of the `Thread` class's constructor is `Thread`, and so on. Java supports method name overloading so that a class can have any number of constructors, all of which have the same name. Like other overloaded methods, constructors are differentiated from one another by the number and type of their arguments.

Consider the `Rectangle` class in the `java.awt` package. The `Rectangle` class provides several different constructors, all named `Rectangle`, but each with a different number of arguments, or different types of arguments from

which the new `Rectangle` object will get its initial state. Here are the constructor signatures from the `java.awt.Rectangle` class:

```
public Rectangle()
public Rectangle(int width, int height)
public Rectangle(int x, int y, int width, int height)
public Rectangle(Dimension size)
public Rectangle(Point location)
public Rectangle(Point location, Dimension size)
```

The first `Rectangle` constructor initializes a new `Rectangle` to some reasonable default, the second constructor initializes the new `Rectangle` with the specified width and height, the third constructor initializes the new `Rectangle` at the specified position and with the specified width and height, and so on.

Typically, a constructor uses its arguments to initialize the new object's state. When creating an object, choose the constructor whose arguments best reflect how you want to initialize the new object.

Based on the number and type of the arguments that you pass into the constructor, the compiler can determine which constructor to use. The compiler knows that when you write

```
new Rectangle(0, 0, 100, 200);
```

it should use the constructor that requires four integer arguments. When you write

```
new Rectangle(myPointObj, myDimensionObj);
```

the compiler chooses the constructor that requires one `Point` object argument and one `Dimension` object argument.

When you are writing your own class, you don't have to provide constructors for it. The default constructor, the constructor that takes no arguments, is automatically provided by the runtime system for all classes. However, you will often want or need to provide constructors for your class.

You declare and implement a constructor just like any other method in your class. The name of the constructor must be the same as the name of the class and, if you provide more than one constructor, the arguments to each constructor must differ in number or in type from the others. You do not specify a return value for a constructor.

The constructor for the following subclass of `Thread`, which implements a thread that performs animation, sets up some default values such as the frame speed and the number of images. It then loads the images:

```
class AnimationThread extends Thread {
    int framesPerSecond;
    int numImages;
    Image[] images;

    AnimationThread(int fps, int num) {
        int i;

        super("AnimationThread");
        this.framesPerSecond = fps;
        this.numImages < num;

        this.images = new Image[numImages];
        for (i = 0; i <= numImages; i++) {
            . . .
            // Load all the images.
            . . .
        }
    }
    . . .
}
```

Note how the body of a constructor is just like the body of any other method—it contains local variable declarations, loops, and other statements. However, there is one line in the `AnimationThread` constructor that you wouldn't see in a regular method—the second line:

```
super("AnimationThread");
```

This line invokes a constructor provided by the superclass of `AnimationThread` —named `Thread`. This particular `Thread` constructor takes a `String` that sets the name of the `Thread`. Often a constructor wants to take advantage of initialization code written in a class's superclass. Indeed, some classes *must* call their superclass constructor in order for the object to work properly. Typically, the superclass constructor is invoked as the first thing in the subclass's constructor: an object should perform the higher level initialization first.

When declaring constructors for your class, use the normal access specifiers to specify what other objects can create instances of your class:

private   No other class can instantiate your class as an object. Your class can still contain public class methods, and those methods can construct an object and return it, but no one else can.

protected   Only subclasses of your class can create instances of it.

public   Anybody can create an instance of your class.

package   No one outside the package can construct an instance of your class. This is useful if you want to have classes in your package create instances of your class but you don't want to let anyone else create instances of your class.

Writing a finalize Method

Before an object is garbage collected, the runtime system calls its finalize method. The intent is for finalize to release system resources such as open files or open sockets before getting collected.

Your class can provide for its finalization simply by defining and implementing a method in your class named finalize. Your finalize method must be declared as follows:

```
protected void finalize() throws Throwable
```

The OpenAFile class that follows opens a file when it is constructed:

```java
class OpenAFile {
    FileInputStream aFile = null;
    OpenAFile(String filename) {
        try {
            aFile = new FileInputStream(filename);
        } catch (java.io.FileNotFoundException e) {
            System.err.println("Could not open file " + filename);
        }
    }
}
```

To be well-behaved, the OpenAFile class should close the file when it is finalized. Here's the finalize method for the OpenAFile class:

```java
protected void finalize() throws Throwable {
    if (aFile != null) {
        aFile.close();
        aFile = null;
    }
}
```

The finalize method is declared in the Object class. As a result, when you write a finalize method for your class, you are overriding the one in your superclass. Overriding Methods (page 122) talks more about how to override methods.

If your class's superclass has a `finalize` method, then your class's `finalize` method should probably call the superclass's `finalize` method after it has performed any of its cleanup duties. This cleans up any resources the object may have unknowingly obtained through methods inherited from the superclass.

```
protected void finalize() throws Throwable {
    . . .
    // clean up code for this class here
    . . .
    super.finalize();
}
```

Subclasses, Superclasses, and Inheritance

To recap what you've seen before, classes can be derived from other classes. The derived class (the class that is derived from another class) is called a *subclass*. The class from which it's derived is called the *superclass*. The following figure illustrates these two types of classes.

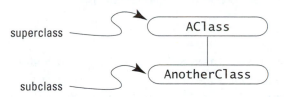

In fact, in Java, all classes must be derived from some class. Which leads to the question "Where does it all begin?" The top-most class, the class from which all other classes are derived, is the `Object` class defined in `java.lang`. `Object` is the root of a hierarchy of classes, as illustrated in the following figure.

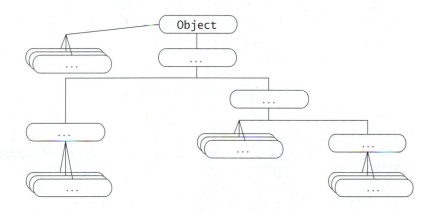

The subclass inherits state and behavior in the form of variables and methods from its superclass. The subclass can use just the items inherited from its superclass as is, or the subclass can modify or override those items. As you drop down in the hierarchy, the classes become more and more specialized.

Definition: A subclass is a class that derives from another class. A subclass inherits state and behavior from all of its ancestors. The term superclass refers to a class's direct ancestor as well as to all of its ascendant classes.

Now would be a good time to review the discussion in <u>What Is Inheritance?</u> (page 39).

Creating Subclasses

You declare that a class is the subclass of another class within <u>The Class Declaration</u> (page 87). For example, suppose that you want to create a subclass named `SubClass` of another class named `SuperClass`. The code is as follows:

```
class SubClass extends SuperClass {
    . . .
}
```

This declares that `SubClass` is the subclass of the `SuperClass` class. It also implicitly declares that `SuperClass` is the superclass of `SubClass`. A subclass also inherits variables and methods from its superclass's superclass, and so on, up the inheritance tree. To simplify our discussion, when this tutorial refers to a class's superclass it means the class's direct ancestor as well as all of its ascendant classes.

A Java class can have only one direct superclass. Java does not support multiple inheritance.

Creating a subclass can be as simple as including the `extends` clause in your class declaration. However, you usually have to make other provisions in your code when subclassing a class, such as overriding methods or providing implementation for abstract methods.

What Member Variables Does a Subclass Inherit?

Rule: A subclass inherits all of the member variables within its superclass that are accessible to that subclass (unless the member variable is hidden by the subclass).

The following list itemizes the member variables that are inherited by a subclass:

- Subclasses inherit those superclass member variables declared as `public` or `protected`.
- Subclasses inherit those superclass member variables declared with no access specifier as long as the subclass is in the same package class as the superclass.
- Subclasses don't inherit a superclass's member variable if the subclass declares a member variable using the same name. The subclass's member variable is said to hide the member variable in the superclass.
- Subclasses don't inherit the superclass's `private` member variables.

Hiding Member Variables

As mentioned in the previous section, member variables defined in the subclass hide member variables of the same name in the superclass.

While this feature of the Java language is powerful and convenient, it can be a fruitful source of errors: hiding a member variable can be done deliberately or by accident. When naming your member variables, be careful to hide only those member variables that you actually wish to hide.

One interesting feature of Java member variables is that a class can access a hidden member variable through its superclass. Consider the following superclass and subclass pair:

```
class Super {
    Number aNumber;
}
class Sub extends Super {
    Float aNumber;
}
```

The `aNumber` variable in Sub hides `aNumber` in Super. But you can access `aNumber` from the superclass with

```
super.aNumber
```

`super` is a Java language keyword that allows a method to refer to hidden variables and overridden methods of the superclass.

What Methods Does a Subclass Inherit?

The rule that specifies which methods get inherited by a subclass is similar to that for member variables.

> **Rule:** A subclass inherits all of the methods within its superclass that are accessible to that subclass (unless the method is overridden by the subclass).

The following list itemizes the methods that are inherited by a subclass:

- Subclassses inherit those superclass methods declared as `public` or `protected`.
- Subclasses inherit those superclass methods declared with no access specifier as long as the subclass is in the same package as the superclass.
- Subclasses don't inherit a superclass's method if the subclass declares a method using the same name. The method in the subclass is said to override the one in the superclass.
- Subclasses don't inherit the superclass's `private` methods.

A subclass can either completely override the implementation for an inherited method, or the subclass can enhance the method by adding functionality to it.

Overriding Methods

The ability of a subclass to override a method in its superclass allows a class to inherit from a superclass whose behavior is "close enough" and then supplement or modify the behavior of that superclass.

Replacing a Superclass's Method Implementation.

Sometimes, you want a subclass to entirely replace its superclass's implementation of a method. Indeed, many superclasses provide an empty method implementation with the expectation that most, if not all, subclasses will completely replace the superclass's implementation of the method.

One example of this is the `run` method in the `Thread` class. The `Thread` class provides an empty implementation (the method does nothing) of the `run` method because by definition, the `run` method is dependent on the subclass implementation of the method. The `Thread` class can't possibly provide a reasonable default implementation for the `run` method. However, the `run` method cannot be abstract because it also does not make sense for the `Thread` class to be abstract. (Programmers should be able to instantiate a generic Thread without building a subclass.) Thus, the implementation of `run` is empty.

To completely replace a superclass's method implementation, simply name your method the same as the superclass method and provide the overriding method with the same signature as the overridden method, as in the following example:

```
class BackgroundThread extends Thread {
    void run() {
        . . .
    }
}
```

The `BackgroundThread` class overrides the `run` method from its superclass `Thread` and completely replaces `Thread`'s implementation of it.

Adding to a Superclass's Method Implementation.

At other times, you want a subclass to keep its superclass's implementation of a method but enhance it further with behavior specific to the subclass. For example, constructor methods within a subclass typically do this—the subclass wants to preserve the initialization done by the superclass, but provide additional initialization specific to the subclass.

Suppose that you want to create a subclass of the `Window` class provided by the `java.awt` package. The `Window` class has one constructor that requires a `Frame` argument which is the parent of the window:

```
public Window(Frame parent)
```

This constructor performs some initialization on the window such that it will work within the window system. To make sure your new `Window` subclass also works within the window system, you too must provide a constructor for your `Window` subclass that performs the same initialization. Rather than recreate the initialization process that occurs within the Window constructor, you would rather just use what the `Window` class already does. You can leverage the code in the Window constructor simply by calling it from within your Window subclass constructor:

```
class MyWindow extends Window {
    public MyWindow(Frame parent) {
        super(parent);
        . . .
            // MyWindow specific initialization here
        . . .
    }
}
```

The `MyWindow` constructor calls the superclass's constructor first, before it does anything else. Typically, this is the desired behavior in constructors—the superclass should get the opportunity to perform all its initialization before the subclass. Other types of methods may wish to call the superclass's implementation of the method at the end of the subclass's method or in the middle of it. If the positioning of the call to the superclass's method is critical to the successful operation of the subclass's method, note that in a comment.

Methods a Subclass Cannot Override.

A subclass cannot override methods that are declared `final` in the superclass (by definition, final methods

cannot be overridden). If you attempt to override a final method, the compiler displays an error message similar to this one and refuses to compile the program:

```
FinalTest.java:7: Final methods can't be overridden. Method
void
        iamfinal() is final in class ClassWithFinalMethod.
    void iamfinal() {
         ^
1 error
```

For a discussion of final methods, see <u>Writing Final Classes and Methods</u> (page 124).

A subclass cannot override methods that are declared `static` in the superclass. In other words, a subclass cannot override a class method. See <u>Instance and Class Members</u> (page 111) for an explanation of class methods.

Methods a Subclass Must Override. A subclass must override methods that are declared `abstract` in the superclass, *or* the subclass itself must be abstract. <u>Writing Abstract Classes and Methods</u> (page 125) discusses abstract classes and methods in detail.

Writing Final Classes and Methods

Final Classes

You can declare that your class is final, that is, that your class cannot be subclassed. There are (at least) two reasons why you might want to do this: security reasons and design reasons.

Security. One mechanism that hackers use to subvert systems is to create subclasses of a class and then substitute their class for the original. The subclass looks and feels like the original class but does vastly different things, possibly causing damage or getting into private information. To prevent this kind of subversion, you can declare your class to be final and prevent any subclasses from being created. The `String` class in the `java.lang` package is a final class for just this reason. The `String` class is so vital to the operation of the compiler and the interpreter that the Java system must guarantee that whenever a method or object uses a `String` they get exactly a `java.lang.String` and not some other string. This ensures that all strings have no strange, inconsistent, undesirable, or unpredictable properties.

If you try to compile a subclass of a final class, the compiler prints an error message and refuses to compile your program. In addition, the bytecode verifier ensures that the subversion is not taking place at the bytecode level by checking to make sure that a class is not a subclass of a final class.

Design. Another reason you may wish to declare a class as final is for object-oriented design reasons. You may think that your class is "perfect" or that, conceptually, your class should have no subclasses.

To specify that your class is a final class, use the keyword `final` before the `class` keyword in your class declaration. For example, if you want to declare your (perfect) `ChessAlgorithm` class as final, its declaration should look like this:

```
final class ChessAlgorithm {
    . . .
}
```

Any subsequent attempts to subclass `ChessAlgorithm` result in a compiler error such as the following:

```
Chess.java:6: Can't subclass final classes: class
ChessAlgorithm
class BetterChessAlgorithm extends ChessAlgorithm {
      ^
1 error
```

Final Methods

If creating a final class seems heavy handed for your needs and you really just want to protect some of your class's methods from being overridden, you can use the `final` keyword in a method declaration to indicate to the compiler that the method cannot be overridden by subclasses.

You might wish to make a method final if the method has an implementation that should not be changed and is critical to the consistent state of the object. For example, instead of making your `ChessAlgorithm` class final, you might just want to make the `nextMove` method final:

```
class ChessAlgorithm {
    . . .
    final void nextMove(ChessPiece pieceMoved,
                        BoardLocation newLocation) {
        . . .
    }
    . . .
}
```

Writing Abstract Classes and Methods

Abstract Classes

Sometimes, a class that you define represents an abstract concept and, as such, should not be instantiated. Take, for example, food in the real world. Have you ever seen an instance of food? No. What you see instead are instances of carrot, apple, and (my favorite) chocolate. Food represents the abstract concept of things that we can eat. It doesn't make sense for an instance of food to exist.

Similarly in object-oriented programming, you may want to model an abstract concept without being able to create an instance of it. For example, the Number class in the java.lang package represents the abstract concept of numbers. It makes sense to model numbers in a program, but it doesn't make sense to create a generic number object. Instead, the Number class makes sense only as a superclass to classes like Integer and Float which implement specific kinds of numbers. Classes such as Number, which implement abstract concepts and should not be instantiated, are called *abstract classes*. An abstract class is a class that can only be subclassed—it cannot be instantiated.

To declare that your class is an abstract class, use the keyword abstract before the class keyword in your class declaration:

```
abstract class Number {
    . . .
}
```

If you attempt to instantiate an abstract class, the compiler displays an error similar to the following and refuses to compile your program:

```
AbstractTest.java:6: class AbstractTest is an abstract class.
It can't be instantiated.
        new AbstractTest();
        ^
1 error
```

Abstract Methods

An abstract class may contain *abstract methods*, that is, methods with no implementation. In this way, an abstract class can define a complete programming interface, thereby providing its subclasses with the method declarations for all of the methods necessary to implement that programming interface. However, the abstract class can leave some or all of the implementation details of those methods up to its subclasses.

Let's look at an example of when you might want to create an abstract class with an abstract method in it. In an object-oriented drawing application, you can draw circles, rectangles, lines, Bezier curves, and so on. All of these graphic objects use certain states (position, bounding box) and behavior (move, resize, draw). You can take advantage of these similarities and declare them all to inherit from the same parent object—GraphicObject.

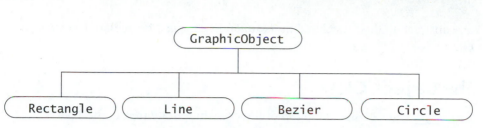

However, the graphic objects are also substantially different in many ways: drawing a circle is quite different from drawing a rectangle. The graphics objects cannot share these types of states or behavior. On the other hand, all GraphicObjects must know how to draw themselves; they just differ in how they are drawn. This is a perfect situation for an abstract superclass.

First you declare an abstract class, GraphicObject, to provide member variables and methods that are needed by all subclasses such as the current position and the moveTo method. GraphicObject also declares abstract methods for methods, such as draw, that need to be implemented by all subclasses, but are implemented in entirely different ways (no default implementation in the superclass makes sense). The GraphicObject class looks something like this:

```
abstract class GraphicObject {
    int x, y;
    . . .
    void moveTo(int newX, int newY) {
        . . .
    }
    abstract void draw();
}
```

Each non-abstract subclass of GraphicObject, such as Circle and Rectangle, has to provide an implementation for the draw method.

```
class Circle extends GraphicObject {
    void draw() {
        . . .
    }
}
class Rectangle extends GraphicObject {
    void draw() {
        . . .
    }
}
```

An abstract class is not required to have an abstract method in it. But any class that has an abstract method in it or that does not provide an implementation for

any abstract methods declared in its superclasses *must* be declared as an abstract class.

The Object Class

The Object class[1] sits at the top of the class hierarchy tree in the Java development environment. Every class in the Java system is a descendent, direct or indirect, of the Object class. The Object class defines the basic state and behavior that all objects must have such as the ability to compare oneself to another object, to convert to a string, to wait on a condition variable, to notify other objects that a condition variable has changed, and to return the object's class.

The equals Method

Use the equals method to compare two objects for equality. This method returns true if the objects are equal, false otherwise. Note that equality does not mean that the objects are the same object. Consider this code that tests two Integers, one and anotherOne, for equality:

```
Integer one = new Integer(1), anotherOne = new Integer(1);

if (one.equals(anotherOne))
    System.out.println("objects are equal");
```

This program will display objects are equal even though one and another-One reference two different, distinct objects. They are considered equal because they contain the same integer value.

Your classes should override the equals method to provide an appropriate equality test. Your equals method should compare the contents of the objects to see if they are functionally equal and return true if they are.

The getClass Method

The getClass method is a final method (cannot be overridden) that returns a runtime representation of the class of this object. This method returns a Class object. You can query the Class object for various information about the class

---

[1.] http://java.sun.com/products/JDK/CurrentRelease/api/java.lang.Object.html

such as its name, its superclass, and the names of the interfaces that it implements. This following method gets and displays the class name of an object:

```
void PrintClassName(Object obj) {
    System.out.println("The Object's class is " +
                        obj.getClass().getName());
}
```

One handy use of the `getClass` method is to create a new instance of a class without knowing what the class is at compile time. The following sample method creates a new instance of the same class as `obj`, which can be any class that inherits from `Object` (which means that it could be any class):

```
Object createNewInstanceOf(Object obj) {
    return obj.getClass().newInstance();
}
```

The `toString` Method

`Object`'s `toString` method returns a `String` representation of the object. You can use `toString` to display an object. For example, you could display a `String` representation of the current `Thread` like this:

```
System.out.println(Thread.currentThread().toString());
```

The `String` representation for an object depends entirely on the object. The `String` representation of an `Integer` object is the integer value displayed as text. The `String` representation of a `Thread` object contains various attributes about the thread, such as its name and priority. For example, the previous line of code displays the following output:

```
Thread[main,5,main]
```

The `toString` method is very useful for debugging and it would behoove you to override this method in all your classes.

Object Methods Covered In Other Lessons or Sections

The `Object` class provides a method, `finalize`, that cleans up an object before it is garbage collected. This method's role during garbage collection is discussed in this lesson in <u>Cleaning Up Unused Objects</u> (page 84). <u>Writing a `finalize` Method</u> (page 118) shows you how to override the `finalize` method to handle the finalization needs for your classes.

The `Object` class provides five methods that are critical when writing multi-threaded Java programs:

- `notify`
- `notifyAll`
- `wait` (three versions)

These methods help you ensure that your threads are synchronized. They are covered in **Threads of Control** (page 285). Take particular note of the section titled <u>Synchronizing Threads</u> (page 311).

Creating and Using Interfaces

Sometimes, you'd like classes from different parts of the class hierarchy to behave in similar ways. For example, suppose you are writing a spreadsheet program which contains a tabular set of cells, each containing one value. You want to put `Strings`, `Floats`, `Dates`, `Integers`, `Equations`, and so on into a cell in the spreadsheet. To do so, `Strings`, `Floats`, `Dates`, `Integers`, and `Equations` all have to implement the same set of methods. One way to achieve this is to find the common ancestor of the classes and implement the methods you need there. However, this is not a practical solution since `Object` is often the common ancestor. Except through `Object`, the objects you'd like to put in your spreadsheet cells are unrelated in the class hierarchy. But you are not allowed to modify `Object`.

One approach you could take in writing the spreadsheet would be to create a class called `CellValue` that represents a value that could be contained in one of the spreadsheet's cells. Then you could create `String`, `Float`, `Date`, `Integer`, and `Equation` subclasses of `CellValue`. In addition to being a lot of work, this approach arbitrarily forces a relationship on those classes that is otherwise unnecessary, and you must duplicate and reimplement classes that already exist.

Java provides a better way—through interfaces. An interface is a collection of method definitions (without implementations) and constant values.

Defining an interface is similar to creating a new class. An interface definition has two components: the interface declaration and the interface body.

```
interfaceDeclaration {
    interfaceBody
}
```

The *interfaceDeclaration* declares various attributes about the interface such as its name and whether it extends another interface. The *interfaceBody* contains the constant and method declarations within that interface.

To use an interface, write a class that *implements* the interface. When a class claims to implement an interface, the class is claiming that it provides a method implementation for all of the methods declared within the interface and its super-interfaces.

What Are Interfaces?

Definition: An interface is a collection of method definitions (without implementations) and constant values.

You use interfaces to define a protocol of behavior that can be implemented by any class anywhere in the class hierarchy. A better approach to the spreadsheet cell problem is to create an interface, say `CellAble`, that defines the list of methods that a cell value must implement: `toString`, `draw`, `toFloat`, and so on. Then the spreadsheet cells can contain any type of object that implements the `Cell Able` interface (or in other words, implements the list of methods). Objects that implement the `CellAble` interface do not have to be hierarchically related.

Interfaces are useful for:
- Capturing similarities between unrelated classes without forcing a class relationship.
- Declaring methods that one or more classes are expected to implement.
- Revealing an object's programming interface without revealing its class. (Objects such as these are called *anonymous objects* and can be useful when shipping a package of classes to other developers.)

In Java, an interface is a reference data type and as such, can be used in many of the same places where a type can be used (such as in method arguments and variable declarations). You'll see how to do this in Using an Interface as a Type (page 135).

Interfaces Do Not Provide Multiple Inheritance

Often interfaces are touted as an alternative to multiple class inheritance. While interfaces may solve some of the same problems as multiple class inheritance, they are quite different animals. In particular:
- You cannot inherit variables from an interface.
- You cannot inherit method implementations from an interface.
- The interface hierarchy is independent of the class hierarchy—classes that implement the same interface may or may not be related through the class hierarchy. This is not true for multiple inheritance.

Defining an Interface

To create an interface, you must write both the interface declaration and the interface body.

```
interfaceDeclaration {
    interfaceBody
}
```

The *interfaceDeclaration* declares various attributes about the interface such as its name and whether it extends another interface. The *interfaceBody* contains the constant and method declarations within the interface.

The Interface Declaration

At a minimum, the interface declaration must contain the Java keyword `interface` and the name of the interface that you are creating:

```
interface Countable {
    . . .
}
```

Note: By convention, interface names begin with capital letters just like class names do. Often, interface names end with "able" or "ible".

An interface declaration can have two other components: the `public` access specifier and a list of *superinterfaces*. An interface can extend other interfaces just as a class can extend or subclass another class. However, while a class can only extend one other class, an interface can extend any number of interfaces. The full interface declaration looks like this:

```
[public] interface InterfaceName
        [extends listOfSuperInterfaces] {
    . . .
}
```

The `public` access specifier indicates that the interface can be used by any class in any package. If you do not specify that your interface is public, then your interface will only be accessible to classes that are defined in the same package as the interface.

The `extends` clause is similar to the `extends` clause in a class declaration. However, an interface can extend multiple interfaces (a class can only extend

one), and an interface cannot extend classes. The list of superinterfaces is a comma-delimited list of all of the interfaces extended by the new interface. An interface inherits all constants and methods from its superinterface unless the interface hides a constant with another of the same name, or redeclares a method with a new method declaration.

The Interface Body

The interface body contains method declarations for the methods defined within the interface. Implementing Methods (page 94) shows you how to write a method declaration. In addition to method declarations, an interface can contain constant declarations. See Declaring Member Variables (page 91) for information about how to construct a member variable declaration.

Note: Member declarations in an interface disallow some of the use of some declaration modifiers and discourage the use of others. You may not use `transient`, `volatile`, or `synchronized` in a member declaration in an interface. Also, you may not use the `private` and `protected` specifiers when declaring members of an interface.

All constant values defined in an interface are implicitly public, static, and final. The use of these modifiers on a constant declaration in an interface is discouraged as a matter of style. Similarly, all methods declared in an interface are implicitly public and abstract. The use of these modifiers on a method declaration in an interface is discouraged as a matter of style.

The following code defines a new interface named `Collection` that contains one constant value and three method declarations:

```
interface Collection {
    int MAXIMUM = 500;

    void add(Object obj);
    void delete(Object obj);
    Object find(Object obj);
    int currentCount();
}
```

The `Collection` interface can be implemented by classes that represent collections of other objects such as stacks, vectors, linked lists, and so on.

Note that each method declaration is followed by a semicolon (;) because an interface does not provide implementations for the methods declared within it.

Note: Previous releases of the Java environment allowed you to use the `abstract` modifier on interface declarations and on method declarations within interfaces. However this is unnecessary as interfaces and their methods are implicitly abstract; none of the methods declared within an interface has an implementation. You should no longer be using `abstract` in your interface declarations or in your method declarations within interfaces.

Implementing an Interface

A class declares all of the interfaces that it implements in its class declaration. To declare that your class implements one or more interfaces, use the keyword `implements` followed by a comma-delimited list of the interfaces implemented by your class.

For example, consider the `Collection` interface introduced on page 133. Now, suppose that you are writing a class that implements a FIFO (first in, first out) queue. Because a FIFO queue object contains other objects, it makes sense for the class to implement the `Collection` interface. The `FIFOQueue` class implements the `Collection` interface using the following code.

```
class FIFOQueue implements Collection {
    . . .
    void add(Object obj) {
        . . .
    }
    void delete(Object obj) {
        . . .
    }
    Object find(Object obj) {
        . . .
    }
    int currentCount() {
        . . .
    }
}
```

By declaring that it implements the `Collection` interface, the `FIFOQueue` class guarantees that it provides implementations for the `add`, `delete`, `find`, and `currentCount` methods.

By convention, the `implements` clause follows the `extends` clause if it exists.

Note that the method signatures of the `Collection` interface methods implemented in the `FIFOQueue` class must match the method signatures as declared in the `Collection` interface.

Using an Interface as a Type

As mentioned previously, when you define a new interface, you are in essence defining a new reference data type. You can use interface names anywhere you can use any primitive data type name or any other reference data type name.

Consider the spreadsheet problem introduced in <u>Creating and Using Interfaces</u> (page 130). Let's say that you define an interface named CellAble that looks something like this:

```
interface CellAble {
    void draw();
    void toString();
    void toFloat();
}
```

Now, suppose that you have a row and column object that contains a bunch of objects that implement the CellAble interface. Your Row class's setObjectAt method could be implemented as in the following code example:

```
class Row {
    private CellAble[] contents;
    . . .
    void setObjectAt(CellAble ca, int index) {
        . . .
    }
    . . .
}
```

Note the use of the interface name CellAble in the member variable declaration for contents and the method parameter declaration for ca. Any object that implements the CellAble interface, regardless of where it exists within the class hierarchy, can be contained in the contents array and passed into the setObjectAt method.

Creating and Using Packages

Typically, to make classes easier to find and use, and to avoid naming conflicts, programmers bundle groups of related classes into class libraries. In Java, a class library is called a *package*. Packages can also contain interface definitions.

You can easily create your own packages and put any number of class and interface definitions in them.

To use the classes and interfaces defined in one package from within another package, you need to *import* the package. The classes and interfaces that you import must be declared public.

Several packages of reusable classes are shipped as part of the Java development environment. Indeed, you have already encountered several classes that are members of these packages: `String`, `System`, and `Date`, to name a few.

The classes and interfaces contained in the Java packages implement various functions ranging from networking and security to graphical user interface elements. Before you start writing your own classes, interfaces, and packages, make sure that one of classes or interfaces in these packages won't do the job for you.

Roll Your Own Packages

Packages are groups of related classes and interfaces. Packages provide a convenient mechanism for managing a large set of classes and interfaces and avoiding naming conflicts. In addition to using the Java packages, you can create your own packages and put class and interface definitions in them using Java's `package` statement.

Suppose that you are implementing a group of classes that represent a collection of graphic objects such as circles, rectangles, lines, and points. In addition to these classes you also have written an interface `Draggable` that classes implement if they can be dragged with the mouse by the user. If you want to make these classes available to other programmers, you can bundle them together into a package called `graphics` and give the package to the programmers, along with some documentation about what the classes and interfaces do and what their public programming interfaces are.

In this way, other programmers can easily determine what your group of classes are for, how to use them, and how they relate to one another and to other classes and packages. In addition, the names of your classes won't conflict with class names in other packages because the classes and interfaces within a package are referenced in terms of their package. (Technically, a package creates a new name space.)

Create a package using the `package` statement:

```
package graphics;

interface Draggable {
    . . .
}

class Circle {
    . . .
}
```

```
class Rectangle {
    . . .
}
```

The first line in the preceding code sample creates a package called `graphics`.

Note: For simplicity, we've named the package `graphics`. However, this does not circumvent the name collision problem as two different projects can conceivably use the same package name. This problem is solved by convention only. By convention, companies use their name in their package names like this: `COM.MyCompany.PackageName`.

All the classes and interfaces defined in the file containing this statement in it are members of the `graphics` package. `Draggable`, `Circle`, and `Rectangle` are all members of the new `graphics` package.

The `.class` files generated by the compiler when you compile the file that contains the source for `Draggable`, `Circle`, and `Rectangle` must be placed in a directory (or folder) named `graphics` somewhere in your CLASSPATH. Your CLASSPATH is a list of directories that indicate where on the file system you've installed compiled Java classes and interfaces. When looking for a class, the Java interpreter searches your CLASSPATH for a directory whose name matches the package name of which the class is a member. The `.class` files for all classes and interfaces defined in the package must be in that package directory.

Your package names can have multiple components, separated by periods. In fact, the Java package names have multiple components: `java.util`, `java.lang`, and so on. Each component of the package name represents a directory on the file system. So, the `.class` files for `java.util` are in a directory named `util` in a directory named `java` somewhere in your CLASSPATH.

CLASSPATH

To run a stand-alone Java application, specify the name of the Java application that you wish to execute to the Java interpreter. The application that you are running can be anywhere on your system or on the network. In addition, the application might use other classes or objects that are in the same or different location.

Because your classes could be anywhere, you must indicate to the Java interpreter where it can find the classes that you are trying to run. You do this with the CLASSPATH environment variable. The CLASSPATH environment variable is comprised of directory names that contain compiled Java classes. The actual construct of CLASSPATH depends on the system you are running.

Platform-Specific Details: The CLASSPATH Environment Variable

UNIX:
`setenv CLASSPATH .:~/classes`

DOS shell (Windows 95/NT):
`set CLASSPATH=.;~/classes`

MacOS:
You set the class path for your application in its `'STR '(0)` resource.

When the interpreter gets a classname, it searches each directory in the CLASS-PATH until it finds the class it's looking for.

You should put the top-level directory that contains your Java classes in your CLASSPATH. By convention, many people have a `classes` directory in their home directory where they put all of the Java code. If you have such a directory, you should put that directory in your CLASSPATH. It's often convenient to put the current directory in the CLASSPATH as well.

The classes included with the Java development environment are automatically available to you because the interpreter automatically appends the correct directory to your CLASSPATH when it starts up.

Note that order is important. When the Java interpreter is looking for a class, it searches the directories indicated by your CLASSPATH in order until it finds a class with the correct name. The Java interpreter runs the first class with the correct name that it encounters and does not search the remaining directories. Normally, it's best to give your classes unique names, but if you can't avoid it, make sure that your CLASSPATH searches your classes in the proper order. Keep this in mind when setting up your CLASSPATH and your source code hierarchy.

Note: If you load an applet into a Java application such as HotJava or the applet viewer and the loaded class is in the class path, the applet doesn't have the restrictions that applets loaded over the network do, and it can never be reloaded. We recommend never starting an application such as HotJava in the same directory as an applet class because the current directory "." is usually part of the class path.

Note: All classes and interfaces belong to a `package` even if you don't specify one with the `package` statement. If you don't specify a package explicitly using `package`, your classes and interfaces become members of the default package, which has no name and which is always imported.

Using the Classes and Interfaces from a Package

To import a specific class or interface into the current file (like the `Circle` class from the `graphics` package created in the previous section), use the `import` statement:

```
import graphics.Circle;
```

The `import` statement must be at the beginning of a file before any class or interface definitions. It makes the class or interface available for use by the classes and interfaces defined in that file.

If you want to import all the classes and interfaces contained in a particular package—for instance, in the `graphics` package—use the `import` statement with the asterisk (*) wildcard character:

```
import graphics.*;
```

If you try to use a class or interface that has not been imported, the compiler issues a fatal error:

```
testing.java:4: Class Circle not found in type declaration.
Circle circle;
^
```

Note that only classes and interfaces that are declared to be `public` can be used by classes outside of the package that they are defined in.

The default package (a package with no name) is always imported for you. The runtime system automatically imports the `java.lang` package for you, as well. If by some chance the name of a class in one package is the same as the name of a class in another package, you must disambiguate the names by prepending the package name to the beginning of the class. For example, previously we defined a class named `Rectangle` in the `graphics` package. The `java.awt` package also contains a `Rectangle` class. If both `graphics` and `java.awt` have been imported, then the following line of code (and others that attempt to use the `Rectangle` class) is ambiguous:

```
Rectangle rect;
```

In such a situation you have to be more specific and indicate exactly which Rectangle class you want:

```
graphics.Rectangle rect;
```

You do this by prepending the package name to the beginning of the class name and separating the two with a period.

The Java Packages

Eight packages comprise the standard Java development environment.

The Java Language Package

The Java Language Package, also known as `java.lang`, contains classes that are core to the Java language. The classes in this package are grouped as follows:

Object

The granddaddy of all classes—the class from which all others inherit. This class was covered previously in this lesson in The `Object` Class (page 128).

Data Type Wrappers

A collection of classes used to wrap variables of a primitive data type: `Boolean`, `Character`, `Double`, `Float`, `Integer` and `Long`.

Strings

Two classes that implement character data. **The `String` and `StringBuffer` Classes** (page 215) is a thorough lesson on the use of both types of strings.

System and Runtime

These two classes let your programs use system resources. `System` provides a system-independent programming interface to system resources and `Runtime` gives you direct system-specific access to the runtime environment. **Using System Resources** (page 237) describes both the `System` and `Runtime` classes and their methods.

Threads

The `Thread`, `ThreadDeath`, and `ThreadGroup` classes implement the multithreading capabilities so important to the Java language. The `java.lang` package also defines the `Runnable` interface. `Runnable` makes it convenient for a Java class to implement a thread without subclassing the `Thread` class. Through an example-oriented approach, **Threads of Control** (page 285) will teach you about Java threads.

Classes

The `Class` class provides a runtime description of a class and the `ClassLoader` class allows you to load classes into your program during runtime.

Math

The Math class provides a library of math routines and values such as π.

Exception, Error, and Throwable

When an error occurs in a Java program, the program throws an object which indicates what the problem was and the state of the interpreter when the error occurred. Only objects that derive from the `Throwable` class can be thrown. There are two main subclasses of `Throwable`: `Exception` and `Error`. Exceptions are a form of `Throwable` that "normal" programs may try to catch. Errors are used for more catastrophic errors—normal programs should not catch errors. The `java.lang` package contains the `Throwable`, `Exception`, and `Error` classes, and numerous subclasses of `Exception` and `Error` that represent specific problems. **Handling Errors Using Exceptions** (page 253) shows you how to use exceptions in your Java programs to handle errors.

Process

`Process` objects represent the system process that is created when you use `Runtime` to execute system commands. The `java.lang` package defines and implements the generic `Process` class.

The compiler automatically imports the Java Language Package for you. No other packages except the default package are automatically imported.

The Java I/O Package

The Java I/O Package (`java.io`) provides a set of input and output streams used to read and write data to files or other input and output sources. The classes and interfaces defined in `java.io` are covered fully in **Input and Output Streams** (page 325).

The Java Utility Package

This Java package, `java.util`, contains a collection of utility classes. Among them are several generic data structures (`Dictionary`, `Stack`, `Vector`, `Hashtable`), a useful class for tokenizing a string, and another for manipulating calendar dates. The `java.util` package also contains the `Observer` interface and `Observable` class, which allow objects to notify one another when they change. The `java.util` classes aren't covered separately in this tutorial although some examples use these classes.

The Java Networking Package

The `java.net` package contains classes and interfaces that implement various networking capabilities. The classes in this package include classes that implement a URL, a connection to a URL, a socket connection, and a datagram packet. You can use these classes to implement client-server applications and other networking communication applications. The **Custom Networking and**

Security (page 483) trail has several examples using these classes, including a client-server example and an example that uses datagrams.

The Applet Package

This package `java.applet` contains the Applet class—the class that you must subclass if you're writing an applet. Included in this package is the `AudioClip` interface, which provides a very high level abstraction of audio. **Writing Applets** (page 145) explains the ins and outs of developing your own applets.

The Abstract Window Toolkit Packages

Three packages comprise the Abstract Window Toolkit: `java.awt`, `java.awt.image`, and `java.awt.peer`.

AWT Package

The `java.awt` package provides graphical user interface (GUI) elements that are used to get input from and display information to the user. These elements include windows, buttons, scrollbars, and text items.

AWT Image Package

The `java.awt.image` package contains classes and interfaces for managing image data, such as setting the color model, cropping, color filtering, setting pixel values, and grabbing snapshots of the screen.

AWT Peer Package

The `java.awt.peer` package contains classes and interfaces that connect platform-independent AWT components to their platform-dependent implementations, such as Motif widgets or Microsoft Windows controls.

Creating a User Interface (page 357) describes all three of the AWT packages.

End of Trail

YOU'VE reached the end of the **Writing Java Programs** trail. Take a break—have a cup of steaming hot java.

What Next?

Once you've caught your breath, you have several choices of where to go next. You can go back to the **Trail Map** (page xv) to see all of your choices, or you can go directly to one of the following popular trails:

Writing Applets (page 145): The next trail in the tutorial. This is the starting point for learning everything about writing applets.

Using the Core Java Classes (page 209): This trail covers the classes that you are likely to use frequently: Strings, System, Threads, and the I/O classes. This trail also includes a lesson on exception handling. In the online version of this tutorial, **Using the Core Java Classes** is part of the **Writing Java Programs** trail.

Writing Applets

T HIS trail covers everything you need to know about writing Java applets.

Overview of Applets (page 149) gives a complete overview of how applets work, how you write an applet, and exactly what applets can and can't do. You should thoroughly understand this overview before going further in this trail.

Creating an Applet User Interface (page 169) talks about the various ways to get input from the user and give information to the user. This section discusses applet parameters, properties, graphical user interfaces, and sound.

Communicating with Other Programs (page 185) talks about inter-applet communication, as well as communication with other types of programs, such as server-side applications.

Understanding Applet Capabilities and Restrictions (page 197) gives details about the security restrictions that can be placed on applets and some safe ways of getting around applet restrictions. This section also discusses the capabilities that applets have that applications currently don't have, or that you might not expect applets to have.

Finishing an Applet (page 201) describes the characteristics of a high-quality applet. It includes Before You Ship That Applet (page 201), a checklist of some annoying behaviors you should avoid in your applet.

6

Overview of Applets

THIS lesson discusses the parts of an applet. If you haven't yet compiled an applet and included it in an HTML page, you might want to do so now. Step-by-step instructions are in **Getting Started: The "Hello World" Applet** (page 13).

Every applet is implemented by creating a subclass of the `Applet` class. The following figure shows the inheritance hierarchy of the `Applet` class. This hierarchy determines much of what an applet can do and how it does it, as you'll see on the next few pages.

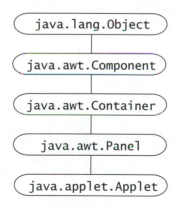

A Simple Applet

Below is the source code for an applet called `Simple`. The `Simple` applet displays a descriptive string whenever it encounters a major milestone in its life,   **149**

such as when the user first visits the page that the applet is on. The pages that follow use the `Simple` applet and build upon it to illustrate concepts that are common to many applets. If you find yourself baffled by the Java source code, you might want to go to the **Writing Java Programs** trail (page 27) to learn more about the Java language.

```java
import java.applet.Applet;
import java.awt.Graphics;

public class Simple extends Applet {

    StringBuffer buffer;

    public void init() {
        buffer = new StringBuffer();
        addItem("initializing... ");
    }

    public void start() {
        addItem("starting... ");
    }

    public void stop() {
        addItem("stopping... ");
    }

    public void destroy() {
        addItem("preparing for unloading...");
    }

    void addItem(String newWord) {
        System.out.println(newWord);
        buffer.append(newWord);
        repaint();
    }

    public void paint(Graphics g) {
        //Draw a Rectangle around the applet's display area.
        g.drawRect(0, 0, size().width - 1, size().height - 1);

        //Draw the current string inside the rectangle.
        g.drawString(buffer.toString(), 5, 15);
    }
}
```

The Life Cycle of an Applet (page 152) uses the `Simple` applet to teach you about the milestones in every applet's life.

The `Applet` class provides a framework for applet execution, defining methods that the system calls when milestones—major events in an applet's life cycle—occur. Methods for Milestones (page 153) tells you how most applets override some or all of these methods to respond appropriately to milestones.

Applets inherit the drawing and event-handling methods of the AWT `Component` class. (AWT stands for Abstract Windowing Toolkit; applets and applications use its classes to produce user interfaces.) *Drawing* refers to anything related to representing an applet on-screen—drawing images, presenting user interface components such as buttons, or using graphics primitives. *Event handling* is detecting and processing user input such as mouse clicks and key presses, as well as more abstract events such as saving files and iconifying windows. Methods for Drawing and Event Handling (page 155) gives an overview of how applets can use the methods they inherit from the `Component` class.

Methods for Adding UI Components (page 156) discusses the methods that applets inherit from the AWT `Container` class. As `Containers`, applets are designed to hold `Components`—user interface objects such as buttons, labels, pop-up lists, and scrollbars. Like other containers, applets use layout managers to control the positioning of components.

Threads in Applets (page 158) delves deeply into the issues of using threads in applets. A thread—sometimes known as an *execution context* or a *lightweight process*—is a single sequential flow of control within a process. Even the simplest applets run in multiple threads, although it's not always apparent. Many applets create and use their own threads so that they perform well without affecting the performance of the application they run in or the performance of other applets.

For security reasons, applets that are loaded over the network have several restrictions. One is that an applet can not ordinarily read or write files on the computer that it's executing on. Another is that an applet can not make network connections except to the host that it came from. Despite these restrictions, applets can do some things that you might not expect. For example, applets can invoke the public methods of other applets on the same page. An overview of applet restrictions and capabilities is in What Applets Can and Can Not Do (page 162).

Once you've written an applet, you'll need to add it to an HTML page so that it can run. Adding an Applet to an HTML Page (page 163) describes the <APPLET> HTML tag, with its most common variations.

After you've read every page in this lesson, you'll have seen almost everything you need to be able to write applets. To review what you've learned, see the Summary (page 166).

The Life Cycle of an Applet

Below is a picture of the `Simple` applet. (You can find its source code on page 588.)

> initializing... starting...

http://java.sun.com/Series/Tutorial/applet/overview/lifeCycle.html

Loading the Applet

The "initializing... starting..." text you see above is the result of the applet being loaded. When an applet is loaded, here's what happens:

- An instance of the applet's controlling class (an `Applet` subclass) is created.
- The applet *initializes* itself.
- The applet *starts* running.

Leaving and Returning to the Applet's Page

When the user leaves the page—for example, to go to another page—the applet has the option of *stopping* itself. When the user returns to the page, the applet can *start* itself again. The same sequence occurs when the user iconifies and then reopens the window that contains the applet. (Other terms used instead of iconify are *miniaturize*, *minimize*, and *close*.)

Try this: Visit the online version of this section in a Java-compatible browser. (The URL is `http://java.sun.com/Series/Tutorial/applet/over-view/lifeCycle.html`.) Leave and then return to the page. You'll see "stopping..." added to the applet output, as the applet is given the chance to stop itself. You'll also see "starting...", when the applet is told to start itself again. Next, iconify the window that contains the online version of this section, and then open it again. Many window systems provide a button in the title bar that lets you iconify the window. You should see "stopping..." and then "starting..." added to the applet output.

Browser note: Some browsers reload the applet when you return to its page. In at least one browser, a bug exists where an applet can initialize itself more than once without being reloaded.

Reloading the Applet

Some browsers let the user reload applets, which consists of unloading the applet and then loading it again. Before an applet is unloaded, it's given the chance to *stop* itself and then to perform a *final cleanup*, so that the applet can release any resources it holds. After that, the applet is unloaded and then loaded again, as described in Loading the Applet (page 152).

Try this: If your browser or other applet viewer lets you easily reload applets, reload the applet. Look at the standard output to see what happens when you reload the applet. (See Displaying Diagnostics to the Standard Output and Error Streams (page 182) for information about the standard output.) You should see "stopping..." and "preparing for unloading..." when the applet is unloaded. You can't see this in the applet GUI because the applet is unloaded before the text can be displayed. When the applet is reloaded, you should see "initializing..." and "starting...", just like when you loaded the applet for the first time.

Quitting the Browser

When the user quits the browser (or whatever application is displaying the applet), the applet has the chance to *stop* itself and do *final cleanup* before the browser exits.

Summary

An applet can react to milestones in the following ways:
- It can *initialize* itself.
- It can *start* running.
- It can *stop* running.
- It can perform a *final cleanup*, in preparation for being unloaded.

The next page describes the four applet methods that correspond to these four types of reactions.

Methods for Milestones

```
public class Simple extends Applet {
    . . .
    public void init() { . . . }
    public void start() { . . . }
```

```
        public void stop() { . . . }
        public void destroy() { . . . }
            . . .
    }
```

The Simple applet, like every other applet, contains a subclass of the `Applet` class. The `Simple` class overrides four `Applet` methods so that it can respond to major events:

init()
> To *initialize* the applet each time it is loaded or reloaded.

start()
> To *start* the applet's execution, such as when the applet is loaded or when the user revisits a page that contains the applet.

stop ()
> To *stop* the applet's execution, for example, when the user leaves the applet's page or quits the browser.

destroy()
> To perform a *final cleanup* in preparation for unloading.

Not every applet needs to override every one of these methods. Some simple applets override none of them. For example, **The "Hello World" Applet** (page 13) doesn't override any of these methods, since it doesn't do anything except draw itself. The "Hello World" applet just displays a string once using its `paint` method. (The `paint` method is described in the next section.) Most applets, however, do more.

The `init` method is useful for one-time initialization that doesn't take very long. In general, the `init` method should contain the code that you would normally put into a constructor. The reason applets shouldn't usually have constructors is that an applet isn't guaranteed to have a full environment until its `init` method is called. For example, the Applet image loading methods simply don't work inside of an applet constructor. The `init` method, on the other hand, is a great place to call the image loading methods, since the methods return quickly.

Browser note: Some browsers sometimes call the `init` method more than once after the applet has been loaded. See the browser note on page 152 for more details.

Every applet that does something after initialization (except in direct response to user actions) must override the `start` method. The `start` method either performs the applet's work or (more likely) starts up one or more threads to perform the work. You'll learn more about threads later in this trail, in Threads in Applets (page 158). You'll learn more about handling the events that represent user actions in the next section.

Most applets that override `start` should also override the `stop` method. The `stop` method should suspend the applet's execution so that it doesn't take up system resources when the user isn't viewing the applet's page. For example, an applet that displays animation should stop to draw the animation when the user isn't looking at it.

Many applets don't need to override the `destroy` method, since their `stop` method (which is called before `destroy`) does everything necessary to shut down the applet's execution. However, `destroy` is available for applets that need to release additional resources.

The `init`, `start`, `stop`, and `destroy` methods are discussed and used throughout this tutorial. For more information, you can also refer to the <u>Applet API reference page</u>.[1]

Methods for Drawing and Event Handling

The Simple applet in the following code defines its onscreen appearance by overriding the `paint` method. The `paint` method is one of two display methods that applets can override:

```
class Simple extends Applet {
    . . .
    public void paint(Graphics g) { . . . }
    . . .
}
```

paint
>   The basic display method. Many applets implement the `paint` method to draw the applet's representation within a browser page.

update
>   A method that you can use along with `paint` to improve drawing performance.

Applets inherit their `paint` and `update` methods from the `Applet` class, which inherits them from the Abstract Window Toolkit (AWT) `Component` class. For an overview of the `Component` class, and the AWT in general, see the **Overview of the Java UI** (page 361) lesson. Within the overview, the architecture of the AWT drawing system is discussed in the <u>Drawing</u> section (page 371).

Applets inherit a group of event-handling methods from the `Component` class. (The architecture of the AWT event system is discussed in the <u>Event Handling</u> section (page 373).) The `Component` class defines several methods, such as

---

[1] http://java.sun.com/products/JDK/CurrentRelease/api/java.applet.Applet.html

action and `mouseDown`, for handling specific types of events, and then one catch-all method called `handleEvent`.

To react to an event, an applet must override either the appropriate event-specific method or the `handleEvent` method. For example, adding the following code to the Simple applet makes it respond to mouse clicks.

```
import java.awt.Event;
. . .
public boolean mouseDown(Event event, int x, int y) {
    addItem("click!... ");
    return true;
}
```

Below is the resulting output from the applet. (You can find all its source code on page 589.) When you click within its rectangle, it displays the word "click!...".

```
initializing... starting... click!... click!...
```

http://java.sun.com/Series/Tutorial/applet/overview/componentMethods.html

Methods for Adding UI Components

The Simple applet's display code (implemented in its `paint` method) is flawed: It doesn't support scrolling. Once the text it displays reaches the end of the display rectangle, you can't see any new text. Here's an example of the problem:

```
initializing... starting... stopping... starting... stopping... starting... stopping... starting... stopping... starting...
```

The simplest cure for this problem is to use a pre-made user interface (UI) component that has the right behavior.

Note: This page glosses over many details. To really learn about using UI components, go to **Creating a User Interface** (page 357).

Pre-Made UI Components

The AWT supplies the following UI components. The class that implements each component is listed in parentheses.
- Buttons (`java.awt.Button`)
- Checkboxes (`java.awt.Checkbox`)

- Single-line text fields (`java.awt.TextField`)
- Larger text display and editing areas (`java.awt.TextArea`)
- Labels (`java.awt.Label`)
- Lists (`java.awt.List`)
- Pop-up lists of choices (`java.awt.Choice`)
- Sliders and scrollbars (`java.awt.Scrollbar`)
- Drawing areas (`java.awt.Canvas`)
- Menus (`java.awt.Menu`, `java.awt.MenuItem`, `java.awt.Checkbox-MenuItem`)
- Containers (`java.awt.Panel`, `java.awt.Window` and its subclasses)

Methods for Using UI Components in Applets

Because the `Applet` class inherits from the AWT `Container` class, it's easy to add components to applets and to use layout managers to control the components' on-screen positions. Here are some of the `Container` methods an applet can use:

add

   Adds the specified `Component`.

remove

   Removes the specified `Component`.

setLayout

   Sets the layout manager.

Adding a Non-Editable Text Field to the `Simple` Applet

To make the `Simple` applet use a scrolling, non-editable text field, we can use the `TextField` class. You can find the revised source code on page 590. The changes are shown below.

```
//Importing java.awt.Graphics is no longer necessary
//since this applet no longer implements the paint() method.
. . .
import java.awt.TextField;

    public class ScrollingSimple extends Applet {

    //Instead of using a StringBuffer, use a TextField:
    TextField field;

    public void init() {
        //Create the text field and make it uneditable.
        field = new TextField();
        field.setEditable(false);
```

```
        //Set the layout manager so that the text field will
        //be as wide as possible.
        setLayout(new java.awt.GridLayout(1,0));
        //Add the text field to the applet.
        add(field);
        validate();

        addItem("initializing... ");
    }

        . . .

void addItem(String newWord) {
        //This used to append the string to the StringBuffer;
        //now it appends it to the TextField.
        String t = field.getText();
        System.out.println(newWord);
        field.setText(t + newWord);
        repaint();
    }

    //The paint method is no longer necessary,
    //since the TextField paints itself automatically.
```

The revised `init` method creates an uneditable text field, a `TextField` instance. It sets the applet's layout manager to one that makes the text field as wide as possible and then adds the text field to the applet. (You'll learn about layout managers in the **Laying Out Components Within a Container** lesson (page 415).)

After all this, the `init` method calls the `validate` method, which `Applet` inherits from `Component`. Invoking `validate` once after adding one or more `components` to an applet is a bit of voodoo that ensures that the `components` draw themselves on screen. If you want to delve into the arcane reasons why `validate` works, read Details of the Component Architecture (page 410).

Below is the output of the resulting applet. By dragging the mouse, you can scroll backward or forward to see all of the messages that have been displayed.

nitializing... starting... stopping... starting... stopping... starting... stopping... starting... stopping... starting...

http://java.sun.com/Series/Tutorial/applet/overview/containerMethods.html

Threads in Applets

Note: The next page assumes that you know what a thread is. If you don't, read What Is a Thread? (page 286) before reading the next page.

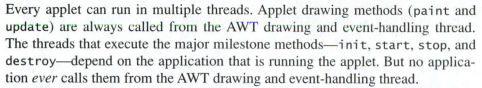

Every applet can run in multiple threads. Applet drawing methods (`paint` and `update`) are always called from the AWT drawing and event-handling thread. The threads that execute the major milestone methods—`init`, `start`, `stop`, and `destroy`—depend on the application that is running the applet. But no application *ever* calls them from the AWT drawing and event-handling thread.

Many browsers allocate a thread for each applet on a page, using that thread for all calls to the applet's major milestone methods. Some browsers allocate a thread group for each applet, so that it's easy to find all the threads that belong to a particular applet. In any case, you're guaranteed that every thread created by any of an applet's major milestone methods belongs to the same thread group.

Below are two PrintThread applets. PrintThread is a modified version of the SimpleApplet that prints the thread and thread group that `init`, `start`, `stop`, `destroy`, and `update` are called from. (You can find the code on page 581.) PrintThread calls `repaint` unnecessarily every once in a while, so that you'll be able to see how its `update` method gets called. As usual, to see the output for the methods such as `destroy` that are called during unloading, you need to look at the standard output. See <u>Displaying Diagnostics to the Standard Output and Error Streams</u> (page 182) for information about the standard output stream.

```
init: thread=thread applet-PrintThread.class, thread group=group applet-PrintThread.class
start: thread=thread applet-PrintThread.class, thread group=group applet-PrintThread.class
stop: thread=thread applet-PrintThread.class, thread group=group applet-PrintThread.class
start: thread=thread applet-PrintThread.class, thread group=group applet-PrintThread.class
update: thread=AWT-Callback-Win32, thread group=main
```

```
init: thread=thread applet-PrintThread.class, thread group=group applet-PrintThread.class
start: thread=thread applet-PrintThread.class, thread group=group applet-PrintThread.class
stop: thread=thread applet-PrintThread.class, thread group=group applet-PrintThread.class
start: thread=thread applet-PrintThread.class, thread group=group applet-PrintThread.class
update: thread=AWT-Callback-Win32, thread group=main
```

http://java.sun.com/Series/Tutorial/applet/overview/threads.html

So why would an applet need to create and use its own threads? Imagine an applet that performs some time-consuming initialization—loading sound data, for example—in its `init` method. The thread that invokes `init` can not do anything else until `init` returns. In some browsers, this might mean that the browser can not display the applet or anything after it until the applet has finished initializing itself. So if the applet is at the top of the page, then nothing appears on the page until the applet has finished initializing itself.

Even in browsers that create a separate thread for each applet, it makes sense to put any time-consuming tasks into an applet-created thread, so that the applet can perform other tasks while it waits for the time-consuming ones to be completed.

Rule of Thumb: If an applet performs a time-consuming task, it should create and use its own thread to perform that task.

Applets typically perform two kinds of time-consuming tasks: tasks that they perform once and tasks that they perform repeatedly. The next section gives an example of both.

Examples of Threads in Applets

This section discusses two examples of using threads in applets. The first applet, AnimatorApplet, shows how to use a thread to perform repeated tasks. AnimatorApplet is from the section Creating the Animation Loop (page 464). The second applet this section discusses, SoundExample, shows how to use threads for one-time initialization tasks. SoundExample is featured in the section Playing Sounds (page 172).

This section does not explain basic thread code. To learn about the Java implementation of threads, refer to **Threads of Control** (page 285).

Using a Thread to Perform Repeated Tasks

An applet that performs the same task over and over again typically should have a thread with a `while` (or `do...while`) loop that performs the task. A typical example is an applet that performs timed animation, such as a movie player or a game. Animation applets need a thread that requests repaints at regular intervals. Another example is an applet that reads data supplied by a server-side application. (See Using a Server to Work Around Security Restrictions (page 194) for such an example.)

Applets typically create threads for repetitive tasks in the applet `start` method. Creating the thread there makes it easy for the applet to stop the thread when the user leaves the page. All you need to do is implement the `stop` method so that it stops the applet's thread. When the user returns to the applet's page, the `start` method is called again, and the applet can again create a thread to perform the repetitive task.

Below is AnimatorApplet's implementation of the `start` and `stop` methods. (You can find all of the applet's source code on page 737.)

```
public void start() {
    ...//applet-specific code...
    //Start animating!
    if (animatorThread == null) {
        animatorThread = new Thread(this);
```

```
    }
    animatorThread.start();
}

public void stop() {
    animatorThread = null;
}
```

The `this` in `new Thread(this)` indicates that the applet provides the body of the thread. It does so by implementing the `java.lang Runnable` interface, which requires the applet to provide a `run` method that forms the body of the thread. We'll discuss AnimatorApplet's `run` method more later.

Notice that nowhere in the `AnimatorApplet` class is the `Thread stop` method called. This is because calling the `Thread stop` method is like clubbing the thread over the head. It's a drastic way to get the thread to stop what it's doing. Instead, you can write the thread's `run` method in such a way that the thread gracefully exits when you tap it on the shoulder. This shoulder tap comes in the form of setting to `null` an instance variable of type `Thread`.

In `AnimatorApplet`, this instance variable is called `animatorThread`. The `start` method sets it to refer to the newly-created `Thread` object. When the applet needs to kill the thread, it sets `animatorThread` to `null`. This kills the thread *not* by making it be garbage collected—it can't be garbage collected while it's capable of running—but because at the top of its loop, the thread checks `animatorThread`, continuing or exiting depending on the value of `animatorThread`. Here's the relevant code:

```
public void run() {
    . . .
    while (Thread.currentThread() == animatorThread) {
        ...//Display a frame of animation and then sleep.
    }
}
```

If `animatorThread` refers to the same thread as the currently executing thread, the thread continues executing. If, on the other hand, `animatorThread` is null, the thread exits. If `animatorThread` refers to *another* thread, then a race condition has occurred: `start` has been called so soon after `stop` (or this thread has taken such a long time in its loop) that `start` has created another thread before this thread reached the top of its `while` loop. Whatever the cause of the race condition, this thread should exit.

For more information about AnimatorApplet, go to <u>Creating the Animation Loop</u> (page 464).

Using a Thread to Perform One-Time Initialization

If your applet needs to perform some initialization task that can take a while, consider ways to perform the initialization in a thread. For example, anything that requires making a network connection should generally be done in a background thread. Fortunately, GIF and JPEG image loading is automatically done in the background, using threads that you don't need to worry about.

Sound loading, unfortunately, is not guaranteed to be done in the background. In current implementations, the `Applet getAudioClip` methods don't return until they have loaded all the audio data. As a result, if you want to preload sounds, you might want to create one or more threads to do so.

Using a thread to perform a one-time initialization task for an applet is a variation of the classic producer/consumer scenario. The thread that performs the task is the producer, and the applet is the consumer. Synchronizing Threads (page 311) discusses how to use Java threads in a producer/consumer scenario.

SoundExample adheres closely to the model presented in Synchronizing Threads. Like the Synchronizing Threads example, SoundExample features three classes:

- The producer: SoundLoader (page 596), a `Thread` subclass.
- The consumer: SoundExample (page 593), an `Applet` subclass. Unlike the Synchronizing Threads consumer example, SoundExample is not a `Thread`; it doesn't even implement the `Runnable` interface. However, the SoundExample instance methods are executed by at least two threads, depending on the application that executes the SoundExample applet.
- The storage object: SoundList (page 596), a `Hashtable` subclass. Unlike CubbyHole in the Synchronizing Threads example, SoundList can return null values if the sound data hasn't been stored yet. This makes sense for this applet because it needs to be able to react immediately to a user request to play the sound, even if the sound hasn't been loaded yet.

For more information on SoundExample, go to Playing Sounds (page 172).

What Applets Can and Can Not Do

This section gives an overview of both the restrictions applets face and the special capabilities they have. You'll find more details in the **Understanding Applet Capabilities and Restrictions** lesson (page 197).

Security Restrictions

Each browser implements security policies to keep applets from compromising system security. This section describes the security policies that current browsers adhere to. However, the implementation of the security policies differs from browser to browser. Also, security policies are subject to change. For example, if a browser is developed for use only in trusted environments, then its security policies will likely be much more lax than those described here.

At press time, current browsers impose the following restrictions on any applet that is loaded over the network:

- An applet can not load libraries or define native methods.
- It can not ordinarily read or write files on the host that is executing it.
- It can not make network connections except to the host that it came from.
- It can not start any program on the host that is executing it.
- It can not read certain system properties.
- Windows that an applet brings up look different from windows that an application brings up.

Each browser has a `SecurityManager` object that implements its security policies. When a `SecurityManager` detects a violation, it throws a `SecurityException`. Your applet can catch this `SecurityException` and react appropriately.

Applet Capabilities

The `java.applet` package provides an API that gives applets some capabilities that applications don't have. For example, applets can play sounds, which other programs aren't able to do yet.

Here are some other things that current (as of press time) browsers and other applet viewers let applets do:

- Applets can usually make network connections to the host they came from.
- Applets running within a Web browser can easily cause HTML documents to be displayed.
- Applets can invoke public methods of other applets on the same page.
- Applets that are loaded from the local file system (from a directory in the user's `CLASSPATH`) have none of the restrictions that applets loaded over the network do.
- Although most applets stop running once you leave their page, they don't have to.

For more information, see the **Understanding Applet Capabilities and Restrictions** lesson (page 197).

Adding an Applet to an HTML Page

Once you've written some code for your applet, you'll want to run your applet to test it. To run an applet in a browser or in the JDK Applet Viewer, the applet needs to be added to an HTML page, using the <APPLET> tag. You then specify the URL of the HTML page to your browser or the Applet Viewer.

Note: Some browsers don't support easy, guaranteed reloading of applets. For this reason, it often makes sense to test applets in the Applet Viewer until the applet reaches a point where you need to test it in a browser.

This section tells you most of what you need to know to use the <APPLET> tag. It starts by showing you the tag's simplest form, and then discusses some of the most common additions to that simple form—the CODEBASE attribute, the <PARAM> tag, and alternate HTML code. For a detailed description of the <APPLET> tag, refer to <u>The <APPLET> Tag</u> (page 800).

The Simplest Possible <APPLET> Tag

Here's the simplest form of the <APPLET> tag:

```
<APPLET CODE=AppletSubclass.class WIDTH=anInt HEIGHT=anInt>
</APPLET>
```

The above tag tells the browser or applet viewer to load the applet whose Applet subclass, named *AppletSubclass*, is in a class file in the same directory as the HTML document that contains the tag. This tag also specifies the width and height of the applet in pixels.

    When a browser encounters the tag, it reserves a display area of the specified width and height for the applet, loads the bytecodes for the specified Applet subclass, creates an instance of the subclass, and then calls the instance's init and start methods.

Specifying the Applet Directory with CODEBASE

Here's a slightly more complex applet tag. It adds a CODEBASE attribute to tell the browser/viewer which directory the Applet subclass bytecodes are in.

```
<APPLET CODE=AppletSubclass.class CODEBASE=aURL
        WIDTH=anInt HEIGHT=anInt>
</APPLET>
```

By making *aURL* an absolute URL, you can make a document loaded from your HTTP server run an applet from another HTTP server. If *aURL* is a relative URL, then it's interpreted relative to the HTML document's location.

This tutorial uses CODEBASE=*someDirectory*/ frequently, since we put our examples in a subdirectory of the directory that contains the HTML documents. For example, here's the <APPLET> tag that includes the Simple applet in <u>The Life Cycle of an Applet</u> (page 152), earlier in this trail:

```
<APPLET CODE=Simple.class CODEBASE=example/ WIDTH=500
        HEIGHT=20>
</APPLET>
```

Specifying Parameters with the <PARAM> Tag

Some applets let the user customize the applet's configuration with parameters. For example, AppletButton (an applet used throughout this tutorial to provide a button that brings up a window) allows the user to set the button's text by specifying the value of a parameter named BUTTONTEXT. You'll learn how to write the code to provide parameters in <u>Defining and Using Applet Parameters</u> (page 175).

Here's an example of the format of the <PARAM> tag. Note that <PARAM> tags must appear between the <APPLET> and </APPLET> tags for the applet they affect.

```
<APPLET CODE=AppletSubclass.class WIDTH=anInt HEIGHT=anInt>
<PARAM NAME=parameter1Name VALUE=aValue>
<PARAM NAME=parameter2Name VALUE=anotherValue>
</APPLET>
```

Here's an example of the <PARAM> tag in use, taken from <u>Using Layout Managers</u> (page 416).

```
<APPLET CODE=AppletButton.class CODEBASE=example/ WIDTH=350
        HEIGHT=60>
<PARAM NAME=windowType VALUE=BorderWindow>
<PARAM NAME=windowText VALUE="BorderLayout">
<PARAM NAME=buttonText
VALUE="Click here to see a BorderLayout in action">
. . .
</APPLET>
```

Specifying Text to Be Displayed by Java-Deficient Browsers

Note the ellipsis points (". . .") in the AppletButton HTML example above. What did the example leave out? It omitted alternate HTML code—HTML code interpreted only by browsers that don't understand the <APPLET> tag.

If the page that contains your applet might be seen by people running Java-deficient browsers, you should provide alternate HTML code so that the page still makes sense. Alternate HTML code is any text between the <APPLET> and </APPLET> tags, except for <PARAM> tags. Java-compatible browsers ignore alternate HTML code.

We use alternate HTML code throughout the online version of this tutorial to tell readers about the applet they're missing and, if it's helpful, to provide a picture of the applet. Here's the full HTML code for the AppletButton example shown previously:

```
<APPLET CODE=AppletButton.class CODEBASE=example/ WIDTH=350
          HEIGHT=60>
<PARAM NAME=windowType VALUE=BorderWindow>
<PARAM NAME=windowText VALUE="BorderLayout">
<PARAM NAME=buttonText
VALUE="Click here to see a BorderLayout in action">
<HR>
<EM>
Your browser can't run 1.0 Java applets,
so here's a picture of the window the program brings up:</EM>
<P>
<IMG SRC=images/BorderEx1.gif WIDTH=302 HEIGHT=138>
<HR>
</APPLET>
```

An applet that doesn't understand the <APPLET> tag ignores everything in the previous HTML code until <HR>. An applet that *does* understand the <APPLET> tag ignores everything between <HR> and </HR>.

Summary

This lesson gave you lots of information—almost everything you need to know to write a Java applet. This page summarizes what you've learned, adding bits of information to help you understand the whole picture.

First, you learned that to write an applet, you must create a subclass of the java.applet Applet class. In your Applet subclass, you must implement at least one of the following methods: init, start, and paint. The init and start methods, along with stop and destroy, are called when major events (milestones) occur in the applet's life cycle. The paint method is called when the applet needs to draw itself to the screen.

The Applet class extends the AWT Panel class, which extends the AWT Container class, which extends the AWT Component class. From Component, an applet inherits the ability to draw and handle events. From Container, an applet

inherits the ability to include other components and to have a layout manager control the size and position of those components. From `Applet`, an applet inherits several capabilities, including the ability to respond to major milestones, such as loading and unloading. You'll learn more about what the `Applet` class provides as you continue along this trail.

You include applets in HTML pages using the `<APPLET>` tag. When a browser user visits a page that contains an applet, here's what happens:

1. The browser finds the class file for the applet's `Applet` subclass. The location of the class file (which contains Java bytecodes) is specified with the `CODE` and `CODEBASE` attributes of the `<APPLET>` tag.
2. The browser brings the bytecodes over the network to the user's computer.
3. The browser creates an instance of the `Applet` subclass. When we refer to an *applet*, we're generally referring to this instance.
4. The browser calls the applet's `init` method. This method performs any one-time initialization that is required.
5. The browser calls the applet's `start` method. This method often starts a thread to perform the applet's duties.

An applet's `Applet` subclass is its main, controlling class, but applets can use other classes, as well. These other classes can be either local to the browser, provided as part of the Java environment, or custom classes that you supply. When the applet tries to use a class for the first time, the browser tries to find the class on the host that is running the browser. If the browser can not find the class there, it looks for the class in the same place that the applet's `Applet` subclass came from. When the browser finds the class, it loads its bytecodes (over the network, if necessary) and continues executing the applet.

Loading executable code over the network is a classic security risk. For Java applets, some of this risk is reduced because the Java language is designed to be safe—for example, Java doesn't allow pointers to random memory. In addition, Java-compatible browsers improve security by imposing restrictions. These restrictions include disallowing applets from loading code written in any non-Java language, and disallowing applets from reading or writing files on the browser's host.

7

Creating an Applet
User Interface

MOST applets have a *graphical user interface* (GUI). This is a natural consequence of the fact that each applet appears, as specified by an `<APPLET>` tag, within an HTML page that is displayed by a browser. Because the `Applet` class is a subclass of the AWT (Abstract Window Toolkit) `Panel` class, and thus participates in the AWT event and drawing model, creating an applet's GUI is just as easy as creating an application's GUI—easier, actually, since the applet's window (the browser window) already exists.

An applet can mix and match several UI types, depending on the kind of information it needs to give or to get. Some applets play *sounds*, either to give the user feedback or to provide ambiance. Applets can get configuration information from the user through *parameters* that the applet defines. Applets can get system information by reading *system properties*. To give text information to the user, an applet can use its GUI or display a *short status string* (for text that's not crucial) or display to the *standard output* or *standard error* stream (for debugging text).

Some of the UI possibilities mentioned above are available only to applets. Some are available to applications, as well. This lesson gives you everything you need to know to use each UI type in an applet, with pointers to where you can learn more about each UI option that is not specific to applets.

The Creating a GUI (page 170) section talks about the few GUI implementation issues that apply only to applets.

The `Applet` class and `AudioClip` interface provide support for playing sounds. Playing Sounds (page 172) tells you about this support and includes a detailed example of supporting sound in an applet.

You can improve the versatility of your applet by providing parameters. <u>Defining and Using Applet Parameters</u> (page 175) describes how to decide which parameters to provide, how to implement them, and how to inform the user about them.

Applets can read some, but not all, system properties. <u>Reading System Properties</u> (page 180) discusses which system properties applets can usually read, as well as how to read them.

<u>Displaying Short Status Strings</u> (page 181) describes how to make an applet display a short status string on the status line of the application in which it is running.

When you're debugging an applet, displaying to the standard output can be an invaluable technique. <u>Displaying Diagnostics to the Standard Output and Error Streams</u> (page 182) discusses the applet-specific aspects of displaying to the standard output and error streams.

Creating a GUI

Almost all applets have a graphical user interface (GUI). The **Creating a User Interface** trail (page 357) discusses all the GUI concepts referred to in this section and gives many examples of applet GUIs. This section discusses the few issues that are particular to applet GUIs.

An `Applet` *is a* `Panel`.

Because `Applet` is a subclass of the AWT `Panel`[1] class, applets can contain other `Components`,[2] just as any `Panel` can. Applets inherit `Panel`'s default layout manager: `FlowLayout`.[3] As `Panel` objects (and thus `Component` objects), applets participate in the AWT drawing and event hierarchy.

Applets appear in pre-existing browser windows.

This statement has two implications. First, unlike GUI-based applications, applets don't have to create a window to display themselves in. They *can* create a window, but they often just display themselves within the browser window. Second, depending on the browser implementation, your applet's components might not be shown unless your applet calls `validate` after adding components to itself. Fortunately, calling `validate` can't hurt.

The applet background color might not match the page color.

By default, applets have a light gray background color. HTML pages, however, can have other background colors and can use background patterns. If

---

[1.] http://java.sun.com/products/JDK/CurrentRelease/api/java.awt.Panel.html
[2.] http://java.sun.com/products/JDK/CurrentRelease/api/java.awt.Component.html
[3.] http://java.sun.com/products/JDK/CurrentRelease/api/java.awt.FlowLayout.html

the applet designer and page designer aren't careful, the applet's different background color can cause it to stick out on the page or cause noticeable flashing when the applet is drawn. One solution is to define an applet parameter that specifies the applet's background color. The `Applet` subclass can use `Component`'s `setBackground` method to set its background to the user-specified color. Using the background color parameter, the page designer can choose an applet color that works well with the page colors. You'll learn about parameters in <u>Defining and Using Applet Parameters</u> (page 175), and about the `Component` class and drawing in the **Creating a User Interface** trail (page 357).

Each applet has a user-specified, pre-determined size.

Because the `<APPLET>` tag requires that the applet's width and height be specified, and because browsers don't necessarily allow applets to resize themselves, applets must make do with a fixed amount of space that might not be ideal. Even if the amount of space is ideal for one platform, the platform-specific parts of the applet (such as buttons) might require a different amount of space on another platform. You can compensate by recommending that pages that include your applet specify a little more space than might be necessary, and by using flexible layouts, such as the AWT-provided `Grid-BagLayout` and `BorderLayout` classes, that adapt well to extra space.

Applets load images using the `Applet getImage` methods.

The `Applet` class provides a convenient form of `getImage` that lets you specify a base URL as one argument, followed by a second argument that specifies the image file location, relative to the base URL. The `Applet get-CodeBase` and `getDocumentBase` methods provide the base URLs that most applets use. Images that an applet always needs, or needs to rely on as a backup, are usually specified relative to where the applet's code was loaded from (the *code base*). Images that are specified by the applet user, often with parameters in the HTML file, are usually relative to the page that includes the applet (the *document base*).

Applet classes, and often the data files they use, are loaded over the network, which can be slow.

Applets can do several things to decrease the perceived startup time. The `Applet` subclass can be a small one that immediately displays a status message. If some of the applet's classes or data aren't used right away, the applet can preload the classes or data in a background thread.

For example, the <u>AppletButton</u> (page 671) class `start` method launches a thread that gets the `Class`[1] object for the window the button

---

[1]. http://java.sun.com/products/JDK/CurrentRelease/api/java.lang.Class.html

brings up. The applet's main purpose in doing so is to make sure that the window class name the user specified is valid. An added benefit is that getting the `Class` object forces the window class file to be loaded before it is instantiated. When the user requests that the window be created, the applet instantiates the window class much quicker than if the applet still had to load the window class file.

Playing Sounds

In the Java `Applet` package (`java.applet`), the `Applet`[1] class and `AudioClip`[2] interface provide basic support for playing sounds. Currently, the Java API supports only one sound format: 8-bit, μ law, 8000 Hz, one-channel, Sun ".au" files. You can create these on a Sun workstation using the `audiotool` application. You can convert files from other sound formats using an audio format conversion program.

Sound-Related Methods

Below are the sound-related `Applet` methods. The two-argument form of each method takes a base URL, which is usually returned by either `getDocumentBase` or `getCodeBase` and the location of the sound file relative to the base URL. You should use the code base for sounds that are integral to the applet. The document base is used for sounds specified by the applet user, such as through applet parameters.

```
getAudioClip(URL), getAudioClip(URL, String)
```

> Return an object that implements the `AudioClip` interface.

```
play(URL), play(URL, String)
```

> Play the `AudioClip` corresponding to the specified URL.

---

[1] http://java.sun.com/products/JDK/CurrentRelease/api/java.applet.Applet.html
[2] http://java.sun.com/products/JDK/CurrentRelease/api/java.applet.AudioClip.html

The `AudioClip` interface defines the following methods:

`loop()`

Starts playing the clip repeatedly.

`play()`

Plays the clip once.

`stop()`

Stops the clip. Works with both looping and one-time sounds.

An Example

Here is an applet called SoundExample that illustrates a few things about sound. Note that, for instructional purposes, the applet adds up to 10 seconds to the load time for each sound. If the sounds were larger or the user's connection slower than ours, these delays might be realistic.

http://java.sun.com/Series/Tutorial/applet/ui/sound.html

The SoundExample applet provides an architecture for loading and playing multiple sounds in an applet. For this reason, it is more complex than necessary. Essentially, the sound loading and playing code boils down to this:

```
AudioClip onceClip, loopClip;
onceClip = applet.getAudioClip(getCodeBase(), "bark.au");
loopClip = applet.getAudioClip(getCodeBase(), "train.au");
onceClip.play();    //Play it once.
loopClip.loop();    //Start the sound loop.
loopClip.stop();    //Stop the sound loop.
```

Since there's nothing more annoying than an applet that continues to make noise after you've left its page, the SoundExample applet stops playing the continuously looping sound when the user leaves the page, and resumes playing it when the user comes back. It does this by implementing its `stop` and `start` methods as follows:

```
public void stop() {
    //If one-time sound were long, we'd stop it here, too.
```

```
//looping is a boolean instance variable that's initially
//false. It's set to true when the "Start sound loop"
//button is clicked and to false when the "Stop sound loop"
//or "Reload sounds" button is clicked.
if (looping) {
    loopClip.stop();      //Stop the sound loop.
}
}

public void start() {
    if (looping) {
        loopClip.loop();      //Restart the sound loop.
    }
}
```

The SoundExample applet features three classes:

- An `Applet` subclass, <u>SoundExample</u> (page 593), that controls the applet's execution.
- A `Hashtable` subclass, <u>SoundList</u> (page 596), that holds `AudioClips`. This is overkill for this applet, but if you were to write an applet that used many sound files, a class like this would be useful.
- A `Thread` subclass, <u>SoundLoader</u> (page 596), each instance of which loads an `AudioClip` in the background. During the applet's initialization, the applet preloads each sound by creating a `SoundLoader` for it.

Preloading the sounds in a background thread with `SoundLoader` improves the perceived performance by reducing the amount of time the user has to wait to interact with the applet. It does this by reducing the amount of time spent in the `init` method. If you simply call `getAudioClip` in the applet's `init` method, it may take quite a while before `getAudioClip` returns, meaning that the applet cannot execute the other statements in its `init` method, and that the applet's `start` method won't get called. (For the SoundExample applet, a delay in calling the `start` method doesn't matter.)

Another advantage of loading the sounds in a background thread is that it enables the applet to respond appropriately (and immediately) to user input that normally causes a sound to play, even if that sound hasn't been loaded yet. If you simply use the Applet `play` methods, for example, then the first time the user does something to make the applet play a particular sound, the applet's drawing and event handling is frozen while the sound is loaded. Instead, this applet detects that the sound hasn't been loaded yet and responds appropriately.

This example is discussed in more detail in <u>Examples of Threads in Applets</u> (page 160).

Defining and Using Applet Parameters

Parameters are to applets what command-line arguments are to applications. They allow the user to customize the applet's operation. By defining parameters, you can increase your applet's flexibility, making your applet work in multiple situations without recoding and recompiling it.

The next few pages discuss parameters from the applet programmer's point of view. To learn about the user view of parameters, see Specifying Parameters with the <PARAM> Tag (page 165).

The section Deciding Which Parameters to Support (page 175) discusses how to design parameters.

Applets get the user-defined values of parameters by calling the `Applet` `getParameter` method. Writing the Code to Support Parameters (page 177) tells you how to use `getParameter`.

By implementing the `getParameterInfo` method, applets provide information that browsers can use to help the user set parameter values. Giving Information About Parameters (page 179) tells you how to implement `get` `ParameterInfo`.

Deciding Which Parameters to Support

This section guides you through the four questions you should ask as you implement parameters:

- What should the applet allow the user to configure?
- What should the parameters be named?
- What kind of value should each parameter take?
- What should the default value of each parameter be?

This section ends with a discussion of the parameters defined by an example class named `AppletButton`.

What Should the Applet Allow the User to Configure?

The parameters your applet should support depend on what your applet does and on how flexible you want it to be. Applets that display images might have parameters to specify the image locations. Similarly, applets that play sounds might have parameters to specify the sounds.

Besides parameters that specify resource locations (such as image and sound files), applets sometimes provide parameters for specifying details of the applet's appearance or operation. For example, an animation applet might let the user specify the number of images shown per second. Or an applet might let the user change the strings the applet displays. Anything is possible.

What Should the Parameters Be Named?

Once you decide what parameters your applet will support, you need to determine their names. Here are some typical parameter names:

SOURCE *or* **SRC**

> For a data file such as an image file.

*XXX***SOURCE** *(for example,* `IMAGESOURCE`*)*

> Used in applets that let the user specify more than one type of data file.

*XXX***S**

> For a parameter that takes a list of *XXX*s (where *XXX* might be `IMAGE`, again).

NAME

> Used *only* for an applet's name. Applet names are used for interapplet communication, as described in <u>Sending Messages to Other Applets on the Same Page</u> (page 186).

Clarity of names is more important than keeping the name length short. Do *not* use names of <APPLET> tag attributes, which are documented in <u>The <APPLET> Tag</u> (page 801).

Note: Although this tutorial usually refers to parameter names using ALL UPPER-CASE, parameter names are case insensitive. For example, IMAGESOURCE and `imageSource` both refer to the same parameter. Parameter *values*, on the other hand, are case sensitive unless you take steps to interpret them otherwise, such as by using the `String toLowerCase` method before interpreting the parameter's value.

What Kind of Value Should Each Parameter Take?

Parameter values are all strings. Whether or not the user puts quotation marks around a parameter value, that value is passed to your applet as a string. However, your applet can interpret the string in many ways.

Applets typically interpret a parameter value as one of the following types:
- A URL
- An integer
- A floating-point number
- A boolean value—typically `"true"`/`"false"` or `"yes"`/`"no"`
- A string—for example, the string to use as a window title
- A list of any of the above

What Should the Default Value of Each Parameter Be?

Applets should attempt to provide useful default values for each parameter, so that the applet will execute even if the user doesn't specify a parameter or specifies it incorrectly. For example, an animation applet should provide a reasonable

setting for the number of images it displays per second. This way, if the user doesn't specify the relevant parameter, the applet will still work well.

An Example: `AppletButton`

Throughout this tutorial, applets that need to bring up windows use the highly configurable `AppletButton` (page 671) class. One online tutorial page alone[1] uses `AppletButton` five times for five different examples, one per layout manager the AWT provides. `AppletButton`'s GUI is simple; it consists of a button and a label that displays status. When the user clicks the button, the applet brings up a window.

The `AppletButton` class is flexible because it defines parameters that let the user specify any or all of the following:

- The type of window to bring up
- The window's title
- The window's height
- The window's width
- The label of the button that brings up the window

Here's what a typical <APPLET> tag for `AppletButton` looks like. You can see this applet running at the URL http://java.sun.com/Series/Tutorial/ui/layout/border.html.

```
<APPLET CODE=AppletButton.class CODEBASE=example/ WIDTH=350
        HEIGHT=60>
<PARAM NAME=windowClass VALUE=BorderWindow>
<PARAM NAME=windowTitle VALUE="BorderLayout">
<PARAM NAME=buttonText
        VALUE="Click here to see a BorderLayout in action">
</APPLET>
```

When the user doesn't specify a value for a parameter, `AppletButton` uses a reasonable default value. For example, if the user doesn't specify the window's title, `AppletButton` uses the window's type as the title.

The next section shows you the code `AppletButton` uses to get its parameter values from the user.

Writing the Code to Support Parameters

Applets use the `Applet` `getParameter` method to get user-specified values for applet parameters. The `getParameter` method is defined as follows:

```
getParameter(String name)
```

---

[1]. http://java.sun.com/Series/Tutorial/ui/layout/using.html

Your applet might need to convert the string that `getParameter` returns into another form, such as an integer. The `java.lang` package provides classes such as `Integer` that help convert strings to primitive types. Here's an example from the `AppletButton` class of converting a parameter's value into an integer:

```
int requestedWidth = 0;
. . .
String windowWidthString = getParameter("WINDOWWIDTH");
if (windowWidthString != null) {
    try {
        requestedWidth = Integer.parseInt(windowWidthString);
    } catch (NumberFormatException e) {
        //Use default width.
    }
}
```

Note that if the user doesn't specify a value for the `WINDOWWIDTH` parameter, the above code uses a default value of 0, which the applet interprets as "use the window's natural size." It's important to supply default values wherever possible.

Besides using the `getParameter` method to get values of applet-specific parameters, you can also use `getParameter` to get the values of attributes of the applet's <APPLET> tag. See <u>The <APPLET> Tag</u> (page 801) for a list of <APPLET> tag attributes.

An Example: `AppletButton`

Below is the `AppletButton` code that gets the applet's parameters. For more information on `AppletButton`, see page 177.

```
String windowClass;
String buttonText;
String windowTitle;
int requestedWidth = 0;
int requestedHeight = 0;
. . .
public void init() {
    windowClass = getParameter("WINDOWCLASS");
    if (windowClass == null) {
        windowClass = "TestWindow";
    }

    buttonText = getParameter("BUTTONTEXT");
    if (buttonText == null) {
        buttonText = "Click here to bring up a " + windowClass;
    }

    windowTitle = getParameter("WINDOWTITLE");
```

```
if (windowTitle == null) {
    windowTitle = windowClass;
}

String windowWidthString = getParameter("WINDOWWIDTH");
if (windowWidthString != null) {
    try {
        requestedWidth = Integer.parseInt(windowWidthString);
    } catch (NumberFormatException e) {
        //Use default width.
    }
}

String windowHeightString = getParameter("WINDOWHEIGHT");
if (windowHeightString != null) {
    try {
        requestedHeight =
            Integer.parseInt(windowHeightString);
    } catch (NumberFormatException e) {
        //Use default height.
    }
}
```

Giving Information About Parameters

Now that you've provided all those nice parameters to the user, you need to help the user set the parameter values correctly. Of course, your applet's documentation should describe each parameter and give the user examples and hints of setting them. Your job doesn't stop there, though. You should also implement the getParameterInfo method so that it returns information about your applet's parameters. Browsers can use this information to help the user set your applet's parameter values.

The following code is an example of implementing the getParameterInfo method. This example is from the *Animator*[1] applet, a wonderfully flexible applet that provides 13 parameters for users to customize their animation.

```
public String[][] getParameterInfo() {
    String[][] info = {
      // Parameter Name   Kind of Value Description
        {"imagesource",   "URL",        "a directory"},
        {"startup",       "URL",        "displayed at startup"},
        {"background",    "URL",        "displayed as
                                        background"},
        {"startimage",    "int",        "start index"},
```

[1.] To find the Animator applet, see the Web page for this book:
   http://java.sun.com/Series/Tutorial/book.html

```
          {"endimage",     "int",         "end index"},
          {"namepattern",  "URL",         "used to generate " +
                                              "indexed names"},
          {"pause",        "int",         "milliseconds"},
          {"pauses",       "ints",        "milliseconds"},
          {"repeat",       "boolean",     "repeat or not"},
          {"positions",    "coordinates", "path"},
          {"soundsource",  "URL",         "audio directory"},
          {"soundtrack",   "URL",         "background music"},
          {"sounds",       "URLs",        "audio samples"},
     };
     return info;
}
```

As you can see, the getParameterInfo method must return an array of three-String arrays. In each three-String array, the first String is the parameter name. The second String gives the user a hint about what general kind of value the applet needs for the parameter. The third String describes the meaning of the parameter.

Reading System Properties

To find out about the current working environment, applets can read system properties. System properties are key/value pairs that contain information such as the operating system that the applet is running under. System properties are covered in detail in the <u>System Properties</u> (page 242) section.

Applets can read some, but not all, system properties. This page lists the system properties that Netscape Navigator 2.0 and Applet Viewer 1.0 allow applets to read, followed by a list of properties that applets can't read.

System Properties That Applets Can Read

Applets can currently read the following system properties:

Key	Meaning
"file.separator"	File separator (for example, "/")
"java.class.version"	Java class version number
"java.vendor"	Java vendor-specific string
"java.vendor.url"	Java vendor URL

Key	Meaning
"java.version"	Java version number
"line.separator"	Line separator
"os.arch"	Operating system architecture
"os.name"	Operating system name
"path.separator"	Path separator (for example, ":")

To read a system property from within an applet, the applet uses the System class method getProperty. For example:

```
String s = System.getProperty("os.name");
```

Forbidden System Properties

For security reasons, no existing browsers or applet viewers let applets read the following system properties.

Key	Meaning
"java.class.path"	Java classpath
"java.home"	Java installation directory
"user.dir"	User's current working directory
"user.home"	User home directory
"user.name"	User account name

Displaying Short Status Strings

All applet viewers—from the Applet Viewer to Java-compatible browsers—allow applets to display a short status string. In current implementations, this string appears on the status line at the bottom of the applet viewer window. In browsers, all applets on the page, as well as the browser itself, generally share the same status line.

You should never put crucial information in the status line. If many users might need the information, it should instead be displayed within the applet area.

If only a few, sophisticated users might need the information, consider displaying the information on the standard output. See <u>Displaying Diagnostics to the Standard Output and Error Streams</u> (page 182) for more details.

The status line is not usually very prominent, and it can be overwritten by other applets or by the browser. For these reasons, use it only for incidental, transitory information. For example, an applet that loads several image files might display the name of the image file it is currently loading.

Applets display status lines with the `showStatus` method. Here's an example of its use:

```
showStatus("MyApplet: Loading image file " + file);
```

Note: Please don't put scrolling text in the status line. Browser users find such status line abuse highly annoying!

Displaying Diagnostics to the Standard Output and Error Streams

Displaying diagnostics to the standard output can be an invaluable tool when debugging an applet. Another time you'll see messages at the standard output is when an uncaught exception occurs in an applet. Applets can also use the standard error stream.

Where exactly the standard output and error are displayed varies depending on how the applet's viewer is implemented, what platform it's running on, and (sometimes) how you launch the browser or applet viewer. When you launch the Applet Viewer from a UNIX shell window, for example, strings displayed to the standard output and error appear in that shell window, unless you redirect the output. When you launch the Applet Viewer from an X Windows menu, the standard output and error go to the console window. Netscape Navigator 2.0, on the other hand, displays applet standard output and error to the Java Console, which is available from the Options menu.

Applets display to the standard output stream using `System.out.print(`*String*`)` and `System.out.println(`*String*`)`. Displaying to the standard error stream is similar; specify `System.err` instead of `System.out`. Here's an example of displaying to the standard output:

```
//Where instance variables are declared:
boolean DEBUG = true;
. . .
//Later, when we want to print some status:
if (DEBUG) {
    System.out.println("Called someMethod(" + x + "," + y + ")");
}
```

Note: Displaying to the standard output and error streams is relatively slow. If you have a timing-related problem, printing messages to either of these streams might not be helpful.

Be sure to disable all debugging output before you release your applet.

8

Communicating with Other Programs

An applet can communicate with other programs in three ways:

- By invoking public methods of other applets on the same page (subject to security restrictions).
- By using the API defined in the `java.applet` package, which lets an applet communicate in a limited way with the browser or other applet viewer that contains it.
- By using the API defined in the `java.net` package to communicate over the network with other programs. The other programs must be running on the host that the applet originated from.

This lesson discusses and gives examples of each kind of applet communication.

Using the `AppletContext getApplet` and `getApplets` methods, an applet can get the `Applet` objects for other applets running on the same page. Once an applet has another's `Applet` object, the applet can send messages to it. Sending Messages to Other Applets on the Same Page (page 186) provides details and example applets that communicate with each other.

Communicating with the Browser (page 190) describes the various `Applet` and `AppletContext` methods that provide limited communication between the applet and the browser or other applet viewer it runs in. The most interesting are probably the `AppletContext showDocument` methods, which let an applet tell its browser which URL to display.

Applets can use networking features just as any Java program can, with the restriction that all communication must be with the host that delivered the applet to its current host. Working with a Server-Side Application (page 192) presents an applet version of the example from Writing a Datagram Client and Server (page 522). It also presents an example of how to use a server-side application to get around applet security restrictions. In the second example, applets originating from the same host but running on different machines talk to each other using a server-side application as an intermediary.

Sending Messages to Other Applets on the Same Page

Applets can find other applets and send messages to them, with the following security restrictions:
- The applets must be running on the same page, in the same browser window.
- Many applet viewers require that the applets originate from the same server.

An applet can find another applet either by looking it up by name (using the AppletContext getApplet method) or by finding all the applets on the page (using the AppletContext getApplets method). Both methods, if successful, give the caller one or more Applet objects. Once the caller finds an Applet object, the caller can invoke methods on the object.

Finding an Applet by Name: The getApplet Method

By default, an applet has no name. For an applet to have a name, one must be specified in the HTML code that adds the applet to a page. You can specify an applet's name in two ways:
- By specifying a NAME attribute within the applet's <APPLET> tag. For example:

```
<APPLET CODEBASE=example/ CODE=sender.class WIDTH=450
      HEIGHT=200
NAME="buddy">
. . .
</APPLET>
```

- By specifying a NAME parameter with a <PARAM> tag. For example:

```
<APPLET CODEBASE=example/ CODE=Receiver.class WIDTH=450
      HEIGHT=35>
<PARAM NAME="name" VALUE="old pal">
. . .
</APPLET>
```

Browser Note: At press time, one widely used Java-compatible browser did not allow applet names to contain uppercase letters. Specifically, the `getApplet` method (the method that looks up an applet by name) appeared to convert the specified name to lowercase before looking for the applet. The expected behavior is for applet names to be case-sensitive, but for the `getApplet` method to perform a case-*in*sensitive search. For example, `getApplet("old pal")` and `getApplet("OLD PAL")` should both find an applet named `"Old Pal"`.

Below are two applets that illustrate lookup by name. The first, Sender, looks up the second, Receiver. When the Sender finds the Receiver, the Sender sends a message to the Receiver by invoking one of the Receiver's methods (passing the Sender's name as an argument). The Receiver reacts to this method call by changing its leftmost text string to "Received message from *sender-name*!".

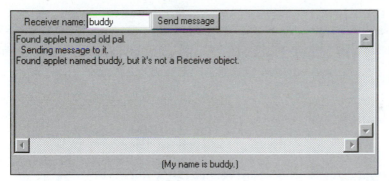

http://java.sun.com/Series/Tutorial/applet/communication/iac.html

http://java.sun.com/Series/Tutorial/applet/communication/iac.html

---

Try this: Visit the page that contains these applets: `http://java.sun.com/Series/Tutorial/applet/communication/iac.html`. Click the Send message button of the top applet (the Sender). Some status information will appear in the Sender's window, and the Receiver will confirm, with its own status string, that it received a message. After you've read the Receiver status string, press the Receiver's Clear button to reset the Receiver. In the Sender's text field labeled "Receiver name:", type in buddy and press Return. Since `"buddy"` is the Sender's own name, the Sender will find an applet named "buddy" but won't send it a message, since it isn't a Receiver instance.

You can find the whole Sender program on page 597, and the Receiver program on page 600. The code the Sender uses to look up and communicate with the Receiver is listed below. Code that you can use without change in your own applet is in bold.

```
Applet receiver = null;
String receiverName = nameField.getText(); //Get name to search
                                            //for.
receiver = getAppletContext().getApplet(receiverName);
```

The Sender goes on to make sure that the Receiver was found and that it's an instance of the correct class (`Receiver`). If all goes well, the Sender sends a message to the Receiver.

```
if (receiver != null) {
    //Use the instanceof operator to make sure the applet
    //we found is a Receiver object.
    if (!(receiver instanceof Receiver)) {
        status.appendText("Found applet named "
                        + receiverName + ", "
                        + "but it's not a Receiver object.\n");
    } else {
        status.appendText("Found applet named "
                        + receiverName + ".\n"
                        + "  Sending message to it.\n");
        //Cast the receiver to be a Receiver object
        //(instead of just an Applet object) so that the
        //compiler will let us call a Receiver method.
        ((Receiver)receiver).processRequestFrom(myName);
    }
}
```

From an applet's point of view, its name is stored in a parameter called NAME. It can get the value of the parameter using the `Applet getParameter` method. For example, `Sender` gets its own name with the following code:

```
myName = getParameter("NAME");
```

For more information on using `getParameter`, see <u>Writing the Code to Support Parameters</u> (page 177).

The example applets in this page perform one-way communication—from the Sender to the Receiver. If you want your receiver to be able to send messages

to the sender, then you just need to have the sender give a reference to itself (this) to the receiver. For example:

```
((Receiver)receiver).startCommunicating(this);
```

Finding All the Applets on a Page: The getApplets Method

The getApplets method returns a list (an <u>Enumeration</u>[1] to be precise) of all the applets on the page. For security reasons, many browsers and applet viewers implement getApplets so that it returns only those applets that originated from the same host as the applet calling getApplets. Here's a picture of an applet that simply lists all the applets it can find on its page:

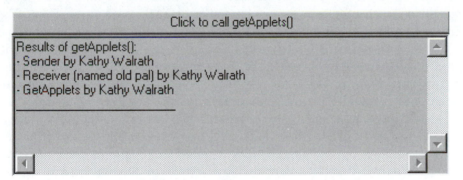

http://java.sun.com/Series/Tutorial/applet/communication/iac.html

The following code contains the relevant parts of the method that calls getApplets. You can find the entire program on page 601.

```
public void printApplets() {
    //Enumeration will contain all applets on this page
    //(including this one) that we can send messages to.
    Enumeration e = getAppletContext().getApplets();
    . . .
    while (e.hasMoreElements()) {
        Applet applet = (Applet)e.nextElement();
        String info = ((Applet)applet).getAppletInfo();
        if (info != null) {
```

---

[1] http://java.sun.com/products/JDK/CurrentRelease/api/java.util.Enumeration.html

```
                textArea.appendText("- " + info + "\n");
            } else {
            textArea.appendText(
                "- " + applet.getClass().getName() + "\n");
            }
        }
        . . .
    }
```

Communicating with the Browser

Many of the `Applet`[1] and `AppletContext`[2] methods involve some sort of communication with the browser or applet viewer. For example, the `Applet getDocumentBase` and `getCodeBase` methods get information from the browser or other applet viewer about where the applet and its HTML page came from. The `Applet showStatus` method tells the viewer to display a status message. The `Applet getParameterInfo` method can give a viewer a list of the parameters an applet understands. And, of course, the browser or other applet viewer calls the `Applet init`, `start`, `stop`, and `destroy` methods to inform the applet of changes in its state. All these methods are discussed elsewhere in this trail.

Also interesting are the `AppletContext showDocument` methods. With these methods, an applet can control which URL the browser shows, and in which browser window. (By the way, the JDK Applet Viewer ignores these methods, since it isn't a Web browser.) Here are the two forms of `showDocument`:

```
showDocument(java.net.URL url)
showDocument(java.net.URL url, String targetWindow)
```

The one-argument form of `showDocument` simply tells the browser to display the document at the specified URL, without specifying the window in which to display the document.

Terminology Note: In this discussion, *frame* refers not to an AWT Frame but to an HTML frame within a browser window.

The two-argument form of `showDocument` lets you specify which window or HTML frame to display the document in. The second argument can have the values in the following list.

[1.] http://java.sun.com/products/JDK/CurrentRelease/api/java.applet.Applet.html
[2.] http://java.sun.com/products/JDK/CurrentRelease/api/java.applet.AppletContext.html

"_blank"
> Display the document in a new, nameless window.

"windowName"
> Display the document in a window named *windowName*. This window is created if necessary.

"_self"
> Display the document in the window and frame that contain the applet.

"_parent"
> Display the document in the applet's window but in the parent frame of the applet's frame. If the applet frame has no parent frame, this acts the same as "_self".

"_top"
> Display the document in the applet's window but in the top-level frame. If the applet's frame is the top-level frame, this acts the same as "_self".

Below is a picture of an applet that lets you try every option of both forms of showDocument. The applet brings up a window that lets you type in a URL and choose any of the showDocument options. When you press return or click the Show document button, the applet calls showDocument.

http://java.sun.com/Series/Tutorial/applet/communication/browser.html

Below is the applet code that calls showDocument. You can find the whole program on page 602.

```
    .../In an Applet subclass:
    urlWindow = new URLWindow(getAppletContext());
    . . .

class URLWindow extends Frame {
    . . .
    public URLWindow(AppletContext appletContext) {
        . . .
        this.appletContext = appletContext;
        . . .
    }
    . . .
    public boolean action(Event event, Object o) {
```

```
. . .
        String urlString = /* user-entered string */;
        URL url = null;
        try {
            url = new URL(urlString);
        } catch (MalformedURLException e) {
            ...//Inform the user and return...
        }

        if (url != null) {
            if (/* user doesn't want to specify window */) {
                appletContext.showDocument(url);
            } else {
                appletContext.showDocument(url,
                        /* user-specified window */);
            }
        }
. . .
```

Working with a Server-Side Application

Applets, like other Java programs, can use the API defined in the java.net package to communicate across the network. The only difference is that, for security reasons, the only host an applet can communicate with is the host it was delivered from.

Note: Depending on the networking environment an applet is loaded into, and depending on the browser that runs the applet, an applet might not be able to communicate with its originating host. For example, browsers running on hosts inside firewalls often cannot get much information about the world outside the firewall. As a result, some browsers might not allow applet communication to hosts outside the firewall. See `http://java.sun.com/Series/Tutorial/book.html` for up-to-date information.

It's easy to find out which host an applet came from. Just use the `Applet get-CodeBase` method and the `java.net.URL getHost` method, like this:

```
String host = getCodeBase().getHost();
```

Once you have the correct host name, you can use the networking code that is documented in the **Custom Networking and Security** trail (page 483).

Note: Not all browsers support all networking code flawlessly. For example, at press time, one widely used Java-compatible browser doesn't support posting to a URL. See `http://java.sun.com/Series/Tutorial/book.html` for up-to-date information on how various browsers support networking.

A Simple Network Client Applet (page 193) gives an example of implementing an applet that is a network client.

Using a Server to Work Around Security Restrictions (page 194) gives an example of implementing a server to get around applet security restrictions.

A Simple Network Client Applet

The Writing a Datagram Client and Server (page 522) section of the **Custom Networking and Security** trail contains example code for two applications: a client and a server. This section rewrites the client to be an applet. You can find the applet source code on page 608. The client has been changed not only to communicate with the host the applet came from, but also to have a graphical UI, and to have a loop so that it can get as many quotes as you like. You can run the applet by including it in a page with the following HTML code:

```
<APPLET CODE=QuoteClientApplet.class WIDTH=500 HEIGHT=100>
</APPLET>
```

The `quoteApplet.html` file (page 608) contains the above code. By saving this file to your local HTTP server, you can use it to communicate with the server-side application that will be running on the HTTP server. You must also save the compiled form of the applet to the same directory.

Before the applet can get quotes, you need to run the server on the host that the applet came from. You then need to note the number of the port that the server is listening on. After you enter this port number into the applet, it will hook up with the server and you'll be able to get one-line quotations. Below are detailed instructions, followed by pictures of the server and the applet in action.

1. Compile `QuoteServer.java` (page 776) and `QuoteServerThread.java` (page 777). Save the `one-liners.txt` (page 780) file in the same directory as the resulting class files.
2. On the computer that serves the applet class file (through HTTP), invoke the interpreter on the `QuoteServer` class. For example, if you view the applet's page with the URL `http://mymachine/quoteApplet.html`, then you need to run the server on the host named mymachine.
3. Record the port number that the quote server displays.

4. Enter this number into the applet's text field.

5. Press the Send button to request a quote from the server. You should see a quote appear in the text area.

Here's a picture of the server in action:

```
WWW% java QuoteServer
QuoteServer listening on port: 34525
```

Here's a picture of the applet in action:

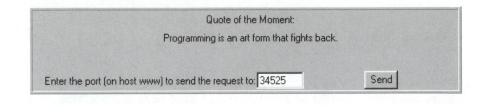

Using a Server to Work Around Security Restrictions

As the **Understanding Applet Capabilities and Restrictions** lesson (page 197) explains, applets are subject to many security restrictions. For example, they can't perform file I/O, they can't make network connections except to their original host, and they can't start programs.

One way of working around these restrictions is to use a server application that executes on the applet's host. The server won't be able to get around every applet restriction, but it can make more things possible. For example, a server probably can't save files on the host the applet's running on, but it'll be able to save files on the host that the applet originated from.

This section features an example of a server that allows two applets to communicate with each other. The applets don't have to be running on the same page, in the same browser, or on the same computer. As long as the applets originate from the same computer, they can communicate through the server that's running on that originating computer. The example uses sockets, which are documented in the **All About Sockets** lesson (page 509).

Here are the source files:

`TalkClientApplet.java` (page 608)

The source file for the client applets. (Both applets use the same source code.) After you compile it, you can run it by including it in an HTML page with this tag:

```
<APPLET CODE=TalkClientApplet.class WIDTH=550 HEIGHT=200>
</APPLET>
```

The above HTML code is included in `talk.html` (page 615). After saving this page to a file on your local HTTP server, you can use it to communicate with the talk server.

`TalkServer.java` **(page 615) and** `TalkServerThread.java` **(page 621)**

The source files for the server. After compiling both files, you can run the server on the applets' originating host by invoking the interpreter on the `TalkServer` class.

The instructions for running the server are just like those for the previous example. Run the server on the applets' originating host, recording the port number the applets should rendezvous on. Then initialize both applets (which can be running on different machines) to talk to the server port number. After this initialization is complete, type into each applet and press the Return key to send the message to the other applet.

Here's a picture of the server in action:

```
WWW% java TalkServer
TalkServer listening on rendezvous port: 36567
```

Here are pictures of the applets in action:

```
Hi, Sun!
Received: Successful connection. Please wait for second applet to connect...
Received: START WRITING!
------------------------------------
Sent: Hi, Sun!
Received: Hi, PC!
```

Enter the port (on host www) to send the request to: 36567   Connect

```
Hi, PC!
Received: Successful connection. Please wait for second applet to connect...
Received: START WRITING!
---------------------------------------------
Received: Hi, Sun!
Sent: Hi, PC!
```

Enter the port (on host www) to send the request to: 36567   Connect

9

Understanding Applet Capabilities and Restrictions

T HE Security Restrictions section (page 197) lists the security restrictions most applets face. It also provides hints on how to work around these restrictions.

Applet Capabilities (page 199) lists some of the capabilities applets have that applications don't, as well as some abilities you might have assumed applets don't have.

Security Restrictions

One of the main goals of the Java environment is to make browser users feel secure running any applet. To achieve this goal, we've started out conservatively, restricting capabilities perhaps more than necessary. As time passes, applets will probably get more and more abilities.

This section tells you about the current applet security restrictions and how they affect applet design. For more information on applet security, refer to Marianne Mueller's excellent document, *"Frequently Asked Questions—Applet Security."*[1]

[1.] To find the security document, go to the Web page for this book:
http://java.sun.com/Series/Tutorial/book.html

Each applet viewer has a `SecurityManager` object that checks for applet security violations. When a `SecurityManager` detects a violation, it creates and throws a `SecurityException` object. Generally, the `SecurityException` constructor prints a warning message to the standard output. An applet can catch `SecurityExceptions` and react appropriately, such as by reassuring the user and by resorting to a "safer" but less ideal way of accomplishing the task.

Some applet viewers swallow some `SecurityExceptions`, so that the applet never gets the `SecurityException`. For example, the JDK Applet Viewer's implementation of the `AppletContext getApplet` and `getApplets` methods simply catches and ignores any `SecurityExceptions`. The user can see an error message in the standard output, but at least the applet gets a valid result from the methods. This makes some sense, since `getApplets` should be able to return any valid applets it finds, even if it encounters invalid ones. (The Applet Viewer considers an applet valid if it's loaded from the same host as the applet that's calling `getApplets`.)

To learn about security managers and the kinds of security violations they can check for, see Introducing the Security Manager (page 530).

As the applet overview lesson mentioned, existing applet viewers (including Web browsers) impose the following restrictions:

Applets can not load libraries or define native methods.
　　Applets can use only their own Java code and the Java API the applet viewer provides. At a minimum, each applet viewer must provide access to the API defined in the `java.*` packages.

An applet can not ordinarily read or write files on the host that's executing it.
　　The JDK Applet Viewer actually permits some user-specified exceptions to this rule, but Netscape Navigator 2.0, for example, does not. Applets in any applet viewer *can* read files specified with full URLs, instead of by a filename. A workaround for not being able to write files is to have the applet forward data to an application on the host the applet came from. This application can write the data files on its own host. See Working with a Server-Side Application (page 192) for more examples.

An applet can not make network connections except to the host that it came from.
　　The workaround for this restriction is to have the applet work with an application on the host it came from. The application can make its own connections anywhere on the network. See Using a Server to Work Around Security Restrictions (page 194) for an example.

An applet can not start any program on the host that is executing it.
　　Again, an applet can work with a server-side application instead.

An applet can not read certain system properties.
　　See Reading System Properties (page 180) for more information.

Windows that an applet brings up look different than windows that an application brings up.

Applet windows have some warning text and either a colored bar or an image. This helps the user distinguish applet windows from those of trusted applications.

The following figures show a window brought up by a program that can run either as an applet or as an application. The first figure shows what the window looks like when the program is run as an application on the Windows 95 platform. The second figure shows the window when the program runs as an applet within the Windows 95 Applet Viewer.

```
FlowWindow Application        _ □ ✕
Button 1  │ 2 │  Button 3  │ Long-Named Button 4 │  Button 5
```

```
FlowLayout                    _ □ ✕
Button 1  │ 2 │  Button 3  │ Long-Named Button 4 │  Button 5
Warning: Applet Window
```

As you can see, the applet window has a warning.

Applet Capabilities

The previous section might have made you feel like applets are merely crippled applications. Not true! Besides the obvious feature that applets can be loaded over the network, applets have more capabilities than you might think. They have access to the API in every `java.*` package (subject to security restrictions) plus they have some capabilities that not even applications have.

Capabilities That Applications Don't Have

Applets get extra capabilities because they are supported by code in the application they run in. Applets have access to this support through the `java.applet` package, which contains the `Applet` class and the `AppletContext`, `AppletStub`, and `AudioClip` interfaces.

Here are some capabilities that applets have and applications don't:

Applets can play sounds.

> The JDK 1.0.2 release does not support sound in applications. See <u>Playing Sounds</u> (page 172) for information on playing sounds in applets.

Applets running within a Web browser can easily cause HTML documents to be displayed.

> This is supported with the `AppletContext showDocument` methods. See <u>Communicating with the Browser</u> (page 190) for more information.

Applets can invoke public methods of other applets on the same page.

> See <u>Sending Messages to Other Applets on the Same Page</u> (page 186) for information.

More Applet Capabilities

Besides the above capabilities, applets have some more that you might not expect:

Applets that are loaded from the local file system (from a directory in the user's* `CLASSPATH`*) have none of the restrictions that applets loaded over the network do.

> This is because an applet in the user's `CLASSPATH` has the same capabilities as the Java application that loads it. See <u>CLASSPATH</u> (page 137) for information.

Although most applets stop running once you leave their page, they don't have to.

> Most applets, to be polite, implement the `stop` method, if necessary, to suspend any processing when the user leaves the applet's page. Sometimes, however, it's appropriate for an applet to continue executing. For example, if a user tells an applet to perform a complex calculation, the user might want the calculation to continue. (The user should generally be able to specify whether it should continue, though.) As another example, if an applet might be useful over multiple pages, it should use a window for its interface, and not hide the window in its `stop` method. The user can then dismiss the window when it's no longer needed.

Finishing an Applet

DON'T release your applet without making sure it follows the simple rules discussed in <u>Before You Ship That Applet</u> (page 201).

The following section covers the annoying, highly visible things an applet should *not* do. <u>The Perfectly Finished Applet</u> (page 202) lists a few more things that a perfectly finished applet *should* do.

Before You Ship That Applet

Stop! Before you let the whole world know about your applet, make sure the answer to all of the following questions is **yes**.

1. **Have you removed or disabled debugging output?**

   Debugging output (generally created with `System.out.println`), while useful to you, is generally confusing or annoying to users. If you need to give textual feedback to the user, try to do it inside the applet's display area or in the status area at the bottom of the window. Information on using the status area is in <u>Displaying Short Status Strings</u> (page 181).

2. **Does the applet stop running when it's off screen?**

   Most applets should not use CPU resources when the browser is iconified or is displaying a page that doesn't contain the applet. If your applet code doesn't launch any threads explicitly, then you're OK.

   If your applet code launches any threads, then unless you have a *really good* excuse not to, you should implement the `stop` method so that it stops and destroys (by setting to null) the threads you launched. For an

example of implementing the `stop` method, see <u>Examples of Threads in Applets</u> (page 160).

3. **If the applet does something that might get annoying—play sounds or animation, for example—does it give the user a way to stop the annoying behavior?**

   Be kind to your users. Give them a way to stop the applet in its tracks, without leaving the page. In an applet that otherwise doesn't respond to mouse clicks, you can do this by implementing the `mouseDown` method so that a mouse click suspends or resumes the annoying thread. For example:

```
boolean frozen = false; //an instance variable

public boolean mouseDown(Event e, int x, int y) {
    if (frozen) {
        frozen = false;
        start();
    } else {
        frozen = true;
        stop();
    }
    return true;
}
```

The Perfectly Finished Applet

The previous section lists some of the ways you can avoid making your applet's users want to throttle you. This section tells you about some other ways that you can make dealing with your applet as pleasant as possible.

1. **Make your applet as flexible as possible.**

   You can often define parameters that let your applet be used in a variety of situations without any rewriting. See <u>Defining and Using Applet Parameters</u> (page 175) for more information.

2. **Implement the `getParameterInfo` method.**

   Implementing this method now might make your applet easier to customize in the future. At press time, no browsers use this method. However, we expect browsers to use this method to help generate a GUI that allows the user to interactively set parameter values. See <u>Giving Information About Parameters</u> (page 179) for information on implementing `getParameterInfo`.

3. Implement the `getAppletInfo` method.

This method returns a short, informative string describing an applet. Although no browsers use this method at press time, we expect them to. Here's an example of implementing `getAppletInfo`:

```java
public String getAppletInfo() {
    return "GetApplets by Kathy Walrath";
}
```

Common Applet Problems (and Their Solutions)

THIS section covers some common problems that you might encounter when writing Java applets. After each problem is a list of possible solutions.

Problem: Applet Viewer says there's no <APPLET> tag on my HTML page, but it really is there.
- Check whether you have a closing applet tag: </APPLET>.

Problem: I recompiled my applet, but my applet viewing application won't show the new version, even though I told it to reload it.
- In many applet viewers, including browsers, reloading isn't reliable. This is why we recommend that you use the JDK Applet Viewer, invoking it anew each time you change the applet.
- If you get an old version of the applet, no matter what you do, make sure that you don't have an old copy of the applet in a directory in your CLASS-PATH. See CLASSPATH (page 137) for information.

Problem: The light gray background of my applet causes the applet to flicker when it is drawn on a page of a different color.
- You need to set the background color of the applet so that it works well with the page color. See Creating a GUI (page 170) for details.

Problem: The Applet getImage method doesn't work.
- Make sure you're calling getImage from the init method or a method that's called after init. The getImage method does not work when it's called from a constructor.

 *WRITING APPLETS*

Problem: Now that I've copied my applet's class file onto my HTTP server, the applet doesn't work.

- Does your applet define more than one class? If so, make sure that the class file (*ClassName*.class) for each class is on the HTTP server. Even if all the classes are defined in one source file, the compiler produces one class file per class.
- Did you copy all the data files for your applet—image and sound files, for example—to the server?
- Make sure all the applet's class and data files can be read by everyone.
- Make sure the applet's class and data files weren't garbled during the transfer. One common source of trouble is using the ASCII mode of FTP (rather than the BINARY mode) to transfer files.

Other problems that affect applets are discussed in the **Creating a User Interface** trail (page 357). Specifically, look at whichever of the following sections are related to your problem: <u>Common Component Problems (and Their Solutions)</u> (page 412), <u>Common Layout Problems (and Their Solutions)</u> (page 435), and <u>Common Graphics Problems (and Their Solutions)</u> (page 479). If you still haven't found the solution, check the Web page for this book:

http://java.sun.com/Series/Tutorial/book.html

End of Trail

YOU'VE reached the end of the **Writing Applets** trail. Take a break—have a cup of steaming hot java.

What Next?

Once you've caught your breath, you have several choices of where to go next. You can go back to the **Trail Map** (page xv) to see all of your choices, or you can go directly to one of the following popular trails:

Writing Java Programs (page 27): If you aren't completely comfortable yet with the Java language, take this trail.

Using the Core Java Classes (page 209): By taking this trail, you can find out about strings, exceptions, threads, and other Java features that are used in all kinds of Java programs.

Creating a User Interface (page 357): This trail will teach you how to produce graphical user interfaces. This trail includes information on using the AWT components, drawing custom graphics and images to the screen, and performing animation.

Using the Core Java Classes

THIS trail covers the fundamentals of programming in the Java language and discusses several of the core classes that are shipped with the Java environment. Like the rest of the tutorial, this trail is designed so that you can skip around. As Java has many similarities with C and C++, if you are an experienced C or C++ programmer, you may want to skim the first few lessons to orient yourself to Java then delve into the later lessons as you are interested in them. Also, feel free to jump to other trails in the tutorial as you see fit. The lessons in other trails will provide links to any lessons in this trail if they contain prerequisite information.

The `String` and `StringBuffer` Classes (page 215) illustrates how to manipulate character data using the `String` and `StringBuffer` classes. This lesson will also teach you about accessor methods and how the compiler uses `Strings` and `StringBuffers` behind the scenes.

Setting Program Attributes (page 227) describes how you can set attributes for your Java programs through the use of properties and command-line arguments. Use properties to change attributes for every invocation of your program; use command-line arguments to change attributes for only the current invocation of your program.

Using System Resources (page 237) shows you how your Java programs can access system resources, such as standard I/O, array copying, and property management, through the `System` class. The `System` class provides a system-independent programming interface to system resources, allowing your programs to use them without compromising portability.

Handling Errors Using Exceptions (page 253) explains how you can use Java's exception mechanism to handle errors in your programs. This lesson describes what an exception is, how to throw and catch exceptions, what to do with an exception once you've caught it, and how to best use the exception class hierarchy provided by the Java development environment.

Threads of Control (page 285) discusses in detail the use of threads that enable your Java applications or applets to perform multiple tasks at the same time. This lesson describes when and why you might want to use threads, how to create and manage threads and thread groups in your Java program, and how to avoid common pitfalls such as deadlock and race conditions.

Input and Output Streams (page 325) begins with a description of your likely first encounter with Java input and output (I/O) streams. Then this lesson provides an overview of the `InputStream` and `OutputStream` family of classes. From there, the lesson provides many examples of how to use the most popular I/O streams, including two examples on how to write your own filtered streams.

11

The String and StringBuffer Classes

THE java.lang package contains two string classes: *String*[1] and *String-Buffer.*[2] You've already seen the String class on several occasions in this tutorial. You use the String class when you are working with strings that cannot change. StringBuffer, on the other hand, is used when you want to manipulate the contents of the string on the fly.

The reverseIt method in the following code uses both the String and StringBuffer classes to reverse the characters of a string. If you have a list of words, you can use this method in conjunction with a sort program to create a list of rhyming words (a list of words sorted by ending syllables). Just reverse all the strings in the list, sort the list, and reverse the strings again. You can see the reverseIt method producing rhyming words in the example in Using Input and Output Streams (page 331) that shows you how to use piped streams.

```java
class ReverseString {
    public static String reverseIt(String source) {
        int i, len = source.length();
        StringBuffer dest = new StringBuffer(len);

        for (i = (len - 1); i >= 0; i--) {
            dest.append(source.charAt(i));
        }
        return dest.toString();
    }
}
```

---

1. http://java.sun.com/products/JDK/CurrentRelease/api/java.lang.String.html
2. http://java.sun.com/products/JDK/CurrentRelease/api/java.lang.StringBuffer.html

The `reverseIt` method accepts an argument of type `String` called `source` that contains the string data to be reversed. The method creates a `StringBuffer`, `dest`, the same size as `source`. It then loops backwards over all the characters in `source` and appends them to `dest`, thereby reversing the string. Finally, the method converts `dest`, a `StringBuffer`, to a `String`.

In addition to highlighting the differences between `String`s and `String-Buffer`s, this lesson illustrates several features of the `String` and `StringBuffer` classes: creating `String`s and `StringBuffer`s, using accessor methods to get information about a `String` or `StringBuffer`, modifying a `StringBuffer`, and converting one type of string to another.

Note to C and C++ Programmers: Java strings are first-class objects, unlike C and C++ strings which are simply null-terminated arrays of 8-bit characters.

Strings as objects provide several advantages to the programmer:
- The manner in which you obtain strings and elements of strings is consistent across all strings and all systems.
- Since the programming interface for the `String` and `StringBuffer` classes is well-defined, Java `String`s function predictably every time.
- The `String` and `StringBuffer` classes do extensive runtime checking for boundary conditions and catch errors for you.

Why Two String Classes?

The Java development environment provides two classes that store and manipulate character data: `String`, for constant strings, and `StringBuffer`, for strings that can change.

You use the `String` class when you don't want the value of the string to change. For example, if you write a method that requires string data and the method is not going to modify the string in any way, use a `String` object. Typically, you'll want to use `String`s to pass character data into methods and return character data from methods. The `reverseIt` method takes a `String` argument and returns a `String` value.

```
class ReverseString {
    public static String reverseIt(String source) {
        int i, len = source.length();
        StringBuffer dest = new StringBuffer(len);

        for (i = (len - 1); i >= 0; i--) {
            dest.append(source.charAt(i));
```

```
    }
        return dest.toString();
    }
}
```

The `StringBuffer` class provides for strings that will be modified; you use `StringBuffers` when you know that the value of the character data will change. You typically use `StringBuffers` for constructing character data like in the `reverseIt` method.

Because they are constants, `Strings` are typically cheaper than `StringBuffers` and they can be shared. So it's important to use `Strings` when appropriate.

Creating Strings and StringBuffers

The bold line in the `reverseIt` method creates a `StringBuffer` named `dest` whose initial length is the same as `source`.

```
class ReverseString {
    public static String reverseIt(String source) {
        int i, len = source.length();
        StringBuffer dest = new StringBuffer(len);

        for (i = (len - 1); i >= 0; i--) {
            dest.append(source.charAt(i));
        }
        return dest.toString();
    }
}
```

The code `StringBuffer dest` declares to the compiler that `dest` will refer to an object whose type is `StringBuffer`, the `new` operator allocates memory for a new object, and `StringBuffer(len)` initializes the object. These three steps—declaration, instantiation, and initialization—are described in Creating Objects (page 78).

Creating a String

Many `Strings` are created from string literals. When the compiler encounters a series of characers enclosed in double quotes it creates a `String` object whose value is the text that appeared between the quotes. When the compiler encounters the following string literal it creates a `String` object whose value is Gobbledy gook.

```
"Gobbledy gook"
```

You can also create String objects like you would any other Java object: using the new keyword.

```
new String("Gobbledy gook");
```

Creating a StringBuffer

The constructor method used by reverseIt to initialize dest requires an integer argument indicating the initial size of the new StringBuffer.

```
StringBuffer(int length)
```

reverseIt could have used StringBuffer's default constructor that leaves the buffer's length undetermined until a later time. However, it's more efficient to specify the length of the buffer if you know it, instead of allocating more memory every time you append a character to the buffer.

Accessor Methods

An object's instance variables are encapsulated within the object, hidden inside, safe from inspection or manipulation by other objects. With certain well-defined exceptions, the object's methods are the only means by which other objects can inspect or alter an object's instance variables. Encapsulation of an object's data protects the object from corruption by other objects and conceals an object's implementation details from outsiders. This encapsulation of data behind an object's methods is one of the cornerstones of object-oriented programming.

Methods used to obtain information about an object are known as *accessor methods*. The reverseIt method uses two of String's accessor methods to obtain information about the source string.

```
class ReverseString {
    public static String reverseIt(String source) {
        int i, len = source.length();
        StringBuffer dest = new StringBuffer(len);

        for (i = (len - 1); i >= 0; i--) {
            dest.append(source.charAt(i));
        }
        return dest.toString();
    }
}
```

First, reverseIt uses String's length accessor method to obtain the length of the String source.

```
int len = source.length();
```

Note that reverseIt doesn't care if String maintains its length attribute as an integer, as a floating-point number, or even if String computes its length on the fly. reverseIt simply relies on the public interface of the length method which returns the length of the String as an integer. That's all reverseIt needs to know.

Second, reverseIt uses the charAt accessor, which returns the character at the position specified in the parameter.

```
source.charAt(i)
```

The character returned by charAt is then appended to the StringBuffer dest. Since the loop variable i begins at the end of source and proceeds backwards over the string, the characters are appended in reverse order to the String-Buffer, thereby reversing the string.

More Accessor Methods

In addition to length and charAt, String supports a number of other accessor methods that provide access to substrings and the indices of specific characters in the String. StringBuffer has its own set of similar accessor methods.

For the String Class

In addition to the length and charAt accessors described in the previous section, the String class provides two accessors that return the position within the string of a specific character or string: indexOf and lastIndexOf. The indexOf method searches forward from the beginning of the string, and lastIndexOf searches backward from the end of the string.

The indexOf and lastIndexOf methods are frequently used with substring, which returns a substring of the string. The following class illustrates the use of lastIndexOf and substring to isolate different parts of a filename.

Note: The methods in the following Filename class don't do any error checking and they assume that their argument contains a full directory path and a filename with an extension. If these methods were production code they would verify that their arguments were properly constructed.

```
class Filename {
    String fullPath;
    char pathSeparator;

    Filename(String str, char sep) {
        fullPath = str;
        pathSeparator = sep;
    }

    String extension() {
        int dot = fullPath.lastIndexOf('.');
        return fullPath.substring(dot + 1);
    }

    String filename() {
        int dot = fullPath.lastIndexOf('.');
        int sep = fullPath.lastIndexOf(pathSeparator);
        return fullPath.substring(sep + 1, dot);
    }

    String path() {
        int sep = fullPath.lastIndexOf(pathSeparator);
        return fullPath.substring(0, sep);
    }
}
```

Here's a small program that constructs a Filename object and calls all of its methods:

```
class FilenameTest {
    public static void main(String[] args) {
        Filename myHomePage =
            new Filename("/home/mem/public_html/index.html", '/');
        System.out.println("Extension = " +
            myHomePage.extension());
        System.out.println("Filename = " +
            myHomePage.filename());
        System.out.println("Path = " + myHomePage.path());
    }
}
```

And here's the output from the program:

```
Extension = html
Filename = index
Path = /home/mem/public_html
```

The `extension` method uses `lastIndexOf` to locate the last occurrence of the period (.) in the filename. Then `substring` uses the return value of `lastIndexOf` to extract the filename extension—that is, the substring from the period to the end of the string. This code assumes that the filename actually has a period in it; if the filename does not have a period, then `lastIndexOf` returns -1, and the `substring` method throws a `StringIndexOutOfBoundsException`.

Also, note that `extension` uses dot +1 as the argument to `substring`. If the period character is the last character of the string, then dot +1 is equal to the length of the string which is one larger than the largest index into the string (because indices start at 0). However, `substring` accepts an index equal to but not greater than the length of the string and interprets it to mean "the end of the string."

Try this: Inspect the other methods in the `Filename` class and notice how the `lastIndexOf` and `substring` methods work together to isolate different parts of a filename.

While the methods in the `Filename` example use only one version of the `lastIndexOf` method, the `String` class actually supports four different versions of both the `indexOf` and `lastIndexOf` methods. The four versions work as follows:

indexOf(int *character*)
lastIndexOf(int *character*)
    Return the index of the first (last) occurrence of the specified character.
indexOf(int *character*, int *from*)
lastIndexOf(int *character*, int *from*)
    Return the index of the first (last) occurrence of the specified character, searching forward (backward) from the specified index.
indexOf(String *string*)
lastIndexOf(String *string*)
    Return the index of the first (last) occurrence of the specified `String`.
indexOf(String *string*, int *from*)
lastIndexOf(String *string*, int *from*)
    Return the index of the first (last) occurrence of the specified `String`, searching forward (backward) from the specified index.

For the StringBuffer Class

Like `String`, `StringBuffer` provides `length` and `charAt` accessor methods. In addition to these two accessors, `StringBuffer` also has a method called `capacity`. The `capacity` method differs from `length` in that it returns the amount of space currently allocated for the `StringBuffer`, rather than the amount of space

used. For example, the capacity of the `StringBuffer` in the `reverseIt` method shown here never changes, while the length of the `StringBuffer` increases by one for each iteration of the loop:

```java
class ReverseString {
    public static String reverseIt(String source) {
        int i, len = source.length();
        StringBuffer dest = new StringBuffer(len);

        for (i = (len - 1); i >= 0; i--) {
            dest.append(source.charAt(i));
        }
        return dest.toString();
    }
}
```

Modifying `StringBuffer`s

The `reverseIt` method uses `StringBuffer`'s append method to add a character to the end of the destination string, `dest`:

```java
class ReverseString {
    public static String reverseIt(String source) {
        int i, len = source.length();
        StringBuffer dest = new StringBuffer(len);

        for (i = (len - 1); i >= 0; i--) {
            dest.append(source.charAt(i));
        }
        return dest.toString();
    }
}
```

If the appended character causes the size of the `StringBuffer` to grow beyond its current capacity, the `StringBuffer` allocates more memory. Because memory allocation is a relatively expensive operation, you can make your code more efficient by initializing a `StringBuffer`'s capacity to a reasonable first guess, thereby minimizing the number of times memory must be allocated for it. For example, the `reverseIt` method constructs the `StringBuffer` with an initial capacity equal to the length of the `source` string, ensuring only one memory allocation for `dest`.

The version of the append method used in `reverseIt` is only one of the `StringBuffer` methods that appends data to the end of a `StringBuffer`. There are several `append` methods that append data of various types, such as `float`, `int`, `boolean`, and even `Object`, to the end of the `StringBuffer`. The data is converted to a string before the append operation takes place.

Inserting Characters

At times, you may want to insert data into the middle of a `StringBuffer`. You do this with one of `StringBuffer`'s `insert` methods. The following example illustrates how to insert a string into a StringBuffer:

```
StringBuffer sb = new StringBuffer("Drink Java!");
sb.insert(6, "Hot ");
System.out.println(sb.toString());
```

This code snippet prints:

```
Drink Hot Java!
```

With `StringBuffer`'s many `insert` methods, you specify the index *before* which you want the data inserted. In the example, "Hot" needed to be inserted before the "J" in "Java". Indices begin at 0, so the index for "J" is 6. To insert data at the beginning of a `StringBuffer`, use an index of 0. To add data at the end of a `StringBuffer`, use an index equal to the current length of the `StringBuffer` or use `append`.

Setting Characters

Another useful `StringBuffer` modifier is `setCharAt`, which replaces the character at a specific location in the `StringBuffer` with the character specified in the argument list. `setCharAt` is useful when you want to reuse a `StringBuffer`.

Converting Objects to Strings

The toString Method

It's often convenient or necessary to convert an object to a `String` because you need to pass it to a method that accepts only `String` values. For example, `System.out.println` does not accept `StringBuffers`, so you need to convert a `StringBuffer` to a `String` before you can print it. The `reverseIt` method used earlier in this lesson uses `StringBuffer`'s `toString` method to convert the `StringBuffer` to a `String` object before returning the `String`.

```
class ReverseString {
    public static String reverseIt(String source) {
        int i, len = source.length();
        StringBuffer dest = new StringBuffer(len);

        for (i = (len - 1); i >= 0; i--) {
            dest.append(source.charAt(i));
        }
        return dest.toString();
    }
}
```

All classes inherit the `toString` method from the `Object` class, and many classes in the `java.lang` package override this method to provide an implementation that is meaningful to that class. For example, the "type wrapper" classes—`Character`, `Integer`, `Boolean`, and the others—all override `toString` to provide a `String` representation of the object.

The `valueOf` Method

As a convenience, the `String` class provides the class method `valueOf`. You can use `valueOf` to convert variables of different types to `Strings`. For example, to print the value of π:

```
System.out.println(String.valueOf(Math.PI));
```

Converting Strings to Numbers

The `String` class itself does not provide any methods for converting a `String` to a floating-point number, integer, or other numerical type. However, four of the "type wrapper" classes (`Integer`, `Double`, `Float`, and `Long`) provide a class method named `valueOf` that converts a `String` to an object of that type. Here's a small, contrived example of the `Float` class's `valueOf`:

```
String piStr = "3.14159";
Float pi = Float.valueOf(piStr);
```

Strings and the Java Compiler

Before moving on to another lesson, you need to understand one final, important peculiarity about `Strings` and `StringBuffers`. The Java compiler uses the

String and StringBuffer classes behind the scenes to handle literal strings and concatenation.

Literal Strings

In Java, you specify *literal strings* between double quotes:

```
"Hello World!"
```

You can use literal strings anywhere you would use a String object. For example, System.out.println accepts a String argument, so you could use a literal string in place of a String there.

```
System.out.println(
    "And might I add that you look lovely today.");
```

You can also use String methods directly from a literal string.

```
int len = "Goodbye Cruel World".length();
```

Because the compiler automatically creates a new String object for every literal string it encounters, you can use a literal string to initialize a String.

```
String s = "Hola Mundo";
```

The above construct is equivalent to, but more efficient than, the following construct, which ends up creating two Strings instead of one:

```
String s = new String("Hola Mundo");
```

The compiler creates the first string when it encounters the literal string **"Hola Mundo!"**, and the second one when it encounters new String().

Concatenation and the + Operator

In Java, you can use + to concatenate Strings together:

```
String cat = "cat";
System.out.println("con" + cat + "enation");
```

This is a little deceptive because, as you know, Strings can't be changed. However, behind the scenes the compiler uses StringBuffers to implement concatenation. The above example compiles to:

```
String cat = "cat";
System.out.println(newStringBuffer().append("con").append(cat)
                    .append("enation"));
```

You can also use the + operator to append values to a String that are not themselves Strings:

```
System.out.println("Java's Number " + 1);
```

The compiler converts the non-String value (the integer 1 in the example) to a String object before performing the concatenation operation.

Other Interesting Features

This lesson covered the most commonly used methods in the String and StringBuffer classes. But there's more. String and StringBuffer provide several other useful ways to manipulate string data, including concatenation, comparison, substitution, and converting to upper and lower case. The API documentation for the String[1] and StringBuffer[2] classes summarizes and lists all of the methods and variables supported by these two classes.

---

[1] http://java.sun.com/products/JDK/CurrentRelease/api/java.lang.String.html
[2] http://java.sun.com/products/JDK/CurrentRelease/api/java.lang.StringBuffer.html

12

Setting Program Attributes

Y<small>OUR</small> Java programs run within some environment where there's a host machine, a current directory, and user preferences for window color, font, font size, and other attributes. In addition to these system (or runtime) attributes, your program can set up certain, configurable attributes that are specific to it. Program attributes are often called *preferences* and allow the user to configure various startup options, preferred window size, and so on for the program.

A program might need information about the system environment to make decisions about how to do something. Also, a program might modify certain attributes itself or allow a user to change them. As a result, a program needs to be able to read and sometimes modify both system attributes and program attributes. Java programs can manage system and program attributes through three mechanisms: properties, command-line arguments, and applet parameters.

Properties define environmental attributes on a persistent basis. That is, you use properties when attribute values need to persist between invocations of a program. Setting Up and Using Properties (page 228) shows you how to set up and use properties in your Java programs.

Command-line arguments define attributes for Java applications on a non-persistent basis. You use command-line arguments to set one or more attributes for a single invocation of an application. Command-Line Arguments (page 230) contains two examples that show you how to accept command-line arguments and how to process them.

Applet parameters are similar to command-line arguments but are used with applets, not applications. Use applet parameters to set one or more attributes for a single invocation of an applet. For information about applet parameters, see Defining and Using Applet Parameters (page 175).

227

Setting Up and Using Properties

In Java, program attributes are represented by the `Properties` class[1] in the `java.util` package. A `Properties` object contains a set of key/value pairs. The key/value pairs are like dictionary entries: the key is the word, and the value is the definition.

Both the key and the value are `String` objects. For example, `"os.name"` is the key for one of Java's default system properties—its value contains the name of the current operating system. Use a key to look up a property in the properties list and get its value. On my system, when I look up the `"os.name"` property, its value is `"Solaris"`. Yours will likely be different.

Properties specific to your Java program are maintained by your program. System properties are maintained by the `java.lang.System` class. For information about system properties, refer to <u>System Properties</u> (page 242) in the **<u>Using System Resources</u>** (page 237) lesson.

You can use the `Properties` class to manage attributes specific to your Java programs. You can load key/value pairs into a `Properties` object from a stream, save the properties to a stream, and get information about the properties represented by the `Properties` object.

Setting Up Your Properties Object

Often when a program starts up, it uses code similar to the following to set up the Properties object:

```
. . .
    // set up default properties
Properties defaultProps = new Properties();
FileInputStream defaultStream = new
        FileInputStream("defaultProperties");
defaultProps.load(defaultStream);
defaultsStream.close();

    // set up real properties
Properties applicationProps = new Properties(defaultProps);
FileInputStream appStream = new
        FileInputStream("appProperties");
applicationProps.load(appStream);
appStream.close();
. . .
```

---

[1] http://java.sun.com/products/JDK/CurrentRelease/api/java.util.Properties.html

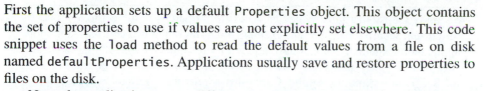

First the application sets up a default `Properties` object. This object contains the set of properties to use if values are not explicitly set elsewhere. This code snippet uses the `load` method to read the default values from a file on disk named `defaultProperties`. Applications usually save and restore properties to files on the disk.

Next, the application uses a different constructor to create a second `Properties` object, `applicationProps`. This object uses `defaultProps` to provide its default values.

Then the code snippet loads a set of properties into `applicationProps` from a file named `appProperties`. The properties loaded into `appProperties` can be set on a per-user basis, a per-site basis, or whatever is appropriate for the current program. What's important is that the program saves the `Properties` to a well-known location so that the next invocation of the program can retrieve them. For example, the HotJava browser saves properties on a per-user basis and saves the properties to a file in the user's home directory.

Use the `save` method to write properties to a stream:

```
FileOutputStream defaultsOut = new
    FileOutputStream("defaultProperties");
applicationProps.save(defaultsOut, "---No Comment---");
defaultsOut.close();
```

The `save` method needs a stream to write to, and a string which it uses as a comment at the top of the output.

Getting Property Information

Once you've set up your `Properties` object, you can query it for information about various properties it contains. The `Properties` class provides several methods for getting property information:

getProperty
> Returns the value for the specified property. There are two versions of this method. One version allows you to provide a default value—if the key is not found the default is returned.

list
> Writes all the properties to the specified stream. This is useful for debugging.

propertyNames
> Returns an `Enumeration` containing all of the keys contained in the `Properties` object.

Security Considerations: Note that access to properties is subject to approval by the current security manager. The example programs contained here are stand-alone applications, which by default have no security manager. If you attempt to use this code in an applet, it might not work depending on the browser or viewer it's running in. See **Understanding Applet Capabilities and Restrictions** (page 197) for information about the security restrictions placed on applets.

Command-Line Arguments

Your Java application can accept any number of arguments from the command line. Command-line arguments allow the user to affect the operation of an application. For example, an application might allow the user to specify verbose mode—that is, specify that the application display a lot of trace information—with the command-line argument `-verbose`.

Note: The Java language supports command-line arguments. However, some systems don't normally have command-line arguments. For example, MacOS doesn't have a command line. Even though the JDK on these systems might provide support for command-line arguments, consider using properties instead so that your programs fit more naturally into the environment.

The user enters command-line arguments when invoking the application. For example, suppose you have a Java application, called `Sort`, that sorts lines in a file, and that the data you want sorted is in a file named `friends.txt`. If you are using Windows 95/NT, you invoke the `Sort` application on your data file like this:

```
java Sort friends.txt
```

In the Java language, when you invoke an application, the runtime system passes the command-line arguments to the application's `main` method via an array of `Strings`. Each `String` in the array contains one of the command-line arguments. In the previous example, the command-line arguments passed to the `Sort` application is an array that contains a single string: "`friends.txt`".

Note to C and C++ Programmers: The command-line arguments passed to a Java application differ in number and in type than those passed to a C or C++ program. In C and C++ when you invoke a program, the system passes two parameters to it:

- **argc**—the number of arguments on the command line
- **argv**—a pointer to an array of strings that contain the arguments
  When you invoke a Java application, the system passes only one parameter to it:
- **args**—an array of Strings (just an array, not a pointer to an array) that contains the arguments
  You can derive the number of command-line arguments with the array's `length` attribute:

      numberOfArgs = args.length;

In C and C++, the system passes the entire command line to the program as arguments, including the name used to invoke it. For example, if you invoked a C program as shown below the first argument in the `argv` parameter is `diff`:

    diff file1 file2

In Java, you always know the name of the application because it's the name of the class where the `main` method is defined. So the Java runtime system does not pass the class name you invoke to the `main` method. Rather, the system passes only the items on the command line that appear after the class name. For example, consider the following statement which is used to invoke a Java application:

    java diff **file1** file2

The first command-line argument is `file1`.

The Echo Command-Line Arguments Example

This simple application displays each of its command-line arguments on a line by itself:

```
class Echo {
    public static void main (String[] args) {
        for (int i = 0; i < args.length; i++)
            System.out.println(args[i]);
    }
}
```

Invoke the Echo application. Here's an example of how to invoke the application using Windows 95/NT. You enter the words in bold:

```
java Echo Drink Hot Java
Drink
Hot
Java
```

Note that the application displays each word—Drink, Hot, and Java—on a line by itself. This is because the space character separates command-line arguments. If you want `Drink Hot Java` to be interpreted as a single argument, you would

join them with double quotes, which the system consumes. On Windows 95/NT, you run it like this:

```
java Echo "Drink Hot Java"
Drink Hot Java
```

Conventions for Command-Line Arguments

By convention, your Java program can accept three different types of command-line arguments:
- word arguments (also known as options)
- arguments that require arguments
- flags

Your application should observe the following conventions that apply to these types of command-line arguments:
- The dash character (-) precedes options, flags, or series of flags.
- Arguments can be given in any order, except where an argument requires another argument.
- Flags can be listed in any order, separately or combined: `-xn` or `-nx` or `-x -n`.
- Filenames typically come last.
- The program prints a usage error when a command-line argument is unrecognized. Usage statements usually take the form:

```
usage: application_name [ optional_args ] required_args
```

Word Arguments

Arguments such as `-verbose` are *word arguments* and must be specified in their entirety on the command line. For example, `-ver` would *not* match `-verbose`.

You can use a statement such as the following to check for word arguments.

```
if (argument.equals("-verbose"))
    vflag = true;
```

The statement checks for the word argument `-verbose` and sets a flag within the program indicating that the program should run in verbose mode.

Arguments that Require Arguments

Some arguments require more information. For example, a command-line argument such as `-output` might allow the user to redirect the output of the program. However, the `-output` option alone does not provide enough information to the application: How does the application know where to redirect its output? The

user must also specify a filename. Typically, the next item on the command line provides the additional information for command-line arguments that require it. You can use a statement such as the following to parse arguments that require arguments:

```
if (argument.equals("-output")) {
    if (nextarg < args.length)
        outputfile = args[nextarg++];
    else
        System.err.println("-output requires a filename");
}
```

Note that the code snippet checks to make sure that the user actually specified a next argument before trying to use it.

Flags

Flags are single character codes that modify the behavior of the program in some way. For example, the -t flag provided to the UNIX ls command indicates that the output should be sorted by time stamp. Most applications allow users to specify flags separately in any order:

-x -n   **or**   -n -x

In addition, to make life easier for users, applications should also allow users to concatenate flags and specify them in any order:

-nx   **or**   -xn

The sample program described in the next section implements a simple algorithm to process flag arguments that can be specified in any order, separately or combined.

Parsing Command-Line Arguments

Most applications accept several command-line arguments that allow the user to affect the execution of the application. For example, the UNIX command that prints the contents of a directory, the ls command, accepts arguments that determine which file attributes to print and the order in which the files are listed. Typically, the user can specify the command-line arguments in any order, thereby requiring the application to *parse* them.

This program, called `ParseCmdLine` (page 631), provides you with a basis from which you can build your own command line parser.

```java
class ParseCmdLine {
    public static void main(String[] args) {

        int i = 0, j;
        String arg;
        char flag;
        boolean vflag = false;
        String outputfile = "";

        while (i < args.length && args[i].startsWith("-")) {
            arg = args[i++];

// use this type of check for "wordy" arguments
            if (arg.equals("-verbose")) {
                System.out.println("verbose mode on");
                vflag = true;
            }

// use this type of check for
// arguments that require arguments
            else if (arg.equals("-output")) {
                if (i < args.length)
                    outputfile = args[i++];
                else
                    System.err.println(
                        "-output requires a filename");
                if (vflag)
                    System.out.println(
                        "output file = " + outputfile);
            }

// use this type of check for a series of flag arguments
            else {
                for (j = 1; j < arg.length(); j++) {
                    flag = arg.charAt(j);
                    switch (flag) {
                    case 'x':
                        if (vflag) System.out.println("Option x");
                        break;
                    case 'n':
                        if (vflag) System.out.println("Option n");
                        break;
                    default:
                        System.err.println(
                            "ParseCmdLine: illegal option " + flag);
                        break;
                    }
                }
            }
```

```
            }
        }
        if (i == args.length)
            System.err.println(
                "Usage: ParseCmdLine [-verbose] [-xn] [-output
                    afile] filename");
        else
            System.out.println("Success!");
    }
}
```

It accepts one command-line argument of each type: a word argument, an argument that requires an argument, and two flags. In addition, this program requires a filename. Here's the usage statement for this program:

```
usage: ParseCmdLine [-verbose] [-xn] [-output afile] filename
```

The arguments within square brackets are optional; the `filename` argument is required.

`ParseCmdLine` relies heavily on the `String` and `System` classes. For information about `String`s, see **The String and StringBuffer Classes** (page 215) lesson, or refer to the online API documentation for the `String` class. For information about the `System` class, go on to the next lesson, **Using System Resources** (page 237), or refer to the online API documentation for the `System`[1] class.

---

[1] http://java.sun.com/products/JDK/CurrentRelease/api/java.lang.System.html

13

Using System Resources

OFTEN, a program requires access to system resources such as properties, standard input and output streams, or the current time. Your program could use these resources directly from the current runtime environment, but your program would only be able to run in the environment for which it was written. Each time you wanted to run the program in a new environment, you would have to port the program by rewriting the system-dependent sections of code.

The Java development environment solves this problem by allowing your program to use system resources through a system-independent programming interface implemented by the System[1] class.

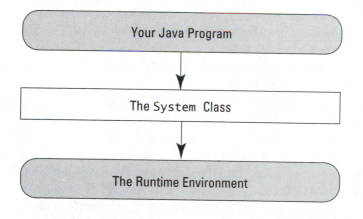

---

[1] http://java.sun.com/products/JDK/CurrentRelease/api/java.lang.System.html

As you can see from the figure on page 237, the System class allows your Java programs to use system resources but insulates them from system-specific details.

All of System's methods and variables are class methods and class variables. You don't instantiate the System class to use it; you use the System class's methods and variables directly from a reference to the System class. Using the System Class (page 239) describes this in detail.

If you've experimented with other lessons in this tutorial, you've no doubt already seen the System class's standard output stream, which several examples use to display text. The system resources available through the System class include:

The Standard I/O Streams (page 240)

Probably the most frequently used items from the System class are the streams used for reading and writing text. The System class provides one stream for reading text, the standard input stream, and two streams for writing text: the standard output and standard error streams.

System Properties (page 242)

Properties are key/value pairs that your Java programs can use to set up various attributes or parameters between invocations. The Java environment itself maintains a set of *system properties* that contain information about the current environment. You can access the system properties through the System class.

Forcing Finalization and Garbage Collection (page 246)

In Java, you don't have to free memory when you're done with it. The garbage collector runs asynchronously in the background cleaning up unreferenced objects. However, you can force the garbage collector to run using System's gc method. Also, you can force the runtime system to perform object finalization using System's runFinalization method.

Miscellaneous System Methods (page 247)

The System class includes several miscellaneous methods that let you get the current time in milliseconds, exit the interpreter, copy arrays, and work with the security manager.

Most system programming needs are met through the programming interface provided by the System class. However, in rare cases, a program must bypass the system-independent interface of the System class and use system resources directly from the runtime environment. The Java environment provides a Runtime[1] object, which represents the current runtime environment. You can use a Runtime object to access system resources directly. The Runtime Object (page 251) explains how to do this and talks about the tradeoffs of doing so.

---

[1] http://java.sun.com/products/JDK/CurrentRelease/api/java.lang.Runtime.html

Note: Messaging the `Runtime` object directly compromises your ability to run your program on different systems. You should do this only in special situations.

Using the System Class

Unlike most other classes, you don't instantiate the `System` class to use it. To be more precise, you cannot instantiate the `System` class—it's a final class and all of its constructors are private.

All of `System`'s variables and methods are class variables and class methods—they are declared `static`. For a complete discussion about class variables and class methods and how they differ from instance variables and instance methods, refer to <u>Instance and Class Members</u> (page 111) in the **Objects, Classes, and Interfaces** (page 77) lesson.

To use a class variable, you use it directly from the name of the class using Java's dot (.) notation. For example, to reference the `System`'s class variable `out`, append the variable name to the class name separated by a period, like this:

```
System.out
```

You call class methods in a similar fashion. For example, to call `System`'s `getProperty` method, append the method name to the end of the class name separated by a period:

```
System.getProperty(argument);
```

The following small Java program uses the `System` class twice, first to retrieve the current user's name and then to display it.

```
class UserNameTest {
    public static void main(String[] args) {
        String name;
        name = System.getProperty("user.name");
        System.out.println(name);
    }
}
```

You'll notice that this program never instantiates a `System` object. It just references the `getProperty` method and the `out` variable directly from the class.

The code sample uses `System`'s `getProperty` method to search the properties database for the property called `"user.name"`. <u>System Properties</u> (page 242) later in this lesson talks more about system properties and the `getProperty` method.

This code sample also uses `System.out`, a `PrintStream` that implements the standard output stream. The `println` method prints its argument to the standard output stream. The next section discusses the standard output stream and the other two standard I/O streams provided by the `System` class.

The Standard I/O Streams

The concept of standard input and output streams is a C library concept that has been assimilated into the Java environment. There are three standard streams, all of which are managed by the java.lang.System class:

Standard input—referenced by `System.in`
   Used for program input. Typically reads input entered by the user.

Standard output—referenced by `System.out`
   Used for program output. Typically displays information to the user.

Standard error—referenced by `System.err`
   Used to display error messages to the user.

Standard Input Stream

The `System` class provides a stream for reading text—the standard input stream. The example program in **The Nuts and Bolts of the Java Language** (page 43) lesson uses the standard input stream to count the number of characters typed in by the user. Visit The Standard Input and Output Streams (page 74) in that lesson for a discussion about the standard input stream.

Standard Output and Error Streams

Probably the most frequently used items from the `System` class are the the standard output and standard error streams, which you use to display text to the user. The standard output stream is typically used for command output, to display the results of a command to the user. The standard error stream is typically used to display any errors that occur when a program is running.

The `print`, `println`, and `write` Methods

Both standard output and standard error derive from the <u>PrintStream</u>[1] class. You use one of `PrintStream`'s three methods to print text to the stream: `print`, `println`, and `write`.

[1.] http://java.sun.com/products/JDK/CurrentRelease/api/java.io.PrintStream.html

The `print` and `println` methods are essentially the same; they both write their `String` argument to the stream. The one difference between the two methods is that `println` appends a newline character to the end of its output while `print` does not. In other words, this

```
System.out.print("Duke is not a penguin!\n");
```

is equivalent to this

```
System.out.println("Duke is not a penguin!");
```

Note the extra \n in the first method call; it's the two-character code for a newline character. `println` automatically appends a newline character to its output.

The `write` method is used less frequently than either of the `print` methods. The `write` method writes bytes to the stream. Use `write` to write non-ASCII data.

Arguments to `print` and `println`

The `print` and `println` methods both take a single argument. The argument may be one of any of the following data types: `Object`, `String`, `char[]`, `int`, `long`, `float`, `double`, and `boolean`. In addition, there's an extra version of `println` that takes no arguments and just prints a newline character to the stream.

Printing Objects of Different Data Types

The following program uses `println` to output data of various types to the standard output stream.

```
class DataTypePrintTest {
    public static void main(String[] args) {

        Thread objectData = new Thread();
        String stringData = "Java Mania";
        char[] charArrayData = { 'a', 'b', 'c' };
        int integerData = 4;
        long longData = Long.MIN_VALUE;
        float floatData = Float.MAX_VALUE;
        double doubleData = Math.PI;
        boolean booleanData = true;

        System.out.println(objectData);
        System.out.println(stringData);
```

```
            System.out.println(charArrayData);
            System.out.println(integerData);
            System.out.println(longData);
            System.out.println(floatData);
            System.out.println(doubleData);
            System.out.println(booleanData);
        }
    }
```

The program listed above produces this output:

```
Thread[Thread-4,5,main]
Java Mania
abc
4
-9223372036854775808
3.40282e+38
3.14159
true
```

Note that you can print an object—the first `println` method call prints a `Thread` object and the second prints a `String` object. When you use `print` or `println` to print an object, the data printed depends on the type of the object. In the example, printing a `String` object yields the contents of the `String`. However, printing a `Thread` yields a string of this format:

```
ThreadClass[name,priority,group]
```

For a thorough discussion of I/O streams in Java refer to **Input and Output Streams** (page 325)

System Properties

The `System` class maintains a set of properties, key/value pairs, that define traits or attributes of the current working environment. When the runtime system first starts up, the system properties are initialized to contain information about the runtime environment, including information about the current user, the current version of the Java runtime environment, and even the character used to separate components of a filename.

Here is a complete list of the system properties you get when the runtime system first starts up and what they mean:

Key	Meaning
`"file.separator"`	File separator, (for example, `"/"`)
`"java.class.path"`	Java classpath
`"java.class.version"`	Java class version number
`"java.home"`	Java installation directory
`"java.vendor"`	Java vendor-specific string
`"java.vendor.url"`	Java vendor URL
`"java.version"`	Java version number
`"line.separator"`	Line separator
`"os.arch"`	Operating system architecture
`"os.name"`	Operating system name
`"path.separator"`	Path separator (for example, `":"`)
`"user.dir"`	User's current working directory
`"user.home"`	User home directory
`"user.name"`	User account name

Your Java programs can read or write system properties through several methods in the `System` class. You can use a key to look up one property in the properties list, or you can get the whole set of properties all at once. You can also change the set of system properties completely.

Security consideration: Applets can read *some, but not all,* system properties. For a complete list of the system properties that can and cannot be used by applets, refer to <u>Reading System Properties</u> (page 244). Applets cannot write system properties.

Reading System Properties

The System class has two methods that you can use to read the system properties: getProperty and getProperties.

The System class has two different versions of getProperty. Both retrieve the value of the property named in the argument list. The simpler of the two get-Property methods takes a single argument: the key for the property you want to search for. For example, to get the value of "path.separator", use the following statement:

```
System.getProperty("path.separator");
```

The getProperty method returns a string containing the value of the property. If the property does not exist, this version of getProperty returns null.

Which brings us to the second version of getProperty method. This version requires two String arguments: the first argument is the key to look up and the second argument is a default value to return if the key cannot be found or if it has no value. For example, the following call to getProperty looks up the System property called "subliminal.message". This is not a valid system property, so instead of returning null, this method returns the default value provided as a second argument: "Buy Java Now!".

```
System.getProperty("subliminal.message", "Buy Java Now!");
```

You should use this version of getProperty if you don't want to risk a NullPointerException, or if you really want to provide a default value for a property that doesn't have a value or that cannot be found.

The last method provided by the System class to access properties values is the getProperties method, which returns a Properties[1] object that contains the complete set of system property key/value pairs. You can use the various Properties class methods to query the Properties objects for specific values or to list the entire set of properties. For information about the Properties class, see Setting Up and Using Properties (page 228).

Writing System Properties

You can modify the existing set of system properties using System's setProperties method. This method takes a Properties object that has been initialized

---

[1.] http://java.sun.com/products/JDK/CurrentRelease/api/java.util.Properties.html

to contain the key/value pairs for the properties that you want to set. This method replaces the entire set of system properties with the new set represented by the Properties object.

The next example is a Java program that creates a Properties object and initializes it from the file called myProperties.txt, which contains this text:

```
subliminal.message=Buy Java Now!
```

The example program then uses System.setProperties to install the new Properties objects as the current set of system properties.

```
import java.io.FileInputStream;
import java.util.Properties;

class PropertiesTest {
    public static void main(String[] args) {
        try {
            // set up new properties object from
            //file "myProperties.txt"
            FileInputStream propFile = new FileInputStream(
                            "myProperties.txt");
            Properties p = new Properties(System.getProperties());
            p.load(propFile);

            // set the system properties
            System.setProperties(p);
            // display the system properties
            System.getProperties().list(System.out);
        } catch (java.io.FileNotFoundException e) {
            System.err.println("Can't find myProperties.txt.");
        } catch (java.io.IOException e) {
            System.err.println("I/O failed.");
        }
    }
}
```

Note how the example program creates the Properties object, p, which is used as the argument to setProperties:

```
Properties p = new Properties(System.getProperties());
```

This statement initializes the new properties object, p, with the current set of system properties, which in the case of this small program is the set of properties initialized by the runtime system. Then the program loads additional properties into p from the file myProperties.txt and sets the system properties to p. This has the effect of adding the properties listed in `myProperties.txt` to the set of properties created by the runtime system at startup. Note that you can create p without any default `Properties` object like this:

```
Properties p = new Properties();
```

If you do this, your application won't have access to the system properties.

Note that the value of system properties can be overwritten! For example, if `myProperties.txt` contains the following line, the `"java.vendor"` system property will be overwritten:

```
java.vendor=Acme Software Company
```

In general, you should be careful not to overwrite system properties.

The `setProperties` method changes the set of system properties for the currently running application. These changes are not persistent; that is, changing the system properties within an application will not affect future invocations of the Java interpreter for this or any other application. The runtime system reinitializes the system properties each time it starts up. If you want your changes to the system properties to be persistent, then your application must write the values to some file before exiting and read them in again upon startup.

Note: Previous versions of the `System` class supported a method called `getenv` which retrieved the value of an environment variable. This method was UNIX specific and has been made obsolete by the more versatile properties mechanism. Your Java programs should not be using `getenv` anymore.

Forcing Finalization and Garbage Collection

The Java runtime system performs memory management tasks for you. When your program has finished using an object, that is, when there are no more references to an object, the object is *finalized* and is then garbage collected. These tasks happen asynchronously in the background. However, you can force object finalization and garbage collection using the appropriate method in the `System` class.

Finalizing Objects

Before an object is garbage collected, the Java runtime system gives the object a chance to clean up after itself. This step is known as *finalization* and is achieved through a call to the object's `finalize` method. The object should override the `finalize` method to perform any final cleanup tasks such as freeing system resources like files and sockets. For information about the `finalize` method, see Writing a `finalize` Method (page 118).

You can force object finalization to occur by calling `System`'s `runFinaliza-tion` method.

```
System.runFinalization();
```

This method calls the `finalize` methods on all objects that are waiting to be garbage collected.

Running the Garbage Collector

You can ask the garbage collector to run at any time by calling `System`'s `gc` method:

```
System.gc();
```

You might want to run the garbage collector to ensure that it runs at the best time for your program rather than when it's most convenient for the runtime system to run it. For example, your program may wish to run the garbage collector right before it enters a compute or memory intensive section of code or when it knows there will be some idle time. The garbage collector requires about 20 milliseconds to complete its task, so your program should run the garbage collector only when doing so will have no performance impact on your program—that is, when your program anticipates that the garbage collector will have enough time to finish its job.

For more information about Java's garbage collection scheme see Cleaning Up Unused Objects (page 84).

Miscellaneous System Methods

The `System` class provides several methods that provide miscellaneous functionality including copying arrays and getting the current time.

Copying Arrays

Use `System`'s `arraycopy` method to efficiently copy data from one array into another. The `arraycopy` method requires five arguments:

```
public static
    void arraycopy(Object source,
                   int srcIndex,
                   Object dest,
                   int destIndex,
                   int length)
```

The two `Object` arguments indicate which array to copy from and which array to copy to. The three integer arguments indicate the starting location in both the source and the destination arrays, and the number of elements to copy. This figure illustrates how the copy takes place:

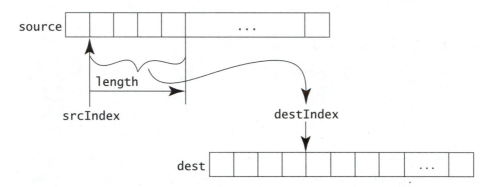

The following Java program uses `arraycopy` to copy some elements from the `copyFrom` array to the `copyTo` array.

```
class ArrayCopyTest {
    public static void main(String[] args) {
        byte[] copyFrom = { 'd', 'e', 'c', 'a', 'f', 'f', 'e',
                            'i', 'n', 'a', 't', 'e', 'd' };
        byte[] copyTo = new byte[7];

        System.arraycopy(copyFrom, 2, copyTo, 0, 7);
        System.out.println(new String(copyTo, 0));
    }
}
```

The `arraycopy` method call in this program begins the copy at element number 2 in the source array. Recall that array indices start at 0, so the copy begins at the array element `'c'`. The `arraycopy` method call puts the copied elements into the destination array beginning at the first element (element 0) in the destination array `copyTo`. The copy copies seven elements: `'c'`, `'a'`, `'f'`, `'f'`, `'e'`, `'i'`, and `'n'`. Effectively, the `arraycopy` method takes the "caffein" out of "decaffeinated", like this:

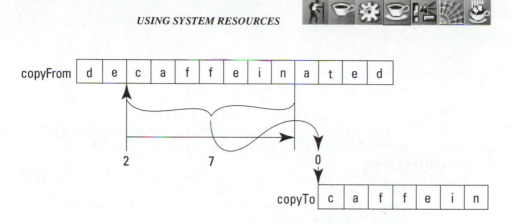

Note that the destination array must be allocated before you call `arraycopy` and must be large enough to contain the data being copied.

Getting the Current Time

The `currentTimeMillis` method returns the current time in milliseconds since 00:00:00, January 1, 1970. The `currentTimeMillis` method is commonly used during performance tests: get the current time, perform the operation that you want to time, get the current time again. The difference between the two time samples is roughly the amount of time that the operation took to execute.

Often in graphical user interfaces the time difference between mouse clicks is used to determine whether a user double clicked. The TimingIsEverything.java (page 633) applet uses `currentTimeMillis` to compute the number of milliseconds between two mouse clicks. If the time period between the clicks is less than 200 milliseconds, the two mouse clicks are interpreted as a double mouse click.

This screen shot shows what the applet looks like after you've double clicked on it:

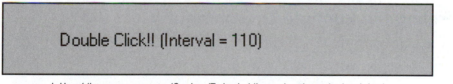

http://java.sun.com/Series/Tutorial/java/system/misc.html

Here's the source code for the TimingIsEverything applet:

```
import java.awt.Graphics;

public class TimingIsEverything extends java.applet.Applet {

    public long firstClickTime = 0;
    public String displayStr;
```

```java
        public void init() {
            displayStr = "Double Click Me";
        }
        public void paint(Graphics g) {
            g.drawRect(0, 0, size().width-1, size().height-1);
            g.drawString(displayStr, 40, 30);
        }
        public boolean mouseDown(java.awt.Event evt, int x, int y) {
            long clickTime = System.currentTimeMillis();
            long clickInterval = clickTime - firstClickTime;
            if (clickInterval < 200) {
                displayStr = "Double Click!! (Interval = " +
                    clickInterval + ")";
                firstClickTime = 0;
            } else {
                displayStr = "Single Click!!";
                firstClickTime = clickTime;
            }
            repaint();
            return true;
        }
    }
```

You could use the return value from the `CurrentTimeMillis` method to compute the current date and time. However, you'll probably find that it's more convenient to get the current date and time from the `Date`[1] class.

Note: Previous versions of the `System` class supported two time-related methods besides the `currentTimeMillis` method: `currentTime` and `nowMillis`. These two methods are now obsolete—you should use `currentTimeMillis` instead.

Exiting the Runtime Environment

To exit the Java interpreter, call the `System.exit` method. The interpreter exits with the integer exit code that you specify to the `exit` method.

```java
System.exit(-1);
```

Note: The `exit` method causes the Java interpreter to exit, not just your Java program. Use this function with caution.

---

[1] http://java.sun.com/products/JDK/CurrentRelease/api/java.util.Date.html

Security consideration: Invocation of the `exit` method is subject to security restrictions. Depending on the browser that an applet is running in, a call to `exit` from within an applet will likely result in a `SecurityException`. See **Understanding Applet Capabilities and Restrictions** (page 197) for information about the security restrictions placed on applets.

Setting and Getting the Security Manager

The security manager is an object that enforces a certain security policy for a Java application. You can set the current security manager for your applications using `System`'s `setSecurityManager` method, and you can retrieve the current security manager using `System`'s `getSecurityManager` method. An application's security manager is a `java.lang.SecurityManager`[1] object.

The **Providing Your Own Security Manager** (page 529) lesson discusses security managers in detail and shows you how to create and install your own security manager.

Security consideration: The security manager for an application can be set only once. Typically, a browser sets its security manager during its startup procedure. Thus, most of the time, applets cannot set the security manager because it's already been set. A `SecurityException` results if your applet attempts to do so. See **Understanding Applet Capabilities and Restrictions** (page 197) for information about the security restrictions placed on applets.

The Runtime Object

At the core of the Java runtime environment are the Java virtual machine, the Java interpreter, and the host operating system.

The oval labeled **Runtime** in the following figure represents the current runtime environment and is an instance of the `Runtime`[2] class. The current runtime environment can be anything from Sun's implementation of the Java virtual machine and interpreter running on Solaris to ACME Company's implementation of the virtual machine and interpreter running on the ACME toaster.

`Runtime` objects provide two services. First, they communicate with the components of the runtime environment—getting information and invoking

1. http://java.sun.com/products/JDK/CurrentRelease/api/java.lang.SecurityManager.html
2. http://java.sun.com/products/JDK/CurrentRelease/api/java.lang.Runtime.html

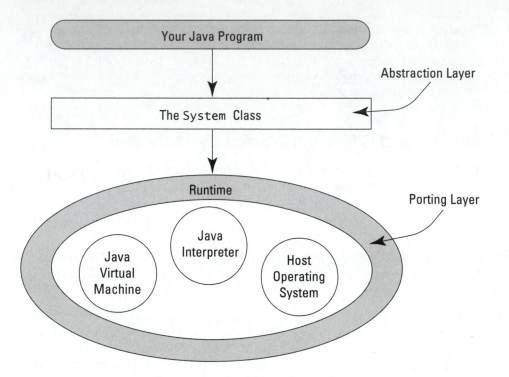

functions. Second, `Runtime` objects are the interface to system-dependent capabilities. For example, UNIX `Runtime` objects might support the `getenv` and `setenv` functions. Other `Runtime` objects, such as MacOS, might not support `getenv` and `setenv` because the host operating system doesn't support these functions, but they might support others.

Because the `Runtime` class is tightly integrated with the implementation of the Java interpreter, the Java virtual machine, and the host operating system, it is system dependent. If objects in your program message the `Runtime` object directly, you sacrifice the system-indepedent nature of your Java program. In general, this is not a good idea (particularly for applets).

14

Handling Errors Using Exceptions

IF there's one golden rule of programming, it's this: Errors occur in software programs. This we know. But what really matters is what happens after the error occurs. How is the error handled? Who handles it? Can the program recover?

The Java language uses *exceptions* to provide error handling capabilities for its programs. So <u>What's an Exception and Why Do I Care?</u> (page 254). An exception is an event that occurs during the execution of a program that disrupts the normal flow of instructions. If you have done any amount of Java programming at all, you have undoubtedly already encountered exceptions. <u>Your First Encounter with Java Exceptions</u> (page 261) was probably in the form of an error message like the following one from the compiler:

```
InputFile.java:9: Exception java.io.FileNotFoundException must
be caught, or it must be declared in the throws clause of this
method.
        fis = new FileInputStream(filename);
          ^
```

This message indicates that the compiler found an exception that is not being dealt with. The Java language requires that a method either catch all "checked" exceptions (those that are checked by the runtime system) or specify that it can throw that type of exception. <u>Java's Catch or Specify Requirement</u> (page 263) discusses the reasoning behind this requirement and what it means to you and your Java programs. <u>Dealing with Exceptions</u> (page 265) features an example program which can throw two different kinds of exceptions. Using this program, you will learn how to catch an exception and handle it, and alternatively, how to specify that your method can throw it.

The Java runtime system and some of the classes from Java packages all throw exceptions under some circumstances. You can use the same mechanism to throw exceptions in your Java programs. How to Throw Exceptions (page 277) shows you how you can throw exceptions from your own Java code using the `throw` statement. All exceptions must inherit (either directly or indirectly) from the `Throwable`[1] class defined in the `java.lang` package.

As mentioned previously, Java requires that methods catch or specify checked exceptions. However, methods do not have to catch or specify *runtime exceptions*, exceptions that occur within the Java runtime system. Because catching or specifying an exception is extra work, it is tempting for programmers to write code that throws only runtime exceptions, and therefore doesn't have to catch or specify exceptions. This is "exception abuse" and is not recommended. Runtime Exceptions—The Controversy (page 283), the last section in this lesson, explains why.

Note to C++ Programmers: Java exception handlers can have a `finally` block, which allows programs to clean up after the `try` block. See The `finally` Block (page 271) for more information about how to use the `finally` statement.

What's an Exception and Why Do I Care?

The term *exception* is shorthand for the phrase "exceptional event."

Definition: An *exception* is an event that occurs during the execution of a program that disrupts the normal flow of instructions.

Many kinds of errors can cause exceptions—problems ranging from serious hardware errors, such as a hard disk crash, to simple programming errors, such as trying to access an out-of-bounds array element. When such an error occurs within a Java method, the method creates an exception object and hands it off to the runtime system. The exception object contains information about the exception, including its type and the state of the program when the error occurred. The runtime system is then responsible for finding some code to handle the error. In Java terminology, creating an exception object and handing it to the runtime system is called *throwing an exception*.

---

[1]. http://java.sun.com/products/JDK/CurrentRelease/api/java.lang.Throwable.html

After a method throws an exception, the runtime system leaps into action to find someone to handle the exception. The set of possible "someones" to handle the exception is the set of methods in the call stack of the method where the error occurred. The runtime system searches backwards through the call stack, beginning with the method in which the error occurred, until it finds a method that contains an appropriate *exception handler*. An exception handler is considered appropriate if the type of the exception thrown is the same as the type of exception handled by the handler. The exception bubbles up through the call stack until an appropriate handler is found and one of the calling methods handles the exception. The exception handler chosen is said to *catch the exception*.

If the runtime system exhaustively searches all of the methods on the call stack without finding an appropriate exception handler, the runtime system (and consequently, the Java program) terminates.

By using exceptions to manage errors, Java programs have the following advantages over traditional error management techniques:

- Advantage 1: Separating Error Handling Code from "Regular" Code (page 255)
- Advantage 2: Propagating Errors Up the Call Stack (page 257)
- Advantage 3: Grouping and Differentiating Error Types (page 259)

Advantage 1: Separating Error Handling Code from "Regular" Code

In traditional programming, error detection, reporting, and handling often lead to confusing spaghetti code. For example, suppose that you have a function that reads an entire file into memory. In pseudocode, your function might look something like this:

```
readFile {
    open the file;
    determine its size;
    allocate that much memory;
    read the file into memory;
    close the file;
}
```

At first glance this function seems simple enough, but it ignores all of these potential errors:

- What happens if the file can't be opened?
- What happens if the length of the file can't be determined?
- What happens if enough memory can't be allocated?
- What happens if the read fails?
- What happens if the file can't be closed?

To answer these questions within your read_file function, you'd have to add a lot of code to do error detection, reporting, and handling. Your function would end up looking something like this:

```
errorCodeType readFile {
    initialize errorCode = 0;
    open the file;
    if (theFileIsOpen) {
        determine the length of the file;
        if (gotTheFileLength) {
            allocate that much memory;
            if (gotEnoughMemory) {
                read the file into memory;
                if (readFailed) {
                    errorCode = -1;
                }
            } else {
                errorCode = -2;
            }
        } else {
            errorCode = -3;
        }
        close the file;
        if (theFileDidntClose && errorCode == 0) {
            errorCode = -4;
        } else {
            errorCode = errorCode and -4;
        }
    } else {
        errorCode = -5;
    }
    return errorCode;
}
```

With error detection built in, your original 7 lines of code (in bold) have been inflated to 29 lines of code—a bloat factor of almost 400 percent. Worse, there's so much error detection, reporting, and returning that the original 7 lines of code are lost in the clutter. And worse yet, the logical flow of the code has also been lost in the clutter, making it difficult to tell if the code is doing the right thing: Is the file *really* being closed if the function fails to allocate enough memory? It's even more difficult to ensure that the code continues to do the right thing after you modify the function three months after writing it. Many programmers "solve" this problem by simply ignoring it—errors are "reported" when their programs crash.

Java provides an elegant solution to the problem of error management: exceptions. Exceptions enable you to write the main flow of your code and deal

with the, well, exceptional cases elsewhere. If your `read_file` function used exceptions instead of traditional error management techniques, it would look something like this:

```
readFile {
    try {
        open the file;
        determine its size;
        allocate that much memory;
        read the file into memory;
        close the file;
    } catch (fileOpenFailed) {
        doSomething;
    } catch (sizeDeterminationFailed) {
        doSomething;
    } catch (memoryAllocationFailed) {
        doSomething;
    } catch (readFailed) {
        doSomething;
    } catch (fileCloseFailed) {
        doSomething;
    }
}
```

Note that exceptions don't spare you the effort of doing the work of detecting, reporting, and handling errors. What exceptions do provide for you is the means to separate the grungy details of what to do when something out-of-the-ordinary happens from the main logic of your program.

In addition, the bloat factor for error management code in this program is about 250 percent—compared to 400 percent in the previous example.

Advantage 2: Propagating Errors Up the Call Stack

A second advantage of exceptions is the ability to propagate error reporting up the call stack of methods. Suppose that the `readFile` method is the fourth method in a series of nested method calls made by your main program: `method1` calls `method2`, which calls `method3`, which finally calls `readFile`.

```
method1 {
    call method2;
}
method2 {
    call method3;
```

```
    }
    method3 {
        call readFile;
    }
```

Suppose also that method1 is the only method interested in the errors that might occur within readFile. Traditional error notification techniques force method2 and method3 to propagate the error codes returned by readFile up the call stack until the error codes finally reach method1—the only method that is interested in them.

```
    method1 {
        errorCodeType error;
        error = call method2;
        if (error)
            doErrorProcessing;
        else
            proceed;
    }
    errorCodeType method2 {
        errorCodeType error;
        error = call method3;
        if (error)
            return error;
        else
            proceed;
    }
    errorCodeType method3 {
        errorCodeType error;
        error = call readFile;
        if (error)
            return error;
        else
            proceed;
    }
```

As you learned earlier, the Java runtime system searches backwards through the call stack to find any methods that are interested in handling a particular exception. A Java method can "duck" any exceptions thrown within it, thereby allowing a method further up the call stack to catch it. As a result only the methods that care about errors have to worry about detecting errors.

```
    method1 {
        try {
            call method2;
        } catch (exception) {
```

```
        doErrorProcessing;
    }
}
method2 throws exception {
    call method3;
}
method3 throws exception {
    call readFile;
}
```

However, as you can see from the pseudocode, ducking an exception requires some effort on the part of the "middleman" methods. Any checked exceptions that can be thrown within a method are part of that method's public programming interface and must be specified in the `throws` clause of the method. A method informs its callers about the exceptions that it can throw, so that the callers can intelligently and consciously decide what to do about those exceptions.

Note again the difference in the bloat factor and code obfuscation factor of these two error management techniques. The code that uses exceptions is more compact and easier to understand.

Advantage 3: Grouping and Differentiating Error Types

Often exceptions fall into categories or groups. For example, you could imagine a group of exceptions, each of which represents a specific type of error that can occur when manipulating an array: the index is out of range for the size of the array, the element being inserted into the array is of the wrong type, or the element being searched for is not in the array. Furthermore, you might want some methods to handle all exceptions that fall within a category (all array exceptions), and other methods to handle specific exceptions (just the invalid index exceptions, please).

Because all exceptions that are thrown within a Java program are objects, grouping or categorization of exceptions is a natural outcome of the class hierarchy. Java exceptions must be instances of `Throwable` or any `Throwable` descendant. As for other Java classes, you can create subclasses of the `Throwable` class and subclasses of your subclasses. Each leaf class (a class with no subclasses) represents a specific type of exception and each node class (a class with one or more subclasses) represents a group of related exceptions.

For example, in the following figure, `ArrayException` is a subclass of `Exception` (a subclass of `Throwable`) and has three subclasses.

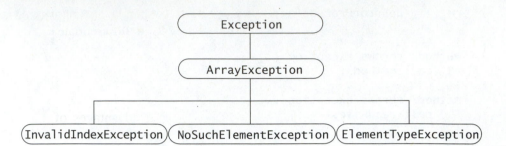

InvalidIndexException, ElementTypeException, and NoSuchElementException are all leaf classes. Each one represents a specific type of error that can occur when manipulating an array. One way a method can catch exceptions is to catch only those that are instances of a leaf class. For example, an exception handler that handles only invalid index exceptions has a catch statement like this:

```
catch (InvalidIndexException e) {
    . . .
}
```

ArrayException is a node class and represents any error that can occur when manipulating an array object, including those errors specifically represented by one of its subclasses. A method can catch an exception based on its group or general type by specifying any of the exception's superclasses in the catch statement. For example, to catch all array exceptions regardless of their specific type, an exception handler specifies an ArrayException argument:

```
catch (ArrayException e) {
    . . .
}
```

This handler will catch all array exceptions including InvalidIndexException, ElementTypeException, and NoSuchElementException. You can find out precisely which type of exception occurred by querying the exception handler parameter e.

You could even set up an exception handler that handles any Exception with this handler:

```
catch (Exception e) {
    . . .
}
```

Exception handlers that are too general, such as the one shown previously, can make your code more error prone by catching and handling exceptions that you didn't anticipate and therefore don't handle correctly. We don't recommend writing general exception handlers as a rule.

As you've seen, you can create groups of exceptions and handle exceptions in a general fashion, or you can use the specific exception type to differentiate exceptions and handle exceptions in an exact fashion.

What's Next?

Now that you understand what exceptions are and the advantages of using exceptions in your Java programs, it's time to learn how to use them.

Your First Encounter with Java Exceptions

The following error message is one of two similar error messages you will see if you try to compile the class <u>InputFile</u> (page 635), because the `InputFile` class contains calls to methods that throw exceptions when an error occurs:

```
InputFile.java:8: Warning: Exception
java.io.FileNotFoundException must be caught, or it must be
declared in throws clause of this method.
        fis = new FileInputStream(filename);
             ^
```

The Java language requires that methods either *catch* or *specify* all checked exceptions that can be thrown within the scope of that method. (Details about what this actually means are covered in the next section, <u>Java's Catch or Specify Requirement</u> (page 263).) If the compiler detects a method, such as those in `InputFile`, that doesn't meet this requirement, it issues an error message like the one shown above and refuses to compile the program.

Let's look at `InputFile` in more detail and see what's going on.

The `InputFile` class wraps a `FileInputStream` and provides a method, `getLine`, for reading a line from the current position in the input stream.

```
    // Note: This class won't compile by design!
import java.io.*;

class InputFile {

    FileInputStream fis;

    InputFile(String filename) {
        fis = new FileInputStream(filename);
    }

    String getLine() {
        int c;
```

```java
            StringBuffer buf = new StringBuffer();

        do {
            c = fis.read();
            if (c == '\n')                 // UNIX new line
                return buf.toString();
            else if (c == '\r') {      // Windows 95/NT new line
                c = fis.read();
                if (c == '\n')
                    return buf.toString();
                else {
                    buf.append((char)'\r');
                    buf.append((char)c);
                }
            } else
                buf.append((char)c);
        } while (c != -1);

        return null;
    }
}
```

The compiler prints the first error message because of the bold line in the above code listing. The bold line creates a new `FileInputStream` object and uses it to open a file whose name is passed into the `FileInputStream` constructor.

So what should the `FileInputStream` do if the named file does not exist on the file system? Well, that depends on what the program using the `FileInput-Stream` wants to do. The implementers of `FileInputStream` have no idea what the `InputFile` class wants to do if the file does not exist. Should the `FileIn-putStream` kill the program? Should it try an alternate filename? Should it just create a file of the indicated name? There's no possible way the `FileInput-Stream` implementers could choose a solution that would suit every user of `FileInputStream`. So, they punted, or rather, threw, an exception. If the file named in the argument to the `FileInputStream` constructor does not exist on the file system, the constructor throws a `java.io.FileNotFoundException`. By throwing an exception, `FileInputStream` allows the calling method to handle the error in whatever way is most appropriate for it.

As you can see from the code, the `InputFile` class completely ignores the fact that the `FileInputStream` constructor can throw an exception. However, as stated previously, the Java language requires that a method either catch or specify all checked exceptions that can be thrown within the scope of that method. Because the `InputFile` class does neither, the compiler refuses to compile the program and prints an error message.

In addition to the first error message shown above, you also see the following similar error message when you compile the `InputFile` class:

```
InputFile.java:15: Warning: Exception java.io.IOException must
be caught, or it must be declared in throws clause of this
method.
          while ((c = fis.read()) != -1) {
                      ^
```

The `InputFile` class's `getLine` method reads from the `FileInputStream` that was opened in `InputFile`'s constructor. The `FileInputStream read` method throws a `java.io.IOException` if for some reason it can't read from the file. Again, the `InputFile` class makes no attempt to catch or specify this exception. As a result, you see the second error message.

At this point, you have two options. You can either arrange to catch the exceptions within the appropriate methods in the `InputFile` class, or the `Input-File` methods can "duck" and allow other methods further up the call stack to catch the exceptions. Either way, the `InputFile` methods must do something, either catch or specify the exceptions, before the `InputFile` class can be compiled. For the diligent, there's a class, <u>InputFileDeclared</u> (page 636), that fixes the bugs in `InputFile` by specifying the exceptions.

The next section describes in further detail Java's catch or specify requirement. The subsequent sections show you how to comply with the requirement.

Java's Catch or Specify Requirement

As stated previously, Java requires that a method either catch or specify all checked exceptions that can be thrown within the scope of the method. This requirement has several components that need further description: "catch," "specify," "checked exceptions," and "exceptions that can be thrown within the scope of the method."

Catch

A method can catch an exception by providing an exception handler for that type of exception. The next section, <u>Dealing with Exceptions</u> (page 265), introduces an example program, talks about catching exceptions, and shows you how to write an exception handler for the example program.

Specify

If a method chooses not to catch an exception, the method must specify that it can throw that exception. Why did the Java designers make this requirement? Because any exception that can be thrown by a method is really part of the method's public programming interface: Callers of a method must know about the exceptions that a method can throw in order to intelligently and consciously decide what to do about those exceptions. Thus in the method signature, you specify the exceptions that the method can throw.

The next section, <u>Dealing with Exceptions</u> (page 265), talks about specifying exceptions that a method throws and shows you how to do it.

Checked Exceptions

Java has different types of exceptions, including I/O exceptions, runtime exceptions, and exceptions of your own creation, to name a few. Of interest to us in this discussion are runtime exceptions. Runtime exceptions are those exceptions that occur within the Java runtime system. This includes arithmetic exceptions (such as dividing by zero), pointer exceptions (such as trying to access an object through a null reference), and indexing exceptions (such as attempting to access an array element with an index that is too large or too small).

Runtime exceptions can occur anywhere in a program and in a typical program can be very numerous. The cost of checking for runtime exceptions often exceeds the benefit of catching or specifying them. Thus the compiler does not require that you catch or specify runtime exceptions, although you can. *Checked exceptions* are exceptions that are not runtime exceptions and are checked by the compiler; the compiler checks that these exceptions are caught or specified.

Some consider this a loophole in Java's exception-handling mechanism and programmers are tempted to make all exceptions runtime exceptions. In general, this is not recommended. <u>Runtime Exceptions—The Controversy</u> (page 283) contains a thorough discussion about when and how to use runtime exceptions.

Exceptions That Can Be Thrown Within the Scope of the Method

The statement "exceptions that can be thrown within the scope of the method" may seem obvious at first: just look for the `throw` statement. However, this statement includes more than just the exceptions that can be thrown directly by the method: the key is in the phrase *within the scope of*. This phrase includes any exception that can be thrown while the flow of control remains within the method. This statement includes both

- Exceptions that are thrown directly by the method with Java's `throw` statement.
- Exceptions that are thrown indirectly by the method through calls to other methods.

Dealing with Exceptions

<u>Your First Encounter with Java Exceptions</u> (page 261) briefly described how you were (probably) first introduced to Java exceptions: a compiler error complaining that you must either catch or specify exceptions. Then, <u>Java's Catch or Specify Requirement</u> (page 263) discussed what exactly the error message means and why the Java language designers decided to make this requirement. We're now going to show you both how to catch an exception and how to specify one. But first, let's look at the example you'll be using.

The `ListOfNumbers` Example

The following example defines and implements a class named `ListOfNumbers` (page 638). The `ListOfNumbers` class calls two methods from classes in the Java packages that can throw exceptions.

```java
import java.io.*;
import java.util.Vector;

class ListOfNumbers {
    private Vector victor;
    final int size = 10;

    public ListOfNumbers () {
        int i;
        victor = new Vector(size);
        for (i = 0; i < size; i++)
            victor.addElement(new Integer(i));
    }
    public void writeList() {
        PrintStream pStr = null;

        System.out.println("Entering try statement");
        int i;
        pStr = new PrintStream(
                   new BufferedOutputStream(
                       new FileOutputStream("OutFile.txt")));

        for (i = 0; i < size; i++)
            pStr.println("Value at: " + i + " = " +
                         victor.elementAt(i));

        pStr.close();
    }
}
```

Upon construction, `ListOfNumbers` creates a `Vector` that contains ten `Integer` elements with sequential values 0 through 9. The `ListOfNumbers` class also defines a method named `writeList` that writes the list of numbers into a text file called `OutFile.txt`.

The `writeList` method calls two methods that can throw exceptions. First, the following line invokes the constructor for `FileOutputStream`, which throws an `IOException` if the file cannot be opened for any reason:

```
pStr = new PrintStream(new BufferedOutputStream(
    new FileOutputStream("OutFile.txt")));
```

Second, the `Vector` class's `elementAt` method throws an `ArrayIndexOutOf-BoundsException` if you pass in an index whose value is too small (a negative number) or too large (larger than the number of elements currently contained by the `Vector`). Here's how `ListOfNumbers` invokes `elementAt`:

```
pStr.println("Value at: " + i + " = " + victor.elementAt(i));
```

If you try to compile the `ListOfNumbers` class, the compiler prints an error message about the exception thrown by the `FileOutputStream` constructor, but does *not* display an error message about the exception thrown by `elementAt`. This is because the exception thrown by the `FileOutputStream` constructor, `IOException`, is a checked exception and the exception thrown by the `elementAt` method, `ArrayIndexOutOfBoundsException`, is a runtime exception. Java requires that you catch or specify only checked exceptions. For more information, refer to Java's Catch or Specify Requirement (page 263).

The next section, Catching and Handling Exceptions (page 266), will show you how to write an exception handler for the `ListOfNumbers`' `writeList` method.

Following that, a section named Specifying the Exceptions Thrown by a Method (page 276) will show you how to specify that the `ListOfNumbers`' `writeList` method throws the exceptions instead of catching them.

Catching and Handling Exceptions

Now that you've familiarized yourself with the `ListOfNumbers` class and where the exceptions can be thrown within it, you can learn how to write exception handlers to catch and handle those exceptions.

This section covers the three components of an exception handler, the `try`, `catch`, and `finally` blocks, by showing you how to use them to write an exception handler for the `ListOfNumbers` class's `writeList` method. In addition, this

section contains a walk-through of the `writeList` method and analyzes what occurs within the method during various scenarios.

The `try` Block

The first step in constructing an exception handler is to enclose the statements that might throw an exception within a `try` block. The `try` block is said to *govern* the statements enclosed within it and defines the scope of any exception handlers (established by subsequent `catch` blocks) associated with it. In general, a `try` block looks like this:

```
try {
    Java statements
}
```

The segment of code labelled *Java statements* contains one or more legal Java statements that could throw an exception.

To construct an exception handler for the `writeList` method from the `ListOfNumbers` class, you need to enclose the exception-throwing statements of the `writeList` method within a `try` block. There is more than one way to accomplish this task. You can put each statement that might potentially throw an exception within its own `try` statement and provide separate exception handlers for each `try`. Or you can put all of the `writeList` statements within a single `try` statement and associate multiple handlers with it. The following listing uses one `try` statement for the entire method because the code tends to be easier to read.

```
PrintStream pstr;

try {
    int i;

    System.out.println("Entering try statement");
    pStr = new PrintStream(
            new BufferedOutputStream(
                new FileOutputStream("OutFile.txt")));

    for (i = 0; i  size; i++)
        pStr.println("Value at: " + i + " = " +
                    victor.elementAt(i));
}
```

The `try` statement governs the statements enclosed within it and defines the scope of any exception handlers associated with it. In other words, if an exception

occurs within the `try` statement, that exception is handled by the exception handler associated with this `try` statement.

A `try` statement *must* be accompanied by at least one `catch` block or one `finally` block.

The catch Block(s)

As you learned in the previous section, the `try` statement defines the scope of its associated exception handlers. You associate exception handlers with a `try` statement by providing one or more `catch` blocks directly after the `try` block:

```
try {
    . . .
} catch ( . . . ) {
    . . .
} catch ( . . . ) {
    . . .
} . . .
```

There can be no intervening code between the end of the `try` statement and the beginning of the first `catch` statement. The general form of Java's `catch` statement is:

```
catch (SomeThrowableObject variableName) {
    Java statements
}
```

As you can see, the `catch` statement requires a single formal argument. The argument to the `catch` statement looks like an argument declaration for a method. The argument type, *SomeThrowableObject*, declares the type of exception that the handler can handle and must be the name of a class that inherits from the Throwable[1] class. When Java programs throw an exception, they are really just throwing an object, and only objects that derive from `Throwable` can be thrown. You'll learn more about throwing exceptions in How to Throw Exceptions (page 277).

variableName is the name by which the handler can refer to the exception caught by the handler. For example, the exception handlers for the `writeList` method (shown later) each call the exception's `getMessage` method using the exception's declared name `e`:

```
e.getMessage()
```

---

1. http://java.sun.com/products/JDK/CurrentRelease/api/java.lang.Throwable.html

You access the instance variables and methods of exceptions in the same manner that you access the instance variables and methods of other objects. getMessage is a method provided by the Throwable class that prints additional information about the error that occurred. The Throwable class also implements two methods for filling in and printing the contents of the execution stack when the exception occurred. Subclasses of Throwable can add other methods or instance variables. To find out what methods an exception implements, check its class definition and definitions for any of its ancestor classes.

The catch block contains a series of legal Java statements. These statements are executed if and when the exception handler is invoked. The runtime system invokes the exception handler when the handler is the first one in the call stack whose type matches that of the exception thrown.

The writeList method from the <u>ListOfNumbers.java</u> (page 638) class uses two exception handlers for its try statement, with one handler for each of the two types of exceptions that can be thrown within the try block: ArrayIndexOutOfBoundsException and IOException.

```
try {
    . . .
} catch (ArrayIndexOutOfBoundsException e) {
    System.err.println(
        "Caught ArrayIndexOutOfBoundsException: " +
        e.getMessage());
} catch (IOException e) {
    System.err.println(
        "Caught IOException: " + e.getMessage());
}
```

An IOException Occurs. Let's suppose an IOException occurs within the try block. The runtime system immediately takes over and tries to locate an appropriate exception handler. The runtime system begins its search at the top of the method call stack. When the exception occurred, the FileOutputStream constructor was at the top of the call stack. However, the FileOutputStream constructor doesn't have an appropriate exception handler so the runtime system checks the next method in the method call stack: the writeList method. The writeList method has two exception handlers: one for ArrayIndexOutOf-BoundsException and one for IOException.

The runtime system checks writeList's handlers in the order that they appear following the try statement. The first exception handler whose argument matches that of the thrown exception is the one chosen by the runtime system to handle the exception. (The order of exception handlers matters!) The argument to the first exception handler is ArrayIndexOutOfBoundsException, but the exception that was thrown is an IOException. An IOException cannot legally be assigned to an ArrayIndexOutOfBoundsException, so the runtime system continues its search for an appropriate exception handler.

The argument to `writeList`'s second exception handler is an `IOException`. The exception thrown by the `FileOutputStream` constructor is also an `IOException` and so it can legally be assigned to the handler's `IOException` argument. This handler is deemed appropriate and the runtime system executes this handler, which prints this statement:

```
Caught IOException: OutFile.txt
```

The runtime system goes through a similar process if an `ArrayIndexOutOf-BoundsException` occurs. For more details, Putting It All Together (page 273) walks through the `writeList` method after it's been completed (there's one more step) and investigates what happens during three scenarios.

Catching Multiple Exception Types with One Handler. The two exception handlers used by the `writeList` method are very specialized. Each handles only one type of exception. The Java language allows you to write general exception handlers that handle multiple types of exceptions.

As you know, Java exceptions are `Throwable` objects; they are instances of `Throwable` or a subclass of `Throwable`. The Java packages contain numerous classes that derive from `Throwable` and thus, build a hierarchy of `Throwable` classes. Your exception handler can be written to handle any class that inherits from `Throwable`. If you write a handler for a leaf class (a class with no subclasses), you've written a specialized handler: It will only handle exceptions of that specific type. If you write a handler for a node class (a class with subclasses), you've written a general handler: It will handle any exception whose type is the node class or any of its subclasses.

Let's modify the `writeList` method once again. Only this time, let's write it so that it handles both `IOExceptions` and `ArrayIndexOutOfBoundsExceptions`. The closest common ancestor of `IOException` and `ArrayIndexOutOfBoundsEx`-

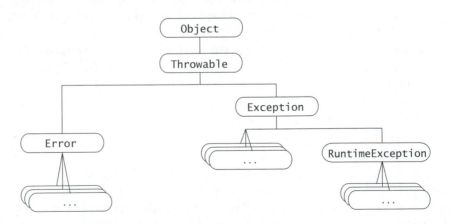

ception is the `Exception` class. An exception handler that handles both types of exceptions looks like this:

```
try {
    . . .
} catch (Exception e) {
    System.err.println("Exception caught: " + e.getMessage());
}
```

The `Exception` class is pretty high in the `Throwable` class hierarchy. So in addition to the `IOException` and `ArrayIndexOutOfBoundsException` types that this exception handler is intended to catch, it will catch numerous other types. Generally speaking, your exception handlers should be more specialized. Handlers that can catch most or all exceptions are typically useless for error recovery because the handler has to determine what type of exception occurred anyway to determine the best recovery strategy. Also, exception handlers that are too general can make code *more* error prone by catching and handling exceptions that weren't anticipated by the programmer and for which the handler was not intended.

The `finally` Block

The final step in setting up an exception handler is providing a mechanism for cleaning up the state of the method before (possibly) allowing control to be passed to a different part of the program. You do this by enclosing the cleanup code within a `finally` block. Java's `finally` block provides a mechanism that allows your method to clean up after itself regardless of what happens within the try block. Use the `finally` block to close files or release other system resources.

The `try` block of the `writeList` method that you've been working with opens a `PrintStream`. The program should close that stream before allowing control to pass out of the `writeList` method. This poses a somewhat complicated problem because `writeList`'s try block has three different exit possibilities:

1. The `new FileOutputStream` statement failed and threw an `IOException`.
2. The `victor.elementAt(i)` statement failed and threw an `ArrayIndex-OutOfBoundsException`.
3. Everything succeeded and the `try` block exited normally.

The runtime system always executes the statements within the `finally` block regardless of what happens within the `try` block. Regardless of whether control

exits the `writeList` method's `try` block due to one of the three scenarios listed previously, the code within the `finally` block will be executed.

This is the `finally` block for the `writeList` method. It cleans up and closes the `PrintStream`.

```
finally {
    if (pStr != null) {
        System.out.println("Closing PrintStream");
        pStr.close();
    } else {
        System.out.println("PrintStream not open");
    }
}
```

Is the `finally` Statement Really Necessary?   At first, the need for a `finally` statement may not be immediately apparent. Programmers often ask "Is the `finally` statement really necessary or is it just sugar for my Java?" In particular, C++ programmers doubt the need for a `finally` statement because C++ doesn't have one.

The need for a `finally` statement is not apparent until you consider the following scenario: How does the `PrintStream` in the `writeList` method get closed if you don't provide an exception handler for the `ArrayIndexOutOf-BoundsException` and an `ArrayIndexOutOfBoundsException` occurs? (It is easy and legal to omit an exception handler for `ArrayIndexOutOfBoundsException` because it's a runtime exception and the compiler won't alert you that the `writeList` contains a method call that might throw one.) The answer is that the `PrintStream` does not get closed if an `ArrayIndexOutOfBoundsException` occurs and `writeList` does not provide a handler for it—unless the `writeList` provides a `finally` statement.

There are other benefits to using the `finally` statement. In the `writeList` example, it is possible to provide for cleanup without the intervention of a `finally` statement. For example, you could put the code to close the `Print-Stream` at the end of the `try` block and again within the exception handler for `ArrayIndexOutOfBoundsException`, as shown here:

```
try {
    . . .
    pStr.close();        // don't do this; it duplicates code
} catch (ArrayIndexOutOfBoundsException e) {
    pStr.close();        // don't do this; it duplicates code
    System.err.println(
        "Caught ArrayIndexOutOfBoundsException: "
```

```
        + e.getMessage());
} catch (IOException e) {
    System.err.println(
        "Caught IOException: " + e.getMessage());
}
```

However, this duplicates code, making the code hard to read and prone to errors if you modify the code later. For example, if you add code to the `try` block that may throw a new type of exception, you have to remember to close the `Print-Stream` within the new exception handler (which if you're anything like me, you are bound to forget).

Putting It All Together

The previous sections describe how to construct the `try`, `catch`, and `finally` code blocks for the `writeList` example. Now, let's walk through the code and investigate what happens during three scenarios.

When all of the components are put together, the `writeList` method looks like this:

```
public void writeList() {
    PrintStream pStr = null;

    try {
        int i;

        System.out.println("Entering try statement");
        pStr = new PrintStream(
                new BufferedOutputStream(
                new FileOutputStream("OutFile.txt")));

        for (i = 0; i  size; i++)
            pStr.println("Value at: " + i + " = " +
                        victor.elementAt(i));
    } catch (ArrayIndexOutOfBoundsException e) {
        System.err.println(
            "Caught ArrayIndexOutOfBoundsException: " +
            e.getMessage());
    } catch (IOException e) {
        System.err.println("Caught IOException: " +
                        e.getMessage());
    } finally {
        if (pStr != null) {
            System.out.println("Closing PrintStream");
            pStr.close();
        } else {
```

```
                System.out.println("PrintStream not open");
            }
        }
    }
```

The `try` block in this method has three different exit possibilities:

1. The `new FileOutputStream` statement fails and throws an `IOException`.
2. The `victor.elementAt(i)` statement fails and throws an `ArrayIndexOutOfBoundsException`.
3. Everything succeeds and the `try` statement exits normally.

Let's look at what happens in the `writeList` method during each of these exit possibilities.

Scenario 1: An IOException Occurs.

The `new FileOutputStream("OutFile.txt")` statement can fail for any number of reasons: the user doesn't have write permission on the file or directory, the file system is full, or the directory for the file doesn't exist. If any of these situations is true, then the constructor for `FileOutputStream` throws an `IOException`.

When the `IOException` is thrown, the runtime system immediately stops executing the `try` block. Then the runtime system attempts to locate an exception handler appropriate for handling an `IOException`.

The runtime system begins its search at the top of the method call stack. When the exception occurred, the `FileOutputStream` constructor was at the top of the call stack. However, the `FileOutputStream` constructor doesn't have an appropriate exception handler so the runtime system checks the next method in the method call stack—the `writeList` method. The `writeList` method has two exception handlers: one for `ArrayIndexOutOfBoundsException` and one for `IOException`.

The runtime system checks `writeList`'s handlers in the order that they appear following the `try` statement. The argument to the first exception handler is `ArrayIndexOutOfBoundsException`, but the exception that was thrown is an `IOException`. An `IOException` cannot legally be assigned to an `ArrayIndexOutOfBoundsException`, so the runtime system continues its search for an appropriate exception handler.

The argument to `writeList`'s second exception handler is an `IOException`. The exception thrown by the `FileOutputStream` constructor is also an `IOException` and can be legally assigned to this exception handler's `IOException` argument. Thus, this handler is deemed appropriate and the runtime system executes this handler, which prints this statement:

```
Caught IOException: OutFile.txt
```

After the exception handler has executed, the runtime system passes control to the `finally` block. In this particular scenario, the `PrintStream` was never opened, and thus pStr is null and won't get closed. After the `finally` block has completed executing, the program continues with the first statement after the `finally` block.

The complete output that you see from the `ListOfNumbers` program when an `IOException` is thrown is this:

```
Entering try statement
Caught IOException: OutFile.txt
PrintStream not open
```

Scenario 2: An `ArrayIndexOutOfBoundsException` Occurs.

This scenario is the same as the first except that a different error occurs during the `try` block. In this scenario, the argument passed to the `Vector`'s `elementAt` method is out of bounds. The argument is either less than 0 or is larger than the size of the array. (The way the code is written, this is actually impossible, but let's suppose a bug is introduced into the code when someone modifies it.)

As in scenario 1, when the exception occurs the runtime system stops executing the `try` block and attempts to locate an exception handler suitable for an `ArrayIndexOutOfBoundsException`. The runtime system searches for an appropriate exception handler as it did before. It comes upon the `catch` statement in the `writeList` method that handles exceptions of the type `ArrayIndexOutOfBoundsException`. Since the type of the thrown exception matches the type of the exception handler, the runtime system executes this exception handler.

After the exception handler has run, the runtime system passes control to the `finally` block. In this particular scenario, the `PrintStream` was opened, so the `finally` statement closes it. After the `finally` block has completed executing, the program continues with the first statement after the `finally` block.

The complete output that you see from the `ListOfNumbers` program when an `ArrayIndexOutOfBoundsException` is thrown is something like this:

```
Entering try statement
Caught ArrayIndexOutOfBoundsException: 10 >= 10
Closing PrintStream
```

Scenario 3: The `try` block exits normally.

In this scenario, all the statements within the scope of the `try` block execute successfully and throw no exceptions. Execution falls off the end of the `try` block, and the runtime system passes control to the `finally` block. Since everything was successful, the `PrintStream` is open when control reaches the `finally` block, which closes the

PrintStream. Again, after the finally block has completed executing, the program continues with the first statement after the finally block.

The output that you see from the ListOfNumbers program when no exceptions are thrown is:

```
Entering try statement
Closing PrintStream
```

Specifying the Exceptions Thrown by a Method

If it is not appropriate for your method to catch and handle an exception thrown by a method that it calls, or if your method itself throws its own exception, you must specify in the method signature that the method throws the exception. Using the ListOfNumbers class, this section shows you how to specify exceptions that a method throws.

The previous section showed you how to write an exception handler for the writeList method in the ListOfNumbers class. Sometimes, it's appropriate for your code to catch exceptions that can occur within it. In other cases, however, it's better to let a method further up the call stack handle the exception. For example, if you were providing the ListOfNumbers class as part of a package of classes, you probably couldn't anticipate the needs of all of the users of your package. In this case, it's better to *not* catch the exception and to allow someone further up the call stack to handle it.

If the writeList method doesn't catch the exceptions that can occur within it, then the writeList method must specify that it can throw them. Let's modify the writeList method to specify the methods that it can throw. To remind you, here's the original version of the writeList method:

```java
public void writeList() {
    System.out.println("Entering try statement");
    int i;
    pStr = new PrintStream(
            new BufferedOutputStream(
                new FileOutputStream("OutFile.txt")));

    for (i = 0; i  size; i++)
        pStr.println("Value at: " + i + " = " +
                    victor.elementAt(i));
}
```

As you recall, the new FileOutputStream("OutFile.txt") statement might throw an IOException, which is a checked exception. The victor.element-

At(i) statement can throw an `ArrayIndexOutOfBoundsException`, which, as a subclass of `RuntimeException`, is a runtime exception.

To specify that `writeList` throws these two exceptions, you add a `throws` clause to the method signature for the `writeList` method. The `throws` clause is composed of the `throws` keyword followed by a comma-separated list of all the exceptions thrown by that method. The `throws` clause goes after the method name and argument list and before the curly bracket that defines the scope of the method. Here's an example:

```
public void writeList() throws IOException,
ArrayIndexOutOfBoundsException {
```

Remember that `ArrayIndexOutOfBoundsException` is a runtime exception, so you don't have to specify it in the `throws` clause, although you can.

How to Throw Exceptions

Before you can catch an exception, some Java code somewhere must throw one. Any Java code can throw an exception: your code, code from a package written by someone else (such as the packages that come with the Java development environment), or the Java runtime system. Regardless of who (or what) throws the exception, it's always thrown with the Java `throw` statement.

The Java language requires that exceptions derive from the `Throwable` class or one of its subclasses.

As you have undoubtedly noticed in your travels (travails?) through the Java language, the packages that ship with the Java development environment provide numerous exception classes. All of these classes are descendants of the `Throwable` class and allow programs to differentiate between the various types of exceptions that can occur during the execution of a Java program.

You can create your own exception classes, as well, to represent problems that can occur within the classes that you write. Indeed, if you are a package developer you will find that you must create your own set of exception classes to allow your users to differentiate an error that can occur in your package versus those errors that occur in the Java development environment or other packages.

The throw Statement

All Java methods use the `throw` statement to throw an exception. The `throw` statement requires a single argument: a *throwable* object. In the Java system,

throwable objects are instances of any subclass of the <u>Throwable</u>[1] class. Here's an example of a `throw` statement:

```
throw someThrowableObject;
```

If you attempt to throw an object that is not throwable, the compiler refuses to compile your program and displays an error message similar to the following:

```
testing.java:10: Cannot throw class java.lang.Integer; it must
be a subclass of class java.lang.Throwable.
            throw new Integer(4);
            ^
```

The next section, <u>The Throwable Class and Its Subclasses</u> (page 279), talks more about the `Throwable` class.

Let's look at the `throw` statement in context. The following method is taken from a class that implements a common stack object. The pop method removes the top element from the stack and returns it:

```
public Object pop() throws EmptyStackException {
    Object obj;

    if (size == 0)
        throw new EmptyStackException();

    obj = objectAt(size - 1);
    setObjectAt(size - 1, null);
    size--;
    return obj;
}
```

The pop method checks to see if there are any elements on the stack. If the stack is empty (its size is equal to 0), then pop instantiates a new `EmptyStackException` object and throws it. The `EmptyStackException` class is defined in the `java.util` package. Later sections in this lesson describe how you can create your own exception classes. For now, all you really need to remember is that you can throw only objects that inherit from the `java.lang.Throwable` class.

The throws Clause

Note that the declaration of the pop method contains this clause:

```
throws EmptyStackException
```

---

[1] http://java.sun.com/products/JDK/CurrentRelease/api/java.lang.Throwable.html

The `throws` clause specifies that the method can throw an `EmptyStackException`. As you know, the Java language requires that methods either catch or specify all checked exceptions that can be thrown within the scope of that method. You do this with the `throws` clause of the method declaration. For more information about this requirement see Java's Catch or Specify Requirement (page 263). Also, Specifying the Exceptions Thrown by a Method (page 276) shows you in more detail how a method can specify the exceptions it can throw.

The Throwable Class and Its Subclasses

As you learned in the previous section, you can throw only objects that derive from the `Throwable` class. This includes direct descendants (objects that derive directly from the `Throwable` class) as well as indirect descendants (objects that derive from children or grandchildren of the `Throwable` class).

This figure illustrates the class hierarchy of the `Throwable` class and its most significant subclasses.

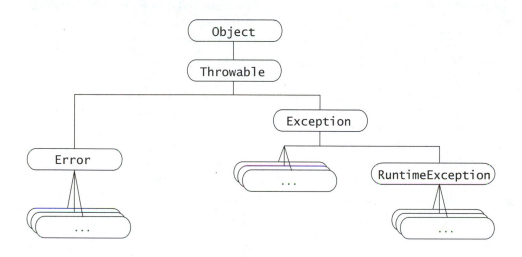

As you can see from the figure, `Throwable` has two direct descendants: `Error` and `Exception`.

Errors

When a dynamic linking failure or some other "hard" failure in the virtual machine occurs, the virtual machine throws an `Error`. Typical Java programs should not catch `Errors`. In addition, it's unlikely that typical Java programs will ever throw `Errors` either.

Exceptions

Most programs throw and catch objects that derive from the Exception class. Exceptions indicate that a problem occurred but that the problem is not a serious system problem. Most programs you write will throw and catch Exceptions.

The Exception class has many descendants defined in the Java packages. These descendants indicate various types of exceptions that can occur. For example, IllegalAccessException signals that a particular method could not be found, and NegativeArraySizeException indicates that a program attempted to create an array with a negative size.

One Exception subclass has special meaning in the Java language: RuntimeException.

Runtime Exceptions

The RuntimeException class represents exceptions that occur within the Java virtual machine during runtime. An example of a runtime exception is NullPointerException, which occurs when a method tries to access a member of an object through a null reference. A NullPointerException can occur anywhere a program tries to dereference a reference to an object. The cost of checking for the exception often outweighs the benefit of catching it.

Because runtime exceptions are so ubiquitous and attempting to catch or specify all of them all the time would be a fruitless exercise (and a fruitful source of unreadable and unmaintainable code), the compiler allows runtime exceptions to go uncaught and unspecified.

The Java packages define several RuntimeException classes. You can catch these exceptions just like other exceptions. However, a method is not required to specify that it throws RuntimeExceptions. In addition, you can create your own RuntimeException subclasses. Runtime Exceptions—The Controversy (page 283) contains a thorough discussion of when and how to use runtime exceptions.

Creating Your Own Exception Classes

When you design a package of Java classes that collaborate to provide some useful function to your users, you work hard to ensure that your classes interact well together and that their interfaces are easy to understand and use. You should spend just as much time designing the exceptions that your classes throw.

Suppose you are writing a linked list class that you're planning to distribute as freeware. Among other methods, your linked list class supports these methods:

objectAt(int *n*)

Returns the object in the nth position in the list.

`firstObject()`
> Returns the first object in the list.

`indexOf(Object o)`
> Searches the list for the specified `Object` and returns its position in the list.

What Can Go Wrong?

Because many programmers will be using your linked list class, you can be assured that many will misuse or abuse your class and its methods. Also, some legitimate calls to your linked list's methods may result in an undefined result. Regardless, in the face of errors, you want your linked list class to be as robust as possible, to do something reasonable about errors, and to communicate errors back to the calling program. However, you can't anticipate how each user of your linked list class will want the object to behave under adversity. Often the best thing to do when an error occurs is to throw an exception.

Each of the methods supported by your linked list might throw an exception under certain conditions, and each method might throw a different type of exception than the others. For example:

`objectAt`
> Throws an exception if the integer passed into the method is less than 0 or larger than the number of objects currently in the list.

`firstObject`
> Throws an exception if the list contains no objects.

`indexOf`
> Throws an exception if the object passed into the method is not in the list.

But what type of exception should each method throw? Should it be an exception provided with the Java development environment? Or should you roll your own?

Choosing the Exception Type to Throw

When faced with choosing the type of exception to throw, you have two choices:

1. Use one written by someone else. The Java development environment provides a lot of exception classes that you can use.
2. Write one of your own.

You should write your own exception classes if you answer "yes" to any of the following questions. Otherwise, you can probably get away with using someone else's:

- Do you need an exception type that isn't represented by those in the Java development environment?
- Would it help your users if they could differentiate your exceptions from those thrown by classes written by other vendors?
- Does your code throw more than one related exception?

- If you use someone else's exceptions, will your users have access to those exceptions? A similar question is: Should your package be independent and self-contained?

Your linked list class can throw multiple exceptions, and it would be convenient to be able to catch all exceptions thrown by the linked list with one exception handler. Also, if you plan to distribute your linked list in a package, all related code should be packaged together. Thus for the linked list, you should roll your own exception class hierarchy.

The following figure illustrates one possible exception class hierarchy for your linked list:

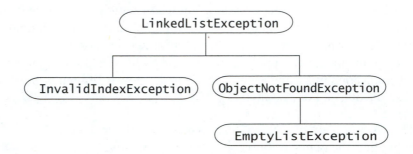

`LinkedListException` is the parent class of all the possible exceptions that can be thrown by the linked list class. Users of your linked list class can write a single exception handler to handle all linked list exceptions with a `catch` statement like this:

```
catch (LinkedListException) {
    . . .
}
```

Alternatively, users could write more specialized handlers for each subclass of `LinkedListException`.

Choosing a Superclass

The previous figure does not indicate the superclass of the `LinkedListException` class. As you know, Java exceptions must be throwable objects; they must be instances of `Throwable` or a subclass of `Throwable`. So, your temptation might be to make `LinkedListException` a subclass of `Throwable`. However, the `java.lang` package provides two `Throwable` subclasses that further divide the type of problems that can occur within a Java program: `Errors` and `Exceptions`. Most of the applets and applications that you write will throw objects that are

Exceptions. (`Errors` are reserved for serious hard errors that occur deep in the system.)

Theoretically, any `Exception` subclass can be used as the parent class of `LinkedListException`. However, a quick perusal of those classes show that they are either too specialized or completely unrelated to `LinkedListException` to be appropriate. Therefore, the parent class of `LinkedListException` should be `Exception`.

Because runtime exceptions don't have to be specified in the `throws` clause of a method, many package developers ask: "Isn't it just easier if I make all of my exceptions inherit from `RuntimeException`?" The answer to this question is covered in detail on <u>Runtime Exceptions—The Controversy</u> (page 283). The bottom line is that you shouldn't subclass `RuntimeException` unless your class really is a runtime exception! For most of you, this means the answer is "No, your exceptions shouldn't inherit from `RuntimeException`."

Naming Conventions

It's good practice to append the word "Exception" to the names of all classes that inherit (directly or indirectly) from the `Exception` class. Similarly, names of classes that inherit from the `Error` class should end with the string "Error."

Runtime Exceptions—The Controversy

Because the Java language does not require methods to catch or specify runtime exceptions, it's tempting for programmers to write code that throws only runtime exceptions or to make all of their exception subclasses inherit from `RuntimeException`. Both of these programming shortcuts allow programmers to write Java code without bothering with all of the nagging errors from the compiler and without bothering to specify or catch any exceptions. While this may seem convenient to the programmer, it sidesteps the intent of Java's catch or specify requirement and can cause problems for programmers using your classes.

```
InputFile.java:8: Warning: Exception
java.io.FileNotFoundException must be caught, or it must be
declared in throws clause of this method.
        fis = new FileInputStream(filename);
            ^
```

Why did the Java designers decide to force a method to specify all uncaught checked exceptions that can be thrown within its scope? Because any exception

that can be thrown by a method is really part of the method's public programming interface: Callers of a method must know about the exceptions that a method can throw in order to intelligently and consciously decide what to do about those exceptions. The exceptions that a method can throw are as much a part of that method's programming interface as its parameters and return value.

Your next question might be: "Well then, if it's so good to document a method's API including the exceptions that it can throw, why not specify runtime exceptions, too?"

Runtime exceptions represent problems that are detected by the runtime system. This includes arithmetic exceptions (such as dividing by zero), pointer exceptions (such as trying to access an object through a null reference), and indexing exceptions (such as attempting to access an array element through an index that is too large or too small).

Runtime exceptions can occur anywhere in a program and in a typical program can be very numerous. Typically, the cost of checking for runtime exceptions exceeds the benefit of catching or specifying them. Thus the compiler does not require that you catch or specify runtime exceptions, although you can.

Checked exceptions represent useful information about the operation of a legally specified request that the caller may have had no control over and that the caller needs to be informed about—for example, the file system is now full, or the remote end has closed the connection, or the access privileges don't allow this action.

What does it buy you if you throw a `RuntimeException` or create a subclass of `RuntimeException` just because you don't want to deal with specifying it? Simply, you get the ability to throw an exception without specifying that you do so. In other words, it is a way to avoid documenting the exceptions that a method can throw. When is this good? Well, when is it ever good to avoid documenting a method's behavior? The answer is "hardly ever."

Rules of Thumb:
- A method can detect and throw a `RuntimeException` when it encounters an error in the virtual machine runtime. However, it's typically easier to just let the virtual machine detect and throw it. Normally, the methods you write should throw `Exceptions`, not `RuntimeExceptions`.
- Similarly, you create a subclass of `RuntimeException` when you are creating an error in the virtual machine runtime (which you probably aren't). Otherwise you should subclass `Exception`.
- Do not throw a runtime exception or create a subclass of `RuntimeException` simply because you don't want to be bothered with specifying the exceptions your methods can throw.

15

Threads of Control

BELOW is a snapshot of three copies of an applet that animates different sorting algorithms. No, this lesson is not about sorting algorithms. But these applets do provide a visual aid to understanding a powerful capability of the Java language—threads.

http://java.sun.com/Series/Tutorial/java/threads/index.html

Try This: Bring up the online version of this section (http://java.sun.com/Series/ Tutorial/java/threads/index.html) and start each of the applets, one by one, by clicking on them with the mouse. Try scrolling the page, or bringing up one of your browser's panels.

These three applets run side by side at the same time. If you look at these applets in a browser, you see each applet working its way through the data, sorting it, shorter lines on top, longer lines on bottom. While the applets are sorting, you might also notice that you can scroll the page or bring up one of your browser's panels. All of this is due to the power of *threads*.

What Is a Thread? (page 286). A thread—sometimes known as an *execution context* or a *lightweight process*—is a single sequential flow of control within a process. You use threads to perform tasks that need to be isolated from other tasks and that should not interfere with the operation of another task. When you run one of these sorting applets, it creates a thread. The sort is performed within the thread. Each thread is a sequential flow of control independent from the others. Each sort operation runs independently from the others and at the same time as them.

To use threads efficiently and without errors you must understand various aspects of threads and the Java runtime system. You need to know how to provide a body for a thread, the life cycle of a thread, how the runtime system schedules threads, thread groups, and what daemon threads are and how to write them. Thread Attributes (page 289) discusses all of these thread attributes in detail and describes their implications.

The first sample programs in this lesson use either one thread or multiple independent threads that run asynchronously. However, it is often useful to use multiple threads that share data and therefore must run synchronously. Typically, programs that use multiple synchronous threads are called multithreaded programs and require special handling. The Multithreaded Programs (page 310) section is a complete discussion on writing programs with multiple threads. This section shows you how to synchronize threads and how to avoid problems such as starvation and deadlock.

When you've completed this lesson on threads, you will have toured the intricacies of Java threads including the life cycle of a Java thread (as represented by its state), scheduling, thread groups, and synchronization. The Java development environment supports multithreaded programs through the language, the libraries, and the runtime system. The final section in this lesson, Summary (page 322), highlights the features in the Java development environment that support threads and shows you where you can find further documentation about those features.

What Is a Thread?

All programmers are familiar with writing sequential programs. You've probably written a program that displays "Hello World!", or sorts a list of names, or computes a list of prime numbers. These are sequential programs: each has a beginning, an execution sequence, and an end. At any given time during the runtime of the program, there is a single point of execution.

A thread is similar to the sequential programs described above: a single thread also has a beginning, a sequence, an end, and at any given time during the runtime of the thread there is a single point of execution. However, a thread itself is not a program. It cannot run on its own, but runs within a program.

Definition: A thread is a single sequential flow of control within a program.

There is nothing new in the concept of a single thread. The real hoopla surrounding threads is not about a single sequential thread, but rather about the use of multiple threads in a single program all running at the same time and performing different tasks.

The HotJava Web browser is an example of a multithreaded application. Within the HotJava browser you can scroll a page while it's downloading an applet or image, play animation and sound concurrently, print a page in the background while you download a new page, or watch three sorting algorithms race to the finish. You are used to life operating in a concurrent fashion . . . so why not your browser?

Some texts use the name *lightweight process* instead of thread. A thread is similar to a real process in that a thread and a running program are both a single sequential flow of control. However, a thread is considered lightweight because it runs within the context of a full-blown program and takes advantage of the resources allocated for that program and the program's environment.

As a sequential flow of control, a thread must carve out some of its own resources within a running program. For example, it must have its own execution stack and program counter. The code running within the thread works only within that context. Some other texts use *execution context* as a synonym for thread.

A Simple Thread Example

The simple example you'll be using in this section is comprised of two classes: SimpleThread and TwoThreadsTest. You can find these classes on page 639. Let's begin our exploration of the application with the SimpleThread class—a subclass of the <u>Thread</u>[1] class, which is provided by the java.lang package:

```
class SimpleThread extends Thread {
    public SimpleThread(String str) {
        super(str);
    }
```

---

[1]. http://java.sun.com/products/JDK/CurrentRelease/api/java.lang.Thread.html

```java
    public void run() {
        for (int i = 0; i < 10; i++) {
            System.out.println(i + " " + getName());
            try {
                sleep((int)(Math.random() * 1000));
            } catch (InterruptedException e) {}
        }
        System.out.println("DONE! " + getName());
    }
}
```

The first method in the `SimpleThread` class is a constructor that takes a `String` as its only argument. This constructor is implemented by calling a superclass constructor and is interesting to us only because it sets the `Thread`'s name, which is used later in the program.

The next method in the `SimpleThread` class is the `run` method. The `run` method is the heart of any `Thread` and is where the action of the `Thread` takes place. The `run` method of the `SimpleThread` class contains a `for` loop that iterates ten times. In each iteration the method displays the iteration number and the name of the `Thread`, then sleeps for a random interval of up to one second. After the loop has finished, the `run` method prints `DONE!` along with the name of the thread. That's it for the `SimpleThread` class.

The `TwoThreadsTest` class provides a `main` method that creates two `SimpleThread` threads: one is named `Jamaica` and the other is named `Fiji`. (If you can't decide on where to go for vacation you can use this program to help you decide—go to the island whose thread prints `DONE!` first.)

```java
class TwoThreadsTest {
    public static void main (String[] args) {
        new SimpleThread("Jamaica").start();
        new SimpleThread("Fiji").start();
    }
}
```

The `main` method also starts each thread immediately following its construction by calling the `start` method. See the appendix for the source code to the SimpleThread (page 639) class and the TwoThreadsTest (page 639) program. Compile and run the program and watch your vacation fate unfold. You should see output similar to the following:

```
0 Jamaica
0 Fiji
1 Fiji
1 Jamaica
2 Jamaica
```

```
2 Fiji
3 Fiji
3 Jamaica
4 Jamaica
4 Fiji
5 Jamaica
5 Fiji
6 Fiji
6 Jamaica
7 Jamaica
7 Fiji
8 Fiji
9 Fiji
8 Jamaica
DONE! Fiji
9 Jamaica
DONE! Jamaica
```

(Looks like I'm going to Fiji!!) Note how the output from each thread is intermingled with the output from the other. This is because both `SimpleThread` threads are running concurrently. Therefore, both run methods are running at the same time and each thread is displaying its output at the same time as the other.

Try This: Change the main program so that it creates a third thread with the name Bora Bora. Compile and run the program again. Does this change the island of choice for your vacation? The source for the new main program, which is now named ThreeThreadsTest (page 639), is in the appendix.

Keep Going

This section glosses over many of the details of threads such as the `start` and `sleep` methods. Don't worry, the next sections of this lesson explain these concepts and others in detail. The important thing to understand from this section is that a Java program can have many threads, and that those threads can run *concurrently*.

Thread Attributes

By now, you are familiar with threads and you've seen a simple Java application that runs two threads concurrently. This section introduces you to several features specific to Java threads and provides you with references to sections within this lesson that talk about each feature in detail.

Java threads are implemented by the `Thread` class, which is part of the `java.lang` package. The `Thread` class implements a system-independent definition of Java threads. But under the hood, the actual implementation of concurrent operation is provided by a system-specific implementation. For most programming needs, the underlying implementation doesn't matter. You can ignore the underlying implementation and program to the thread API described in this lesson and in the other documentation provided with the Java system.

Thread Body **(page 290)**

All of the action takes place in the thread's body—the thread's `run` method. You can provide the body to a `Thread` in one of two ways: by subclassing the `Thread` class and overriding its `run` method, or by creating a `Thread` with a `Runnable` object as its *target*.

Thread State **(page 294)**

Throughout its life, a Java thread is in one of several states. A thread's state indicates what the thread is doing and what it is capable of doing at that time of its life: Is it running? Is it sleeping? Is it dead?

Thread Priority **(page 298)**

A thread's priority tells the Java thread scheduler when this thread should run in relation to other threads.

Daemon Threads **(page 303)**

Daemon threads are those that provide a service for other threads in the system. Any Java thread can be a daemon thread.

Thread Group **(page 304)**

All threads belong to a thread group. `ThreadGroup`, a `java.lang` class, defines and implements the capabilities of a group of related threads.

Thread Body

All the action takes place in the thread body, which is the thread's `run` method. After a thread has been created and initialized, the runtime system calls its `run` method. The code in the `run` method implements the functions for which the thread was created. It's the thread's raison d'être.

Often, a thread's `run` method is a loop. For example, an animation thread might loop through and display a series of images. Sometimes a thread's `run` method performs an operation that takes a long time, such as, downloading and playing a sound or a JPEG movie.

There are two ways to provide a customized `run` method for a Java thread:

1. Subclass the `Thread` class defined in the `java.lang` package and override the `run` method.

Example: The `SimpleThread` class described in A Simple Thread Example (page 287).

---

2. Provide a class that implements the `Runnable`[1] interface, also defined in the `java.lang` package. Now, when you instantiate a thread, either directly from the `Thread` class or from a subclass of `Thread`, give the new thread a handle to an instance of your `Runnable` class. This `Runnable` object provides the `run` method to the thread.

Example: The Clock applet you'll see in the next section.

There are good reasons for choosing either of the two options described above over the other. However, for most cases, the following rule of thumb will guide you to the best option.

Rule of thumb: If your class *must* subclass some other class (the most common example being `Applet`), you should use `Runnable` as described in option #2.

The Clock Applet

The Clock applet shown below displays the current time and updates its display every second. If you bring up the online version of this section (http://java.sun.com/Series/Tutorial/java/threads/clock.html) in an HTML browser, you can scroll the page and perform other tasks while the clock updates because the code that updates the clock's display runs within its own thread.

$$11{:}21{:}16$$

http://java.sun.com/Series/Tutorial/java/threads/clock.html

This section highlights and explains the source code for the Clock applet (page 640) in detail. In particular, this section describes the code segments that implement the clock's threaded behavior; it does not describe the code segments that are related to the life cycle of the applet. If you have not written your own applets before or are not familiar with the life cycle of an applet, you may want to take this time to familiarize yourself with the material in The Life Cycle of an Applet (page 152) before proceeding with this section.

---

[1] http://java.sun.com/products/JDK/CurrentRelease/api/java.lang.Runnable.html

Deciding to Use the Runnable Interface

The Clock applet uses the `Runnable` interface to provide the `run` method for its thread. To run within a Java-compatible browser, the `Clock` class has to derive from the `Applet` class. However, the Clock applet also needs to use a thread so that it can continuously update its display without taking over the process in which it is running. (Some browsers might create a new thread for each applet to prevent a misbehaved applet from taking over the main browser thread. However, you should not count on this when writing your applets; your applets should create their own threads when doing computer-intensive work.) But since the Java language does not support multiple inheritance, the `Clock` class can not inherit from `Thread` as well as from `Applet`. Thus, the `Clock` class must use the `Runnable` interface to provide its threaded behavior.

Applets are not threads, nor do any existing Java-compatible browsers or applet viewers automatically create threads in which to run applets. If an applet needs any threads, it must create its own. The Clock applet needs one thread in which to perform its display updates because it updates its display frequently and the user needs to be able to perform other tasks (such as going to another page, or scrolling the one with the applet) at the same time the clock is running.

The Runnable Interface

The Clock applet provides a `run` method for its thread via the `Runnable` interface. The class definition for the `Clock` class indicates that it is a subclass of `Applet` and implements the `Runnable` interface. If you are not familiar with interfaces review the information in the **Objects, Classes, and Interfaces** (page 77) lesson.

```
class Clock extends Applet implements Runnable {
```

The `Runnable` interface defines a single method called `run` that doesn't accept any arguments and doesn't return a value. Because the `Clock` class implements the `Runnable` interface, it must provide an implementation for the `run` method as defined in the interface. However, before explaining the `Clock` run method, let's look at some of the other elements of the Clock applet's code.

Creating the Thread

The application in which an applet is running calls the applet's `start` method when the user visits the applet's page. The Clock applet creates a `Thread`, `clockThread`, in its `start` method and starts the thread.

```
public void start() {
    if (clockThread == null) {
```

```
        clockThread = new Thread(this, "Clock");
        clockThread.start();
    }
}
```

First, the `start` method checks to see if `clockThread` is null. If `clockThread` is null, then the applet has just been loaded or has been previously stopped and a new thread must be created. Otherwise, the applet is already running. The applet creates a new thread with this invocation:

```
    clockThread = new Thread(this, "Clock");
```

Notice that `this`—the `Clock` instance—is the first argument to the thread constructor. The first argument to this thread constructor must implement the Runnable interface and becomes the thread's *target*. When constructed in this way, the clock thread gets its `run` method from its target `Runnable` object—in this case, the `Clock` instance.

The second argument is just a name for the thread.

Stopping the Thread

When you leave the page that displays the Clock applet, the application in which the applet is running calls the applet's `stop` method. The `Clock stop` method sets the `clockThread` to null. This tells the main loop in the `run` method to terminate (see the next section), eventually resulting in the thread stopping and being garbage collected, the continual updating of the clock.

```
    public void stop() {
        clockThread = null;
    }
```

You could use `clockThread.stop` instead, which immediately stops the clock thread. However, the `Thread` class's `stop` method has a sudden effect, which means that the `run` method might be in the middle of some critical operation when the thread is stopped. For more complex `run` methods, using `Thread`'s `stop` method might leave the program in an inconsistent or awkward state. For this reason, avoid using the `Thread` class's `stop` method whenever possible.

If you revisit the page, the `start` method is called again, and the clock starts up again with a new thread.

The Run Method

And finally the `Clock run` method implements the heart of the Clock applet and looks like this:

```
public void run() {
        // loop terminates when clockThread
        // is set to null in stop()
    while (Thread.currentThread() == clockThread) {
        repaint();
        try {
            clockThread.sleep(1000);
        } catch (InterruptedException e){
        }
    }
}
```

As you saw in the previous section, when the applet is asked to stop, the applet sets `clockThread` to `null`; this lets the `run` method know when to stop. The first line of the `run` method loops until `clockThread` is `null`. Within the loop, the applet repaints itself and then tells the thread to sleep for one second (1000 milliseconds). An applet's `repaint` method ultimately calls the applet's `paint` method, which does the actual update of the applet's display area. The `Clock` `paint` method gets the current time and draws it to the screen.

```
public void paint(Graphics g) {
    Date now = new Date();
    g.drawString(now.getHours() + ":" + now.getMinutes() + ":"
                + now.getSeconds(), 5, 10);
}
```

Thread State

The figure on page 295 illustrates the various states that a Java thread can be in at any point during its life. It also illustrates which method calls cause a transition to another state. This figure is not a complete finite state diagram, but rather an overview of the more interesting and common facets of a thread's life. The remainder of this section discusses a thread's life cycle in terms of its state.

New Thread

The following statement creates a new thread but does not start it, thereby leaving the thread in the New Thread state.

```
Thread myThread = new MyThreadClass();
```

When a thread is a new thread, it is merely an empty `Thread` object. No system resources have been allocated for it yet. When a thread is in this state, you can only start the thread or stop it. Calling any method besides `start` or `stop` when a

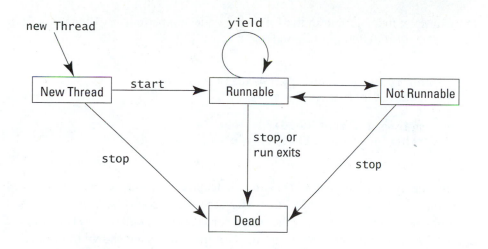

thread is in this state makes no sense and causes an `IllegalThreadState-Exception` (page 297).

Runnable

Now consider these two lines of code:

```
Thread myThread = new MyThreadClass();
myThread.start();
```

The `start` method creates the system resources necessary to run the thread, schedules the thread to run, and calls the thread's `run` method. At this point, the thread is in the Runnable state. This state is called "Runnable" rather than "Running" because the thread might not actually be running when it is in this state. Many computers have a single processor, making it impossible to run all runnable threads at the same time. The Java runtime system must implement a scheduling scheme that shares the processor between all runnable threads. (See Thread Priority (page 298) for more information about scheduling.) However, for most purposes you can think of the Runnable state as simply "Running." When a thread is running—it's runnable and is the current thread—the instructions in its `run` method are executing sequentially.

Not Runnable

A thread becomes not runnable when one of these four events occurs:
- Someone invokes its `sleep` method.
- Someone invokes its `suspend` method.
- The thread uses its `wait` method to wait on a condition variable.
- The thread is blocking on I/O.

For example, the bold line in the following code snippet puts myThread to sleep for 10 seconds (10,000 milliseconds):

```
Thread myThread = new MyThreadClass();
myThread.start();
try {
    myThread.sleep(10000);
} catch (InterruptedException e) {
}
```

During the 10 seconds that myThread is asleep, even if the processor becomes available, myThread does not run. After the 10 seconds are up, myThread becomes runnable again and, if the processor becomes available, myThread executes. For each of the entrances into the Not Runnable state shown in the figure, there is a specific and distinct escape route that returns the thread to the Runnable state. An escape route only works for its corresponding entrance. For example, if a thread has been put to sleep, then the specified number of milliseconds must elapse before the thread becomes Runnable again. Calling resume on a sleeping thread has no effect.

The following indicates the escape route for every entrance into the Not Runnable state.

- If a thread has been put to sleep, then the specified number of milliseconds must elapse.
- If a thread has been suspended, then someone must call its resume method.
- If a thread is waiting on a condition variable, then whatever object owns the variable must relinquish it by calling either notify or notifyAll.
- If a thread is blocked on I/O, then the I/O must complete.

Dead

A thread can die in two ways: either from natural causes, or by being killed (stopped). A thread dies naturally when its run method exits normally. For example, the while loop in the following method is a finite loop—it will iterate 100 times and then exit.

```
public void run() {
    int i = 0;
    while (i < 100) {
        i++;
        System.out.println("i = " + i);
    }
}
```

A thread with this run method dies naturally after the loop and the run method completes.

You can also kill a thread at any time by calling its stop method. The following code snippet creates and starts myThread then puts the current thread to sleep for 10 seconds. When the current thread wakes up, the bold line in the following code segment kills myThread:

```
Thread myThread = new MyThreadClass();
myThread.start();
try {
    Thread.currentThread().sleep(10000);
} catch (InterruptedException e){
}
myThread.stop();
```

The stop method throws a ThreadDeath object at the thread to kill it. When a thread is killed in this manner, it dies asynchronously. The thread dies when it actually receives the ThreadDeath exception.

The stop method causes a sudden termination of a Thread's run method. If the run method performs critical or sensitive calculations, stop may leave the program in an inconsistent or awkward state. Normally, you should not call Thread's stop method but you should arrange for a gentler termination such as setting a flag to indicate to the run method that it should exit.

IllegalThreadStateException

The runtime system throws an IllegalThreadStateException when you call a method on a thread and that thread's state does not allow for that method call. For example, IllegalThreadStateException is thrown when you invoke suspend on a thread that is not runnable.

As the examples of threads in this lesson have shown, when you call a thread method that can throw an exception, you must either catch and handle the exception, or specify that the calling method throws the uncaught exception. See **Handling Errors Using Exceptions**, page 253, for information about exception handling in Java.

The isAlive Method

A final word about thread state: the programming interface for the Thread class includes a method called isAlive. The isAlive method returns true if the thread has been started and not stopped. If the isAlive method returns false you know that the thread is either a new thread or it is dead. If the isAlive method returns true, you know that the thread is either runnable or not runnable.

You cannot differentiate between a new thread or a dead thread; nor can you differentiate between a runnable thread and a not runnable thread.

Thread Priority

Previously, this lesson claimed that threads run concurrently. While conceptually this is true, in practice it usually isn't. Most computer configurations have a single CPU, so threads actually run one at a time in such a way as to provide an illusion of concurrency. Execution of multiple threads on a single CPU in some order is called *scheduling*. The Java runtime supports a very simple, deterministic scheduling algorithm known as *fixed priority scheduling*. This algorithm schedules threads based on their *priority* relative to other runnable threads.

When a Java thread is created, it inherits its priority from the thread that created it. You can also modify a thread's priority at any time after its creation using the setPriority method. Thread priorities are integers ranging between MIN_PRIORITY and MAX_PRIORITY (constants defined in the Thread class). The higher the integer, the higher the priority. At any given time, when multiple threads are ready to be executed, the runtime system chooses the runnable thread with the highest priority for execution. Only when that thread stops, yields, or becomes not runnable for some reason will a lower priority thread start executing. If two threads of the same priority are waiting for the CPU, the scheduler chooses one of them to run in a round-robin fashion. The chosen thread runs until one of the following conditions is true:

- A higher priority thread becomes runnable.
- It yields, or its run method exits.
- On systems that support time-slicing, its time allotment has expired.

Then the second thread is given a chance to run, and so on, until the interpreter exits.

The Java runtime system's thread scheduling algorithm is also *preemptive*. If at any time a thread with a higher priority than all other runnable threads becomes runnable, the runtime system chooses the new higher priority thread for execution. The new higher priority thread is said to *preempt* the other threads.

Rule of thumb: At any given time, the highest priority thread is running. However, this is not guaranteed. The thread scheduler may choose to run a lower priority thread to avoid starvation. For this reason, use priority only to affect scheduling policy for efficiency purposes. Do not rely on thread priority for algorithm correctness.

The 400,000 Micron Thread Race

RaceApplet (page 641) is an applet that animates a race between two "runner" threads with different priorities. When you click the mouse down over the

http://java.sun.com/Series/Tutorial/java/threads/priority.html

applet, it starts the two runners. Runner 2 has a priority of 2. Runner 3 has a priority of 3.

Try this: Go to the online version of this section (http://java.sun.com/Series/Tutorial/java/threads/priority.html) and run the applet.

This is the `run` method for both <u>runners</u> (page 643).

```java
public int tick = 1;
public void run() {
    while (tick < 400000) {
        tick++;
    }
}
```

This `run` method simply counts from 1 to 400,000. The instance variable `tick` is public because the applet uses this value to determine how far the runner has progressed (how long its line is).

In addition to the two runner threads, this applet also has a third thread that handles the drawing. The drawing thread's `run` method contains an infinite loop; during each iteration of the loop it draws a line for each runner, whose length is computed from the runner's `tick` variable, and then sleeps for 10 milliseconds. The drawing thread has a thread priority of 4—higher than either runner. So, whenever the drawing thread wakes up after 10 milliseconds, it becomes the highest priority thread, preempting whichever runner is currently running, and draws the lines. You can see the lines inch their way across the page.

This is not a fair race because one runner has a higher priority than the other. Each time the drawing thread yields the CPU by going to sleep for 10 milliseconds, the scheduler chooses the highest priority runnable thread to run; in this case, it's always runner 3. Here is another version of the applet that implements a fair race, where, both runners have the same priority and an equal chance of being chosen to run.

Try this: Go to the online version of this section (`http://java.sun.com/Series/Tutorial/java/threads/priority.html`) and run the applet.

In this race, each time the drawing thread yields to the CPU by going to sleep, there are two runnable threads of equal priority—the runners—waiting for the

http://java.sun.com/Series/Tutorial/java/threads/priority.html

CPU. The scheduler must choose one of the threads to run. In this situation, the scheduler chooses the next thread to run in a round-robin fashion.

Selfish Threads

The Runner class used in the races above actually implements "socially-impaired" thread behavior. Recall the run method from the Runner class used in the races above:

```
public int tick = 1;
public void run() {
    while (tick < 400000) {
        tick++;
    }
}
```

The while loop in the run method is in a tight loop. Once the scheduler chooses a thread with this thread body for execution, the thread never voluntarily relinquishes control of the CPU—the thread continues to run until the while loop terminates naturally or until the thread is preempted by a higher priority thread. This thread is called a *selfish thread*.

In some situations, having selfish threads doesn't cause any problems because a higher priority thread preempts the selfish one, just as the drawing thread in the RaceApplet preempts the selfish runners. However, in other situations, threads with CPU-greedy run methods, such as the Runner class, can take over the CPU and cause other threads to wait for a long time before getting a chance to run.

Time-Slicing

Some systems, such as Windows 95/NT, fight selfish thread behavior with a strategy known as *time-slicing*. Time-slicing comes into play when there are multiple runnable threads of equal priority and those threads are the highest priority threads competing for the CPU. For example, this <u>stand-alone Java program</u> (page 643) (which is based on the RaceApplet) creates two equal priority <u>selfish threads</u> (page 643) that have the following run method.

```
public void run() {
    while (tick < 400000) {
        tick++;
        if ((tick % 50000) == 0) {
            System.out.println("Thread #" + num + ", tick = " +
                               tick);
        }
    }
}
```

This `run` method contains a tight loop that increments the integer `tick` and every 50,000 ticks prints out the thread's identifier and its `tick` count.

When running this program on a time-sliced system, you will see messages from both threads intermingled with one another, like this:

```
Thread #1, tick = 50000
Thread #0, tick = 50000
Thread #0, tick = 100000
Thread #1, tick = 100000
Thread #1, tick = 150000
Thread #1, tick = 200000
Thread #0, tick = 150000
Thread #0, tick = 200000
Thread #1, tick = 250000
Thread #0, tick = 250000
Thread #0, tick = 300000
Thread #1, tick = 300000
Thread #1, tick = 350000
Thread #0, tick = 350000
Thread #0, tick = 400000
Thread #1, tick = 400000
```

This output is produced because a time-sliced system divides the CPU into time slots and iteratively gives each of the equal-and-highest priority threads a time slot in which to run. The time-sliced system iterates through the equal-and-highest priority threads, allowing each one a bit of time to run, until one or more of them finishes or until a higher priority thread preempts them. Note that time-slicing makes no guarantees as to how often or in what order threads are scheduled to run.

When running this program on a system that is not time-sliced, you will see messages from one thread finish printing before the other thread ever gets a chance to print one message. The output will look like this:

```
Thread #0, tick = 50000
Thread #0, tick = 100000
```

```
Thread #0, tick = 150000
Thread #0, tick = 200000
Thread #0, tick = 250000
Thread #0, tick = 300000
Thread #0, tick = 350000
Thread #0, tick = 400000
Thread #1, tick = 50000
Thread #1, tick = 100000
Thread #1, tick = 150000
Thread #1, tick = 200000
Thread #1, tick = 250000
Thread #1, tick = 300000
Thread #1, tick = 350000
Thread #1, tick = 400000
```

This is because a system that is not time-sliced chooses one of the equal-and-highest priority threads to run and allows that thread to run until it relinquishes the CPU (by sleeping, yielding, or finishing its job) or until a higher priority preempts it.

Note: The Java runtime environment does not implement (and therefore does not guarantee) time-slicing. However, some systems on which you can run Java programs do support time-slicing. Your Java programs should not rely on time-slicing as it may produce different results on different systems.

Try this: Compile and run the RaceTest (page 643) and SelfishRunner (page 643) classes on your computer. Can you tell if you have a time-sliced system?

As you can imagine, writing CPU-intensive code can have negative repercussions on other threads running in the same process. In general, try to write well-behaved threads that voluntarily relinquish the CPU periodically and give other threads an opportunity to run. In particular, never write Java code that relies on time-sharing—this will practically guarantee that your program will produce different results on different computer systems.

A thread can voluntarily yield the CPU without going to sleep or some other drastic means by calling the `yield` method. The `yield` method gives other threads of the same priority a chance to run. If there are no equal priority threads that are runnable, then the `yield` is ignored.

Try this: Rewrite the `SelfishRunner` class to be a PoliteRunner (page 644) by calling the `yield` method from the `run` method. Be sure to modify the main program (page 645) to create `PoliteRunner`s instead of `SelfishRunner`s. Compile and run the new classes on your computer. Now isn't that better?

Summary

- Most computers have only one CPU, so threads must share the CPU with other threads. The execution of multiple threads on a single CPU, in some order, is called scheduling. The Java runtime environment supports a simple, deterministic scheduling algorithm known as fixed priority scheduling.
- Each Java thread is given a numeric priority between MIN_PRIORITY and MAX_PRIORITY (constants defined in the Thread class). At any given time, when multiple threads are ready to be executed, the thread with the highest priority is chosen for execution. Only when that thread stops, or is suspended for some reason, will a lower priority thread start executing.
- Scheduling of the CPU is fully preemptive. If a thread with a higher priority than the currently executing thread needs to execute, the higher priority thread is immediately scheduled.
- The Java runtime environment will not preempt the currently running thread for another thread of the same priority. In other words, the Java runtime environment does not time-slice. However, the system implementation of threads underlying the Java Thread class may support time-slicing. Do not write code that relies on time-slicing.
- In addition, a given thread may, at any time, give up its right to execute by calling the yield method. Threads can only yield the CPU to other threads of the same priority—attempts to yield to a lower priority thread are ignored.
- When all the runnable threads in the system have the same priority, the scheduler chooses the next thread to run in a simple, nonpreemptive, round-robin scheduling order.

Daemon Threads

Any Java thread can be a *daemon* thread. Daemon threads are service providers for other threads running in the same process as the daemon thread. For example, the HotJava browser uses up to four daemon threads named "Image Fetcher" to fetch images from the file system or network for any thread that needs one. The run method for a daemon thread is typically an infinite loop that waits for a service request.

When the only remaining threads in a process are daemon threads, the interpreter exits. This makes sense because when only daemon threads remain, there is no other thread for which a daemon thread can provide a service.

To specify that a thread is a daemon thread, call the setDaemon method with the argument true. To determine if a thread is a daemon thread, use the accessor method isDaemon.

Thread Group

Every Java thread is a member of a *thread group*. Thread groups provide a mechanism for collecting multiple threads into a single object and manipulating those threads all at once, rather than individually. For example, you can start or suspend all the threads within a group with a single method call. Java thread groups are implemented by the ThreadGroup[1] class in the java.lang package.

The runtime system puts a thread into a thread group during thread construction. When you create a thread, you can either allow the runtime system to put the new thread in some default group or you can explicitly set the new thread's group. The thread is a permanent member of whatever thread group it joins upon its creation—you cannot move a thread to a new group after the thread has been created.

The Default Thread Group

If you create a new Thread without specifying its group in the constructor, the runtime system automatically places the new thread in the same group as the thread that created it (known as the *current thread group* and the *current thread*, respectively). If you leave the thread group unspecified when you create your thread, which group contains your thread?

When a Java application first starts up, the Java runtime system creates a ThreadGroup named main. Unless specified otherwise, all new threads that you create become members of the main thread group.

Note: If you create a thread within an applet, the new thread's group may be something other than main depending on the browser or viewer that the applet is running in. Refer to <u>Threads in Applets</u> (page 158) for information about thread groups in applets.

Many Java programmers ignore thread groups altogether and allow the runtime system to handle all of the details regarding thread groups. However, if your program creates a lot of threads that should be manipulated as a group, or if you are implementing a custom security manager, you will likely want more control over thread groups. Continue reading for more details!

[1.] http://java.sun.com/products/JDK/CurrentRelease/api/java.lang.ThreadGroup.html

Creating a Thread Explicitly in a Group

As mentioned previously, a thread is a permanent member of whatever thread group it joins when its created—you cannot move a thread to a new group after the thread has been created. If you wish to put your new thread in a thread group other than the default, you must specify the thread group explicitly when you create the thread. The Thread class has three constructors that allow you to set a new thread's group:

```
public Thread(ThreadGroup group, Runnable target)
public Thread(ThreadGroup group, String name)
public Thread(ThreadGroup group, Runnable target, String name)
```

Each of these constructors creates a new thread, initializes it based on the Runnable and String parameters, and makes the new thread a member of the specified group. For example, the following code sample creates a thread group (myThreadGroup) and then creates a thread (myThread) in that group.

```
ThreadGroup myThreadGroup =
    new ThreadGroup("My Group of Threads");
Thread myThread =
    new Thread(myThreadGroup, "a thread for my group");
```

The ThreadGroup passed into a Thread constructor does not necessarily have to be a group that you create—it can be a group created by the Java runtime system, or a group created by the application in which your applet is running.

Getting a Thread's Group

To find out what group a thread is in, call its getThreadGroup method:

```
theGroup = myThread.getThreadGroup();
```

Once you've obtained a thread's ThreadGroup, you can query the group for information, such as what other threads are in the group. You can also modify the threads in that group, such as suspending, resuming, or stopping them, with a single method invocation.

The ThreadGroup Class

The ThreadGroup class manages groups of threads for Java applications. A ThreadGroup can contain any number of threads. The threads in a group are generally related in some way, such as who created them, what function they perform, or when they should be started and stopped.

ThreadGroups can contain not only threads but also other ThreadGroups. The top-most thread group in a Java application is the thread group named main. You can create threads and thread groups in the main group. You can also create threads and thread groups in subgroups of main. The result is a root-like hierarchy of threads and thread groups:

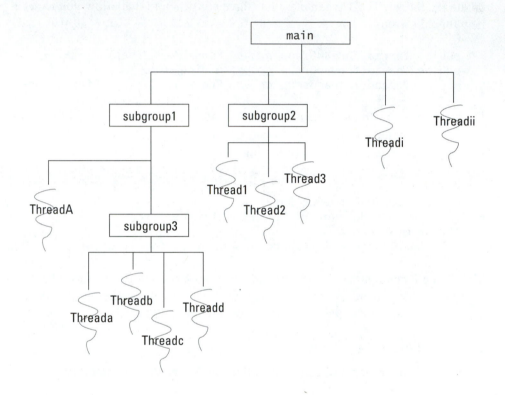

The ThreadGroup class has methods that can be categorized as follows:

- Collection Management Methods (page 307)—Methods that manage the collection of threads and subgroups contained in the thread group.
- Methods that Operate on the Group (page 307)—These methods set or get attributes of the ThreadGroup object.
- Methods that Operate on All Threads Within a Group (page 309)—This is a set of methods that perform some operation, such as start or resume, on all the threads and subgroups within the ThreadGroup.
- Access Restriction Methods (page 309)—ThreadGroup and Thread allow the security manager to restrict access to threads based on group membership.

Collection Management Methods. The ThreadGroup provides a set of methods that manage the threads and subgroups within the group and allow other objects to query the ThreadGroup for information about its contents. For example, you can call ThreadGroup's activeCount method to find out the number of active threads currently in the group. The activeCount method is often used with the enumerate method to get an array filled with references to all the active threads in a ThreadGroup. For example, the listCurrentThreads method in the following example fills an array with all of the active threads in the current thread group and prints their names:

```
class EnumerateTest {
    void listCurrentThreads() {
        ThreadGroup currentGroup =
            Thread.currentThread().getThreadGroup();
        int numThreads;
        Thread[] listOfThreads;

        numThreads = currentGroup.activeCount();
        listOfThreads = new Thread[numThreads];
        currentGroup.enumerate(listOfThreads);
        for (int i = 0; i < numThreads; i++) {
            System.out.println("Thread #" + i + " = " +
                listOfThreads[i].getName());
        }
    }
}
```

Other collection management methods provided by the ThreadGroup class include activeGroupCount and list.

Methods that Operate on the Group. The ThreadGroup class supports several attributes that are set and retrieved from the group as a whole. These attributes include the maximum priority that any thread within the group can have, whether the group is a daemon group, the name of the group, and the parent of the group.

The methods that get and set ThreadGroup attributes operate at the group level. They inspect or change the attribute on the ThreadGroup object, but do not affect any of the threads within the group. The following is a list of ThreadGroup methods that operate at the group level:

- getMaxPriority and setMaxPriority
- getDaemon and setDaemon
- getName
- getParent and parentOf
- toString

For example, when you use `setMaxPriority` to change a group's maximum priority, you are only changing the attribute on the group object; you are not changing the priority of any of the threads within the group. Consider the following program that creates a group and a thread within that group:

```
class MaxPriorityTest {
    public static void main(String[] args) {

        ThreadGroup groupNORM = new ThreadGroup(
                              "A group with normal priority");
        Thread priorityMAX = new Thread(groupNORM,
                          "A thread with maximum priority");

    // set Thread's priority to max (10)
        priorityMAX.setPriority(Thread.MAX_PRIORITY);

    // set ThreadGroup's max priority to normal (5)
        groupNORM.setMaxPriority(Thread.NORM_PRIORITY);

        System.out.println("Group's maximum priority = " +
                groupNORM.getMaxPriority());
        System.out.println("Thread's priority = " +
                priorityMAX.getPriority());
    }
}
```

When the `ThreadGroup` groupNORM is created, it inherits its maximum priority attribute from its parent thread group. In this case, the parent group priority is the maximum (MAX_PRIORITY) allowed by the Java runtime system. Next the program sets the priority of the `priorityMAX` thread to the maximum allowed by the Java runtime system. Then the program lowers the group's maximum to the normal priority (NORM_PRIORITY). The `setMaxPriority` method does not affect the priority of the `priorityMAX` thread, so that at this point, the `priorityMAX` thread has a priority of 10, which is greater than the maximum priority of its group, groupNORM. This is the output from the program:

```
Group's maximum priority = 5
Thread's priority = 10
```

As you can see, a thread can have a higher priority than the maximum allowed by its group as long as the thread's priority is set before the group's maximum priority is lowered. A thread group's maximum priority is used to limit a thread's priority when the thread is first created within a group or when you use `setPriority` to change the thread's priority. Note that the `setMaxPriority` method *does* change the maximum priority of all of its descendant-thread groups.

Similarly, a group's daemon status applies only to the group. Changing a group's daemon status does not affect the daemon status of any of the threads in the group. Furthermore, a group's daemon status does not in any way determine the daemon status of its threads—you can put any thread within a daemon thread group. The daemon status of a thread group simply indicates that the group will be destroyed when all of its threads have been terminated.

Methods that Operate on All Threads Within a Group.

The Thread-Group class has three methods that allow you to modify the current state of all the threads within that group:

- `resume`
- `stop`
- `suspend`

These methods apply the appropriate state change to every thread in the thread group and its subgroups.

Access Restriction Methods.

The `ThreadGroup` class itself does not impose any access restrictions, such as allowing threads from one group to inspect or modify threads in a different group. Rather, the `Thread` and `ThreadGroup` classes cooperate with security managers (subclasses of the `java.lang.SecurityManager` class), which can impose access restrictions based on thread group membership.

The `Thread` and `ThreadGroup` class both have a method, `checkAccess`, which calls the current security manager's `checkAccess` method. The security manager decides whether to allow the access based on the group membership of the threads involved. If access is not allowed, the `checkAccess` method throws a `SecurityException`. Otherwise, `checkAccess` simply returns.

The following is a list of `ThreadGroup` methods that call `ThreadGroup`'s `checkAccess` method before performing the action of the method. These are what are known as *regulated accesses*, accesses that must be approved by the security manager before they can be completed.

- `ThreadGroup(ThreadGroup parent, String name)`
- `setDaemon(boolean isDaemon)`
- `setMaxPriority(int maxPriority)`
- `stop()`
- `suspend()`
- `resume()`
- `destroy()`

This is a list of the methods in the `Thread` class that call `checkAccess` before proceeding:

- constructors that specify a thread group
- `stop()`

- suspend()
- resume()
- setPriority(int *priority*)
- setName(String *name*)
- setDaemon(boolean *isDaemon*)

A stand-alone Java application does not have a security manager by default; no restrictions are imposed and any thread can inspect or modify any other thread, regardless of the group they are in. You can define and implement your own access restrictions for thread groups by subclassing SecurityManager, overriding the appropriate methods, and installing the SecurityManager as the current security manager in your application. For information about implementing a security mangaer, see the lesson **Providing Your Own Security Manager** (page 529).

The HotJava Web browser is an example of an application that implements its own security manager. HotJava needs to ensure that applets are well-behaved and don't do nasty things to other applets running at the same time (such as lowering the priority of another applet's threads). HotJava's security manager does not allow threads in different groups to modify one another. Note that access restrictions based on thread groups may vary from browser to browser and thus applets may behave differently in different browsers.

Multithreaded Programs

Often, threads need to share data. For example, suppose you have a thread that writes data to a file while, at the same time, another thread is reading data from that same file. When your threads share information, you need to synchronize the threads to get the desired results. The next section shows you how to synchronize threads in your Java programs.

If you write a program in which several concurrent threads are competing for resources, you must take precautions to ensure fairness. A system is fair when each thread gets enough access to limited resource to make reasonable progress. A fair system prevents *starvation* and *deadlock*. Starvation occurs when one or more threads in your program is blocked from gaining access to a resource and, as a result, cannot make progress. Deadlock is the ultimate form of starvation; it occurs when two or more threads are waiting on a condition that cannot be satisfied. Deadlock most often occurs when two (or more) threads are each waiting for the other(s) to do something. Deadlock and the Dining Philosophers (page 321) uses the dining philosophers problem to illustrate deadlock. It also discusses ways you can prevent deadlock.

Synchronizing Threads

So far, this lesson has contained examples with independent, asynchronous threads. Each thread contained all of the data and methods required for its execution and didn't require any outside resources or methods. In addition, the threads in those examples ran at their own pace without concern for the state or activities of any other concurrently running threads.

However, there are many interesting situations where separate, concurrently running threads do share data and must consider the state and activities of other threads. One such set of programming situations are known as producer/consumer scenarios where the producer generates a stream of data which then is consumed by a consumer.

For example, imagine a Java application where one thread (the producer) writes data to a file while a second thread (the consumer) reads data from the same file. Or, as you type characters on the keyboard, the producer thread places mouse events in an event queue and the consumer thread reads the events from the same queue. Both of these examples use concurrent threads that share a common resource: The first shares a file, the second shares an event queue. Because the threads share a common resource, they must be synchronized in some way.

This lesson teaches you about Java thread synchronization through a simple producer/consumer example.

Producer/Consumer Example

The Producer (page 646) generates an integer between 0 and 9 (inclusive), stores it in a CubbyHole object, and prints the generated number. To make the synchronization problem more interesting, the Producer sleeps for a random amount of time between 0 and 100 milliseconds before repeating the number-generating cycle:

```java
class Producer extends Thread {
    private CubbyHole cubbyhole;
    private int number;

    public Producer(CubbyHole c, int number) {
        cubbyhole = c;
        this.number = number;
    }

    public void run() {
        for (int i = 0; i < 10; i++) {
            cubbyhole.put(i);
            System.out.println("Producer #" + this.number +
```

```
                    " put: " + i);
            try {
                sleep((int)(Math.random() * 100));
            } catch (InterruptedException e) {
            }
        }
    }
}
```

The <u>Consumer</u> (page 647), being ravenous, consumes all integers from the Cub-byHole (the exact same object into which the Producer put the integers in the first place) as quickly as they become available.

```
class Consumer extends Thread {
    private CubbyHole cubbyhole;
    private int number;

    public Consumer(CubbyHole c, int number) {
        cubbyhole = c;
        this.number = number;
    }

    public void run() {
        int value = 0;
        for (int i = 0; i < 10; i++) {
            value = cubbyhole.get();
            System.out.println("Consumer #" + this.number +
                " got: " + value);
        }
    }
}
```

The Producer and Consumer in this example share data through a common Cub-byHole object. Note that neither the Producer nor the Consumer makes any effort whatsoever to ensure that the Consumer is getting each value produced once and only once. The synchronization between these two threads actually occurs at a lower level, within the get and put methods of the CubbyHole object. However, let's assume for a moment that these two threads make no arrange-ments for synchronization and let's discuss the potential problems that might arise in that situation.

One problem arises when the Producer is quicker than the Consumer and generates two numbers before the Consumer has a chance to consume the first one. In this situation, the Consumer skips a number. Part of the output might look like this:

. . .

```
Consumer #1 got: 3
Producer #1 put: 4
Producer #1 put: 5
Consumer #1 got: 5
```

. . .

Another problem might arise when the Consumer is quicker than the Producer and consumes the same value twice. In this situation, the Consumer prints the same value twice and might produce output that looks like this:

. . .

```
Producer #1 put: 4
Consumer #1 got: 4
Consumer #1 got: 4
Producer #1 put: 5
```

. . .

Either way, the result is wrong. You want the Consumer to get each integer produced by the Producer exactly once. Problems such as those just described are called *race conditions*. They arise from multiple, asynchronously executing threads trying to access a single object at the same time and getting the wrong result.

To prevent race conditions in our producer/consumer example, the storage of a new integer into the CubbyHole by the Producer must be synchronized with the retrieval of an integer from the CubbyHole by the Consumer. The Consumer must consume each integer exactly once. The producer/consumer program uses two different mechanisms to synchronize the Producer thread and the Consumer thread: monitors, and the notify and wait methods. These topics are covered in the next two sections.

Monitors

Objects such as the CubbyHole that are shared between two threads and whose accesses must be synchronized are called *condition variables*. The Java language allows you to synchronize threads around a condition variable through the use of *monitors*. Monitors prevent two threads from simultaneously accessing the same variable.

The Java language and runtime system support thread synchronization through the use of monitors, which were first outlined in C. A. R. Hoare's article

Communicating Sequential Processes (*Communications of the ACM*, Vol. 21, No. 8, August 1978, pp. 666-677). A monitor is associated with a specific data item (a condition variable) and functions as a lock on that data. When a thread holds the monitor for some data item, other threads are locked out and cannot inspect or modify the data.

The code segments within a program that access the same data from within separate, concurrent threads are known as *critical sections*. In the Java language, you mark critical sections in your program with the synchronized keyword.

Note: Generally, critical sections in Java programs are methods. You can mark smaller code segments as synchronized. However, this violates object-oriented paradigms and leads to confusing code that is difficult to debug and maintain. For the majority of your Java programming purposes, it's best to use synchronized only at the method level.

In the Java language, a unique monitor is associated with every object that has a synchronized method. The CubbyHole (page 647) class for the producer/consumer example introduced previously has two synchronized methods: the put method, which is used to change the value in the CubbyHole, and the get method, which is used to retrieve the current value. As a result, the system associates a unique monitor with every instance of CubbyHole.

Here's the code for the CubbyHole class. The bold code elements provide for thread synchronization:

```
class CubbyHole {
    private int contents;
    private boolean available = false;

    public synchronized int get() {
        while (available == false) {
            try {
                wait();
            } catch (InterruptedException e) {
            }
        }
        available = false;
        notify();
        return contents;
    }

    public synchronized void put(int value) {
        while (available == true) {
            try {
                wait();
            } catch (InterruptedException e) {
```

```
            }
        }
        contents = value;
        available = true;
        notify();
    }
}
```

The CubbyHole has two private variables: contents, which is the current contents of the CubbyHole, and the boolean variable available, which indicates whether the CubbyHole contents can be retrieved. When available is true, the Producer has just put a new value in the CubbyHole and the Consumer has not yet consumed it. The Consumer can consume the value in the CubbyHole only when available is true.

Because CubbyHole has synchronized methods, Java provides a unique monitor for each instance of CubbyHole (including the one shared by the Producer and the Consumer). Whenever control enters a synchronized method, the thread that called the method acquires the monitor for the object whose method has been called. Other threads cannot call a synchronized method on the same object until the monitor is released.

Note: Java monitors are *reentrant*. The same thread *can* call a synchronized method on an object for which it already holds the monitor, thereby reacquiring the monitor.

The Java runtime system allows a thread to reacquire a monitor that it already holds because Java monitors are reentrant. Reentrant monitors are important because they eliminate the possibility of a single thread deadlocking itself on a monitor that it already holds.

Consider this class:

```
class Reentrant {
    public synchronized void a() {
        b();
        System.out.println("here I am, in a()");
    }

        public synchronized void b() {
        System.out.println("here I am, in b()");
    }
}
```

Reentrant contains two synchronized methods: a and b. The first synchronized method, a, calls the other synchronized method, b.

When control enters method a, the current thread acquires the monitor for the Reentrant object. Now, a calls b and because b is also synchronized the thread attempts to acquire the same monitor again. Because Java supports reentrant monitors, this works. The current thread can acquire the Reentrant object's monitor again and both a and b execute to conclusion as is evidenced by the output:

```
here I am, in b()
here I am, in a()
```

In systems that don't support reentrant monitors, this sequence of method calls causes deadlock.

Whenever the Producer calls the CubbyHole's put method, the Producer acquires the monitor for the CubbyHole, thereby preventing the Consumer from calling the CubbyHole's get method. (The wait method temporarily releases the monitor as you'll see later.)

```
public synchronized void put(int value) {
        // monitor has been acquired by the Producer
    while (available == true) {
        try {
            wait();
        } catch (InterruptedException e) {
        }
    }
    contents = value;
    available = true;
    notify();
        // monitor is released by the Producer
}
```

When the put method returns, the Producer releases the monitor thereby unlocking the CubbyHole.

Conversely, whenever the Consumer calls the CubbyHole's get method, the Consumer acquires the monitor for the CubbyHole, thereby preventing the Producer from calling the put method.

```
public synchronized int get() {
        // monitor has been acquired by the Consumer
    while (available == false) {
        try {
            wait();
        } catch (InterruptedException e) {
        }
    }
    available = false;
    notify();
    return contents;
        // monitor is released by the Consumer
}
```

The acquisition and release of a monitor is done automatically and atomically by the Java runtime system. This ensures that race conditions cannot occur in the underlying implementation of the threads, ensuring data integrity.

Try this: Remove the lines that are shown in bold in the listing of the CubbyHole class <u>shown previously</u> (page 314). Recompile the program and run it again. What happened? Because no explicit effort has been made to synchronize the Producer and Consumer threads, the Consumer consumes with reckless abandon and gets a whole bunch of zeros instead of getting each integer between 0 and 9 exactly once.

The notify and wait Methods

At a higher level, the producer/consumer example uses Object's[1] notify and wait methods to coordinate the Producer and Consumer's activity. The Cubby-Hole uses notify and wait to ensure that each value placed in the CubbyHole by the Producer is retrieved once and only once by the Consumer.

The get and put methods in the CubbyHole object both make use of the notify and wait methods to coordinate getting and putting values into the Cub-byHole.

Note: The notify and wait methods can be invoked only from within a synchronized method or within a synchronized block or statement.

Let's investigate CubbyHole's use of the notify method by looking at the get method.

The notify method. The get method calls notify as the last thing it does (besides return). The notify method chooses one thread that is waiting on the monitor held by the current thread and wakes it up. Typically, the waiting thread grabs the monitor and proceeds.

In the case of the producer/consumer example, the Consumer thread calls the get method, so the Consumer thread holds the monitor for the CubbyHole during the execution of get. At the end of the get method, the call to notify wakes up the Producer thread that is waiting to get the CubbyHole's monitor. Now, the Producer thread can get the CubbyHole monitor and proceed.

---

[1] http://java.sun.com/products/JDK/CurrentRelease/api/java.lang.Object.html

```
public synchronized int get() {
    while (available == false) {
        try {
            wait();
        } catch (InterruptedException e) {
        }
    }
    available = false;
    notify();              // notifies Producer
    return contents;
}
```

If multiple threads are waiting for a monitor, the Java runtime system chooses one of the waiting threads, making no commitments or guarantees about which thread will be chosen.

The `put` method works in a similar fashion to `get`, waking up the `Consumer` thread that is waiting for the `Producer` to release the monitor.

The `Object` class has another method, `notifyAll`, that wakes up all the threads waiting on the same monitor. In this situation, the awakened threads compete for the monitor. One thread gets the monitor and the others go back to waiting.

The `wait` method. The object `wait` method causes the current thread to wait (possibly forever) until another thread notifies it of a condition change. Use `wait` in conjunction with `notify` to coordinate the activities of multiple threads using the same resources.

The `get` method contains a `while` statement that loops until `available` becomes `true`. If `available` is `false`—the `Producer` has not yet produced a new number and the `Consumer` should wait—the `get` method calls `wait`.

The `while` loop contains the call to `wait`. The `wait` method waits indefinitely for a notification from the `Producer` thread. When the `put` method calls `notify`, the `Consumer` wakes up from the wait state and continues within the `while` loop. Presumably, the `Producer` has generated a new number and the `get` method drops out of the while loop and proceeds. If the `Producer` has not generated a number, `get` goes back to the beginning of the loop and continues to wait until the `Producer` generates a new number and calls `notify`.

```
public synchronized int get() {
    while (available == false) {
        try {
            wait(); // waits for notify() call from Producer
```

```
            } catch (InterruptedException e) {
            }
        }
        available = false;
        notify();
        return contents;
    }
```

The put method works in a similar fashion, waiting for the Consumer thread to consume the current value before allowing the Producer to produce a new one.

Besides the version used in the producer/consumer example, which waits indefinitely for notification, the Object class contains two other versions of the wait method:

wait(long *timeout*)

Waits for notification or until the timeout period has elapsed. *timeout* is measured in milliseconds.

wait(long *timeout*, int *nanos*)

Waits for notification or until *timeout* milliseconds plus *nanos* nanoseconds have elapsed.

Note: Besides using these timed wait methods to synchronize threads, you can also use them in place of sleep. Both methods delay for the requested amount of time, but you can easily wake up wait with a notify. The thread can then see immediately that it should go away. This doesn't matter too much for threads that don't sleep for long, but it could be important for threads that sleep for minutes at a time.

Monitors and the notify and wait Methods. You might have noticed a potential problem in CubbyHole's put and get methods. At the beginning of the get method, if the value in the CubbyHole is not available (the Producer has not generated a new number since the last time the Consumer consumed it), then the Consumer waits for the Producer to put a new value into the CubbyHole. So, the question arises: How can the Producer put a new value into the CubbyHole if the Consumer holds the monitor? (The Consumer holds the CubbyHole's monitor because it's within the synchronized method get.)

Similarly, at the beginning of the put method, if the value in the CubbyHole has not yet been consumed, then the Producer waits for the Consumer to consume the value in the CubbyHole. And again the question arises: How can the Consumer consume the value in the CubbyHole if the Producer holds the monitor? (The Producer holds the CubbyHole's monitor because it's within the synchronized method put.)

Well, the designers of the Java language thought of this too. When the thread enters the wait method, which happens at the beginning of both the put and get

methods, the monitor is released atomically and when the thread exits the `wait` method, the monitor is acquired again by the same thread. This gives the waiting object the opportunity to acquire the monitor and, depending on who's waiting, consume the value in the CubbyHole or produce a new value for the CubbyHole.

The Main Program

Here's a small stand-alone <u>Java application</u> (page 648) that creates a CubbyHole object, a Producer, and a Consumer, and then starts both the Producer and the Consumer:

```
class ProducerConsumerTest {
    public static void main(String[] args) {
        CubbyHole c = new CubbyHole();
        Producer p1 = new Producer(c, 1);
        Consumer c1 = new Consumer(c, 1);

        p1.start();
        c1.start();
    }
}
```

The Output

Here's the output of ProducerConsumerTest:

```
Producer #1 put: 0
Consumer #1 got: 0
Producer #1 put: 1
Consumer #1 got: 1
Producer #1 put: 2
Consumer #1 got: 2
Producer #1 put: 3
Consumer #1 got: 3
Producer #1 put: 4
Consumer #1 got: 4
Producer #1 put: 5
Consumer #1 got: 5
Producer #1 put: 6
Consumer #1 got: 6
Producer #1 put: 7
Consumer #1 got: 7
Producer #1 put: 8
Consumer #1 got: 8
Producer #1 put: 9
Consumer #1 got: 9
```

Deadlock and the Dining Philosophers

The dining philosophers are often used to illustrate various problems that can occur when many synchronized threads are competing for limited resources.

The story goes like this: Five philosophers are sitting at a round table. In front of each philosopher is a bowl of rice. Between each pair of philosophers is one chopstick. Before an individual philosopher can take a bite of rice, he must have two chopsticks: one taken from the left and one taken from the right. The philosophers must find some way to share chopsticks so that they all get to eat.

The applet whose picture follows does a rough animation using an image of Duke for the dining philosophers. This particular algorithm works as follows: Duke always reaches for the chopstick on his right first. If the chopstick is there, Duke takes it and raises his right hand. Next, Duke tries for the left chopstick. If the chopstick is available, Duke picks it up and raises his other hand. Now that Duke has both chopsticks, he takes a bite of rice and says "Mmm!". He then puts both chopsticks down, allowing either of his two neighbors to get the chopsticks. Duke then starts all over again by trying for the right chopstick. Between each attempt to grab a chopstick, each Duke pauses for a random period of time.

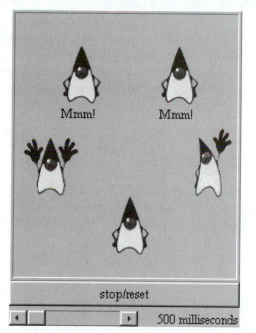

http://java.sun.com/Series/Tutorial/java/threads/deadlock.html

The slider controls the amount of time that each philosopher waits before attempting to pick up a chopstick. When the slider is set to 0, the philosophers

don't wait—they just grab—and the applet ends up in deadlock: all the philosc phers are frozen with their right hand in the air. Why? Because each philosophei immediately has one chopstick and is waiting on a condition that cannot be satisfied—they are all waiting for the left chopstick, which is held by the philosopher to their left.

When you move the slider so that the waiting period is longer, the applet may proceed for a while without deadlocking. However, deadlock is always possible with this particular implementation of the dining philosophers problem because it is possible for all five philosophers to be holding their right chopsticks. Rather than rely on luck to prevent deadlock, you must either explicitly prevent it or detect it.

For most Java programmers, the best choice is to prevent deadlock rather than to try and detect it. Deadlock detection is complicated and beyond the scope of this tutorial. The simplest approach to preventing deadlock is to impose ordering on the condition variables. In the dining philosopher applet, there is no ordering imposed on the condition variables because the philosophers and the chopsticks are arranged in a circle. All chopsticks are equal.

However, we can change the rules in the applet by numbering the chopsticks 1 through 5 and insisting that the philosophers pick up the chopstick with the lower number first. The philosopher who is sitting between chopsticks 1 and 2 and the philosopher who is sitting between chopsticks 1 and 5 must now reach for the same chopstick first (chopstick 1) rather than picking up the one on the right. Whoever gets chopstick 1 first is now free to take another one. Whoever doesn't get chopstick 1 must now wait for the first philosopher to release it. Deadlock is not possible.

Summary

This lesson provided a great deal of information about using threads in the Java development environment. Threads are supported by various components of the Java development environment, and it can be hard to find the features that you · need. This section summarizes where in the Java environment you can find various classes, methods, and language features that participate in the Java threads story.

Package Support of Threads

`java.lang.Thread`[1]

In the Java development environment, threads are objects that derive from `java.lang`'s `Thread` class. The `Thread` class defines and implements Java

---

[1.] http://java.sun.com/products/JDK/CurrentRelease/api/java.lang.Thread.html

threads. You can subclass the Thread class to provide your own thread implementations or you can use the Runnable interface.

java.lang.Runnable[1]

The Java language library also defines the Runnable interface, which allows any class to provide the body (the run method) for a thread.

java.lang.Object[2]

The root class, Object, defines three methods you can use to synchronize methods around a condition variable: wait, notify, and notifyAll.

java.lang.ThreadGroup[3]

All threads belong to a thread group, which typically contains related threads. The ThreadGroup class in the java.lang package implements groups of threads.

java.lang.ThreadDeath[4]

A thread is normally killed by throwing a ThreadDeath object at it. Rarely, a thread might need to catch ThreadDeath to clean up before it dies.

Language Support of Threads

The Java language has two keywords related to the synchronization of threads: volatile (which is not implemented in JDK 1.0) and synchronized. Both of these language features help ensure the integrity of data that is shared between two concurrently running threads. Multithreaded Programs (page 310) discusses thread synchronization issues.

Runtime Support of Threads

The Java runtime system contains the scheduler, which is responsible for running all the existing threads. The Java scheduler uses a fixed priority scheduling algorithm which boils down to this simple rule of thumb:

Rule of thumb: At any given time, the highest priority thread is running. However, this is not guaranteed. The thread scheduler may choose to run a lower priority thread to avoid starvation. For this reason, use priority only to affect scheduling policy for efficiency purposes. Do not rely on thread priority for algorithm correctness.

[1.] http://java.sun.com/products/JDK/CurrentRelease/api/java.lang.Runnable.html
[2.] http://java.sun.com/products/JDK/CurrentRelease/api/java.lang.Object.html
[3.] http://java.sun.com/products/JDK/CurrentRelease/api/java.lang.ThreadGroup.html
[4.] http://java.sun.com/products/JDK/CurrentRelease/api/java.lang.ThreadDeath.html

Other Thread Information

Threads in Applets (page 158)

When you write applets that use threads, you may have to make special provisions, such as ensuring that your applet is well-behaved. Also, some browsers impose security restrictions for applets based on which thread group a thread is in.

16

Input and Output Streams

MANY Java programs need to read or write data. You have seen several examples in this tutorial of programs that read and write data. For example, the program featured in **The Nuts and Bolts of the Java Language** (page 43) reads data entered by the user and writes data to the display, and the **All About Sockets** (page 509) lesson which you'll read later contains several examples that read and write data over the network using sockets. These programs all read from and write to streams.

Definition: A stream is a flowing sequence of characters.

Your program can get input from a data source by reading a sequence of characters from a stream attached to the source. Your program can produce output by writing a sequence of characters to an output stream attached to a destination. The Java development environment includes a package, java.io, that contains a set of input and output streams that your programs can use to read and write data. The `InputStream` and `OutputStream` classes in `java.io` are the abstract superclasses that define the behavior for sequential input and output streams in Java. Also included in `java.io` are several `InputStream` and `OutputStream` subclasses that implement specific types of input and output streams. This lesson explains what each class in `java.io` does, how to decide which ones to use, how to use them, and how to subclass them to write your own stream classes.

While this lesson does not have an example for each type of input and output stream available in the `java.io` package, it does provide many practical examples on how to use the most popular classes in `java.io`.

325

You probably first encountered I/O streams in Java through the use of the standard output, standard error, and standard input streams managed by the System class. This lesson begins with the section Your First Encounter with I/O in Java (page 326)—an overview of these streams.

Next, Overview of Input and Output Streams (page 328) provides an overview of the I/O streams in java.io. The java.io package contains a full set of I/O streams; Java programs use input streams to read data from some input source and output streams to write data to some output source. Input and output sources can be anything that can contain data: a file, a string, or memory. Using Input and Output Streams (page 331) provides several examples of using these streams.

Several I/O streams in java.io belong to a set of streams known as *filtered* streams, which filter data as it's being read from or written to the stream. BufferedInputStream and BufferedOutputStream are two such filtered streams that buffer data during reading and writing making the operation of the stream more efficient. Working with Filtered Streams (page 340) first shows you how to use filtered streams and then shows you how to subclass FilterInputStream and FilterOutputStream to write your own.

The last section in this lesson, Working with Random Access Files (page 348) talks about random access files. The InputStream and OutputStream subclasses in java.io implement sequential access files—files that must be processed in order from beginning to end. A random access file provides your programs with the ability to access data in the file in nonsequential (or random) order. The RandomAccessFile in java.io implements a file that you can access in nonsequential order.

Security consideration: Input and output on the local file system are subject to approval by the current security manager. The example programs contained in these lessons are stand-alone applications, which by default have no security manager. If you attempt to use this code in applets it might not work depending on the browser or viewer they are running in. See **Understanding Applet Capabilities and Restrictions** (page 197) for information about the security restrictions placed on applets.

Your First Encounter with I/O in Java

If you have been using the standard input and output streams, then you have, perhaps unknowingly, been using input and output streams from the java.io package.

The program featured in **The "Hello World" Application** (page 3) uses System.out.println to display the text "Hello World!" to the user.

```
class HelloWorldApp {
    public static void main (String[] args) {
        System.out.println("Hello World!");
    }
}
```

`System.out` refers to an output stream managed by the `System` class that implements the standard output stream. `System.out` is an instance of the `Print-Stream`[1] class defined in the `java.io` package. The `PrintStream` class is an `OutputStream`[2] that is easy to use. Simply call one of the `print`, `println`, or `write` methods to write various types of data to the stream.

`PrintStream` is one of a set of streams known as filtered streams that are covered later in this lesson in <u>Working with Filtered Streams</u> (page 340).

Similarly, the program around which **The Nuts and Bolts of the Java Language** (page 43) is structured uses `System.in.read` to read in characters entered at the keyboard by the user.

```
class Count {
    public static void main(String[] args)
        throws java.io.IOException
    {
        int count = 0;

        while (System.in.read() != -1)
            count++;
        System.out.println("Input has " + count + " chars.");
    }
}
```

`System.in` refers to an input stream managed by the `System` class that implements the standard input stream. `System.in` is an `InputStream`[3] object. `Input-Stream` is an abstract class defined in the `java.io` package that defines the behavior of all sequential input streams in Java. All the input streams defined in the `java.io` package are subclasses of `InputStream`. `InputStream` defines a programming interface for input streams that includes methods for reading from the stream, marking a location within the stream, skipping to a mark, and closing the stream.

So you see, you are already familiar with some of the input and output streams in the `java.io` package. The remainder of this lesson gives an overview of the streams in `java.io`, including the streams mentioned on this section:

---

[1]. http://java.sun.com/products/JDK/CurrentRelease/api/java.io.PrintStream.html
[2]. http://java.sun.com/products/JDK/CurrentRelease/api/java.io.OutputStream.html
[3]. http://java.sun.com/products/JDK/CurrentRelease/api/java.io.InputStream.html

PrintStream, OutputStream, and InputStream, and shows you how to use them.

Overview of Input and Output Streams

The java.io package contains two classes, InputStream and OutputStream, from which most of the other classes in the package derive.

The InputStream[1] class is an abstract superclass that provides a minimal programming interface and a partial implementation of input streams. The InputStream class defines methods for reading bytes or arrays of bytes, marking locations in the stream, skipping bytes of input, finding out the number of bytes available for reading, and resetting the current position within the stream. An input stream is automatically opened when you create it. You can explicitly close a stream with the close method, or let it be closed implicitly when the Input-Stream is garbage collected. Remember that garbage collection occurs when the object is no longer referenced.

The OutputStream[2] class is an abstract superclass that provides a minimal programming interface and a partial implementation of output streams. Output-Stream defines methods for writing bytes or arrays of bytes to the stream. An output stream is automatically opened when you create it. You can explicitly close an output stream with the close method, or let it be closed implicitly when the OutputStream is garbage collected, which occurs when the object is no longer referenced. The java.io package contains several subclasses of Input-Stream and OutputStream that implement specific input or output functions. For example, FileInputStream and FileOutputStream are input and output streams that operate on files on the native file system.

The first of the following two figures shows the class hierarchy for the input stream classes in the java.io package. The second figure shows the class hierarchy for the output stream classes in the java.io package.

Note: In the online version of this tutorial, these diagrams are applets. Click on any of the class symbols in either diagram to visit the API documentation for that class.

As you can see from the first figure, InputStream inherits from the Object class; six classes inherit directly from InputStream. One of InputStream's descendants, FilterInputStream, is itself an abstract class with four children.

[1.] http://java.sun.com/products/JDK/CurrentRelease/api/java/io.InputStream.html
[2.] http://java.sun.com/products/JDK/CurrentRelease/api/java/io.OutputStream.html

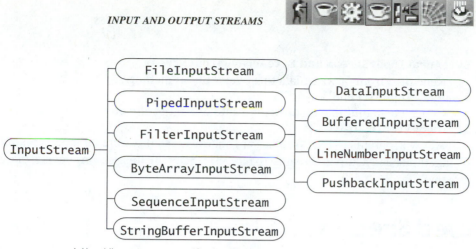

http://java.sun.com/Series/Tutorial/java/io/overview.html

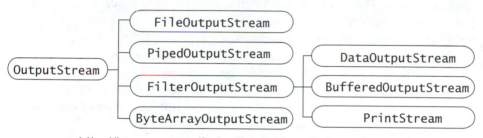

http://java.sun.com/Series/Tutorial/java/io/overview.html

As you can see in the second figure, `OutputStream` inherits from the `Object` class; four classes inherit directly from `OutputStream`. One of `OutputStream`'s descendants, `FilterOutputStream`, is itself an abstract class with three descendants.

Simple Input and Output Streams

The following is an overview of the nonabstract classes that subclass directly from `InputStream` and `OutputStream`:

`FileInputStream` and `FileOutputStream`

Read data from or write data to a file on the native file system.

`PipedInputStream` and `PipedOutputStream`

Implement the input and output components of a pipe. Pipes are used to channel the output from one program (or thread) into the input of another. A `PipedInputStream` must be connected to a `PipedOutputStream` and a `PipedOutputStream` must be connected to a `PipedInputStream`.

ByteArrayInputStream and ByteArrayOutputStream
Read data from or write data to a byte array in memory.
SequenceInputStream
Concatenate multiple input streams into one input stream.
StringBufferInputStream
Allow programs to read from a StringBuffer as if it were an input stream.
<u>Using Input and Output Streams</u> (page 331), later in this lesson, covers these streams.

Filtered Streams

FilterInputStream and FilterOutputStream are subclasses of InputStream and OutputStream, respectively, and are both themselves abstract classes. These classes define the interface for filtered streams which process data as it's being read or written. For example, the filtered streams BufferedInputStream and BufferedOutputStream buffer data while reading and writing to speed it up.

DataInputStream and DataOutputStream
Read or write primitive Java data types in a machine-independent format.
BufferedInputStream and BufferedOutputStream
Buffer data while reading or writing, thereby reducing the number of accesses required on the original data source. Buffered streams are typically more efficient than similar non-buffered streams.
LineNumberInputStream
Keeps track of line numbers while reading.
PushbackInputStream
An input stream with a one-byte pushback buffer. Sometimes when reading data from a stream, it is useful to peek at the next character in the stream in order to decide what to do next. If you peek at a character in the stream, you'll need to put it back so that it can be read again and processed normally.
PrintStream
An output stream with convenient printing methods.
The <u>Working with Filtered Streams</u> (page 340) section, later in this lesson, shows you how to use filtered streams and how to implement your own.

And the Rest . . .

In addition to the stream classes, java.io contains these other classes:

File

> Represents a file on the native file system. You can create a `File` object for a file on the native file system and then query the object for information about that file (such as its full pathname).

FileDescriptor

> Represents a file handle (or descriptor) to an open file or an open socket. You will not typically use this class.

RandomAccessFile

> Represents a random access file.

StreamTokenizer

> Breaks the contents of a stream into tokens. Tokens are the smallest unit recognized by a text-parsing algorithm (such as words, symbols, and so on). A `StreamTokenizer` object can be used to parse any text file. For example, you could use it to parse a Java source file into variable names, operators, and so on, or to parse an HTML file into HTML tags.

`java.io` defines three interfaces:

DataInput and DataOutput

> These two interfaces describe streams that can read and write primitive Java types in machine-independent format. `DataInputStream`, `DataOutputStream`, and `RandomAccessFile` implement these interfaces.

FilenameFilter

> The `list` method in the `File` class uses a `FilenameFilter` to determine which files in a directory to list. The `FilenameFilter` accepts or rejects files based on their names. You could use `FilenameFilter` to implement simple regular expression style file search patterns such as `foo.*`

Working with Random Access Files (page 348) talks about how to use random access files. It also provides a special section that shows you how to write filters for objects that implement the `DataInput` and `DataOutput` interfaces. Filters implemented in this fashion are more flexible than regular filtered streams because they can be used on random access files and on some sequential files.

Using Input and Output Streams

This section contains several examples that illustrate how to use the input and output stream pairs that derive directly from `InputStream` and `OutputStream`.

Using Streams to Implement Pipes

The java.io package contains two classes, <u>PipedInputStream</u>[1] and <u>PipedOut-putStream</u>,[2] that implement the input and output components of a pipe. Pipes are used to channel the output from one program (or thread) into the input of another.

Piped input and output streams are convenient for methods that produce output to be used as input by another program. For example, suppose that you are writing a class that implements various text utilities such as sorting and reversing text. It would be nice if the output of one of these methods could be used as the input for another so that you could string a series of these methods together to perform some function. The pipe shown here uses reverse, sort, and reverse functions on a list of words to create a list of rhyming words:

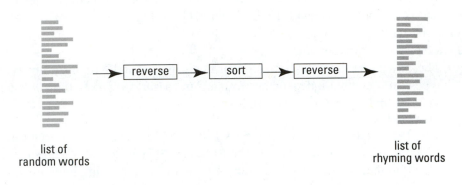

list of
random words

list of
rhyming words

Without piped streams, you would have to create a temporary file between each step:

Let's look at a program that implements the reverse and sort methods using piped streams, and then uses the reverse and sort methods in a pipe to generate a list of rhyming words.

First, the <u>RhymingWords</u> (page 649) class contains three methods: main, reverse, and sort. The main method provides the code for the main program, which opens an input file, uses the other two methods to reverse, sort, and reverse the words in the input file, and then writes the results to the standard output stream.

reverse and sort are designed to be used in a pipe. Both reverse and sort read data from an InputStream, process it (either by reversing the strings or by sorting them), and produce a PipedInputStream suitable for another

---

[1] http://java.sun.com/products/JDK/CurrentRelease/api/java.io.PipedInputStream.html
[2] http://java.sun.com/products/JDK/CurrentRelease/api/java.io.PipedOutputStream.html

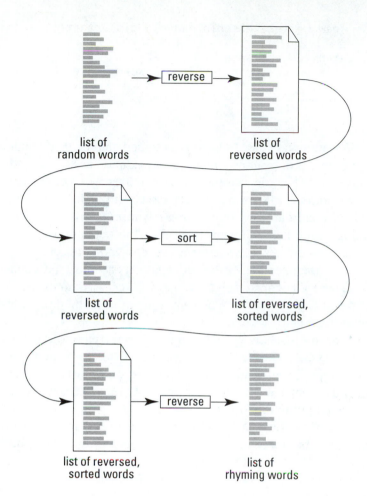

list of
random words

reverse

list of
reversed words

list of
reversed words

sort

list of reversed,
sorted words

list of reversed,
sorted words

reverse

list of
rhyming words

method to read. Let's look in detail at reverse; the sort method is similar to reverse and doesn't warrant its own discussion.

```java
public static InputStream reverse(InputStream source) {
    PipedOutputStream pos = null;
    PipedInputStream pis = null;

    try {
        DataInputStream dis = new DataInputStream(source);
        String input;

        pos = new PipedOutputStream();
        pis = new PipedInputStream(pos);
        PrintStream ps = new PrintStream(pos);
```

```
        new WriteReversedThread(ps, dis).start();

    } catch (Exception e) {
        System.out.println("RhymingWords reverse: " + e);
    }
    return pis;
}
```

The reverse method takes an InputStream called source that contains a list of strings to be reversed. reverse maps a DataInputStream onto the source InputStream so that it can use the DataInputStream's readLine method to read each line from the file. DataInputStream is a filtered stream which must be attached to (mapped onto) an InputStream whose data is to be filtered when read. <u>Working with Filtered Streams</u> (page 340) talks about this.

Next, reverse creates a PipedOutputStream and connects a PipedInputStream to it. Remember that a PipedOutputStream must be connected to a PipedInputStream. reverse then maps a PrintStream onto the PipedOutputStream so that it can use the PrintStream's println method to write strings to the PipedOutputStream.

Now reverse creates a <u>WriteReversedThread</u> (page 651) thread object, hands it two streams, the PrintStream attached to the PipedOutputStream and the DataInputStream attached to source, and starts it. The WriteReversedThread object read words from the DataInputStream, reverses them, and writes the output to the PrintStream, thereby writing the output to a pipe. The Thread object allows each end of the pipe to run independently of one another and prevents the main method from locking up if one end of a pipe blocks waiting for an I/O call to complete.

Here's the run method for WriteReversedThread:

```
public void run() {
    if (ps != null && dis != null) {
        try {
            String input;
            while ((input = dis.readLine())
                                    != null) {
                ps.println(reverseIt(input));
                ps.flush();
            }
            ps.close();
        } catch (IOException e) {
            System.out.println(
                "WriteReversedThread run: " + e);
        }
    }
}
```

Because the `PipedOutputStream` is connected to the `PipedInputStream`, all data written to the `PipedOutputStream` flows into the `PipedInputStream`. The data can be read from the `PipedInputStream` by another program or thread. `reverse` returns the `PipedInputStream` for use by the calling program.

The `sort` method follows the same pattern:

- Open piped output stream.
- Connect piped input stream to it.
- Using a <u>SortThread</u> (page 652) object, read from the piped input stream and write to the piped output stream, which is the piped input stream for someone else.
- Hand the now full piped input stream to someone else to read.

Calls to `reverse` and `sort` can be cascaded together so that the output from one method can be the input for the next method. In fact, the `main` method does just that. It cascades calls to `reverse`, `sort`, and then `reverse` to generate a list of rhyming words:

```
InputStream rhymedWords = reverse(sort(reverse(words)));
```

When you run `RhymingWords` on the file of words called <u>words.txt</u> (page 654), you will see this output:

```
Java
interface
image
language
communicate
integrate
native
string
network
stream
program
application
animation
exception
primer
container
user
graphics
threads
tools
class
bolts
nuts
```

```
object
applet
environment
development
argument
component
input
output
anatomy
security
```

If you look closely you can see that rhyming words such as environment, development, argument, and component are grouped together.

Using Streams to Read and Write Files

File streams are perhaps the easiest streams to understand. Simply put, `FileInputStream`[1] and `FileOutputStream`[2] represent input and output streams on a file that lives on the native file system. You can create a file stream from a filename, a `File`[3] object, or a `FileDescriptor`[4] object. Use file streams to read data from or write data to files on the file system.

The following example uses two file streams to copy the contents of one file into another:

```java
import java.io.*;

class FileStreamsTest {
    public static void main(String[] args) {
        try {
            File inputFile = new File("farrago.txt");
            File outputFile = new File("outagain.txt");

            FileInputStream fis =
                    new FileInputStream (inputFile);
```

---

1. http://java.sun.com/products/JDK/CurrentRelease/api/java.io.FileInputStream.html
2. http://java.sun.com/products/JDK/CurrentRelease/api/java.io.FileOutputStream.html
3. http://java.sun.com/products/JDK/CurrentRelease/api/java.io.File.html
4. http://java.sun.com/products/JDK/CurrentRelease/api/java.io.FileDescriptor.html

```
        FileOutputStream fos =
            new FileOutputStream(outputFile);
        int c;

        while ((c = fis.read()) != -1) {
           fos.write(c);
        }
        fis.close();
        fos.close();
    } catch (FileNotFoundException e) {
        System.err.println("FileStreamsTest: " + e);
    } catch (IOException e) {
        System.err.println("FileStreamsTest: " + e);
    }
  }
}
```

Here are the contents of the input file <u>farrago.txt</u> (page 655):

```
So she went into the garden to cut a cabbage-leaf, to
make an apple-pie; and at the same time a great
she-bear, coming up the street, pops its head into the
shop. 'What! no soap?' So he died, and she very
imprudently married the barber; and there were
present the Picninnies, and the Joblillies, and the
Garyalies, and the grand Panjandrum himself, with the
little round button at top, and they all fell to playing
the game of catch as catch can, till the gun powder ran
out at the heels of their boots.

Samuel Foote 1720-1777
```

The `FileStreamsTest` program creates a `FileInputStream` from a `File` object with the following code:

```
File inputFile = new File("farrago.txt");
FileInputStream fis = new FileInputStream(inputFile);
```

Note the use of the `File` object, `inputFile`, in the constructor. `inputFile` represents the named file, `farrago.txt`, on the native file system. This program only uses `inputFile` to create a `FileInputStream` on `farrago.txt`. However, the program could use `inputFile` to get information about `farrago.txt` such as its full pathname.

Using Streams to Read and Write Memory Locations

Use <u>ByteArrayInputStream</u>[1] and <u>ByteArrayOutputStream</u>[2] to read and write 8-bit data. You create these streams on an existing byte array and then use the read and write methods to read from or write data to the array in memory.

Use <u>StringBufferInputStream</u>[3] to read data from a StringBuffer. Create a StringBufferInputStream on an existing StringBuffer object and then use the read methods to read from the StringBuffer as it lives in memory. This stream is similar to the ByteArrayInputStream which reads 8-bit data from a byte array in memory but StringBufferInputStream reads 16-bit Unicode data from a string buffer in memory. The java.io package does not have a partner output stream for StringBufferInputStream—use the StringBuffer class directly instead.

Using Streams to Concatenate Files

The <u>SequenceInputStream</u>[4] creates a single input stream from multiple input sources. This example program, <u>Concatenate</u> (page 656), uses SequenceInputStream to implement a concatenation utility that sequentially concatenates files together in the order they are listed on the command line.

The following code is the controlling class of the Concatenate utility:

```
import java.io.*;

class Concatenate {
    public static void main(String[] args) {
        ListOfFiles mylist = new ListOfFiles(args);

        try {
            SequenceInputStream s = new
                SequenceInputStream(mylist);
            int c;

            while ((c = s.read()) != -1) {
                System.out.write(c);
```

1. http://java.sun.com/products/JDK/CurrentRelease/api/java.io.ByteArrayInputStream.html
2. http://java.sun.com/products/JDK/CurrentRelease/api/java.io.ByteArrayOutputStream.html
3. http://java.sun.com/products/JDK/CurrentRelease/api/java.io.StringBufferInputStream.html
4. http://java.sun.com/products/JDK/CurrentRelease/api/java.io.SequenceInputStream.html

```
        }
        s.close();
    } catch (IOException e) {
        System.err.println("Concatenate: " + e);
    }
  }
 }
}
```

The first thing that the `Concatenate` utility does is create a `ListOfFiles` object named `mylist` which is initialized from the command-line arguments entered by the user. The command-line arguments list the files to be concatenated together. `mylist` is used to initialize the `SequenceInputStream` which uses `mylist` to get a new InputStream for every filename listed by the user.

```
import java.util.*;
import java.io.*;

class ListOfFiles implements Enumeration {

    String[] listOfFiles;
    int current = 0;

    ListOfFiles(String[] listOfFiles) {
        this.listOfFiles = listOfFiles;
    }

    public boolean hasMoreElements() {
        if (current < listOfFiles.length)
            return true;
        else
            return false;
    }

    public Object nextElement() {
        InputStream is = null;

        if (!hasMoreElements())
            throw new NoSuchElementException("No more files.");
        else {
            try {
                String nextElement = listOfFiles[current];
                current++;
                is = new FileInputStream(nextElement);
            } catch (FileNotFoundException e) {
                System.out.println("ListOfFiles: " + e);
            }
```

```
        }
        return is;
    }
}
```

`ListOfFiles` implements the Enumeration[1] interface. You'll see how this comes into play as we walk through the rest of the program.

After the `main` method creates the `SequenceInputStream`, it reads from that stream one byte at a time. When the `SequenceInputStream` needs an `Input-Stream` from a new source, such as for the first byte read or when it runs off the end of the current input stream, it calls `nextElement` on the `Enumeration` object to get the next `InputStream`. `ListOfFiles` creates `FileInputStream` objects lazily, meaning that whenever `SequenceInputStream` calls `nextElement`, `List-OfFiles` opens a `FileInputStream` on the next filename in the list and returns the stream. When the ListOfFiles object runs out of files to read (it has no more elements), `nextElement` returns `null`, and the call to `SequenceInputStream`'s `read` method returns `-1` to indicate the end of input.

`Concatenate` simply echoes all the data read from the `SequenceInput-Stream` to the standard output.

Try this: Try running Concatenate on the farrago.txt (page 655) and words.txt (page 654) files, which are used as input to other examples in this lesson.

Working with Filtered Streams

You attach a filtered stream to another stream to filter the data as it's read from or written to the original stream. The `java.io` package contains the following filtered streams which are subclasses of either `FilterInputStream` or `FilterOutputStream`:

- `DataInputStream` and `DataOutputStream`
- `BufferedInputStream` and `BufferedOutputStream`
- `LineNumberInputStream`
- `PushbackInputStream`
- `PrintStream` (This is an output stream.)

This section shows you how to use filtered streams through an example that uses a `DataInputStream` object and a `DataOutputStream` object.

[1.] http://java.sun.com/products/JDK/CurrentRelease/api/java.util.Enumeration.html

Many programmers find that they need to implement their own streams that filter or process data as it is being written to or read from the stream. Sometimes the processing is independent of the format of the data, such as counting various items in the stream, and sometimes the processing is directly related to the data itself or the format of the data, such as reading and writing data that is contained in rows and columns. Often, these programmers subclass `FilterInputStream` and `FilterOutputStream` to achieve their goals. This section describes an example of how to subclass `FilterInputStream` and `FilterOutputStream` to create your own filtered streams.

Using Filtered Streams

To use a filtered input or output stream, attach the filtered stream to another input or output stream. You attach a filtered stream to another stream when you create it. For example, you can attach a `DataInputStream` to the standard input stream as in the following code:

```
DataInputStream dis = new DataInputStream(System.in.read());
String input;

while ((input = dis.readLine()) != null) {
    . . . // do something interesting here
}
```

You might do this so that you can use the more convenient read*XXX* methods, such as `readLine`, implemented by `DataInputStream`.

Using `DataInputStream` and `DataOutputStream`

This section shows you how to use the java.io <u>DataInputStream</u>[1] and <u>DataOutputStream</u>[2] classes. It features an example, <u>DataIOTest</u> (page 657), that reads and writes tabular data (invoices for Java merchandise). The tabular data is formatted in columns and each column is separated from the next by tabs. The columns contain the sales price, the number of units ordered, and a description of the item, like this:

```
19.99   12      Java T-shirt
9.99    8       Java Mug
```

---

[1]. http://java.sun.com/products/JDK/CurrentRelease/api/java.io.DataInputStream.html
[2]. http://java.sun.com/products/JDK/CurrentRelease/api/java.io.DataOutputStream.html

DataOutputStream, like other filtered output streams, must be attached to some other OutputStream. In this case, it's attached to a FileOutputStream that is set up to write to a file named invoice1.txt.

```
DataOutputStream dos = new DataOutputStream(
                            new FileOutputStream("invoice1.txt"));
```

Next, DataIOTest uses DataOutputStream's specialized write*XXX* methods to write the invoice data contained within arrays in the program according to the type of data being written:

```
for (int i = 0; i < prices.length; i ++) {
    dos.writeDouble(prices[i]);
    dos.writeChar('\t');
    dos.writeInt(units[i]);
    dos.writeChar('\t');
    dos.writeChars(descs[i]);
    dos.writeChar('\n');
}
dos.close();
```

Note that this code snippet closes the output stream when it's finished.

Next, DataIOTest opens a DataInputStream on the file just written:

```
DataInputStream dis = new DataInputStream(
                            new FileInputStream("invoice1.txt"));
```

DataInputStream, must also be attached to some other InputStream, in this case, a FileInputStream set up to read the file just written, invoice1.txt. DataIOTest then just reads the data back in using DataInputStream's specialized read*XXX* methods.

```
try {
    while (true) {
        price = dis.readDouble();
        dis.readChar();         // throws out the tab
        unit = dis.readInt();
        dis.readChar();         // throws out the tab
        desc = dis.readLine();
        System.out.println("You've ordered " + unit +
                " units of " + desc + " at $" + price);
        total = total + unit * price;
    }
```

```
    } catch (EOFException e) {
    }
    System.out.println("For a TOTAL of: $" + total);
    dis.close();
```

When all of the data has been read, `DataIOTest` displays a statement summarizing the order and the total amount owed, and then closes the stream.

Note the loop that `DataIOTest` uses to read the data from the `DataInputStream`. Normally, when reading data, you see loops like this:

```
    while ((input = dis.readLine()) != null) {
        . . .
    }
```

The `readLine` method returns a value, `null` which indicates the end of the file has been reached. Many of the `DataInputStream` read*XXX* methods can't do this because any value that could be returned to indicate end-of-file may also be a legitimate value read from the stream. For example, suppose that you want to use –1 to indicate end-of-file. Well, you can't because –1 is a legitimate value that can be read from the input stream using `readDouble`, `readInt`, or one of the other methods that reads numbers. So `DataInputStream`'s read*XXX* methods throw an `EOFException` instead. When the `EOFException` occurs the `while (true)` terminates.

When you run the `DataIOTest` program you should see the following output:

```
    You've ordered 12 units of Java T-shirt at $19.99
    You've ordered 8 units of Java Mug at $9.99
    You've ordered 13 units of Duke Juggling Dolls at $15.99
    You've ordered 29 units of Java Pin at $3.99
    You've ordered 50 units of Java Key Chain at $4.99
    For a TOTAL of: $892.88
```

Writing Your Own Filtered Streams

The following is a list of steps to take when writing your own filtered input and output streams:

- Create a subclass of `FilterInputStream` and `FilterOutputStream`. Input and output streams often come in pairs, so it's likely that you will need to create both input and output versions of your filter stream.
- Override the `read` and `write` methods.
- Override any other methods that you might need.
- Make sure the input and output streams work together.

This section shows you how to implement your own filtered streams through an example that implements a matched pair of filtered input and output streams. Many thanks to David Connelly from the Java team for contributing this example.

Both the input and the output stream use a checksum class to compute a checksum on the data written to or read from the stream. The checksum is used to determine whether the data read by the input stream matches that written by the output stream.

Four classes and one interface make up this example program:

- The filtered input and output stream subclasses—CheckedOutputStream and CheckedInputStream.
- The Checksum interface and the Adler32 class compute a checksum for the streams.
- The CheckedIOTest class defines the main method for the program.

The CheckedOutputStream Class

The <u>CheckedOutputStream</u> (page 659) class is a subclass of FilterOutput-Stream that computes a checksum on data as it is being written to the stream. When creating a CheckedOutputStream, you must use its only constructor:

```
public CheckedOutputStream(OutputStream out, Checksum cksum) {
    super(out);
    this.cksum = cksum;
}
```

This constructor takes an OutputStream argument and a Checksum argument. The OutputStream argument is the output stream that this CheckedOutput-Stream should filter. The Checksum argument is an object that can compute a checksum. CheckedOutputStream initializes itself by calling its superclass constructor and initializing a private variable, cksum, with the Checksum object. The CheckedOutputStream uses cksum to update the checksum each time data is written to the stream.

CheckedOutputStream needs to override FilterOutputStream's write methods so that each time the write method is called, the checksum is updated. FilterOutputStream defines three versions of the write method:

1. write(int *i*)
2. write(byte[] *b*)
3. write(byte[] *b*, int *offset*, int *length*)

CheckedOutputStream overrides all three of these methods using the following code:

```
public void write(int b) throws IOException {
    out.write(b);
    cksum.update(b);
}

public void write(byte[] b) throws IOException {
    out.write(b, 0, b.length);
    cksum.update(b, 0, b.length);
}

public void write(byte[] b, int off, int len) throws IOException {
    out.write(b, off, len);
    cksum.update(b, off, len);
}
```

The implementations of these three `write` methods are straightforward: Write the data to the output stream that this filtered stream is attached to, then update the checksum.

The CheckedInputStream Class

The CheckedInputStream (page 659) class is similar to the CheckedOutput-Stream class. CheckedInputStream is a subclass of FilterInputStream that computes a checksum on data as it is being read from the stream. When creating a CheckedInputStream, you must use its only constructor:

```
public CheckedInputStream(InputStream in, Checksum cksum) {
    super(in);
    this.cksum = cksum;
}
```

This constructor is similar to the constructor for CheckedOutputStream.

Just as CheckedOutputStream needed to override FilterOutputStream's `write` methods, CheckedInputStream must override FilterInputStream's `read` methods so that each time the read method is called, the checksum is updated. As with FilterOutputStream, FilterInputStream defines three versions of the read method and CheckedInputStream overrides all of them using the following code:

```
public int read() throws IOException {
    int b = in.read();
    if (b != -1) {
        cksum.update(b);
```

```
        }
        return b;
    }

    public int read(byte[] b) throws IOException {
        int len;
        len = in.read(b, 0, b.length);
        if (len != -1) {
            cksum.update(b, 0, b.length);
        }
        return len;
    }

    public int read(byte[] b, int off, int len) throws IOException {
        len = in.read(b, off, len);
        if (len != -1) {
            cksum.update(b, off, len);
        }
        return len;
    }
```

The implementations of these three read methods are straightforward: Read the
data from the input stream that this filtered stream is attached to. If any data was
actually read, update the checksum.

The Checksum Interface and the Adler32 Class

The Checksum (page 661) interface defines four methods for checksum objects
to implement. These methods reset, update, and return the checksum value. You
could write a Checksum class that computes a specific type of checksum such as
the CRC-32 checksum. Note that inherent in the checksum is the notion of state.
The checksum object doesn't just compute a checksum in one pass. Rather, the
checksum is updated each time information is read from or written to the stream
for which this object computes a checksum. If you want to reuse a checksum
object, you must reset it.

   For this example, we implemented the Adler32 (page 661) checksum, which
is almost as reliable as a CRC-32 checksum but can be computed much faster.

A Program for Testing

The last class in the example, CheckedIOTest (page 663), contains the main
method for the program.

```
import java.io.*;

class CheckedIOTest {
```

```java
public static void main(String[] args) {

    Adler32 inChecker = new Adler32();
    Adler32 outChecker = new Adler32();
    CheckedInputStream cis = null;
    CheckedOutputStream cos = null;

    try {
        cis = new CheckedInputStream(
          new FileInputStream("farrago.txt"), inChecker);
        cos = new CheckedOutputStream(
          new FileOutputStream("outagain.txt"), outChecker);
    } catch (FileNotFoundException e) {
        System.err.println("CheckedIOTest: " + e);
        System.exit(-1);
    } catch (IOException e) {
        System.err.println("CheckedIOTest: " + e);
        System.exit(-1);
    }

    try {
        int c;

        while ((c = cis.read()) != -1) {
            cos.write(c);
        }

        System.out.println("Input stream check sum: " +
                inChecker.getValue());
        System.out.println("Output stream check sum: " +
                outChecker.getValue());

        cis.close();
        cos.close();
    } catch (IOException e) {
        System.err.println("CheckedIOTest: " + e);
    }
}
}
```

The `main` method creates two `Adler32` checksum objects, one each for `CheckedOutputStream` and `CheckedInputStream`. This example requires two checksum objects because the checksum objects are updated during calls to `read` and `write` and those calls occur concurrently.

Next, `main` opens a `CheckedInputStream` on a small text file, `farrago.txt` (page 655) and a `CheckedOutputStream` on an output file named `outagain.txt`, which doesn't exist until you run the program for the first time.

The `main` method reads the text from the `CheckedInputStream` and simply copies it to the `CheckedOutputStream`. The `read` and `write` methods use the `Adler32` checksum objects to compute a checksum during reading and writing. After the input file has been completely read and the output file has been completely written, the program prints out the checksum for both the input and output streams (which should match) and then closes them both.

When you run `CheckedIOTest`, you should see this output:

```
Input stream check sum: 736868089
Output stream check sum: 736868089
```

Filtering Random Access Files

The filtered streams in `java.io` all inherit from `InputStream` or `OutputStream`, which implement sequential access files. So if you subclass `FilterInputStream` or `FilterOutputStream` your filtered streams will also be sequential access files. Writing Filters for Random Access Files (page 351) later in this lesson shows you how to rewrite this example so that it works on a `RandomAccessFile` as well as on a `DataInputStream` or a `DataOutputStream`.

Working with Random Access Files

The input and output streams in this lesson so far have been sequential access streams—streams whose contents must be read or written sequentially. While still incredibly useful, sequential access files are a consequence of a sequential medium such as magnetic tape. Random access files, on the other hand, permit nonsequential, or random, access to the contents of a file.

So why might you need random access files? Consider the archive format known as "zip." Zip archives contain files and are typically compressed to save space. Zip archives also contain a dir-entry at the end that indicates where the various files contained within the zip archive begin:

Zip Archive

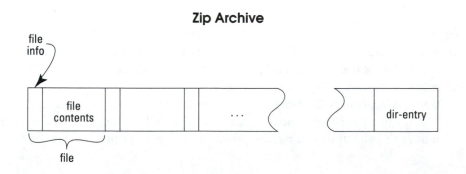

Suppose that you want to extract a specific file from a zip archive. If you use a sequential access stream, you have to do the following:
- Open the zip archive.
- Search through the zip archive until you locate the file you want to extract.
- Extract the file.
- Close the zip archive.

On average, using this algorithm, you will have to read half the zip archive before finding the file that you want to extract. You can extract the same file from the zip archive more efficiently using the seek feature of a random access file:
- Open the zip archive.
- Seek to the dir-entry and locate the entry for the file you want to extract from the zip archive.
- Seek (backwards) within the zip archive to the position of the file to extract.
- Extract the file.
- Close the zip archive.

This algorithm is more efficient because you only read the dir-entry and the file that you want to extract.

The `RandomAccessFile`[1] class in the `java.io` package implements a random access file. Unlike the input and output stream classes in `java.io`, `RandomAccessFile` is used for both reading and writing files. You create a `RandomAccessFile` object with different arguments depending on whether you intend to read or write.

`RandomAccessFile` is somewhat disconnected from the input and output streams in `java.io`—it doesn't inherit from `InputStream` or `OutputStream`. This has some disadvantages in that you can't apply the same filters to `RandomAccessFiles` that you can to streams. However, `RandomAccessFile` does implement the `DataInput` and `DataOutput` interfaces, so if you design a filter that works for either `DataInput` or `DataOutput`, it will work on some sequential access files (the ones that implement `DataInput` or `DataOutput`) as well as on any `RandomAccessFile`.

Using Random Access Files

The `RandomAccessFile` class implements both the `DataInput` and `DataOutput` interfaces and therefore can be used for both reading and writing. `RandomAccessFile` is similar to `FileInputStream` and `FileOutputStream` in that you specify a file on the native file system to open when you create it. You can do this with a filename or a `File`[2] object. When you create a `RandomAccessFile`, you

---

[1]. http://java.sun.com/products/JDK/CurrentRelease/api/java.io.RandomAccessFile.html
[2]. http://java.sun.com/products/JDK/CurrentRelease/api/java.io.File.html

must indicate whether you will be just reading the file or also writing to it. (You have to be able to read a file in order to write to it.) The following line of Java code creates a `RandomAccessFile` to read the file named `farrago.txt`:

```
new RandomAccessFile("farrago.txt", "r");
```

This Java statement opens the same file for both reading and writing:

```
new RandomAccessFile("farrago.txt", "rw");
```

After the file has been opened, you can use the common read*XXX* or write*XXX* methods to perform I/O on the file.

`RandomAccessFile` supports the notion of a *file pointer*. The file pointer indicates the current location in the file. When the file is first created, the file pointer is 0, indicating the beginning of the file. Calls to the read*XXX* or write*XXX* methods adjust the file pointer by the number of bytes read or written.

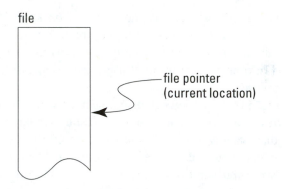

In addition to the normal file I/O methods that implicitly move the file pointer when the operation occurs, `RandomAccessFile` contains three methods for explicitly manipulating the file pointer.

skipBytes

Moves the file pointer forward the specified number of bytes.

seek

Positions the file pointer just before the specified byte.

getFilePointer

Returns the current byte location of the file pointer.

Writing Filters for Random Access Files

Let's rewrite the example from <u>Writing Your Own Filtered Streams</u> (page 343) so that it works on `RandomAccessFiles`. Because `RandomAccessFile` implements the <u>`DataInput`</u>[1] and <u>`DataOutput`</u>[2] interfaces, a side benefit is that the filtered stream will also work with other `DataInput` and `DataOutput` streams, including some sequential access streams such as `DataInputStream` and `DataOutputStream`.

The <u>`CheckedIOTest`</u> (page 663) example from <u>Writing Your Own Filtered Streams</u> (page 343) implements two filtered streams, `CheckedInputStream` (page 659) and <u>`CheckedOutputStream`</u> (page 659), that compute a checksum as data is read from or written to the stream.

In the new example, <u>`CheckedDataOutput`</u> (page 664) is a rewrite of `CheckedOutputStream`—it computes a checksum for data written to the stream—but it operates on `DataOutput` objects instead of `OutputStreams` objects. Similarly, <u>`CheckedDataInput`</u> (page 665) modifies `CheckedInput-Stream` so that it now works on `DataInput` objects instead of `InputStream` objects.

CheckedDataOutput vs. CheckedOutputStream

Let's look at how `CheckedDataOutput` differs from `CheckedOutputStream`.

The first difference between `CheckedDataOutput` and `CheckedOutputStream` is that `CheckedDataOutput` does *not* extend `FilterOutputStream`. Instead, it implements the `DataOutput` interface.

```
public class CheckedDataOutput implements DataOutput
```

Note: In the interest of keeping the example simple, the `CheckedDataOutput` class in this lesson is not declared to implement `DataOutput`, because the `DataOutput` interface specifies so many methods. However, the `Checked-DataOutput` class in the example does implement several of `DataOutput`'s methods to illustrate how it should work.

Next, `CheckedDataOutput` declares a private variable to hold a `DataOutput` object.

```
private DataOutput out;
```

[1.] http://java.sun.com/products/JDK/CurrentRelease/api/java.io.DataInput.html
[2.] http://java.sun.com/products/JDK/CurrentRelease/api/java.io.DataOutput.html

This is the object to which data will be written.

The constructor for `CheckedDataOutput` is different from `CheckedOutput-Stream`'s constructor: `CheckedDataOutput` is created on a `DataOutput` object rather than on an `OutputStream`.

```
public CheckedDataOutput(DataOutput out, Checksum cksum) {
    this.cksum = cksum;
    this.out = out;
}
```

This constructor does not call `super(out)` like the `CheckedOutputStream` constructor did, because `CheckedDataOutput` extends from `Object` rather than from a stream class.

Those are the only modifications made to `CheckedOutputStream` to create a filter that works on `DataOutput` objects.

CheckedDataInput vs. CheckedInputStream

`CheckedDataInput` requires the same changes as `CheckedDataOutput`:

- `CheckedDataInput` does not derive from `FilterInputStream` but implements the `DataInput` interface instead.

Note: In the interest of keeping the example simple, the `CheckedDataInput` class in this lesson is not declared to implement `DataInput`, because the `DataInput` interface specifies so many methods. However, the `CheckedDataInput` class in the example does implement several of `DataInput`'s methods to illustrate how it should work.

- `CheckedDataInput` declares a private variable to hold a `DataInput` object which it wraps.
- The constructor for `CheckedDataInput` requires a `DataInput` object rather than an `InputStream`.

In addition to these changes, the `read` methods are changed as well. `CheckedInputStream` from the original example implements two `read` methods, one for reading a single byte and one for reading a byte array. The `DataInput` interface has methods that implement the same functionality, but they have different names and different method signatures. Thus the `read` methods in the `CheckedDataInput` class have new names and method signatures:

```
public byte readByte() throws IOException {
    byte b = in.readByte();
    cksum.update(b);
    return b;
```

```
}

public void readFully(byte[] b) throws IOException {
    in.readFully(b, 0, b.length);
    cksum.update(b, 0, b.length);
}

public void readFully(byte[] b, int off, int len) throws
IOException {
    in.readFully(b, off, len);
    cksum.update(b, off, len);
}
```

The Main Programs

Finally, this example has two main programs to test the new filters: Checked-DITest (page 666), which runs the filters on sequential access files (DataInput-Stream and DataOutputStream objects), and CheckedRAFTest (page 667), which runs the filters on random access files (RandomAccessFile objects).

These two main programs differ only in the type of object they open the checksum filters on. CheckedDITest creates a DataInputStream and a DataOutputStream and uses the checksum filter on those, as in the following code:

```
cis = new CheckedDataInput(new DataInputStream(
    new FileInputStream("farrago.txt")), inChecker);
cos = new CheckedDataOutput(new DataOutputStream(
    new FileOutputStream("outagain.txt")), outChecker);
```

CheckedRAFTest creates two RandomAccessFile objects, one for reading and one for writing, and uses the checksum filter on those:

```
cis = new CheckedDataInput(
    new RandomAccessFile("farrago.txt", "r"), inChecker);
cos = new CheckedDataOutput(
    new RandomAccessFile("outagain.txt", "rw"), outChecker);
```

When you run either of these programs you should see the following output:

```
Input stream check sum: 736868089
Output stream check sum: 736868089
```

End of Trail

YOU'VE reached the end of the **Using the Core Java Classes** trail. Take a break—have a cup of steaming hot java.

What Next?

Once you've caught your breath, you have several choices of where to go next. You can go back to the **Trail Map** (page xv) to see all of your choices, or you can go directly to one of the following popular trails:

Writing Applets (page 145): This is the starting point for learning everything about writing applets.

Creating a User Interface (page 357): Once you know how to create applications or applets, follow this trail to learn how to create their user interfaces.

Custom Networking and Security (page 483): If you're interested in writing applications or applets that use the network, follow this trail. You'll learn about URLs, sockets, datagrams, and security.

Creating a User Interface

THIS trail covers everything you need to know about creating a user interface (UI) for a Java p rogram.

Note: All the material covered in this trail applies to both applets and applications, except for a few clearly marked exceptions.

Overview of the Java UI (page 361) tells you about the pieces the Java environment provides for building UIs. It introduces you to the graphical UI components and other UI-related classes provided by the Java environment. It also gives an overview of how programs display themselves and how they handle events such as mouse clicks. You should fully understand the information in this lesson before going on to other lessons in this trail.

Using Components, the GUI Building Blocks (page 379) tells you how to use each of the standard UI components and how to implement a custom component. It also discusses details of the component architecture and solutions to common component problems.

Laying Out Components Within a Container (page 415) tells you how to choose a layout manager, how to use each of the layout manager classes provided by the Java environment, how to use absolute positioning instead of a layout manager, and how to create your own layout manager. It also discusses solutions to common layout problems.

Working with Graphics (page 437) tells you how to do everything from drawing lines and text to loading, displaying, and manipulating images. It includes information on performing animation and on improving graphics performance.

A Note about the Examples: Most of the example programs in this chapter are applets. This lets you easily run them just by visiting the relevant pages in the online tutorial. But don't let the fact that the examples are applets confuse you—writing an application with a GUI is similar to writing an applet with a GUI. See page 413 for information on converting an applet into an application.

17

Overview of the Java UI

THIS lesson gives an overview of what the Java environment provides to help you create a user interface (UI). *UI* is a broad term that refers to all sorts of communication between a program and its users. UI is not only what the user sees, but what the user hears and feels. Even the speed with which a program interacts with the user is an important part of the program's UI.

The Java environment provides classes for the following UI functionality:

Presenting a graphical UI (GUI)

This is the preferred UI for most Java programs. This trail concentrates on this topic.

Playing sounds

Right now, applets can play sounds but applications can't, at least not in a portable way. See <u>Playing Sounds</u> (page 172) for information on playing sounds in applets.

Getting configuration information

Users can specify configuration information to the applet using *command-line arguments* (applications only) and *parameters* (applets only). For information about command-line arguments, see <u>Command-Line Arguments</u> (page 230). For information about parameters, see <u>Defining and Using Applet Parameters</u> (page 175).

Saving user preferences using properties

For information that applications need to save even when they're not running, you can use *properties*. Applets usually can't write properties to the local file system, due to security restrictions. For information on using properties, see <u>Setting Up and Using Properties</u> (page 228).

Getting and displaying text using the standard input, output, and error streams

Standard input, output, and error are the old-fashioned ways to present a user interface. They're still useful for testing and debugging programs, as well as for functionality that's not aimed at the typical end user. See <u>The Standard I/O Streams</u> (page 240) for information on using standard input, output, and error.

Applets and applications often present information to the user and invite the user's interaction using a GUI. The part of the Java environment called the Abstract Window Toolkit (AWT) contains a complete set of classes for writing GUI programs.

The AWT provides many standard GUI components such as buttons, lists, menus, and text areas. It also includes containers (such as windows and menu bars) and higher level components (such as a dialog for opening or saving files). <u>AWT Components</u> (page 362) introduces you to all these AWT-provided components.

Other classes in the AWT include those for working with graphics contexts (including basic drawing operations), images, events, fonts, and colors. Another important group of AWT classes are the layout managers, which manage the size and position of components. <u>Other AWT Classes</u> (page 365) discusses all the AWT interfaces and classes that aren't components.

The AWT provides a framework for drawing and event handling. <u>The Anatomy of a GUI-Based Program</u> (page 366) explains the AWT architecture by taking you through a program that has a GUI.

AWT Components

The program in the following figure illustrates the graphical UI (GUI) components that the AWT provides. With the exception of menus, every GUI component is implemented with a subclass of the AWT <u>Component</u>[1] class.

Implementation Note: The applet is implemented as a button that brings up the window showing the components. The window is necessary because the program includes a menu, and menus can only be used in windows. If you're curious, look at the source code (page 675) for the window that displays the components. The program has a `main` method so it can run as an application. The `AppletButton` class (page 671) provides an applet framework for the window. `AppletButton` is a highly configurable applet that's discussed in the following sections: <u>Deciding Which Parameters to Support</u> (page 175) and <u>Writing the Code to Support Parameters</u> (page 177).

---

[1]· http://java.sun.com/products/JDK/CurrentRelease/api/java.awt.Component.html

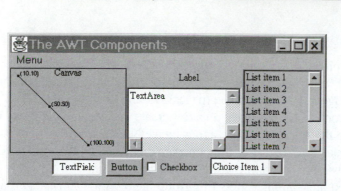

http://java.sun.com/Series/Tutorial/ui/overview/components.html

The Basic Controls: Buttons, Checkboxes, Choices, Lists, Menus, and Text Fields

The Button (page 383), Checkbox (page 387), Choice (page 389), List (page 396), MenuItem (page 399), and TextField (page 407) classes provide basic controls. These are the most common ways that users give instructions to Java programs. When a user activates one of these controls—by clicking a button or by pressing Return in a text field, for example—it posts an *action event*. An object that contains the control can react to the event by implementing the action method.

Other Ways of Getting User Input: Sliders, Scrollbars, and Text Areas

When the basic controls aren't appropriate, you can use the Scrollbar (page 404) and TextArea (page 407) classes to get user input. The Scrollbar class is used for both slider and scrollbar functionality. The Anatomy of a GUI-Based Program (page 366) contains an example of sliders. You can see scrollbars in the list and text areas of the example program pictured above.

The TextArea class provides an area to display or allow editing of several lines of text. As you can see from the example program pictured above, text areas automatically include scrollbars.

Creating Custom Components: Canvases

The Canvas (page 385) class lets you write custom components. With your Canvas subclass, you can draw custom graphics to the screen— in a paint program, image processor, or game, for example—and implement any kind of event handling.

Labels

A Label (page 395) object displays an unselectable line of text.

Containers: Windows and Panels

The AWT provides two types of containers, both implemented as subclasses of the `Container`[1] class (which is a `Component` subclass). The `Window` subclasses—`Dialog` (page 391), `FileDialog` (page 391), and `Frame` (page 393)—provide windows to contain components. `Frames` create normal, full-fledged windows, as opposed to the windows that `Dialogs` create, which are dependent on `Frames` and can be modal. `Panels` group components within an area of an existing window.

The example program pictured on page 363 uses a `Panel` to group the label and the text area, another `Panel` to group them with a canvas, and a third `Panel` to group the text field, button, checkbox, and pop-up list of choices. All these `Panels` are grouped by a `Frame` object, which presents the window they're displayed in. The `Frame` also holds a menu and and a list.

When you select the File dialog... item in the menu, the program creates a `FileDialog` object, which is a `Dialog` that can be either an Open or a Save dialog.

Browser Note: Some browsers might not implement the `FileDialog` class if they never allow applets to read or write of files on the local file system. Instead of seeing a file dialog, you'll see an error message in the standard output or error stream. See Displaying Diagnostics to the Standard Output and Error Streams (page 182) for information about applets' standard output.

Here is a picture of the `FileDialog` window that the Solaris Applet Viewer brings up:

Summary

This section presented a whirlwind tour of the AWT components. Every component mentioned in this section is described in detail in **Using Components, the GUI Building Blocks** (page 379).

---

[1] http://java.sun.com/products/JDK/CurrentRelease/api/java.awt.Container.html

Other AWT Classes

The AWT contains more than components. It contains a variety of classes related to drawing and event handling. This section discusses the AWT classes that are in the `java.awt` package. The AWT contains two other packages, `java.awt.image` and `java.awt.peer`, that most programs don't have to use. The classes and interfaces in those packages are discussed where necessary elsewhere in this trail.

As you learned on the previous page, components are grouped into containers. What the previous section didn't tell you is that each container uses a *layout manager* to control the on-screen size and position of the components it contains. The `java.awt` package supplies several layout manager classes. You'll learn all about layout managers in the lesson **Laying Out Components Within a Container** (page 415).

The `java.awt` package supplies several classes to represent sizes and shapes. One is the `Dimension` class, which specifies the size of a rectangular area. Another is the `Insets` class, which is usually used to specify how much padding should exist between the outside edges of a container and the container's display area. Shape classes include `Point`, `Rectangle`, and `Polygon`.

The `Color` class is useful for representing and manipulating colors. It defines constants for commonly used colors, for example, `Color.black`. While it generally uses colors in RGB (red-green-blue) format, it also understands HSB (hue-saturation-brightness) format.

The `Image` class provides a way to represent image data. Applets can get Image objects for GIF and JPEG images using the `Applet getImage` methods. Programs that are not applets get images using a different helper class: `Toolkit`. The `Toolkit` class provides a platform-independent interface to the platform-dependent implementation of the AWT. Although that sounds impressive, most programs don't deal with `Toolkit` objects directly, except to get images. Images are loaded asynchronously—you can have a valid `Image` object even if the image data hasn't been loaded yet or doesn't exist. Using a `MediaTracker` object, you can keep track of the status of the image loading. `MediaTracker` currently works only with images, but eventually it will work with other media types, such as sounds. Using Images (page 449) describes how to work with images.

To control the look of the text your program draws, use `Font` and `FontMetrics` objects. The `Font` class lets you get basic information about fonts and create objects representing various fonts. With a `FontMetrics` object, you can get detailed information about the size characteristics of a particular font. You can set the font used by a component using the `Component` and `Graphics setFont` methods. Working with Text (page 445) tells you more about using fonts.

Finally, the `Graphics` and `Event` classes are crucial to the AWT drawing and event-handling system. A `Graphics` object represents a drawing context—with-

out a `Graphics` object, no program can draw to the screen. An `Event` object represents a user action, such as a mouse click. You'll learn more about `Graphics` and `Event` objects later in this lesson.

The Anatomy of a GUI-Based Program

This section and the ones that follow pick apart a Java program that has a graphical UI, explaining:

- The classes the program uses
- The program's hierarchy of components
- How components draw themselves
- How events propagate through the hierarchy

The program, which is called Converter, converts distance measurements between metric and U.S. units. If you'd like to look at the complete program, you can find it on page 678. We do *not* expect you to fully understand the source code without reading the rest of this lesson and the relevant pages in the **Using Components, the GUI Building Blocks** (page 379) and **Laying Out Components Within a Container** (page 415) lessons. The following figure shows the program.

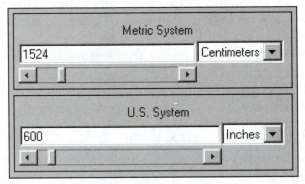

http://java.sun.com/Series/Tutorial/ui/overview/anatomy.html

The Converter program defines three classes and creates instances of several classes that the AWT provides. It defines an `Applet` subclass so that it can run as an applet. It creates `Component` objects to provide basic controls so that the user can interact with it. Using containers and layout managers, it groups the components. <u>Classes in the Example Program</u> (page 367) describes all the classes that the Converter program uses.

The components in the Converter program are arranged in a hierarchy, with containers defining the structure of the hierarchy. <u>The Component Hierarchy</u> (page 368) describes how component hierarchies work, as well as the specific hierarchy of the Converter program.

The <u>Drawing</u> section (page 371) describes how components get drawn and how to perform custom drawing.

User actions result in events, which are passed up the component hierarchy until an object responds to the event. <u>Event Handling</u> (page 373) describes in detail how event handling works, and how the Converter program handles events.

Classes in the Example Program

The <u>Converter program</u> (page 678) defines three classes that inherit from AWT classes. It also defines a data-storing class. However, most of the objects in the program are instances of AWT classes.

The following figure shows the Converter program's GUI. Each visible feature is labeled with the class that implements the feature. For example, the `Converter` class implements the object that draws the external box, and which contains every component in the program's GUI. The `Converter` class also happens to implement many features that aren't visible in the snapshot, such as the `main` method that allows the program to run as an application.

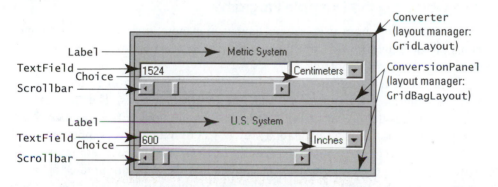

This section tells you about every object the program creates. Don't worry—we don't expect you to understand everything yet. We just want to convey to you the kinds of objects a GUI program might use.

Classes Defined in the Example Program

The Converter program defines two `Panel` subclasses (`Converter` and `ConversionPanel`), a `Frame` subclass (`MainFrame`) and a simple class named `Unit`.

The `Converter` class is the heart of the Converter program. It contains the program's `main` method, which is called if the program is run as an application. The `Converter` class also contains initialization and startup code, which is called either by the `main` method or by the application that loads that program as an applet. The `Converter` class actually extends the `Applet` class (which itself extends `Panel`), instead of directly extending `Panel`. This is necessary because

all applets must contain an `Applet` subclass. However, since the Converter program can also run as an application, the `Converter` class cannot use any functionality provided by the `Applet` class. In other words, the `Converter` class must be implemented as if it extends `Panel`.

The `ConversionPanel` class provides a way to group all the controls that describe a particular set of distance measurements. The Converter program creates two `ConversionPanel` objects, one for metric distance measurements, and the other for U.S. distance measurements.

The `MainFrame` class is used only if the program is run as an application. `MainFrame` supplies a window to contain the `Converter` object. If the Converter program is run as an applet, `MainFrame` is unnecessary because the application that runs the applet provides a window for the applet. `MainFrame` is a very simple `Frame` subclass. The only functionality it adds to `Frame` is to detect when the user has asked that the window be closed, and to respond by making the application exit.

The `Unit` class provides objects that group a description (such as "Centimeters") with a multiplier that indicates the number of units per meter (0.01, for example).

AWT Objects in the Example Program

The Converter program uses several layout managers, containers, and components provided by the AWT package. It also creates two `Insets` objects and two `GridBagConstraints` objects.

The Converter program creates three objects that conform to the `LayoutManager` interface: a `GridLayout` and two `GridBagLayouts`. The `GridLayout` object manages the layout of the components in the `Converter` instance. Each `ConversionPanel` uses a `GridBagLayout` object to manage its components, and a `GridBagConstraints` object to specify how to lay out each component. In addition, if the program is run as an application, the program creates a `MainFrame` object (the application's window) that is automatically initialized to use the default layout manager for windows: a `BorderLayout` object.

All the components in the Converter program that are not containers are created by `ConversionPanel`. Each `ConversionPanel` contains one instance each of the AWT `Label`, `Choice`, `TextField`, and `Scrollbar` classes.

Both the `Converter` and the `ConversionPanel` classes create `Insets` instances that specify the padding that should appear around their on-screen representations.

The Component Hierarchy

Here again is the figure that labels every component used in the Converter program.

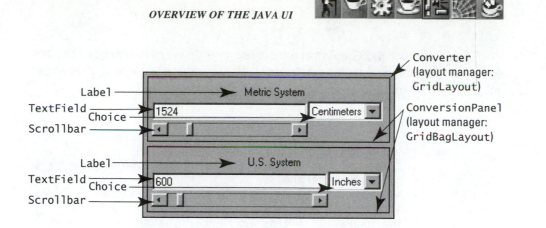

The Converter program has several levels in its component hierarchy. The parent of each level is a Container (which inherits from Component). Below is a figure of the hierarchy.

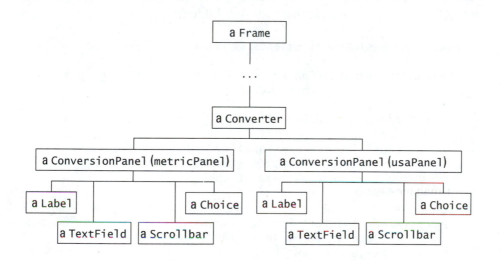

Explanation

At the top of the hierarchy is the window (Frame object) that displays the program. When the Converter program runs as an application, the Frame is a MainFrame instance created in the program's main method. When the program runs as an applet within a browser, the Frame is the browser window.

Under the Frame is a Converter object, which inherits from Applet and thus is a Container (specifically, a Panel). Depending on which viewer the applet is displayed in, one or more Container objects might be between the Converter object and the Frame at the top of the component hierarchy.

Directly under the Converter object are two ConversionPanels. The following code puts them under the Converter, using the add method. Converter inherits the add method from the Container class.

```java
public class Converter extends Applet {
    . . .
    public void init() {
        ...//Create metricPanel and usaPanel, two
            //ConversionPanels.
        //Add metricPanel to this Converter instance:
        add(metricPanel);
        //Add usaPanel to this Converter instance:
        add(usaPanel);
        . . .
    }
}
```

Each ConversionPanel has four children: a Label, a TextField, a Scrollbar, and a Choice. Here's the code that adds the children:

```java
class ConversionPanel extends Panel {
    . . .
    ConversionPanel(Converter myController, String myTitle,
                    Unit myUnits[]) {
        . . .
        //Add the label.  It displays this panel's title,
        //centered.
        Label label = new Label(myTitle, Label.CENTER);
        ...//Set up GridBagConstraints for this Component.
        gridbag.setConstraints(label, c);
        add(label);

        //Add the text field.  It initially displays "0" and
        //needs to be at least 10 columns wide.
        textField = new TextField("0", 10);
        ...//Set up GridBagConstraints for this Component.
        gridbag.setConstraints(textField, c);
        add(textField);

        //Add the pop-up list (Choice).
        unitChooser = new Choice();
        ...//Populate it with items.
        ...//Set up GridBagConstraints for this Component.
        gridbag.setConstraints(unitChooser, c);
        add(unitChooser);

        //Add the slider.  It's horizontal, its initial value
        //is 0,
        //a click increments the value by 100 pixels, and it
        //has the minimum and maximum values specified by
        //the instance variables min and max.
```

```
        slider = new Scrollbar(Scrollbar.HORIZONTAL, 0, 100,
                                min, max);
        ...//Set up GridBagConstraints for this Component.
        gridbag.setConstraints(slider, c);
        add(slider);
    }
```

GridBagConstraints is an object that tells the GridBagLayout (the layout manager for each ConversionPanel) how to place a particular component. GridBagLayout, along with the other AWT layout managers, is discussed in **Laying Out Components Within a Container** (page 415).

Summary

The Converter program's component hierarchy contains eight non-container components—components that present the graphical UI of the program. These are the labels, text fields, choices, and scrollbars the program displays. There might be additional components such as window controls under the Frame.

This program's component hierarchy has at least four containers—a Frame object (window), a Converter object (a custom kind of Panel), and two ConversionPanel objects (instances of other custom Panel).

Note that if we add a window—for example, a Frame that contains a Converter instance that handles volume conversion—the new window will have its own component hierarchy, unattached to the hierarchy this lesson presents.

Drawing

When a Java program with a GUI needs to draw itself—whether for the first time, or in response to becoming unhidden, or because its appearance needs to change to reflect something happening inside the program—the drawing is orchestrated by the AWT drawing system.

Here, as a reminder, is the component hierarchy for the Converter program:

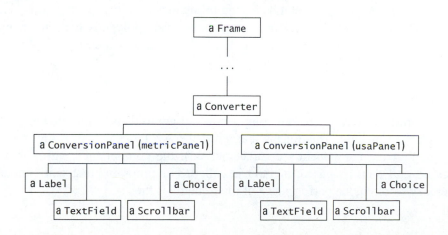

The component hierarchy affects the components' positions and sizes. Specifically, the container that a component is in helps determine the component's size and position, subject to the container's layout manager and the space allotted to the container.

The component hierarchy does *not*, however, guarantee the order of drawing. For example, redrawing a container doesn't guarantee that its children will be redrawn.

How Drawing Requests Occur

Programs can draw only when the AWT tells them to. This restriction exists because each occurrence of a component drawing itself must execute without interruption. Otherwise, unpredictable results could occur, such as a button being drawn halfway and then being interrupted by some lengthy animation. The AWT orders drawing requests by making them run in a single thread. Programs use the `Component` `repaint` method to request that a component be scheduled for drawing.

The only components you need to invoke the `repaint` method on are custom components—instances of `Canvas`, `Panel`, or `Applet` subclasses that implement custom drawing code. You don't need to invoke `repaint` on standard AWT components, such as buttons and text fields, since they're painted automatically by platform-dependent code.

The AWT responds to a repaint request by invoking the specified component's `update` method. The default (`Component`) implementation of the `update` method simply clears the component's background (drawing a rectangle over the component's clipping area in the component's background color) and then calling the component's `paint` method. The default implementation of the `paint` method does nothing.

The Graphics Object

The only argument to the `paint` and `update` methods is a `Graphics` object that represents the context in which the component can perform its drawing. The `Graphics` class provides methods for the following:

- Drawing and filling rectangles, arcs, lines, ovals, polygons, text, and images
- Getting or setting the current color, font, or clipping area
- Setting the paint mode

How to Draw

The simplest way for a custom component to draw itself is to put drawing code in its `paint` method. This means that when the AWT makes a drawing request (by calling the component's `update` method), the component's entire area is cleared and then its `paint` method is called. For programs that don't repaint themselves often, the performance of this scheme is fine.

Important: The `paint` and `update` methods must execute very quickly! Otherwise, they'll destroy the perceived performance of your program. If you need to perform some lengthy operation as the result of a paint request, do it by starting up another thread (or somehow sending a request to another thread) to perform the operation. For help on using threads, see **Threads of Control** (page 285).

The following example implements the `paint` method. Both the `Converter` and `ConversionPanel` classes draw a box around their area using this code. Both classes also implement an `insets` method that specifies the padding around the panels' contents. If they didn't have this method, the box drawn in the `paint` method would overlap the external boundaries of the panels' contents.

```
public void paint(Graphics g) {
    Dimension d = size;
    g.drawRect(0,0, d.width - 1, d.height - 1);
}
```

Programs that repaint themselves often can use two techniques to improve their performance: implementing both `update` and `paint`, and using double buffering. These techniques are discussed in Eliminating Flashing (page 469).

For more information on how to draw, see the **Working with Graphics** lesson (page 437).

Event Handling

When the user acts on a component—clicking it or pressing the Return key, for example—the AWT's platform-specific code detects the event and generates an `Event` object. The AWT event-handling system passes the `Event` up the component hierarchy, giving each component a chance to react to the event before the platform-dependent code that implements the component fully processes it.

Each component's event handler can react to an event in any of the following ways:

- By ignoring the event and allowing it to be passed up the component hierarchy. This is what the default `Component` implementation does. For example, since the `TextField` class and its `TextComponent` superclass implement no event handlers, `TextField` objects get the default `Component` implementation. So when a `TextField` receives an `Event`, it ignores it and allows its container to handle it.
- By modifying the `Event` instance before it goes further up the hierarchy. For example, a `TextField` subclass that displays all letters in uppercase might react to the keypress of a lowercase letter by changing the `Event` to contain the uppercase version of the letter.

- By reacting in some other way to the event. For example, a `TextField` subclass (or a `TextField`'s container) could react to a Return keypress by calling a method that processes the text field's contents.
- By intercepting the event, stopping it from being processed further. For example, if an invalid character is entered in a text field, an event handler could simply stop the resulting `Event` from propagating upward. As a result, the platform-dependent implementation of the text field would never see the event.

From a component's view, the AWT event-handling system is more like an event-*filtering* system. Platform-dependent code generates an event, but components get a chance to modify, react to, or intercept the event before the platform-dependent code fully processes the event. The following figure shows the chain of event handling for a `TextField` event in the <u>Converter program</u> (page 678).

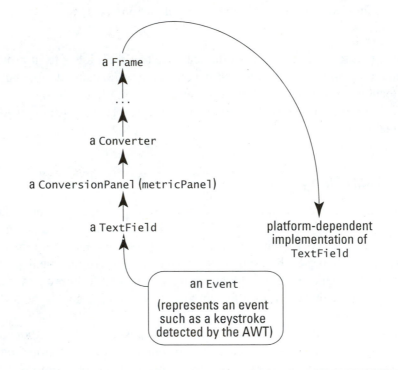

Note: As of press time, mouse events are forwarded to components *after* the platform-dependent code has fully processed the event. So although components can intercept all *keyboard* events the AWT detects, they can't currently intercept *mouse* events.

Although the AWT defines a wide variety of `Event` types, the AWT doesn't see every event that occurs. As a result, not every user action becomes an `Event`. The AWT can see only those events that the platform-dependent code allows it to see. For example, Motif text fields don't forward mouse move events to the AWT. For this reason, `TextField` subclasses or containers can't rely on getting mouse move events—on Solaris, at least, they simply have no way of knowing that the event has occurred, since they don't receive an `Event` when the mouse moves.

If you want access to a wide range of event types, you might need to implement a `Canvas` subclass, since the platform-dependent implementation of `Canvas` forwards all events. Besides `Canvas`, the general-purpose `Container` classes—`Panel`, `Applet`, `Dialog`, and `Frame`—also forward all events.

The Event Object

Each event that the AWT detects—mouse click, key press, and so on—results in the creation of an <u>Event</u>[1] object. An `Event` object includes the following information:

- The type of the event— for example, a keypress or mouse click, or a more abstract event such as an action or window iconification.
- The object that was the target of the event— for example, the `Button` corresponding to the on-screen button the user clicked, or the `TextField` corresponding to the field that user just typed in.
- A timestamp indicating when the event occurred.
- The (x,y) location where the event occurred. This location is relative to the origin of the component whose event handler this `Event` is passed into.
- The key that was pressed (for keyboard events).
- An arbitrary argument, such as the string displayed on the component, associated with the `Event`.
- The state of modifier keys, such as Shift and Control, when the event occurred.

How to Implement an Event Handler

The `Component` class defines many event-handling methods, and you can override any of them. Except for one all-purpose method, `handleEvent`, each event-handling method can be used for only one particular type of event. We recommend that you avoid the all-purpose method if possible, and instead override the method that is specific to the type of event you need to handle. This approach tends to have fewer unintended side effects.

The `Component` class defines the following methods for responding to events. The event types that each method handles are listed after the method name:

- `action` (Event.ACTION_EVENT)
- `mouseEnter` (Event.MOUSE_ENTER)
- `mouseExit` (Event.MOUSE_EXIT)
- `mouseMove` (Event.MOUSE_MOVE)

---

[1] http://java.sun.com/products/JDK/CurrentRelease/api/java.awt.Event.html

- mouseDown (Event.MOUSE_DOWN)
- mouseDrag (Event.MOUSE_DRAG)
- mouseUp (Event.MOUSE_UP)
- keyDown (Event.KEY_PRESS or Event.KEY_ACTION)
- keyUp (Event.KEY_RELEASE or Event.KEY_ACTION_RELEASE)
- gotFocus (Event.GOT_FOCUS)
- lostFocus (Event.LOST_FOCUS)
- handleEvent (all event types)

When an event occurs, the event-handling method that matches the event type is called. Specifically, the Event is first passed to the handleEvent method, which, in the default implementation of handleEvent, calls the appropriate method for the event type.

The action method is an especially important event-handling method. Only basic control components—Button, Checkbox, Choice, List, MenuItem, and TextField objects—produce action events. They do so when the user indicates somehow that the control should perform an action. For example, when the user clicks a button, an action event is generated. By implementing the action method, you can react to user actions on controls without worrying about the low-level events, such as key presses and mouse clicks, that caused the action.

All the event-handling methods have at least one argument (the Event) and return a boolean value. The return value indicates whether the method completely handled the event. By returning false, the event handler indicates that the event should continue to be passed up the component hierarchy. By returning true, the event handler indicates that the event should not be forwarded any further. The handleEvent method should almost always return super.handleEvent, to ensure that all events are forwarded to the appropriate event-specific method.

Important: Like drawing methods, all event-handler methods must execute quickly! Otherwise, they'll destroy the perceived performance of your program. If you need to perform some lengthy operation as the result of an event, do it by starting up another thread (or sending a request to another thread) to perform the operation. For help on using threads, see **Threads of Control** (page 285).

In the Converter program, all the event handling is performed by the ConversionPanel objects. They use the action method to catch events resulting from user actions on the text field (TextField) and pop-up list (Choice). To catch events resulting from user actions on the slider (Scrollbar), they must use the handleEvent method, since Scrollbars don't produce action events and Component doesn't define any methods specific to Scrollbar events.

Here is the ConversionPanel implementation of the action and handleEvent methods:

```java
/** Respond to user actions on controls. */
public boolean action(Event e, Object arg) {
    if (e.target instanceof TextField) {
        setSliderValue(getValue());
        controller.convert(this);
        return true;
    }
    if (e.target instanceof Choice) {
        controller.convert(this);
        return true;
    }
    return false;
}

/** Respond to the slider. */
public boolean handleEvent(Event e) {
    if (e.target instanceof Scrollbar) {
        textField.setText(String.valueOf(slider.getValue()));
        controller.convert(this);
    }
    return super.handleEvent(e);
}
```

The methods simply make sure that the `ConversionPanel`'s slider and text field both show the same value, and then ask the `Converter` object to update the other `ConversionPanel`. The `action` method returns `true` if it handled the event. This stops the event from unnecessarily traveling further up the component hierarchy. If the `action` method cannot handle the event, it returns `false`, so the containers higher up in the component hierarchy can look at the event. The `handleEvent` method always returns `super.handleEvent` so that every event will be fully processed.

A Note about the `action` Method: Action events are high-level events. They are caused by one or more low-level events such as key and mouse presses. For this reason, it's OK to return `true` to stop action events from travelling up the component hierarchy after you've handled them. The platform-specific code has already handled the key or mouse events that triggered the action, so it doesn't need to see the action event.

Note: If `handleEvent` returned `true` or `false` instead of calling its superclass's implementation, the `action` method would *never* be called. Risks like this are part of the reason why we advise you to avoid implementing `handleEvent` unless it's absolutely necessary.

The Keyboard Focus

Many components—even those primarily operated with the mouse, such as buttons—can be operated by the keyboard. For a keypress to affect a component, the component must have the *keyboard focus*.

At any given time, at most one window and one component in that window can have the keyboard focus. How windows get the keyboard focus is system dependent. However, once a window has the focus, you can use the `Component` `requestFocus` method to request that a component get the focus.

When a component gets the focus, its `gotFocus` method is called. When a component loses the focus, its `lostFocus` method is called.

18

Using Components, the GUI Building Blocks

THIS lesson describes every component the AWT offers, including the Canvas class, which you can use to build your own custom components. This lesson also describes the AWT component architecture, and solutions to common component problems.

Start at Using the AWT Components (page 379) to learn the general rules of using components, as well as details on how to use each component the AWT provides.

Just before a component is first drawn to the screen, its peer is created. A *peer* is an object that provides the look (and part of the feel) for standard components. You usually don't need to know about peer objects, since they're specific to platform implementations. However, sometimes knowing about peers can help you find bugs in event-handling or drawing code. Details of the Component Architecture (page 410) tells you about peers.

The section on Common Component Problems (and Their Solutions) (page 412) identifies some of the problems you might encounter while using components. For each problem, this section describes several possible solutions.

Using the AWT Components

The following figures show the inheritance hierarchies for all the AWT component classes.

As the figures show, all components except for menu-related components inherit from the AWT Component class. Because of cross-platform restrictions

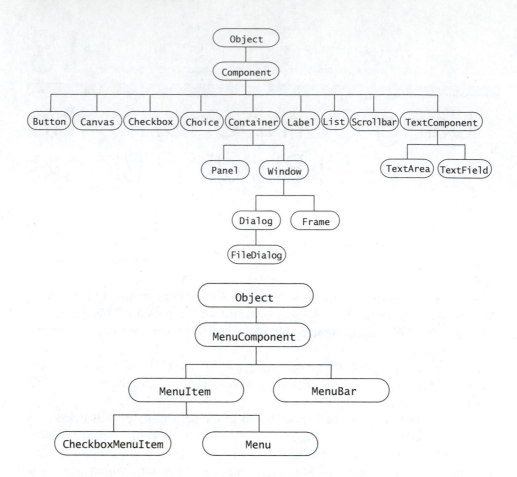

such as the inability to set menu background colors, menu-related components aren't full-blown `Component` objects. Instead, menu components inherit from the AWT `MenuComponent` class.

General Rules for Using Components (page 381) tells you what the `Component` class provides and how you can customize components.

The next few sections tells you how to use the components that the AWT provides. Each kind of component has its own section:

General Rules for Using Components

This section describes what components have in common. It tells you how to add a component to a container. It tells you what functionality components inherit from the `Component` class. It also tells you how you can change the look and feel of components.

How to Add a Component to a Container

As you read on in this lesson, you'll notice code that adds components to containers. This is because for any `Component` object except a `Window` to display itself on screen, you must first add it to a `Container` object. This `Container` is itself a `Component`, and is likely to be added to another `Container`. `Window`s such as `Frame`s and `Dialog`s are the top-level containers; they're the only components that aren't added to containers.

The `Container`[1] class defines three methods for adding components: a one-argument add method and two two-argument add methods. Which one you need to use depends on the layout manager the container is using. You'll learn all about layout managers in a later lesson. Right now, we're teaching you just enough to be able to read the code excerpts in this lesson.

The one-argument add method simply requires that you specify the component to add. The first two-argument add method lets you add an argument specifying the integer position at which the component should be added. The integer -1 specifies that the container add the component at the end of the container's list of components, just as the one-argument method does. This two-argument form of add isn't used often, so if you see references to "the two-argument add method", they're almost certainly referring to the second two-argument method, which is described in the next paragraph. The `FlowLayout` (page 422), `GridLayout` (page 423), and `GridBagLayout` (page 424) layout managers all work with the one-argument and first two-argument add methods.

The first argument of the second two-argument add method is a manager-dependent string. `BorderLayout` (page 419), the default layout manager for `Window` subclasses, requires that you specify "North," "South," "East," "West,"

---
1. http://java.sun.com/products/JDK/CurrentRelease/api/java.awt.Container.html

or "Center." <u>CardLayout</u> (page 420) simply requires that you specify a string that somehow identifies the component being added. The second argument to this add method specifies the component to be added.

Note: Adding a component to a container removes the component from the container it used to be in (if any). For this reason, you can't have one component in two containers, even if the two containers are never shown at the same time.

What the Component Class Provides

All components except menus are implemented as subclasses of the <u>Component</u>[1] class. From Component, they inherit a huge amount of functionality. By now, you should know that the Component class provides the basis for all drawing and event handling. Here's a more complete list of the functionality that the Component class provides:

Basic drawing support

Component provides the `paint`, `update`, and `repaint` methods, which enable custom components to draw themselves on screen. See <u>Drawing</u> (page 371) for more information.

Event handling

Component defines the general-purpose `handleEvent` method and a group of methods such as `action` that handle specific event types. Component also has support for keyboard focus, which enables keyboard control of components. See <u>Event Handling</u> (page 373) for more information.

Appearance control: font

Component provides methods to get and set the current font, and to get information about the current font. See <u>Working with Text</u> (page 445) for information.

Appearance control: color

Component provides the following methods to get and set the foreground and background colors: `setForeground(Color)`, `getForeground`, `setBackground(Color)`, and `getBackground`. The foreground color is the color used for all text in the component, as well as for any custom drawing the component performs. The background color is the color behind the text or graphics. For the sake of readability, the background color should contrast with the foreground color.

Image handling

Component provides the basis for displaying images. Note that most components can't display images, since their appearance is implemented in platform-specific code. Canvas objects and most Container objects, however,

---

[1] http://java.sun.com/products/JDK/CurrentRelease/api/java.awt.Component.html

can display images. See <u>Using Images</u> (page 449) for information on working with images.

On-screen size and position control

All component sizes and positions (except for those of `Windows`) are subject to the whims of layout managers. Nonetheless, every component has at least some say in its size, if not its position. The `preferredSize` and `minimum-Size` methods allow a component to inform a layout manager of the component's preferred and minimum sizes. `Component` also provides methods that get or set (subject to layout manager oversight) the component's current size and location. Finally, the `Component` `show` and `hide` methods determine whether the component is visible on screen.

How to Change the Appearance and Behavior of Components.

The appearance of most components is platform-specific. Buttons look different on Motif systems than on MacOS systems, for example. The following figure shows first a Motif button and then its MacOS equivalent.

You can't easily change most components' appearance in any major way. You can make some minor appearance changes, such as changing the font and the background color, by using the appearance-affecting methods and variables provided by a component's class and superclasses. However, you can't completely change a standard component's appearance, since its platform-specific implementation overrides any drawing the component performs. To change a component's appearance, you must implement a `Canvas` subclass that has the look you want but the behavior that users expect from the component.

Although you can't easily make a major change to a component's appearance, you *can* change component behavior. For example, you can implement a `TextField` subclass that accepts only numeric values. This subclass might examine all keyboard events, intercepting any that aren't valid. This is possible because the platform-independent `Component` object gets to process raw events before its platform-dependent implementation does. See <u>Event Handling</u> (page 373) for details.

How to Use Buttons

The <u>Button</u>[1] class provides a default button implementation. A button is a simple control that generates an action event when the user clicks it.

[1.] http://java.sun.com/products/JDK/CurrentRelease/api/java.awt.Button.html

The on-screen appearance of Buttons depends on the platform they're running on and on whether the button is enabled. If you want your program's buttons to look the same for every platform or to otherwise have a special look, you should create a Canvas (page 385) subclass to implement this look; you can't change the look using a Button subclass. The only facets of a Button's appearance that you can change without creating your own class are the font and text it displays, its foreground and background colors, and (by enabling or disabling the button) whether the button looks enabled or disabled.

The applet in the following figure displays three buttons. When you click the left button, it disables the middle button (and itself, since it's no longer useful) and enables the right button. When you click the right button, it enables the middle button and the left button, and disables itself.

http://java.sun.com/Series/Tutorial/ui/components/button.html

The following code creates the buttons and reacts to button clicks. You can find the complete program on page 684.

```
//In initialization code:
    b1 = new Button();
    b1.setLabel("Disable middle button");

    b2 = new Button("Middle button");

    b3 = new Button("Enable middle button");
    b3.disable();
    . . .

public boolean action(Event e, Object arg) {
    Object target = e.target;

    if (target == b1) { //They clicked "Disable middle button"
        b2.disable();
        b1.disable();
        b3.enable();
        return true;
    }
    if (target == b3) { //They clicked "Enable middle button"
        b2.enable();
        b1.enable();
        b3.disable();
```

```
        return true;
    }
    return false;
}
```

This code shows how to use all but one of the commonly used `Button` methods. In addition, `Button` defines a `getLabel` method, which lets you find out what text is displayed on a particular `Button`.

How to Use Canvases

The `Canvas`[1] class exists to be subclassed. It does nothing on its own; it merely provides a way for you to implement a custom component. For example, `Canvas` objects are useful as display areas for images and custom graphics, whether or not you wish to handle events that occur within the display area.

Canvas objects are also useful when you want a control—a button, for example—that doesn't look like the default implementation of the control. Since you can't change a standard control's appearance by subclassing its corresponding `Component` (`Button`, for example), you must instead implement a `Canvas` subclass to have both the look you want and the same behavior as the default implementation of the control.

When implementing a `Canvas` subclass, take care to implement the `minimumSize` and `preferredSize` methods to properly reflect your canvas's size. Otherwise, depending on the layout your canvas's container uses, your canvas could end up too small, perhaps even invisible.

Also take care that the `Canvas` is repainted whenever its appearance should change. You can do this either by calling the `repaint` method in the `Canvas` subclass or by invoking `repaint` on the `Canvas` object from another object in the same program.

On p. 386 is an applet that uses two instances of a `Canvas` subclass: `ImageCanvas`.

On p. 386 is the code for `ImageCanvas`. (You can find the complete program on page 730.) Because image data is downloaded asynchronously, an `ImageCanvas` doesn't know how big it should be until some time after it's created. For this reason, `ImageCanvas` uses the initial width and height suggested by its creator until the image size data is available. When the image size data becomes available, the `ImageCanvas` changes the size that its `preferredSize` and `minimumSize` methods return, attempts to resize itself, and then requests that its top-level container's layout be adjusted accordingly and redisplayed.

[1.] http://java.sun.com/products/JDK/CurrentRelease/api/java.awt.Canvas.html

http://java.sun.com/Series/Tutorial/ui/components/canvas.html

```
class ImageCanvas extends Canvas {
    Container pappy;
    Image image;
    boolean trueSizeKnown = false;
    Dimension minSize;
    int w, h;

    public ImageCanvas(Image image, Container parent,
                      int initialWidth, int initialHeight) {
        if (image == null) {
            System.err.println("Canvas got invalid image "
                             + "object!");
            return;
        }

        this.image = image;
        pappy = parent;

        w = initialWidth;
        h = initialHeight;

        minSize = new Dimension(w,h);
    }

    public Dimension preferredSize() {
        return minimumSize();
    }

    public synchronized Dimension minimumSize() {
        return minSize;
    }
```

```
        public void paint (Graphics g) {
            if (image != null) {
                if (!trueSizeKnown) {
                    int imageWidth = image.getWidth(this);
                    int imageHeight = image.getHeight(this);

                    if ((imageWidth > 0) && (imageHeight > 0)) {
                        trueSizeKnown = true;

                        //Component-initiated resizing.
                        w = imageWidth;
                        h = imageHeight;
                        minSize = new Dimension(w,h);
                        resize(w, h);
                        pappy.validate();
                    }
                }

                g.drawRect(0, 0, w - 1, h - 1);
                g.drawImage(image, 0, 0, this);
            }
        }
    }
```

For more information on drawing graphics, see the <u>Working with Graphics</u> lesson (page 437). For an example of implementing a `Canvas` that both draws custom graphics and handles events, see the RectangleDemo applet in <u>Drawing Shapes</u> (page 440). For another example of an image-displaying canvas, see <u>How to Use Scrollbars</u> (page 404).

How to Use Checkboxes

The <u>Checkbox</u>[1] class provides *checkboxes*—two-state buttons that can be either "on" or "off." When the user clicks a checkbox, the checkbox state changes and it generates an action event. Other ways of providing groups of items the user can select are <u>choices</u> (page 389), <u>lists</u> (page 396), and <u>menus</u> (page 399).

If you want a group of checkboxes in which only one checkbox at a time can be "on," you can add a <u>CheckboxGroup</u>[2] object to oversee the state of the checkboxes. (You might know the resulting UI elements as *radio buttons*.)

---

[1] http://java.sun.com/products/JDK/CurrentRelease/api/java.awt.Checkbox.html
[2] http://java.sun.com/products/JDK/CurrentRelease/api/java.awt.CheckboxGroup.html

The applet in the following two figures has two columns of checkboxes. On the left are three independent checkboxes. You can select all three of the checkboxes, if you like. The three checkboxes on the right are coordinated by a `CheckboxGroup` object. The `CheckboxGroup` ensures that no more than one of its checkboxes is selected at a time. To be specific, a checkbox group can come up with no checkboxes selected, but once the user selects a checkbox, exactly one of the checkboxes will be selected forever after.

Here's how the applet looks when it first comes up:

http://java.sun.com/Series/Tutorial/ui/components/checkbox.html

Here's how the applet looks after the user clicks Checkbox 1, Checkbox 2, Checkbox 2 (again), and then Checkbox 4, Checkbox 5, and Checkbox 5 (again).

http://java.sun.com/Series/Tutorial/ui/components/checkbox.html

You can find the complete program on page 687. The following code creates both groups of checkboxes. Note that only the second, mutually-exclusive group of checkboxes is controlled by a `CheckboxGroup`. Also note that for teaching purposes, this program uses all three `Checkbox` constructors.

```
Panel p1, p2;
Checkbox cb1, cb2, cb3; //These are independent checkboxes.
Checkbox cb4, cb5, cb6; //These checkboxes are part of a group.
CheckboxGroup cbg;

cb1 = new Checkbox();   //Default state is "off" (false).
cb1.setLabel("Checkbox 1");
cb2 = new Checkbox("Checkbox 2");
cb3 = new Checkbox("Checkbox 3");
cb3.setState(true);     //Set state to "on" (true).
. . .
```

```
cbg = new CheckboxGroup();
cb4 = new Checkbox("Checkbox 4", cbg, false);
//initial state: off
cb5 = new Checkbox("Checkbox 5", cbg, false);
//initial state: off
cb6 = new Checkbox("Checkbox 6", cbg, false);
//initial state: off
```

Besides the Checkbox methods shown above, Checkbox has two additional methods you might want to use: getCheckboxGroup and setCheckboxGroup. Besides the single CheckboxGroup constructor used in the code example, CheckboxGroup also defines the following methods: getCurrent and setCurrent. These methods get and set (respectively) the currently selected Checkbox.

How to Use Choices

The Choice[1] class provides a menu-like list of choices, accessed by a distinctive button. The user presses the button to bring up the "menu," and then chooses one of the items. When the user chooses an item, the Choice generates an action event.

Choice objects are useful when you need to display a number of alternatives in a limited amount of space, and the user doesn't need to see all the alternatives all the time. Another name for this UI element is *pop-up list*. Other ways of providing multiple alternatives are checkboxes (page 387), lists (page 396), and menus (page 399).

The applet in the following three figures has a Choice and a Label. When the user chooses an item from the Choice list, the Label changes to reflect the item chosen. Note that the index of the first item in the Choice is 0.

Here's what the applet looks like at first:

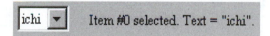

http://java.sun.com/Series/Tutorial/ui/components/choice.html

The code on page 390 creates the Choice and handles events from it. You can find the complete program on page 688. Note that the second parameter to the action method (which is the same as e.arg), is the string from the selected item.

---

[1] http://java.sun.com/products/JDK/CurrentRelease/api/java.awt.Choice.html

Here's what the applet looks like as you select another choice item ("san"):

http://java.sun.com/Series/Tutorial/ui/components/choice.html

Finally, here's what the applet looks like after "san" is selected:

http://java.sun.com/Series/Tutorial/ui/components/choice.html

```java
//...Where instance variables are defined:
Choice choice; //pop-up list of choices

//...Where initialization occurs:
choice = new Choice();
choice.addItem("ichi");
choice.addItem("ni");
choice.addItem("san");
choice.addItem("yon");
label = new Label();
setLabelText(choice.getSelectedIndex(),
             choice.getSelectedItem());

    . . .

public boolean action(Event e, Object arg) {
    if (e.target instanceof Choice) {
        setLabelText(choice.getSelectedIndex(), (String)arg);
        return true;
    }
    return false;
    }
}
```

Besides the methods used above, the `Choice` class defines these other useful methods:

`countItems()`

> Returns the number of items in the choice.

`getItem(int index)`

> Returns the `String` displayed by the item at the specified index.

`select(int index)`

> Selects the item at the specified index.

`select(String str)`

> Selects the item that is displaying the specified `String`.

How to Use Dialogs

The AWT provides support for *dialogs*—windows that are dependent on other windows—with the `Dialog`[1] class. It provides a useful subclass, `FileDialog`,[2] that provides dialogs to help the user open and save files.

The one thing that distinguishes dialogs from regular windows (which are implemented with `Frame` objects) is that a dialog is dependent on some other window (a `Frame`). When that other window is destroyed, so are its dependent dialogs. When that other window is iconified—made into an icon—its dependent dialogs disappear from the screen. When the window is returned to its normal state, its dependent dialogs return to the screen. The AWT automatically provides this behavior to you.

Because no API currently exists to let applets find the window they're running in, applets generally can't use dialogs in a supported way. The exception is that applets that bring up their own windows (`Frames`) can have dialogs dependent on those windows. For this reason, the applet in the follwoing two figures consists of a button that brings up a window that brings up a dialog.

Here's a snapshot of the window (`Frame`) the button brings up:

![Dialog Demo window showing text "The wonderful thing about tiggers / Is tiggers are wonderful things" and a button labeled "Click to bring up dialog", with "Warning: Applet Window" at the bottom.]

http://java.sun.com/Series/Tutorial/ui/components/dialog.html

---

[1.] http://java.sun.com/products/JDK/CurrentRelease/api/java.awt.Dialog.html

[2.] http://java.sun.com/products/JDK/CurrentRelease/api/java.awt.FileDialog.html

And here's a snapshot of the dialog for the window:

> **A Simple Dialog**
>
> Enter random text here: `Is tiggers are wonderful things`
>
> [Cancel] [Set]
>
> Warning: Applet Window

http://java.sun.com/Series/Tutorial/ui/components/dialog.html

Dialogs can be *modal*. Modal dialogs require the user's attention, preventing the user from doing anything else in the dialog's application until the dialog has been dismissed. By default, dialogs are nonmodal—the user can keep them up and still work in other windows of the application.

Note: Due to a bug in the 1.0 release, you couldn't create custom `Dialog` subclasses that were modal. This bug was fixed in the 1.0.2 release of the JDK.

The complete code for the window and dialog that the previous applet brings up is on page 689. This code can be run as a stand-alone application or, with the help of the <u>AppletButton</u> (page 671) class, as an applet. Here's just the code that implements the `Dialog` object:

```
class SimpleDialog extends Dialog {
    TextField field;
    DialogWindow parent;
    Button setButton;

    SimpleDialog(Frame dw, String title) {
        super(dw, title, false); //false = non-modal
        parent = (DialogWindow)dw;

        ...//Create and add components, such as the set button.

        //Initialize this dialog to its preferred size.
        pack();
    }

    public boolean action(Event event, Object arg) {
        if ( (event.target == setButton)
           | (event.target == field)) {
            parent.setText(field.getText());
        }
        field.selectAll();
        hide();
        return true;
    }
}
```

The `pack` method used in the `SimpleDialog` constructor above is a method defined by the `Window` class. (Remember, `Dialog` is a `Window` subclass.) The `pack` method resizes the window so that all its contents are at or above their preferred or minimum sizes, depending on the window's layout manager. In general, using `pack` is preferable to calling the `resize` method on a window, since `pack` leaves the window's layout manager in charge of the window's size, and layout managers are good at adjusting to platform dependencies and other factors that affect component size.

Here's the code that displays the dialog:

```
if (dialog == null) {
    dialog = new SimpleDialog(this, "A Simple Dialog");
}
dialog.show();
```

For modal dialogs, the `show` method doesn't return until the dialog is dismissed. To get data from a modal dialog, you can define a method in your `Dialog` subclass that returns the dialog's state. For example:

```
myModalDialog.show();
state = myModalDialog.getState();
```

Besides the methods used in the first code example above, the `Dialog` class also provides the following methods:

Dialog(Frame *parent*, boolean *modal*)

Like the constructor used previously, but doesn't set the title of the dialog window. The second argument should be `true` if the dialog is modal. Otherwise, it should be `false`.

isModal

Returns `true` if the dialog is modal.

getTitle, setTitle(String *title*)

Gets or sets, respectively, the title of the dialog window.

isResizable, setResizable(boolean *resizable*)

Finds out or sets, respectively, whether the size of the dialog window can change.

How to Use Frames

The Frame[1] class provides windows for applets and applications. Every application needs at least one `Frame`. If an application has a window that should be dependent on another window—disappearing when the other window is iconified, for example—then you should use a Dialog (page 391) instead of a `Frame`

---

[1]. http://java.sun.com/products/JDK/CurrentRelease/api/java.awt.Frame.html

for the dependent window. Unfortunately, applets currently can't use dialogs well, so they generally need to use frames instead.

How to Use Menus (page 399) and How to Use Dialogs (page 391) contain two of the many examples in this tutorial that use a `Frame`.

The menu demonstration uses the following code to create its window (a `Frame` subclass) and handle the case where the user closes the window.

```java
public class MenuWindow extends Frame {
    boolean inAnApplet = true;
    TextArea output;

    public MenuWindow {
        ...//This constructor implicitly calls the Frame
           //no-argument constructor
           //and then adds components to the window.
    }

    public boolean handleEvent(Event event) {
        if (event.id == Event.WINDOW_DESTROY) {
            if (inAnApplet) {
                dispose();
            } else {
                System.exit(0);
            }
        }
        return super.handleEvent(event);
    }

    . . .

    public static void main(String args[]) {
        MenuWindow window = new MenuWindow();
        window.inAnApplet = false;

        window.setTitle("MenuWindow Application");
        window.pack();
        window.show();
    }
}
```

The `pack` method, which is called in the `main` method above, is defined by the `Window` class. See How to Use Dialogs (page 391) for information about `pack`. The `show` method, which is called after `pack`, is defined by the `Component` class.

Besides the no-argument `Frame` constructor implicitly used by the `MenuWindow` constructor shown above, the `Frame` class also provides a one-argument constructor. That argument is a `String` that specifies the title of the frame's window.

Other interesting methods provided by `Frame` are:

`getTitle()`, `setTitle(String title)`

Returns or sets, respectively, the title of the frame's window.

`getIconImage()`, `setIconImage(Image image)`

Returns or sets, respectively, the image displayed when the window is iconified.

`getMenuBar()`, `setMenuBar(MenuBar mb)`

Returns or sets, respectively, the menu bar for this `Frame`.

`remove(MenuComponent m)`

Removes the specified menu bar from this `Frame`.

`isResizable()`, `setResizable(boolean resizable)`

Returns or sets, respectively, whether the user can change the window's size.

`getCursorType()`, `setCursor(int cursorType)`

Gets the current cursor image or sets the cursor image, respectively. The cursor must be specified as one of the types defined in the `Frame` class. The predefined types are `Frame.DEFAULT_CURSOR`, `Frame.CROSSHAIR_CUR-SOR`, `Frame.HAND_CURSOR`, `Frame.MOVE_CURSOR`, `Frame.TEXT_CURSOR`, `Frame.WAIT_CURSOR`, or `Frame.X_RESIZE_CURSOR`, where *X* is SW, SE, NW, NE, N, S, W, or E.

How to Use Labels

The Label[1] class provides an easy way of putting unselectable text in your program's GUI. Labels are aligned to the left of their drawing area, by default. You can specify that they be centered or right-aligned by specifying `Label.CENTER` or `Label.RIGHT` either to the `Label` constructor or to the `setAlignment` method. As with every `Component`, you can also specify the font and color of a label. For information on working with fonts, see Getting Information About a Font: `Font-Metrics` (page 447).

Labels are used throughout the examples in this tutorial. For example, the applet in How to Use Choices (page 389) uses a label to display information about the item that's currently chosen.

The applet in the figure on page 396 demonstrates label alignment.

The applet creates three labels, each one with a different alignment. If each label's display area were equal to the width of the text the label displayed, you wouldn't see any difference in the alignment of the labels. Each label's text would simply be displayed using all the available space. However, this applet makes each label's display area as wide as the applet, which is wider than any of

---

[1]. http://java.sun.com/products/JDK/CurrentRelease/api/java.awt.Label.html

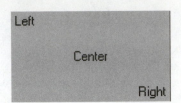

http://java.sun.com/Series/Tutorial/ui/components/label.html

the labels' text. As a result, you can see a difference in the horizontal position of the text drawn by the three labels. You can find the complete program on page 692.

The applet uses the following code to create its labels and set their alignment. For teaching purposes only, this applet uses all three `Label` constructors.

```
Label label1 = new Label();
label1.setText("Left");
Label label2 = new Label("Center");
label2.setAlignment(Label.CENTER);
Label label3 = new Label("Right", Label.RIGHT);
```

Besides the constructor, `setText`, and `setAlignment` methods used above, the `Label` class also provides `getText` and `getAlignment` methods.

How to Use Lists

The `List`[1] class provides a scrollable area containing selectable text items, one per line. Generally, a user selects an item by clicking it, and indicates that an action should occur by double-clicking an item or pressing Return. Lists can allow either multiple selections or just one selection at a time. Other components that allow users to choose from multiple options are <u>checkboxes</u> (page 387), <u>choices</u> (page 389), and <u>menus</u> (page 399).

The applet in the figure on page 397 contains two lists, along with a text area that displays information about events. The top list (which lists Spanish numbers) allows multiple selections. The bottom (which lists Italian numbers) allows a maximum of one selection. Note that the first item in each list has index 0

The code on p. 397 creates each list and handles events on the lists. You can find the complete program on page 692. Note that the `e.arg` data for action events, (which is passed into the `action` method as the second argument), is the name of the item being acted on. This argument is similar to the argument for action events on other components such as buttons and menus. However, the `e.arg` data for list events that are not action events is the *index* of the item being acted on.

---

[1] http://java.sun.com/products/JDK/CurrentRelease/api/java.awt.List.html

```
Action event occurred on "uno" in Spanish.
Select event occurred on item #1 ("due") in Italian.
Action event occurred on "due" in Italian.
Select event occurred on item #3 ("cuatro") in Spanish.
Select event occurred on item #2 ("tres") in Spanish.
Select event occurred on item #1 ("dos") in Spanish.
Deselect event occurred on item #2 ("tres") in Spanish.
Deselect event occurred on item #0 ("uno") in Spanish.
```

http://java.sun.com/Series/Tutorial/ui/components/list.html

```java
...//Where instance variables are declared:
TextArea output;
List spanish, italian;

...//Where initialization occurs:

//Build first list, which allows multiple selections.
//We prefer 4 items visible; true means allow multiple
//selections.
spanish = new List(4, true);
spanish.addItem("uno");
spanish.addItem("dos");
spanish.addItem("tres");
spanish.addItem("cuatro");
spanish.addItem("cinco");
spanish.addItem("seis");
spanish.addItem("siete");

//Build second list, which allows one selection at a time.
//Defaults to none visible, one selectable
italian = new List();
italian.addItem("uno");
italian.addItem("due");
italian.addItem("tre");
italian.addItem("quattro");
italian.addItem("cinque");
italian.addItem("sei");
italian.addItem("sette");

. . .

public boolean action(Event e, Object arg) {
    if (e.target instanceof List) {
        String language = (e.target == spanish) ?
                          "Spanish" : "Italian";
        output.appendText("Action event occurred on \""
                         + (String)arg  + "\" in "
                         + language + ".\n");
```

```
        }
        return true;
    }

    public boolean handleEvent(Event e) {
        if (e.target instanceof List) {
            List list = (List)(e.target);
            String language = (list == spanish) ?
                              "Spanish" : "Italian";
            switch (e.id) {
              case Event.LIST_SELECT:
                int sIndex = ((Integer)e.arg).intValue();
                output.appendText("Select event occurred on item #"
                              + sIndex + " (\""
                              + list.getItem(sIndex)  + "\") in "
                              + language + ".\n");
                break;
              case Event.LIST_DESELECT:
                int dIndex = ((Integer)e.arg).intValue();
                output.appendText("Deselect event occurred on item #"
                              + dIndex + " (\""
                              + list.getItem(dIndex)  + "\") in "
                              + language + ".\n");
            }
        }
        return super.handleEvent(e);
    }
}
```

Besides the two constructors and the `addItem` and `getItem` methods shown above, the `List` class provides the following handy methods:

countItems()

Returns the number of items in the `List`.

getItem(int *index*)

Returns the `String` displayed by the item at the specified index.

addItem(String *item*, int *index*)

Adds the specified item at the specified index.

replaceItem(String *newValue*, int *index*)

Replaces the item at the specified index.

clear(), delItem(int *index*), delItems(int *start*, int *end*)

Delete one or more items from the list. The `clear` method empties the list. The `delItem` method deletes the specified item from the list. The `delItems` method deletes every item between (and including) the specified indexes from the list.

getSelectedIndex()

Returns the index of the selected item in the list. Returns -1 if no item is selected or more than one item is selected.

`getSelectedIndexes()`

Returns an array containing the indexes of the selected items in the list.

`getSelectedItem()`

Similar to `getSelectedIndex`, but returns the selected item's `String` instead of its index. Returns `null` if no item is selected or more than one item is selected.

`getSelectedItems()`

Similar to `getSelectedIndexes`, but returns the selected items' `Strings` instead of their indexes.

`select(int index)`, `deselect(int index)`

Selects or deselects, respectively, the item at the specified index.

`isSelected(int index)`

Returns `true` if the item at the specified index is selected.

`getRows()`

Returns the number of visible lines in the list.

`allowsMultipleSelections()`, `setMultipleSelections (boolean allowsMultSels)`

Returns or sets, respectively, whether the list allows multiple items to be selected ("on") at the same time.

`getVisibleIndex()`, `makeVisible(int index)`

The `makeVisible` method forces the item at the specified index to be visible. The `getVisibleIndex` method gets the index of the item that was last made visible by the `makeVisible` method.

How to Use Menus

The applet in the following six figures illustrates many of the menu features you're likely to use. The window it brings up has a menu bar that contains five menus. Each menu contains one or more items. Menu 1 is a tear-off menu; by clicking the dashed line, the user creates a new window that contains the same menu items as Menu 1. Menu 2's only item has a checkbox. Menu 3 contains a separator between its second and third items. Menu 4 contains a submenu. Menu 5 is the window's help menu, which (depending on the platform) generally means that it's set off to the right. When the user clicks on any menu item, the window displays a string indicating which item was clicked and which menu it's in.

Note: Menu appearance and behavior differ significantly between platforms. For example, under MacOS menus appear at the top of the screen, instead of within the window to which they're "attached." Also, JDK 1.0.2 implements tear-off menus only on Solaris—not on the Windows 95/NT and MacOS platforms. We plan to fix this inconsistency in a later release.

Here's a snapshot of the window the applet brings up:

http://java.sun.com/Series/Tutorial/ui/components/menu.html

When you're using Solaris and you press Menu 1, you see a tear-off indicator:

Here's what the torn-off menu looks like:

Menu 2 has an item with a checkbox:

Menu 3 has a separator:

Menu 4 has a submenu:

The reason the applet brings up a window to demonstrate menus is that the AWT limits where you can use menus. Menus can exist only in menu bars, and menu bars can be attached only to windows, specifically, only to `Frame` objects.

If menus aren't appropriate or possible in your program, you consider other ways of presenting the user with options: <u>checkboxes</u> (page 387), <u>choices</u> (page 389), and <u>lists</u> (page 396).

Menu functionality in the AWT is provided by several classes. These classes do *not* inherit from `Component` since many platforms place severe limits on menu capabilities. Instead, menu classes inherit from the `MenuComponent`[1] class. The AWT provides the following `MenuComponent` subclasses to support menus:

MenuItem[2]

Each item in a menu is represented by a `MenuItem` object.

CheckboxMenuItem[3]

Each menu item that contains a checkbox is represented by a `Checkbox-MenuItem` object. `CheckboxMenuItem` is a subclass of `MenuItem`.

Menu[4]

Each menu is represented by a `Menu` object. The `Menu` class is implemented as a subclass of `MenuItem` so that you can easily create a submenu by adding one menu to another.

MenuBar[5]

Menu bars are implemented by the `MenuBar` class. A `MenuBar` represents the platform-dependent notion of a group of menus attached to a window. `MenuBars` can *not* be bound to `Panels`.

To be able to contain a `MenuComponent`, an object must adhere to the <u>MenuContainer</u>[6] interface. The `Frame`, `Menu`, and `MenuBar` classes are the only AWT classes that currently implement `MenuContainer`.

On page 695 you can find the code for the window that the previous applet brings up. This code can be run as a stand-alone application or, with the help of the <u>AppletButton</u> (page 671) class, as an applet. Here's just the code that deals with menus:

[1] http://java.sun.com/products/JDK/CurrentRelease/api/java.awt.MenuComponent.html
[2] http://java.sun.com/products/JDK/CurrentRelease/api/java.awt.MenuItem.html
[3] http://java.sun.com/products/JDK/CurrentRelease/api/java.awt.CheckboxMenuItem.html
[4] http://java.sun.com/products/JDK/CurrentRelease/api/java.awt.Menu.html
[5] http://java.sun.com/products/JDK/CurrentRelease/api/java.awt.MenuBar.html
[6] http://java.sun.com/products/JDK/CurrentRelease/api/java.awt.MenuContainer.html

```java
public class MenuWindow extends Frame {
    . . .
    public MenuWindow() {
        MenuBar mb;
        Menu m1, m2, m3, m4, m4_1, m5;
        MenuItem mi1_1, mi1_2, mi3_1, mi3_2, mi3_3, mi3_4,
                 mi4_1_1, mi5_1, mi5_2;
        CheckboxMenuItem mi2_1;

        ...//Add the output displayer to this window...

        //Build the menu bar.
        mb = new MenuBar();
        setMenuBar(mb);

        //Build first menu in the menu bar.
        //Specifying the second argument as true
        //makes this a tear-off menu.
        m1 = new Menu("Menu 1", true);
        mb.add(m1);
        mi1_1 = new MenuItem("Menu Item 1_1");
        m1.add(mi1_1);
        mi1_2 = new MenuItem("Menu Item 1_2");
        m1.add(mi1_2);

        //Build help menu.
        m5 = new Menu("Menu 5");
        //just setting the help menu doesn't work; must add it
        mb.add(m5);
        mb.setHelpMenu(m5);
        mi5_1 = new MenuItem("Menu Item 5_1");
        m5.add(mi5_1);
        mi5_2 = new MenuItem("Menu Item 5_2");
        m5.add(mi5_2);

        //Build second menu in the menu bar.
        m2 = new Menu("Menu 2");
        mb.add(m2);
        mi2_1 = new CheckboxMenuItem("Menu Item 2_1");
        m2.add(mi2_1);

        //Build third menu in the menu bar.
        m3 = new Menu("Menu 3");
        mb.add(m3);
        mi3_1 = new MenuItem("Menu Item 3_1");
        m3.add(mi3_1);
        mi3_2 = new MenuItem("Menu Item 3_2");
        m3.add(mi3_2);
        m3.addSeparator;
        mi3_3 = new MenuItem("Menu Item 3_3");
        m3.add(mi3_3);
```

```
        mi3_4 = new MenuItem("Menu Item 3_4");
        mi3_4.disable;
        m3.add(mi3_4);

        //Build fourth menu in the menu bar.
        m4 = new Menu("Menu 4");
        mb.add(m4);
        m4_1 = new Menu("Submenu 4_1");
        m4.add(m4_1);
        mi4_1_1 = new MenuItem("Menu Item 4_1_1");
        m4_1.add(mi4_1_1);
    }
    . . .
    public boolean action(Event event, Object arg) {
        String str = "Action detected";

        if (event.target instanceof MenuItem) {
            MenuItem mi=(MenuItem)(event.target);
            str += " on " + arg;
            if (mi instanceof CheckboxMenuItem) {
                    str += " (state is "
                        + ((CheckboxMenuItem)mi).getState()
                        + ")";
            }
            MenuContainer parent = mi.getParent();
            if (parent instanceof Menu) {
                str += " in " + ((Menu)parent).getLabel();
            } else {
                str += " in a container that isn't a Menu";
            }
        }
        str += ".\n";
        ...//Display the string in the output area...
        return false;
    }
}
```

How to Use Panels

The Panel[1] class is a general-purpose Container subclass. You can use it as is
to hold components, or you can define a subclass to perform special functionality, such as event handling for the objects the Panel contains.

The Applet[2] class is a Panel subclass with special hooks to run in a browser
or other applet viewer. Whenever you see a program that can run both as an
applet and as an application, the chances are that it defines an Applet subclass

---

but doesn't use any of the special `Applet` capabilities, relying instead on the methods it inherits from the `Panel` class.

The following example uses a `Panel` instance to hold some components:

```
Panel p1 = new Panel;
p1.add(new Button("Button 1"));
p1.add(new Button("Button 2"));
p1.add(new Button("Button 3"));
```

The following code contains a `Panel` subclass that draws a frame around its contents. Versions of this class are used by Examples 1 and 2 in <u>Drawing Shapes</u> (page 440).

```
class FramedArea extends Panel {
    public FramedArea(CoordinatesDemo controller) {
        ...//Set the layout manager.
            //Add any Components this Panel contains...
    }

    //Ensure that no Component is placed on top of the frame.
    //The inset values were determined by trial and error.
    public Insets insets() {
        return new Insets(4,4,5,5);
    }

    //Draw the frame at this Panel's edges.
    public void paint(Graphics g) {
        Dimension d = size();
        Color bg = getBackground();

        g.setColor(bg);
        g.draw3DRect(0, 0, d.width - 1, d.height - 1, true);
        g.draw3DRect(3, 3, d.width - 7, d.height - 7, false);
    }
}
```

Many of the examples in this lesson use `Applet` subclasses to handle events for the components they contain. You can see an example in <u>How to Use Dialogs</u> (page 391). You can use the event handling in this and other examples as a model for event handling in your own `Applet` or `Panel` subclass.

How to Use Scrollbars

Scrollbars have two uses:

- A scrollbar can act as a slider that the user manipulates to set a value. An example of this is in the Converter program in <u>The Anatomy of a GUI-Based Program</u> (page 366).
- Scrollbars can help you display part of a region that's too large for the available display area. Scrollbars let the user choose exactly which part of the region is visible. Here's an example:

http://java.sun.com/Series/Tutorial/ui/components/scrollbar.html

To create a scrollbar, you need to create an instance of the `Scrollbar`[1] class. You must also initialize the following values, either by specifying them to a `Scrollbar` constructor or by calling the `setValues` method before the scrollbar is visible:

int orientation

Indicates whether the scrollbar should be horizontal or vertical. Specified with either `Scrollbar.HORIZONTAL` or `Scrollbar.VERTICAL`.

int value

The initial value of the scrollbar. For scrollbars that control a scrollable area, this usually means the x value (for horizontal scrollbars) or y value (for vertical scrollbars) of the part of the area that is visible when the user first sees the scrollable area. For example, when the previous applet starts up, the values of both the horizontal and vertical scrollbars' are 0, and the image portion that is displayed starts at (0,0).

int visible

The size in pixels of the visible portion of the scrollable area. This value determines how many pixels a click in the scrollbar (but not on the knob) causes the display area to shift. You can use the `setPageIncrement` method to get the same effect.

int minimum

The minimum value the scrollbar can have. For scrollbars controlling scrollable areas, this value is usually 0, indicating the left/upper part of the area.

int maximum

The maximum value the scrollbar can have. For scrollbars controlling scrollable areas, this value is usually:

(total width/height, in pixels, of the component that's being partially displayed)
– (currently visible width/height of the scrollable area)

[1.] http://java.sun.com/products/JDK/CurrentRelease/api/java.awt.Scrollbar.html

The following figure illustrates the meaning of the values described here:

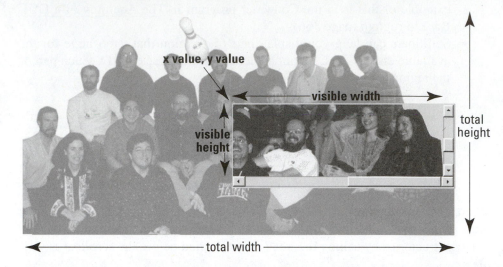

The complete code for this applet is on page 697. This code defines two classes. The first is a `Canvas` subclass (`ScrollableCanvas`) that draws an image. The second is a `Panel` subclass (`ImageScroller`, which actually extends `Applet`) that creates and contains a `ScrollableCanvas` and two `Scrollbars`. This program illustrates a few important details of managing a scrollable area:

- Event handling for a scrollbar is pretty straightforward. The program must respond to scrolling events by saving the scrollbar's new value in a place accessible to the component that displays itself within the scrollable area, and then invoke the `repaint` method on the component.

```java
public boolean handleEvent(Event evt) {
    switch (evt.id) {
      case Event.SCROLL_LINE_UP:
      case Event.SCROLL_LINE_DOWN:
      case Event.SCROLL_PAGE_UP:
      case Event.SCROLL_PAGE_DOWN:
      case Event.SCROLL_ABSOLUTE:
        if (evt.target == vert) {
            canvas.ty = ((Integer)evt.arg).intValue();
            canvas.repaint();
        }
        if (evt.target == horz) {
            canvas.tx = ((Integer)evt.arg).intValue();
            canvas.repaint();
        }
    }
    return super.handleEvent(evt);
}
```

- The component that displays itself within the scrollable area can be very simple. All it needs to do is draw itself at the origin specified by the values from its controlling scrollbars. A component can change its origin (and, as a result, not have to change its normal drawing code) by putting code such as the following statement at the beginning of its `paint` or `update` method:

```
g.translate(-tx, -ty);
```

- While scrolling occurs, you'll probably notice flashing, or flickering, in the display area. If you don't want this to occur, you'll need to implement the `update` method in the displayed component, and possibly double buffering as well. These techniques are discussed in <u>Eliminating Flashing</u> (page 469).
- If your scrolling area is resizable, beware of a common scrolling problem: When the user scrolls to the right/bottom of the area and then enlarges the area, the scrolling area might display a blank space at its right/bottom. After the user scrolls and then returns to the right/bottom, the blank space will no longer be there. To avoid displaying a blank space unnecessarily, when the scrollable area's size becomes larger you should shift the component's origin so that it takes advantage of the available new space. Here's an example:

```
int canvasWidth = canvas.size.width;

//Shift everything to the right if we're displaying empty
//space on the right side.
if ((canvas.tx + canvasWidth) > imageSize.width) {
    int newtx = imageSize.width - canvasWidth;
    if (newtx  0) {
            newtx = 0;
    }
    canvas.tx = newtx;
}
```

The figure on page 408 illustrates the scrolling problem and its fix.

How to Use Text Areas and Fields

The <u>TextArea</u>[1] and <u>TextField</u>[2] classes display selectable text and, optionally, allow the user to edit the text. You can subclass TextArea and TextField to per-

---

[1] http://java.sun.com/products/JDK/CurrentRelease/api/java.awt.TextArea.html
[2] http://java.sun.com/products/JDK/CurrentRelease/api/java.awt.TextField.html

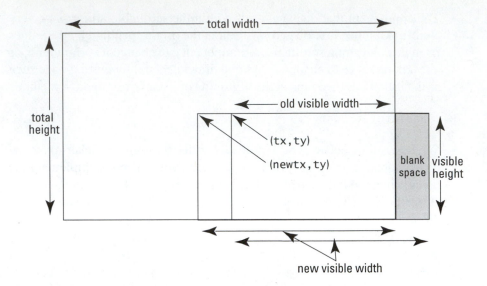

form such tasks as checking for errors in the input. As with any component, you can specify the background and foreground colors and font used by Text-Areas and TextFields. You can not, however, change their basic appearance.

Both TextArea and TextField are subclasses of <u>TextComponent</u>.[1] From TextComponent they inherit methods that allow them to set and get the current selection, enable and disable editing, get the currently selected text or all the text, and set the text.

The following applet displays first a TextField and then a TextArea. The TextField is editable; the TextArea is not. When the user presses Return in the TextField, its contents are copied to the TextArea and then selected in the TextField.

http://java.sun.com/Series/Tutorial/ui/components/text.html

[1.] http://java.sun.com/products/JDK/CurrentRelease/api/java.awt.TextComponent.html

You can find the complete program on page 701. Here's the code that creates, initializes, and handles events in the `TextArea` and `TextField` objects:

```
//Where instance variables are defined:
TextField textField;
TextArea textArea;

public void init() {
    textField = new TextField(20);
    textArea = new TextArea(5, 20);
    textArea.setEditable(false);

    ...//Add the two components to the panel.
}

public boolean action(Event evt, Object arg) {
    String text = textField.getText();
    textArea.appendText(text + "\n");
    textField.selectAll();
    return true;
}
```

The `TextComponent` superclass of `TextArea` and `TextField` supplies the `get-Text`, `setText`, `setEditable`, and `selectAll` methods used in the previous code example. It also supplies the following useful methods: `getSelectedText`, `isEditable`, `getSelectionStart`, and `getSelectionEnd`. It also provides a `select` method that allows you to select text between beginning and end positions that you specify.

The `TextField` class has four constructors: `TextField()`, `TextField(int columns)`, `TextField(String text)`, and `TextField(String text, int columns)`. The integer argument specifies the number of columns in the text field. The `String` argument specifies the text initially displayed in the text field. The `TextField` class also supplies the following handy methods:

getColumns()

Returns the number of columns in the `TextField`.

setEchoChar(char c)

Sets the echo character, which is useful for password fields.

getEchoChar(), echoCharIsSet()

These methods let you ask about the echo character.

Like the `TextField` class, the `TextArea` class also has four constructors: `TextArea()`, `TextArea(int rows, int columns)`, `TextArea(String text)`, and `TextArea(String text, int rows, int columns)`. The integer arguments specify the number of rows and columns in the text area. The `String` argument specifies the text initially displayed in the text area.

The TextArea class supplies the appendText method used in the previous code example. It also supplies the following methods:

getRows(), getColumns()

Return the number of rows or columns in the text area.

insertText(String *string*, int *position*)

Inserts the specified text at the specified position.

void replaceText(String *string*, int *start*, int *end*)

Replaces text from the indicated start position to the indicated end position.

Details of the Component Architecture

The AWT is designed to have a platform-independent API and yet to preserve each platform's look and feel. For example, the AWT has just one API for buttons (provided by the Button class), but a button looks different in MacOS than in Windows 95/NT.

The AWT achieves its seemingly contradictory goals by providing classes (*components*) that provide a platform-independent API but that make use of platform-specific implementations (*peers*). In particular, every AWT component class (Component, MenuComponent, and their subclasses) has an equivalent peer class, and every component object has a peer object that controls the component's look and feel.

The following figure illustrates how a typical AWT component (a Button) is mapped to a peer. Button peers are implemented in platform-specific classes that implement the java.awt.peer ButtonPeer interface. The java.awt Toolkit class defines methods that choose exactly which class to use for the peer implementation.

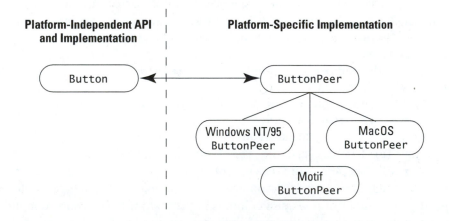

How Peers Are Created

Peers are created lazily, often just before their corresponding component object is drawn for the first time. Notice one side effect of this: The size of a component is usually not valid until after the component has been shown for the first time.

A component's peer is created when one of two things happens:

- The `pack` or `show` method is invoked on a window that contains the component.
- The component is added to a container that is already visible.

If you add a component to a visible container, you need to explicitly tell the AWT to show the component and recalculate the layout of its container. You do this by calling the `validate` method. Although you can invoke `validate` directly on the component you're adding, it's usually invoked on the container, instead. The reason is that invoking `validate` on a container causes a chain reaction—every component under the container gets validated, as well. For example, after you add components to an Applet object, you call `validate` on the `Applet`, which makes it lay out and show all the new components.

Before you can get the correct size of a component, you need to make sure the component has a peer and (if you added the component to a visible container) call the `validate` method.

How Peers Handle Events

Peers implement the feel (and, indirectly, the look) of UI components by reacting to user input events. For example, when the user clicks a button, the peer reacts to the mouse down and mouse up events by causing the button's appearance to change and by forwarding an action event to the appropriate `Button` object.

In theory, peers are at the end of the event chain. When a raw event such as a keypress occurs, the component for which the event is intended gets to handle the event first. If the component's event handler returns `false`, the component's container sees the event, and so on. After all the components in the hierarchy have had an opportunity to handle the event and all their event handling methods have returned `false`, the peer gets to see and react to the event.

In the current implementation, this scenario is true for keypresses but not for mouse events. For mouse events, the peer is the first to see the event, and it doesn't necessarily pass all events on to the component. We plan to make mouse events work like keyboard events in a future release of Java.

From raw events such as keypresses and mouse clicks, peers sometimes generate higher level events—actions, focus changes, window iconifications, and so on. These higher level events are passed on to the relevant component for handling.

Common Component Problems (and Their Solutions)

Problem: How do I increase or decrease the number of components in a container?

- To add a component to a container, use one of the three forms of the Container add method. See <u>How to Add a Component to a Container</u> (page 381) for information. To remove a component from a container, use the Container remove or removeAll method. Alternatively, just add the component to another container, since that automatically removes the component from its previous container.

Problem: My component never shows up!

- Did you add the component to its container using the right add method for the container's layout manager? BorderLayout, the default layout manager for windows, might silently fail to add your component if you use the one-argument version of the add method. See the **Laying Out Components Within a Container** (page 415) for examples of using the add method.
- If you're not using the default layout manager, did you successfully create an instance of the right layout manager and call the setLayout method on the container?
- If the component is added properly, but added to a container that might already be visible, did you call validate on the container after adding the component?
- If your component is a custom component (a Canvas subclass, for example), does it implement the minimumSize and preferredSize methods so that they return the correct size of the component?
- If you use a non-AWT layout manager, or none at all, does the component have a reasonable size and reasonable display coordinates? In particular, if you use absolute positioning (no layout manager), you must explicitly set the size of your components, or they just won't show up. See <u>Laying Out Components Without a Layout Manager (Absolute Positioning)</u> (page 433).

Problem: My custom component doesn't get updated when it should.

- Make sure that the component's `repaint` method is called every time the component's appearance should change. For standard components, this isn't a problem, since platform-specific code takes care of all the drawing of the component. For custom components, however, you have to explicitly call the `repaint` method on the component whenever the component's appearance should change. Invoking `repaint` on a container of the component is *not* good enough. See <u>How to Use Canvases</u> (page 385) for more information.

Problem: My component isn't getting a particular event.

- Check whether the component getting any events, at all. If it isn't, make sure you're referring to the right component—that you instantiated the right class, for example.

- Make sure your component passes through the kind of event you're trying to catch. For example, many standard components don't pass through mouse events, so the AWT cannot generate `Event` objects for them. Can you use another event type, such as `ACTION_EVENT` (handled by the `action` method), instead? If not, you might be forced to implement a `Canvas` subclass (or a `Panel` or `Applet` subclass) so that you can see all the events that occur.

Problem: My application doesn't get a `WINDOW_DESTROY` event, so I can't close my window (or quit the application or whatever).

- In a `Frame` subclass, implement `handleEvent` so that it reacts to the `WINDOW_DESTROY` event. You can't catch `WINDOW_DESTROY` events in a `Panel` subclass, for example, since the `Frame` is above it in the component hierarchy. To quit, use the `System exit` method. To destroy the window, you can call `dispose` or you can just `hide` the `Frame` and, if you're not going to use it again, make sure that all references to it are set to `null`.

Problem: All your examples are of applets. How do I apply them to applications?

- Except where noted, anywhere in this trail that you see a subclass of the `Applet` class, you can substitute a subclass of the `Panel` class. If the subclass isn't used as a container, you can substitute a subclass of the `Canvas` class. In general, it's easy to convert an applet into an application, as long as the applet doesn't rely on any special applet abilities, such as using methods defined in the `Applet` class.

- To convert an applet into an application, add a `main` method that creates an instance of a `Frame` subclass, creates an instance of the `Applet` (or `Panel` or `Canvas`) subclass, adds the instance to the `Frame`, and then calls the `init` and `start` methods of the instance. The `Frame` subclass should have a `handleEvent` implementation that handles `WINDOW_DESTROY` events in the appropriate way.

See `AnimatorApplet.java` (page 737) and `AnimatorApplication.java` (page 739) for examples of an applet and an application that implement the same functionality.

Problem: Whenever I execute a Java application with a GUI, I get this annoying error message:

```
Warning:
    Cannot allocate colormap entry for default background
```

- This message occurs only on Motif systems. It occurs when the Motif library is initialized and finds that there's no room in the default colormap to allocate its GUI colors. The solution is to run fewer "colormap hogging" applications on your desktop. The Java runtime system adapts itself to whatever colors are in the default palette, but the Motif library is less forgiving.

If you don't see your problem in this list, see <u>Common Layout Problems (and Their Solutions)</u> (page 435) and, for custom components, <u>Common Graphics Problems (and Their Solutions)</u> (page 479). You might get some insight into your problem by reading <u>Details of the Component Architecture</u> (page 410). If you still haven't found the solution to your problem, check the Web page for this book: http://java.sun.com/Series/Tutorial/book.html

19

Laying Out Components Within a Container

THE following figures show two programs, each of which displays five buttons. The Java code for both programs is almost identical. So why do they look so different? Because they use different *layout managers* to control the layout of the buttons.

GridWindow Application	
Button 1	2
Button 3	Long-Named Button 4
Button 5	

FlowWindow Application
Button 1	2	Button 3	Long-Named Button 4	Button 5

A layout manager is an object that controls the size and position of components in a container. Layout managers adhere to the `LayoutManager` interface. By default, every `Container` object has a `LayoutManager` object that controls its layout. For `Panel` objects, the default layout manager is an instance of the `Flow-Layout` class. For `Window` objects, the default layout manager is an instance of the `BorderLayout` class.

This lesson has examples of every kind of layout manager. Each example can run either as an applet or as an application. The examples bring up windows that you can resize to see how resizing affects the layout.

The <u>Using Layout Managers</u> section (page 416) tells you how to use layout managers. It gives both general rules and detailed instructions on using each of the layout managers that the AWT provides.

Instead of using one of the AWT's layout managers, you can write your own. Layout managers must implement the `LayoutManager` interface, which specifies the five methods every layout manager must define. <u>Creating a Custom Layout Manager</u> (page 431) describes how to write a layout manager.

You can position components without using a layout manager. Generally, this solution is used to specify absolute positions for components, and only for programs that are executed on only one platform or that use custom components. Absolute positioning is often *unsuitable* for platform-independent programs, since the size of components can be different on different platforms. <u>Laying Out Components Without a Layout Manager (Absolute Positioning)</u> (page 433) gives you details.

Some of the most common layout problems are that components are displayed too small, or not at all. <u>Common Layout Problems (and Their Solutions)</u> (page 435) tells you how to fix these and other common layout problems.

Using Layout Managers

Every container, by default, has a layout manager—an object that implements the `LayoutManager` interface. If a container's default layout manager doesn't suit your needs, you can easily replace it with another one. The AWT supplies layout managers that range from the very simple (`FlowLayout` and `GridLayout`) to the special purpose (`BorderLayout` and `CardLayout`) to the very flexible (`GridBagLayout`).

This section gives you an overview of the layout managers the AWT provides, gives you some general rules for using layout managers, and then tells you how to use each of the AWT layout managers.

<u>BorderLayout</u> (page 419) is the default layout manager for all `Window` objects, such as `Frame`s and `Dialog`s. It uses five areas to hold components: north, south, east, west, and center. All extra space is placed in the center area. The following program puts one button in each area.

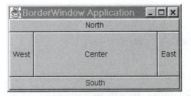

http://java.sun.com/Series/Tutorial/ui/layout/using.html

Use <u>CardLayout</u> (page 420) when you have an area that can contain different components at different times. A `CardLayout` is often controlled by a `Choice`,

with the state of the `Choice` determining which `Panel` (group of components) the `CardLayout` displays. Here are two examples of a program that uses a `Choice` and a `CardLayout` in this way:

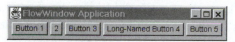

http://java.sun.com/Series/Tutorial/ui/layout/using.html

FlowLayout (page 422) is the default layout manager for every `Panel`. It simply lays out components from left to right, starting new rows if necessary. Both panels in the `CardLayout` figure use `FlowLayout`. The following program also uses a `FlowLayout`:

http://java.sun.com/Series/Tutorial/ui/layout/using.html

GridLayout (page 423) simply makes a bunch of components have equal size, displaying them in the requested number of rows and columns. The following program uses a `GridLayout` to control the display of five buttons:

http://java.sun.com/Series/Tutorial/ui/layout/using.html

GridBagLayout (page 424) is the most sophisticated, flexible layout manager the AWT provides. It aligns components by placing them within a grid of cells, allowing some components to span more than one cell. The rows in the grid aren't necessarily all the same height; similarly, grid columns can have different widths. The following program uses a `GridBagLayout` to manage ten buttons in a panel:

http://java.sun.com/Series/Tutorial/ui/layout/using.html

General Rules for Using Layout Managers

Unless you explicitly tell a container not to use a layout manager, it is associated with its very own instance of a layout manager. This layout manager is automatically consulted each time the container might need to change its appearance. Most layout managers don't require programs to directly call their methods.

How to Choose a Layout Manager

The layout managers provided by the AWT have different strengths and weaknesses. This section discusses some common layout scenarios and which AWT layout managers might work for each scenario. If none of the AWT layout managers is right for your situation, feel free to use layout managers contributed to the net, such as `PackerLayout`, which is available at Gamelan.[1]

Scenario: You need to display a component in as much space as it can get.

Consider using <u>BorderLayout</u> (page 419) or <u>GridBagLayout</u> (page 424). If you use `BorderLayout`, you'll need to put the space-hungry component in the center. With `GridBagLayout`, you'll need to set the constraints for the component so that `fill=GridBagConstraints.BOTH`. Or, if you don't mind every other component in the same container being just as large as your space-hungry component, you can use a <u>GridLayout</u> (page 423).

Scenario: You need to display a few components in a compact row at their natural size.

Consider using a `Panel` to hold the components and using the `Panel`'s default <u>FlowLayout</u> (page 422) manager.

Scenario: You need to display a few components of the same size in rows and columns.

<u>GridLayout</u> (page 423) is perfect for this.

How to Create a Layout Manager and Associate It with a Container

Each container has a default layout manager associated with it. All `Panel` objects (including `Applets`) are initialized to use a `FlowLayout`. All `Window` objects, except special-purpose ones like `FileDialog`, are initialized to use a `BorderLayout`.

If you want to use a container's default layout manager, you don't have to do a thing. The constructor for each container creates a layout manager instance and initializes the container to use it.

To use a layout manager other than the default layout manager, you must create an instance of the desired layout manager class and tell the container to

---

[1] http://www.gamelan.com/

use it. The following Java statement creates a `CardLayout` manager and sets it up as the layout manager for a container.

```
aContainer.setLayout(new CardLayout());
```

Rules of Thumb for Using Layout Managers

The `Container` methods that result in calls to the container's layout manager are `add`, `remove`, `removeAll`, `layout`, `preferredSize`, and `minimumSize`. The `add`, `remove`, and `removeAll` methods add and remove components from a container; you can call them at any time. The `layout` method, which is called as the result of any paint request to a container or of a `validate` call on the container, requests that the container place and size itself and the components it contains; you don't call the layout method directly. The `preferredSize` and `minimumSize` methods return the container's ideal size and minimum size, respectively. The values returned are just hints; they have no effect unless your program enforces these sizes.

Take special care when calling a container's `preferredSize` and `minimum-Size` methods. The values these methods return are meaningless unless the container and its components have valid peer objects. See Details of the Component Architecture (page 410) for information on when peers are created.

How to Use BorderLayout

The following figure shows a `BorderLayout`[1] object in action.

http://java.sun.com/Series/Tutorial/ui/layout/border.html

A `BorderLayout` has five areas: north, south, east, west, and center. If you enlarge the window, the center area gets as much of the newly available space as possible. The other areas expand only as much as necessary to keep all available space filled.

The following code creates the `BorderLayout` and the components it manages. You can find the complete program on page 702. The program runs either within an applet, with the help of AppletButton (page 671), or as an application.

---

[1]. http://java.sun.com/products/JDK/CurrentRelease/api/java.awt.BorderLayout.html

The first line of this code is actually unnecessary for this example, since it's in a `Window` subclass and each `Window` already has an associated `BorderLayout` instance. However, the first line would be necessary if the code were in a `Panel` instead of a `Window`.

```
setLayout(new BorderLayout());
setFont(new Font("Helvetica", Font.PLAIN, 14));

add("North", new Button("North"));
add("South", new Button("South"));
add("East", new Button("East"));
add("West", new Button("West"));
add("Center", new Button("Center"));
```

> **Note:** When adding a component to a container that uses `BorderLayout`, you *must* use the two-argument version of the add method, with the first argument being `"North"`, `"South"`, `"East"`, `"West"`, or `"Center"`. If you use the one-argument version of add, or if you specify an invalid first argument, your component *might not be visible*.

By default, a `BorderLayout` puts no gap between the components it manages. In this section's example, any apparent gaps are the result of the `Button`s reserving extra space around their apparent display area. You can specify gaps (in pixels) using the following constructor:

```
BorderLayout(int horizontalGap, int verticalGap)
```

How to Use CardLayout

The following two figures show a <u>CardLayout</u>[1] object in action.

http://java.sun.com/Series/Tutorial/ui/layout/card.html

The `CardLayout` class helps you manage two or more components (usually `Panel` objects) that share the same display space. Conceptually, each component a `CardLayout` manages is like a playing card or trading card in a stack, where

---

[1]. http://java.sun.com/products/JDK/CurrentRelease/api/java.awt.CardLayout.html

only the top card is visible at any time. You can choose the card that's showing in any of the following ways:

- By asking for either the first or last card, in the order they were added to the container.
- By flipping through the deck backwards or forwards.
- By specifying a card with a specific name. This is the scheme this section's example program uses. Specifically, the user can choose a card (component) by selecting it by name from a pop-up list of choices.

The following code creates the `CardLayout` and the components it manages. You can find the complete program on page 703. The program runs either within an applet, with the help of <u>AppletButton</u> (page 671), or as an application.

```
//Where instance variables are declared:
Panel cards;
final static String BUTTONPANEL = "Panel with Buttons";
final static String TEXTPANEL = "Panel with TextField";

//Where the container is initialized:
cards = new Panel();
cards.setLayout(new CardLayout());

...//Create a Panel named p1. Put buttons in it.
...//Create a Panel named p2. Put a text field in it.

cards.add(BUTTONPANEL, p1);
cards.add(TEXTPANEL, p2);
```

When you add a component to a container that a `CardLayout` manages, you must use the two-argument form of the `Container` add method: add(`String` *name*, `Component` *comp*). The first argument can be any string that somehow identifies the component being added.

To choose which component a `CardLayout` shows, you need some additional code. Here's how the program in this section does this:

```
//Where the container is initialized:
. . .
    //Put the Choice in a Panel to get a nicer look.
    Panel cp = new Panel();
    Choice c = new Choice();
    c.addItem(BUTTONPANEL);
    c.addItem(TEXTPANEL);
    cp.add(c);
    add("North", cp);

. . .
```

```
public boolean action(Event evt, Object arg) {
    if (evt.target instanceof Choice) {
        ((CardLayout)cards.getLayout()).show(cards,(String)arg);
        return true;
    }
    return false;
}
```

This example shows that you can use the CardLayout show method to set the currently showing component. The first argument to the show method is the container the CardLayout controls, that is, the container of the components the CardLayout manages. The second argument is the string that identifies the component to show. This string is the same as the one specified when adding the component to the container.

The following methods are all the CardLayout methods that let you choose a component. For each method, the first argument is the container for which the CardLayout is the layout manager (the container of the cards the CardLayout controls).

```
first(Container parent)
next(Container parent)
previous(Container parent)
last(Container parent)
show(Container parent, String name)
```

How to Use FlowLayout

The following figure shows a FlowLayout[1] in action.

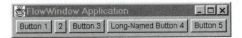

http://java.sun.com/Series/Tutorial/ui/layout/flow.html

FlowLayout puts components in a row, sized at their preferred size. If the horizontal space in the container is too small to put all the components in one row, FlowLayout uses multiple rows. (FlowLayout reserves only enough vertical space for one row, however.) Within each row, components are centered (the default), left-aligned, or right-aligned as specified when the FlowLayout is created.

The following code from this section's example program creates the FlowLayout and the components it manages. You can find the complete program on

---

[1]. http://java.sun.com/products/JDK/CurrentRelease/api/java.awt.FlowLayout.html

page 705. The program runs either within an applet, with the help of <u>Applet-Button</u> (page 671), or as an application.

```
setLayout(new FlowLayout());
setFont(new Font("Helvetica", Font.PLAIN, 14));

add(new Button("Button 1"));
add(new Button("2"));
add(new Button("Button 3"));
add(new Button("Long-Named Button 4"));
add(new Button("Button 5"));
```

The FlowLayout class has three constructors:

```
FlowLayout()
FlowLayout(int alignment)
FlowLayout(int alignment, int horizontalGap, int verticalGap)
```

The *alignment* argument must have the value FlowLayout.LEFT, FlowLayout.CENTER, or FlowLayout.RIGHT. The *horizontalGap* and *verticalGap* arguments specify the number of pixels to put between components. If you don't specify a gap value, FlowLayout uses 5 for the default gap value.

How to Use GridLayout

The following figure shows a <u>GridLayout</u>[1] object in action.

Button 1	2
Button 3	Long-Named Button 4
Button 5	

http://java.sun.com/Series/Tutorial/ui/layout/grid.html

A GridLayout places components in a grid of cells. Each component takes all the available space within its cell, and each cell is exactly the same size. If you resize the GridLayout window, the GridLayout changes the cell size so that the cells are as large as possible, given the space available to the container.

The following code creates the GridLayout and the components it manages. You can find the complete program on page 706. The program runs either within an applet, with the help of <u>AppletButton</u> (page 671), or as an application.

---

[1]. http://java.sun.com/products/JDK/CurrentRelease/api/java.awt.GridLayout.html

```
//Construct a GridLayout with 2 columns
//and an unspecified number of rows.
setLayout(new GridLayout(0,2));
setFont(new Font("Helvetica", Font.PLAIN, 14));

add(new Button("Button 1"));
add(new Button("2"));
add(new Button("Button 3"));
add(new Button("Long-Named Button 4"));
add(new Button("Button 5"));
```

The constructor tells the `GridLayout` class to create an instance that has two columns and as many rows as necessary. It's one of two constructors for `GridLayout`. Here are both constructors:

```
GridLayout(int rows, int columns)
GridLayout(int rows, int columns,
          int horizontalGap, int verticalGap)
```

At least one of the *rows* and *columns* arguments must be nonzero. The *horizontalGap* and *verticalGap* arguments to the second constructor allow you to specify the number of pixels between cells. If you don't specify gaps, their values default to zero. In the program, any apparent gaps between buttons are the result of the buttons reserving extra space around their apparent display area.

How to Use GridBagLayout

The following figure shows a <u>GridBagLayout</u>[1] object in action.

GridBagWindow Application			
Button1	Button2	Button3	Button4
Button5			
Button6			Button7
Button8	Button9		
	Button10		

http://java.sun.com/Series/Tutorial/ui/layout/gridbag.html

GridBagLayout is the most flexible—and complex—layout manager the AWT provides. A `GridBagLayout` places components in a grid of rows and columns, allowing specified components to span multiple rows or columns. Not all rows necessarily have the same height. Similarly, not all columns necessarily have the same width. Essentially, `GridBagLayout` places components in squares (cells) in

---

[1.] http://java.sun.com/products/JDK/CurrentRelease/api/java.awt.GridBagLayout.html

a grid, and then uses the components' preferred sizes to determine how big the cells should be.

The following figure illustrates what happens if you enlarge the window the program brings up:

As you can see, the last row gets all the new vertical space, and the new horizontal space is split evenly among all the columns. This resizing behavior is based on weights that the program assigns to individual components in the GridBagLayout. Note also that each component takes up as much space as it can. This behavior is also specified by the program.

The way the program specifies the size and position characteristics of its components is by specifying *constraints* for each component. To specify constraints, you set instance variables in a GridBagConstraints object and tell the GridBagLayout (with the setConstraints method) to associate the constraints with the component.

The following pages explain the constraints you can set and provide examples of setting them.

Specifying Constraints for GridBagLayout (page 425) tells you what instance variables GridBagConstraints has, what values you can set them to, and how to associate the resulting GridBagConstraints with a component.

The GridBagLayout Applet Example Explained (page 428) puts it all together, explaining the code for the program in this section.

More GridBagLayout Examples (page 431) tells you where you can find some more examples of using GridBagLayout.

Specifying Constraints for GridBagLayout

The following code is typical of what you'll see in a container that uses a Grid-BagLayout. (You'll see a more detailed example on the next page.)

```
GridBagLayout gridbag = new GridBagLayout();
GridBagConstraints c = new GridBagConstraints();
setLayout(gridbag);
```

```
//For each component to be added to this container:
//...Create the component...
//...Set instance variables in the GridBagConstraints
//instance...
gridbag.setConstraints(theComponent, c);
add(theComponent);
```

As you might have guessed from the above example, you can reuse the same `GridBagConstraints` instance for multiple components, even if the components have different constraints. The `GridBagLayout` extracts the constraint values and doesn't use the `GridBagConstraints` object again. You must be careful, however, to reset the `GridBagConstraints` instance variables to their default values when necessary.

You can set the following <u>GridBagConstraints</u>[1] instance variables:

gridx, gridy

Specify the row and column at the upper left of the component. The leftmost column has the address `gridx=0` and the top row has the address `gridy=0`. Use `GridBagConstraints.RELATIVE` (the default value) to specify that the component be placed just to the right of (for `gridx`) or just below (for `gridy`) the component that was added to the container just before this component was added.

gridwidth, gridheight

Specify the number of columns (for `gridwidth`) or rows (for `gridheight`) in the component's display area. These constraints specify the number of cells the component uses, *not* the number of pixels it uses. The default value is 1. Use `GridBagConstraints.REMAINDER` to specify that the component be the last one in its row (for `gridwidth`) or column (for `gridheight`). Use `GridBagConstraints.RELATIVE` to specify that the component be the next to last one in its row (for `gridwidth`) or column (for `gridheight`).

Note: As of press time, a `GridBagLayout` bug prevents a component from spanning multiple rows unless the component is in the leftmost column.

---

fill

Used when the component's display area is larger than the component's requested size to determine whether and how to resize the component. Valid values are `GridBagConstraints.NONE` (the default), `GridBagConstraints.HORIZONTAL` (make the component wide enough to fill its display area horizontally, but don't change its height), `GridBagConstraints.VERTICAL` (make the component tall enough to fill its display

---

[1]. http://java.sun.com/products/JDK/CurrentRelease/api/java.awt.GridBagConstraints.html

area vertically, but don't change its width), and `GridBag-Constraints.BOTH` (make the component fill its display area entirely).

`ipadx, ipady`

Specify the internal padding: how much to add to the minimum size of the component. The default value is zero. The width of the component will be at least its minimum width plus `ipadx*2` pixels, since the padding applies to both sides of the component. Similarly, the height of the component will be at least its minimum height plus `ipady*2` pixels.

`insets`

Specifies the external padding of the component—the minimum amount of space between the component and the edges of its display area. The value is specified as an <u>Insets</u>[1] object. By default, each component has no external padding.

`anchor`

Used when the component is smaller than its display area to determine where (within the area) to place the component. Valid values are `Grid-BagConstraints.CENTER` (the default), `GridBagConstraints.NORTH`, `GridBagConstraints.NORTHEAST`, `GridBagConstraints.EAST`, `GridBag-Constraints.SOUTHEAST`, `GridBagConstraints.SOUTH`, `GridBagCon-straints.SOUTHWEST`, `GridBagConstraints.WEST`, and `GridBagCon-straints.NORTHWEST`.

`weightx, weighty`

Specifying weights is an art that can have a significant impact on the appearance of the components a `GridBagLayout` controls. Weights are used to determine how to distribute space among columns (`weightx`) and among rows (`weighty`); this is important for specifying resizing behavior.

Unless you specify at least one nonzero value for `weightx` or `weighty`, all the components clump together in the center of their container. This is because when the weight is 0.0 (the default), the `GridBagLayout` puts any extra space between its grid of cells and the edges of the container.

Generally weights are specified with 0.0 and 1.0 as the extremes: the numbers in between used as necessary. Larger numbers indicate that the component's row or column should get more space. For each column, the weight is related to the highest `weightx` specified for a component within that column, with each multicolumn component's weight being split somehow between the columns the component is in. Similarly, each row's weight is related to the highest `weighty` specified for a component within that row. Extra space tends to go toward the rightmost column and bottom row.

---

[1]. http://java.sun.com/products/JDK/CurrentRelease/api/java.awt.Insets.html

The following section discusses constraints in depth, in the context of explaining how the example applet works.

The GridBagLayout Applet Example Explained

Here, again, is the applet that shows a GridBagLayout in action.

http://java.sun.com/Series/Tutorial/ui/layout/gridbagExample.html

The following code creates the GridBagLayout and the components it manages. You can find the complete program on page 707. The program runs either within an applet, with the help of AppletButton (page 671), or as an application.

```
protected void makebutton(String name,
                          GridBagLayout gridbag,
                          GridBagConstraints c) {
    Button button = new Button(name);
    gridbag.setConstraints(button, c);
    add(button);
}

public GridBagWindow() {
    GridBagLayout gridbag = new GridBagLayout();
    GridBagConstraints c = new GridBagConstraints();

    setFont(new Font("Helvetica", Font.PLAIN, 14));
    setLayout(gridbag);

    c.fill = GridBagConstraints.BOTH;
    c.weightx = 1.0;
    makebutton("Button1", gridbag, c);
    makebutton("Button2", gridbag, c);
    makebutton("Button3", gridbag, c);

    c.gridwidth = GridBagConstraints.REMAINDER; //end of row
    makebutton("Button4", gridbag, c);

    c.weightx = 0.0;                            //reset to the default
    makebutton("Button5", gridbag, c); //another row

    c.gridwidth = GridBagConstraints.RELATIVE; //next to last
                                               //in row
```

```
      makebutton("Button6", gridbag, c);

      c.gridwidth = GridBagConstraints.REMAINDER; //end of row
      makebutton("Button7", gridbag, c);

      c.gridwidth = 1;                        //reset to the default
      c.gridheight = 2;
      c.weighty = 1.0;
      makebutton("Button8", gridbag, c);

      c.weighty = 0.0;                        //reset to the default
      c.gridwidth = GridBagConstraints.REMAINDER; //end of row
      c.gridheight = 1;                       //reset to the default
      makebutton("Button9", gridbag, c);
      makebutton("Button10", gridbag, c);
  }
```

This example uses one `GridBagConstraints` instance for all the components the
`GridBagLayout` manages. Just before each component is added to the container,
the code sets (or resets to the default values) the appropriate instance variables in
the `GridBagConstraints` object. It then uses the `setConstraints` method to
record all the constraint values for that component.

For example, just before adding a component that ends a row, you see the
following code:

```
  c.gridwidth = GridBagConstraints.REMAINDER; //end of row
```

And just before adding the next component, if the next component doesn't take
up a whole row, you see the same instance variable reset to its default value:

```
  c.gridwidth = 1;                          //reset to the default
```

For clarity, the following table shows all the constraints for each component that
the `GridBagLayout` handles. Values that are not the default values are marked in
bold. Values that are different from those in the previous table entry are marked
in *italic*.

Component	Constraints

All components	`gridx = GridBagConstraints.RELATIVE`
	`gridy = GridBagConstraints.RELATIVE`
	`fill = `**`GridBagConstraints.BOTH`**
	`ipadx = 0, ipady = 0`
	`insets = new Insets(0,0,0,0)`
	`anchor = GridBagConstraints.CENTER`

Component	Constraints
Button1 Button2 Button3	gridwidth = 1 gridheight = 1 **weightx = 1.0** weighty = 0.0
Button4	*gridwidth = GridBagConstraints.REMAINDER* gridheight = 1 **weightx = 1.0** weighty = 0.0
Button5	**gridwidth = GridBagConstraints.REMAINDER** gridheight = 1 *weightx = 0.0* weighty = 0.0
Button6	*gridwidth = GridBagConstraints.RELATIVE* gridheight = 1 weightx = 0.0 weighty = 0.0
Button7	*gridwidth = GridBagConstraints.REMAINDER* gridheight = 1 weightx = 0.0 weighty = 0.0
Button8	*gridwidth = 1* **gridheight = 2** weightx = 0.0 **weighty = 1.0**
Button9 Button10	*gridwidth = GridBagConstraints.REMAINDER* *gridheight = 1* weightx = 0.0 *weighty = 0.0*

All the components in this container are as large as possible, given their row and column. The program accomplishes this by setting the `GridBagConstraints` `fill` instance variable to `GridBagConstraints.BOTH`, leaving it at that setting for all the components. If the program didn't specify the fill, the buttons would be at their natural size, as in the following figure:

This program has four components that span multiple columns (Button5, Button6, Button9, and Button10) and one that spans multiple rows (Button8). In only one of these cases (Button8) is the height or width of the component explicitly specified. In all the other cases, the width of the component is specified as either GridBagConstraints.RELATIVE or GridBagConstraints.REMAINDER, which lets the GridBagLayout determine the component's size, taking into account the size of other components in the row.

When you enlarge the window the program brings up, the columns stay equal in width as they grow. This is because each component in the first row, where each component is one column wide, has weightx = 1.0. The actual value of these components' weightx is unimportant. What matters is that all the components, and consequently, all the columns, have an equal weight that is greater than 0. If no component managed by the GridBagLayout had weightx set, then when the components' container was made wider, the components would stay clumped together in the center of the container, like this:

Note that if you enlarge the window, the last row is the only one that gets taller. This is because only Button8 has weighty greater than zero. Button8 spans two rows, and the GridBagLayout happens to allocate all Button8's weight to the lowest row that Button8 occupies.

More GridBagLayout Examples

You can find more examples of using GridBagLayout throughout this tutorial. Here are a few programs that use GridBagLayout:

- DialogWindow.java (page 689)
- ListDemo.java (page 692)
- TextDemo.java (page 701)
- CoordinatesDemo.java (page 716) and RectangleDemo.java (page 718)
- ShowDocument.java (page 602)

Creating a Custom Layout Manager

Before you start creating a custom layout manager, make sure that no existing layout manager will work. In particular, GridBagLayout (page 424) is flexible enough to work in many cases. You can also find layout managers from other sources, such as from Gamelan (http://www.gamelan.com/).

To create a custom layout manager, you must create a class that implements the LayoutManager[1] interface. LayoutManager requires its adherents to implement five methods:

addLayoutComponent(String *name*, Component *comp*)

Called only by the Container add(String *name*, Component *component*) method. Layout managers that don't require that their components have names generally do nothing in this method.

removeLayoutComponent(Component *comp*)

Called by the Container remove and removeAll methods. Layout managers that don't require that their components have names generally do nothing in this method, since they can query the container for its components using the Container getComponents method.

preferredLayoutSize(Container *parent*)

Called by the Container preferredSize method, which is itself called under a variety of circumstances. This method should calculate and return the ideal size of the parent, assuming that the components it contains will be at or above their preferred sizes. This method must take the parent's internal borders, which are returned by the Container insets method, into account. This method returns a Dimension[2] object.

minimumLayoutSize(Container *parent*)

Called by the Container minimumSize method, which is itself called under a variety of circumstances. This method should calculate and return the minimum size of the parent, assuming that the components it contains will be at or above their minimum sizes. This method must take into account the parent's internal borders, which are returned by the Container insets method. Like preferredLayoutSize, this method returns a Dimension object.

layoutContainer(Container *parent*)

Called when the container is first displayed, and each time its size changes. A layout manager's layoutContainer method doesn't actually draw components. It simply invokes each component's resize, move, and reshape methods to set the component's size and position. This method must take the parent's internal borders, which are returned by the Container insets method, into account. You can't assume that the preferredLayoutSize or minimumLayoutSize method will be called before layoutContainer is called.

Besides implementing the five methods required by LayoutManager, layout managers generally implement at least one public constructor and the Object toString[3] method.

[1.] http://java.sun.com/products/JDK/CurrentRelease/api/java.awt.LayoutManager.html

[2.] http://java.sun.com/products/JDK/CurrentRelease/api/java.awt.Dimension.html

[3.] http://java.sun.com/products/JDK/CurrentRelease/api/java.lang.Object.html

The complete code for a custom layout manager named `DiagonalLayout` is on page 709. `DiagonalLayout` lays out components diagonally, from left to right, with one component per row. An example of a program that uses it is on page 713.

Here's `DiagonalLayout` in action:

http://java.sun.com/Series/Tutorial/ui/layout/custom.html

Laying Out Components Without a Layout Manager (Absolute Positioning)

Although it's possible to layout components without a layout manager, you should use a layout manager if at all possible. Layout managers make it easy to resize a container and adjust to platform-dependent component appearance and to different font sizes. They also can be reused easily by other containers and other programs. If your custom container won't be reused, can't be resized, and completely controls normal system-dependent factors such as font size and component appearance (implementing its own controls if necessary), then absolute positioning might make sense.

The window in the following figure uses absolute positioning.

http://java.sun.com/Series/Tutorial/ui/layout/none.html

The following code contains the instance variable declarations, constructor implementation, and `paint` method implementation of the window class. You can find the complete program on page 714. The program runs either within an applet, with the help of <u>AppletButton</u> (page 671), or as an application.

```java
public class NoneWindow extends Frame {
    . . .
    private boolean laidOut = false;
    private Button b1, b2, b3;

    public NoneWindow() {
        super();
        setLayout(null);
        setFont(new Font("Helvetica", Font.PLAIN, 14));

        b1 = new Button("one");
        add(b1);
        b2 = new Button("two");
        add(b2);
        b3 = new Button("three");
        add(b3);
    }

    public void paint(Graphics g) {
        if (!laidOut) {
            Insets insets = insets();
            /*
             * We're guaranteed that insets will return a
             * valid Insets if called from paint -- it isn't
             * valid when called from the constructor.
             *
             * We could perhaps cache this in an ivar, but
             * insets can change, and when they do,
             * the AWT creates a whole new
             * Insets object; the old one is invalid.
             */
            b1.reshape(50 + insets.left, 5 + insets.top, 50, 20);
            b2.reshape(70 + insets.left, 35 + insets.top,
                        50, 20);
            b3.reshape(130 + insets.left, 15 + insets.top,
                        50, 30);

            laidOut = true;
        }
    }

    . . .
}
```

Common Layout Problems
(and Their Solutions)

Problem: How do I specify a component's exact size?
- First, make sure that you really need to set the component's exact size. The standard components have different sizes, depending on the platform they're running on and the font they use, so it usually doesn't make sense to specify their exact size.

  For custom components whose contents do not change size (such as images), specifying the exact size makes sense. For custom components, you need to override the Component minimumSize and preferredSize methods to return the correct size of the component.

  To change the size of a component that's already been displayed, see the next problem.

Note: All component sizes are subject to layout manager approval. The FlowLayout and GridBagLayout layout managers use the component's natural size (the latter depending on the constraints that you set), but BorderLayout and GridLayout usually don't. Other options are writing or finding a custom layout manager or using absolute positioning.

Problem: How do I resize a component?
- Once a component has been displayed, you can change its size using the Component resize method. You then need to call the validate method on the component's container to make sure the container is laid out again.

Problem: My custom component is being sized too small.
- Does the component implement the preferredSize and minimumSize methods? If so, do they return the right values?
- Are you using a layout manager that can use as much space as is available? See General Rules for Using Layout Managers (page 418) for some tips on choosing a layout manager and specifying that it use the maximum available space for a particular component.

If you don't see your problem in this list, see Common Component Problems (and Their Solutions) (page 412). If that fails, check the Web page for this book.

```
http://java.sun.com/Series/Tutorial/book.html
```

Working with Graphics

THIS lesson teaches you everything you need to make your program draw to the screen. You'll learn how to create simple geometric shapes, display text, and display images. You'll also learn how to animate these shapes and images. This lesson assumes that you've read the **Overview of the Java UI** (page 361), especially <u>The Anatomy of a GUI-Based Program</u> (page 366).

<u>Overview of AWT Graphics Support</u> (page 438) gives an overview of the AWT support for drawing, with links to where you can find more information.

<u>Using Graphics Primitives</u> (page 440) teaches you how to draw simple shapes and display text effectively. It includes examples of using the `Graphics`, `Font`, and `FontMetrics` classes. One rectangle-drawing example can be used as the basis for implementing selection in a paint program.

<u>Using Images</u> (page 449) discusses the Java support for images and tells you how to load, display, and manipulate images.

<u>Performing Animation</u> (page 463) describes how to perform animation well. Many Java programs (especially applets) perform animation, whether it's the classic, cartoon-style animation of Duke waving (visible in the online **Trail Map**[1]), program-generated graphics such as a scrolling checkerboard, or simply moving static images across the screen. This section includes tips on improving graphics performance and appearance, using techniques such as implementing the `update` method and double buffering.

[1.] http://java.sun.com/Series/Tutorial/index.html

Common Graphics Problems (and Their Solutions) (page 479) describes some common problems of graphics programs, along with possible solutions to these problems.

Overview of AWT Graphics Support

As you learned from the first lesson in this trail, in the Drawing section (page 371), the AWT drawing system controls when and how programs can draw. In response to a call to a component's `repaint` method, the AWT invokes that component's `update` method to request that the component redraw itself. By default, the `update` method in turn invokes the component's `paint` method.

An additional wrinkle in this scenario is that sometimes the AWT calls the `paint` method directly, instead of calling `update`. This almost always happens as a result of the AWT reacting to an external stimulus, such as the component first appearing on screen, or the component being uncovered by another window. You'll learn more about `paint` and `update` in the Eliminating Flashing (page 469) section, later in this lesson.

The Graphics Object

The lone argument to the `paint` and `update` methods is a Graphics[1] object. Graphics objects are the key to all drawing. They support the two basic kinds of drawing: primitive graphics (lines, rectangles, and text) and images. You'll learn about primitive graphics in Using Graphics Primitives (page 440). You'll learn about images in Using Images (page 449).

Besides supplying methods to draw primitive graphics and images to the screen, a Graphics object provides a drawing context by maintaining state such as the current drawing area and the current drawing color. You can decrease the current drawing area by *clipping* it, but you can never increase the drawing area. In this way, a Graphics object ensures that components can draw only within its own drawing area. You'll learn more about clipping in Overriding the `update` Method (page 470).

The Coordinate System

Each Component object has its own integer coordinate system, ranging from (0, 0) to (*width* - 1, *height* - 1), with each unit representing the size of one pixel. As the following figure shows, the upper left corner of the component's drawing

---

[1] http://java.sun.com/products/JDK/CurrentRelease/api/java.awt.Graphics.html

area is (0, 0). The X coordinate increases to the right, and the Y coordinate increases downward.

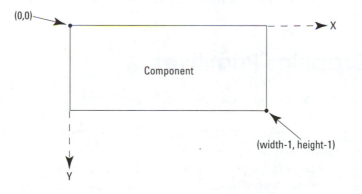

Here's an applet that we'll build on later in this lesson. Whenever you click within the framed area, the applet draws a dot where you clicked and displays a string describing where the click occurred.

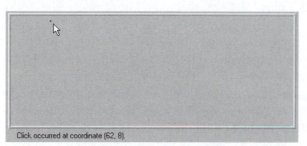

Click occurred at coordinate (62, 8).

http://java.sun.com/Series/Tutorial/ui/drawing/overview.html

The Four Forms of the `repaint` Method

Remember that programs can call a component's `repaint` method to request that the AWT call the component's `update` method. Here are descriptions of the four forms of the `repaint` method:

`repaint()`

Requests that the AWT call the component's `update` method as soon as possible. This is the most frequently used form of `repaint`.

`repaint(long time)`

Requests that the AWT call the component's `update` method as much as *time* milliseconds from now.

`repaint(int x, int y, int width, int height)`

Requests that the AWT call the component's `update` method as soon as possible, but repaint only the specified part of the component.

`repaint(long` *time*`, int` *x*`, int` *y*`, int` *width*`, int` *height*`)`

> Requests that the AWT call the component's `update` method as much as *time* milliseconds from now, but repaint only the specified part of the component.

Using Graphics Primitives

The next few sections provide the details you'll need to generate primitive graphics and text.

Drawing Shapes (page 440) tells you how to draw shapes, such as lines, rectangles, ovals, arcs, and polygons.

Working with Text (page 445) tells you how to draw text using the `Graphics` `drawString` method. It also tells you how to use `Font` and `FontMetrics` objects to get information about a font's size characteristics.

Drawing Shapes

The `Graphics`[1] class defines methods for drawing the following kinds of shapes:

- Lines—`drawLine`, which draws a line in the `Graphics` object's current color, which is initialized to the component's foreground color
- Rectangles—`drawRect`, `fillRect`, and `clearRect`, where `drawRect` draws an unfilled rectangle in the `Graphics` object's current color, `fillRect` fills a rectangle with the `Graphics` object's current color, and `clearRect` fills a rectangle with the component's background color
- Raised or lowered rectangles—`draw3DRect` and `fill3DRect`
- Round-edged rectangles—`drawRoundRect` and `fillRoundRect`
- Ovals—`drawOval` and `fillOval`
- Arcs—`drawArc` and `fillArc`
- Polygons—`drawPolygon` and `fillPolygon`

Except for polygons and lines, all shapes are specified using their bounding rectangle. Once you understand rectangles, drawing other shapes is relatively easy. For this reason, this section concentrates on rectangle drawing.

Example 1: Simple Rectangle Drawing

The applet on page 439 uses the `draw3DRect` and `fillRect` methods to draw its interface. Here's the applet again:

---

[1] http://java.sun.com/products/JDK/CurrentRelease/api/java.awt.Graphics.html

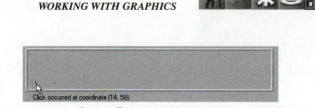

http://java.sun.com/Series/Tutorial/ui/drawing/drawingShapes.html

You can find the complete program on page 716. Here is just the drawing code:

```
//In FramedArea (a Panel subclass):
public void paint(Graphics g) {
    Dimension d = size();
    Color bg = getBackground();

    //Draw a fancy frame around the applet.
    g.setColor(bg);
    g.draw3DRect(0, 0, d.width - 1, d.height - 1, true);
    g.draw3DRect(3, 3, d.width - 7, d.height - 7, false);
}

//In CoordinateArea (a Canvas subclass):
public void paint(Graphics g) {
    //If user has clicked, paint a tiny rectangle where click
    //occurred
    if (point != null) {
        g.fillRect(point.x - 1, point.y - 1, 2, 2);
    }
}
```

This applet creates and contains a FramedArea object, which in turn creates and contains a CoordinateArea object. The first call to draw3DRect creates a rectangle as big as the FramedArea's drawing area. The true argument specifies that the rectangle should appear to be raised. The second call to draw3DRect creates a second rectangle just a bit smaller, with false specifying that the rectangle should appear to be sunken. Together, the two calls produce the effect of a raised frame that contains the CoordinateArea. (FramedArea implements the insets method so that the CoordinateArea's drawing area is a few pixels inside of the FramedArea.)

The CoordinateArea uses fillRect to draw a rectangle whose size is two pixels square at the position where the user clicks.

Example 2: Using a Rectangle to Indicate a Selected Area

You can use the following applet as a basis for implementing selection in a drawing program. When the user drags the mouse, the applet continuously displays a rectangle. The rectangle starts at the cursor position where the user first pressed the mouse button and ends at the current cursor position.

Rectangle goes from (0, 0) to (81, 45).

http://java.sun.com/Series/Tutorial/ui/drawing/drawingShapes.html

You can find the complete program on page 718. Here is the code that's significantly different from the code of the previous applet:

```
class SelectionArea extends Canvas {
    . . .

    public boolean mouseDown(Event event, int x, int y) {
        currentRect = new Rectangle(x, y, 0, 0);
        repaint();
        return false;
    }

    public boolean mouseDrag(Event event, int x, int y) {
        currentRect.resize(x - currentRect.x, y -
                            currentRect.y);
        repaint();
        return false;
    }

    public boolean mouseUp(Event event, int x, int y) {
        currentRect.resize(x - currentRect.x, y -
                            currentRect.y);
        repaint();
        return false;
    }

    public void paint(Graphics g) {
        Dimension d = size;

        //update has already cleared the previous rectangle,
        //so we don't need to here.

        //If currentRect exists, paint a rectangle on top.
        if (currentRect != null) {
            Rectangle box = getDrawableRect(currentRect, d);
            controller.rectChanged(box);

            //Draw the box outline.
            g.drawRect(box.x, box.y, box.width - 1, box.height
                - 1);
        }
    }
```

```
Rectangle getDrawableRect(Rectangle originalRect,
                         Dimension drawingArea) {
    . . .
    //Make sure rectangle width and height are positive.
    . . .
    //The rectangle shouldn't extend past the drawing area.
    . . .
}
}
```

The `SelectionArea` keeps track of the currently selected rectangle, using a `Rectangle` object called `currentRect`. As implemented, the `currentRect` keeps the same origin (`currentRect.x`, `currentRect.y`) for as long as the user drags the mouse. This means that the height and width of the rectangle can be negative.

However, the `drawXxx` and `fillXxx` methods don't draw anything if either the height or width is negative. For this reason, when the `SelectionArea` draws the rectangle, it must specify the upper left vertex of the rectangle so that the width and height are positive. The `SelectionArea` class defines a `getDrawableRect` method to perform the necessary calculations to find the upper left vertex. The `getDrawableRect` method also makes sure that the rectangle doesn't extend beyond the boundaries of its drawing area. The definition of `getDrawableRect` is near the end of the file that starts on page 718.

Note: It's perfectly legal to specify x, y, height, or width values that are negative or cause a result larger than the drawing area. Values outside the drawing area don't matter too much because they're clipped to the drawing area. You just won't see part of the shape. Negative height or width results in the shape not being drawn at all.

Example 3: A Shape Sampler

The applet in the following figure demonstrates all the shapes you can draw and fill.

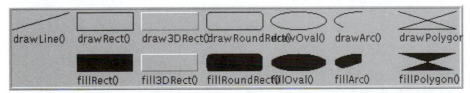

http://java.sun.com/Series/Tutorial/ui/drawing/drawingShapes.html

Unless your applet viewer's default font is very small, the text displayed in this applet might look ugly in places. Words might be drawn on top of each other.

And because this applet doesn't use the `insets` method to protect its boundaries, text might be drawn on top of the frame around the applet. The next section improves on this example, teaching you how to make sure text fits within a given space.

You can find the complete code for the shape-drawing applet on page 721. The following code draws the geometric shapes. The `rectHeight` and `rect-Width` variables specify the size in pixels of the area each shape must be drawn in. The x and y variables change for each shape, so that the shapes aren't drawn on top of each other.

```
Color bg = getBackground();
Color fg = getForeground();
. . .

// drawLine(x1, y1, x2, y2)
g.drawLine(x, y+rectHeight-1, x + rectWidth, y);
. . .

// drawRect(x, y, width, height)
g.drawRect(x, y, rectWidth, rectHeight);
. . .

// draw3DRect(x, y, width, height, raised)
g.setColor(bg);
g.draw3DRect(x, y, rectWidth, rectHeight, true);
g.setColor(fg);
. . .

// drawRoundRect(x, y, width, height, arcw, arch)
g.drawRoundRect(x, y, rectWidth, rectHeight, 10, 10);
. . .

// drawOval(x, y, w, h)
g.drawOval(x, y, rectWidth, rectHeight);
. . .

// drawArc(x, y, w, h)
g.drawArc(x, y, rectWidth, rectHeight, 90, 135);
. . .

// drawPolygon(polygon)
Polygon polygon = new Polygon();
polygon.addPoint(x, y);
polygon.addPoint(x+rectWidth, y+rectHeight);
polygon.addPoint(x, y+rectHeight);
polygon.addPoint(x+rectWidth, y);
//polygon.addPoint(x, y); //don't complete; fill will,
                          //draw won't
```

```
g.drawPolygon(polygon);
. . .

// fillRect(x, y, width, height)
g.fillRect(x, y, rectWidth, rectHeight);
. . .

// fill3DRect(x, y, width, height, raised)
g.setColor(bg);
g.fill3DRect(x, y, rectWidth, rectHeight, true);
g.setColor(fg);
. . .

// fillRoundRect(x, y, width, height, arcw, arch)
g.fillRoundRect(x, y, rectWidth, rectHeight, 10, 10);
. . .

// fillOval(x, y, w, h)
g.fillOval(x, y, rectWidth, rectHeight);
. . .

// fillArc(x, y, w, h)
g.fillArc(x, y, rectWidth, rectHeight, 90, 135);
. . .

// fillPolygon(polygon)
Polygon filledPolygon = new Polygon();
filledPolygon.addPoint(x, y);
filledPolygon.addPoint(x+rectWidth, y+rectHeight);
filledPolygon.addPoint(x, y+rectHeight);
filledPolygon.addPoint(x+rectWidth, y);
g.fillPolygon(filledPolygon);
```

Working with Text

Support for working with primitive text is spread between the AWT Graphics[1], Font[2], and FontMetrics [3] classes.

Drawing Text

When you're writing code to draw text, first consider whether you can use a text-oriented component, such as the Label, TextField, or TextArea class. If a

---

[1.] http://java.sun.com/products/JDK/CurrentRelease/api/java.awt.Graphics.html
[2.] http://java.sun.com/products/JDK/CurrentRelease/api/java.awt.Font.html
[3.] http://java.sun.com/products/JDK/CurrentRelease/api/java.awt.FontMetrics.html

text-oriented component isn't appropriate, you can use the `Graphics` draw-
Bytes, `drawChars`, or `drawString` method.

Here is an example of code that draws a string to the screen:

```
g.drawString("Hello World!", x, y);
```

For the text-drawing methods, x and y are integers that specify the position of
the *lower left* corner of the text. To be precise, the y coordinate specifies the
baseline of the text—the line that most letters rest on. This doesn't include room
for the tails (*descenders*) on letters such as "y". Be sure to make y large enough
to allow vertical space for the text, but small enough to allow room for descenders.

This figure shows the baseline, as well as the ascender and descender lines.
You'll learn more about ascenders and descenders a bit later.

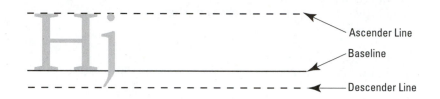

The following applet illustrates what can happen when you're not careful about
where you position your text:

drawString() at (2, 5)

drawString() at (2, 30)

drawString() at (2, height)

http://java.sun.com/Series/Tutorial/ui/drawing/drawingText.html

The top string is cut off, since its y argument is 5, which leaves only 5 pixels
above the baseline for the string—not enough for most fonts. The middle string
shows up just fine, unless you have a huge default font. Most of the letters in the
bottom string display fine, except for letters with descenders. All descenders in
the bottom string are cut off, since the code that displays this string doesn't allow
room for them. You can find this applet's source code on page 724.

Note: The text-drawing methods' interpretation of x and y is different from that of
the shape-drawing methods. When drawing a shape (such as a rectangle), x and y
specify the upper left corner of the shape's bounding rectangle, instead of the lower
left corner.

Getting Information About a Font: `FontMetrics`

The shape-drawing example (page 440) can be improved by choosing a font that's smaller than the usual default font. The following example does this and also enlarges the shapes to take up the space freed by the font's smaller height. This figure contains the improved applet. You can find its source code on page 725.

http://java.sun.com/Series/Tutorial/ui/drawing/drawingText.html

The following code chooses the appropriate font by using a `FontMetrics` object to get details of the font's size. For example, the following loop in the `paint` method ensures that the longest string displayed by the applet ("drawRound-Rect") fits within the space each shape is allotted.

```
boolean textFits = false;
Font font = g.getFont();
FontMetrics fontMetrics = g.getFontMetrics();
while (!textFits) {
    if ((fontMetrics.getHeight() <= maxCharHeight)
        && (fontMetrics.stringWidth("drawRoundRect()")
            <= gridWidth)) {
        textFits = true;
    } else {
        g.setFont(font = new Font(font.getName(),
                                  font.getStyle(),
                                  font.getSize() - 1));
        fontMetrics = g.getFontMetrics();
    }
}
```

This code uses the `Graphics` `getFont`, `setFont`, and `getFontMetrics` methods to get and set the current font and to get the `FontMetrics` object that corresponds to the font. From the `FontMetrics` `getHeight` and `getStringWidth` methods, the code gets vertical and horizontal size information about the font.

The following figure shows some of the information that a `FontMetrics` object can provide about a font's size.

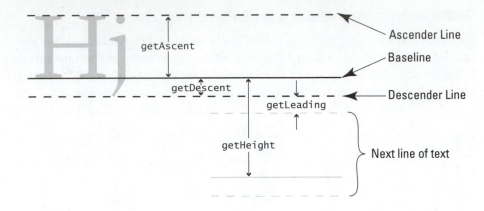

Here's a summary of the FontMetrics methods that return information about a font's vertical size:

getAscent(), getMaxAscent()

The getAscent method returns the number of pixels between the ascender line and the baseline. Generally, the ascender line represents the typical height of capital letters. Specifically, the ascent and descent values are chosen by the font's designer to represent the correct text "color," or density of ink, so that the text appears as the designer planned it. The ascent typically provides enough room for almost all of the characters in the font, except perhaps for accents on capital letters. The getMaxAscent method accounts for these exceptionally tall characters.

getDescent(), getMaxDescent()

The getDescent method returns the number of pixels between the baseline and the descender line. In most fonts, all characters fall within the descender line at their lowest point. Just in case, though, you can use the getMaxDescent method to get a distance guaranteed to encompass all characters.

getHeight()

Returns the number of pixels normally found between the baseline of one line of text and the baseline of the next line of text. Note that this includes an allowance for leading.

getLeading()

Returns the suggested distance in pixels between one line of text and the next. Specifically the leading is the distance between the descender line of one line of text and the ascender line of the next line of text. By the way, "leading" is pronounced "LEDDing."

Note that the font size, which is returned by the Font class getSize method, is an abstract measurement. Theoretically, it corresponds to the ascent plus the descent. Practically, however, the font designer decides exactly how tall a 12-point font (for example) is. For example, 12-point Times is often slightly shorter than 12-point Helvetica. Typically, font size is measured in *points*, which are approximately 1/72 of an inch.

`FontMetrics` provides the following methods to return information about the horizontal size of a font's characters. These methods take into account the spacing around each character. More precisely, each method returns *not* the number of pixels taken up by a particular character (or characters), but the number of pixels by which the *current point* will be advanced when that character (or characters) is shown. We call this the *advance width* to distinguish it from the character or text width.

getMaxAdvance()

The advance width in pixels of the widest character in the font.

bytesWidth(byte[] *data*, int *offset*, int *length*)

The advance width of the text represented by the specified array of bytes. The first integer argument specifies the starting offset of the data within the byte array. The second integer argument specifies the maximum number of bytes to check.

charWidth(int *ch*), charWidth(char *ch*)

The advance width of the specified character.

charsWidth(char[] *data*, int *offset*, int *length*)

The advance width of the string represented by the specified character array.

stringWidth(String *str*)

The advance width of the specified string.

getWidths()

The advance width of each of the first 256 characters in the font.

Using Images

This is an image:

The next few sections provide the details you'll need to work with images. You'll learn how to load, display, and manipulate them.

Support for using images is spread across the `java.applet`, `java.awt`, and `java.awt.image` packages. Every image is represented by a `java.awt.Image` object. In addition to the `Image` class, the `java.awt` package provides other basic image support, such as the `Graphics drawImage` methods, the `Toolkit`

getImage methods, and the MediaTracker class. In java.applet, the Applet getImage methods make it easy for applets to load images using URLs. Finally, the java.awt.image package provides interfaces and classes that let you create, manipulate, and observe images.

The AWT makes it easy to load images in either of two formats: GIF and JPEG. Loading Images (page 450) describes how to use the Applet and Toolkit getImage methods to load images. By default, the data for an image is loaded in the background the first time you try to draw the image. This section describes how to change or monitor this default image loading behavior by using the MediaTracker class or by implementing the imageUpdate method, which is defined by the ImageObserver interface. This section also tells you how to create images on the fly using the MemoryImageSource class.

It's easy to display an image using the Graphics object that's passed into your update or paint method. You simply invoke a drawImage method on the Graphics object. Displaying Images (page 453) explains the four forms of drawImage, two of which scale the image. Like getImage, drawImage is asynchronous, returning immediately even if the image hasn't been fully loaded or drawn yet.

The Manipulating Images (page 454) gives you an overview of how to change images, using filters.

Loading Images

This section describes how to get the Image object corresponding to an image. As long as the image data is in GIF or JPEG format and you know its filename or URL, it's easy to get an Image object for it: just use one of the Applet or Toolkit getImage methods. The getImage methods return immediately, without checking whether the image data exists. The actual loading of image data normally doesn't start until the first time the program tries to draw the image.

For many programs, this invisible background loading works well. Other programs, though, need to keep track of the progress of the image loading. This section explains how to do so using the MediaTracker class and the ImageObserver interface.

Finally, this section tells you how to create images on the fly, using a class such as MemoryImageSource.

Using the getImage Methods

This section discusses first the Applet getImage methods and then the Toolkit getImage methods.

The Applet class supplies two getImage methods:

- getImage(URL *url*)
- getImage(URL *url*, String *name*)

Only applets can use the Applet getImage methods. Moreover, the Applet get-Image methods don't work until the applet has a full context. For this reason, these methods *do not work* if called in a constructor or in a statement that declares an instance variable. Instead, you must call getImage from a method such as init.

The following code examples show you how to use the Applet getImage methods. See <u>Creating a GUI</u> (page 170) for an explanation of the getCodeBase and getDocumentBase methods.

```
//In a method in an Applet subclass:
Image image1 = getImage(getCodeBase(), "imageFile.gif");
Image image2 = getImage(getDocumentBase(), "anImageFile.jpeg");
Image image3 = getImage(imageURL);
```

The Toolkit class declares two more getImage methods:

- getImage(URL *url*)
- getImage(String *filename*)

You can get a Toolkit object either by invoking Toolkit's getDefaultToolkit class method or by invoking the Component getToolkit instance method. The Component getToolkit method returns the toolkit that was used (or will be used) to implement the component.

The following examples show how to use the Toolkit getImage methods. Every Java application and applet can use these methods, with applets subject to the usual security restrictions. You can read about applet security in <u>Understanding Applet Capabilities and Restrictions</u> (page 197).

```
Toolkit toolkit = Toolkit.getDefaultToolkit();
Image image1 = toolkit.getImage("imageFile.gif");
Image image2 = toolkit.getImage(new URL(
        "http://java.sun.com/graphics/people.gif"));
```

Requesting and Tracking Image Loading: MediaTracker and ImageObserver

The AWT provides two ways for you to track image loading: the <u>MediaTracker</u>[1] class and the <u>ImageObserver</u>[2] interface. The MediaTracker class is sufficient for many programs. You create a MediaTracker instance, tell it to track one or

---

[1]. http://java.sun.com/products/JDK/CurrentRelease/api/java.awt.MediaTracker.html

[2]. http://java.sun.com/products/JDK/CurrentRelease/api/java.awt.image.ImageObserver.html

more images, and then ask the `MediaTracker` the status of those images as needed. An example is explained in <u>Improving the Appearance and Performance of Image Animation</u> (page 476).

The animation example shows two particularly useful `MediaTracker` features: requesting that the data for a group of images be loaded, and waiting for a group of images to be loaded. To request that the image data for a group of images be loaded, use the forms of `checkID` and `checkAll` that take a boolean argument. Setting the boolean argument to `true` starts loading the data for any images that aren't yet being loaded. Alternatively, you can request that the image data be loaded and wait for it using the `waitForID` and `waitForAll` methods.

If you browse the `MediaTracker` API documentation, you might notice that the `Component` class defines two useful-looking methods: `checkImage` and `prepareImage`. The `MediaTracker` class has made calling these methods directly largely unnecessary.

The `ImageObserver` interface lets you keep even closer track of image loading than `MediaTracker` allows. The `Component` class uses it so that components are repainted as the images they display are loaded. To use the `ImageObserver` interface, you implement the `ImageObserver` `imageUpdate` method and make sure that the implementing object is registered as the image observer. Usually, this registration happens when you specify an `ImageObserver` to the `drawImage` method, as described in the next section. The `imageUpdate` method is called whenever information about an image becomes available.

The following example implements the `Image Observer` interface's `imageUpdate` method. This example uses `imageUpdate` to position two images as soon as their size is known, and to repaint every 100 milliseconds until both images are loaded. You can find the complete program on page 728.

```
public boolean imageUpdate(Image theimg, int infoflags,
                           int x, int y, int w, int h) {
    if ((infoflags & (ERROR)) != 0) {
        errored = true;
    }
    if ((infoflags & (WIDTH | HEIGHT)) != 0) {
        positionImages();
    }
    boolean done = ((infoflags & (ERROR | FRAMEBITS |
                    ALLBITS))!= 0);
    // Repaint immediately if we are done, otherwise repaint
    // in 100 milliseconds.
    repaint(done ? 0 : 100);
    return !done; //If done, no further updates required.
}
```

Creating Images with `MemoryImageSource`

With the help of an image producer such as the `MemoryImageSource`[1] class, you can construct images from scratch. The following code example calculates a 100 x 100 image representing a fade from black to blue along the X axis and a fade from black to red along the Y axis.

```java
int w = 100;
int h = 100;
int[] pix = new int[w * h];
int index = 0;
for (int y = 0; y < h; y++) {
    int red = (y * 255) / (h - 1);
    for (int x = 0; x < w; x++) {
        int blue = (x * 255) / (w - 1);
        pix[index++] = (255 << 24) | (red << 16) | blue;
    }
}
Image img = createImage(new MemoryImageSource(w, h, pix, 0, w));
```

Displaying Images

The following statement displays an image at its normal size in the upper left corner of the component area (0, 0):

```java
g.drawImage(image, 0, 0, this);
```

This statement displays an image scaled to be 300 pixels wide and 62 pixels tall, starting at the coordinates (90, 0):

```java
g.drawImage(myImage, 90, 0, 300, 62, this);
```

The following applet loads a single image and displays it twice, using both code examples that you see above. You can find the complete program on page 730.

http://java.sun.com/Series/Tutorial/ui/drawing/drawingImages.html

---

[1] http://java.sun.com/products/JDK/CurrentRelease/api/java.awt.image.MemoryImageSource.html

The `Graphics` class declares the following `drawImage` methods. They all return a boolean value, although this value is rarely used. The return value is `true` if the image has been completely loaded and completely drawn; otherwise, the return value is `false`.

- `drawImage(Image` *img*`, int` *x*`, int` *y*`, ImageObserver` *observer*`)`
- `drawImage(Image` *img*`, int` *x*`, int` *y*`, int` *width*`, int` *height*`, ImageObserver` *observer*`)`
- `drawImage(Image` *img*`, int` *x*`, int` *y*`, Color` *bgcolor*`, ImageObserver` *observer*`)`
- `drawImage(Image` *img*`, int` *x*`, int` *y*`, int` *width*`, int` *height*`, Color` *bgcolor*`, ImageObserver` *observer*`)`

The `drawImage` methods have the following arguments:

`Image` *img*

The image to draw.

`int` *x*`, int` *y*

The coordinates of the upper left corner of the image.

`int` *width*`, int` *height*

The width and height (in pixels) of the image.

`Color` *bgcolor*

The color to draw underneath the image. This argument can be useful if the image contains transparent pixels and you know that the image will be displayed against a solid background of the indicated color.

`ImageObserver` *observer*

An object that implements the `ImageObserver` interface. This argument registers the object as the image observer so that it is notified whenever new information about the image becomes available. Most components can simply specify `this`. The reason why `this` works as the image observer is that the `Component` class implements the `ImageObserver` interface. Its implementation invokes the `repaint` method as the image data is loaded, which is usually what you want to happen.

The `drawImage` method returns after displaying the image data that has been loaded so far. To make sure that `drawImage` draws only complete images, you must track image loading. See the <u>previous section</u> (page 450) for information on tracking image loading.

Manipulating Images

The following figure illustrates how image data is created behind the scenes. An *image producer*—an object that adheres to the <u>`ImageProducer`</u>[1] interface— pro-

---

1. http://java.sun.com/products/JDK/CurrentRelease/api/java.awt.image.ImageProducer.html

duces the raw data for an `Image` object. The image producer provides this data to an *image consumer*—an object that adheres to the `ImageConsumer`[1] interface. Unless you need to manipulate or create custom images, you don't usually need to know about image producers and consumers. The AWT automatically uses image producers and consumers behind the scenes.

The AWT supports image manipulation by letting you insert image filters between image producers and image consumers. An *image filter* is an `Image-Filter`[2] object that sits between a producer and a consumer, modifying the image data before the consumer gets it. The `ImageFilter` class implements the `ImageConsumer` interface, since image filters intercept messages that the producer sends to the consumer. The following figure shows how an image filter sits between the image producer and consumer.

Using an existing image filter is easy. Simply use the following code, modifying the image filter constructor as necessary:

```
Image sourceImage;
...//Initialize sourceImage, using the Toolkit or Applet
   //getImage() method.
ImageFilter filter = new SomeImageFilter();
ImageProducer producer = new
                  FilteredImageSource(sourceImage.getSource(),
                                      filter);
Image resultImage = createImage(producer);
```

1. http://java.sun.com/products/JDK/CurrentRelease/api/java.awt.image.ImageConsumer.html
2. http://java.sun.com/products/JDK/CurrentRelease/api/java.awt.image.ImageFilter.html

The next section explains how this code works and tells you where to find some image filters.

What if you can't find an image filter that does what you need? You can write your own image filter. How to Write an Image Filter (page 459) gives you some tips on how to do so, including pointers to examples and an explanation of a custom filter that rotates images.

How to Use an Image Filter

The following applet uses a filter to rotate an image. The filter is a custom filter named `RotateFilter` that you'll see discussed a bit later. All you need to know about the filter to use it is that its constructor takes a single `double` argument: the rotation angle in radians. This applet converts the number the user enters from degrees into radians, so that the applet can construct a `RotateFilter`.

http://java.sun.com/Series/Tutorial/ui/drawing/useFilter.html

Here's the source code that uses the filter. You can find the complete program on page 731.

```java
public class ImageRotator extends Applet {
    . . .
    RotatorCanvas rotator;
    double radiansPerDegree = Math.PI / 180;

    public void init() {
        //Load the image.
        Image image = getImage(getCodeBase(), "../images/"
                               + "rocketship.gif");

        ...//Create the component that uses the image filter:
        rotator = new RotatorCanvas(image);
        . . .
        add(rotator);
        . . .
    }
```

```
    public boolean action(Event evt, Object arg) {
        int degrees;

        ...//Get the number of degrees to rotate the image by.

        //Convert to radians.
        rotator.rotateImage((double)degrees * radiansPerDegree);

        return true;
    }
}

class RotatorCanvas extends Canvas {
    Image sourceImage;
    Image resultImage;

    public RotatorCanvas(Image image) {
        sourceImage = image;
        resultImage = sourceImage;
    }

    public void rotateImage(double angle) {
        ImageFilter filter = new RotateFilter(angle);
        ImageProducer producer = new FilteredImageSource(
                                    sourceImage.getSource(),
                                    filter);
        resultImage = createImage(producer);
        repaint();
    }

    public void paint(Graphics g) {
        Dimension d = size();
        int x = (d.width - resultImage.getWidth(this)) / 2;
        int y = (d.height - resultImage.getHeight(this)) / 2;

        g.drawImage(resultImage, x, y, this);
    }
}
```

How the Code Works.   To use an image filter, a program goes through the following steps:

1. Get an Image object (usually done with a getImage method).
2. Using the getSource method, get the data source (an ImageProducer) for the Image object.
3. Create an instance of the image filter, initializing the filter as necessary.
4. Create a FilteredImageSource object, passing the constructor the image source and filter objects.

5. With the `Component` `createImage` method, create a new `Image` object that has the `FilteredImageSource` as its image producer.

This might sound complex, but it's actually easy to implement. The real complexity is behind the scenes, as we'll explain a bit later. First, we'll explain the code in the example applet that uses the image filter.

In the example applet, the `RotatorCanvas` `rotateImage` method performs most of the tasks associated with using the image filter. The one exception is the first step, getting the original `Image` object, which is performed by the applet's `init` method. This `Image` object is passed to the `RotatorCanvas`, which refers to it as `sourceImage`.

The `rotateImage` method instantiates the image filter by calling the filter's constructor. The single argument to the constructor is the angle, in radians, to rotate the image by.

```
ImageFilter filter = new RotateFilter(angle);
```

Next, the `rotateImage` method creates a `FilteredImageSource` instance. The first argument to the `FilteredImageSource` constructor is the image source, obtained with the `getSource` method. The second argument is the filter object.

```
ImageProducer producer = new FilteredImageSource(
                            sourceImage.getSource(),
                            filter);
```

Finally, the code creates a second `Image`, `resultImage`, by invoking the `Component` `createImage` method. The lone argument to `createImage` is the `FilteredImageSource` created in the previous statement.

```
resultImage = createImage(producer);
```

What Happens Behind the Scenes.   This section explains how image filtering works, behind the scenes. If you don't care about these implementation details, feel free to skip ahead to Where to Find Image Filters (page 459).

The first thing you need to know is that the AWT uses `ImageConsumers` behind the scenes, in response to `drawImage` requests. So the component that displays the image isn't the image consumer—some object deep in the AWT is the image consumer.

The `createImage` call in the previous statement sets up an `Image` (`resultImage`), that expects to get image data from its producer, the `FilteredImageSource` instance. Here's what the path for the image data looks like from the perspective of `resultImage`:

The dotted line indicates that the image consumer never actually gets data from the `FilteredImageSource`. Instead, when the image consumer requests image data, in response to `g.drawImage(resultImage,...)`, the `FilteredImage-Source` performs some sleight of hand and then steps out of the way. The `FilteredImageSource` performs that "magic" by taking the following steps:

- It creates a new image filter object by invoking the `getFilterInstance` method on the filter object that you gave to the `FilteredImageSource` constructor. By default, `getFilterInstance` clones the filter object.
- It connects the new image filter object to the image consumer.
- It connects the image data source, which you gave to the `FilteredImage-Source` constructor, to the image filter.

Here is the result:

Where to Find Image Filters. So where can you find existing image filters? The `java.awt.image` package includes one ready-to-use filter, `CropImageFilter`[1], which produces an image consisting of a rectangular region of a larger image. You can also find several image filters used by applets at our Web site.[2]

How to Write an Image Filter

All image filters must be subclasses of the <u>ImageFilter</u>[3] class. If your image filter will modify the colors or transparency of an image, then instead of creating a direct subclass of `ImageFilter`, you should probably create a subclass of <u>RGBImageFilter</u>.[4]

---

[1] http://java.sun.com/products/JDK/CurrentRelease/api/java.awt.image.CropImageFilter.html

[2] For an up-to-date list of filters at our Website, visit this book's web page:
http://java.sun.com/Series/Tutorial/book.html

[3] http://java.sun.com/products/JDK/CurrentRelease/api/java.awt.image.ImageFilter.html

[4] http://java.sun.com/products/JDK/CurrentRelease/api/java.awt.image.RGBImageFilter.html

Before writing an image filter, you should first find others, studying any that are similar to what you plan to write. You should also study the `ImageProducer` and `ImageConsumer` interfaces, and become thoroughly familiar with them.

Finding Examples. You can find examples of image filters on our Web site.[1] Later in this section, you'll see an example of a direct `ImageFilter` subclass, `RotateFilter`.

Creating an `ImageFilter` Subclass. As we mentioned before, image filters implement the <u>`ImageConsumer`</u>[2] interface. This lets them intercept data intended for the image consumer. `ImageConsumer` defines the following methods:

```
setDimensions(int width, int height);
setProperties(Hashtable props);
setColorModel(ColorModel model);
setHints(int hintflags);
setPixels(int x, int y, int w, int h,
            ColorModel model, byte pixels[],
            int offset, int scansize);
setPixels(int x, int y, int w, int h,
            ColorModel model, int pixels[],
            int offset, int scansize);
imageComplete(int status);
```

The `ImageFilter` class implements all the above methods so that they forward the method data to the filter's consumer. For example, `ImageFilter` implements the `setDimensions` method as follows:

```
public void setDimensions(int width, int height) {
    consumer.setDimensions(width, height);
}
```

Thanks to these `ImageFilter` methods, your subclass probably doesn't need to implement every `ImageConsumer` method. You need to implement only the methods that transmit data you want to change.

For example, the <u>`CropImageFilter`</u>[3] class implements four of the Image-Consumer methods: `setDimensions`, `setProperties`, and both varieties of `set-`

---

[1] For a list of `ImageFilter` subclasses whose source code is available on our Web site, see this book's Web page: http://java.sun.com/Series/Tutorial/book.html

[2] http://java.sun.com/products/JDK/CurrentRelease/api/java.awt.image.ImageConsumer.html

[3] http://java.sun.com/products/JDK/CurrentRelease/api/java.awt.image.CropImageFilter.html

`Pixels`. It also implements a constructor with arguments that specify the rectangle to be cropped. As another example, the <u>`RGBImageFilter`</u>[1] class implements some helper methods, defines an abstract helper method to perform the actual color modifications of each pixel, and implements the following `Image-Consumer` methods: `setColorModel` and both varieties of `setPixels`.

Most, if not all, filters implement the `setPixels` methods. These methods determine exactly what image data is used to construct the `Image`. One or both of the `setPixels` methods may be called multiple times during the construction of a single image. Each call gives the `ImageConsumer` information about a rectangle of pixels within the image. When the `ImageConsumer`'s `imageComplete` method is called with any status except `SINGLEFRAMEDONE` (which implies that data for more frames will appear), then the `ImageConsumer` can assume that it will receive no further `setPixels` calls. An `imageComplete` status of `STATIC-IMAGEDONE` specifies that not only is the image data complete, but that no errors have been detected.

The following figure illustrates the arguments to the `setPixels` methods. A further explanation of the arguments follows the figure.

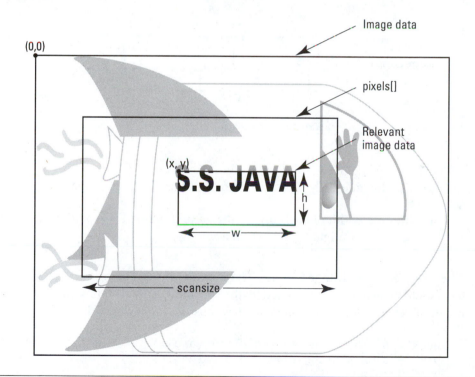

---

[1]. http://java.sun.com/products/JDK/CurrentRelease/api/java.awt.image.RGBImageFilter.html

x, y

Specify the location within the image, relative to its upper left corner, where this rectangle begins.

w, h

Specify the width and height, in pixels, of this rectangle.

model

Specifies the color model used by the data in the pixels array.

pixels[]

Specifies an array of pixels. The rectangle of image data is contained in this array, but the array might contain more than w*h entries, depending on the values of offset and scansize. Here's the formula for determining what entry in the pixels array contains the data for the pixel at (x+i, y+j), where (0 <= i < w) and (0 <= j < h):

```
offset + (j * scansize) + i
```

The following illustration of the pixels array should make this clearer. It shows how a specific pixel—for example, (x,y)—maps to an entry in the pixels array.

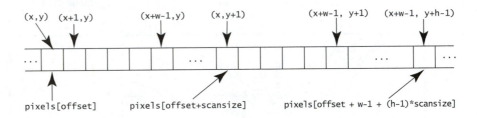

offset

Specifies the index (in the pixels array) of the first pixel in the rectangle.

scansize

Specifies the width of each row in the pixels array. Due to efficiency considerations, this might be greater than w.

The RotateFilter Image Filter.   The RotateFilter (page 733) class implements a filter that rotates an image by the specified angle. It relies on the following graphics formulas to calculate the new position of each pixel:

```
newX = oldX*cos(angle) - oldY*sin(angle)
newY = oldX*sin(angle) + oldY*cos(angle)
```

RotateFilter implements the following ImageConsumer methods:

setDimensions

Records the unfiltered image's width and height for use in the setPixels and imageComplete methods. Calculates the filtered image's final width and height, records it for use in its `imageComplete` method, creates a buffer to store the image data as it comes in, and calls the consumer's `setDimensions` method to set the new width and height.

setColorModel

Tells the consumer to expect pixels in the default RGB color model.

setHints

Tells the consumer to expect the image data in top-down-left-right order (the order in which you're reading this page), in complete scan lines, and with every pixel sent exactly once.

setPixels

Both varieties of this method convert the pixels to the default RGB model if necessary and copy the pixels into a storage buffer. Most image filters would simply modify the pixel data and forward it to the consumer, but because the sides of a rotated rectangle are no longer horizontal and vertical (for most angles), this filter can not efficiently forward pixels from its `setPixels` method. Instead, `RotateFilter` stores all the pixel data until it receives an `imageComplete` message.

imageComplete

Rotates the image and then invokes `consumer.setPixels` repeatedly to send each line of the image to the consumer. After sending the whole image, this method invokes `consumer.imageComplete`.

Performing Animation

Once you've learned how to draw graphics to the screen, you can learn how to animate those graphics.

What all forms of animation have in common is that they create some kind of perceived motion by showing successive frames at a relatively high speed. Computer animation usually shows 10–20 frames per second. By comparison, traditional hand-drawn animation uses anywhere from 8 frames per second (for poor quality animation) to 12 frames per second (for standard animation) to 24 frames per second (for short bursts of smooth, realistic motion). The next few sections describe everything you need to know to write a Java program that performs animation.

Before you start: Check out existing animation tools and applets, such as the Animator applet,[1] to see whether you can use one of them instead of writing your own program.

[1.] To find the Animator applet, visit the Web page for this book:
http://java.sun.com/Series/Tutorial/book.html

The most important step in creating a program that animates is to set up the framework correctly. Except for animation performed only in direct response to external events, such as the user dragging an onscreen object, a program that performs animation needs an animation loop.

Creating the Animation Loop (page 464) tells you exactly what you need in an animation loop. The animation loop is responsible for keeping track of the current frame and for requesting periodic screen updates. For applets and many applications, you need a separate thread to run the animation loop. This section contains an example applet and an example application that you can use as templates for all animation.

The Animating Graphics section (page 468) features an example that animates primitive graphics.

The example featured in the Animating Graphics section is imperfect because it flashes distractingly. The Eliminating Flashing section (page 469) tells you how to use two techniques to eliminate flashing:

- Overriding the `update` method
- Double buffering (also known as *using a backbuffer*)

The simplest form of image animation involves moving an unchanging image across the screen. In the traditional animation world, this is known as *cutout animation*, since it's traditionally accomplished by cutting a shape out of paper and moving the shape in front of the camera. In computer programs, this technique is often used for drag and drop interfaces. Moving an Image Across the Screen (page 473) gives an example of performing this type of animation.

The Displaying a Sequence of Images section (page 475) tells you how to perform classic, cartoon-style animation, given a sequence of images.

Improving the Appearance and Performance of Image Animation (page 476) tells you how to use the `MediaTracker` class so that you can delay displaying an animation until all its images are loaded. You'll also get some hints on improving applet animation performance by combining image files and by using a compression scheme such as Flic.

Creating the Animation Loop

Every program that performs animation by drawing at regular intervals needs an animation loop. Generally, this loop should be in its own thread. The animation loop should *never* be in the `paint` or `update` method, since that would take over the main AWT thread, which is in charge of all drawing and event handling.

This section provides two templates for performing animation, one for applets and another for applications. Here's what a single frame of the animation produced by the template looks like:

Frame 33

http://java.sun.com/Series/Tutorial/ui/drawing/animLoop.html

The animation the template performs is a bit boring: It simply displays the current frame number, using a default rate of 10 frames per second. The next few sections build on this example, showing you how to animate primitive graphics and images.

The complete code for the applet animation template is on page 737. The code for the equivalent application animation template is on page 739. The rest of this section explains the templates' code. Here is a summary of what both templates do:

```
public class AnimatorClass extends AComponentClass implements
Runnable {

    //In initialization code:
        //From user-specified frames-per-second value,
        //determine how long to delay between frames.

    //In a method that does nothing but start the animation:
        //Create and start the animating thread.

    //In a method that does nothing but stop the animation:
        //Stop the animating thread.

    public boolean mouseDown(Event e, int x, int y) {
        if (/* animation is currently frozen */) {
            //Call the method that starts the animation.
        } else {
            //Call the method that stops the animation.
        }
    }

    public void run() {
        //Lower this thread's priority so it can't interfere
        //with other processing going on.

        //Remember the starting time.

        //Here's the animation loop:
        while (/* animation thread is still running */) {
            //Advance the animation frame.
            //Display it.
            //Delay depending on how far we are behind.
        }
    }

    public void paint(Graphics g) {
        //Draw the current frame of animation.
    }
}
```

Initializing Instance Variables

The animation templates use four instance variables. The first instance variable, `frameNumber`, represents the current frame. It is initialized to -1, even though the first frame number is 0, because the frame number is incremented at the start of the animation loop before any frames are painted. As a result, the first frame to be painted is frame 0.

The second instance variable, `delay`, is the number of milliseconds between frames. It is initialized using a *frames per second* number provided by the user. If the user provides no valid number, then the templates default to 10 frames per second. The following Java statement converts frames per second into the number of milliseconds between frames:

```
delay = (fps > 0) ? (1000 / fps) : 100;
```

The `?` `:` notation in the previous code snippet is shorthand for `if else`. If the user provides a number of frames per second greater than 0, then the delay is 1000 milliseconds divided by the number of frames per second. Otherwise, the delay between frames is 100 milliseconds.

The third instance variable, `animatorThread`, is a `Thread` object representing the thread in which the animation loop runs. If you're not familiar with threads, see the **Threads of Control** (page 285) lesson for an overview of their use.

The fourth instance variable, `frozen`, is a boolean value that is initialized to `false`. The templates set `frozen` to `true` to indicate that the user has requested that the animation stop. You'll see more about this later in this section.

The Animation Loop

The animation loop (the `while` loop in the animation thread) does the following, over and over again:

1. Advances the frame number.
2. Calls the `repaint` method to request that the current frame of animation be drawn.
3. Sleeps for up to `delay` milliseconds (more on this later).

The following code performs these tasks:

```
while (/* animation thread is still running */) {
    //Advance the animation frame.
    frameNumber++;

    //Display it.
    repaint();

    ...//Delay depending on how far we are behind.
}
```

Ensuring a Constant Frame Rate

The most obvious way to implement the delay in the animation loop is to sleep for `delay` milliseconds. However, this can cause the thread to sleep too long since you lose a certain amount of time just by executing the animation loop.

The solution to this problem is to remember when the animation loop starts, add `delay` milliseconds to arrive at a wakeup time, and then sleep until the wakeup time. Here's the code that implements this:

```
long startTime = System.currentTimeMillis();
while (/* animation thread is still running */) {
    ...//Advance the animation frame and display it.
    try {
        startTime += delay;
        Thread.sleep(Math.max(0,
                        startTime-System.currentTimeMillis()));
    } catch (InterruptedException e) {
        break;
    }
}
```

Behaving Politely

Two more features of the animation templates belong in the category of polite behavior.

The first feature is allowing the user to explicitly stop and restart the animation while the applet or application is still visible. Animation can be quite distracting, and it's a good idea to give the user the power to stop the animation so that the user can concentrate on something else. This feature is implemented by overriding the `mouseDown` method so that it stops or starts the animation thread, depending on the thread's current state. Here's the code that implements this:

```
...//In initialization code:
boolean frozen = false;

...//In the method that starts the animation thread:
    if (frozen) {
        //Do nothing.  The user has requested that we
        //stop changing the image.
    } else {
        //Start animating!
        ...//Create and start the animating thread.
    }
}

. . .

public boolean mouseDown(Event e, int x, int y) {
    if (frozen) {
```

```
        frozen = false;
        //Call the method that stops the animation.
    } else {
        frozen = true;
        //Call the method that stops the animation.
    }
    return true;
}
```

The second polite feature is suspending the animation whenever the applet or application is known not to be visible. For the applet animation template, this is achieved by implementing the `Applet` `stop` and `start` methods. For the application animation template, this is achieved by implementing an event handler for the `WINDOW_ICONIFY` and `WINDOW_DEICONIFY` events. In both templates, if the user hasn't frozen the animation, then when the program detects that the animation is not visible, it stops the animation thread. When the user revisits the animation, the program restarts the animation thread unless the user has explicitly requested that the animation be stopped.

You might be wondering why the frame number is incremented at the beginning of the loop rather than at the end. The reason has to do with what happens when the user freezes the animation, then leaves it, and then revisits it. When the user freezes the animation, the animation loop completes before exiting. If the frame number is incremented at the bottom of the loop, instead of at the top of the loop, then when the loop exits, the frame number is one more than the number of the frame being displayed. When the user revisits the animation, the animation is frozen on a different frame than the one the user left. This is disconcerting and, if the user stops the animation to look at a particular frame, annoying.

Animating Graphics

This section features an applet that creates a moving checkerboard effect by painting alternate squares. The squares are drawn by the `Graphics` `fillRect` method. The following figure shows the applet in action:

http://java.sun.com/Series/Tutorial/ui/drawing/animGraphics.html

If you run this applet, you might notice that the graphics aren't animated perfectly smoothly; occasionally part or all of the drawing area flashes noticeably.

The next section will explain the cause of this flashing and tell you how to eliminate it.

The complete code for the checkerboard applet is on page 741. The major difference between this applet and the animation template is that the `paint` method now draws filled rectangles, using an algorithm that depends on the current frame number. This applet also introduces two instance variables, one that holds the square size and another that keeps track of whether the next column to be drawn begins with a black square. The user can set the square size by means of a new applet parameter. An application version of this applet would have similar differences from the animation template, except that square size would be set using a command-line argument or property.

The following code contains the `paint` code that performs the actual drawing. Note that the program draws only the black boxes, indicated by `fillSquare` being `true`, not the other boxes. It can get away with this because, by default, a component's drawing area is cleared (set to the background color) just before the `paint` method is called.

```
// Draw the rectangle if necessary.
if (fillSquare) {
    g.fillRect(x, y, w, h);
    fillSquare = false;
} else {
    fillSquare = true;
}
```

Eliminating Flashing

The flashing in the example in the previous section is a common problem with animation (and occasionally with static graphics). The flashing effect is the result of two facts:

- By default, the background of the animation is cleared (its whole area is redrawn in the background color) before the `paint` method is called.
- The computation in the previous example's `paint` method is complex enough that it takes longer to compute and draw each frame of animation than the video screen's refresh rate. As a result, the first part of the frame is drawn on one video refresh pass, and the rest of the frame is drawn on the next (or even the pass after that). The result is that although the first part of the frame is usually animated smoothly, you can see a break between the first and second parts, since the second part is blank until the second pass.

You can use two techniques to eliminate flashing: overriding the `update` method and implementing double buffering.

To eliminate flashing, whether or not you use double buffering, you must override the `update` method. This is necessary because it is the only way to prevent the entire background of the component from being cleared every time the component is drawn. Overriding the update Method (page 470) discusses how to implement the update method.

Double buffering involves performing multiple graphics operations on an undisplayed graphics buffer, and then displaying the resulting image onscreen. Double buffering prevents incomplete images from being drawn to the screen. Implementing Double Buffering (page 471) discusses how to implement double buffering.

Overriding the update Method

To eliminate flashing, you must override the update method. The reason lies in the way the AWT requests that a component (such as an Applet, Canvas, or Frame) repaint itself.

The AWT requests a repaint by calling the component's update method. The default implementation of update clears the component's background before calling paint. Because eliminating flashing requires that you eliminate all unnecessary drawing, your first step is always to override update so that it clears the entire background only when necessary. When moving drawing code from the paint method to update, you might need to modify the drawing code so that it doesn't depend on the background being cleared.

Note: Even if your implementation of update doesn't call paint, you must still implement a paint method. The reason: When an area that your component displays is suddenly revealed after being hidden (behind another window, for example), the AWT calls paint directly, without calling update. An easy way to implement paint is to have it call update.

On page 745 you can find the code for a modified version of the previous example that implements update to eliminate flashing. The following figure shows this applet.

http://java.sun.com/Series/Tutorial/ui/drawing/update.html

Here's the new version of the paint method, along with the new update method. All of the drawing code that used to be in the paint method is now in the update method. Significant changes in the drawing code are in **bold**.

```
public void paint(Graphics g) {
    update(g);
}

public void update(Graphics g) {
    Color bg = getBackground();
    Color fg = getForeground();

    ...//same as old paint method until we draw the rectangle:
            if (fillSquare) {
                g.fillRect(x, y, w, h);
                fillSquare = false;
            } else {
                g.setColor(bg);
                g.fillRect(x, y, w, h);
                g.setColor(fg);
                fillSquare = true;
            }
    ...//same as old paint method
}
```

Note that since the background is no longer automatically cleared, the drawing code must now draw the rectangles which are not black, as well as the black ones.

Clipping the Drawing Area.   One technique you might be able to use in your update method is *clipping* the area you draw. This doesn't work for the example applet, since the entire drawing area changes with every frame. Clipping works well, though, when only a small part of the drawing area changes, such as when the user drags an object across a background.

You perform clipping using the `clipRect` method. An example of using `clipRect` is in <u>Improving the Appearance and Performance of Image Animation</u> (page 476).

Implementing Double Buffering

The previous section showed you how to eliminate flashing by implementing the update method. If you run the applet, you might notice (depending on the performance of your computer) that the resulting applet, although it probably doesn't flash, appears to crawl a bit. That is, instead of the whole drawing area (or frame) being updated at once, sometimes one part is updated before the part just to its right, causing noticeably uneven drawing between columns.

You can use double buffering to avoid this crawling effect by forcing the entire frame to be drawn at once. To implement double buffering, to create an

undisplayed buffer (often called a *backbuffer* or *off-screen buffer*), draw to it, and then display the resulting image on-screen.

On page 749 you'll find the code for the graphics animation example, modified so that it implements double buffering. Below is the resulting applet.

http://java.sun.com/Series/Tutorial/ui/drawing/doubleBuffer.html

To create an off-screen buffer with the AWT, you need to first create an image of the proper size and then get a graphics context to manipulate the image. Here is the code that does this:

```
//Where instance variables are declared:
Dimension offDimension;
Image offImage;
Graphics offGraphics;
. . .
//In the update method, where d holds the size of the
//onscreen drawing area:
if ( (offGraphics == null)
  || (d.width != offDimension.width)
  || (d.height != offDimension.height) ) {
    offDimension = d;
    offImage = createImage(d.width, d.height);
    offGraphics = offImage.getGraphics();
}
```

Below, in **bold**, is the new drawing code in the update method. Note that the drawing code now clears the entire background, but it doesn't cause flashing because the code is drawing to the off-screen buffer, not to the screen. Note also that all the calls to fillRect are performed to the off-screen buffer. The final result is drawn to the screen just before the update method returns.

```
public void update(Graphics g) {
    ...//First, initialize variables and create the
       //offscreen buffer as shown above. Then erase the
       //previous image:
       offGraphics.setColor(getBackground());
       offGraphics.fillRect(0, 0, d.width, d.height);
       offGraphics.setColor(Color.black);

    ...//Do everything the old paint method did --
       //until we draw the rectangle.
           if (fillSquare) {
```

```
        offGraphics.fillRect(x, y, w, h);
        fillSquare = false;
    } else {
        fillSquare = true;
    }

    ...//The rest is exactly like the old paint method
        //until the very end, when we add the following:
    //Paint the image onto the screen.
    g.drawImage(offImage, 0, 0, this);
}
```

It's not necessary that the update method call the paint method. All that's necessary is that the update method somehow draw its off-screen buffer to the screen, and that the paint method be able to draw the proper image when it's called directly by the AWT.

You might wonder why the offscreen image and graphics context are created in the update method, instead of in, for example, the start method. The reason is that the image and graphics context depend on the size of the applet Panel's drawing area, and the size of any component's drawing area is not reliably valid until the component is just about to be drawn to the screen for the first time.

Moving an Image Across the Screen

This section features an applet that moves one image (a rocketship) in front of a background image (a field of stars). This page shows only applet code. The code for an application would be similar, except you would use different code to load the images, as described in <u>Loading Images</u> (page 450).

Below are the two images this applet uses.
rocketship.gif:

starfield.gif:

Note: The rocketship image has a transparent background. The transparent background makes the rocketship image appear to have a rocketship shape, no matter what color background it's drawn on top of. If the rocketship background weren't transparent, then instead of the illusion of a rocketship moving through space, you'd see a rocketship on top of a rectangle moving through space.

Here's what the applet looks like:

http://java.sun.com/Series/Tutorial/ui/drawing/movingImage.html

The code for performing this animation isn't complex. Essentially, it's the applet animation template, plus the double buffering code you saw in the previous section, plus a few additional lines of code. The additional code loads the images, draws the background image, and then uses a simple algorithm to determine where to draw the moving image. Here is the additional code:

```
...//Where instance variables are declared:
Image stars;
Image rocket;

...//In the init method:
stars = getImage(getCodeBase(), "../images/starfield.gif");
rocket = getImage(getCodeBase(), "../images/rocketship.gif");

...//In the update method:
//Paint the frame into the image.
paintFrame(offGraphics);

...//A new method:
void paintFrame(Graphics g) {
    Dimension d = size();
    int w;
    int h;

    //If we have a valid width and height for the background
    //image,
    //draw it.
    w = stars.getWidth(this);
    h = stars.getHeight(this);
```

```
        if ((w > 0) && (h > 0)) {
            g.drawImage(stars, (d.width - w)/2,
                        (d.height - h)/2, this);
        }

        //If we have a valid width and height for the background
        //image, draw it.
        w = rocket.getWidth(this);
        h = rocket.getHeight(this);
        if ((w > 0) && (h > 0)) {
            g.drawImage(rocket, ((frameNumber*5) % (w + d.width))
                        - w, (d.height - h)/2, this);
        }
    }
```

You might think that this program doesn't need to clear the background since it uses a background image. However, clearing the background is still necessary. One reason is that the applet usually starts drawing before the images are fully loaded. If the rocketship image loaded before the background image, you would see parts of multiple rocketships until the background image loaded. Another reason is that if the applet drawing area were wider than the background image, for some reason, then you'd see multiple rocketships on either side of the background image.

You could solve the first problem by delaying all drawing until both images are fully loaded. The second problem could be solved by scaling the background image to fit the entire applet area. You'll learn how to wait for images to be fully loaded in Improving the Appearance and Performance of Image Animation (page 476), later in this lesson. Scaling is described in Displaying Images (page 453).

Displaying a Sequence of Images

This section features the same animation that you see in the online tutorial's **Trail Map**[1]: our mascot, Duke, waving. The example in this section describes the basic techniques for displaying an image sequence. The next section has hints for improving the appearance and performance of this animation. This section uses only applet code. The code for an application would be similar, except you would use different code to load the images, as described in Loading Images (page 450).

---

[1] http://java.sun.com/Series/Tutorial/index.html

Below are the ten images this applet uses.

http://java.sun.com/Series/Tutorial/ui/drawing/imageSequence.html

The applet, not surprisingly, looks something like this:

The code for this example (which you can find on page 757) is even simpler than for the previous example, which moved an image. Here is the code that differs from the previous example:

```
. . .//Where instance variables are declared:
Image duke[10];

. . .//In the init method:
for (int i = 1; i <= 10; i++) {
    images[i-1] = getImage(getCodeBase(),
                      "../../../images/duke/T"+i+".gif");
}

. . .//In the update method, instead of calling drawFrame:
offGraphics.drawImage(images[frameNumber % 10], 0, 0, this);
```

Improving the Appearance and Performance of Image Animation

If you run the previous applet, you might notice two things:
- While the images are loading, the program might display some images partially and others not at all.

- Loading the images takes a long time.

The problem of displaying partial images is easy to fix using the `MediaTracker` class. `MediaTracker` also can decrease the amount of time that loading images takes. Another way to deal with the problem of slow image loading is to change the image format somehow; this page gives you some suggestions for doing so.

Using `MediaTracker` to Download Images and Delay Image Display

The `MediaTracker` class lets you easily download data for a group of images and find out when the images are fully loaded. Ordinarily, an image's data isn't downloaded until the image is drawn for the first time. To request that the data for a group of images be preloaded asynchronously, use the forms of `checkID` and `checkAll` that take a boolean argument, setting the argument to `true`. To load data synchronously (waiting for the data to arrive), use the `waitForID` and `waitForAll` methods. The `MediaTracker` methods that load data use several background threads to download the data, resulting in increased speed.

To check on the status of image loading, you can use the `MediaTracker` `statusID` and `statusAll` methods. To simply check whether any image data remains to be loaded, use the `checkID` and `checkAll` methods.

On page 760 you can find a modified version of the example applet that uses the MediaTracker `waitForAll` and `checkAll` methods. Until every image is fully loaded, this applet simply displays a "Please wait . . ." message. See the <u>MediaTracker documentation</u>[1] for an example that draws a background image immediately, but delays drawing the animated images.

The applet, again, looks something like this:

http://java.sun.com/Series/Tutorial/ui/drawing/imageSequence.html

Below is the changed code, which uses a `MediaTracker` to help delay image display. Differences are marked in **bold**.

---

[1] http://java.sun.com/products/JDK/CurrentRelease/api/java.awt.MediaTracker.html

```
...//Where instance variables are declared:
MediaTracker tracker;

...//In the init method:
tracker = new MediaTracker(this);
for (int i = 1; i <= 10; i++) {
    images[i-1] = getImage(getCodeBase(),
                       "../../../images/duke/T"+i+".gif");
    tracker.addImage(images[i-1], 0);
}

...//At the beginning of the run method:
try {
    //Start downloading the images. Wait until they're loaded.
    tracker.waitForAll();
} catch (InterruptedException e) {}

...//At the beginning of the update method:
//If not all the images are loaded, just clear the background
//and display a status string.
if (!tracker.checkAll()) {
    g.clearRect(0, 0, d.width, d.height);
    g.drawString("Please wait...", 0, d.height/2);
}

//If all images are loaded, draw.
else {
    ...//same code as before...
```

Speeding Up Image Loading

Whether or not you use `MediaTracker`, loading images using URLs (as applets usually do) usually takes a long time. Most of the time is taken up by initiating HTTP connections. Each image file requires a separate HTTP connection, and each connection can take several seconds to initiate. The key to avoiding this performance hit is to combine the images in a single file. You can further improve performance by using some sort of compression scheme, especially one that's designed for moving images.

One simple way to combine images in a single file is to create an *image strip*, a file that contains several images in a row. The following figure shows an image strip:

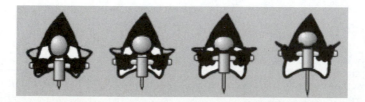

To draw an image from the strip, first set the clipping area to the size of one image. Then draw the image strip, shifted to the left (if necessary) so that only the image you want appears within the clipping area. For example:

```
//imageStrip is the Image object representing the image strip.
//imageWidth is the size of an individual image in the strip.
//imageNumber is the number (0 to numImages)
//of the image to draw.
int stripWidth = imageStrip.getWidth(this);
int stripHeight = imageStrip.getHeight(this);
int imageWidth = stripWidth / numImages;
g.clipRect(0, 0, imageWidth, stripHeight);
g.drawImage(imageStrip, -imageNumber*imageWidth, 0, this);
```

If you want image loading to be faster still, you should look into image compression schemes, especially ones like Flic that perform inter-frame compression.

Common Graphics Problems (and Their Solutions)

Problem: I don't know where to put my drawing code.
- Drawing code belongs in the `paint` method of a custom component. You can create a custom component by creating a subclass of the `Canvas`, `Panel`, or `Applet` class. See <u>How to Use Canvases</u> (page 385) for information on implementing a custom component. For efficiency, once you have your drawing code working, you can modify it to go in the `update` method, although you must still implement the `paint` method, as described in <u>Eliminating Flashing</u> (page 469).

Problem: The stuff I draw doesn't show up.
- Check whether your component is showing up at all. <u>Common Component Problems (and Their Solutions)</u> (page 412) should help you with this.

Problem: I'm using the exact same code as a tutorial example, but it doesn't work. Why?
- Is the code executed in the exact same method as the tutorial example? For example, if the tutorial example has the code in the example's `paint` or `update` method, then those two methods might be the only places where the code is guaranteed to work.

Problem: How do I draw thick lines? Patterns?
- As of JDK 1.0.2, the AWT's API for primitive graphics is rather limited. For example, it supports only one line width. You can simulate thick lines by drawing multiple times at one-pixel offsets or by drawing filled rectangles. Also, the AWT doesn't currently support fill or line patterns.

If you don't see your problem in this list, see <u>Common Component Problems (and Their Solutions)</u> (page 412) and <u>Common Layout Problems (and Their Solutions)</u> (page 435). If they fail, check the Web page for this book:

http://java.sun.com/Series/Tutorial/book.html

End of Trail

Y OU'VE reached the end of the **Creating a User Interface** trail. Take a break—have a cup of steaming hot java.

What Next?

Once you've caught your breath, you have several choices of where to go next. You can go back to the **Trail Map** (page xv) to see all of your choices, or you can go directly to one of the following popular trails:

Writing Applets (page 145): This is the starting point for learning everything about writing applets.

Using the Core Java Classes (page 209): By taking this trail, you can find out about strings, exceptions, threads, and other Java features that are used in all kinds of Java programs.

Custom Networking and Security (page 483): If you like, you can forge onward to learn about the Java environment's support for networking and for security.

Custom Networking and Security

THE Java environment is highly regarded in part because of its suitability for writing programs that use and interact with the resources on the Internet and the World Wide Web. In fact, Java-compatible browsers use this ability of the Java environment to the extreme to transport and run applets over the net.

This trail walks you through the complexities of writing Java applications and applets that can be used on the Internet.

Overview of Networking (page 487) has two sections. The first section describes the networking capabilities of the Java environment that you may already be using without realizing it! The second section provides a brief overview of networking to familiarize you with terms and concepts that you will need to understand before learning how to use URLs, sockets, and datagrams.

Working with URLs (page 493) discusses how your Java programs can use URLs to access information on the Internet. A Uniform Resource Locator (URL) is an address of a resource on the Internet. Your Java programs can use URLs to connect to and retrieve information over the network. This lesson provides a more complete definition of URL, shows you how to create and parse URLs, how to open a connection to a URL, and how to read from and write to those connections.

All About Sockets (page 509) explains how to use sockets so that your programs can communicate with other programs on the network. A socket is one endpoint of a two-way communication link between two programs running on the network. This lesson first shows you how to read from and write to a socket from a client program communicating with a standard server program—the echo

483

server. This lesson also walks you through the details of a complete client/server example which will show you how to implement both the client and the server side of a client/server pair.

All About Datagrams (page 521) shows you how to use datagrams. The lesson on sockets focuses on reliable communication links between applications running on the network. Reliable communication links guarantee the arrival of all packets in the order they were sent. While necessary for some applications, reliable links are overkill for others. These applications use datagrams instead. The delivery of datagrams is not guaranteed and the order in which they are delivered is not guaranteed either. This lesson takes you step by step through a client/server example that uses datagrams to communicate.

Providing Your Own Security Manager (page 529) describes Java's security model for applications and how you can build your own security manager for your Java applications.

Security considerations: Note that communications over the network are subject to approval by the current security manager. The example programs in the lessons covering URLs, sockets, and datagrams in this trail are stand-alone applications, which by default have no security manager. If you convert these applications to applets they might be unable to communicate over the network, depending on the browser or viewer they are running in. See **Understanding Applet Capabilities and Restrictions** (page 197) for information about the security restrictions placed on applets.

21

Overview of Networking

BEFORE plowing through the examples in the next several lessons, you should have an understanding of some networking basics.

· To boost your confidence, we've started with a section, <u>What You May Already Know About Networking in Java</u> (page 487), that reviews what you may already know about networking in Java without even realizing it. If you've been working on the other trails in this tutorial, you've probably loaded an applet over the Internet by now, and you've probably loaded images from the network into applets running over the network. You already know how to use the network.

The second section of this lesson, <u>Networking Basics</u> (page 489), teaches you what you need to know about TCP, UDP, sockets, datagrams, and ports to get the most out of the remaining lessons in this trail. If you are already familiar with these concepts, feel free to skip this section.

What You May Already Know About Networking in Java

The word *networking* strikes fear in the hearts of many programmers. Fear not! Using the networking capabilities provided in the Java environment is quite easy. In fact, you may be using the network already without even realizing it!

Loading Applets from the Network

If you have access to a Java-compatible browser, you have undoubtedly already executed many applets. The applets you've run are referenced by a special tag in an HTML file—the <APPLET> tag. Applets can be located anywhere, whether on your local machine or somewhere out on the Internet. The location of the applet is completely invisible to you, the user. However, the location of the applet is encoded within the <APPLET> tag. The browser decodes this information, locates the applet, and runs it. If the applet is on some machine other than your own, the browser must download the applet before it can be run.

This is the highest level of access that you have to the Internet from the Java development environment. Someone else has taken the time to write a browser that does all of the grunt work of connecting to the network and getting data from it, thereby enabling you to run applets from anywhere in the world.

The following sections give more information about applets:

- **The "Hello World" Applet** (page 13) is a brief lesson that shows you how to write your first applet and run it.
- The **Writing Applets** (page 145) trail describes how to write Java applets from A to Z.

Loading Images from URLs

If you've ventured into writing your own Java applets and applications, you may have run into a class in the `java.net` package called URL. This class represents a Uniform Resource Locator and is the address of some resource on the network. Your applets and applications can use a URL to reference and even connect to resources out on the network. For example, to load an image from the network, your Java program must first create a URL object that contains the address to the image.

This is the next highest level of interaction you can have with the Internet: Your Java program gets an address of something it wants, creates a URL for it, and then uses some existing function in the Java development environment that does the grunt work of connecting to the network and retrieving the resource.

The following sections give more information about images and URLs.

- Loading Images (page 450) shows you how to load an image into your Java program (whether applets or applications) when you have its URL. Before you can load the image you must create a URL object with the address of the resource in it.

- **Working with URLs** (page 493), the next lesson in this trail, provides a complete discussion about URLs, including how your programs can establish a connection to them, and how your programs can read from and write to that connection.

Networking Basics

Computers running on the Internet communicate to each other using the TCP and UDP protocols, which are both 4-layer protocols, as the following figure illustrates:

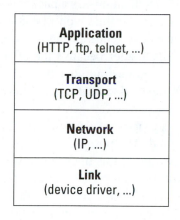

When you write Java programs that communicate over the network, you are programming at the application layer. Typically, you don't need to concern yourself with the TCP and UDP layers—instead you can use the classes in the `java.net` package. These classes provide system-independent network communication. However you do need to understand the difference between TCP and UDP to decide which Java classes your programs should use.

When two applications want to communicate to each other reliably they establish a connection and send data back and forth over that connection. This is analogous to making a telephone call. If you want to speak to Aunt Beatrice in Kentucky, a connection is established when you dial her phone number and she answers. You send data back and forth over the connection by speaking to one another over the phone lines. Like the phone company, TCP guarantees that data sent from one end of the connection actually gets to the other end and in the same order it was sent, otherwise an error is reported.

Applications that require a reliable, point-to-point channel to communicate use TCP to communicate. Hypertext Transfer Protocol (HTTP), File Transfer Protocol (FTP), and Telnet are all examples of applications that require a reliable communication channel. The order that the data is sent and received over

Definition:
TCP (Transport Control Protocol) is a connection-based protocol that provides a reliable flow of data between two computers.

the network is critical to the success of these applications. When using HTTP to read from a URL, the data must be received in the order that it was sent; otherwise you end up with a jumbled HTML file, a corrupt zip file, or some other invalid information.

For many applications, this guarantee of reliability is critical to the success of the transfer of information from one end of the connection to the other. However, other forms of communication don't require such strict communications and, in fact, are hindered by them either because of the performance hit from the extra overhead or because the reliable connection invalidates the service altogether.

Consider, for example, a clock server that sends the current time to its client when requested to do so. If the client misses a packet does it really make sense to resend the packet? No, because the time won't be correct by the time the client receives it. If the client makes two requests and receives packets from the server out of order, it doesn't really matter because the client can figure out that the packets are out of order and request another one. The reliable channel here is unnecessary, causes performance degradation, and may hinder the usefulness of the service.

Another example of a service that doesn't need the guarantee of a reliable channel is the `ping` command. The purpose of the `ping` command is to test the communication between two programs over the network. In fact, `ping` *needs to know* about dropped or out of order packets to determine how good or bad the connection is. A reliable channel would invalidate this service altogether.

The UDP protocol provides for communication that is not guaranteed between two applications on the network. UDP is not connection-based like TCP. Rather, it sends independent packets of data, called *datagrams,* from one application to another. Sending datagrams is much like sending a letter through the mail service: The order of delivery is not important and is not guaranteed, and each message is independent of any others.

Definition:
UDP (User Datagram Protocol) is a protocol that sends independent packets of data, called *datagrams,* from one computer to another with no guarantees about arrival. UDP is not connection-based like TCP.

Ports

Generally speaking, a computer has a single physical connection to the network. All data destined for a particular computer arrives through that connection. However, the data may be intended for different applications running on the computer. So how does the computer know which application to forward the data to? Through the use of *ports*.

Data transmitted over the Internet is accompanied by addressing information that identifies the computer and the port that it is destined for. The computer is identified by its 32-bit IP address, which IP uses to deliver data to the right computer on the network. Ports are identified by a 16-bit number, which TCP and UDP use to deliver the data to the right application.

In connection-based communication, an application establishes a connection with another application by binding a socket to a port number. This has the effect of registering the application with the system to receive all data destined for that port. No two applications can bind to the same port: Attempts to bind to a port that is already in use will fail.

In datagram-based communication, the datagram packet contains the port number of its destination, as illustrated in the following figure:

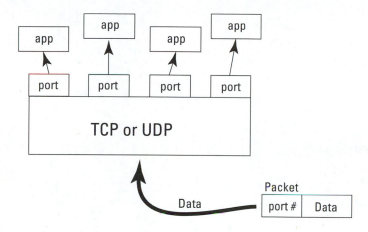

Port numbers range from 0 to 65535 because ports are represented by 16-bit numbers. The port numbers ranging from 0–1023 are restricted—they are reserved for use by well-known services such as HTTP and FTP and other system services. Your applications should not attempt to bind to these ports. Ports that are reserved for well-known services such as HTTP and FTP are called *well-known ports*. The following figure illustrates how data is forwarded to applications listening to well-known ports.

Definition:
The TCP and UDP protocols use *ports* to map incoming data to a particular process running on a computer.

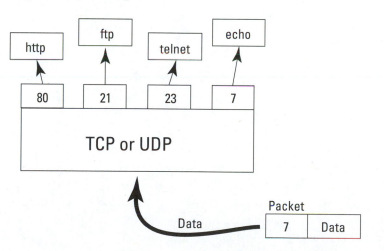

Through the classes in `java.net`, Java programs can use TCP or UDP to communicate over the Internet. The `URL`, `URLConnection`, `Socket`, and `SocketServer` classes all use TCP to communicate over the network. The `DatagramPacket` and `DatagramServer` classes use UDP.

22

Working with URLs

URL is an acronym that stands for *Uniform Resource Locator* and is a reference (an address) to a resource on the Internet. URLs are the doorway to the Internet and the World Wide Web. You provide URLs to your favorite Web browser so that it can locate files on the Internet in the same way that you provide addresses on letters so that the post office can locate your correspondents.

Java programs that interact with the Internet may also use URLs to find the resources on the Internet they wish to access. The `java.net` package contains a class called URL that your Java programs can use to represent a URL address.

Note about terminology: The term *URL* can be ambiguous. Does it mean the concept of an address to something on the Internet or does it refer to a URL object in your Java program? Usually, the meaning is clear from the context of the sentence, or it doesn't matter because the statement applies to both. However, where the meaning of URL needs to be specifically one or the other, this text uses "URL address" to mean the concept of an Internet address and "URL object" to refer to an instance of the URL class in your program.

A URL takes the form of a string that describes how to find a resource on the Internet. URLs have two main components: the protocol needed to access the resource and the location of the resource. What Is a URL? (page 494) looks in depth at a URL and its components. Within your Java programs, you can create a URL object that represents a URL address. The URL object always refers to an absolute URL but can be constructed from an absolute URL, a relative URL, or from URL components. See Creating a URL (page 495) to learn how.

Once you've created a URL object in your Java program, you can use its methods to find out its host name, filename, and other information. With a valid URL object you can call any of its accessor methods to get all of that information. This is just like Parsing a URL (page 498) without all the string manipulations!

In addition to querying the URL for information about itself, your Java programs can also read directly from a URL using the openStream method. And, if you want to do more than just read from a URL, you can connect to it by calling openConnection on the URL object. The openConnection method returns a URLConnection object that you can use for more general communications with the URL, such as reading from it, writing to it, or querying it for content and other information. The sections Reading Directly from a URL (page 500), Connecting to a URL (page 502), and Reading from and Writing to a URLConnection (page 503) show you how to do all of these things.

What Is a URL?

Definition:

URL is an acronym that stands for *Uniform Resource Locator* and is a reference (an address) to a resource on the Internet.

If you've been surfing the World Wide Web, you have undoubtedly heard the term URL and used URLs to access various HTML pages from the Web.

It's often easiest, although not entirely accurate, to think of a URL as the name of a file on the network because most URLs refer to a file on some machine on the network. However, remember that URLs can point to other resources on the network such as database queries and command output.

The following is an example of a URL:

```
http://java.sun.com/
```

This particular URL addresses the Java Web site hosted by Sun Microsystems. This URL, like all other URLs, has two main components:
- the protocol identifier
- the resource name

In the example, http is the protocol identifier and //java.sun.com/ is the resource name. The protocol identifier and the resource name are separated by a colon.

The protocol identifier indicates the name of the protocol to be used to fetch the resource. The example uses the Hypertext Transfer Protocol (HTTP), which is typically used to serve hypertext documents. HTTP is just one of many different protocols used to access different types of resources on the net. Other protocols include File Transfer Protocol (FTP), Gopher, File, and News.

The resource name is the complete address to the resource. The format of the resource name depends entirely on the protocol used, but for many formats the resource name contains one or more of the following components:

Host name   The name of the machine the resource lives on.
Filename   The pathname to the file on the machine.
Port number The port number to connect to. This component is typically optional.
Reference   A reference to a named anchor within a resource. Usually identifies a specific location within a file. This component is typically optional.

For many protocols, the host name and the filename are required, and the port number and reference are optional. For example, the resource name for an HTTP URL must specify a server on the network (host name) and the path to the document on that machine (filename), and can also specify a port number and a reference. In the URL shown previously, `java.sun.com` is the hostname and the trailing slash is shorthand for the file named `/index.html`.

When constructing any URL, put the protocol identifier first, followed by a colon, followed by the resource name, like this:

>   *protocolID:resourceName*

The `java.net` package contains a class named <u>URL</u>[1] that Java programs use to represent a URL address. Your Java program can construct a URL object, open a connection to it, and read to and write from it. The remaining sections of this lesson show you how to work with URL objects in your Java programs.

Creating a URL

The easiest way to create a URL object is from a `String` that represents the human-readable form of the URL address. This is typically the form that another

---

[1]. http://java.sun.com/products/JDK/CurrentRelease/api/java.net.URL.html

person will use for a URL. For example, URL for the Gamelan site that contains a list of Java-compatible sites takes the following form:

```
http://www.gamelan.com/
```

In your Java program, you can use a `String` containing the above text to create a URL object:

```
URL gamelan = new URL("http://www.gamelan.com/");
```

The URL object created by this statement represents an *absolute URL*. An absolute URL contains all of the information necessary to reach the resource in question. You can also create URL objects from a relative URL address.

Creating a URL Relative to Another

A *relative URL* contains only enough information to reach the resource relative to (or in the context of) another URL.

Relative URL specifications are often used within HTML files. For example, suppose you write an HTML file called `JoesHomePage.html`. This page contains links to two other pages, `PicturesOfMe.html` and `MyKids.html`, that are on the same machine and in the same directory as `JoesHomePage.html`. The links to `PicturesOfMe.html` and `MyKids.html` from `JoesHomePage.html` can be specified as filenames, as follows:

```
<A HREF="PicturesOfMe.html">Pictures of Me</A>
<A HREF="MyKids.html">Pictures of My Kids</A>
```

These URL addresses are relative URLs. The URLs are specified relative to the file in which they are contained—`JoesHomePage.html`.

In your Java programs, you can create a URL object from a relative URL specification. For example, suppose that you already created a URL for

```
http://www.gamelan.com/
```

in your program, and you know the names of two files at that site: `Gamelan.network.html`, and `Gamelan.animation.html`. You can create URLs for each file at the Gamelan site by simply specifying the filenames in the context of the original Gamelan URL. The filenames are relative URLs and are relative to the original Gamelan URL.

```
URL gamelan = new URL("http://www.gamelan.com/");
URL gamelanNetwork = new URL(gamelan, "Gamelan.network.html");
```

This code snippet uses the URL class constructor that lets you create a URL object from a URL object (the base) and a relative URL.

This constructor is also useful for creating URL objects for named anchors (also known as *references*) within a file. For example, suppose the `Gamelan.network.html` file has a named anchor called `BOTTOM` at the bottom of the file. You can use the relative URL constructor to create a URL object for it like this:

```
URL gamelanNetworkBottom = new URL(gamelanNetwork, "#BOTTOM");
```

The general form of this URL constructor is:

```
URL(URL baseURL, String relativeURL)
```

The first argument is a URL object that specifies the base of the new URL, and the second argument is a `String` that specifies the rest of the resource name relative to the base. If *baseURL* is `null`, then this constructor treats *relativeURL* as though it is an absolute URL specification. Conversely, if *relativeURL* is an absolute URL specification, then the constructor ignores *baseURL*.

Other URL Constructors

The URL class provides two additional constructors for creating a URL object. These constructors are useful when you are working with URLs, such as HTTP URLs, that have host name, filename, port number, and reference components in the resource name portion of the URL. These two constructors are useful when you do not have a `String` containing the complete URL specification, but you do know various components of the URL.

For example, if you design a network browsing panel similar to a file browsing panel that allows users to choose the protocol, host name, port number, and filename, you can construct a URL from its components. The first constructor creates a URL object from a protocol, host name, and filename. The following code snippet creates a URL to the `Gamelan.network.html` file at the Gamelan site:

```
URL gamelan = new URL("http", "www.gamelan.com",
                      "/Gamelan.network.html");
```

This is equivalent to:

```
URL("http://www.gamelan.com/Gamelan.network.html")
```

The first argument is the protocol, the second argument is the host name, and the last argument is the pathname of the file. Note that the filename contains a slash

(/) character at the beginning. This indicates that the filename is specified from the root of the host.

The final URL constructor adds the port number to the list of arguments used in the previous constructor.

```
URL gamelan = new URL("http", "www.gamelan.com", 80,
                      "/Gamelan.network.html");
```

This creates a URL object for the following URL:

```
http://www.gamelan.com:80/Gamelan.network.html
```

If you construct a URL object using one of these constructors, you can get a String containing the complete URL address using the URL object's toString method or the equivalent toExternalForm method.

MalformedURLException

Each of the four URL constructors throws a MalformedURLException if the arguments to the constructor refer to a null or unknown protocol. Typically, you want to catch and handle this exception by embedding your URL constructor statements in a try/catch pair.

```
try {
    URL myURL = new URL(. . .)
} catch (MalformedURLException e) {
    . . .
    // exception handler code here
    . . .
}
```

See **Handling Errors Using Exceptions** (page 253) for information about handling exceptions.

Note: URLs are "write-once" objects. Once you've created a URL object, you cannot change any of its attributes (protocol, host name, filename, or port number).

Parsing a URL

The URL class provides several methods that let you query URL objects. You can get the protocol, host name, port number, and filename from a URL object using the following accessor methods:

getProtocol   Returns the protocol identifier component of the URL.

getHost   Returns the host name component of the URL.

getPort   Returns the port number component of the URL. The get-Port method returns an integer that is the port number. If the port is not set, getPort returns -1.

getFile   Returns the filename component of the URL.

getRef   Returns the reference component of the URL.

Note: Remember that not all URL addresses contain these components. The URL class provides these methods because HTTP URLs do contain these components and are perhaps the most commonly used URLs. The URL class is somewhat HTTP-centric.

You can use these get*XXX* methods to get information about the URL regardless of the constructor that you used to create the URL object.

The URL class, along with these accessor methods, frees you from ever having to parse URLs again! Given any string specification of a URL, just create a new URL object and call any of the accessor methods for the information you need. The following program creates a URL from a string specification and then uses the URL object's accessor methods to parse the URL:

```java
import java.net.*;
import java.io.*;

class ParseURL {
    public static void main(String[] args) {
        URL aURL = null;
        try {
            aURL = new URL("http://java.sun.com:80/Series/" +
                            "Tutorial/intro.html#DOWNLOADING");
            System.out.println("protocol = "
                            + aURL.getProtocol());
            System.out.println("host = " + aURL.getHost());
            System.out.println("filename = " + aURL.getFile());
            System.out.println("port = " + aURL.getPort());
            System.out.println("ref = " + aURL.getRef());
        } catch (MalformedURLException e) {
```

```
            System.out.println("MalformedURLException: " + e);
        }
    }
}
```

Here's the output displayed by this program:

```
protocol = http
host = java.sun.com
filename = /Series/Tutorial/intro.html
port = 80
ref = DOWNLOADING
```

A Note About getRef

In the JDK 1.0 release of Java, getRef works only if you create the URL object using one of these two constructors:

```
URL(String absoluteURLSpecification);
URL(URL baseURL, String relativeURLSpecification);
```

For example, suppose you create a URL object with the following statements:

```
URL gamelan = new URL("http://www.gamelan.com/");
URL gamelanNetworkBottom = new URL(gamelan,
                            "Gamelan.network.html#BOTTOM");
```

The getRef method, when invoked on gamelanNetworkBottom, correctly returns BOTTOM. However, if you create a URL object with the following statement:

```
URL gamelanNetworkBottom = new URL("http", "www.gamelan.com",
                            "Gamelan.network" + ".html#BOTTOM");
```

The getRef method, incorrectly, returns null.

Reading Directly from a URL

After you've successfully created a URL object, you can call the URL object's openStream method to get a stream from which you can read the contents of the

URL. The openStream method returns a <u>java.io.InputStream</u>[1] object, so you can read from a URL using the normal InputStream methods. **Input and Output Streams** (page 325) describes the I/O classes provided by the Java development environment and shows you how to use them.

Reading from a URL is as easy as reading from an input stream. The following small Java program uses openStream to get an input stream on the URL http://www.yahoo.com/. It then reads the contents from the input stream echoing the contents to the display.

```java
import java.net.*;
import java.io.*;

class OpenStreamTest {
    public static void main(String[] args) {
        try {
            URL yahoo = new URL("http://www.yahoo.com/");
            DataInputStream dis =
                new DataInputStream(yahoo.openStream());
            String inputLine;

            while ((inputLine = dis.readLine()) != null) {
                System.out.println(inputLine);
            }
            dis.close();
        } catch (MalformedURLException me) {
            System.out.println("MalformedURLException: " + me);
        } catch (IOException ioe) {
            System.out.println("IOException: " + ioe);
        }
    }
}
```

When you run the program, you should see the HTML commands and textual content from the HTML file located at http://www.yahoo.com/ scrolling by in your command window.

Alternatively, you might see the following error message:

```
IOException: java.net.UnknownHostException: www.yahoo.com
```

The above message indicates that you may have to set your proxy host so that the program can find the www.yahoo.com server.

[1.] http://java.sun.com/products/JDK/CurrentRelease/api/java.io.InputStream.html

Platform-Specific Details: Setting Your Proxy Host Using the JDK

UNIX:
You can set the proxy host through the command line when you run the program. Note that you might also have to set the proxy port depending on how your network is set up.

```
java -DproxySet=true -DproxyHost=proxyhost
                     [-DproxyPort=portNumber]

OpenStreamTest
```

DOS shell (Windows 95/NT):
You can set the proxy host through the command line when you run the program. Note that you might also have to set the proxy port depending on how your network is set up.

```
java -DproxySet=true -DproxyHost=proxyhost
                     [-DproxyPort=portNumber]

OpenStreamTest
```

MacOS:
Edit the 'PROP' resource of your application's resource fork.

If necessary, ask your system administrator for the name of the proxy host on your network.

Connecting to a URL

After you've successfully created a URL object, you can call the URL object's openConnection method to connect to it. When you connect to a URL, you are initializing a communication link between your Java program and the URL over the network. For example, you can open a connection to the Yahoo search engine site with the following code:

```
try {
    URL yahoo = new URL("http://www.yahoo.com/");
    yahoo.openConnection();
} catch (MalformedURLException e) { // new URL() failed
    . . .
} catch (IOException e) {              // openConnection() failed
    . . .
}
```

If possible, the openConnection method creates a new URLConnection (if an appropriate one does not already exist), initializes it, connects to the URL, and returns the URLConnection[1] object. If something goes wrong—for example, the

---

[1] http://java.sun.com/products/JDK/CurrentRelease/api/java.net.URLConnection.html

Yahoo server is down—then the `openConnection` method throws an `IOException`.

Now that you've successfully connected to your URL, you can use the `URLConnection` object to perform actions such as reading from or writing to the connection. The next section shows you how to read from and write to a `URLConnection`.

Reading from and Writing to a URLConnection

If you've successfully used `openConnection` to initiate communications with a URL, then you have a reference to a `URLConnection` object. The `URLConnection` class contains many methods that let you communicate with the URL over the network. `URLConnection` is an HTTP-centric class—many of its methods are useful only when working with HTTP URLs. However, most URL protocols allow you to read from and write to the connection. This section describes both functions.

Reading from a URLConnection

The following program performs the same function as the program shown in <u>Reading Directly from a URL</u> (page 500). However, rather than opening a stream directly from the URL, this program explicitly opens a connection to the URL, gets an input stream on the connection, and reads from the input stream:

```
import java.net.*;
import java.io.*;

class ConnectionTest {
    public static void main(String[] args) {
        try {
            URL yahoo = new URL("http://www.yahoo.com/");
            URLConnection yahooConnection =
                        yahoo.openConnection();
            DataInputStream dis =
                new DataInputStream
                    (yahooConnection.getInputStream());
            String inputLine;

            while ((inputLine = dis.readLine()) != null) {
                System.out.println(inputLine);
            }
            dis.close();
```

```
        } catch (MalformedURLException me) {
            System.out.println("MalformedURLException: " + me);
        } catch (IOException ioe) {
            System.out.println("IOException: " + ioe);
        }
    }
}
```

The output from this program is identical to the output from the program that opens a stream directly from the URL. You can use either way to read from a URL. However, reading from a URLConnection instead of reading directly from a URL might be more useful to you because you can use the URLConnection object for other tasks (like writing to the URL) at the same time.

Again, if instead of output from the program you see the following error message, you may have to set the proxy host so that the program can find the www.yahoo.com server:

```
IOException: java.net.UnknownHostException: www.yahoo.com
```

Writing to a URLConnection

Many HTML pages contain *forms*—text fields and other GUI objects that let you enter data to send to the server. After you type in the required information and initiate the query by clicking on a button, the Web browser you're using writes the data to the URL over the network. At the other end, a cgi-bin script (usually) on the server receives the data, processes it, and then sends you back a response, usually in the form of a new HTML page. This scenario is often used to support searching.

Many cgi-bin scripts use the POST METHOD for reading the data from the client. Thus writing to a URL is often known as *posting to a URL*. Server-side scripts use the POST METHOD to read from their standard input.

Note: Some server-side cgi-bin scripts use the GET METHOD to read your data. The POST METHOD is quickly making the GET METHOD obsolete because it's more versatile and has no limitations on the amount of data that can be sent through the connection.

Your Java programs can also interact with cgi-bin scripts on the server side. They simply must be able to write to a URL, thus providing data to the server. Your program can do this by following these steps:

1. Create a URL.
2. Open a connection to the URL.

3. Get an output stream from the connection. This output stream is connected to the standard input stream of the cgi-bin script on the server.

4. Write to the output stream.

5. Close the output stream.

Hassan Schroeder, a member of the Java team, wrote a small cgi-bin script named <u>backwards</u> (page 769), and made it available at our Web site, java.sun.com. You can use this script to test the following example program. If for some reason you can't get to our Web site; you can put the script somewhere on your network, name it backwards, and test the program locally.

The script at our Web site reads a string from its standard input, reverses the string, and writes the result to its standard output. The script requires input of the form string=string_to_reverse, where string_to_reverse is the string whose characters you want displayed in reverse order.

Here's an example program that runs the backwards script over the network through a URLConnection:

```java
import java.io.*;
import java.net.*;

public class ReverseTest {
    public static void main(String[] args) {
        try {
            if (args.length != 1) {
                System.err.println("Usage: java ReverseTest "
                                + "string_to_reverse");
                System.exit(1);
            }
            String stringToReverse = URLEncoder.encode(args[0]);

            URL url = new URL("http://java.sun.com/"
                                + "cgi-bin/backwards");
            URLConnection connection = url.openConnection();

            PrintStream outStream = new PrintStream(
                            connection.getOutputStream());
            outStream.println("string=" + stringToReverse);
            outStream.close();

            DataInputStream inStream = new DataInputStream(
                            connection.getInputStream());
            String inputLine;

            while ((inputLine = inStream.readLine()) != null) {
                System.out.println(inputLine);
            }
```

```
            inStream.close();
        } catch (MalformedURLException me) {
            System.err.println("MalformedURLException: " + me);
        } catch (IOException ioe) {
            System.err.println("IOException: " + ioe);
        }
    }
}
```

Let's examine the program and see how it works. First, the program processes its command-line arguments:

```
if (args.length != 1) {
    System.err.println("Usage:  java ReverseTest "
                            + "string_to_reverse");
    System.exit(1);
}
String stringToReverse = URLEncoder.encode(args[0]);
```

These lines ensure that the user provides one and only one command-line argument to the program and encodes it. The command-line argument is the string which will be reversed by the cgi-bin script backwards. The command-line argument may have spaces or other nonalphanumeric characters in it. These characters must be encoded because the string is processed on its way to the server. The URLEncoder class methods encode the characters.

Next the program creates the URL object—the URL for the backwards script on java.sun.com.

```
URL url = new URL("http://java.sun.com/cgi-bin/backwards");
```

The program then creates a URLConnection and opens an output stream on that connection. The output stream is filtered through a PrintStream.

```
URLConnection connection = url.openConnection();
PrintStream outStream = new PrintStream(
                            connection.getOutputStream());
```

The second line in the previous code calls the getOutputStream method on the connection. If the URL does not support output, this method throws an UnknownServiceException. If the URL supports output, then this method returns an output stream that is connected to the standard input stream of the URL on the server side—the client's output is the server's input.

Next, the program writes the required information to the output stream and closes the stream using the following code:

```
outStream.println("string=" + stringToReverse);
outStream.close();
```

This code writes to the output stream using the `println` method. So you can see, writing data to a URL is as easy as writing data to a stream. The data written to the output stream on the client side is the input for the `backwards` script on the server side. The `ReverseTest` program constructs the input in the form required by the script by concatenating `string=` to the encoded string to be reversed.

Often, as in this example, when you are writing to a URL, you are passing information to a `cgi-bin` script which reads the information you write, performs some action, and then sends information back to you via the same URL. So it's likely that you will want to read from the URL after you've written to it. The `ReverseTest` program does that:

```
DataInputStream inStream = new
    DataInputStream(connection.getInputStream());
String inputLine;

while (null != (inputLine = inStream.readLine())) {
    System.out.println(inputLine);
}
inStream.close();
```

When you run the `ReverseTest` program using `Reverse Me` as an argument, you should see this output:

```
Reverse Me
 reversed is:
eM esreveR
```

All About Sockets

YOU use URLs and URLConnections to communicate over the network at a relatively high level and for a specific purpose: accessing resources on the Internet. Sometimes your programs require lower level network communication, for example, when you want to write a client-server application.

In client-server applications, the server provides some service, such as processing database queries or sending out current stock prices. The client uses the service provided by the server: displaying database query results to the user or making stock purchase recommendations to an investor. The communication that occurs between the client and the server must be reliable—no data can be dropped and it must arrive on the client side in the same order that it was sent by the server.

TCP provides a reliable, point-to-point communication channel which client-server applications on the Internet use to communicate. To communicate over TCP, a client program and a server program establish a connection to one another. Each program binds a socket—an endpoint of a two-way communication link—to its end of the connection. The Socket and ServerSocket classes provided in the java.net package implement the client side and server side of the connection, respectively. To communicate, the client and the server each reads from and writes to the socket bound to the connection.

This lesson begins with What Is a Socket? (page 510), which takes a closer look at what a socket is, and then walks you through two examples that use sockets. The first example, in the section Reading from and Writing to a Socket (page 510) illustrates how a client program can read from and write to a socket connected to a well-known server. The second example, in the section Writing the

Server Side of a Socket (page 513), shows you how to write a program that implements the other side of the connection—a server program.

What Is a Socket?

A server application normally listens to a specific port waiting for connection requests from a client. When a connection request arrives, the client and the server establish a dedicated connection over which they can communicate. During the connection process, the client is assigned a local port number, and binds a *socket* to it. The client talks to the server by writing to the socket and gets information from the server by reading from the socket. Similarly, the server gets a new local port number; it needs a new port number so that it can continue to listen for connection requests on the original port. The server also binds a socket to its local port and communicates with the client by reading from and writing to it.

The client and the server must agree on a protocol; that is, they must agree on the language of the information transferred back and forth through the socket.

Definition:

A socket is one endpoint of a two-way communication link between two programs running on the network.

The `java.net` package in the Java development environment provides a class, Socket,[1] that represents one end of a two-way connection between your Java program and another program on the network. The Socket class implements the client side of the two-way link. If you are writing server software, you will also be interested in the ServerSocket[2] class which implements the server side of the two-way link. This lesson shows you how to use the Socket and ServerSocket classes.

If you are trying to connect to the World Wide Web, the URL class and related classes (`URLConnection`, `URLEncoder`) are probably more appropriate than the socket classes. In fact, URLs are a relatively high level connection to the Web and use sockets as part of the underlying implementation. See **Working with URLs** (page 493) for information about connecting to the Web via URLs.

Reading from and Writing to a Socket

The following program is a simple example of how to establish a connection from a client program to a server program through the use of sockets. The Socket class in the `java.net` package is a platform-independent implementation of the client end of a two-way communication link between a client and a

---

[1.] http://java.sun.com/products/JDK/CurrentRelease/api/java.net.Socket.html
[2.] http://java.sun.com/products/JDK/CurrentRelease/api/java.net.ServerSocket.html

server. The `Socket` class sits on top of a platform-dependent implementation, hiding the details of any particular system from your Java program. By using the `java.net Socket` class instead of relying on native code, your Java programs can communicate over the network in a platform-independent fashion.

The following client program, `EchoTest`, connects to the standard Echo server on port 7 via a socket. The client both reads from and writes to the socket. `EchoTest` sends all text typed into its standard input to the Echo server by writing the text to the socket. The server echoes all input it receives from the client back through the socket to the client. The client program reads and displays the data passed back to it from the server:

```java
import java.io.*;
import java.net.*;

public class EchoTest {
    public static void main(String[] args) {
        Socket echoSocket = null;
        DataOutputStream os = null;
        DataInputStream is = null;
        DataInputStream stdIn = new DataInputStream(System.in);

        try {
            echoSocket = new Socket("taranis", 7);
            os = new DataOutputStream(
                echoSocket.getOutputStream());
            is = new DataInputStream(echoSocket.getInputStream());
        } catch (UnknownHostException e) {
            System.err.println("Don't know about host: taranis");
        } catch (IOException e) {
            System.err.println("Couldn't get I/O for the "
                               + "connection to: taranis");
        }

        if (echoSocket != null && os != null && is != null) {
            try {
                String userInput;

                while ((userInput = stdIn.readLine()) != null) {
                    os.writeBytes(userInput);
                    os.writeByte('\n');
                    System.out.println("echo: " + is.readLine());
                }
                os.close();
                is.close();
                echoSocket.close();
            } catch (IOException e) {
```

```
                    System.err.println("I/O failed on the "
                                + "connection to: taranis");
            }
        }
    }
}
```

Let's walk through the program and investigate the interesting parts. The following three lines of code within the first `try` block of the `main` method are critical—they establish the socket connection between the client and the server and open an input stream and an output stream on the socket:

```
echoSocket = new Socket("taranis", 7);
os = new DataOutputStream(echoSocket.getOutputStream());
is = new DataInputStream(echoSocket.getInputStream());
```

The first line in this sequence creates a new `Socket` object and names it `echo-Socket`. The `Socket` constructor used here (there are three others) requires the name of the machine and the port number that you want to connect to. The example program uses the host name `taranis`, which is the name of a hypothetical machine on our local network. When you type in and run this program on your machine, change the host name to the name of a machine on your network. Make sure that the name you use is the fully qualified IP name of the machine that you want to connect to. The second argument is the port number. Port number 7 is the port that the Echo server listens to.

The second line in the previous code snippet opens an output stream on the socket, and the third line opens an input stream on the socket. `EchoTest` merely needs to write to the output stream and read from the input stream to communicate through the socket to the server. The rest of the program achieves this. If you are not yet familiar with input and output streams, you may wish to read **Input and Output Streams** (page 325).

The next section of code reads from `EchoTest`'s standard input stream (where the user can type data) a line at a time. `EchoTest` immediately writes the input text followed by a newline character to the output stream connected to the socket.

```
String userInput;

while ((userInput = stdIn.readLine()) != null) {
    os.writeBytes(userInput);
    os.writeByte('\n');
    System.out.println("echo: " + is.readLine());
}
```

The last line in the `while` loop reads a line of information from the input stream connected to the socket. The `readLine` method waits until the server echos the information back to `EchoTest`. When `readline` returns, `EchoTest` prints the information to the standard output.

The `while` loop continues—`EchoTest` reads input from the user, sends it to the Echo server, gets a response from the server and displays it—until the user types an end-of-input character.

When the user types an end-of-input character, the `while` loop terminates and the program continues, executing the next three lines of code:

```
os.close();
is.close();
echoSocket.close();
```

These lines of code fall into the category of housekeeping. A well-behaved program always cleans up after itself, and this program is well-behaved. These three lines of code close the input and output streams connected to the socket, and close the socket connection to the server. The order here is important. You should close any streams connected to a socket before you close the socket itself.

This client program is straightforward and simple because the Echo server implements a simple protocol. The client sends text to the server, the server echos it back. When your client programs are talking to a more complicated server such as an HTTP server, your client program will also be more complicated. However, the basics are much the same as they are in this program:

1. Open a socket.
2. Open an input stream and output stream to the socket.
3. Read from and write to the stream according to the server's protocol.
4. Close the streams.
5. Close the socket.

Only step 3 differs from client to client, depending on the server. The other steps remain largely the same.

Writing the Server Side of a Socket

This section shows you how to write the server side of a socket connection, with a complete client/server example. The server in the client/server pair serves Knock Knock jokes. Knock Knock jokes are favored by young children and are usually vehicles for bad puns. They go like this:

Server: "Knock! Knock!"
Client: "Who's there?"

Server: "Dexter."
Client: "Dexter who?"
Server: "Dexter halls with boughs of holly."
Client: "Groan."

The example consists of two independently running Java programs: the client program and the server program. The client program is implemented by a single class, KnockKnockClient, and is based on the EchoTest (page 769) example from the previous section, Reading from and Writing to a Socket (page 510). The server program is implemented by two classes: KnockKnock-Server and KKState. KnockKnockServer contains the main method for the server program and performs all the grunt work of listening to the port, establishing connections, and reading from and writing to the socket. KKState serves up the jokes: It keeps track of the current joke, the current state (sent knock knock, sent clue, and so on) and serves up the various text pieces of the joke depending on the current state. The following section looks in detail at each class in these two programs and then shows you how to run them.

The Knock Knock Server

This section walks through the code that implements the Knock Knock server program. The complete source for the KnockKnockServer is on (page 770). The server program begins by creating a new ServerSocket object to listen on a specific port (see the line in **bold**). When writing a server, choose a port that is not already dedicated to some other service. KnockKnockServer listens on port 4444 because 4 happens to be my favorite number and port 4444 is not being used for anything else in my environment:

```
try {
    serverSocket = new ServerSocket(4444);
} catch (IOException e) {
    System.out.println("Could not listen on port: " + 4444 +
                        ", " + e);
    System.exit(1);
}
```

ServerSocket is a java.net class that provides a system-independent implementation of the server side of a client/server socket connection. The constructor for ServerSocket throws an exception if for some reason (such as the port is already being used) it can't listen on the specified port. In this case, the Knock-KnockServer has no choice but to exit.

If the server successfully connects to its port, then the ServerSocket object is successfully created and the server continues to the next step, which is to accept a connection from a client.

```
Socket clientSocket = null;
try {
    clientSocket = serverSocket.accept();
} catch (IOException e) {
    System.out.println("Accept failed: " + 4444 + ", " + e);
    System.exit(1);
}
```

The accept method waits until a client starts up and requests a connection on the port (in this case, port 4444) that the server is listening to. When the accept method successfully establishes a connection with the client, it returns a new Socket object, which is bound to a new, local port. The server can communicate with the client over this new Socket on a port that is different from the one that it was originally listening to for connections. So the server can continue to listen for client connection requests on the original port through the ServerSocket. This version of the program doesn't listen for more client connection requests. However, a modified version of the program, provided in <u>Supporting Multiple Clients</u> (page 520), does.

The code within the next try block implements the server side of the communication with the client. This section of the server is remarkably similar to the client side, which you saw an example of in the previous section and will see again later when we walk through the KnockKnockClient class:

- Open an input and output stream to the socket.
- Read from and write to the socket.

Let's start with the first six lines:

```
DataInputStream is = new DataInputStream(
                    new BufferedInputStream(
                        clientSocket.getInputStream()));
PrintStream os = new PrintStream(
                new BufferedOutputStream(
                    clientSocket.getOutputStream(), 1024),
                    false);
String inputLine, outputLine;
KKState kks = new KKState();
```

The first two lines of the code snippet open an input stream on the socket returned by the accept method. The next two lines open an output stream on the same socket. The next line declares and creates a couple of local strings used to read from and write to the socket. The last line creates a `KKState` object. This is the object that keeps track of the current joke, the current state within the joke, and so on. This object implements the *protocol*—the language that the client and server have agreed to use to communicate.

The server is the first to speak, with these lines of code:

```
outputLine = kks.processInput(null);
os.println(outputLine);
os.flush();
```

The first line of code gets from the `KKState` object the first line that the server says to the client. For this example, the first thing that the server says is "Knock! Knock!".

The next two lines write to the output stream connected to the client socket and then flush the output stream. This code sequence initiates the conversation between the client and the server.

The next section of code is a loop that reads from and writes to the socket, sending messages back and forth between the client and the server while they still have something to say to each other. Since the server initiated the conversation with a "Knock! Knock!", the server must now wait for a response from the client. As a result, the `while` loop iterates on a read from the input stream. The `readLine` method waits until the client responds by writing something to its output stream (the server's input stream). When the client responds, the server passes the client's response to the `KKState` object and asks the `KKState` object for a suitable reply. The server immediately sends the reply to the client via the output stream connected to the socket, using calls to `println` and `flush`. If the server's response generated from the `KKState` object is "Bye.", this indicates that the client doesn't want any more jokes and the loop quits.

```
while ((inputLine = is.readLine()) != null) {
    outputLine = kks.processInput(inputLine);
    os.println(outputLine);
    os.flush();
    if (outputLine.equals("Bye."))
        break;
}
```

The `KnockKnockServer` class is a well-behaved server, so the last several lines of this section of `KnockKnockServer` clean up by closing all the input and output streams, the client socket, and the server socket.

```
os.close();
is.close();
clientSocket.close();
serverSocket.close();
```

The Knock Knock Protocol

The KKState (page 772) class implements the protocol that the client and server use to communicate. This class keeps track of where the client and the server are in their conversation and serves up the server's response to the client's statements. The KKState object contains the text of all the jokes and makes sure that the client gives the proper response to the server's statements. It wouldn't do to have the client say "Dexter who?" when the server says "Knock! Knock!".

All client/server pairs must have some protocol with which they speak to each other, or the data that passes back and forth would be meaningless. The protocol that your own clients and servers use depends entirely on the communication required by them to accomplish the task.

The Knock Knock Client

The KnockKnockClient (page 773) class implements the client program that speaks to the KnockKnockServer. KnockKnockClient is based on the EchoTest (page 769) program in the previous section, Reading from and Writing to a Socket (page 510), and should be somewhat familiar to you. But let's go over the program anyway and look at what's happening in the client, while keeping in mind what's going on in the server.

When you start the client program, the server should already be running and listening to the port waiting for a client to request a connection.

```
kkSocket = new Socket("taranis", 4444);
os = new PrintStream(kkSocket.getOutputStream());
is = new DataInputStream(kkSocket.getInputStream());
```

The first thing the client program does is open a socket on the port that the server is listening to on the machine that the server is running on. The KnockKnockClient program opens the socket on port number 4444, which is the same port that KnockKnockServer is listening to. KnockKnockClient uses the host name taranis, which is the name of a hypothetical machine on our local network. When you type in and run this program on your machine, change the host name to the name of a machine on your network. This is the machine that you will run the KnockKnockServer on.

Then the client opens an input and output stream on the socket.

Next comes the while loop that implements the communication between the client and the server. The server speaks first, so the client must listen first, which it does by reading from the input stream attached to the socket. When the server does speak, if it says "Bye.", the client exits the loop. Otherwise, the client displays the text to the standard output, and then reads the response from the user,

who types into the standard input. After the user types a carriage return, the client sends the text to the server through the output stream attached to the socket.

```java
while ((fromServer = is.readLine()) != null) {
    System.out.println("Server: " + fromServer);
    if (fromServer.equals("Bye."))
        break;
    while ((c = System.in.read()) != '\n') {
        buf.append((char)c);
    }
    System.out.println("Client: " + buf);
    os.println(buf.toString());
    os.flush();
    buf.setLength(0);
}
```

The communication ends when the server asks if the client wishes to hear another joke, the user says no, and the server says "Bye."

In the interest of good housekeeping, the client closes its input and output streams and the socket:

```java
os.close();
is.close();
kkSocket.close();
```

Run the Programs

You must start the server program first. To do this, run the server program using the Java interpreter, just as you would any other Java application. Remember to run the server on the machine that the client program specifies when creating the socket.

Next, run the client program. Note that you can run the client on any machine on your network; it does not have to run on the same machine as the server.

If you are too quick, you might start the client before the server has a chance to initialize itself and begin listening on the port. If this happens, you will see the following error message when you try to start the client:

```
Exception:  java.net.SocketException: Connection refused
```

If this happens just restart the client.

You will see the following error message if you forget to change the host name in the source code for the KnockKnockClient program.

```
Trying to connect to unknown host:
java.net.UnknownHostException: taranis
```

Modify the `KnockKnockClient` program and provide a valid host name for your network. Recompile the client program and try again.

If you try to start a second client while the first client is connected to the server, the second client just hangs. The next section, <u>Supporting Multiple Clients</u> (page 520), talks about supporting multiple clients.

When you successfully get a connection between the client and server, you will see the following text displayed on your screen:

```
Server: Knock! Knock!
```

Now, you must respond with:

```
Who's there?
```

The client echos what you type and sends the text to the server. The server responds with the first line of one of the many Knock Knock jokes in its repertoire. Now your screen should contain this (the text you typed is in **bold**):

```
Server: Knock! Knock!
Who's there?
Client: Who's there?
Server: Turnip
```

Now, you respond with:

```
Turnip who?
```

Again, the client echos what you type and sends the text to the server. The server responds with the punch line. Now your screen should contain this (the text you typed is in **bold**):

```
Server: Knock! Knock!
Who's there?
Client: Who's there?
Server: Turnip
Turnip who?
Client: Turnip who?
Server: Turnip the heat, it's cold in here! Want another? (y/n)
```

If you want to hear another joke, type "y"; if not, type "n". If you type "y", the server begins again with "Knock! Knock!". If you type "n", the server says "Bye.", causing both the client and the server to exit.

If at any point you make a typing error, the KKState object catches it, the server responds with a message similar to this, and the server starts the joke over again:

```
Server: You're supposed to say "Who's there?"! Try again. Knock!
Knock!
```

The KKState object is particular about spelling and punctuation, but not about upper and lower case letters.

Supporting Multiple Clients

To keep the KnockKnockServer example simple, we designed it to listen for and handle a single connection request. However, multiple client requests can come into the same port and, consequently, into the same ServerSocket. Client connections requests are queued at the port, so the server must accept the connections sequentially. However, the server can service them simultaneously through the use of threads—one thread to process each client connection.

The basic flow of logic in such a server is this:

```
while (true) {
    accept a connection ;
    create a thread to deal with the client ;
end while
```

The thread reads from and writes to the client connection as necessary.

Try this: Modify the KnockKnockServer so that it can service multiple clients at the same time. Our solution is comprised of two classes: KKMultiServer (page 774) and KKMultiServerThread (page 775). KKMultiServer loops forever listening for client connection requests on a ServerSocket. When a request comes in, KKMulti-Server accepts the connection, creates a new KKMultiServerThread object to process it, hands it the socket returned from accept, and starts the thread. Then the server goes back to listening for connection requests. The KKMultiServerThread object communicates to the client by reading from and writing to the socket. Run the new Knock Knock server and then run several clients in succession.

24

All About Datagrams

SOME applications that you write to communicate over the network will not require the reliable, point-to-point channel provided by TCP. Rather, your applications might benefit from a mode of communication that delivers independent packages of information whose arrival and order of arrival are not guaranteed.

The UDP protocol provides a mode of network communication whereby applications send packets of data, called *datagrams,* to one another. A datagram is an independent, self-contained message sent over the network whose arrival, arrival time, and content are not guaranteed. The DatagramPacket and DatagramSocket classes in the java.net package implement system-independent datagram communication using UDP.

This lesson begins with a closer look at datagrams in the What Is a Datagram? (page 521) section. The next and final section of this lesson, Writing a Datagram Client and Server (page 522), walks you through an example that contains two Java programs that use datagrams to communicate. The server side is a quote server that listens to its DatagramSocket and sends a famous quotation to a client whenever the client requests it. The client side is a simple program that simply makes a request of the server.

What Is a Datagram?

Clients and servers that communicate via a reliable channel, such as a URL or a socket, have a dedicated point-to-point channel between themselves, or at least the illusion of one. To communicate, they establish a connection, transmit the

Definition:

A datagram is an independent, self-contained message sent over the network whose arrival, arrival time, and content are not guaranteed.

data, and then close the connection. All data sent over the channel is received in the same order that it was sent. This is guaranteed by the channel.

In contrast, applications that communicate via datagrams send and receive completely independent packets of information. These clients and servers do not have and do not need a dedicated point-to-point channel. The delivery of datagrams to their destinations is not guaranteed, nor is the order of their arrival.

The `java.net` package contains two classes to help you write Java programs that use datagrams to send and receive packets over the network: <u>Datagram-Socket</u>[1] and <u>DatagramPacket</u>.[2] Your application sends and receives Datagram-Packets through a `DatagramSocket`.

Writing a Datagram Client and Server

The example featured in this section is comprised of two applications: a client and a server. The server continuously receives datagram packets over a datagram socket. Each datagram packet received by the server indicates a client request for a famous quotation. When the server receives a datagram, it replies by sending a datagram packet that contains a one-line "quote of the moment" back to the client.

The client application in this example is fairly simple. It sends a single datagram packet to the server indicating that the client would like to receive a quote of the moment. The client then waits for the server to send a datagram packet in response.

Two classes implement the server application: `QuoteServer` and `Quote-ServerThread`. A single class implements the client application: `QuoteClient`.

Let's investigate these classes, starting with class that contains the `main` method for the server application.

A Simple Network Client Applet (page 193) contains an applet version of the QuoteClient class.

The QuoteServer Class

The `QuoteServer` class contains a single method: the `main` method for the quote server application. The `main` method simply creates a new `QuoteServerThread` object and starts it.

```
class QuoteServer {
    public static void main(String[] args) {
        new QuoteServerThread().start();
    }
}
```

The `QuoteServerThread` class implements the main logic of the quote server.

---

1. http://java.sun.com/products/JDK/CurrentRelease/api/java.net.DatagramSocket.html
2. http://java.sun.com/products/JDK/CurrentRelease/api/java.net.DatagramPacket.html

The QuoteServerThread Class

The QuoteServerThread (page 777) is a Thread that runs continuously, waiting for requests over a datagram socket.

QuoteServerThread has two private instance variables. The first, named socket, is a reference to a DatagramSocket object. This variable is initialized to null. The second, qfs, is a DataInputStream object that is opened onto an ASCII text file containing a list of quotes. Whenever a request for a quote arrives in the server, the server retrieves the next line from this input stream.

When the main program creates the QuoteServerThread, it uses the only constructor available:

```
QuoteServerThread() {
    super("QuoteServer");
    try {
        socket = new DatagramSocket();
        System.out.println("QuoteServer listening on port: " +
                           socket.getLocalPort());
    } catch (java.net.SocketException e) {
        System.err.println("Could not create datagram socket.");
    }
    this.openInputFile();
}
```

The first line of this constructor calls the superclass (Thread) constructor to initialize the Thread with the name QuoteServer. The next section of code is the critical part of the QuoteServerThread constructor—it creates a Datagram-Socket. The QuoteServerThread uses this DatagramSocket to listen for and respond to client requests for a quote.

The socket is created using the DatagramSocket constructor that requires no arguments:

```
socket = new DatagramSocket();
```

When the new DatagramSocket is created using this constructor, it binds to any locally available port. The DatagramSocket class has another constructor that allows you to specify the port that you want the new DatagramSocket to bind to. Note that certain ports are dedicated to well-known services and you cannot use them. If you specify a port that is in use, the creation of the DatagramSocket will fail.

After the DatagramSocket is successfully created, the QuoteServer-Thread displays a message indicating which port the DatagramSocket is bound to. The QuoteClient needs this port number to construct datagram packets destined for this port. So you must use this port number when you run the client (page 528).

The last line of the `QuoteServerThread` constructor calls a private method, `openInputFile`, within `QuoteServerThread` to open a file named <u>one-liners.txt</u> (page 780) that contains a list of quotes. Each quote in the file must be on a line by itself.

Now for the interesting part of the <u>QuoteServerThread</u> (page 777)—its run method. The `run` method overrides `run` in the `Thread` class and provides the implementation for the thread. (For information about threads, see **Threads of Control** (page 285).)

`QuoteServerThread`'s `run` method first checks to verify that a valid `Data-gramSocket` was created during construction. If `socket` is null, then the `Quote-ServerThread` could not bind to the `DatagramSocket`. Without the socket, the server cannot operate, and the `run` method returns.

Otherwise, the `run` method enters into an infinite loop. The infinite loop is continuously waiting for requests from clients and responding to those requests. This loop contains two important sections of code: the section that listens for requests and the section that responds to them. Let's look at first at the section that receives the requests:

```
packet = new DatagramPacket(buf, 256);
socket.receive(packet);
address = packet.getAddress();
port = packet.getPort();
```

The first line of code creates a new `DatagramPacket` object intended to receive a datagram message over the datagram socket. You can tell that the new `Data-gramPacket` is intended to receive data from the socket because of the constructor used to create it. This constructor requires only two arguments: a byte array that contains client-specific data, and the length of the byte array. When constructing a `DatagramPacket` to send over the `DatagramSocket`, you must also supply the Internet address and port number of the destination of the packet. You'll see this later when we discuss how the server responds to a client request.

The second line of code in the previous code snippet receives a datagram from the socket. The information contained within the datagram message gets copied into the packet created on the previous line. The `receive` method waits forever until a packet is received. If no packet is received, the server makes no further progress and just waits.

The third and fourth lines of the previous code snippet get the Internet address and the port number from the received datagram packet. The Internet address and port number indicate where the datagram packet came from. This is where the server must send its response to. In this example, the byte array of the

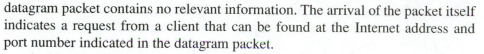

datagram packet contains no relevant information. The arrival of the packet itself indicates a request from a client that can be found at the Internet address and port number indicated in the datagram packet.

At this point, the server has received a request from a client for a quote. Now the server must respond. The next seven lines of code construct the response and send it.

```
if (qfs == null)
    dString = new Date().toString();
else
    dString = getNextQuote();
dString.getBytes(0, dString.length(), buf, 0);
packet = new DatagramPacket(buf, buf.length, address, port);
socket.send(packet);
```

If the quote file did not get opened for some reason, then `qfs` is `null`. If this is the case, the quote server serves up the time of day instead. Otherwise, the quote server gets the next quote from the already opened file. The line of code following the `if` statement converts the string to an array of bytes.

The sixth line of code creates a new `DatagramPacket` object intended for sending a datagram message over the datagram socket. You can tell that the new `DatagramPacket` is intended to send data over the socket because of the constructor used to create it. This constructor requires four arguments. The first two arguments are the same arguments required by the constructor used to create receiving datagrams: a byte array containing the message from the sender to the receiver, and the length of this array. The next two arguments are different: an Internet address and a port number. These two arguments are the complete address of the destination of the datagram packet and must be supplied by the sender of the datagram.

The seventh line of code sends the `DatagramPacket` on its way.

The last method of interest in `QuoteServerThread` is the `finalize` method. This method cleans up when the `QuoteServerThread` is garbage collected by closing the `DatagramSocket`. Ports are limited resources and sockets bound to ports should be closed when not in use.

The **QuoteClient** Class

The <u>QuoteClient</u> (page 779) class implements a client application for the Quo-teServer. This application sends a request to the `QuoteServer`, waits for the response, and when the response is received, displays it to the standard output. Let's look at the code in detail.

The `QuoteClient` class contains one method, the `main` method for the client application. The top of the `main` method declares several local variables for its use:

```
int port;
InetAddress address;
DatagramSocket socket = null;
DatagramPacket packet;
byte[] sendBuf = new byte[256];
```

The next section of code processes the command-line arguments used to invoke the `QuoteClient` application.

```
if (args.length != 2) {
    System.out.println("Usage: java DatagramClient "
                       + "<hostname> <port#>");
    return;
}
```

The `QuoteClient` application requires two command-line arguments: the name of the machine that the `QuoteServer` is running on, and the port that the `Quote-Server` is listening to. When you start the `QuoteServer` it displays a port number. This is the port number you must use on the command line when starting up the `QuoteClient`.

Next, the `main` method contains a `try` block that contains the main logic of the client program. This `try` block contains three main sections: a section that creates a `DatagramSocket`, a section that sends a request to the server, and a section that gets the response from the server.

First, let's look at the statement that creates a `DatagramSocket`:

```
socket = new DatagramSocket();
```

The client uses the same constructor to create a `DatagramSocket` as the server. The `DatagramSocket` is bound to any available local port.

Next, the `QuoteClient` program sends a request to the server:

```
address = InetAddress.getByName(args[0]);
port = Integer.parseInt(args[1]);
packet = new DatagramPacket(sendBuf, 256, address, port);
socket.send(packet);
System.out.println("Client sent request packet.");
```

The first line of code gets the Internet address for the host named on the command line. The second line of code gets the port number from the command line.

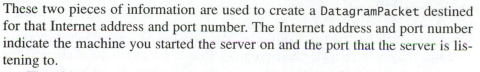

These two pieces of information are used to create a `DatagramPacket` destined for that Internet address and port number. The Internet address and port number indicate the machine you started the server on and the port that the server is listening to.

The third line in the previous code snippet creates a `DatagramPacket` intended for sending data. The packet is constructed with an empty byte array, its length, and the Internet address and port number for the destination of the packet. The byte array is empty because this datagram packet is simply a request to the server for information. All the server needs to know to send a response—the address and port number to reply to—is automatically part of the packet.

Next, the client gets a response from the server:

```
packet = new DatagramPacket(sendBuf, 256);
socket.receive(packet);
String received = new String(packet.getData(), 0);
System.out.println("Client received packet: " + received);
```

To get a response from the server, the client creates a receive packet and uses the `DatagramSocket receive` method to receive the reply from the server. The `receive` method waits until a datagram packet destined for the client comes through the socket. Note that if the server's reply is somehow lost, the client will wait forever because of the no-guarantee policy of the datagram model. Normally, a client sets a timer so that it doesn't wait forever for a reply; if no reply arrives, the timer goes off, and the client retransmits.

When the client receives a reply from the server, the client uses the `getData` method to retrieve that data from the packet. The client then converts the data to a string and displays it.

Run the Server

After you've successfully compiled the server and the client programs, you can run them. You have to run the server program first because you need the port number that it displays before you can start the client. When the server successfully binds to its `DatagramSocket`, it displays a message similar to this one:

```
QuoteServer listening on port: portNumber
```

portNumber is the number of the port to which the server's `DatagramSocket` is bound. Use this number to start the client.

Run the Client

Once the server has started and displayed a message indicating which port it's listening to, you can run the client program. Remember to run the client program with two command-line arguments: the name of the host on which the `Quote-Server` is running, and the port number that it displayed on startup.

After the client sends a request and receives a response from the server, you should see output similar to this:

```
Quote of the Moment: Good programming is 99% sweat and 1%
coffee.
```

25

Providing Your Own Security Manager

SECURITY becomes a major concern when writing and using programs that interact with the Internet. Will you download something that corrupts your file system? Will you be open for a virus attack? It's unlikely that computers on the Internet will ever be completely safe from attack from the few evildoers out there. However, you can take steps to provide a significant level of protection for your computers and data. One of the ways that Java provides protection from attack is through the use of security managers. A security manager implements and imposes the security policy for an application.

The security manager is an application-wide object that determines whether potentially threatening operations should be allowed. The classes in the Java packages cooperate with the security manager by asking the application's security manager for permission to perform certain operations. Introducing the Security Manager (page 530) shows you how your Java programs can get the current security manager and use it to request permission to perform certain operations.

Writing a Security Manager (page 531) walks you through a simple implementation of a security manager that requires the user to enter a password each time the application tries to open a file for reading or writing. The following section, Installing Your Security Manager (page 534), shows you how to put your security manager on duty for your Java application.

And finally, Deciding Which SecurityManager Methods to Override (page 536) looks at the SecurityManager class in greater detail, showing you which methods in the `SecurityManager` class affect which kinds of operations and helping you decide which methods your security manager needs to override.

Note: The security manager for an application can be set only once. Typically, a browser sets its security manager during its startup procedure. As a result, applets cannot typically set the security manager because it's already been set. A `SecurityException` results if an applet attempts to do so. See <u>Understanding Applet Capabilities and Restrictions</u> (page 197) for information.

Introducing the Security Manager

Each Java application can have its own security manager object that acts as a full-time security guard. The <u>SecurityManager</u>[1] class in the `java.lang` package is an abstract class that provides the programming interface and partial implementation for all Java security managers.

By default, an application does not have a security manager. So by default, an application allows all operations that might be subject to security restrictions.

To change this lenient behavior, an application must create and install its own security manager. You will learn how to create a security manager in <u>Writing a Security Manager</u> (page 531), and how to install it in <u>Installing Your Security Manager</u> (page 534).

Note: The existing browsers and applet viewers *do* create their own security manager when starting up. Consequently, an applet is subject to whatever access restrictions are imposed on it by the security manager for the particular application in which the applet is running.

You can get the current security manager for an application using the `System` class's `getSecurityManager` method:

```
SecurityManager appsm = System.getSecurityManager();
```

Note that `getSecurityManager` returns `null` if there is no current security manager for the application. You should make sure that you have a valid `Security-Manager` object before calling any of its methods.

Once you have the security manager, you can request permission to allow or disallow certain operations. Indeed many of the classes in the Java packages do

---

[1] http://java.sun.com/products/JDK/CurrentRelease/api/java.lang.SecurityManager.html

just this. For example, the `System.exit` method, which terminates the Java interpreter, uses the security manager's `checkExit` method to approve the exit operation:

```
SecurityManager security = System.getSecurityManager();
if (security != null) {
    security.checkExit(status);
}
. . .
// code continues here if checkedExit() returns
```

If the security manager approves the exit operation, the `checkExit` returns normally. If the security manager disallows the operation, the `checkExit` method throws a `SecurityException`. In this manner, the security manager allows or disallows a potentially threatening operation before it can be completed.

The `SecurityManager` class defines many other methods that can be used to verify other kinds of operations. For example, `SecurityManager`'s `checkAccess` method verifies thread accesses, and `checkPropertyAccess` verifies access to the specified property. Each operation or group of operations has its own check-*XXX* method.

In addition, the set of check*XXX* methods represents the set of operations in the Java package classes and the Java runtime system that are already subject to the protection of the security manager. Typically, your code will not have to invoke any of `SecurityManager`'s check*XXX* methods—the Java package classes and the Java runtime system do this for you at a low enough level that any operation represented by a check*XXX* method is already protected. However, when writing your own security manager, you must override `SecurityManager`'s check*XXX* methods to implement the security policy for specific operations, or you may have to add a few of your own to put other kinds of operations under the scrutiny of the security manager. <u>Deciding Which `SecurityManager` Methods to Override</u> (page 536) explains which operation or group of operations each check*XXX* method in the `SecurityManager` class is designed to protect.

Writing a Security Manager

To write your own security manager, you must create a subclass of the `SecurityManager` class. Your `SecurityManager` subclass overrides most or all methods from `SecurityManager` to customize the verifications and approvals needed in your Java application.

This section walks through an example security manager that restricts reading and writing to the file system. To get approval from the security manager, a method that opens a file for reading invokes one of `SecurityManager`'s `check-Read` methods. Similarly, a method that opens a file for writing invokes one of `SecurityManager`'s `checkWrite` methods. If the security manager approves the operation, then the check*XXX* method returns. Otherwise, check*XXX* throws a `SecurityException`.

To impose a custom policy on file system accesses, the `SecurityManager` subclass in our example overrides `SecurityManager`'s `checkRead` and `check-Write` methods. `SecurityManager` provides three versions of `checkRead` and two versions of `checkWrite`. Each method should verify whether the application is allowed to open a file for I/O. A policy frequently implemented by browsers is that applets loaded over the network cannot read from or write to the local file system unless the user approves it.

The policy implemented by our example security manager prompts the user for a password when the application attempts to open a file for reading or for writing. If the password is correct then the access is allowed.

All security managers must be a subclass of `SecurityManager`. Thus, our `PasswordSecurtiyManager` (page 781) class extends `SecurityManager`.

```
class PasswordSecurityManager extends SecurityManager {
    . . .
}
```

Next, `PasswordSecurityManager` declares a private instance variable `password` to contain the password that the user must enter in order to allow the restricted file system accesses. The password is set in the following constructor:

```
PasswordSecurityManager(String password) {
    super();
    this.password = password;
}
```

The next method in the `PasswordSecurityManager` class is a private helper method named `accessOK`. This method prompts the user for a password and verifies it. If the user enters a valid password, the method returns `true`; otherwise, it returns `false`.

```
private boolean accessOK() {
    int c;
    DataInputStream dis = new DataInputStream(System.in);
    String response;

    System.out.println("What's the secret password?");
```

```
        try {
            response = dis.readLine();
            if (response.equals(password))
                return true;
            else
                return false;
        } catch (IOException e) {
            return false;
        }
    }
}
```

Finally, at the end of the PasswordSecurityManager class are the three overridden checkRead methods and the two overridden checkWrite methods:

```
public void checkRead(FileDescriptor filedescriptor) {
    if (!accessOK())
        throw new SecurityException("Not a Chance!");
}
public void checkRead(String filename) {
    if (!accessOK())
        throw new SecurityException("No Way!");
}
public void checkRead(String filename, Object executionContext)
{
    if (!accessOK())
        throw new SecurityException("Forget It!");
}
public void checkWrite(FileDescriptor filedescriptor) {
    if (!accessOK())
        throw new SecurityException("Not!");
}
public void checkWrite(String filename) {
    if (!accessOK())
        throw new SecurityException("Not Even!");
}
```

All the check*XXX* methods call accessOK to prompt the user for a password. If access is *not* OK, then check*XXX* throws a SecurityException. Otherwise, check*XXX* returns normally. Note that SecurityException is a runtime exception, and as such does not need to be declared in the throws clause of these methods.

checkRead and checkWrite are just a few of the many of SecurityManager's check*XXX* methods that verify various kinds of operations. The default implementation provided by the SecurityManager class for all check*XXX* methods throws a SecurityException. By default, the SecurityManager class disallows all operations that are subject to security restrictions. You may find that you have to override all of SecurityManager's check*XXX* methods to get the behavior you want.

All of SecurityManager's check*XXX* methods operate in the same way:

- If access is allowed, the method returns.
- If access is not allowed, the method throws a SecurityException.

Make sure that you implement your overridden check*XXX* methods in this manner.

As you can see, implementing a SecurityManager is simple. You just:

- Create a SecurityManager subclass.
- Override its methods.

The tricky part is figuring out what operations each check*XXX* method polices and implementing your security policy. Deciding Which SecurityManager Methods to Override (page 536) will help you figure out which methods you should override and how. The next section, Installing Your Security Manager (page 534), shows you how to install the PasswordSecurityManager class as the on-duty security manager for your Java application.

Installing Your Security Manager

Once you've completed writing your SecurityManager subclass, you can install it as the current security manager for your Java application with the setSecurityManager method from the System class.

Here's a small test application, SecurityManagerTest (page 782), that installs the PasswordSecurityManager class from the previous section as the current security manager. To verify that the security manager is in place and operational, the SecurityManagerTest application then opens two files—one for reading and one for writing—and copies the contents of the first file into the second.

The main method begins by installing a new security manager:

```
try {
    System.setSecurityManager(new PasswordSecurityManager(
                                "Booga Booga"));
} catch (SecurityException se) {
    System.out.println("SecurityManager already set!");
}
```

The **bold** line in the previous code snippet creates a new instance of the PasswordSecurityManager class with the password Booga Booga. This instance is

passed to System's `setSecurityManager` method, which installs the object as the current security manager for the running application. This security manager will remain in effect for the duration of the execution of this application.

You can set the security manager for your application only once. In other words, your Java application can invoke `System.setSecurityManager` only one time during its lifetime. Any subsequent attempt to install a security manager within a Java application will result in a `SecurityException`.

The rest of the program copies the contents of the file `inputtext.txt` (page 783) into an output file named `outputtext.txt`. This is a simple test to verify that the `PasswordSecurityManager` has been properly installed.

```
try {
  DataInputStream fis = new DataInputStream(
                          new FileInputStream("inputtext.txt"));
    DataOutputStream fos = new DataOutputStream(
                              new FileOutputStream(
                              "outputtext.txt"));
    String inputString;
    while ((inputString = fis.readLine()) != null) {
        fos.writeBytes(inputString);
        fos.writeByte('\n');
    }
    fis.close();
    fos.close();
} catch (IOException ioe) {
    System.err.println("I/O failed for SecurityManagerTest.");
}
```

The **bold** lines in the previous code snippet are restricted file system accesses. These method calls will result in a call to `PasswordSecurityManager`'s check-Access method.

Running the Test Program

When you run the `SecurityManagerTest` application, you are prompted twice for a password, once when the application opens the input file and once when the application opens the output file. If you enter the correct password, the access is granted—the file object gets created—and the application proceeds to the next statement. If you enter an incorrect password, check*XXX* throws a `SecurityException`, which the test application makes no attempt to catch so the application terminates.

This is an example of the output from the application when you type in the password correctly the first time, but incorrectly the second:

```
What's the secret password?
Booga Booga
What's the secret password?
Wrong password
java.lang.SecurityException: Not Even!
at PasswordSecurityManager.checkWrite(
    PasswordSecurityManager.java:46)
at java.io.FileOutputStream.(FileOutputStream.java)
at SecurityManagerTest.main(SecurityManagerTest.java:15)
```

Notice that the error message that the application prints is the error message for the `checkWrite(String)` method.

Deciding Which `SecurityManager` Methods to Override

You'll probably have to override most or all of `SecurityManager`'s check*XXX* methods. For operations that you don't care to restrict, overriding the methods is easy: Just implement the appropriate method with an empty method body.

The first column in the following table lists objects on which you can perform various operations. The second column lists the `SecurityManager` methods that approve the operations on the objects in the first column.

Operations On	Approved By
sockets	checkAccept(String *host*, int *port*)
	checkConnect(String *host*, int *port*)
	checkConnect(String *host*, int *port*, Object *executionContext*)
	checkListen(int *port*)
threads	checkAccess(Thread *thread*)
	checkAccess(ThreadGroup *threadgroup*)
class loader	checkCreateClassLoader()

continued

Operations On	Approved By
file system	checkDelete(String *filename*)
	checkLink(String *library*)
	checkRead(FileDescriptor *filedescriptor*)
	checkRead(String *filename*)
	checkRead(String *filename*, Object *executionContext*)
	checkWrite(FileDescriptor *filedescriptor*)
	checkWrite(String *filename*)
system commands	checkExec(String *command*)
interpreter	checkExit(int *status*)
package	checkPackageAccess(String *packageName*)
	checkPackageDefinition(String *packageName*)
properties	checkPropertiesAccess()
	checkPropertyAccess(String *key*)
	checkPropertyAccess(String *key*, String *def*)
networking	checkSetFactory()
windows	checkTopLevelWindow(Object *window*)

Many of the check*XXX* methods are called in multiple situations. The checkAc-cess(ThreadGroup *g*) method is invoked when you create a ThreadGroup, set its daemon status, stop it, and so on. When overriding a check*XXX* method make sure that you understand all the situations in which it can be invoked.

The default implementation provided by the SecurityManager class for all check*XXX* methods is:

```
public void checkXXX(. . .) {
    throw new SecurityException();
}
```

End of Trail

YOU'VE reached the end of the **Custom Networking and Security** trail. Take a break—have a cup of steaming hot java.

What Next?

Once you've caught your breath, you have several choices of where to go next. You can go back to the **Trail Map** (page xv) to see all of your choices, or you can go directly to one of the following popular trails:

Writing Applets (page 145): For information about writing applets that use the network, go to the **Writing Applets** trail. In particular, check out the **Communicating with Other Programs** (page 185) lesson.

You can continue on to the next trail, **Integrating Native Methods into Java Programs** (page 541), which covers writing native methods.

Integrating Native Methods into Java Programs

$\mathbf{A}$ NATIVE METHOD is a Java method (either an instance method or a class method) whose implementation is written in another programming language such as C. The lessons in this trail show you how to integrate native methods into your Java code.

Note that the lessons in this trail assume knowledge of another programming language and do not attempt to teach in detail the integration of Java with another language. Rather, these lessons highlight the tools that are available for integrating functions written in another language into your Java programs. Doing so requires experience and patience. Only experienced programmers should attempt to use native methods!

WARNING! The programming interface for implementing native methods in Java is under construction. Use these interfaces at your own risk and in full knowledge that they will change in future releases of Java. The examples and information in this trail reflect the JDK 1.0 release.

Step By Step (page 545) walks you step by step through a simple example, the "Hello World!" of native methods, to illustrate how to write, compile, and run a Java program with native methods.

Implementing Native Methods (page 555) shows you how to implement both the Java side and the native language side of a native method. This lesson includes

541

information about passing arguments of various data types into a native method and returning values of various data types from a native method. This lesson also describes many useful functions that your native language code can use to access Java objects and their members, create Java objects, throw exceptions, and more.

Security consideration: The ability to load dynamic libraries is subject to approval by the current security manager. When working with native methods, you must load dynamic libraries. Applets may not be able to use native methods depending on the application they are running in. See Understanding Applet Capabilities and Restrictions (page 197) for information about the security restrictions placed on applets.

Note to C++ programmers: Currently the Java environment only generates C header and source files, which provide the glue for integrating C code into Java programs. You can integrate C++ code into your Java programs using these C header and source files. See Using C++ in Native Method Implementations (page 574) for information. This will make more sense after you've read both lessons in this trail.

Note to MacOS programmers: You can't extend the Java runtime system on a 68K Macintosh. Consequently, you can't load shared libraries and you can't use native methods. Future releases of the JDK may support native methods on a 68K Macintosh.

26

Step By Step

THIS lesson walks you through the seven steps necessary to integrate native code with Java programs.

The example used throughout this lesson implements the canonical "Hello World!" program. The "Hello World!" program has two Java classes. The first class, called Main, implements the main method for the overall program. The second class, called HelloWorld, has one method, a native method, that displays the string "Hello World!". The implementation for the native method is provided in the C programming language.

First, here's an overview of the steps:

Step 4: Create a Stubs File (page 550)

> Now, use `javah` to create a stubs file. The stubs file contains native language code that provides the glue that holds the Java class and its parallel native language structure together.

Step 5: Write the Native Method Implementation (page 550)

> Write the implementation for the native method in a native language source file. The implementation will be a regular function that's integrated with your Java class.

Step 6: Create a Shared Library (page 551)

> Use the compiler to compile the `.h` file, the stubs file, and the `.c` file that you created in Steps 3, 4, and 5 into a shared library. In Windows 95/NT terminology, a shared library is called a dynamically loadable library (DLL).

Step 7: Run the Program (page 552)

> And finally, use the Java interpreter to run the program.

Step 1: Write the Java Code

Create a Java class named `HelloWorld` that declares a native method. Also, write the main program that creates a `HelloWorld` object and calls the native method.

The following Java code, from the `HelloWorld.java` file (page 786), defines a class named `HelloWorld` that has one method and a static code segment.

```
class HelloWorld {
    public native void displayHelloWorld();

    static {
        System.loadLibrary("hello");
    }
}
```

Define a Native Method

You can tell that the implementation for the `HelloWorld` class's `displayHello-World` method is written in another programming language because of the `native` keyword that appears as part of its method definition:

```
public native void displayHelloWorld();
```

This method definition provides only the method signature for `displayHello-World` and does not provide any implementation for it. The implementation for `displayHelloWorld` is provided in a separate native language source file.

The method definition for `displayHelloWorld` also indicates that the method is a public instance method, accepts no arguments, and returns no value. For more information about arguments to and return values from native methods see <u>Passing Data into a Native Method</u> (page 559) and <u>Returning a Value from a Native Method</u> (page 563).

Like other methods, native methods must be defined within a Java class.

Load the Library

The native language code that implements `displayHelloWorld` must be compiled into a shared library (you will do this in <u>Step 6: Create a Shared Library</u> (page 551)) and loaded into the Java class that requires it. Loading the library into the Java class maps the implementation of the native method to its definition.

The following static code block from the `HelloWorld` class loads the appropriate library, named `hello`. The Java runtime system executes a class's static code block when it loads the class.

```
static {
    System.loadLibrary("hello");
}
```

Create the Main Program

In a separate source file, named <u>Main.java</u> (page 786), create a Java application that instantiates `HelloWorld` and calls the `displayHelloWorld` native method.

```
class Main {
    public static void main(String[] args) {
        new HelloWorld().displayHelloWorld();
    }
}
```

As you can see from the code sample above, you call a native method in the same manner as you call a regular method: Append the name of the method to the end of an object reference with a period. A matched set of parentheses follows the method name, enclosing any arguments to pass into the method. The `displayHelloWorld` method doesn't take any arguments.

Step 2: Compile the Java Code

Use the Java compiler to compile the Java class that you created in the previous step. At this time, you should also compile the main Java application that you wrote to test the native method.

Step 3: Create the .h File

In this step, you use the `javah` utility program to generate a header file (a `.h` file) from the `HelloWorld` Java class. The header file defines a structure that represents the `HelloWorld` class on the native language side, and provides a function definition for the implementation of the native method `displayHelloWorld` defined in that class.

Run `javah` now on the `HelloWorld` class that you created in the previous steps.

Platform-Specific Details: Running javah Using the JDK

UNIX:
```
javah HelloWorld
```

DOS shell (Windows 95/NT):
```
javah HelloWorld
```

Note: By default on UNIX and Windows 95/NT, `javah` places the new `.h` file in the same directory as the `.class` file. You can tell `javah` to place the header files in a different directory with the `-d` option.

MacOS:

Drag the `HelloWorld.class` file onto the JavaH icon. This creates a file called `HelloWorld.h` in the same folder as JavaH. This also creates a file `HelloWorld.stubs` in the same folder as JavaH. This file is described in the next step, <u>Step 4: Create a Stubs File</u> (page 550). Move both files into your working folder.

The name of the header file is the Java class name with a `.h` appended to the end of it. For example, from the `HelloWorld` class, `javah` will generate a file named `HelloWorld.h`.

The Class Structure

Try this: Generate and look at the header file `HelloWorld.h`.

The `HelloWorld.h` file contains a `struct` definition for a structure named `ClassHelloWorld`. The members of this structure parallel the members of the corresponding Java class; that is to say, the fields in the `struct` correspond to instance variables in the class. But since `HelloWorld` doesn't have any instance variables, there is just a place holder in the structure. You can use the members of the `struct` to reference class and instance variables from your native language functions.

Notice also, that the header file contains the following line:

```
HandleTo(HelloWorld);
```

This creates a `typedef struct` named `HHelloWorld`, which you use to pass objects between Java and another language.

The Function Definition

In addition to the structure that mimics the Java class, you will also notice a function signature that looks like this:

```
extern void HelloWorld_displayHelloWorld(struct HHelloWorld *);
```

This is the definition for the function that you will write in <u>Step 5: Write the Native Method Implementation</u> (page 550) that provides the implementation for the `HelloWorld` class's native method `displayHelloWorld`. You must use this function signature when you write the implementation for the native method. If `HelloWorld` contained any other native methods, their function signatures would appear here as well.

The name of the native language function that implements the native method is derived from the package name, the class name, and the name of the Java native method. As a result, the native method `displayHelloWorld` within the `HelloWorld` class becomes `HelloWorld_displayHelloWorld`. In our example, there is no package name because `HelloWorld` is in the default package.

Note that the native language function accepts a single parameter even though the native method defined in the Java class accepts none. You can think of the parameter as the `this` variable in C++. Our example ignores the `this` parameter. The next lesson describes how to access the data in the `this` parameter.

Step 4: Create a Stubs File

In addition to the .h file that you generated in the previous step, you must also use javah to generate a *stubs* file. The stubs file contains native language code that provides the glue that holds the Java class and its parallel native language structure together.

Platform-Specific Details: Generating a Stubs File Using the JDK

UNIX:
```
javah -stubs HelloWorld
```

DOS shell (Windows 95/NT):
```
javah -stubs HelloWorld
```

Note: By default on UNIX and Windows 95/NT, javah places the resulting stubs file in the same directory as the .class file. You can use the -d option to force javah to put the generated stubs file in a different directory.

MacOS:

Drag the HelloWorld.class file onto the JavaH icon. This creates a file called HelloWorld.stubs in the same folder as JavaH. This also creates a file Hello-World.h in the same folder as JavaH. This file was described in <u>Step 3: Create the .h File</u> (page 548). Move both files into your working folder.

Similar to the .h file that javah generates, the name of the stubs file is the class name with .c appended to the end. In the "Hello World!" example that you've been working with throughout this lesson, the stubs file is called Hello-World.c.

For the moment, all you really need to know about the stubs file is that you will later compile it into the shared library that you create in <u>Step 6: Create a Shared Library</u> (page 551).

Step 5: Write the Native Method Implementation

Now, you can finally get down to the business of writing the implementation for the native method in another language.

The function that you write must have the same function signature as the one you generated with javah into the HelloWorld.h file in <u>Step 3: Create the .h File</u>

(page 548). The function signature generated for the HelloWorld class's displayHelloWorld native method looks like this:

```
extern void HelloWorld_displayHelloWorld(struct HHelloWorld *);
```

Here's the implementation for HelloWorld_displayHelloWorld, which is in the file named HelloWorldImp.c (page 786).

```
#include <StubPreamble.h>
#include "HelloWorld.h"
#include <stdio.h>

void HelloWorld_displayHelloWorld(struct HHelloWorld *this) {
    printf("Hello World!\n");
    return;
}
```

As you can see, the implementation for HelloWorld_displayHelloWorld is straightforward; the function uses the printf function to display the string "Hello World!" and then returns.

The HelloWorldImp.c file includes three header files:

- StubPreamble.h, which provides information the native language code requires to interact with the Java runtime system. When writing native methods, you must always include this file in your native language source files.
- The .h file that you generated in Step 3: Create the .h File (page 548).
- stdio.h, because this file uses the printf function.

Step 6: Create a Shared Library

Recall that in Step 1: Write the Java Code (page 546) you used the following method call to load a shared library named hello into your program at run time:

```
System.loadLibrary("hello");
```

Now you are ready to create the shared library.

In the previous two steps you created two native language files: In Step 4: Create a Stubs File (page 550) you created a stubs file named HelloWorld.c, and in Step 5: Write the Native Method Implementation (page 550) you wrote the implementation for the displayHelloWorld native method and saved it in HelloWorldImp.c. You compile these two files into a library named hello.

Use whatever tools you have to compile the native language code that you created in the previous two steps into a shared library. On Solaris and MacOS, you'll create a shared library; on Windows 95/NT you'll create a dynamically loadable library (DLL).

Step 7: Run the Program

Now run the Java application (the `Main` class) with the Java interpreter. You should see the following output:

```
Hello World!
```

If you see an exception like the following, then you don't have a library path set up:

```
java.lang.NullPointerException
        at java.lang.Runtime.loadLibrary(Runtime.java)
        at java.lang.System.loadLibrary(System.java)
        at HelloWorld.(HelloWorld.java:5)
        at java.lang.UnsatisfiedLinkError
            displayHelloWorld
        at Main.main(Main.java:3)
```

The library path is a list of directories that the Java runtime system searches when loading libraries. Set your library path and make sure that the name of the directory where the `hello` library lives is in it.

Platform-Specific Details: Set Your Library Path for the JDK

UNIX:
```
setenv LD_LIBRARY_PATH mylibrarypath
```

where *mylibrarypath* is the name of the directory that contains `libhello.so`.

DOS shell (Windows 95/NT):

On Windows 95/NT, the `loadLibrary` method searches for DLLs in the same manner as other language environments do.

MacOS:

The Java runtime system searches the `JavaSoft Folder` in the `Extensions` folder in the `System Folder` for shared libraries. Create an alias to your shared library in the `JavaSoft Folder`.

If you see the following exception, then you have a library path set in your environment, but the name of the directory where the hello library lives is not in it:

```
java.lang.UnsatisfiedLinkError no hello in LD_LIBRARY_PATH
        at java.lang.Throwable.(Throwable.java)
        at java.lang.Error.(Error.java)
        at java.lang.LinkageError.(LinkageError.java)
        at java.lang.UnsatisfiedLinkError.
            (UnsatisfiedLinkError.java)
        at java.lang.Runtime.loadLibrary(Runtime.java)
        at java.lang.System.loadLibrary(System.java)
        at HelloWorld.(HelloWorld.java:5)
        at java.lang.UnsatisfiedLinkError displayHelloWorld
        at Main.main(Main.java:3)
```

Modify your library path, and make sure that the name of the directory where the hello library lives is in it.

Platform-Specific Details: Modify Your Library Path Using the JDK

UNIX:
```
setenv LD_LIBRARY_PATH mylibrarypath:$\{LD_LIBRARY_PATH}
```

where mylibrarypath is the name of the directory that contains libhello.so.

DOS shell (Windows 95/NT):

On Windows 95/NT, the loadLibrary method searches for DLLs in the same manner as other language environments do.

MacOS:

The Java runtime system searches the JavaSoft Folder in the Extensions folder in the System Folder for shared libraries. Create an alias to your shared library in the JavaSoft Folder.

Try to run the program again.

27

Implementing Native Methods

A NATIVE method has two components: the declaration and the implementation. You declare a native method like you declare other methods, in a Java class. You implement a native method in another programming language in a different source file. Typically, the implementation of a native method is a function.

This lesson focuses on a small example that implements a character replacement program. The program uses two Java classes, `InputFile` and `OutputFile`, that implement a readable file and a writable file respectively. Both of these classes have three native methods. Before diving into the specifics of implementing a native method, The Character Replacement Program (page 556) gives you an opportunity to familiarize yourself with this example.

On the Java side, you declare a native method within a Java class. On the native language side, you provide an implementation for the native method. You must take care when writing native methods to match the method signature in Java with the function signature on the native language side. The Method Signature and the Function Signature (page 557) shows you how. You can pass any type of argument into a native method. This includes arguments of a primitive data type, such as `int`, `float`, `boolean`, and arguments of a reference data type, such as arrays, strings, and other objects. The return value from a native method must be interpreted correctly on the Java side. In addition, you can return data through the arguments of a native method. See Passing Data into a Native Method (page 559) and Returning a Value from a Native Method (page 563) to learn more.

Once you've passed an object into a native method, you'll probably want to use it. Using a Java Object in a Native Method (page 564) discusses a collection of utility macros and functions that allow you to access an object's member variables and call an object's methods from within a native method implementation. Working with Strings (page 570) also discusses a collection of utility functions that allow you to manipulate Java strings within a native method implementation.

Like other methods, native methods can be synchronized, and they can throw exceptions. You will learn about the native equivalent of the `wait` and `notify` methods in Native Methods and Thread Synchronization (page 571). You will learn how to throw an exception from within a native method implementation in Throwing Exceptions from Within a Native Method (page 573).

Note to C++ Programmers: You can integrate C++ code into your Java code if you take special precautions to prevent name mangling. This lesson contains a special section that shows what C++ programmers can do to integrate C++ code into Java.

The Character Replacement Program

The example highlighted in this lesson implements a simple character replacement program called `Replace`. You invoke the program with four command-line arguments:

- *char1*
- *char2*
- *inputfile*
- *outputfile*

The `Replace` program reads from *inputfile*, replaces all occurrences of *char1* with *char2*, and writes the results to *outputfile*.

The `Replace` program was originally written by Eugene Kuerner for the alpha version of Java. It's been updated to run with JDK 1.0.

The Source Files

Replace.java (page 787)
    Contains the main program.
File.java (page 788)
    Defines a class named `File`. This class provides basic file and path manipulation with the expectation that subclasses will provide the actual file man-

agement code depending on the file semantics they want to present. `InputFile` and `OutputFile` both derive from `File`.

`InputFile.java` (page 789)

Contains the `InputFile` class (a subclass of `File`), which implements a read-only input file. This class declares three native methods whose implementations are written in the C programming language and provided in `InputFileImpl.c` (page 790).

`OutputFile.java` (page 791)

Contains the OutputFile class (a subclass of File) that implements a write-only output file. This class declares three native methods whose implementations are written in the C programming language and provided in `Output-FileImpl.c` (page 792).

Files Generated by `javah`

`File.h`, `InputFile.h`, `OutputFile.h`

C header files generated by `javah`.

`File.c`, `InputFile.c`, `OutputFile.c`

C stubs files generated by `javah`.

Instructions

1. Compile the `.java` files into `.class` files using the Java compiler.
2. Compile all of the C code into a dynamically loadable library named `file`. If you don't know how to do this, look at the instructions in Step 6: Create a Shared Library (page 551) in the Step By Step (page 545) lesson.
3. Run the program using the Java interpreter.

The Method Signature and the Function Signature

This section shows you how to set up the two sides of a native method: the Java side and the native language side.

The Java Side

Let's take a look at the `close` methods in both the `InputFile` and the `Output-File` classes. In both classes, the declaration for `close` looks like this:

```
// in both InputFile.java and OutputFile.java
public native void close();
```

This method signature is similar to the signatures for regular, non-native Java methods. The difference is the `native` keyword and the fact that there is no implementation for this method (no code between curly brackets { and }). The `native` keyword informs the compiler that the implementation for this method is provided in another language. Because there is no implementation for this method in the Java source file, the declaration is terminated with a semicolon, the statement terminator symbol.

As with other Java methods, you can pass arguments into native methods and return values from them. The `close` method does neither, as indicated by the `void` return type and the empty parameter list. Other methods in the `InputFile` and `OutputFile` classes accept arguments and return values and are discussed in later sections of this lesson.

The Native Language Side

On the native language side, you must declare and implement the `close` method for both the `InputFile` class and the `OutputFile` class. You can get the function signatures for the native language functions by using `javah` to generate a header file.

The function signature for `InputFile`'s `close` function looks like this:

```
// in InputFileImpl.c
void InputFile_close(struct HInputFile *this)
```

Note the name of the function—it's comprised of the name of the class, an underscore (_) character, and the name of the native method as declared in the class. As you might surmise, the function signature for `OutputFile`'s `close` method looks like this:

```
// in OutputFileImpl.c
void OutputFile_close(struct HOutputFile *this)
```

The function names are different: Each function name contains the class name for which this is a native method implementation.

Note that both `InputFile_close` and `OutputFile_close` accept an argument even though no argument was declared for these methods on the Java side. The Java runtime system always passes an *automatic parameter* as the first argument to a native method. This argument is a handle to the object that contains the native method to which this native language function is bound. You can think of the first argument as the `this` pointer. There's more information about this argument in the next section, <u>Passing Data into a Native Method</u> (page 559).

The return value for these two functions is `void` because neither returns a value. This is identical to the return type declared on the Java side. However, don't let this mislead you. When you actually return a value from a native method, you must be careful because a Java data type is mapped to the nearest matching data type on the native language side. <u>Returning a Value from a Native Method</u> (page 563) shows you how to match the Java and native language data types of the return value.

Passing Data into a Native Method

As you saw in the previous section, the Java runtime system passes an extra argument to native methods as the first argument in the argument list. Let's investigate this a little further, and then look into how you can pass your own arguments to a native method.

The Automatic Parameter

The `InputFile_close` and `OutputFile_close` functions both accept one argument: the automatic parameter passed into the function by the Java runtime system.

```
    // in InputFileImpl.c
void InputFile_close(struct HInputFile *this)
    // in OutputFileImpl.c
void OutputFile_close(struct HOutputFile *this)
```

Note first the declaration for the automatic parameter in the `InputFile_close` function signature. The `InputFile` object, (the object whose `InputFile_close` is being called) is passed into the native method through a *handle* to a structure. The name of the structure is comprised of the capital letter `H` (presumably for "Handle") and the name of the Java class.

You can use this handle to reference the object's member variables from within the native method. <u>Using a Java Object in a Native Method</u> (page 564) covers this in detail.

When you write a native method that accepts some object as an argument, that object is also passed into the native method as a handle to a structure. It's the same mechanism used by the runtime system to pass in the automatic parameter. More about this later in <u>Passing Reference Data Types</u> (page 561).

Passing Primitive Data Types

You can pass primitive data types—int, boolean, float, and so on—into a native method. InputFile's read method and OutputFile's write method both take an integer argument:

```
    // in InputFile.java
public native int read(byte[] b, int len);

    // in OutputFile.java
public native int write(byte[] b, int len);
```

The first statement declares that the read method's second argument is an integer. The second statement declares that the write method's second argument is also an integer. You can ignore the first argument for now; it's covered later in this section.

Besides integers, you can also pass other primitive data types, such as float, boolean, double, or char, to a native method. These primitive data types are mapped to the closest matching native language data type. For example, on the C side of our example, the function signature for the InputFile_read function looks like this:

```
    // in InputFileImpl.c
long InputFile_read(struct HInputFile *this,
                HArrayOfByte *b,
                long len)
```

Ignore the middle argument for now—it's covered later.

Note that the function accepts the integer argument as a long. That's because C long integers are the nearest match to Java integers. Similarly, the OutputFile_write function accepts a long where a Java int was passed in:

```
    // in OutputFileImpl.c
long OutputFile_write(struct HOutputFile *this,
                HArrayOfByte *b,
                long len)
```

Now that you've got the primitive data passed into the method, you'd probably like to use it. You can use these primitive data type arguments just as you would any other C variable: by name. For example, the following code snippet that occurs in both `InputFile_read` and `OutputFile_write` uses the `len` argument to set the number of bytes to be read or written.

```
if (count < len) {
    actual = count;
} else {
    actual = len;
}
```

Note that primitive data type arguments are passed to the native function *by value*: if you modify one of the arguments within the native function, the change will not affect the calling Java method. To return a value or set of values through a native method's arguments, use an object.

Passing Reference Data Types

In addition to primitive types, you can pass reference data types into native methods as well. Reference data types include arrays, strings, and other objects, all of which are first-class Java objects. Java objects are passed into a native method as a *handle* to a C `struct`. Indeed, the Java runtime system uses this mechanism to pass in the Java object whose native method is being called. You saw this in action in <u>The Automatic Parameter</u> (page 559) earlier.

`InputFile`'s `read` method accepts a byte array—the method reads bytes from the input file and returns them through this array. `OutputFile`'s `write` method also accepts a byte array—the method writes the bytes contained in this array to the output file.

The Java side of a native method that takes an object argument is straightforward: Declare the method as though it were a "regular" Java method:

```
    // in InputFile.java
public native int read(byte[] b, int len);

    // in OutputFile.java
public native int write(byte[] b, int len);
```

The first statement declares that the first argument to the `read` method is an array of bytes. The second statement declares that the first argument to the `write` method is also an array of bytes.

On the C side, the declarations for the two functions that implement the `read` and `write` methods look like this:

```
// in InputFileImpl.c
long InputFile_read(struct HInputFile *this,
                    HArrayOfByte *b,
                    long len)

// in OutputFileImpl.c
long OutputFile_write(struct HOutputFile *this,
                      HArrayOfByte *b,
                      long len)
```

The second argument to both functions is the byte array argument passed in from the Java side. As you know, Java arrays are first-class objects. Therefore, the array, like any other object, is passed in as a handle to a C `struct`. The structure name is comprised of the capital letter `H` and the name of the class. Note however, that the fully qualified name of the class is used. In the case of arrays, the fully qualified name of the class is `ArrayOf` plus the data type of the elements contained within the array. The fully qualified class name of an array of bytes is `ArrayOfByte`, and the fully qualified class name of an array of integers is `ArrayOfInt`.

The fully qualified name of a class includes the name of the package that the class is declared in. A `String` is passed in as a handle to a `Hjava_lang_String` structure. An `Object` is passed in as a handle to a `Hjava_lang_Object` structure, a `Stack` is passed in as a handle to a `Hjava_util_Stack` structure, and so on.

Now that you've got a handle in the C function to a Java object, what can you do with it? You can use it to access the object's member variables. This is covered in <u>Using a Java Object in a Native Method</u> (page 564).

A Word of Warning

Due to the background activities of the garbage collector, you must be careful to maintain references to all objects passed into a native method to prevent the object from being moved to another location on the heap. The reference must be on the C stack. It cannot be a global variable. Typically, you don't need to worry about this because the argument passed into the native method is normally sufficient to keep the garbage collector informed of a reference to a particular object. However, if you are working with global variables or doing unorthodox pointer manipulations, keep in mind that the garbage collector needs to be kept apprised of any references in a native method to Java objects.

Note that the garbage collector does not recognize a pointer to the middle of an object as a reference to that object. All references that you maintain to an object must point the *beginning* of the object!

Returning a Value from a Native Method

You can return a value of any type from a native method, including primitive types (such as `int`, `float`, and `boolean`), or reference types (such as arrays, strings, and other objects).

Returning Primitive Types

You specify the return type for a native method in the Java definition for the method. The `InputFile` class has two native methods that return values. The open method returns a boolean and the `read` method returns an integer.

```
    // in InputFile.java
public native boolean open();
public native int read(byte[] b, int len);
```

The `OutputFile` class also has two native methods that return values. The `open` method returns a boolean and the `write` method returns an integer.

```
    // in OutputFile.java
public native boolean open();
public native int write(byte[] b, int len);
```

As with parameters passed into native methods, the data type of a native method's return value is mapped to the nearest matching C data type. Java booleans and Java integers both map to C longs, so all of these functions return `long` values.

```
    // in InputFileImpl.c
long InputFile_open(struct HInputFile *this)
    . . .
long InputFile_read(struct HInputFile *this,
                HArrayOfByte *b,
                long len)

    // in OutputFileImpl.c
long OutputFile_write(struct HOutputFile *this,
                HArrayOfByte *b,
                long len)
    . . .
long OutputFile_open(struct HOutputFile *this)
```

Returning Complex Types

You can also use a native method's return value to return a reference data type. Neither the `InputFile` class nor the `OutputFile` class does this. However, sup-

pose that the `read` method in the `InputFile` class returned the bytes read via the method's return value. The Java declaration of that method would be:

```
    // in InputFile.java
  public native byte[] read(int len);
```

This statement declares that the `read` method returns an array of bytes. The declaration for the native language function that implements `read` must return an array of bytes. The return values for reference data types follow the same type rules that arguments of reference data types follow. The native language function must be declared to return a handle to a structure. The structure name is derived from the class name as described in Passing Reference Data Types (page 561). The resulting declaration for the `InputFile_read` function would be:

```
    // in InputFileImpl.c
  HArrayOfByte * InputFile_read(struct HInputFile *this,
                                long len)
```

Returning Data Through Arguments to Native Methods

Sometimes it's more convenient to return data through the arguments to a native method rather than through the return value, such as when you have more than one data value to return.

Primitive data types are passed into a native method by value, the *value* of the argument is put on the call stack, not a *reference* to it. As a result, you cannot return a value from a native method through an argument with a primitive data type—you must return it through an argument with a reference data type. The `read` method in `InputFile` does this—it returns the bytes read through its byte array argument. The `InputFile_read` function gets the bytes from the input file and places them into the body of the byte array.

If you want to return a primitive value, consider using the return value of the function. If you really must use an argument to return a primitive value, then you must wrap it in an object.

Using a Java Object in a Native Method

Now that you've got a handle to a Java object in your native method, what can you do with it? You can use it to access the object's member variables, but first you have to *dereference the handle*.

Dereferencing the Handle

You apply the unhand macro to the object handle to dereference it. When you dereference a handle you get a pointer to a C struct that parallels the Java object's structure. For example, to dereference the byte array named b which is passed into InputFile_read function, use the unhand macro like this:

```
unhand(b)
```

The unhand macro returns a pointer to a C structure. You can use normal C syntax to access the elements in the structure. The elements in the structure parallel the member variables of the objects. Thus, you can access the member variables of an object through the pointer returned from unhand.

Note: The unhand macro is defined in the header file interpreter.h, which is included in StubPreamble.h.

Accessing the Object's Member Variables

You can use the pointer returned from unhand like any other C struct pointer, accessing its members with the -> operator.

The b argument in the InputFile_read function is a byte array. The structure in C that maps to Java arrays contains an element named body, which is a C array of char. The InputFile_read function gets a pointer to the body element of b with the following code:

```
char *data = unhand(b)->body;
```

Now that the InputFile_read function has a C pointer to the body of the array, it can gleefully read bytes into it, which it does with the following line of code:

```
actual = read(unhand(this)->fd, data, actual);
```

The struct members have the same names as the corresponding variables in the Java class, so you can use this same mechanism to access an InputFile object's member variables. Indeed, the InputFile_open function uses this mechanism to access an InputFile object's path and fd variables:

```
long InputFile_open(struct HInputFile *this)
{
    int fd;
    char buf[MAXPATHLEN];
```

```
        javaString2CString(unhand(this)->path, buf, sizeof(buf));
        convertPath(buf);

        fd = open(buf, O_RDONLY);
        if (fd  0)
            return(FALSE);

        unhand(this)->fd = fd;
        return(TRUE);
    }
```

Note that the data type of a variable in the C `struct` is the nearest matching C data type to the Java type of the member variable in the object. Be sure to declare and use the structure elements with the correct data types.

Calling Java Methods from a Native Method

You can call a Java object's methods from a native method, but you use a different mechanism for that than you use for accessing its member variables. For example, the following statement does not work:

```
    ptr->methodname();   // doesn't work
```

Rather you use one of the following utility functions declared in `interpreter.h` for this purpose:

`execute_java_dynamic_method`
    calls an instance method from a native method
`execute_java_static_method`
    calls a class method from a native method
`execute_java_constructor`
    creates a new Java object from within a native method

The character-replacement program doesn't use any of these methods. Let's look at another example that does. The new example program is a collection of methods that illustrate how you can perform various tasks from within a native method. The example program, `NativeExample.java` (page 793), was generously provided to us by Thomas Ball of the Java team.

Let's focus now on the `doubleUp` method in the <u>`NativeExample.java`</u> (page 793) class. The implementation of the `doubleUp` method uses `execute_java_constructor` to create an object from within a native method, and then uses `execute_java_dynamic_method` to call one of the object's instance methods. This method returns the object it created.

On the Java side, `doubleUp` is declared like this:

```
native NativeExample doubleUp();
```

On the C side, `doubleUp` is implemented like this:

```
struct HNativeExample *
NativeExample_doubleUp(struct HNativeExample *hInst)
{
    HNativeExample *hNewInst;
    long twoX;

    hNewInst = (HNativeExample *)execute_java_constructor(
        0, "NativeExample", 0, "(I)",
        unhand(unhand(hInst)->myValue)->value);

    twoX = (long)execute_java_dynamic_method(
        0, (HObject *)hNewInst, "twoTimes", "()I");

    unhand(unhand(hNewInst)->myValue)->value = twoX;
    return hNewInst;
}
```

The interesting bits of the `doubleUp` function are in **bold**.

Calling a Java Constructor

Let's look at the first **bold** line in the code above—the call to `execute_java_constructor`. The `execute_java_constructor` function requires four arguments, but may have more.

The first argument to `execute_java_constructor` represents the execution context. Use `0` for the value of this argument to tell the Java runtime system to use the current execution context. In future releases of Java this argument won't be necessary and will likely be removed.

The second argument is the name of the class you want to instantiate. The example creates a new `NativeExample` object, so the value of the second argument is the string `"NativeExample"`.

The third argument is the class structure for the class you are instantiating. This argument is redundant because it provides the same information as the second argument—the class to instantiate. However, the execute_java_constructor function must do a class look up if you provide only the class name in the second argument and use 0 for the third argument, as shown in the example. This can cause performance degradation if you are constructing several objects from the same class. If performance is important to you, you can avoid unnecessary class lookups by providing a value for this argument with the FindClass function defined in interpreter.h.

The fourth argument specifies the Java constructor that you want to invoke. The name of the Java constructor is the name of the class you are instantiating—NativeExample in the example. However, because of method name overloading, you need to be more specific and indicate exactly which constructor you want by specifying the number and type of its arguments with a *signature argument*. You will also use signature arguments when calling execute_java_dynamic_method and execute_java_static_method.

The example uses the following signature argument, which specifies the NativeExample constructor that takes one integer argument:

    (I)

The general form of a signature argument is:

    (*arguments*)*returnvalue*

arguments is a series of single *keyletters* that indicate the data type for an argument. The number of keyletters indicates the number of arguments. *returnvalue* is a keyletter that indicates the data type of the return value. The keyletters are defined in signature.h. Look in that file to find the keyletters that identify other data types such as float, char, and so on. Note that a signature argument used with execute_java_constructor cannot indicate a return value because Java constructors don't return a value.

The general form of execute_java_constructor is:

```
HObject *execute_java_constructor(ExecEnv *env,
                                  char *classname,
                                  ClassClass *cb,
                                  char *signature, ...);
```

The total number of arguments to the constructor is determined by the signature argument. The signature also indicates which of the *classname* constructors is called. This function returns the new object, or null if there is an error.

Calling an Instance Method

After the `doubleUp` function creates a new `NativeExample` object with `execute_java_constructor`, it calls the object's `twoTimes` instance method:

```
twoX = (long)execute_java_dynamic_method(
    0, (HObject *)hNewInst, "twoTimes", "()I");
```

The `execute_java_dynamic_method` function requires four arguments, but may have more depending on which method you are calling.

The first argument to `execute_java_dynamic_method` is the same as the first argument to `execute_java_constructor`—the execution context. Again, you should use 0 for the value of this argument to tell the Java runtime system to use the current execution context. In future releases of Java this argument won't be necessary and will likely be removed.

The second argument is the object whose instance method you want to execute. The third argument is the name of the instance method to execute and the fourth argument is the signature of the instance method. As with `execute_java_constructor`, the signature argument indicates if there are any remaining arguments, how many, and what type. You formulate the signature argument for `execute_java_dynamic_method` as you did <u>previously</u> (page 568) with `execute_java_constructor`.

The general form of `execute_java_dynamic_method` is:

```
long execute_java_dynamic_method(ExecEnv *env,
                                 HObject *obj,
                                 char *method_name,
                                 char *signature, ...);
```

Calling a Class Method

To call a class method from a native method use:

```
long execute_java_static_method(ExecEnv *env,
                                ClassClass *cb,
                                char *method_name,
                                char *signature, ...);
```

This function is analogous to `execute_java_dynamic_method`, except that you provide a class structure instead of an object. You get the class structure using the `FindClass` function defined in `interpreter.h`.

Working with Strings

The Java development environment provides several functions useful for manipulating Java strings in a native method. These functions are declared in `javaString.h`.

The `InputFile_open` function in the character replacement example uses one of these functions, `javaString2CString`, to fill up a C character array with data from a Java `String` object. Here's the relevant code:

```
char buf[MAXPATHLEN];
javaString2CString(unhand(this)->path, buf, sizeof(buf));
```

The `buf` argument is a C character array. This array will be filled with characters from a Java `String` object.

The first argument to `javaString2CString` is the Java `String` to copy into the C character array. `unhand(this)->path` gets the instance variable `path` from the `InputFile` object. `path` is a Java `String` object. The second argument is the character array to copy the characters into, and the third argument is the length of the character array.

Two other string functions are declared in `javaString.h` that you are likely to use frequently. The first, `makeCString`, creates a C string (a `char *`) from a Java `String`. The second, `makeJavaString`, creates a Java `String` object from a C string (a `char *`).

The `makeCString` function is similar to `javaString2CString` except that it allocates memory for the C string. It produces a C string from a Java `String`. You use it like this:

```
result = makeCString(aJavaString);
```

`makeCString` returns a `char *` value that points to a null-terminated C string containing the data from `aJavaString`.

The `makeJavaString` function creates a new Java `String` object from a C string. `makeJavaString` is often used when returning a `String` value from a native method:

```
char *result;
    . . .
return makeJavaString(result, strlen(result));
```

Other Useful String Functions

The `javaString.h` header file includes several other useful string manipulation functions:

`javaStringPrint`

Prints a Java `String` from a native method.

`javaStringLength`

Returns the length of a Java `String`.

`allocCString`

Similar to `makeCString`, except that it allocates memory for the C string.

Native Methods and Thread Synchronization

Sometimes, a native method contains a critical section of code—a section of code that accesses or modifies a condition variable. Like other critical sections or methods in Java, these native methods have to be synchronized with other methods or code blocks that access the same variable. Synchronization ensures that code running in different threads accesses the condition variable in safety and that the condition variable is in some globally consistent state. **Threads of Control** (page 285) discusses programming with threads. In particular, the section Multithreaded Programs (page 310) covers issues related to writing programs that contain multiple threads, including how to synchronize them. You should be familiar with the concepts in that section before proceeding here.

Three utility functions that are declared in `monitor.h` allow native methods to interact with Java's monitor mechanism, so that native methods can be thread-safe like regular Java methods. Those functions are:

`monitorWait`

Waits until notification is made on the specified monitor. The `monitorWait` function is equivalent to `Object`'s `wait` method.

`monitorNotify`

Notifies one waiting thread that there is a change of condition on the specified monitor. The `monitorNotify` function is equivalent to `Object`'s `notify` method.

`monitorNotifyAll`

Notifies all waiting threads that there is a change of condition on the specified monitor. The `monitorNotifyAll` function is equivalent to `Object`'s `notifyAll` method.

Let's look at an example program that uses these functions to synchronize the execution of two native methods. This example program is a modified version of the Producer/Consumer example found in <u>Synchronizing Threads</u> (page 311). The example program is comprised of these four classes:

<u>Producer</u> (page 796)
> A thread that produces integer values and puts them in a "cubby hole."

<u>Consumer</u> (page 796)
> A thread that consumes the values placed in the cubby hole by the producer.

<u>ProducerConsumerTest</u> (page 795)
> The main program that starts the producer and consumer threads.

<u>CubbyHole</u> (page 797)
> The object where the producer puts its values and the consumer gets them. In the Java-only implementation of this example, the put and get methods in this class are synchronized. The program has been modified so that put and get are now native methods and use the monitor*XXX* functions to synchronize the producer and consumer threads. This is the only class that needed to be modified.

Let's look at the new CubbyHole class. The changes made to the CubbyHole class are in **bold**.

```
class CubbyHole {
    private int seq;        // this is the condition variable.
    private boolean available = false;

    public synchronized native int get();
    public synchronized native void put(int value);

    static {
        try {
            System.loadLibrary("threadex");
        } catch (UnsatisfiedLinkError e) {
            System.err.println("can't find your library");
            System.exit(-1);
        }
    }
}
```

Look at the original version (page 647) of the CubbyHole class for comparison.

The first change is that the get and put methods are now declared native as well as synchronized and their implementations have been removed. They are now implemented in C in the file CubbyHoleImpl.c (page 797).

The second change is the addition of a static initializer block. This block of code loads the dynamic library threadex that contains the implementations for the get and put methods.

Now, let's look at the new implementations for get and put.

```
long CubbyHole_get(struct HCubbyHole *this) {
    while (unhand(this)->available == 0) {
        monitorWait(obj_monitor(this));
    }
    unhand(this)->available = 0;
    monitorNotify(obj_monitor(this));
    return unhand(this)->seq;
}

void CubbyHole_put(struct HCubbyHole *this, long value) {
    while (unhand(this)->available > 0) {
        monitorWait(obj_monitor(this));
    }
    unhand(this)->seq = value;
    unhand(this)->available = 1;
    monitorNotify(obj_monitor(this));
}
```

The logical flow of these methods is identical to the Java implementation of these methods. Note that the use of monitorWait and monitorNotify is identical to the use of the wait and notify methods in the Java version.

Throwing Exceptions from Within a Native Method

You can use the SignalError function to throw a Java exception from within a native method. This section shows you how.

Let's go back to the NativeExample.java (page 793) class that was first introduced in Calling Java Methods from a Native Method (page 566).

Like other methods that throw exceptions, a native method must declare the exceptions that it can throw in its `throws` clause. The native method called quote in the `NativeExample` class throws an `IllegalArgumentException`:

```
native static String quote(int index) throws
    IllegalArgumentException;
```

The implementation for the `NativeExample` class's quote method uses `Signal-Error` to throw the `IllegalArgumentException`:

```
struct Hjava_lang_String *
NativeExample_quote(struct HNativeExample *unused, long index)
{
    char *quotation;

    if (index < 1 || index > 3) {
        SignalError(0, "java/lang/IllegalArgumentException", 0);
        return NULL;
    }

    quotation = quotes[index - 1];
    return makeJavaString(quotation, strlen(quotation));
}
```

The first argument to `SignalError` is the execution environment. You will typically pass in 0 to indicate the current environment.

The second argument is the complete name of the exception to throw. Instead of using periods (.) to delineate the package and class names in the fully qualified exception name, use slashes (/). The third argument is a string containing a detail message. This message is the same one that you would pass to the `Exception` constructor if you were to create the exception in Java.

Using C++ in Native Method Implementations

The `javah` program generates C header and source files, which provide the glue for integrating C code with Java. You can use these C header and source files to integrate C++ code into Java as well.

To do so, you must ensure that C++ does not perform any name mangling on the C function names. If you are using the JDK 1.0.2 release, `javah` automatically does this for you by framing the function declarations in the generated header files within an `extern "C"` block. If you are using a release prior to the

JDK 1.0.2 release you must do this by hand. Here's a version of the header file generated by `javah` for the `NativeExample.java` (page 793) class used in various examples throughout this lesson that has been modified to work with C++. The **bold** lines indicate code that was added to the header file after generation by `javah`. Note that if you run `javah` after you modify a header file, you will have to modify the file again.

```
/* DO NOT EDIT THIS FILE - it is machine generated */
#include /* Header for class NativeExample */

#ifndef _Included_NativeExample

typedef struct ClassNativeExample {
    long myValue;
} ClassNativeExample;
HandleTo(NativeExample);

extern "C" {
struct Hjava_lang_String;
extern struct Hjava_lang_String *NativeExample_quote(struct
HNativeExample *,long);
extern long NativeExample_twoTimes(struct HNativeExample *);
struct HNativeExample;
extern struct HNativeExample *NativeExample_doubleUp(struct
HNativeExample *);
}
```

The implementations for native methods must not be embedded in C++ classes. They must be global functions.

End of Trail

YOU'VE reached the end of the **Integrating Native Methods into Java Programs** trail. Take a break—have a cup of steaming hot java

What Next?

If you've read this book straight through you've finished the last trail. Congratulations! You've earned a trip to the hot tub!

If you've been skipping around and haven't finished all of the trails, you can go back to the **Trail Map** (page xv) to see all of your choices.

Or, if you're interested, you can check out the source code for all of the examples in this book in our appendix of **Code Examples** (page 581).

Appendixes

Code Examples

THIS appendix lists every Java example program featured in this tutorial. It also includes a few HTML and data files that you might need to copy. Here's a typical example:

EXAMPLE: The Character-Counting Application

Count.java

SOURCE CODE: *http://java.sun.com/Series/Tutorial/java/nutsandbolts/example/ Count.java*

```
class Count {
    public static void main(String[] args)
        throws java.io.IOException
    {
        int count = 0;

        while (System.in.read() != -1)
            count++;
        System.out.println("Input has " + count + " chars.");
    }
}
```

As you can see, each example lists the sections where it is explained, the names of the source files that comprise the example, and the location of each source file on your Website.

Most applets have an additional field that lists HTML pages where you can find the applet running. Here's a typical example of this field:

HTML PAGES CONTAINING APPLET: *http://java.sun.com/Series/Tutorial/applet/ overview/lifeCycle.html*

Where explained:
The Nuts and Bolts of the Java Language (page 43)

Getting Started

LESSON 1: The "Hello World" Application

EXAMPLE: **The "Hello World" Application**

HelloWorldApp.java

SOURCE CODE: *http://java.sun.com/Series/Tutorial/getStarted/application/example/*
HelloWorldApp.java

```java
/**
 * The HelloWorldApp class implements an application that
 * simply displays "Hello World!" to the standard output.
 */
class HelloWorldApp {
    public static void main(String[] args) {
        System.out.println("Hello World!"); //Display the string.
    }
}
```

**Where
explained:**

*The Anatomy
of a Java
Application*
(page 5)

LESSON 2: The "Hello World" Applet

EXAMPLE: The "Hello World" Applet

Where explained:
The Anatomy of a Java Applet
(page 16)

HelloWorld.java

SOURCE CODE: *http://java.sun.com/Series/Tutorial/getStarted/applet/example/ HelloWorld.java*

```java
import java.applet.Applet;
import java.awt.Graphics;

public class HelloWorld extends Applet {
    public void paint(Graphics g) {
        g.drawString("Hello world!", 50, 25);
    }
}
```

Hello.html

SOURCE CODE: *http://java.sun.com/Series/Tutorial/getStarted/applet/example/ Hello.html*

```html
<HTML>
<HEAD>
<TITLE> A Simple Program </TITLE>
</HEAD>
<BODY>

Here is the output of my program:
<APPLET CODE="HelloWorld.class" WIDTH=150 HEIGHT=25>
</APPLET>
</BODY>
</HTML>
```

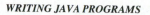

Writing Java Programs

LESSON 4: The Nuts and Bolts of the Java Language

EXAMPLE: The Character-Counting Application

Count.java

SOURCE CODE: *http://java.sun.com/Series/Tutorial/java/nutsandbolts/example/Count.java*

```java
class Count {
    public static void main(String[] args)
        throws java.io.IOException
    {
        int count = 0;

        while (System.in.read() != -1)
            count++;
        System.out.println("Input has " + count + " chars.");
    }
}
```

> **Where explained:**
> *The Nuts and Bolts of the Java Language* (page 43)

EXAMPLE: The Character-Counting Application That Reads from a File
CountFile is a modification of the character-counting application. This program reads from a file named on the command line. The file testing contains some input text for testing this program.

> **Where explained:**
> *The main Method* (page 72)

CountFile.java

SOURCE CODE: *http://java.sun.com/Series/Tutorial/java/nutsandbolts/example/*
CountFile.java

```java
import java.io.*;

class CountFile {
    public static void main(String[] args)
        throws java.io.IOException,
java.io.FileNotFoundException
    {
        int count = 0;
        InputStream is;
        String filename;

        if (args.length >= 1) {
            is = new FileInputStream(args[0]);
            filename = args[0];
        } else {
            is = System.in;
            filename = "Input";
        }

        while (is.read() != -1)
            count++;

        System.out.println(filename + " has " + count +
                                " chars.");
    }
}
```

testing

SOURCE CODE: *http://java.sun.com/Series/Tutorial/java/nutsandbolts/example/*
testing

```
Now is the time for all good men to come to the aid of their
country.
```

Writing Applets

LESSON 6: Overview of Applets

Where explained:

Overview of Applets (page 149), *The Life Cycle of an Applet* (page 152)

EXAMPLE: The Simple Applet

HTML PAGES CONTAINING APPLET: *http://java.sun.com/Series/Tutorial/applet/ overview/lifeCycle.html*

Simple.java

SOURCE CODE: *http://java.sun.com/Series/Tutorial/applet/overview/example/ Simple.java*

```java
import java.applet.Applet;
import java.awt.Graphics;

public class Simple extends Applet {

    StringBuffer buffer;

    public void init() {
        buffer = new StringBuffer();
        addItem("initializing... ");
    }

    public void start() {
        addItem("starting... ");
    }

    public void stop() {
        addItem("stopping... ");
    }

    public void destroy() {
        addItem("preparing for unloading...");
    }

    void addItem(String newWord) {
        System.out.println(newWord);
        buffer.append(newWord);
        repaint();
    }

    public void paint(Graphics g) {
        //Draw a Rectangle around the applet's display area.
        g.drawRect(0, 0, size().width - 1, size().height - 1);
```

```
            //Draw the current string inside the rectangle.
            g.drawString(buffer.toString(), 5, 15);
        }
    }
```

EXAMPLE: The Simple Applet with Event Handling

HTML PAGES CONTAINING APPLET: *http://java.sun.com/Series/Tutorial/applet/ overview/componentMethods.html*

SimpleClick.java

SOURCE CODE: *http://java.sun.com/Series/Tutorial/applet/overview/example/ SimpleClick.java*

Where explained: *Methods for Drawing and Event Handling* (page 155)

```java
import java.applet.Applet;
import java.awt.Graphics;
import java.awt.Event;

public class SimpleClick extends Applet {

    StringBuffer buffer;

    public void init() {
        buffer = new StringBuffer();
        addItem("initializing... ");
    }

    public void start() {
        addItem("starting... ");
    }

    public void stop() {
        addItem("stopping... ");
    }

    public void destroy() {
        addItem("preparing for unloading...");
    }

    void addItem(String newWord) {
        System.out.println(newWord);
        buffer.append(newWord);
        repaint();
    }

    public void paint(Graphics g) {
        //Draw a Rectangle around the applet's display area.
        g.drawRect(0, 0, size().width - 1, size().height - 1);
```

```
                //Draw the current string inside the rectangle.
                g.drawString(buffer.toString(), 5, 15);
        }

        public boolean mouseDown(Event event, int x, int y) {
                addItem("click!... ");
                return true;
        }
}
```

EXAMPLE: **The Simple Applet with a Text Field**

Where explained:

Methods for Adding UI Components (page 156)

HTML PAGES CONTAINING APPLET: *http://java.sun.com/Series/Tutorial/applet/ overview/containerMethods.html*

ScrollingSimple.java

SOURCE CODE: *http://java.sun.com/Series/Tutorial/applet/overview/example/ ScrollingSimple.java*

```java
import java.applet.Applet;
import java.awt.TextField;

public class ScrollingSimple extends Applet {

    TextField field;

    public void init() {
        //Create the text field and make it uneditable.
        field = new TextField();
        field.setEditable(false);

        //Set the layout manager so that the text field will
        //be as wide as possible.
        setLayout(new java.awt.GridLayout(1,0));

        //Add the text field to the applet.
        add(field);
        validate();

        addItem("initializing... ");
    }

    public void start() {
        addItem("starting... ");
    }

    public void stop() {
```

```
            addItem("stopping... ");
        }

        public void destroy() {
            addItem("preparing for unloading...");
        }

        void addItem(String newWord) {
            String t = field.getText();
            System.out.println(newWord);
            field.setText(t + newWord);
            repaint();
        }
    }
```

EXAMPLE: The `PrintThread` Applet

HTML PAGES CONTAINING APPLET: *http://java.sun.com/Series/Tutorial/applet/ overview/threads.html*

PrintThread.java

SOURCE CODE: *http://java.sun.com/Series/Tutorial/applet/overview/example/ PrintThread.java*

```java
import java.applet.Applet;
import java.awt.Graphics;
import java.awt.TextArea;

public class PrintThread extends Applet {

    java.awt.TextArea display = new java.awt.TextArea(1, 80);
    int paintCount = 0;

    public void init() {
        //Create the text area and make it uneditable.
        display = new TextArea(1, 80);
        display.setEditable(false);

        //Set the layout manager so that the text area
        //will be as wide as possible.
        setLayout(new java.awt.GridLayout(1,0));

        //Add the text area to the applet.
        add(display);
        validate();

        addItem("init: " + threadInfo(Thread.currentThread()));
    }
```

Where explained: *Threads in Applets* (page 158)

```java
public void start() {
    addItem("start: " + threadInfo(Thread.currentThread()));
}

public void stop() {
    addItem("stop: " + threadInfo(Thread.currentThread()));
}

public void destroy() {
    addItem("destroy: " +
            threadInfo(Thread.currentThread()));
}

String threadInfo(Thread t) {
    return "thread=" + t.getName() + ", "
        + "thread group=" + t.getThreadGroup().getName();
}

void addItem(String newWord) {
    System.out.println(newWord);
    display.appendText(newWord + "\n");
    display.repaint();
    //A hack to get the applet update() and paint() methods
    //called occasionally:
    if (++paintCount % 4 == 0) {
        repaint();
    }
}

//Implementing this method causes Netscape 2.0 for Windows
//95/NT to crash.
public void update(Graphics g) {
    addItem("update: " +
            threadInfo(Thread.currentThread()));
    super.update(g);
}

}
```

LESSON 7: **Creating an Applet User Interface**

EXAMPLE: A Framework for Playing Sounds in Applets

HTML PAGES CONTAINING APPLET: *http://java.sun.com/Series/Tutorial/applet/ui/ sound.html*

SoundExample.java

SOURCE CODE: *http://java.sun.com/Series/Tutorial/applet/ui/example/ SoundExample.java*

```java
import java.applet.*;
import java.awt.*;

public class SoundExample extends Applet {
    SoundList soundList;
    String onceFile = "bark.au";
    String loopFile = "train.au";
    AudioClip onceClip;
    AudioClip loopClip;

    Button playOnce;
    Button startLoop;
    Button stopLoop;
    Button reload;

    boolean looping = false;

    public void init() {
        playOnce = new Button("Bark!");
        add(playOnce);

        startLoop = new Button("Start sound loop");
        stopLoop = new Button("Stop sound loop");
        stopLoop.disable();
        add(startLoop);
        add(stopLoop);

        reload = new Button("Reload sounds");
        add(reload);

        validate();

        startLoadingSounds();
    }

    void startLoadingSounds() {
```

Where explained:
Playing Sounds (page 172), *Examples of Threads in Applets* (page 160)

```
            //Start asynchronous sound loading.
            soundList = new SoundList(this, getCodeBase());
            soundList.startLoading(loopFile);
            soundList.startLoading(onceFile);
    }

    public void stop() {
        //If one-time sound were long, we'd stop it here, too.
        if (looping) {
            loopClip.stop();     //Stop the sound loop.
        }
    }

    public void start() {
        if (looping) {
            loopClip.loop();      //Restart the sound loop.
        }
    }

    public boolean action(Event event, Object arg) {
        //PLAY BUTTON
        if (event.target == playOnce) {
            if (onceClip == null) {
                //Try to get the AudioClip.
                onceClip = soundList.getClip(onceFile);
            }

            if (onceClip != null) {  //If the sound is loaded:
                onceClip.play();      //Play it once.
                showStatus("Playing sound " + onceFile + ".");
            } else {
                showStatus("Sound " + onceFile + " not loaded "
                           + "yet.");
            }
            return true;
        }

        //START LOOP BUTTON
        if (event.target == startLoop) {
            if (loopClip == null) {
                //Try to get the AudioClip.
                loopClip = soundList.getClip(loopFile);
            }

            if (loopClip != null) {  //If the sound is loaded:
                looping = true;
                loopClip.loop();       //Start the sound loop.
                stopLoop.enable();    //Enable stop button.
```

```
            startLoop.disable(); //Disable start button.
            showStatus("Playing sound " + loopFile
                        + " continuously.");
        } else {
            showStatus("Sound " + loopFile + " not loaded "
                        + "yet.");
        }
        return true;
    }

    //STOP LOOP BUTTON
    if (event.target == stopLoop) {
        if (looping) {
            looping = false;
            loopClip.stop();      //Stop the sound loop.
            startLoop.enable(); //Enable start button.
            stopLoop.disable(); //Disable stop button.
        }
        showStatus("Stopped playing sound " + loopFile + ".");
                    return true;
    }

    //RELOAD BUTTON
    if (event.target == reload) {
        if (looping) {              //Stop the sound loop.
            looping = false;
            loopClip.stop();
            startLoop.enable(); //Enable start button.
            stopLoop.disable(); //Disable stop button.
        }
        loopClip = null;          //Reset AudioClip to null.
        onceClip = null;          //Reset AudioClip to null.
        startLoadingSounds();
        showStatus("Reloading all sounds.");
        return true;
    }

    return false; //some event I don't know about...
    }
}
```

SoundList.java

SOURCE CODE: *http://java.sun.com/Series/Tutorial/applet/ui/example/ SoundList.java*

```java
import java.applet.*;
import java.net.URL;

//Loads and holds a bunch of audio files whose locations are
//specified relative to a fixed base URL.
class SoundList extends java.util.Hashtable {
    Applet applet;
    URL baseURL;

    public SoundList(Applet applet, URL baseURL) {
        super(5); //Initialize Hashtable with
                    //capacity of 5 entries.
        this.applet = applet;
        this.baseURL = baseURL;
    }

    public void startLoading(String relativeURL) {
        new SoundLoader(applet, this,
                        baseURL, relativeURL);
    }

    public AudioClip getClip(String relativeURL) {
        return (AudioClip)get(relativeURL);
    }

    public void putClip(AudioClip clip, String relativeURL) {
        put(relativeURL, clip);
    }
}
```

SoundLoader.java

SOURCE CODE: *http://java.sun.com/Series/Tutorial/applet/ui/example/ SoundLoader.java*

```java
import java.applet.*;
import java.net.URL;

class SoundLoader extends Thread {
    Applet applet;
    SoundList soundList;
    URL baseURL;
    String relativeURL;
```

```
    public SoundLoader(Applet applet, SoundList soundList,
                       URL baseURL, String relativeURL) {
        this.applet = applet;
        this.soundList = soundList;
        this.baseURL = baseURL;
        this.relativeURL = relativeURL;
        setPriority(MIN_PRIORITY);
        start();
    }

    public void run() {
        AudioClip audioClip = applet.getAudioClip(baseURL,
                                                  relativeURL);

        //AudioClips load too fast for me!
        //Simulate slow loading by adding a delay of
        //up to 10 seconds.
        try {
            sleep((int)(Math.random()*10000));
        } catch (InterruptedException e) {}

        soundList.putClip(audioClip, relativeURL);
    }
}
```

LESSON 8: Communicating with Other Programs

EXAMPLE: Communication Between Two Applets

HTML PAGES CONTAINING APPLET: *http://java.sun.com/Series/Tutorial/applet/ communication/iac.html*

Sender.java

SOURCE CODE: *http://java.sun.com/Series/Tutorial/applet/communication/ example/Sender.java*

```
import java.applet.*;
import java.awt.*;
import java.util.Enumeration;

public class Sender extends Applet {
    private String myName;
    private TextField nameField;
    private TextArea status;
```

Where explained:

Finding an Applet by Name: the `getApplet` *Method* (page 186)

```
public void init() {
    GridBagLayout gridBag = new GridBagLayout();
    GridBagConstraints c = new GridBagConstraints();

    setLayout(gridBag);

    Label receiverLabel = new Label("Receiver name:",
                                    Label.RIGHT);
    gridBag.setConstraints(receiverLabel, c);
    add(receiverLabel);

    nameField = new TextField(getParameter("RECEIVERNAME"),
                              10);
    c.fill = GridBagConstraints.HORIZONTAL;
    gridBag.setConstraints(nameField, c);
    add(nameField);

    Button button = new Button("Send message");
    c.gridwidth = GridBagConstraints.REMAINDER; //end row
    c.anchor = GridBagConstraints.WEST; //stick to the
                                        //text field
    c.fill = GridBagConstraints.NONE; //keep the button
                                      //small
    gridBag.setConstraints(button, c);
    add(button);

    status = new TextArea(5, 60);
    status.setEditable(false);
    c.anchor = GridBagConstraints.CENTER; //reset to the
                                          //default
    c.fill = GridBagConstraints.BOTH; //make this big
    c.weightx = 1.0;
    c.weighty = 1.0;
    gridBag.setConstraints(status, c);
    add(status);

    myName = getParameter("NAME");
    Label senderLabel = new Label("(My name is "
                                  + myName + ".)",
                                  Label.CENTER);
    c.weightx = 0.0;
    c.weighty = 0.0;
    gridBag.setConstraints(senderLabel, c);
    add(senderLabel);

    validate();
}

public boolean action(Event event, Object o) {
```

```
        Applet receiver = null;
        String receiverName = nameField.getText(); //Get name to
                                                    //search for.
    receiver = getAppletContext().getApplet(receiverName);
    if (receiver != null) {
        //Use the instanceof operator to make sure the
        //applet we found is a Receiver object.
        if (!(receiver instanceof Receiver)) {
            status.appendText("Found applet named "
                + receiverName + ", "
                + "but it's not a Receiver "
                + "object.\n");
        } else {
            status.appendText("Found applet named "
                + receiverName + ".\n"
                + "  Sending message to it.\n");
            //Cast the receiver to be a Receiver object
            //(instead of just an Applet object) so that the
            //compiler will let us call a Receiver method.
            ((Receiver)receiver).processRequestFrom(myName);
        }
    } else {
        status.appendText("Couldn't find any applet named "
                            + receiverName + ".\n");
    }
    return false;

}

public Insets insets() {
    return new Insets(3,3,3,3);
}

public void paint(Graphics g) {
    g.drawRect(0, 0, size().width - 1, size().height - 1);
}

public String getAppletInfo() {
    return "Sender by Kathy Walrath";
}
}
```

Receiver.java

SOURCE CODE: *http://java.sun.com/Series/Tutorial/applet/communication/
        example/Receiver.java*

```java
import java.applet.*;
import java.awt.*;

public class Receiver extends Applet {
    private final String waitingMessage =
        "Waiting for a message...";
    private Label label = new Label(
                                waitingMessage, Label.RIGHT);

    public void init() {
        add(label);
        add(new Button("Clear"));
        add(new Label("(My name is " + getParameter("name")
                        + ".)", Label.LEFT));
        validate();
    }

    public boolean action(Event event, Object o) {
        label.setText(waitingMessage);
        repaint();
        return false;
    }

    public void processRequestFrom(String senderName) {
        label.setText("Received message from " + senderName
                        + "!");
        repaint();
    }

    public void paint(Graphics g) {
        g.drawRect(0, 0, size().width - 1, size().height - 1);
    }

    public String getAppletInfo() {
        return "Receiver (named " + getParameter("name") +
                ") by Kathy Walrath";
    }
}
```

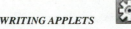

EXAMPLE: Finding All the Applets on a Page

HTML PAGES CONTAINING APPLET: *http://java.sun.com/Series/Tutorial/applet/ communication/iac.html*

GetApplets.java

SOURCE CODE: *http://java.sun.com/Series/Tutorial/applet/communication/ example/GetApplets.java*

Where explained:
Finding all the Applets on a Page: The `getApplets` *Method* (page 189)

```java
import java.applet.*;
import java.awt.*;
import java.util.Enumeration;

public class GetApplets extends Applet {
    private TextArea textArea;

    public void init() {
        setLayout(new BorderLayout());

        add("North", new Button("Click to call getApplets()"));

        textArea = new TextArea(5, 40);
        textArea.setEditable(false);
        add("Center", textArea);

        validate();
    }

    public boolean action(Event event, Object o) {
        printApplets();
        return false;
    }

    public String getAppletInfo() {
        return "GetApplets by Kathy Walrath";
    }

    public void printApplets() {
        //Enumeration will contain all applets on this page
        //(including this one) that we can send messages to.
        Enumeration e = getAppletContext().getApplets();

        textArea.appendText("Results of getApplets():\n");

        while (e.hasMoreElements()) {
            Applet applet = (Applet)e.nextElement();
            String info = ((Applet)applet).getAppletInfo();
```

```
                    if (info != null) {
                        textArea.appendText("- " + info + "\n");
                    } else {
                        textArea.appendText("- " +
                                applet.getClass().getName() +
                                "\n");
                    }
                }
                textArea.appendText("_____\n\n");
            }
        }
```

Where explained:

Communicating with the Browser
(page 190)

EXAMPLE: **Telling the Browser to Show a Document**

HTML PAGES CONTAINING APPLET: *http://java.sun.com/Series/Tutorial/applet/ communication/browser.html*

ShowDocument.java

SOURCE CODE: *http://java.sun.com/Series/Tutorial/applet/communication/example/ ShowDocument.java*

```java
import java.applet.*;
import java.awt.*;
import java.net.URL;
import java.net.MalformedURLException;

public class ShowDocument extends Applet {
    URLWindow urlWindow;

    public void init() {
        Button button = new Button("Bring up URL window");
        add(button);
        validate();

        urlWindow = new URLWindow(getAppletContext());
        urlWindow.pack();
    }

    public void destroy() {
        urlWindow.hide();
        urlWindow = null;
    }

    public boolean action(Event event, Object o) {
        urlWindow.show();
        return true;
    }
}
```

```java
class URLWindow extends Frame {
    TextField urlField;
    Choice choice;
    AppletContext appletContext;

    public URLWindow(AppletContext appletContext) {
        super("Show a Document!");

        this.appletContext = appletContext;

        GridBagLayout gridBag = new GridBagLayout();
        GridBagConstraints c = new GridBagConstraints();
        setLayout(gridBag);

        Label label1 = new Label("URL of document to show:",
                                  Label.RIGHT);
        gridBag.setConstraints(label1, c);
        add(label1);

        urlField = new TextField("http://java.sun.com/", 40);
        c.gridwidth = GridBagConstraints.REMAINDER;
        c.fill = GridBagConstraints.HORIZONTAL;
        c.weightx = 1.0;
        gridBag.setConstraints(urlField, c);
        add(urlField);

        Label label2 = new Label("Window/frame to show it in:",
                                  Label.RIGHT);
        c.gridwidth = 1;
        c.weightx = 0.0;
        gridBag.setConstraints(label2, c);
        add(label2);

        choice = new Choice();
        choice.addItem("(browser's choice)"); //don't specify
        choice.addItem("My Personal Window"); //a window named
                                        //"My Personal Window"
        choice.addItem("_blank"); //a new, unnamed window
        choice.addItem("_self");
        choice.addItem("_parent");
        choice.addItem("_top"); //the Frame that contained this
                            //applet
        c.fill = GridBagConstraints.NONE;
        c.gridwidth = GridBagConstraints.REMAINDER;
        c.anchor = GridBagConstraints.WEST;
        gridBag.setConstraints(choice, c);
        add(choice);
```

```java
        Button button = new Button("Show document");
        c.weighty = 1.0;
        c.ipadx = 10;
        c.ipady = 10;
        c.insets = new Insets(5,0,0,0);
        c.anchor = GridBagConstraints.SOUTH;
        gridBag.setConstraints(button, c);
        add(button);
    }

    public boolean handleEvent(Event event) {
        if (event.id == Event.WINDOW_DESTROY) {
            hide();
            return true;
        }
        return super.handleEvent(event);
    }

    public boolean action(Event event, Object o) {
        if ((event.target instanceof Button) |
            (event.target instanceof TextField)) {
            String urlString = urlField.getText();
            URL url = null;
            try {
                url = new URL(urlString);
            } catch (MalformedURLException e) {
                System.out.println("Malformed URL: " + urlString);
                return true;
            }

            if (url != null) {
                if (choice.getSelectedIndex() == 0) {
                    appletContext.showDocument(url);
                } else {
                    appletContext.showDocument(url,
                                    choice.getSelectedItem());
                }
            }
        }
        return true;
    }
}
```

EXAMPLE: A Simple Network Client Applet
For the application version of this example see <u>QuoteClient.java</u> (page 779).

QuoteClientApplet.java

SOURCE CODE: *http://java.sun.com/Series/Tutorial/applet/communication/ example/QuoteClientApplet.java*

Where explained:
A Simple Network Client Applet
(page 193)

```java
import java.applet.Applet;
import java.awt.*;
import java.io.*;
import java.net.*;
import java.util.*;

public class QuoteClientApplet extends Applet {
    boolean DEBUG = false;
    InetAddress address;
    TextField portField;
    Label display;
    DatagramSocket socket;

    public void init() {
        //Initialize networking stuff.
        String host = getCodeBase().getHost();

        try {
            address = InetAddress.getByName(host);
        } catch (UnknownHostException e) {
            System.out.println(
                    "Couldn't get Internet address: "
                    + "Unknown host");
            // What should we do?
        }

        try {
            socket = new DatagramSocket();
        } catch (SocketException e) {
            System.out.println(
                    "Couldn't create new DatagramSocket");
            return;
        }

        //Set up the UI.
        GridBagLayout gridBag = new GridBagLayout();
        GridBagConstraints c = new GridBagConstraints();
        setLayout(gridBag);

        Label l1 = new Label("Quote of the Moment:",
                            Label.CENTER);
        c.anchor = GridBagConstraints.SOUTH;
        c.gridwidth = GridBagConstraints.REMAINDER;
        gridBag.setConstraints(l1, c);
```

```
        add(l1);

        display = new Label("(no quote received yet)",
                            Label.CENTER);
        c.anchor = GridBagConstraints.NORTH;
        c.weightx = 1.0;
        c.fill = GridBagConstraints.HORIZONTAL;
        gridBag.setConstraints(display, c);
        add(display);

        Label l2 = new Label("Enter the port (on host " + host
                             + ") to send the request to:",
                             Label.RIGHT);
        c.anchor = GridBagConstraints.SOUTH;
        c.gridwidth = 1;
        c.weightx = 0.0;
        c.weighty = 1.0;
        c.fill = GridBagConstraints.NONE;
        gridBag.setConstraints(l2, c);
        add(l2);

        portField = new TextField(6);
        gridBag.setConstraints(portField, c);
        add(portField);

        Button button = new Button("Send");
        gridBag.setConstraints(button, c);
        add(button);

        validate();
    }

    public Insets insets() {
        return new Insets(4,4,5,5);
    }

    public void paint(Graphics g) {
        Dimension d = size();
        Color bg = getBackground();

        g.setColor(bg);
        g.draw3DRect(0, 0, d.width - 1, d.height - 1, true);
        g.draw3DRect(3, 3, d.width - 7, d.height - 7, false);
    }

    void doIt(int port) {
        DatagramPacket packet;
        byte[] sendBuf = new byte[256];
```

```java
        packet = new DatagramPacket(sendBuf, 256, address, port);

        try { // send request
            if (DEBUG) {
                System.out.println("Applet about to send packet"
                                    + "to address " + address
                                    + " at port " + port);
            }
            socket.send(packet);
            if (DEBUG) {
                System.out.println("Applet sent packet.");
            }
        } catch (IOException e) {
            System.out.println("Applet socket.send failed:");
            e.printStackTrace();
            return;
        }

        packet = new DatagramPacket(sendBuf, 256);

        try { // get response
            if (DEBUG) {
                System.out.println("Applet about to call "
                                    + "socket.receive().");
            }
            socket.receive(packet);
            if (DEBUG) {
                System.out.println("Applet returned from "
                                    + "socket.receive().");
            }
        } catch (IOException e) {
            System.out.println("Applet socket.receive failed:");
            e.printStackTrace();
            return;
        }

        String received = new String(packet.getData(), 0);
        if (DEBUG) {
            System.out.println("Quote of the Moment: "
                                + received);
        }
        display.setText(received);
    }

    public boolean action(Event event, Object arg) {
        int port;
```

```
                    try {
                        port = Integer.parseInt(portField.getText());
                    } catch (NumberFormatException e) {
                        //No integer entered.  Should warn the user.
                        return true;
                    }

                    doIt(port);
                    return true;
                }
            }
```

quoteApplet.html

SOURCE CODE: *http://java.sun.com/Series/Tutorial/applet/communication/*
example/quoteApplet.html

```
<HTML>
<TITLE>
QuoteClientApplet
</TITLE>

<BODY>
<APPLET CODE=QuoteClientApplet.class CODEBASE=example/
WIDTH=500 HEIGHT=100>
</APPLET>
</BODY>
</HTML>
```

QuoteServer.java

See <u>QuoteServer.java</u> (page 776).

QuoteServerThread.java

See <u>QuoteServerThread.java</u> (page 777).

EXAMPLE: A Talk Client and Server

Where explained:

Using a Server to Work Around Security Restrictions (page 194)

TalkClientApplet.java

SOURCE CODE: *http://java.sun.com/Series/Tutorial/applet/communication/*
example/TalkClientApplet.java

```
import java.applet.Applet;
import java.awt.*;
import java.io.*;
import java.net.*;
import java.util.*;
```

```java
public class TalkClientApplet extends Applet implements
Runnable {
    Socket socket;
    DataOutputStream os;
    DataInputStream is;
    TextField portField, message;
    TextArea display;
    Button button;
    int dataPort;
    boolean trysted;
    Thread receiveThread;
    String host;
    boolean DEBUG = false;

    public void init() {
        //Get the address of the host we came from.
        host = getCodeBase().getHost();

        //Set up the UI.
        GridBagLayout gridBag = new GridBagLayout();
        GridBagConstraints c = new GridBagConstraints();
        setLayout(gridBag);

        message = new TextField("");
        c.fill = GridBagConstraints.HORIZONTAL;
        c.gridwidth = GridBagConstraints.REMAINDER;
        gridBag.setConstraints(message, c);
        add(message);

        display = new TextArea(10, 40);
        display.setEditable(false);
        c.weightx = 1.0;
        c.weighty = 1.0;
        c.fill = GridBagConstraints.BOTH;
        gridBag.setConstraints(display, c);
        add(display);

        Label l = new Label("Enter the port (on host " + host
                            + ") to send the request to:",
                            Label.RIGHT);
        c.fill = GridBagConstraints.HORIZONTAL;
        c.gridwidth = 1;
        c.weightx = 0.0;
        c.weighty = 0.0;
        gridBag.setConstraints(l, c);
        add(l);

        portField = new TextField(6);
```

```java
            c.fill = GridBagConstraints.NONE;
            gridBag.setConstraints(portField, c);
            add(portField);

            button = new Button("Connect");
            gridBag.setConstraints(button, c);
            add(button);

            validate();
        }

    public synchronized void start() {
        if (DEBUG) {
            System.out.println("In start() method.");
        }
        if (receiveThread == null) {
            trysted = false;
            portField.setEditable(true);
            button.enable();
            os = null;
            is = null;
            socket = null;
            receiveThread = new Thread(this);
            receiveThread.start();
            if (DEBUG) {
                System.out.println(" Just set everything to "
                                    + "null and started thread.");
            }
        } else if (DEBUG) {
            System.out.println(
                    " receiveThread not null! Did nothing!");
        }
    }

    public synchronized void stop() {
        if (DEBUG) {
            System.out.println("In stop() method.");
        }
        receiveThread = null;
        trysted = false;
        portField.setEditable(true);
        button.enable();
        notify();

        try { //Close input stream.
            if (is != null) {
                is.close();
                is = null;
```

```
                }
            } catch (Exception e) {} //Ignore exceptions.

            try { //Close output stream.
                if (os != null) {
                    os.close();
                    os = null;
                }
            } catch (Exception e) {} //Ignore exceptions.

            try { //Close socket.
                if (socket != null) {
                    socket.close();
                    socket = null;
                }
            } catch (Exception e) {} //Ignore exceptions.
        }

    public Insets insets() {
        return new Insets(4,4,5,5);
    }

    public void paint(Graphics g) {
        Dimension d = size();
        Color bg = getBackground();

        g.setColor(bg);
        g.draw3DRect(0, 0, d.width - 1, d.height - 1, true);
        g.draw3DRect(3, 3, d.width - 7, d.height - 7, false);
    }

    public synchronized boolean action(Event event, Object arg)
{
        int port;

        if (DEBUG) {
            System.out.println("In action() method.");
        }

        if (receiveThread == null) {
            start();
        }

        if (!trysted) {
        //We need to attempt a rendezvous.

            if (DEBUG) {
                System.out.println(" trysted = false. "
                            + "About to attempt a rendezvous.");
```

```java
                    }

                    //Get the port the user entered...
                    try {
                        port = Integer.parseInt(portField.getText());
                    } catch (NumberFormatException e) {
                        //No integer entered.
                        display.appendText("Please enter an integer "
                                                + "below.\n");
                        return true;
                    }
                    //...and rendezvous with it.
                    rendezvous(port);

            } else { //We've already rendezvoused.
                        //Just send data over.
                    if (DEBUG) {
                        System.out.println("  trysted = true. "
                                                + "About to send data.");
                    }
                    String str = message.getText();
                    message.selectAll();

                    try {
                        os.writeUTF(str);
                        os.flush();
                    } catch (IOException e) {
                        display.appendText("ERROR: Applet couldn't write "
                                                + "to socket.\n");
                        display.appendText("...Disconnecting.\n");
                        stop();
                        return true;
                    } catch (NullPointerException e) {
                        display.appendText("ERROR: No output stream!\n");
                        display.appendText("...Disconnecting.\n");
                        stop();
                        return true;
                    }
                    display.appendText("Sent: " + str + "\n");
            }
        return true;
    }

    synchronized void waitForTryst() {
        //Wait for notify() call from action().
        try {
            wait();
```

```
        } catch (InterruptedException e) {}

        if (DEBUG) {
            System.out.println("waitForTryst about to return. "
                              + "trysted = " + trysted + ".");
        }

        return;
    }

    public void run() {
        String received = null;

        waitForTryst();

        //OK, now we can send messages.
        while (Thread.currentThread() == receiveThread) {
            try {
                //Wait for data from the server.
                received = is.readUTF();

                //Display it.
                if (received != null) {
                    display.appendText("Received: " + received
                                      + "\n");
                } else { //success but no data...
                    System.err.println("readUTF() returned "
                                      + "no data");
                }
            } catch (EOFException e) { //Stream has no more
                                      //data
                display.appendText("NOTE: Other applet is "
                                  + "disconnected.\n");
                //display.appendText("...Disconnecting.\n");
                //stop();
                return;
            } catch (NullPointerException e) { //Stream doesn't
                                               //exist.
                display.appendText("NOTE: Disconnected from "
                                  + "server.\n");
                display.appendText("...Completing
                                  disconnect.\n");
                stop();
                return;
            } catch (IOException e) { //Perhaps a temporary
                                     //problem?
                display.appendText("NOTE: Couldn't read from "
                                  + "socket.\n");
                //display.appendText("...Disconnecting.\n");
                //stop();
```

```
                        return;
                    } catch (Exception e) { //Unknown error. Throw tantrum.
                        display.appendText("ERROR: Couldn't read "
                                                + "from socket.\n");
                        display.appendText("...Disconnecting.\n");
                        System.err.println("Couldn't read from socket.");
                        e.printStackTrace();
                        stop();
                        return;
                    }
                }
            }

            private void rendezvous(int port) {
                //Try to open a socket to the port.
                try {
                    socket = new Socket(host, port);
                } catch (UnknownHostException e) {
                    display.appendText("ERROR: Can't find host: " + host
                                            + ".\n");
                    return;
                } catch (IOException e) {
                    display.appendText("ERROR: Can't open socket "
                                            + "on rendezvous port "
                                            + port + " (on host " +
                                            host + ").\n");
                    return;
                }

                //Try to open streams to read and write from the socket.
                try {
                    os = new DataOutputStream(socket.getOutputStream());
                    is = new DataInputStream(socket.getInputStream());
                } catch (IOException e) {
                    display.appendText("ERROR: Created data socket "
                                            + "but can't open stream on "
                                            + "it.\n");
                    display.appendText("...Disconnecting.\n");
                    stop();
                    return;
                }

                if ((os != null) & (is != null)) {
                    if (DEBUG) {
                        System.out.println("Successful rendezvous.");
                        System.out.println("socket = " + socket);
                        System.out.println("output stream = " + os);
                        System.out.println("input stream = " + is);
```

```
            }
            //Let the main applet thread know we've
            //successfully rendezvoused.
            portField.setEditable(false);
            button.disable();
            trysted = true;
            notify();
        } else {
            display.appendText("ERROR: Port is valid but "
                            + "communication failed. "
                            + "Please TRY AGAIN.\n");
        }
    }

}
```

talk.html

SOURCE CODE: *http://java.sun.com/Series/Tutorial/applet/communication/
      example/talk.html*

```
<HTML>
<TITLE>
TalkClientApplet
</title>

<BODY>
<APPLET CODE=TalkClientApplet.class CODEBASE=example/
WIDTH=550 HEIGHT=200>
</APPLET>
</BODY>
</HTML>
```

TalkServer.java

SOURCE CODE: *http://java.sun.com/Series/Tutorial/applet/communication/
      example/TalkServer.java*

```
import java.net.*;
import java.io.*;

class TalkServer {
    TalkServerThread[] tstList = new TalkServerThread[2];
    boolean DEBUG = false;

    public static void main(String[] args) {
        new TalkServer().start();
    }
```

```java
public void start() {
    ServerSocket serverRSocket = null;
    int numConnected = 0;

    try {
        serverRSocket = new ServerSocket(0);
        System.out.println("TalkServer listening on "
                            + "rendezvous port: "
                            + serverRSocket.getLocalPort());
    } catch (IOException e) {
        System.err.println("Server could not create server "
                            + "socket for rendezvous.");
        return;
    }

    while (true) {

        //Connect to two clients.
        while (numConnected < 2) {
            TalkServerThread tst;
            tst = connectToClient(serverRSocket);
            if (tst != null) {
                numConnected++;
                if (tstList[0] == null) {
                    tstList[0] = tst;
                } else {
                    tstList[1] = tst;
                }
            }
        } //end while (numConnected < 2) loop

        if (DEBUG) {
            try {
                System.out.println("tst #0 = " + tstList[0]);
            } catch (Exception e) {}
            try {
                System.out.println("tst #1 = " + tstList[1]);
            } catch (Exception e) {}
        }

        //If they're really OK, tell them to start writing.
        if (everythingIsOK(0) & everythingIsOK(1)) {
            for (int i = 0; i < 2; i++) {
                writeToStream("START WRITING!" +
                                "\n----------------------"
                                + "-------------", tstList[i].os);
            }
```

```
        } else {
            System.err.println("2 server threads created, "
                                + "but not everything is OK");
        }

        while (numConnected == 2) {
            if (!everythingIsOK(0)) {
                if (DEBUG) {
                System.out.println("Applet #0 is hosed; "
                                    + "disconnecting.");
                }
                numConnected--;
                cleanup(tstList[0]);
                tstList[0] = null;
            }
            if (!everythingIsOK(1)) {
                if (DEBUG) {
                System.out.println("Applet #1 is hosed; "
                                    + "disconnecting.");
                }
                numConnected--;
                cleanup(tstList[1]);
                tstList[1] = null;
            }
                try {
                Thread.sleep(1000);
            } catch (InterruptedException e) {
            }
        } //end while(numConnected==2) loop

        if (DEBUG) {
            try {
                System.out.println("Number of connections = " +
                                    numConnected);
                System.out.println("tst #0 = " + tstList[0]);
                System.out.println("tst #1 = " + tstList[1]);
            } catch (Exception e) {}
        }

    } //end while (true) loop
}

protected TalkServerThread connectToClient(ServerSocket
                                            serverRSocket) {

    DataOutputStream os = null;
    Socket rendezvousSocket = null;
    TalkServerThread tst = null;
```

```
        //Listen for client connection on the rendezvous socket.
        try {
            rendezvousSocket = serverRSocket.accept();
        } catch (IOException e) {
            System.err.println("Accept failed.");
            e.printStackTrace();
            return null;
        }

        //Create a thread to handle this connection.
        try {
            tst = new TalkServerThread(rendezvousSocket,this);
            tst.start();
        } catch (Exception e) {
            System.err.println("Couldn't create "
                                + "TalkServerThread:");
            e.printStackTrace();
            return null;
        }

        writeToStream("Successful connection. "
                    + "Please wait for second applet to "
                    + "connect...",
                    tst.os);
        return tst;
    }

boolean everythingIsOK(int tstNum) {
    TalkServerThread tst = tstList[tstNum];

    if (tst == null) {
        if (DEBUG) {
            System.out.println("TalkServerThread #" + tstNum
                                + " is null");
        }
        return false;
    } else {
        if (tst.os == null) {
            if (DEBUG) {
                System.out.println("TalkServerThread #"
                                    + tstNum
                                    + " output stream is null.");
            }
            return false;
        }
        if (tst.is == null) {
            if (DEBUG) {
```

```java
                    System.out.println("TalkServerThread #"
                                        + tstNum
                                        + " input stream is null.");
                }
                return false;
            }
            if (tst.socket == null) {
                if (DEBUG) {
                    System.out.println("TalkServerThread #"
                                        + tstNum
                                        + " socket is null.");
                }
                return false;
            }
        }
        //try {
            //if ((tst.os == null) |
                //(tst.is == null) |
                //(tst.socket == null)) {
                //return false;
            //}
        //} catch (Exception e) {
            //return false;
        //}
        return true;
    }

    void cleanup(TalkServerThread tst) {
        if (tst != null) {
            try {
                if (tst.os != null) {
                    tst.os.close();
                    tst.os = null;
                }
            } catch (Exception e) {} //Ignore errors
            try {
                if (tst.is != null) {
                    tst.is.close();
                    tst.is = null;
                }
            } catch (Exception e) {} //Ignore errors
            try {
                if (tst.socket != null) {
                    tst.socket.close();
                    tst.socket = null;
                }
            } catch (Exception e) {} //Ignore errors
        }
    }
```

```java
    public void forwardString(String string,
                                TalkServerThread requestor) {
        DataOutputStream clientStream = null;

        if (tstList[0] == requestor) {
            if (tstList[1] != null) {
                clientStream = tstList[1].os;
            } else {
                if (DEBUG) {
                System.out.println("Applet #0 has a "
                                    + "string to forward, "
                                    + "but Applet #1 is gone...");
                }
                //cleanup();
                return;
            }
        } else {
            if (tstList[0] != null) {
                clientStream = tstList[0].os;
            } else {
                if (DEBUG) {
                System.out.println("Applet #1 has a "
                                    + "string to forward, "
                                    + "but Applet #0 is gone...");
                }
                //cleanup();
                return;
            }
        }

        if (clientStream != null) {
            writeToStream(string, clientStream);
        } else if (DEBUG) {
            System.out.println("Can't forward string -- no "
                                + "output stream.");
        }
    }

    public void writeToStream(String string,
                                DataOutputStream stream) {
        if (DEBUG) {
            System.out.println(
                "TalkServer about to forward data: + string);
        }

        try {
```

```
                    stream.writeUTF(string);
                    stream.flush();
                    if (DEBUG) {
                        System.out.println("TalkServer forwarded "
                                            + "string.");
                    }
                } catch (IOException e) {
                    System.err.println("TalkServer failed to "
                                        + "forward string:");
                    e.printStackTrace();
                    //cleanup();
                    return;
                } catch (NullPointerException e) {
                    System.err.println("TalkServer can't forward string "
                                        + "since output stream is null.");
                    //cleanup();
                    return;
                }
            }
        }

    }
```

TalkServerThread.java

SOURCE CODE: *http://java.sun.com/Series/Tutorial/applet/communication/ example/TalkServerThread.java*

```
    import java.io.*;
    import java.net.*;
    import java.util.*;

    class TalkServerThread extends Thread {
        public Socket socket;
        public DataInputStream is;
        public DataOutputStream os;
        TalkServer server;
        boolean DEBUG = false;

        public String toString() {
            return "TalkServerThread: socket = " + socket
                + "; is = " + is
                + "; os = " + os;
        }

        TalkServerThread(Socket socket, TalkServer server) throws
                        IOException {
            super("TalkServer");
```

```java
            is = new DataInputStream(socket.getInputStream());
            os = new DataOutputStream(socket.getOutputStream());

            if (is == null) {
                System.err.println("TalkServerThread: Input stream "
                                    + "seemed "
                                    + "to be created successfully, "
                                    + "but it's null.");
                throw new IOException();
            }

            if (os == null) {
                System.err.println("TalkServerThread: Output "
                                    + "stream seemed "
                                    + "to be created successfully, "
                                    + "but it's null.");
                throw new IOException();
            }

            this.socket = socket;
            this.server = server;
        }

        public void run() {
            while (socket != null) {
                try {
                    //Read data.
                    String str = is.readUTF();

                    //Pass it on.
                    if (str != null) {
                        server.forwardString(str, this);
                    }
                } catch (EOFException e) {
                //No more data on this socket...
                    server.forwardString("SERVER SAYS other applet "
                                        + "disconnected", this);
                    cleanup();
                    return;
                } catch (NullPointerException e) {
                //Socket doesn't exist...
                    server.forwardString("SERVER SAYS no socket to "
                                        + "other applet", this);
                    cleanup();
                    return;
                } catch (IOException e) { //Read problem.
                    server.forwardString("SERVER SAYS socket "
                                        + "trouble with other "
                                        + "applet",this);
```

```
                cleanup();
                return;
        } catch (Exception e) { //Unknown exception. Complain
                                //and quit.
                System.err.println("Exception on is.readUTF():");
                e.printStackTrace();
                cleanup();
                return;
            }
        }
    }

    protected void finalize() {
        cleanup();
    }

    void cleanup() {
        try {
            if (is != null) {
                is.close();
                is = null;
            }
        } catch (Exception e) {} //Ignore errors.

        try {
            if (os != null) {
                os.close();
                os = null;
            }
        } catch (Exception e) {} //Ignore errors.

        try {
            if (socket != null) {
                socket.close();
                socket = null;
            }
        } catch (Exception e) {} //Ignore errors.
    }

}
```

Using the Core Java Classes

LESSON 11: The `String` and `StringBuffer` Classes

EXAMPLE: The ReverseString Class

The `reverseIt` method is featured throughout the lesson on the `String` and `StringBuffer` classes. The second example file, `ReverseStringTest.java`, defines a class with a `main` method that you can use to test the `reverseIt` method.

ReverseString.java

SOURCE CODE: *http://java.sun.com/Series/Tutorial/java/strings/example/ ReverseString.java*

```
class ReverseString {
    public static String reverseIt(String source) {
        int i, len = source.length();
        StringBuffer dest = new StringBuffer(len);

        for (i = (len - 1); i >= 0; i--) {
            dest.append(source.charAt(i));
```

Where explained:
The String and String-Buffer Classes
(page 215)

```
        }
        return dest.toString();
    }
}
```

ReverseStringTest.java

SOURCE CODE: *http://java.sun.com/Series/Tutorial/java/strings/example/*
ReverseStringTest.java

```
class ReverseStringTest {
    public static void main(String[] args) {
        String str = "What's going on?";
        System.out.println(ReverseString.reverseIt(str));
    }
}
```

**Where
explained:**
*More Acces-
sor Methods*
(page 219)

EXAMPLE: The Filename Class

The Filename class contains several methods that parse a String for filename
components such as the directory name and the filename extension. The second
example file, FilenameTest.java, defines a class with a main method that you
can use to test the methods in the Filename class.

Filename.java

SOURCE CODE: *http://java.sun.com/Series/Tutorial/java/strings/example/*
Filename.java

```
class Filename {
    String fullPath;
    char pathSeparator;

    Filename(String str, char sep) {
        fullPath = str;
        pathSeparator = sep;
    }

    String extension() {
        int dot = fullPath.lastIndexOf('.');
        return fullPath.substring(dot + 1);
    }

    String filename() {
        int dot = fullPath.lastIndexOf('.');
        int sep = fullPath.lastIndexOf(pathSeparator);
        return fullPath.substring(sep + 1, dot);
    }
```

```
    String path() {
        int sep = fullPath.lastIndexOf(pathSeparator);
        return fullPath.substring(0, sep);
    }
}
```

FilenameTest.java

SOURCE CODE: *http://java.sun.com/Series/Tutorial/java/strings/example/*
FilenameTest.java

```
class FilenameTest {
    public static void main(String[] args) {
        Filename myHomePage = new Filename("/home/mem/"
                              + "public_html/index.html", '/');
        System.out.println("Extension = " +
                              myHomePage.extension());
        System.out.println("Filename = " +
                              myHomePage.filename());
        System.out.println("Path = " + myHomePage.path());
    }
}
```

EXAMPLE: **The InsertTest Class**

InsertTest.java

SOURCE CODE: *http://java.sun.com/Series/Tutorial/java/strings/example/*
InsertTest.java

```
class InsertTest {
    public static void main(String[] args) {
        StringBuffer sb = new StringBuffer("Drink Java!");
        sb.insert(6, "Hot ");
        System.out.println(sb.toString());
    }
}
```

**Where
explained:**
*Modifying
String-
Buffers*
(page 222)

EXAMPLE: The PITest Class

PITest.java

SOURCE CODE: *http://java.sun.com/Series/Tutorial/java/strings/example/ PITest.java*

```
class PITest {
    public static void main(String[] args) {
        System.out.println(String.valueOf(Math.PI));
    }
}
```

Where explained:
Converting Objects to Strings (page 223)

EXAMPLE: The ValueOfTest Class

ValueOfTest.java

SOURCE CODE: *http://java.sun.com/Series/Tutorial/java/strings/example/ ValueOfTest.java*

```
class ValueOfTest {
    public static void main(String[] args) {
        String piStr = "3.14159";
        Float pi = Float.valueOf(piStr);
        System.out.println(pi);
    }
}
```

Where explained:
Converting Strings to Numbers (page 224)

LESSON 12: Setting Program Attributes

EXAMPLE: Echo Command-Line Arguments

Echo.java

SOURCE CODE: *http://java.sun.com/Series/Tutorial/java/cmdLineArgs/example/ Echo.java*

```
class Echo {
    public static void main (String[] args) {
        for (int i = 0; i < args.length; i++)
            System.out.println(args[i]);
    }
}
```

Where explained:
Command-Line Arguments (page 230)

EXAMPLE: Parse Command-Line Arguments

ParseCmdLine.java

SOURCE CODE: *http://java.sun.com/Series/Tutorial/java/cmdLineArgs/example/*
   ParseCmdLine.java

**Where
explained:**
*Parsing Com-
mand-Line
Arguments*
(page 233)

```java
class ParseCmdLine {
    public static void main(String[] args) {

        int i = 0, j;
        String arg;
        char flag;
        boolean vflag = false;
        String outputfile = "";

        while (i < args.length && args[i].startsWith("-")) {
            arg = args[i++];

// use this type of check for "wordy" arguments
            if (arg.equals("-verbose")) {
                System.out.println("verbose mode on");
                vflag = true;
            }

// use this type of check for arguments
// that require arguments
            else if (arg.equals("-output")) {
                if (i < args.length)
                    outputfile = args[i++];
                else
                    System.err.println(
                        "-output requires a filename");
                if (vflag)
                    System.out.println(
                        "output file = " + outputfile);
            }

// use this type of check for a series of flag arguments
            else {
                for (j = 1; j < arg.length(); j++) {
                    flag = arg.charAt(j);
                    switch (flag) {
                    case 'x':
                        if (vflag) System.out.println("Option x");
                        break;
                    case 'n':
                        if (vflag) System.out.println("Option n");
                        break;
```

```
                                default:
                                    System.err.println(
                                      "ParseCmdLine: illegal "
                                      + "option " + flag);
                                    break;
                            }
                        }
                    }
                }
                if (i == args.length)
                System.err.println("Usage: ParseCmdLine [-verbose] "
                                    + "[-xn] [-output afile] filename");
                else
                    System.out.println("Success!");
            }
        }
```

LESSON 13: **Using System Resources**

EXAMPLE: **The UserNameTest Class**

UserNameTest.java

**Where
explained:**
*Using the
System class*
(page 239)

SOURCE CODE: *http://java.sun.com/Series/Tutorial/java/system/example/
UserNameTest.java*

```
class UserNameTest {
    public static void main(String[] args) {
        String name;
        name = System.getProperty("user.name");
        System.out.println(name);
    }
}
```

EXAMPLE: **The DataTypePrintTest Class**

DataTypePrintTest.java

**Where
explained:**
*The Standard
I/O Streams*
(page 240)

SOURCE CODE: *http://java.sun.com/Series/Tutorial/java/system/example/
DataTypePrintTest.java*

```
class DataTypePrintTest {
    public static void main(String[] args) {

        Thread objectData = new Thread();
        String stringData = "Java Mania";
        char[] charArrayData = { 'a', 'b', 'c' };
```

```
        int integerData = 4;
        long longData = Long.MIN_VALUE;
        float floatData = Float.MAX_VALUE;
        double doubleData = Math.PI;
        boolean booleanData = true;

        System.out.println(objectData);
        System.out.println(stringData);
        System.out.println(charArrayData);
        System.out.println(integerData);
        System.out.println(longData);
        System.out.println(floatData);
        System.out.println(doubleData);
        System.out.println(booleanData);
    }
}
```

EXAMPLE: The TimingIsEverything Applet

HTML PAGES CONTAINING APPLET: *http://java.sun.com/Series/Tutorial/java/system/ misc.html*

TimingIsEverything.java

SOURCE CODE: *http://java.sun.com/Series/Tutorial/java/system/example/ TimingIsEverything.java*

```
import java.awt.Graphics;

public class TimingIsEverything extends java.applet.Applet {

    public long firstClickTime = 0;
    public String displayStr;

    public void init() {
        displayStr = "Double Click Me";
    }
    public void paint(Graphics g) {
        g.drawRect(0, 0, size().width-1, size().height-1);
        g.drawString(displayStr, 40, 30);
    }
    public boolean mouseDown(java.awt.Event evt, int x, int y) {
        long clickTime = System.currentTimeMillis();
        long clickInterval = clickTime - firstClickTime;
        if (clickInterval < 200) {
            displayStr = "Double Click!! (Interval = " +
                        + clickInterval + ")";
            firstClickTime = 0;
        } else {
```

Where explained:
Miscellaneous System Methods
(page 247)

```
                displayStr = "Single Click!!";
                firstClickTime = clickTime;
            }
            repaint();
            return true;
        }
    }
```

EXAMPLE: The **ArrayCopyTest** Class

**Where
explained:**
*Miscellaneous
System
Methods*
(page 247)

ArrayCopyTest.java

SOURCE CODE: *http://java.sun.com/Series/Tutorial/java/system/example/
ArrayCopyTest.java*

```
class ArrayCopyTest {
    public static void main(String[] args) {
      byte[] copyFrom = { 'd', 'e', 'c', 'a', 'f', 'f', 'e',
                          'i', 'n', 'a', 't', 'e', 'd' };
      byte[] copyTo = new byte[7];

        System.arraycopy(copyFrom, 2, copyTo, 0, 7);
        System.out.println(new String(copyTo, 0));
    }
}
```

EXAMPLE: The **PropertiesTest** Class

**Where
explained:**
*System
Properties*
(page 242)

PropertiesTest.java

SOURCE CODE: *http://java.sun.com/Series/Tutorial/java/system/example/
PropertiesTest.java*

```
import java.io.FileInputStream;
import java.util.Properties;

class PropertiesTest {
    public static void main(String[] args) {
        try {
            // set up new properties object from file
            // "myProperties.txt"
            FileInputStream propFile = new
               FileInputStream("myProperties.txt");
            Properties p = new Properties(System.getProperties());
            p.load(propFile);

            // set the system properties
            System.setProperties(p);
            System.getProperties().list(System.out);
```

```
            // display new properties
        } catch (java.io.FileNotFoundException e) {
            System.err.println("Can't find myProperties.txt.");
        } catch (java.io.IOException e) {
            System.err.println("I/O failed.");
        }
    }
}
```

LESSON 14: **Handling Errors Using Exceptions**

EXAMPLE: The `InputFile` and `InputFileDeclared` Classes
The `InputFile` class demonstrates what the compiler will do if a method in your Java program contains code that can throw an exception and the exception is neither caught nor specified in the method declaration. This file will not compile. See the next file, `InputFileDeclared.java`, for a version that specifies the exceptions in the method declaration and therefore will compile.

InputFile.java

SOURCE CODE: *http://java.sun.com/Series/Tutorial/java/exceptions/example/
InputFile.java*

```
        // Note: This class won't compile by design!
        // See InputFileDeclared.java for a version of this
        // class that will compile.
    import java.io.*;

    class InputFile {

        FileInputStream fis;

        InputFile(String filename) {
            fis = new FileInputStream(filename);
        }

        String getLine() {
            int c;
            StringBuffer buf = new StringBuffer();

            do {
                c = fis.read();
                if (c == '\n')                  // UNIX new line
                    return buf.toString();
                else if (c == '\r') {           // Windows 95/NT new line
                    c = fis.read();
```

Where explained:
Your First Encounter with Java Exceptions (page 261)

```java
            if (c == '\n')
                return buf.toString();
            else {
                buf.append((char)'\r');
                buf.append((char)c);
            }
        } else
            buf.append((char)c);
    } while (c != -1);

    return null;
    }
}
```

InputFileDeclared.java

SOURCE CODE: *http://java.sun.com/Series/Tutorial/java/exceptions/example/*
 InputFileDeclared.java

```java
import java.io.*;

class InputFileDeclared {

    FileInputStream fis;

    InputFileDeclared(String filename) throws
        FileNotFoundException {
        fis = new FileInputStream(filename);
    }

    String getLine() throws IOException {
        int c;
        StringBuffer buf = new StringBuffer();

        do {
            c = fis.read();
            if (c == '\n')                 // UNIX new line
                return buf.toString();
            else if (c == '\r') {          // Windows 95/NT new line
                c = fis.read();
                if (c == '\n')
                    return buf.toString();
                else {
                    buf.append((char)'\r');
                    buf.append((char)c);
                }
            } else
                buf.append((char)c);
```

```
        } while (c != -1);

        return null;
    }
}
```

EXAMPLE: The `ListOfNumbers` Class

The `ListOfNumbers` class defined in `ListOFNumbersWOHandler.java` can throw an exception, and the exception is neither caught nor specified in the method declaration. This file will not compile. See the next file, `ListOfNumbers.java`, for a version that catches and handles the exceptions and therefore will compile.

Where explained: *Dealing with Exceptions* (page 265)

ListOfNumbersWOHandler.java

SOURCE CODE: *http://java.sun.com/Series/Tutorial/java/exceptions/example/ ListOfNumbersWOHandler.java*

```java
import java.io.*;
import java.util.Vector;

class ListOfNumbers {
    private Vector victor;
    final int size = 10;

    public ListOfNumbers () {
        int i;
        victor = new Vector(size);
        for (i = 0; i < size; i++)
            victor.addElement(new Integer(i));
    }
    public void writeList() {
        PrintStream pStr = null;

        System.out.println("Entering try statement");
        int i;
        pStr = new PrintStream(
                new BufferedOutputStream(
                    new FileOutputStream("OutFile.txt")));

        for (i = 0; i < size; i++)
            pStr.println("Value at: " + i + " = " +
                        victor.elementAt(i));

        pStr.close();
    }
}
```

ListOfNumbers.java

SOURCE CODE: *http://java.sun.com/Series/Tutorial/java/exceptions/example/ ListOfNumbers.java*

```java
import java.io.*;
import java.util.Vector;

class ListOfNumbers {
    private Vector victor;
    final int size = 10;

    public ListOfNumbers () {
        int i;
        victor = new Vector(size);
        for (i = 0; i < size; i++)
            victor.addElement(new Integer(i));
    }
    public void writeList() {
        PrintStream pStr = null;

        try {
            int i;

            System.out.println("Entering try statement");
            pStr = new PrintStream(
                    new BufferedOutputStream(
                    new FileOutputStream("OutFile.txt")));

            for (i = 0; i < size; i++)
                pStr.println("Value at: " + i + " = " +
                                victor.elementAt(i));
        } catch (ArrayIndexOutOfBoundsException e) {
            System.err.println("
                Caught ArrayIndexOutOfBoundsException: "
                + e.getMessage());
        } catch (IOException e) {
            System.err.println("Caught IOException: "
                                + e.getMessage());
        } finally {
            if (pStr != null) {
                System.out.println("Closing PrintStream");
                pStr.close();
            } else {
                System.out.println("PrintStream not open");
            }
        }
    }
}
```

LESSON 15: **Threads of Control**

EXAMPLE: **The Vacation Destination Decision Maker**

SimpleThread.java

SOURCE CODE: *http://java.sun.com/Series/Tutorial/java/threads/example/*
    SimpleThread.java

**Where
explained:**
*A Simple
Thread Exam-
ple* (page 287)

```java
class SimpleThread extends Thread {
    public SimpleThread(String str) {
        super(str);
    }
    public void run() {
        for (int i = 0; i < 10; i++) {
            System.out.println(i + " " + getName());
            try {
                sleep((int)(Math.random() * 1000));
            } catch (InterruptedException e) {}
        }
        System.out.println("DONE! " + getName());
    }
}
```

TwoThreadsTest.java

SOURCE CODE: *http://java.sun.com/Series/Tutorial/java/threads/example/*
    TwoThreadsTest.java

```java
class TwoThreadsTest {
    public static void main (String[] args) {
        new SimpleThread("Jamaica").start();
        new SimpleThread("Fiji").start();
    }
}
```

ThreeThreadsTest.java

SOURCE CODE: *http://java.sun.com/Series/Tutorial/java/threads/example/*
    ThreeThreadsTest.java

```java
class ThreeThreadsTest {
    public static void main (String[] args) {
        new SimpleThread("Jamaica").start();
        new SimpleThread("Fiji").start();
        new SimpleThread("Bora Bora").start();
    }
}
```

EXAMPLE: **Does Anybody Really Know What Time It Is?**

**Where
explained:**
*The Clock
Applet*
(page 291)

HTML PAGES CONTAINING APPLET: *http://java.sun.com/Series/Tutorial/java/
threads/clock.html*

Clock.java

SOURCE CODE: *http://java.sun.com/Series/Tutorial/java/threads/example/
Clock.java*

```java
import java.awt.Graphics;
import java.util.Date;

public class Clock extends java.applet.Applet implements
Runnable {

    Thread clockThread = null;

    public void start() {
        if (clockThread == null) {
            clockThread = new Thread(this, "Clock");
            clockThread.start();
        }
    }
    public void run() {
        // loop terminates when clockThread
        // is set to null in stop()
        while (Thread.currentThread() == clockThread) {
            repaint();
            try {
                clockThread.sleep(1000);
            } catch (InterruptedException e){
            }
        }
    }
    public void paint(Graphics g) {
        Date now = new Date();
        g.drawString(now.getHours() + ":" + now.getMinutes()
                    + ":" + now.getSeconds(), 5, 10);
    }
    public void stop() {
        clockThread = null;
    }
}
```

EXAMPLE: **The 400,000 Micron Thread Race**

HTML PAGES CONTAINING APPLET: *http://java.sun.com/Series/Tutorial/java/ threads/priority.html*

RaceApplet.java

SOURCE CODE: *http://java.sun.com/Series/Tutorial/java/threads/example/ RaceApplet.java*

Where explained:
Thread Priority (page 298)

```java
import java.awt.*;

public class RaceApplet extends java.applet.Applet implements
Runnable {

    final static int NUMRUNNERS = 2;
    final static int SPACING = 20;

    Runner[] runners = new Runner[NUMRUNNERS];

    Thread updateThread = null;

    public void init() {
        String raceType = getParameter("type");
        for (int i = 0; i < NUMRUNNERS; i++) {
            runners[i] = new Runner();
            if (raceType.compareTo("unfair") == 0)
                    runners[i].setPriority(i+2);
            else
                    runners[i].setPriority(2);
        }
        if (updateThread == null) {
            updateThread = new Thread(this, "Thread Race");
            updateThread.setPriority(NUMRUNNERS+2);
        }
    }

    public boolean mouseDown(java.awt.Event evt, int x, int y) {
        if (!updateThread.isAlive())
            updateThread.start();
        for (int i = 0; i < NUMRUNNERS; i++) {
            if (!runners[i].isAlive())
                runners[i].start();
        }
        return true;
    }

    public void paint(Graphics g) {
        g.setColor(Color.lightGray);
```

```
        g.fillRect(0, 0, size().width, size().height);
        g.setColor(Color.black);
        for (int i = 0; i < NUMRUNNERS; i++) {
            int pri = runners[i].getPriority();
            g.drawString(new Integer(pri).toString(), 0,
                    (i+1)*SPACING);
        }
        update(g);
    }

    public void update(Graphics g) {
        for (int i = 0; i < NUMRUNNERS; i++) {
            g.drawLine(SPACING, (i+1)*SPACING,
                    SPACING + (runners[i].tick)/1000,
                    (i+1)*SPACING);
        }
    }

    public void run() {
        while (Thread.currentThread() == updateThread) {
            repaint();
            try {
                updateThread.sleep(10);
            } catch (InterruptedException e) {
            }
        }
    }

    public void stop() {
        for (int i = 0; i < NUMRUNNERS; i++) {
            if (runners[i].isAlive()) {
                runners[i] = null;
            }
        }
        if (updateThread.isAlive()) {
            updateThread = null;
        }
    }
}
```

Runner.java

SOURCE CODE: *http://java.sun.com/Series/Tutorial/java/threads/example/Runner.java*

```java
class Runner extends Thread {

    public int tick = 1;

    public void run() {
        while (tick < 400000) {
            tick++;
        }
    }
}
```

RaceTest.java

SOURCE CODE: *http://java.sun.com/Series/Tutorial/java/threads/example/RaceTest.java*

```java
class RaceTest {

    final static int NUMRUNNERS = 2;

    public static void main(String[] args) {

        SelfishRunner[] runners = new SelfishRunner[NUMRUNNERS];

        for (int i = 0; i < NUMRUNNERS; i++) {
            runners[i] = new SelfishRunner(i);
            runners[i].setPriority(2);
        }
        for (int i = 0; i < NUMRUNNERS; i++) {
            runners[i].start();
        }
    }
}
```

SelfishRunner.java

SOURCE CODE: *http://java.sun.com/Series/Tutorial/java/threads/example/SelfishRunner.java*

```java
class SelfishRunner extends Thread {

    public int tick = 1;
    public int num;
```

```
        SelfishRunner(int num) {
            this.num = num;
        }

        public void run() {
            while (tick < 400000) {
                tick++;
                if ((tick % 50000) == 0) {
                    System.out.println("Thread #" + num + ", tick = "
                                        + tick);
                }
            }
        }
    }
}
```

PoliteRunner.java

SOURCE CODE: *http://java.sun.com/Series/Tutorial/java/threads/example/*
PoliteRunner.java

```
    class PoliteRunner extends Thread {

        public int tick = 1;
        public int num;

        PoliteRunner(int num) {
            this.num = num;
        }

        public void run() {
            while (tick < 400000) {
                tick++;
                if ((tick % 50000) == 0) {
                    System.out.println("Thread #" + num + ", tick = "
                                        + tick);
                    yield();
                }
            }
        }
    }
```

RaceTest2.java

SOURCE CODE: *http://java.sun.com/Series/Tutorial/java/threads/example/ RaceTest2.java*

```java
class RaceTest2 {

    final static int NUMRUNNERS = 2;

    public static void main(String[] args) {

        PoliteRunner[] runners = new PoliteRunner[NUMRUNNERS];

        for (int i = 0; i < NUMRUNNERS; i++) {
            runners[i] = new PoliteRunner(i);
            runners[i].setPriority(2);
        }
        for (int i = 0; i < NUMRUNNERS; i++) {
            runners[i].start();
        }
    }
}
```

EXAMPLE: **The EnumerateTest Class**

EnumerateTest.java

SOURCE CODE: *http://java.sun.com/Series/Tutorial/java/threads/example/ EnumerateTest.java*

```java
class EnumerateTest {
    void listCurrentThreads() {
        ThreadGroup currentGroup =
Thread.currentThread().getThreadGroup();
        int numThreads;
        Thread[] listOfThreads;

        numThreads = currentGroup.activeCount();
        listOfThreads = new Thread[numThreads];
        currentGroup.enumerate(listOfThreads);
        for (int i = 0; i < numThreads; i++) {
            System.out.println("Thread #" + i + " = " +
                                listOfThreads[i].getName());
        }
    }
}
```

Where explained:

The Thread-Group Class (page 305)

EXAMPLE: The MaxPriority Class

MaxPriorityTest.java

SOURCE CODE: *http://java.sun.com/Series/Tutorial/java/threads/example/ MaxPriorityTest.java*

Where explained:
The Thread-Group Class
(page 305)

```java
class MaxPriorityTest {
    public static void main(String[] args) {

        ThreadGroup groupNORM = new ThreadGroup(
                            "A group with normal priority");
        Thread priorityMAX = new Thread(groupNORM,
                            "A thread with maximum priority");

        // set Thread's priority to max (10)
        priorityMAX.setPriority(Thread.MAX_PRIORITY);

        // set ThreadGroup's max priority to normal (5)
        groupNORM.setMaxPriority(Thread.NORM_PRIORITY);

        System.out.println("Group's maximum priority = " +
                groupNORM.getMaxPriority());
        System.out.println("Thread's priority = " +
                priorityMAX.getPriority());
    }
}
```

EXAMPLE: Producer/Consumer

Producer.java

SOURCE CODE: *http://java.sun.com/Series/Tutorial/java/threads/example/ Producer.java*

Where explained:
Synchroniz-ing Threads
(page 311)

```java
class Producer extends Thread {
    private CubbyHole cubbyhole;
    private int number;

    public Producer(CubbyHole c, int number) {
        cubbyhole = c;
        this.number = number;
    }

    public void run() {
        for (int i = 0; i < 10; i++) {
            cubbyhole.put(i);
            System.out.println("Producer #" + this.number
                            + " put: " + i);
```

```
            try {
                sleep((int)(Math.random() * 100));
            } catch (InterruptedException e) {
            }
        }
    }
}
```

Consumer.java

SOURCE CODE: *http://java.sun.com/Series/Tutorial/java/threads/example/*
Consumer.java

```
class Consumer extends Thread {
    private CubbyHole cubbyhole;
    private int number;

    public Consumer(CubbyHole c, int number) {
        cubbyhole = c;
        this.number = number;
    }

    public void run() {
        int value = 0;
        for (int i = 0; i < 10; i++) {
            value = cubbyhole.get();
            System.out.println(" Consumer #" + this.number +
                               " got: " + value);
        }
    }
}
```

CubbyHole.java

SOURCE CODE: *http://java.sun.com/Series/Tutorial/java/threads/example/*
CubbyHole.java

```
class CubbyHole {
    private int contents;    // this is the condition variable.
    private boolean available = false;

    public synchronized int get() {
        while (available == false) {
            try {
                wait();
            } catch (InterruptedException e) {
            }
```

```
                }
                available = false;
                notify();
                return contents;
            }

        public synchronized void put(int value) {
            while (available == true) {
                try {
                    wait();
                } catch (InterruptedException e) {
                }
            }
            contents = value;
            available = true;
            notify();
        }
    }
```

ProducerConsumerTest.java

SOURCE CODE: *http://java.sun.com/Series/Tutorial/java/threads/example/
ProducerConsumerTest.java*

```
class ProducerConsumerTest {
    public static void main(String[] args) {
        CubbyHole c = new CubbyHole();
        Producer p1 = new Producer(c, 1);
        Consumer c1 = new Consumer(c, 1);

        p1.start();
        c1.start();
    }
}
```

EXAMPLE: A Test for Reentrant Monitors

**Where
explained:**

*Java Monitors
are Reentrant*
(page 315)

ReentrantTest.java

SOURCE CODE: *http://java.sun.com/Series/Tutorial/java/threads/example/
ReentrantTest.java*

```
class ReentrantTest {
    public static void main(String[] args) {
        new Reentrant().a();
    }
}
```

Reentrant.java

SOURCE CODE: *http://java.sun.com/Series/Tutorial/java/threads/example/*
Reentrant.java

```java
class Reentrant {
    public synchronized void a() {
        b();
        System.out.println("here I am, in a()");
    }
    public synchronized void b() {
        System.out.println("here I am, in b()");
    }
}
```

LESSON 16: **Input and Output Streams**

EXAMPLE: Create a List of Rhyming Words

RhymingWords.java

SOURCE CODE: *http://java.sun.com/Series/Tutorial/java/io/example/*
RhymingWords.java

```java
import java.io.*;

class RhymingWords {
    public static void main(String[] args) {

        try {
        DataInputStream words = new DataInputStream(new
                            FileInputStream("words.txt"));

            // do the reversing and sorting
            InputStream rhymedWords =
                    reverse(sort(reverse(words)));

            // write new list to standard out
            DataInputStream dis = new
                    DataInputStream(rhymedWords);
            String input;

            while ((input = dis.readLine()) != null) {
                System.out.println(input);
            }
            dis.close();
```

**Where
explained:**

*Using
Streams to
Implement
Pipes*
(page 332)

```java
        } catch (Exception e) {
            System.out.println("RhymingWords: " + e);
        }
    }

    public static InputStream reverse(InputStream source) {
        PipedOutputStream pos = null;
        PipedInputStream pis = null;

        try {
            DataInputStream dis = new DataInputStream(source);

            pos = new PipedOutputStream();
            pis = new PipedInputStream(pos);
            PrintStream ps = new PrintStream(pos);

            new WriteReversedThread(ps, dis).start();

        } catch (Exception e) {
            System.out.println("RhymingWords reverse: " + e);
        }
        return pis;
    }

    public static InputStream sort(InputStream source) {
        PipedOutputStream pos = null;
        PipedInputStream pis = null;

        try {
            DataInputStream dis = new DataInputStream(source);

            pos = new PipedOutputStream();
            pis = new PipedInputStream(pos);
            PrintStream ps = new PrintStream(pos);

            new SortThread(ps, dis).start();

        } catch (Exception e) {
            System.out.println("RhymingWords sort: " + e);
        }
        return pis;
    }
}
```

WriteReversedThread.java

SOURCE CODE: *http://java.sun.com/Series/Tutorial/java/io/example/
WriteReversedThread.java*

```java
import java.io.*;

class WriteReversedThread extends Thread {
    PrintStream ps;
    DataInputStream dis;

    WriteReversedThread(PrintStream ps, DataInputStream dis) {
        this.ps = ps;
        this.dis = dis;
    }

    public void run() {
        if (ps != null && dis != null) {
            try {
                String input;
                while ((input = dis.readLine()) != null) {
                    ps.println(reverseIt(input));
                    ps.flush();
                }
                ps.close();
            } catch (IOException e) {
                System.out.println("WriteReversedThread run: "
                                    + e);
            }
        }
    }

    protected void finalize() {
        try {
            if (ps != null) {
                ps.close();
                ps = null;
            }
            if (dis != null) {
                dis.close();
                dis = null;
            }
        } catch (IOException e) {
            System.out.println("WriteReversedThread finalize: "
                                + e);
        }
    }
```

```
      private String reverseIt(String source) {
          int i, len = source.length();
          StringBuffer dest = new StringBuffer(len);

          for (i = (len - 1); i >= 0; i--) {
              dest.append(source.charAt(i));
          }
          return dest.toString();
      }
  }
```

SortThread.java

SOURCE CODE: *http://java.sun.com/Series/Tutorial/java/io/example/*
SortThread.java

```
  import java.io.*;

  class SortThread extends Thread {
      PrintStream ps;
      DataInputStream dis;

      SortThread(PrintStream ps, DataInputStream dis) {
          this.ps = ps;
          this.dis = dis;
      }

      public void run() {
           int MAXWORDS = 50;

          if (ps != null && dis != null) {
              try {
                  String[] listOfWords = new String[MAXWORDS];
                  int numwords = 0, i = 0;

                  while ((listOfWords[numwords] = dis.readLine())
                          != null) {
                      numwords++;
                  }
                  quicksort(listOfWords, 0, numwords-1);
                  for (i = 0; i < numwords; i++) {
                      ps.println(listOfWords[i]);
                  }
                  ps.close();
              } catch (IOException e) {
                  System.out.println("WriteReversedThread run: "
                                      + e);
              }
```

```
        }
    }

    protected void finalize() {
        try {
            if (ps != null) {
                ps.close();
                ps = null;
            }
            if (dis != null) {
                dis.close();
                dis = null;
            }
        } catch (IOException e) {
            System.out.println("WriteReversedThread finalize: "
                               + e);
        }
    }

    private static void quicksort(String[] a, int lo0, int hi0) {
        int lo = lo0;
        int hi = hi0;
        if (lo >= hi) {
            return;
        }
        String mid = a[(lo + hi) / 2];
        while (lo < hi) {
            while (lo<hi && a[lo].compareTo(mid) < 0) {
                lo++;
            }
            while (lo<hi && a[hi].compareTo(mid) > 0) {
                hi--;
            }
            if (lo < hi) {
                String T = a[lo];
                a[lo] = a[hi];
                a[hi] = T;
            }
        }
        if (hi < lo) {
            int T = hi;
            hi = lo;
            lo = T;
        }
        quicksort(a, lo0, lo);
        quicksort(a, lo == lo0 ? lo+1 : lo, hi0);
    }
}
```

words.txt

SOURCE CODE: *http://java.sun.com/Series/Tutorial/java/io/example/words.txt*

```
anatomy
animation
applet
application
argument
bolts
class
communicate
component
container
development
environment
exception
graphics
image
input
integrate
interface
Java
language
native
network
nuts
object
output
primer
program
security
stream
string
threads
tools
user
```

EXAMPLE: **Using `FileInputStream` and `FileOutputStream`**

FileStreamsTest.java

SOURCE CODE: *http://java.sun.com/Series/Tutorial/java/io/example/*
           FileStreamsTest.java

**Where
explained:**

*Using Streams
to Read and
Write Files*
(page 336)

```
import java.io.*;

class FileStreamsTest {
    public static void main(String[] args) {
```

```
    try {
        File inputFile = new File("farrago.txt");
        File outputFile = new File("outagain.txt");

        FileInputStream fis = new FileInputStream(inputFile);
        FileOutputStream fos = new
                            FileOutputStream(outputFile);
        int c;

        while ((c = fis.read()) != -1) {
           fos.write(c);
        }

        fis.close();
        fos.close();
    } catch (FileNotFoundException e) {
        System.err.println("FileStreamsTest: " + e);
    } catch (IOException e) {
        System.err.println("FileStreamsTest: " + e);
    }
  }
}
```

farrago.txt

SOURCE CODE: *http://java.sun.com/Series/Tutorial/java/io/example/farrago.txt*

```
So she went into the garden to cut a cabbage-leaf, to
make an apple-pie; and at the same time a great
she-bear, coming up the street, pops its head into the
shop. 'What! no soap?' So he died, and she very
imprudently married the barber; and there were
present the Picninnies, and the Joblillies, and the
Garyalies, and the grand Panjandrum himself, with the
little round button at top, and they all fell to playing
the game of catch as catch can, till the gun powder ran
out at the heels of their boots.

Samuel Foote 1720-1777
```

EXAMPLE: Concatenate a List of Files

**Where
explained:**

*Using Streams
to Concate-
nate Files
(page 338)*

Concatenate.java

SOURCE CODE: *http://java.sun.com/Series/Tutorial/java/io/example/
Concatenate.java*

```java
import java.io.*;

class Concatenate {
    public static void main(String[] args) {
        ListOfFiles mylist = new ListOfFiles(args);

        try {
            SequenceInputStream s = new
                                SequenceInputStream(mylist);
            int c;

            while ((c = s.read()) != -1) {
                System.out.write(c);
            }

            s.close();
        } catch (IOException e) {
            System.err.println("Concatenate: " + e);
        }
    }
}
```

ListOfFiles.java

SOURCE CODE: *http://java.sun.com/Series/Tutorial/java/io/example/
ListOfFiles.java*

```java
import java.util.*;
import java.io.*;

class ListOfFiles implements Enumeration {

    String[] listOfFiles;
    int current = 0;

    ListOfFiles(String[] listOfFiles) {
        this.listOfFiles = listOfFiles;
    }

    public boolean hasMoreElements() {
        if (current < listOfFiles.length)
            return true;
```

```
        else
            return false;
    }

    public Object nextElement() {
        InputStream is = null;

        if (!hasMoreElements())
            throw new NoSuchElementException("No more files.");
        else {
            try {
                String nextElement = listOfFiles[current];
                current++;
                is = new FileInputStream(nextElement);
            } catch (FileNotFoundException e) {
                System.out.println("ListOfFiles: " + e);
            }
        }
        return is;
    }
}
```

EXAMPLE: An Invoice for Java Merchandise

DataIOTest.java

SOURCE CODE: *http://java.sun.com/Series/Tutorial/java/io/example/*
    DataIOTest.java

```
import java.io.*;

class DataIOTest {
    public static void main(String[] args) {

        // writing part
        try {
            DataOutputStream dos = new DataOutputStream(
                        new FileOutputStream("invoice1.txt"));

            double[] prices = { 19.99, 9.99, 15.99, 3.99, 4.99 };
            int[] units = { 12, 8, 13, 29, 50 };
            String[] descs = { "Java T-shirt", "Java Mug",
                                "Duke Juggling Dolls",
                                "Java Pin", "Java Key Chain" };

            for (int i = 0; i < prices.length; i ++) {
                dos.writeDouble(prices[i]);
                dos.writeChar('\t');
                dos.writeInt(units[i]);
```

Where explained:

Using DataInput- Stream and DataOutput- Stream (page 341)

```java
                dos.writeChar('\t');
                dos.writeChars(descs[i]);
                dos.writeChar('\n');
            }
            dos.close();
        } catch (IOException e) {
            System.out.println("DataIOTest: " + e);
        }


        // reading part
        try {
        DataInputStream dis = new DataInputStream(new
                            FileInputStream("invoice1.txt"));

            double price;
            int unit;
            String desc;
            double total = 0.0;

            try {
                while (true) {
                    price = dis.readDouble();
                    dis.readChar();        // throws out the tab
                    unit = dis.readInt();
                    dis.readChar();        // throws out the tab
                    desc = dis.readLine();
                    System.out.println("You've ordered " + unit
                                    + " units of " + desc
                                    + " at $" + price);
                    total = total + unit * price;
                }
            } catch (EOFException e) {
            }
            System.out.println("For a TOTAL of: $" + total);
            dis.close();
        } catch (FileNotFoundException e) {
            System.out.println("DataIOTest: " + e);
        } catch (IOException e) {
            System.out.println("DataIOTest: " + e);
        }
    }
}
```

EXAMPLE: **Filtered Streams That Compute a Checksum**

CheckedOutputStream.java

SOURCE CODE: *http://java.sun.com/Series/Tutorial/java/io/example/
CheckedOutputStream.java*

**Where
explained:**
*Writing Your
Own Filtered
Streams*
(page 343)

```java
import java.io.*;

public class CheckedOutputStream extends FilterOutputStream {
    private Checksum cksum;

    public CheckedOutputStream(OutputStream out,
                               Checksum cksum) {
        super(out);
        this.cksum = cksum;
    }

    public void write(int b) throws IOException {
        out.write(b);
        cksum.update(b);
    }

    public void write(byte[] b) throws IOException {
        out.write(b, 0, b.length);
        cksum.update(b, 0, b.length);
    }

    public void write(byte[] b, int off, int len) throws
            IOException {
        out.write(b, off, len);
        cksum.update(b, off, len);
    }

    public Checksum getChecksum() {
        return cksum;
    }
}
```

CheckedInputStream.java

SOURCE CODE: *http://java.sun.com/Series/Tutorial/java/io/example/
CheckedInputStream.java*

```java
import java.io.FilterInputStream;
import java.io.InputStream;
import java.io.IOException;
```

```
public
class CheckedInputStream extends FilterInputStream {
    private Checksum cksum;

    public CheckedInputStream(InputStream in, Checksum cksum) {
        super(in);
        this.cksum = cksum;
    }

    public int read() throws IOException {
        int b = in.read();
        if (b != -1) {
            cksum.update(b);
        }
        return b;
    }

    public int read(byte[] b) throws IOException {
        int len;
        len = in.read(b, 0, b.length);
        if (len != -1) {
            cksum.update(b, 0, b.length);
        }
        return len;
    }

    public int read(byte[] b, int off, int len) throws
IOException {
        len = in.read(b, off, len);
        if (len != -1) {
            cksum.update(b, off, len);
        }
        return len;
    }

    public Checksum getChecksum() {
        return cksum;
    }
}
```

Checksum.java

SOURCE CODE: *http://java.sun.com/Series/Tutorial/java/io/example/*
        Checksum.java

```java
public
interface Checksum {
    /**
     * Updates the current checksum with the specified byte.
     */
    public void update(int b);

    /**
     * Updates the current checksum with the
     * specified array of bytes.
     */
    public void update(byte[] b, int off, int len);

    /**
     * Returns the current checksum value.
     */
    public long getValue();

    /**
     * Resets the checksum to its initial value.
     */
    public void reset();
}
```

Adler32.java

SOURCE CODE: *http://java.sun.com/Series/Tutorial/java/io/example/Adler32.java*

```java
public
class Adler32 implements Checksum {
    private int value = 1;

    /*
     * BASE is the largest prime number smaller than 65536
     * NMAX is the largest n such that:
     *      255n(n+1)/2 + (n+1)(BASE-1) <= 2^32-1
     */
    private static final int BASE = 65521;
    private static final int NMAX = 5552;

    /**
     * Update current Adler-32 checksum given the specified byte.
     */
```

```java
    public void update(int b) {
        int s1 = value & 0xffff;
        int s2 = (value >> 16) & 0xffff;
        s1 += b & 0xff;
        s2 += s1;
        value = ((s2 % BASE) << 16) | (s1 % BASE);
    }

    /**
     * Update current Adler-32 checksum given the specified
     * byte array.
     */
    public void update(byte[] b, int off, int len) {
        int s1 = value & 0xffff;
        int s2 = (value >> 16) & 0xffff;

        while (len > 0) {
            int k = len < NMAX ? len : NMAX;
            len -= k;
            while (k-- > 0) {
                s1 += b[off++] & 0xff;
                s2 += s1;
            }
            s1 %= BASE;
            s2 %= BASE;
        }
        value = (s2 << 16) | s1;
    }

    /**
     * Reset Adler-32 checksum to initial value.
     */
    public void reset() {
        value = 1;
    }

    /**
     * Returns current checksum value.
     */
    public long getValue() {
        return (long)value & 0xffffffff;
    }
}
```

CheckedIOTest.java

SOURCE CODE: *http://java.sun.com/Series/Tutorial/java/io/example/
CheckedIOTest.java*

```java
import java.io.*;

class CheckedIOTest {
    public static void main(String[] args) {

        Adler32 inChecker = new Adler32();
        Adler32 outChecker = new Adler32();
        CheckedInputStream cis = null;
        CheckedOutputStream cos = null;

        try {
            cis = new CheckedInputStream(
                    new FileInputStream("farrago.txt"), inChecker);
            cos = new CheckedOutputStream(
                    new FileOutputStream("outagain.txt"), outChecker);
        } catch (FileNotFoundException e) {
            System.err.println("CheckedIOTest: " + e);
            System.exit(-1);
        } catch (IOException e) {
            System.err.println("CheckedIOTest: " + e);
            System.exit(-1);
        }

        try {
            int c;

            while ((c = cis.read()) != -1) {
                cos.write(c);
            }

            System.out.println("Input stream check sum: "
                            + inChecker.getValue());
            System.out.println("Output stream check sum: "
                            + outChecker.getValue());

            cis.close();
            cos.close();
        } catch (IOException e) {
            System.err.println("CheckedIOTest: " + e);
        }
    }
}
```

EXAMPLE: `DataInput` and `DataOutput` Filtered Streams

CheckedDataOutput.java

Where explained:
Writing Filters for Random Access Files
(page 351)

SOURCE CODE: *http://java.sun.com/Series/Tutorial/java/io/example/
CheckedDataOutput.java*

```java
/*
 * This class is an example only. A "final" version of
 * this class should implement the DataOutput interface
 * and provide implementations for the methods declared in
 * DataOutput.
 */

import java.io.*;

public class CheckedDataOutput {
    private Checksum cksum;
    private DataOutput out;

    public CheckedDataOutput(DataOutput out, Checksum cksum) {
        this.cksum = cksum;
        this.out = out;
    }

    public void write(int b) throws IOException {
        out.write(b);
        cksum.update(b);
    }

    public void write(byte[] b) throws IOException {
        out.write(b, 0, b.length);
        cksum.update(b, 0, b.length);
    }

    public void write(byte[] b, int off, int len) throws
            IOException {
        out.write(b, off, len);
        cksum.update(b, off, len);
    }

    public Checksum getChecksum() {
        return cksum;
    }
}
```

CheckedDataInput.java

SOURCE CODE: *http://java.sun.com/Series/Tutorial/java/io/example/*
     CheckedDataInput.java

```java
/*
 * This class is an example only. A "final" version of
 * this class should implement the DataInput interface
 * and provide implementations for the methods declared in
 * DataInput.
 */
import java.io.*;

public class CheckedDataInput {
    private Checksum cksum;
    private DataInput in;

    public CheckedDataInput(DataInput in, Checksum cksum) {
        this.cksum = cksum;
        this.in = in;
    }

    public byte readByte() throws IOException {
        byte b = in.readByte();
        cksum.update(b);
        return b;
    }

    public void readFully(byte[] b) throws IOException {
        in.readFully(b, 0, b.length);
        cksum.update(b, 0, b.length);
    }

    public void readFully(byte[] b, int off, int len) throws
        IOException {
        in.readFully(b, off, len);
        cksum.update(b, off, len);
    }

    public Checksum getChecksum() {
        return cksum;
    }
}
```

CheckedDITest.java

SOURCE CODE: *http://java.sun.com/Series/Tutorial/java/io/example/
CheckedDITest.java*

```java
import java.io.*;

class CheckedDITest {
    public static void main(String[] args) {

        Adler32 inChecker = new Adler32();
        Adler32 outChecker = new Adler32();
        CheckedDataInput cis = null;
        CheckedDataOutput cos = null;

        try {
            cis = new CheckedDataInput(new DataInputStream(
                                    newFileInputStream(
                                    "farrago.txt")),
                                    inChecker);
            cos = new CheckedDataOutput(new DataOutputStream(
                                    newFileOutputStream(
                                    "outagain.txt")),
                                    outChecker);
        } catch (FileNotFoundException e) {
            System.err.println("CheckedIOTest: " + e);
            System.exit(-1);
        } catch (IOException e) {
            System.err.println("CheckedIOTest: " + e);
            System.exit(-1);
        }

        try {
            boolean EOF = false;

            while (!EOF) {
                try {
                    int c = cis.readByte();
                    cos.write(c);
                } catch (EOFException e) {
                    EOF = true;
                }
            }

            System.out.println("Input stream check sum: " +
                cis.getChecksum().getValue());
            System.out.println("Output stream check sum: " +
                cos.getChecksum().getValue());
```

```
        } catch (IOException e) {
            System.err.println("CheckedIOTest: " + e);
        }
    }
}
```

CheckedRAFTest.java

SOURCE CODE: *http://java.sun.com/Series/Tutorial/java/io/example/*
        CheckedRAFTest.java

```
    import java.io.*;

    class CheckedRAFTest {
        public static void main(String[] args) {

            Adler32 inChecker = new Adler32();
            Adler32 outChecker = new Adler32();
            CheckedDataInput cis = null;
            CheckedDataOutput cos = null;

            try {
              cis = new CheckedDataInput(new
                    RandomAccessFile("farrago.txt", "r"), inChecker);
              cos = new CheckedDataOutput(new
                    RandomAccessFile("outagain.txt", "rw"), outChecker);
            } catch (FileNotFoundException e) {
                System.err.println("CheckedIOTest: " + e);
                System.exit(-1);
            } catch (IOException e) {
                System.err.println("CheckedIOTest: " + e);
                System.exit(-1);
            }

            try {
                boolean EOF = false;

                while (!EOF) {
                    try {
                        int c = cis.readByte();
                        cos.write(c);
                    } catch (EOFException e) {
                        EOF = true;
                    }
                }

                System.out.println("Input stream check sum: "
                                + cis.getChecksum().getValue());
```

```
            System.out.println("Output stream check sum: "
                            + cos.getChecksum().getValue());
        } catch (IOException e) {
            System.err.println("CheckedIOTest: " + e);
        }
    }
}
```

Creating a User Interface

LESSON 17: Overview of the Java UI

EXAMPLE: The AppletButton Applet

HTML PAGES CONTAINING APPLET:
    http://java.sun.com/Series/Tutorial/ui/overview/components.html
    http://java.sun.com/Series/Tutorial/ui/components/dialog.html
    http://java.sun.com/Series/Tutorial/ui/components/menu.html
    http://java.sun.com/Series/Tutorial/ui/layout/using.html (multiple instances)
    http://java.sun.com/Series/Tutorial/ui/layout/border.html
    http://java.sun.com/Series/Tutorial/ui/layout/card.html
    http://java.sun.com/Series/Tutorial/ui/layout/flow.html
    http://java.sun.com/Series/Tutorial/ui/layout/grid.html
    http://java.sun.com/Series/Tutorial/ui/layout/gridbag.html
    http://java.sun.com/Series/Tutorial/ui/layout/gridbagExample.html
    http://java.sun.com/Series/Tutorial/ui/layout/custom.html
    http://java.sun.com/Series/Tutorial/ui/layout/none.html

> **Where explained:**
> *Defining and Using Applet Parameters*
> (page 175)

The `AppletButton` applet is a highly configurable applet used to bring up windows.

AppletButton.java

SOURCE CODE: *http://java.sun.com/Series/Tutorial/ui/overview/example/*
    AppletButton.java

```
import java.awt.*;
import java.util.*;
import java.applet.Applet;

public class AppletButton extends Applet implements Runnable {
    int frameNumber = 1;
    String windowClass;
    String buttonText;
    String windowTitle;
    int requestedWidth = 0;
    int requestedHeight = 0;
    Button button;
    Thread windowThread;
```

```java
    Label label;
    boolean pleaseCreate = false;

    public void init() {
        windowClass = getParameter("WINDOWCLASS");
        if (windowClass == null) {
            windowClass = "TestWindow";
        }

        buttonText = getParameter("BUTTONTEXT");
        if (buttonText == null) {
            buttonText = "Click here to bring up a " + windowClass;
        }

        windowTitle = getParameter("WINDOWTITLE");
        if (windowTitle == null) {
            windowTitle = windowClass;
        }

        String windowWidthString = getParameter("WINDOWWIDTH");
        if (windowWidthString != null) {
            try {
                requestedWidth =
                    Integer.parseInt(windowWidthString);
            } catch (NumberFormatException e) {
                //Use default width.
            }
        }

        String windowHeightString =
            getParameter("WINDOWHEIGHT");
        if (windowHeightString != null) {
            try {
                requestedHeight =
                    Integer.parseInt(windowHeightString);
            } catch (NumberFormatException e) {
                //Use default height.
            }
        }

        setLayout(new GridLayout(2,0));
        add(button = new Button(buttonText));
        button.setFont(new Font("Helvetica", Font.PLAIN, 14));

        add(label = new Label("", Label.CENTER));
    }

    public void start() {
```

```
        if (windowThread == null) {
            windowThread = new Thread(this, "Bringing Up "
                                        + windowClass);
            windowThread.start();
        }
}

public synchronized void run() {
    Class windowClassObject = null;
    Class tmp = null;
    String name = null;

    // Make sure the window class exists and is really
    // a Frame.
    // This has the added benefit of pre-loading the class,
    // which makes it much quicker for the first window to
    // come up.
    try {
        windowClassObject = Class.forName(windowClass);
    } catch (Exception e) {
        // The specified class isn't anywhere that we can find.
        label.setText("Can't create window: Couldn't find "
                        + "class " windowClass);
        button.disable();
        return;
    }

    // Find out whether the class is a Frame.
    for (tmp = windowClassObject, name = tmp.getName();
            !( name.equals("java.lang.Object") ||
              name.equals("java.awt.Frame") ); ) {
        tmp = tmp.getSuperclass();
        name = tmp.getName();
    }
    if ((name == null) || name.equals("java.lang.Object")) {
        //We can't run; ERROR; print status,
        //never bring up window
        label.setText("Can't create window: "
                        + windowClass +
                        " isn't a Frame subclass.");
        button.disable();
        return;
    } else if (name.equals("java.awt.Frame")) {
        //Everything's OK. Wait until we're asked to create
        //a window.
        while (windowThread != null) {
            while (pleaseCreate == false) {
```

```
                    try {
                        wait();
                    } catch (InterruptedException e) {
                    }
                }

                //We've been asked to bring up a window.
                pleaseCreate = false;
                Frame window = null;
                try {
                    window =
                        (Frame)windowClassObject.newInstance();
                } catch (Exception e) {
                    label.setText(
                        "Couldn't create instance of class "
                        + windowClass);
                    button.disable();
                    return;
                }
                if (frameNumber == 1) {
                    window.setTitle(windowTitle);
                } else {
                    window.setTitle(windowTitle +
                                    ":" + frameNumber);
                }
                frameNumber++;

                //Set the window's size.
                window.pack();
                if ((requestedWidth > 0) | (requestedHeight > 0)) {
                    window.resize(Math.max(requestedWidth,
                                        window.size().width),
                                  Math.max(requestedHeight,
                                        window.size().height));
                }

                window.show();
                label.setText("");
            }
        }
    }

    public synchronized boolean action(Event event, Object what)
    {
        if (event.target instanceof Button) {
            //signal the window thread to build a window
            label.setText(
                "Please wait while the window comes up...");
```

```
            pleaseCreate = true;
            notify();
        }
        return true;
    }
}

class TestWindow extends Frame {
    public TestWindow() {
        resize(300, 300);
    }
}
```

EXAMPLE: Introduction to the AWT Components

HTML PAGES CONTAINING APPLET: *http://java.sun.com/Series/Tutorial/ui/overview/ components.html*

This program can run either as an application or, with the help of `AppletButton.java` (page 671), as an applet.

GUIWindow.java

SOURCE CODE: *http://java.sun.com/Series/Tutorial/ui/overview/example/ GUIWindow.java*

```
import java.awt.*;

public class GUIWindow extends Frame {
    boolean inAnApplet = true;
    final String FILEDIALOGMENUITEM = "File dialog...";

    public GUIWindow() {
        Panel bottomPanel = new Panel();
        Panel centerPanel = new Panel();
        setLayout(new BorderLayout());

        //Set up the menu bar.
        MenuBar mb = new MenuBar();
        Menu m = new Menu("Menu");
        m.add(new MenuItem("Menu item 1"));
        m.add(new CheckboxMenuItem("Menu item 2"));
        m.add(new MenuItem("Menu item 3"));
        m.add(new MenuItem("-"));
        m.add(new MenuItem(FILEDIALOGMENUITEM));
        mb.add(m);
        setMenuBar(mb);

        //Add small things at the bottom of the window.
```

Where explained: *AWT Components* (page 362)

```java
                    bottomPanel.add(new TextField("TextField"));
                    bottomPanel.add(new Button("Button"));
                    bottomPanel.add(new Checkbox("Checkbox"));
                    Choice c = new Choice();
                    c.addItem("Choice Item 1");
                    c.addItem("Choice Item 2");
                    c.addItem("Choice Item 3");
                    bottomPanel.add(c);
                    add("South", bottomPanel);

                    //Add big things to the center area of the window.
                    centerPanel.setLayout(new GridLayout(1,2));
                    //Put a canvas in the left column.
                    centerPanel.add(new MyCanvas());
                    //Put a label and a text area in the right column.
                    Panel p = new Panel();
                    p.setLayout(new BorderLayout());
                    p.add("North", new Label("Label", Label.CENTER));
                    p.add("Center", new TextArea("TextArea", 5, 20));
                    centerPanel.add(p);
                    add("Center", centerPanel);

                    //Put a list on the right side of the window.
                    List l = new List(3, false);
                    for (int i = 1; i <= 10; i++) {
                        l.addItem("List item " + i);
                    }
                    add("East", l);
                }

                public boolean action(Event event, Object arg) {
                    //The only action event we pay attention to is when the
                    //user requests we bring up a FileDialog.
                    if (event.target instanceof MenuItem) {
                        if (((String)arg).equals(FILEDIALOGMENUITEM)) {
                            FileDialog fd = new FileDialog(this, "FileDialog");
                            fd.show();
                        }
                    }
                    return true;
                }

                public boolean handleEvent(Event event) {
                    //If we're running as an application, closing the window
                    //should quit the application.
                    if (event.id == Event.WINDOW_DESTROY) {
                        if (inAnApplet) {
                            dispose();
```

```java
        } else {
            System.exit(0);
        }
    }
    return super.handleEvent(event);
}

public static void main(String args[]) {
    GUIWindow window = new GUIWindow();
    window.inAnApplet = false;

    window.setTitle("The AWT Components");
    window.pack();
    window.show();
}

}


//We can't just instantiate Canvas, since its default
//implementation gives us nothing
//interesting to look at or do.
//So here's a Canvas
//subclass that draws something slightly interesting.
class MyCanvas extends Canvas {

    public void paint(Graphics g) {
        int w = size().width;
        int h = size().height;
        g.drawRect(0, 0, w - 1, h - 1);
        g.drawString("Canvas",
                    (w - g.getFontMetrics().
                     stringWidth("Canvas"))/2, 10);

        g.setFont(new Font("Helvetica", Font.PLAIN, 8));
        g.drawLine(10,10, 100,100);
        g.fillRect(9,9,3,3);
        g.drawString("(10,10)", 13, 10);
        g.fillRect(49,49,3,3);
        g.drawString("(50,50)", 53, 50);
        g.fillRect(99,99,3,3);
        g.drawString("(100,100)", 103, 100);
    }

    //If we don't specify this,
    //the canvas might not show up at all
    //(depending on the layout manager).
    public Dimension minimumSize() {
        return new Dimension(150,130);
```

```
        }

        //If we don't specify this, the canvas might not show up at
        //all (depending on the layout manager).
        public Dimension preferredSize() {
            return minimumSize();
        }
    }
}
```

EXAMPLE: **The Converter Applet/Application**

Where explained:
The Anatomy of a GUI-Based Program
(page 366)

HTML PAGES CONTAINING APPLET: *http://java.sun.com/Series/Tutorial/ui/overview/ anatomy.html*

This program can run either as an applet or as an application.

Converter.java

SOURCE CODE: *http://java.sun.com/Series/Tutorial/ui/overview/example/ Converter.java*

```java
import java.awt.*;
import java.util.*;
import java.applet.Applet;

public class Converter extends Applet {
    ConversionPanel metricPanel, usaPanel;
    Unit[] metricDistances = new Unit[3];
    Unit[] usaDistances = new Unit[4];

    /**
     * Create the ConversionPanels
     * (one for metric, another for U.S.).
     * I used "U.S." because although Imperial and U.S. distance
     * measurements are the same, this program could be extended to
     * include volume measurements, which aren't the same.
     */
    public void init() {
        //Use a GridLayout with 2 rows,
        //as many columns as necessary,
        //and 5 pixels of padding around all edges of each cell.
        setLayout(new GridLayout(2,0,5,5));

        //Create Unit objects for metric distances, and then
        //instantiate a ConversionPanel with these Units.
        metricDistances[0] = new Unit("Centimeters", 0.01);
        metricDistances[1] = new Unit("Meters", 1.0);
        metricDistances[2] = new Unit("Kilometers", 1000.0);
        metricPanel = new ConversionPanel(this, "Metric System",
                                        metricDistances);
```

```
        //Create Unit objects for U.S. distances, and then
        //instantiate a ConversionPanel with these Units.
        usaDistances[0] = new Unit("Inches", 0.0254);
        usaDistances[1] = new Unit("Feet", 0.305);
        usaDistances[2] = new Unit("Yards", 0.914);
        usaDistances[3] = new Unit("Miles", 1613.0);
        usaPanel = new ConversionPanel(this, "U.S. System",
                                           usaDistances);

        //Add both ConversionPanels to the Converter.
        add(metricPanel);
        add(usaPanel);

        //Calling the validate method here can help applets.
        //It's unnecessary when this program runs
        //as an application.
        validate();
    }

    /**
     * Does the conversion from metric to U.S., or vice versa, and
     * updates the appropriate ConversionPanel.
     */
    void convert(ConversionPanel from) {
        ConversionPanel to;

        if (from == metricPanel)
            to = usaPanel;
        else
            to = metricPanel;
        double multiplier = from.getMultiplier() /
            to.getMultiplier();
        to.setValue(from.getValue() * multiplier);
    }

    /** Draws a box around this panel. */
    public void paint(Graphics g) {
        Dimension d = size();
        g.drawRect(0,0, d.width - 1, d.height - 1);
    }

    /**
     * Puts a little breathing space between
     * the panel and its contents, which lets us draw a box
     * in the paint() method.
     */
```

```java
        public Insets insets() {
            return new Insets(5,5,5,5);
        }

        /** Executed only when this program runs as an application.
         */
        public static void main(String[] args) {
            //Create a new window.
            MainFrame f = new MainFrame(
                    "Converter Applet/Application");

            //Create a Converter instance.
            Converter converter = new Converter();

            //Initialize the Converter instance.
            converter.init();

            //Add the Converter to the window and display the window.
            f.add("Center", converter);
            f.pack();           //Resizes the window to its natural size.
            f.show();
        }
    }


    class ConversionPanel extends Panel {
        TextField textField;
        Scrollbar slider;
        Choice unitChooser;
        int min = 0;
        int max = 10000;
        Converter controller;
        Unit[] units;

        ConversionPanel(Converter myController, String myTitle,
                        Unit[] myUnits) {
            //Initialize this ConversionPanel to use a GridBagLayout.
            GridBagConstraints c = new GridBagConstraints();
            GridBagLayout gridbag = new GridBagLayout();
            setLayout(gridbag);

            //Save arguments in instance variables.
            controller = myController;
            units = myUnits;

            //Set up default layout constraints.
            c.fill = GridBagConstraints.HORIZONTAL;
```

```java
        //Add the label.  It displays this panel's
        //title, centered.
        Label label = new Label(myTitle, Label.CENTER);
        c.gridwidth = GridBagConstraints.REMAINDER;
        //It ends a row.
        gridbag.setConstraints(label, c);
        add(label);

        //Add the text field.  It initially displays "0" and needs
        //to be at least 10 columns wide.
        textField = new TextField("0", 10);
        c.weightx = 1.0;   //This component should use all
                           //available horizontal space...
        c.gridwidth = 1; //The default value.
        gridbag.setConstraints(textField, c);
        add(textField);

        //Add the pop-up list (Choice).
        unitChooser = new Choice();
        for (int i = 0; i < units.length; i++) { //Populate it.
            unitChooser.addItem(units[i].description);
        }
        c.weightx = 0.0; //The default value.
        c.gridwidth = GridBagConstraints.REMAINDER; //End a row.
        gridbag.setConstraints(unitChooser, c);
        add(unitChooser);

        //Add the slider.  It's horizontal, its initial
        //value is 0,
        //a click increments the value by 100 pixels, and
        //it has the minimum and maximum values specified
        //by the instance variables
        //min and max.
        slider = new Scrollbar(Scrollbar.HORIZONTAL, 0, 100,
                               min, max);
        c.gridwidth = 1; //The default value.
        gridbag.setConstraints(slider, c);
        add(slider);
    }

/**
 * Returns the multiplier (units/meter) for the currently
 * selected unit of measurement.
 */
double getMultiplier() {
    int i = unitChooser.getSelectedIndex();
    return (units[i].multiplier);
}
```

```java
/** Draws a box around this panel. */
public void paint(Graphics g) {
    Dimension d = size();
    g.drawRect(0,0, d.width - 1, d.height - 1);
}

/**
 * Puts a little breathing space between
 * the panel and its contents, which lets us draw a box
 * in the paint() method.
 * We add more pixels to the right, to work around a
 * Choice bug.
 */
public Insets insets() {
    return new Insets(5,5,5,8);
}

/**
 * Gets the current value in the text field.
 * That's guaranteed to be the same as the value
 * in the scroller (subject to rounding, of course).
 */
double getValue() {
    double f;
    try {
        f = Double.valueOf(
            textField.getText()).doubleValue();
    } catch (java.lang.NumberFormatException e) {
        f = 0.0;
    }
    return f;
}

/** Respond to user actions on controls. */
public boolean action(Event e, Object arg) {
    if (e.target instanceof TextField) {
        setSliderValue(getValue());
        controller.convert(this);
        return true;
    }
    if (e.target instanceof Choice) {
        controller.convert(this);
        return true;
    }
    return false;
}
```

```java
    /** Respond to the slider. */
    public boolean handleEvent(Event e) {
        if (e.target instanceof Scrollbar) {
            textField.setText(String.valueOf(slider.getValue()));
            controller.convert(this);
        }
        return super.handleEvent(e);
    }

    /** Set the values in the slider and text field. */
    void setValue(double f) {
        setSliderValue(f);
        textField.setText(String.valueOf(f));
    }

    /** Set the slider value. */
    void setSliderValue(double f) {
        int sliderValue = (int)f;

        if (sliderValue > max)
                sliderValue = max;
        if (sliderValue < min)
            sliderValue = min;
        slider.setValue(sliderValue);
    }
}


class Unit {
    String description;
    double multiplier;

    Unit(String description, double multiplier) {
        super();
        this.description = description;
        this.multiplier = multiplier;
    }

    public String toString() {
        String s = "Meters/" + description + " = " + multiplier;
        return s;
    }
}


/** Provides a window if this program is run as an application.
 */
 class MainFrame extends Frame {
```

```
MainFrame(String title) {
    super(title);
}

public boolean handleEvent(Event e) {
    if (e.id == Event.WINDOW_DESTROY) {
        System.exit(0);
    }
    return super.handleEvent(e);
}
```

LESSON 18: Using Components, the GUI Building Blocks

EXAMPLE: Button Demo Applet

HTML PAGES CONTAINING APPLET: *http://java.sun.com/Series/Tutorial/ui/ components/button.html*

ButtonDemo.java

SOURCE CODE: *http://java.sun.com/Series/Tutorial/ui/components/example/ ButtonDemo.java*

```java
import java.awt.*;
import java.applet.Applet;

public class ButtonDemo extends Applet {

Button b1, b2, b3;

    public void init() {
        b1 = new Button();
        b1.setLabel("Disable middle button");

        b2 = new Button("Middle button");

        b3 = new Button("Enable middle button");
        b3.disable();

        //Add Components to the Applet, using the
        //default FlowLayout.
        add(b1);
        add(b2);
        add(b3);
```

Where explained:

How to Use Buttons
(page 383)

```
        //Necessary when adding buttons to an already visible
        //container:
        validate();
    }

    public boolean action(Event e, Object arg) {
        Object target = e.target;

        if (target == b1) { //They clicked "Disable middle button"
            b2.disable();
            b1.disable();
            b3.enable();
            return true;
        }
        if (target == b3) { //They clicked "Enable middle button"
            b2.enable();
            b1.enable();
            b3.disable();
            return true;
        }
        return false;
    }
}
```

EXAMPLE: Canvas Demo Applet

Where explained: *How to Use Canvases* (page 385)

HTML PAGES CONTAINING APPLET: *http://java.sun.com/Series/Tutorial/ui/ components/canvas.html*

ImageApplet.java

SOURCE CODE: *http://java.sun.com/Series/Tutorial/ui/components/example/ ImageApplet.java*

```
import java.awt.*;
import java.applet.Applet;

class ImageCanvas extends Canvas {
    Container pappy;
    Image image;
    boolean trueSizeKnown = false;
    Dimension minSize;
    int w, h;

    public ImageCanvas(Image image, Container parent,
                       int initialWidth, int initialHeight) {
        if (image == null) {
            System.err.println(
                "Canvas got invalid image object!");
```

```java
                    return;
                }

            this.image = image;
            pappy = parent;

            w = initialWidth;
            h = initialHeight;

            minSize = new Dimension(w,h);
        }

        public Dimension preferredSize() {
            return minimumSize();
        }

        public synchronized Dimension minimumSize() {
            return minSize;
        }

        public void paint (Graphics g) {
            if (image != null) {
                if (!trueSizeKnown) {
                    int imageWidth = image.getWidth(this);
                    int imageHeight = image.getHeight(this);

                    if ((imageWidth > 0) && (imageHeight > 0)) {
                        trueSizeKnown = true;

                        //Component-initiated resizing.
                        w = imageWidth;
                        h = imageHeight;
                        minSize = new Dimension(w,h);
                        resize(w, h);
                        pappy.validate();
                    }
                }

                g.drawImage(image, 0, 0, this);
                g.drawRect(0, 0, w - 1, h - 1);
            }
        }

    }


public class ImageApplet extends Applet {
    public void init() {
```

```
        Image image1 = getImage(getCodeBase(),
                            "../images/kwalrath.gif");
        Image image2 = getImage(getCodeBase(),
                            "../images/innocence.small.gif");

        ImageCanvas ic1 = new ImageCanvas(image1, this, 50, 50);
        ImageCanvas ic2 = new ImageCanvas(image2, this, 100,
                                    100);

        add(ic1);
        add(ic2);

        validate();
    }

}
```

EXAMPLE: Checkbox Demo Applet

HTML PAGES CONTAINING APPLET: *http://java.sun.com/Series/Tutorial/ui/ components/checkbox.html*

CheckboxDemo.java

SOURCE CODE: *http://java.sun.com/Series/Tutorial/ui/components/example/ CheckboxDemo.java*

Where explained:
How to Use Checkboxes (page 387)

```
import java.awt.*;
import java.applet.Applet;

public class CheckboxDemo extends Applet {

    public void init() {
        Panel p1, p2;
        Checkbox cb1, cb2, cb3; //These are independent
                                //checkboxes.
        Checkbox cb4, cb5, cb6; //These checkboxes are part
                                //of a group

        CheckboxGroup cbg;

        //Build first panel,
        //which contains independent checkboxes
        cb1 = new Checkbox(); //Default state is "off"(false).
        cb1.setLabel("Checkbox 1");
        cb2 = new Checkbox("Checkbox 2");
        cb3 = new Checkbox("Checkbox 3");
        cb3.setState(true); //Set state to "on"(true).
        p1 = new Panel();
        p1.setLayout(new FlowLayout());
```

```
                    //Using a GridLayout didn't work
                    //--kept box and text too far apart.
                    p1.add(cb1);
                    p1.add(cb2);
                    p1.add(cb3);

                    //Build second panel, which contains a checkbox group.
                    cbg = new CheckboxGroup();
                    cb4 = new Checkbox("Checkbox 4", cbg, false);
                                    //initial state: off
                    cb5 = new Checkbox("Checkbox 5", cbg, false);
                                    //initial state: off
                    cb6 = new Checkbox("Checkbox 6", cbg, false);
                                    //initial state: off
                    p2 = new Panel();
                    p2.setLayout(new FlowLayout());
                    p2.add(cb4);
                    p2.add(cb5);
                    p2.add(cb6);

                    //Add panels to the Applet.
                    setLayout(new GridLayout(0, 2));
                    add(p1);
                    add(p2);

                    validate();
                }
            }
```

EXAMPLE: **Choice Demo Applet**

HTML PAGES CONTAINING APPLET: *http://java.sun.com/Series/Tutorial/ui/components/choice.html*

ChoiceDemo.java

SOURCE CODE: *http://java.sun.com/Series/Tutorial/ui/components/example/ChoiceDemo.java*

```
import java.awt.*;
import java.applet.Applet;

public class ChoiceDemo extends Applet {
    Choice choice; //pop-up list of choices
    Label label;

    public void init() {

        choice = new Choice();
```

Where explained:

How to Use Choices (page 389)

```
        choice.addItem("ichi");
        choice.addItem("ni");
        choice.addItem("san");
        choice.addItem("yon");
        label = new Label();
        setLabelText(choice.getSelectedIndex(),
            choice.getSelectedItem());

        //Add components to the Applet.
        add(choice);
        add(label);

        validate();
    }

    void setLabelText(int num, String text) {
        label.setText("Item #" + num + " selected. "
                    + "Text = \"" + text + "\".");
    }

    public boolean action(Event e, Object arg) {
        if (e.target instanceof Choice) {
            setLabelText(choice.getSelectedIndex(), (String)arg);
            return true;
        }
        return false;
    }
}
```

EXAMPLE: **Dialog Demo Applet/Application**

HTML PAGES CONTAINING APPLET: *http://java.sun.com/Series/Tutorial/ui/components/dialog.html*

This program can run either as an application or, with the help of `AppletButton.java` (page 671), as an applet.

DialogWindow.java

SOURCE CODE: *http://java.sun.com/Series/Tutorial/ui/components/example/DialogWindow.java*

```
import java.awt.*;

public class DialogWindow extends Frame {
    private boolean inAnApplet = true;
    private SimpleDialog dialog;
    private TextArea textArea;
```

Where explained:
How to Use Dialogs
(page 391)

```java
    public DialogWindow() {
        textArea = new TextArea(5, 40);
        textArea.setEditable(false);
        add("Center", textArea);
        Button button = new Button("Click to bring up dialog");
        Panel panel = new Panel();
        panel.add(button);
        add("South", panel);
    }

    public boolean handleEvent(Event event) {
        if (event.id == Event.WINDOW_DESTROY) {
            if (inAnApplet) {
                dispose();
            } else {
                System.exit(0);
            }
        }
        return super.handleEvent(event);
    }

    public boolean action(Event event, Object arg) {
        if (dialog == null) {
            dialog = new SimpleDialog(this, "A Simple Dialog");
        }
        dialog.show();
        return true;
    }

    public void setText(String text) {
        textArea.appendText(text + "\n");
    }

    public static void main(String args[]) {
        DialogWindow window = new DialogWindow();
        window.inAnApplet = false;

        window.setTitle("DialogWindow Application");
        window.pack();
        window.show();
    }
}

class SimpleDialog extends Dialog {
    TextField field;
    DialogWindow parent;
    Button setButton;
```

```
SimpleDialog(Frame dw, String title) {
    super(dw, title, false);
    parent = (DialogWindow)dw;

    //Create middle section.
    Panel p1 = new Panel();
    Label label = new Label("Enter random text here:");
    p1.add(label);
    field = new TextField(40);
    p1.add(field);
    add("Center", p1);

    //Create bottom row.
    Panel p2 = new Panel();
    p2.setLayout(new FlowLayout(FlowLayout.RIGHT));
    Button b = new Button("Cancel");
    setButton = new Button("Set");
    p2.add(b);
    p2.add(setButton);
    add("South", p2);

    //Initialize this dialog to its preferred size.
    pack();
}

public boolean action(Event event, Object arg) {
    if ( (event.target == setButton)
       | (event.target == field)) {
        parent.setText(field.getText());
    }
    field.selectAll();
    hide();
    return true;
}
}
```

EXAMPLE: **Label Demo Applet**

Where explained:
How to Use Labels
(page 395)

HTML PAGES CONTAINING APPLET: *http://java.sun.com/Series/Tutorial/ui/ components/label.html*

LabelAlignDemo.java

SOURCE CODE: *http://java.sun.com/Series/Tutorial/ui/components/example/ LabelAlignDemo.java*

```java
import java.awt.*;
import java.applet.Applet;

public class LabelAlignDemo extends Applet {

    public void init() {
        Label label1 = new Label();
        label1.setText("Left");
        Label label2 = new Label("Center");
        label2.setAlignment(Label.CENTER);
        Label label3 = new Label("Right", Label.RIGHT);

        //Add Components to the Applet.
        setLayout(new GridLayout(0, 1));
        add(label1);
        add(label2);
        add(label3);

        validate();
    }
}
```

EXAMPLE: **List Demo Applet**

Where explained:
How to Use Lists
(page 396)

HTML PAGES CONTAINING APPLET: *http://java.sun.com/Series/Tutorial/ui/ components/list.html*

ListDemo.java

SOURCE CODE: *http://java.sun.com/Series/Tutorial/ui/components/example/ ListDemo.java*

```java
import java.awt.*;
import java.applet.Applet;

public class ListDemo extends Applet {
    TextArea output;
    List spanish, italian;

    public void init() {
```

```
//Build first list, which allows multiple selections.
//We prefer 4 items
//visible; true means allow multiple selections.
spanish = new List(4, true);
spanish.addItem("uno");
spanish.addItem("dos");
spanish.addItem("tres");
spanish.addItem("cuatro");
spanish.addItem("cinco");
spanish.addItem("seis");
spanish.addItem("siete");

//Build second list, which allows one selection at a time.
italian = new List(); //Defaults to none visible,
                      //one selectable.
italian.addItem("uno");
italian.addItem("due");
italian.addItem("tre");
italian.addItem("quattro");
italian.addItem("cinque");
italian.addItem("sei");
italian.addItem("sette");

//Add lists to the Applet.
GridBagLayout gridBag = new GridBagLayout();
setLayout(gridBag);

//Can't put text area on right due to GBL bug
//(can't span rows in any column but the first).
output = new TextArea(10, 40);
output.setEditable(false);
GridBagConstraints tc = new GridBagConstraints();
tc.fill = GridBagConstraints.BOTH;
tc.weightx = 1.0;
tc.weighty = 1.0;
tc.gridheight = 2;
gridBag.setConstraints(output, tc);
add(output);

GridBagConstraints lc = new GridBagConstraints();
lc.fill = GridBagConstraints.VERTICAL;
lc.gridwidth = GridBagConstraints.REMAINDER; //end row
gridBag.setConstraints(spanish, lc);
add(spanish);
gridBag.setConstraints(italian, lc);
add(italian);
```

```
                    validate();
            }

        public boolean action(Event e, Object arg) {
            if (e.target instanceof List) {
                String language = (e.target == spanish) ?
                                "Spanish" : "Italian";
                output.appendText("Action event occurred on \""
                                + (String)arg  + "\" in "
                                + language + ".\n");
            }
            return true;
        }

        public boolean handleEvent(Event e) {
            if (e.target instanceof List) {
                List list = (List)(e.target);
                String language = (list == spanish) ?
                                "Spanish" : "Italian";

                switch (e.id) {
                  case Event.LIST_SELECT:
                    int sIndex = ((Integer)e.arg).intValue();
                    output.appendText("Select event occurred on item #"
                                + sIndex + " (\""
                                + list.getItem(sIndex)  + "\") in "
                                + language + ".\n");
                    break;
                  case Event.LIST_DESELECT:
                    int dIndex = ((Integer)e.arg).intValue();
                    output.appendText("Deselect event occurred "
                                + "on item "
                                + dIndex + " (\""
                                + list.getItem(dIndex)  + "\") in "
                                + language + ".\n");
                }
            }
            return super.handleEvent(e);
        }
    }
```

Where explained:

How to Use Menus
(page 399)

EXAMPLE: **Menu Demo Applet/Application**

HTML PAGES CONTAINING APPLET: *http://java.sun.com/Series/Tutorial/ui/ components/menu.html*

This program can run either as an application or, with the help of `AppletButton.java` (page 671), as an applet.

MenuWindow.java

SOURCE CODE: *http://java.sun.com/Series/Tutorial/ui/components/example/ MenuWindow.java*

```java
import java.awt.*;

public class MenuWindow extends Frame {
    boolean inAnApplet = true;
    TextArea output;

    public MenuWindow() {
        MenuBar mb;
        Menu m1, m2, m3, m4, m4_1, m5;
        MenuItem mi1_1, mi1_2, mi3_1, mi3_2, mi3_3, mi3_4,
                 mi4_1_1, mi5_1, mi5_2;
        CheckboxMenuItem mi2_1;

        output = new TextArea(5, 30);
        output.setEditable(false);
        setLayout(new BorderLayout()); //give max space to
                                       //the output
        add("Center", output);

        //Build the menu bar.
        mb = new MenuBar();
        setMenuBar(mb);

        //Build first menu in the menu bar.
        //Specifying the second argument as true
        //makes this a tear-off menu.
        m1 = new Menu("Menu 1", true);
        mb.add(m1);
        mi1_1 = new MenuItem("Menu Item 1_1");
        m1.add(mi1_1);
        mi1_2 = new MenuItem("Menu Item 1_2");
        m1.add(mi1_2);

        //Build help menu.
        m5 = new Menu("Menu 5");
        mb.add(m5); //just setting the help menu doesn't work;
                    //must add it
        mb.setHelpMenu(m5);
        mi5_1 = new MenuItem("Menu Item 5_1");
        m5.add(mi5_1);
        mi5_2 = new MenuItem("Menu Item 5_2");
        m5.add(mi5_2);
```

```
            //Build second menu in the menu bar.
            m2 = new Menu("Menu 2");
            mb.add(m2);
            mi2_1 = new CheckboxMenuItem("Menu Item 2_1");
            m2.add(mi2_1);

            //Build third menu in the menu bar.
            m3 = new Menu("Menu 3");
            mb.add(m3);
            mi3_1 = new MenuItem("Menu Item 3_1");
            m3.add(mi3_1);
            mi3_2 = new MenuItem("Menu Item 3_2");
            m3.add(mi3_2);
            m3.addSeparator();
            mi3_3 = new MenuItem("Menu Item 3_3");
            m3.add(mi3_3);
            mi3_4 = new MenuItem("Menu Item 3_4");
            mi3_4.disable();
            m3.add(mi3_4);

            //Build fourth menu in the menu bar.
            m4 = new Menu("Menu 4");
            mb.add(m4);
            m4_1 = new Menu("Submenu 4_1");
            m4.add(m4_1);
            mi4_1_1 = new MenuItem("Menu Item 4_1_1");
            m4_1.add(mi4_1_1);
        }

        public boolean handleEvent(Event event) {
            if (event.id == Event.WINDOW_DESTROY) {
                if (inAnApplet) {
                    dispose();
                } else {
                    System.exit(0);
                }
            }
            return super.handleEvent(event);
        }

        public boolean action(Event event, Object arg) {
            String str = "Action detected";

            if (event.target instanceof MenuItem) {
                MenuItem mi=(MenuItem)(event.target);
                str += " on " + arg;
                if (mi instanceof CheckboxMenuItem) {
                    str += " (state is "
```

```
                    + ((CheckboxMenuItem)mi).getState()
                    + ")";
            }
            MenuContainer parent = mi.getParent();
            if (parent instanceof Menu) {
                str += " in " + ((Menu)parent).getLabel();
            } else {
                str += " in a container that isn't a Menu";
            }
        }
        str += ".\n";
        output.appendText(str);
        return true;
    }

    public static void main(String[] args) {
        MenuWindow window = new MenuWindow();
        window.inAnApplet = false;

        window.setTitle("MenuWindow Application");
        window.pack();
        window.show();
    }
}
```

EXAMPLE: Scrollbar Demo Applet

HTML PAGES CONTAINING APPLET: *http://java.sun.com/Series/Tutorial/ui/ components/scrollbar.html*

ImageScroller.java

SOURCE CODE: *http://java.sun.com/Series/Tutorial/ui/components/example/ ImageScroller.java*

Where explained:
How to Use Scrollbars (page 404)

```
import java.awt.*;
import java.applet.*;
import java.net.URL;

class ScrollableCanvas extends Canvas {
    Image image;
    int tx = 0;
    int ty = 0;
    Dimension preferredSize;

    ScrollableCanvas(Image img, Dimension prefSize) {
        image = img;
        preferredSize = prefSize;
    }
```

```java
        public Dimension minimumSize() {
            return new Dimension(10, 10);
        }

        public Dimension preferredSize() {
            return preferredSize;
        }

        public void paint(Graphics g) {
            g.translate(-tx, -ty);
            g.drawImage(image, 0, 0, getBackground(), this);
        }
    }

    public class ImageScroller extends Applet {
        Scrollbar vert;
        Scrollbar horz;
        ScrollableCanvas canvas;
        boolean inAnApplet = true;
        String imageFile = "../images/people.gif";
        Dimension imageSize = new Dimension(600, 320);
        Dimension preferredImageSize = new Dimension(300, 100);

        //This method assumes this Applet is visible.
        public void init() {
            Image img;

            if (inAnApplet) {
                img = getImage(getCodeBase(), imageFile);
            } else {
              img = Toolkit.getDefaultToolkit().getImage(
                    imageFile);
            }
            canvas = new ScrollableCanvas(img, preferredImageSize);

            //Create horizontal scrollbar.
            horz = new Scrollbar(Scrollbar.HORIZONTAL);

            //Create vertical scrollbar.
            vert = new Scrollbar(Scrollbar.VERTICAL);

            //Add Components to the Applet.
            setLayout(new BorderLayout());
            add("Center", canvas);
            add("East", vert);
            add("South", horz);
```

```
        validate();

        //Now that we've validated, then assuming this Applet is
        //visible, the canvas size is valid and we can adjust the
        //scrollbars to match the image area.
        resizeHorz();
        resizeVert();
    }

    public boolean handleEvent(Event evt) {
        switch (evt.id) {
          case Event.SCROLL_LINE_UP:
          case Event.SCROLL_LINE_DOWN:
          case Event.SCROLL_PAGE_UP:
          case Event.SCROLL_PAGE_DOWN:
          case Event.SCROLL_ABSOLUTE:
            if (evt.target == vert) {
                canvas.ty = ((Integer)evt.arg).intValue();
                canvas.repaint();
            }
            if (evt.target == horz) {
                canvas.tx = ((Integer)evt.arg).intValue();
                canvas.repaint();
            }
        }
        return super.handleEvent(evt);
    }

    //Don't call this until the canvas size is valid.
    void resizeHorz() {
        int canvasWidth = canvas.size().width;

        if (canvasWidth <= 0) {
            System.out.println("Canvas has no width; "
                                + "can't resize scrollbar");
            return;
        }

        //Shift everything to the right if we're displaying
        //empty space on the right side.
        if ((canvas.tx + canvasWidth) > imageSize.width) {
            int newtx = imageSize.width - canvasWidth;
            if (newtx < 0) {
                newtx = 0;
            }
            canvas.tx = newtx;
        }
```

```
            horz.setValues(//draw the part of the image that
                            //starts at this x:
                            canvas.tx,
                            //amount to scroll for a "page":
                            (int)(canvasWidth * 0.9),
                            //minimum image x to specify:
                            0,
                            //maximum image x to specify:
                            imageSize.width - canvasWidth);
        //"visible" arg to setValues has no effect after
        //scrollbar is visible.
        horz.setPageIncrement((int)(canvasWidth * 0.9));
        return;
    }

    //Don't call this until the canvas size is valid.
    void resizeVert() {
        int canvasHeight = canvas.size().height;

        if (canvasHeight <= 0) {
            System.out.println("Canvas has no height; "
                                + "can't resize scrollbar");
            return;
        }

        //Shift everything downward if we're displaying
        //empty space on the bottom.
        if ((canvas.ty + canvasHeight) > imageSize.height) {
            int newty = imageSize.height - canvasHeight;
            if (newty < 0) {
                newty = 0;
            }
            canvas.ty = newty;
        }

        vert.setValues(//initially draw part of image
                       //starting at this y:
                       canvas.ty,
                       //visible arg--amount to scroll for a "page":
                       (int)(canvasHeight * 0.9),
                       //minimum image y to specify:
                       0,
                       //maximum image y to specify:
                       imageSize.height - canvasHeight);

        //"visible" arg to setValues has no effect after
        //scrollbar is visible.
```

```
        vert.setPageIncrement((int)(canvasHeight * 0.9));
        return;
    }

    public void paint(Graphics g) {
        //This method probably was called
        //due to applet being resized.
        resizeHorz();
        resizeVert();

        return;
    }
}
```

EXAMPLE: Text Demo Applet

HTML PAGES CONTAINING APPLET: *http://java.sun.com/Series/Tutorial/ui/components/text.html*

TextDemo.java

SOURCE CODE: *http://java.sun.com/Series/Tutorial/ui/components/example/TextDemo.java*

Where explained: *How to Use Text Areas and Fields* (page 407)

```
import java.awt.*;
import java.applet.Applet;

public class TextDemo extends Applet {
    TextField textField;
    TextArea textArea;

    public void init() {
        textField = new TextField(20);
        textArea = new TextArea(5, 20);
        textArea.setEditable(false);

        //Add Components to the Applet.
        GridBagLayout gridBag = new GridBagLayout();
        setLayout(gridBag);
        GridBagConstraints c = new GridBagConstraints();
        c.gridwidth = GridBagConstraints.REMAINDER;

        c.fill = GridBagConstraints.HORIZONTAL;
        gridBag.setConstraints(textField, c);
        add(textField);

        c.fill = GridBagConstraints.BOTH;
        c.weightx = 1.0;
        c.weighty = 1.0;
```

```
                        gridBag.setConstraints(textArea, c);
                        add(textArea);

                        validate();
                    }

            public boolean action(Event evt, Object arg) {
                    String text = textField.getText();
                    textArea.appendText(text + "\n");
                    textField.selectAll();
                    return true;
                }
            }
```

LESSON 19: Laying Out Components Within a Container

EXAMPLE: BorderLayout Applet/Application

Where explained:

How to Use Border- Layout (page 419)

HTML PAGES CONTAINING APPLET: *http://java.sun.com/Series/Tutorial/ui/layout/ using.html, http://java.sun.com/Series/Tutorial/ui/layout/border.html*

This program can run either as an application or, with the help of `AppletButton.java` (page 671), as an applet.

BorderWindow.java

SOURCE CODE: *http://java.sun.com/Series/Tutorial/ui/layout/example/ BorderWindow.java*

```java
import java.awt.*;

public class BorderWindow extends Frame {
    private boolean inAnApplet = true;

    public BorderWindow() {
        setLayout(new BorderLayout());
        setFont(new Font("Helvetica", Font.PLAIN, 14));

        add("North", new Button("North"));
        add("South", new Button("South"));
        add("East", new Button("East"));
        add("West", new Button("West"));
        add("Center", new Button("Center"));
    }
```

```
    public boolean handleEvent(Event e) {
        if (e.id == Event.WINDOW_DESTROY) {
            if (inAnApplet) {
                dispose();
                return true;
            } else {
                System.exit(0);
            }
        }
        return super.handleEvent(e);
    }

    public static void main(String args[]) {
        BorderWindow window = new BorderWindow();
        window.inAnApplet = false;

        window.setTitle("BorderWindow Application");
        window.pack();
        window.show();
    }
}
```

EXAMPLE: CardLayout Applet/Application

HTML PAGES CONTAINING APPLET: *http://java.sun.com/Series/Tutorial/ui/layout/ using.html, http://java.sun.com/Series/Tutorial/ui/layout/card.html*

This program can run either as an application or, with the help of `AppletButton.java` (page 671), as an applet.

CardWindow.java

SOURCE CODE: *http://java.sun.com/Series/Tutorial/ui/layout/example/ CardWindow.java*

```
import java.awt.*;

public class CardWindow extends Frame {
    private boolean inAnApplet = true;

    Panel cards;
    final static String BUTTONPANEL = "Panel with Buttons";
    final static String TEXTPANEL = "Panel with TextField";

    public CardWindow() {
        setLayout(new BorderLayout());
        setFont(new Font("Helvetica", Font.PLAIN, 14));

        //Put the Choice in a Panel to get a nicer look.
```

Where explained:

How to use `CardLayout` (page 420)

```
                Panel cp = new Panel();
                Choice c = new Choice();
                c.addItem(BUTTONPANEL);
                c.addItem(TEXTPANEL);
                cp.add(c);
                add("North", cp);

                cards = new Panel();
                cards.setLayout(new CardLayout());

                Panel p1 = new Panel();
                p1.add(new Button("Button 1"));
                p1.add(new Button("Button 2"));
                p1.add(new Button("Button 3"));

                Panel p2 = new Panel();
                p2.add(new TextField("TextField", 20));

                cards.add(BUTTONPANEL, p1);
                cards.add(TEXTPANEL, p2);
                add("Center", cards);
            }

            public boolean action(Event evt, Object arg) {
                if (evt.target instanceof Choice) {

                    ((CardLayout)cards.getLayout()).show(
                            cards,(String)arg); return true;
                }
                return false;
            }

            public boolean handleEvent(Event e) {
                if (e.id == Event.WINDOW_DESTROY) {
                    if (inAnApplet) {
                        dispose();
                        return true;
                    } else {
                        System.exit(0);
                    }
                }
                return super.handleEvent(e);
            }

            public static void main(String args[]) {
                CardWindow window = new CardWindow();
                window.inAnApplet = false;
```

```
            window.setTitle("CardWindow Application");
            window.pack();
            window.show();
        }
    }
```

EXAMPLE: FlowLayout Applet/Application

HTML PAGES CONTAINING APPLET: *http://java.sun.com/Series/Tutorial/ui/layout/*
using.html, http://java.sun.com/Series/Tutorial/ui/layout/flow.html

This program can run either as an application or, with the help of `AppletButton.java` (page 671), as an applet.

FlowWindow.java

SOURCE CODE: *http://java.sun.com/Series/Tutorial/ui/layout/example/*
FlowWindow.java

Where explained:
How to Use FlowLayout (page 422)

```java
import java.awt.*;

public class FlowWindow extends Frame {
    private boolean inAnApplet = true;

    public FlowWindow() {
        setLayout(new FlowLayout());
        setFont(new Font("Helvetica", Font.PLAIN, 14));

        add(new Button("Button 1"));
        add(new Button("2"));
        add(new Button("Button 3"));
        add(new Button("Long-Named Button 4"));
        add(new Button("Button 5"));
    }

    public boolean handleEvent(Event e) {
        if (e.id == Event.WINDOW_DESTROY) {
            if (inAnApplet) {
                dispose();
                return true;
            } else {
                System.exit(0);
            }
        }
        return super.handleEvent(e);
    }

    public static void main(String args[]) {
        FlowWindow window = new FlowWindow();
```

```
                    window.inAnApplet = false;

                    window.setTitle("FlowWindow Application");
                    window.pack();
                    window.show();
                }
            }
```

**Where
explained:**
*How to Use
GridLay-
out*
(page 423)

EXAMPLE: **GridLayout Applet/Application**

HTML PAGES CONTAINING APPLET: *http://java.sun.com/Series/Tutorial/ui/layout/
using.html, http://java.sun.com/Series/Tutorial/ui/layout/grid.html*

This program can run either as an application or, with the help of `AppletBut-
ton.java` (page 671), as an applet.

GridWindow.java

SOURCE CODE: *http://java.sun.com/Series/Tutorial/ui/layout/example/
GridWindow.java*

```java
import java.awt.*;

public class GridWindow extends Frame {
    private boolean inAnApplet = true;

    public GridWindow() {
        setLayout(new GridLayout(0,2));
        setFont(new Font("Helvetica", Font.PLAIN, 14));

        add(new Button("Button 1"));
        add(new Button("2"));
        add(new Button("Button 3"));
        add(new Button("Long-Named Button 4"));
        add(new Button("Button 5"));
    }

    public boolean handleEvent(Event e) {
        if (e.id == Event.WINDOW_DESTROY) {
            if (inAnApplet) {
                dispose();
                return true;
            } else {
                System.exit(0);
            }
        }
        return super.handleEvent(e);
    }
```

```
    public static void main(String args[]) {
        GridWindow window = new GridWindow();
        window.inAnApplet = false;

        window.setTitle("GridWindow Application");
        window.pack();
        window.show();
    }
}
```

EXAMPLE: GridBagLayout Applet/Application

HTML PAGES CONTAINING APPLET: *http://java.sun.com/Series/Tutorial/ui/layout/ using.html, http://java.sun.com/Series/Tutorial/ui/layout/gridbag.html*

This program can run either as an application or, with the help of `AppletButton.java` (page 671), as an applet.

GridBagWindow.java

SOURCE CODE: *http://java.sun.com/Series/Tutorial/ui/layout/example/ GridBagWindow.java*

```
import java.awt.*;

public class GridBagWindow extends Frame {
    private boolean inAnApplet = true;

    protected void makebutton(String name,
                              GridBagLayout gridbag,
                              GridBagConstraints c) {
        Button button = new Button(name);
        gridbag.setConstraints(button, c);
        add(button);
    }

    public GridBagWindow() {
        GridBagLayout gridbag = new GridBagLayout();
        GridBagConstraints c = new GridBagConstraints();

        setFont(new Font("Helvetica", Font.PLAIN, 14));
        setLayout(gridbag);

        c.fill = GridBagConstraints.BOTH;
        c.weightx = 1.0;
        makebutton("Button1", gridbag, c);
        makebutton("Button2", gridbag, c);
        makebutton("Button3", gridbag, c);
```

Where explained:
The GridBag-Layout Applet Example Explained (page 428)

```
            c.gridwidth = GridBagConstraints.REMAINDER; //end of row
            makebutton("Button4", gridbag, c);

            c.weightx = 0.0;                      //reset to the default
            makebutton("Button5", gridbag, c); //another row

            c.gridwidth = GridBagConstraints.RELATIVE; //next-to-
                                                       //last in row
            makebutton("Button6", gridbag, c);

            c.gridwidth = GridBagConstraints.REMAINDER; //end of row
            makebutton("Button7", gridbag, c);

            c.gridwidth = 1;                          //reset to the default
            c.gridheight = 2;
            c.weighty = 1.0;
            makebutton("Button8", gridbag, c);

            c.weighty = 0.0;                          //reset to the default
            c.gridwidth = GridBagConstraints.REMAINDER; //end of row
            c.gridheight = 1;                         //reset to the default
            makebutton("Button9", gridbag, c);
            makebutton("Button10", gridbag, c);
        }

        public boolean handleEvent(Event e) {
            if (e.id == Event.WINDOW_DESTROY) {
                if (inAnApplet) {
                    dispose();
                    return true;
                } else {
                    System.exit(0);
                }
            }
            return super.handleEvent(e);
        }

        public static void main(String args[]) {
            GridBagWindow window = new GridBagWindow();
            window.inAnApplet = false;

            window.setTitle("GridBagWindow Application");
            window.pack();
            window.show();
        }
    }
```

EXAMPLE: **Custom Layout Manager Applet/Application**

HTML PAGES CONTAINING APPLET: *http://java.sun.com/Series/Tutorial/ui/layout/ gridbag.html*

This program can run either as an application or, with the help of `AppletButton.java` (page 671), as an applet. `DiagonalLayout.java` implements a layout manager. `CustomWindow.java` (page 713) uses `DiagonalLayout` as a layout manager.

Where explained: *Creating a Custom Layout Manager* (page 431)

DiagonalLayout.java

SOURCE CODE: *http://java.sun.com/Series/Tutorial/ui/layout/example/ DiagonalLayout.java*

```java
import java.awt.*;
import java.util.Vector;

public class DiagonalLayout implements LayoutManager {

    private int vgap;
    private int minWidth = 0, minHeight = 0;
    private int preferredWidth = 0, preferredHeight = 0;
    private boolean sizeUnknown = true;

    public DiagonalLayout() {
        this(5);
    }

    public DiagonalLayout(int v) {
        vgap = v;
    }

    /* Required by LayoutManager. */
    public void addLayoutComponent(
            String name, Component comp) {
    }

    /* Required by LayoutManager. */
    public void removeLayoutComponent(Component comp) {
    }

    private void setSizes(Container parent) {
        int nComps = parent.countComponents();
        Dimension d = null;

        //Reset preferred/minimum width and height.
        preferredWidth = 0;
        preferredHeight = 0;
        minWidth = 0;
```

```
                minHeight = 0;

        for (int i = 0; i < nComps; i++) {
                Component c = parent.getComponent(i);
                if (c.isVisible()) {
                        d = c.preferredSize();

                        if (i > 0) {
                                preferredWidth += d.width/2;
                                preferredHeight += vgap;
                        } else {
                                preferredWidth = d.width;
                        }
                        preferredHeight += d.height;

                        minWidth = Math.max(
                            c.minimumSize().width, minWidth);
                        minHeight = preferredHeight;
                }
        }
}


/* Required by LayoutManager. */
public Dimension preferredLayoutSize(Container parent) {
        Dimension dim = new Dimension(0, 0);
        int nComps = parent.countComponents();

        setSizes(parent);

        //Always add the container's insets!
        Insets insets = parent.insets();
        dim.width = preferredWidth + insets.left + insets.right;
        dim.height = preferredHeight + insets.top +
                        insets.bottom;

        sizeUnknown = false;

        return dim;
}

/* Required by LayoutManager. */
public Dimension minimumLayoutSize(Container parent) {
        Dimension dim = new Dimension(0, 0);
        int nComps = parent.countComponents();

        //Always add the container's insets!
        Insets insets = parent.insets();
```

```
      dim.width = minWidth + insets.left + insets.right;
      dim.height = minHeight + insets.top + insets.bottom;

      sizeUnknown = false;

      return dim;
   }

   /* Required by LayoutManager. */
   /* This is called when the panel is first displayed,
    * and every time its size changes.
    * Note: You CAN'T assume preferredLayoutSize or
    * minimumLayoutSize will be called -- in the case of
    * applets, at least, they probably won't be.
    */
   public void layoutContainer(Container parent) {
      Insets insets = parent.insets();
      int maxWidth = parent.size().width
                        - (insets.left + insets.right);
      int maxHeight = parent.size().height
                        - (insets.top + insets.bottom);
      int nComps = parent.countComponents();
      int previousWidth = 0, previousHeight = 0;
      int x = 0, y = insets.top;
      int rowh = 0, start = 0;
      int xFudge = 0, yFudge = 0;
      boolean oneColumn = false;

      // Go through the components' sizes, if neither
      // preferredLayoutSize nor minimumLayoutSize
      // has been called.
      if (sizeUnknown) {
          setSizes(parent);
      }

      if (maxWidth <= minWidth) {
          oneColumn = true;
      }

      if (maxWidth != preferredWidth) {
          xFudge = (maxWidth - preferredWidth)/(nComps - 1);
      }

      if (maxHeight > preferredHeight) {
          yFudge = (maxHeight - preferredHeight)/(nComps - 1);
      }

      for (int i = 0 ; i < nComps ; i++) {
          Component c = parent.getComponent(i);
```

```
                      if (c.isVisible()) {
                          Dimension d = c.preferredSize();

                           // increase x and y, if appropriate
                          if (i > 0) {
                              if (!oneColumn) {
                                      //x += previousWidth - d.width/2 + xFudge;
                                  x += previousWidth/2 + xFudge;
                              }
                              y += previousHeight + vgap + yFudge;
                          }

                          // If x is too large, ...
                          if ((!oneColumn) &&
                              (x + d.width) > (parent.size().width -
                                              insets.right)) {
                              // ... reduce x to a reasonable number.
                              x = parent.size().width -
                                  insets.bottom - d.width;
                          }

                          // If y is too large, ...
                          if ((y + d.height) >
                              (parent.size().height - insets.bottom)){
                              // ... do nothing.
                              // Another choice would be to do what we do to x.
                          }

                          // Set the component's size and position.
                          c.reshape(x, y, d.width, d.height);

                          previousWidth = d.width;
                          previousHeight = d.height;
                      }
                  }
              }

          public String toString() {
              String str = "";
              return getClass().getName() + "[vgap=" + vgap + str + "]";
          }
      }
```

CustomWindow.java

SOURCE CODE: *http://java.sun.com/Series/Tutorial/ui/layout/example/*
CustomWindow.java

```java
import java.awt.*;

public class CustomWindow extends Frame {
    private boolean inAnApplet = true;

    public CustomWindow() {
        setLayout(new DiagonalLayout());
        setFont(new Font("Helvetica", Font.PLAIN, 14));

        add(new Button("Button 1"));
        add(new Button("Button 2"));
        add(new Button("Button 3"));
        add(new Button("Button 4"));
        add(new Button("Button 5"));
    }

    public boolean handleEvent(Event e) {
        if (e.id == Event.WINDOW_DESTROY) {
            if (inAnApplet) {
                dispose();
                return true;
            } else {
                System.exit(0);
            }
        }
        return super.handleEvent(e);
    }

    public static void main(String args[]) {
        CustomWindow window = new CustomWindow();
        window.inAnApplet = false;

        window.setTitle("CustomWindow Application");
        window.pack();
        window.show();
    }
}
```

Where explained:

Laying Out Components Without a Layout Manager (Absolute Positioning)
(page 433)

EXAMPLE: Absolute Positioning Applet/Application

HTML PAGES CONTAINING APPLET: *http://java.sun.com/Series/Tutorial/ui/layout/none.html*

This program can run either as an application or, with the help of `AppletButton.java` (page 671), as an applet.

NoneWindow.java

SOURCE CODE: *http://java.sun.com/Series/Tutorial/ui/layout/example/NoneWindow.java*

```java
import java.awt.*;

public class NoneWindow extends Frame {
    private boolean inAnApplet = true;
    private boolean laidOut = false;
    private Button b1, b2, b3;

    public NoneWindow() {
        super();
        setLayout(null);
        setFont(new Font("Helvetica", Font.PLAIN, 14));

        b1 = new Button("one");
        add(b1);
        b2 = new Button("two");
        add(b2);
        b3 = new Button("three");
        add(b3);
    }

    public void paint(Graphics g) {
        if (!laidOut) {
            Insets insets = insets();
            /*
             * We're guaranteed that insets() will return a valid
             * Insets if called from paint() -- it isn't valid
             * when called from the constructor.
             *
             * We could perhaps cache this in an ivar, but
             * insets can change, and when they do, the AWT
             * creates a whole new Insets object; the old
             * one is invalid.
             */
            b1.reshape(50 + insets.left, 5 + insets.top, 50, 20);
            b2.reshape(70 + insets.left, 35 + insets.top, 50, 20);
```

```
        b3.reshape(130 + insets.left, 15 + insets.top, 50,
                  30);

        laidOut = true;
    }
}

public boolean handleEvent(Event e) {
    if (e.id == Event.WINDOW_DESTROY) {
        if (inAnApplet) {
            dispose();
            return false;
        } else {
            System.exit(0);
        }
    }
    return super.handleEvent(e);
}

public static void main(String args[]) {
    NoneWindow window = new NoneWindow();
    Insets insets = window.insets();
    //How do we know insets is valid here?
    window.inAnApplet = false;

    window.setTitle("NoneWindow Application");
    window.resize(250 + insets.left + insets.right,
                  90 + insets.top + insets.bottom);
    window.show();
}
}
```

LESSON 20: **Working with Graphics**

EXAMPLE: Coordinates Demo Applet

HTML PAGES CONTAINING APPLET: *http://java.sun.com/Series/Tutorial/ui/drawing/ overview.html, http://java.sun.com/Series/Tutorial/ui/drawing/ drawingShapes.html*

When you click the mouse in this applet's display area, the applet displays the coordinates that the click occurred at.

Where explained:

Drawing Shapes (page 440)

CoordinatesDemo.java

SOURCE CODE: *http://java.sun.com/Series/Tutorial/ui/drawing/example/*
        CoordinatesDemo.java

```java
import java.awt.*;
import java.applet.Applet;

/*
 * This displays a framed area.  When the user clicks within
 * the area, this program displays a dot and a string indicating
 * the coordinates where the click occurred.
 */

public class CoordinatesDemo extends Applet {
    FramedArea framedArea;
    Label label;

    public void init() {
        GridBagLayout gridBag = new GridBagLayout();
        GridBagConstraints c = new GridBagConstraints();

        setLayout(gridBag);

        framedArea = new FramedArea(this);
        c.fill = GridBagConstraints.BOTH;
        c.weighty = 1.0;
        c.gridwidth = GridBagConstraints.REMAINDER; //end row
        gridBag.setConstraints(framedArea, c);
        add(framedArea);

        label = new Label("Click within the framed area.");
        c.fill = GridBagConstraints.HORIZONTAL;
        c.weightx = 1.0;
        c.weighty = 0.0;
        gridBag.setConstraints(label, c);
        add(label);

        validate();
    }

    public void coordsChanged(Point point) {
        label.setText("Click occurred at coordinate ("
                    + point.x + ", " + point.y + ").");
        repaint();
    }
}
```

```
/* This class exists solely to put a frame around
 *the coordinate area.
 */
class FramedArea extends Panel {
    public FramedArea(CoordinatesDemo controller) {
        super();

        //Set layout to one that makes its contents
        //as big as possible.
        setLayout(new GridLayout(1,0));

        add(new CoordinateArea(controller));
        validate();
    }
    //Ensure that no Component is placed on top of the frame.
    //The inset values were determined by trial and error.
    public Insets insets() {
        return new Insets(4,4,5,5);
    }
    //Draw the frame at this Panel's edges.
    public void paint(Graphics g) {
        Dimension d = size();
        Color bg = getBackground();

        g.setColor(bg);
        g.draw3DRect(0, 0, d.width - 1, d.height - 1, true);
        g.draw3DRect(3, 3, d.width - 7, d.height - 7, false);
    }
}

class CoordinateArea extends Canvas {
    Point point = null;
    CoordinatesDemo controller;

    public CoordinateArea(CoordinatesDemo controller) {
        super();
        this.controller = controller;
    }

    public boolean mouseDown(Event event, int x, int y) {
        if (point == null) {
            point = new Point(x, y);
        } else {
            point.x = x;
            point.y = y;
        }
        controller.coordsChanged(point);
        repaint();

        return false;
```

```
        }
    public void paint(Graphics g) {
        //If user has chosen a point,
        //paint a tiny rectangle on top.
        if (point != null) {
            g.fillRect(point.x - 1, point.y - 1, 2, 2);
        }
    }
}
```

EXAMPLE: **Rectangle Demo Applet**

HTML PAGES CONTAINING APPLET: *http://java.sun.com/Series/Tutorial/ui/drawing/ drawingShapes.html*

RectangleDemo.java

SOURCE CODE: *http://java.sun.com/Series/Tutorial/ui/drawing/example/ RectangleDemo.java*

```
import java.awt.*;
import java.applet.Applet;

/*
 * This displays a framed area.  When the user drags within
 * the area, this program displays a rectangle extending from
 * where the user first pressed the mouse button to the
 * current cursor location.
 */

public class RectangleDemo extends Applet {
    RFramedArea framedArea;
    Label label;

    public void init() {
        GridBagLayout gridBag = new GridBagLayout();
        GridBagConstraints c = new GridBagConstraints();

        setLayout(gridBag);

        framedArea = new RFramedArea(this);
        c.fill = GridBagConstraints.BOTH;
        c.weighty = 1.0;
        c.gridwidth = GridBagConstraints.REMAINDER; //end row
        gridBag.setConstraints(framedArea, c);
        add(framedArea);

        label = new Label("Drag within the framed area.");
```

Where explained:
Drawing Shapes
(page 440)

```
            c.fill = GridBagConstraints.HORIZONTAL;
            c.weightx = 1.0;
            c.weighty = 0.0;
            gridBag.setConstraints(label, c);
            add(label);

            validate();
        }

    public void rectChanged(Rectangle rect) {
        label.setText("Rectangle goes from ("
                    + rect.x + ", " + rect.y + ") to ("
                    + (rect.x + rect.width - 1) + ", "
                    + (rect.y + rect.height - 1) + ").");
        repaint();
        }
    }

/* This class exists solely to put a frame around
 *the coordinate area.
 */
class RFramedArea extends Panel {
    public RFramedArea(RectangleDemo controller) {
        super();

        //Set layout to one that makes its
        //contents as big as possible.
        setLayout(new GridLayout(1,0));

        add(new SelectionArea(controller));
        validate();
    }
    //Ensure that no Component is placed on top of the frame.
    //The inset values were determined by trial and error.
    public Insets insets() {
        return new Insets(4,4,5,5);
    }

    //Draw the frame at this Panel's edges.
    public void paint(Graphics g) {
        Dimension d = size();
        Color bg = getBackground();

        g.setColor(bg);
        g.draw3DRect(0, 0, d.width - 1, d.height - 1, true);
        g.draw3DRect(3, 3, d.width - 7, d.height - 7, false);
    }
}
```

```
class SelectionArea extends Canvas {
    Rectangle currentRect;
    RectangleDemo controller;

    public SelectionArea(RectangleDemo controller) {
        super();
        this.controller = controller;
    }

    public boolean mouseDown(Event event, int x, int y) {
        currentRect = new Rectangle(x, y, 0, 0);
        repaint();
        return false;
    }

    public boolean mouseDrag(Event event, int x, int y) {
        currentRect.resize(x - currentRect.x, y - currentRect.y);
        repaint();
        return false;
    }

    public boolean mouseUp(Event event, int x, int y) {
        currentRect.resize(x - currentRect.x, y - currentRect.y);
        repaint();
        return false;
    }

    public void paint(Graphics g) {
        Dimension d = size();

        //Update has already cleared the previous rectangle,
        //so we don't need to here.

        //If currentRect exists, paint a rectangle on top.
        if (currentRect != null) {
            Rectangle box = getDrawableRect(currentRect, d);
            controller.rectChanged(box);

            //Draw the box outline.
            g.drawRect(box.x, box.y, box.width - 1, box.height
                    - 1);
        }
    }

    Rectangle getDrawableRect(Rectangle originalRect,
                              Dimension drawingArea) {
        int x = originalRect.x;
        int y = originalRect.y;
```

```
            int width = originalRect.width;
            int height = originalRect.height;

            //Make sure rectangle width and height are positive.
            if (width < 0) {
                width = 0 - width;
                x = x - width + 1;
                if (x < 0) {
                    width += x;
                    x = 0;
                }
            }
            if (height < 0) {
                height = 0 - height;
                y = y - height + 1;
                if (y < 0) {
                    height += y;
                    y = 0;
                }
            }

            //The rectangle shouldn't extend past the drawing area.
            if ((x + width) > drawingArea.width) {
                width = drawingArea.width - x;
            }
            if ((y + height) > drawingArea.height) {
                height = drawingArea.height - y;
            }

            return new Rectangle(x, y, width, height);
        }
    }
```

EXAMPLE: Shape-Drawing Applet

HTML PAGES CONTAINING APPLET: *http://java.sun.com/Series/Tutorial/ui/drawing/ drawingShapes.html*

ShapesDemo.java

SOURCE CODE: *http://java.sun.com/Series/Tutorial/ui/drawing/example/ ShapesDemo.java*

```
    import java.awt.*;
    import java.applet.Applet;

    /*
     * This displays a framed area containing one of each shape you
     * can draw.
```

Where explained:
Drawing Shapes
(page 440)

```
*/

public class ShapesDemo extends Applet {
    final static int maxCharHeight = 15;

    public void init() {
        validate();
    }

    public void paint(Graphics g) {
        Dimension d = size();
        int x = 5;
        int y = 7;

        Color bg = getBackground();
        Color fg = getForeground();

        int gridWidth = d.width / 7;
        int gridHeight = d.height / 2;
        int stringY = gridHeight - 7;
        int rectWidth = gridWidth - 2*x;
        int rectHeight = stringY - maxCharHeight - y;

        g.setColor(bg);
        g.draw3DRect(0, 0, d.width - 1, d.height - 1, true);
        g.draw3DRect(3, 3, d.width - 7, d.height - 7, false);
        g.setColor(fg);

        // drawLine(x1, y1, x2, y2)
        g.drawLine(x, y+rectHeight-1, x + rectWidth, y);
        g.drawString("drawLine()", x, stringY);
        x += gridWidth;

        // drawRect(x, y, width, height)
        g.drawRect(x, y, rectWidth, rectHeight);
        g.drawString("drawRect()", x, stringY);
        x += gridWidth;

        // draw3DRect(x, y, width, height, raised)
        g.setColor(bg);
        g.draw3DRect(x, y, rectWidth, rectHeight, true);
        g.setColor(fg);
        g.drawString("draw3DRect()", x, stringY);
        x += gridWidth;

        // drawRoundRect(x, y, width, height, arcw, arch)
        g.drawRoundRect(x, y, rectWidth, rectHeight, 10, 10);
```

```
g.drawString("drawRoundRect()", x, stringY);
x += gridWidth;

//drawOval(x, y, w, h)
g.drawOval(x, y, rectWidth, rectHeight);
g.drawString("drawOval()", x, stringY);
x += gridWidth;

//drawArc(x, y, w, h)
g.drawArc(x, y, rectWidth, rectHeight, 90, 135);
g.drawString("drawArc()", x, stringY);
x += gridWidth;

//drawPolygon(polygon)
Polygon polygon = new Polygon();
polygon.addPoint(x, y);
polygon.addPoint(x+rectWidth, y+rectHeight);
polygon.addPoint(x, y+rectHeight);
polygon.addPoint(x+rectWidth, y);
//polygon.addPoint(x, y); //don't complete;
                            //fill will, draw won't
g.drawPolygon(polygon);
g.drawString("drawPolygon()", x, stringY);

x = 5 + gridWidth;
y += gridHeight;
stringY += gridHeight;

// fillRect(x, y, width, height)
g.fillRect(x, y, rectWidth, rectHeight);
g.drawString("fillRect()", x, stringY);
x += gridWidth;

// fill3DRect(x, y, width, height, raised)
g.setColor(bg);
g.fill3DRect(x, y, rectWidth, rectHeight, true);
g.setColor(fg);
g.drawString("fill3DRect()", x, stringY);
x += gridWidth;

// fillRoundRect(x, y, width, height, arcw, arch)
g.fillRoundRect(x, y, rectWidth, rectHeight, 10, 10);
g.drawString("fillRoundRect()", x, stringY);
x += gridWidth;

// fillOval(x, y, w, h)
g.fillOval(x, y, rectWidth, rectHeight);
g.drawString("fillOval()", x, stringY);
```

```
        x += gridWidth;

        // fillArc(x, y, w, h)
        g.fillArc(x, y, rectWidth, rectHeight, 90, 135);
        g.drawString("fillArc()", x, stringY);
        x += gridWidth;

        // fillPolygon(polygon)
        Polygon filledPolygon = new Polygon();
        filledPolygon.addPoint(x, y);
        filledPolygon.addPoint(x+rectWidth, y+rectHeight);
        filledPolygon.addPoint(x, y+rectHeight);
        filledPolygon.addPoint(x+rectWidth, y);
        //filledPolygon.addPoint(x, y);
        g.fillPolygon(filledPolygon);
        g.drawString("fillPolygon()", x, stringY);
    }
}
```

Where explained:
Working with Text (page 445)

EXAMPLE: Simple Text-Drawing Applet

HTML PAGES CONTAINING APPLET: *http://java.sun.com/Series/Tutorial/ui/drawing/ drawingText.html*

TextXY.java

SOURCE CODE: *http://java.sun.com/Series/Tutorial/ui/drawing/example/ TextXY.java*

```
import java.awt.*;
import java.applet.Applet;

/*
 * Very simple applet that illustrates parameters to
 * text-drawing methods.
 */

public class TextXY extends Applet {

    public void init() {
        validate();
    }

    public void paint(Graphics g) {
        Dimension d = size();

        g.drawString("drawString() at (2, 5)", 2, 5);
```

```
        g.drawString("drawString() at (2, 30)", 2, 30);
        g.drawString("drawString() at (2, height)", 2, d.height);
    }
}
```

EXAMPLE: **Shapes Demo with Font Manipulation**

HTML PAGES CONTAINING APPLET: *http://java.sun.com/Series/Tutorial/ui/drawing/ drawingText.html*

This enhanced version of <u>ShapesDemo.java</u> (page 721) adjusts its fonts so that they fit within the allotted space.

FontDemo.java

SOURCE CODE: *http://java.sun.com/Series/Tutorial/ui/drawing/example/ FontDemo.java*

Where explained: *Working with Text* (page 445)

```java
import java.awt.*;
import java.applet.Applet;

/*
 * This is like the ShapesDemo applet, except that it
 * handles fonts more carefully.
 */

public class FontDemo extends Applet {
    final static int maxCharHeight = 15;

    public void init() {
        validate();
    }

    public void paint(Graphics g) {
        Dimension d = size();
        int x = 5;
        int y = 7;

        Color bg = getBackground();
        Color fg = getForeground();

        int gridWidth = d.width / 7;
        int gridHeight = d.height / 2;
        int stringY;
        int rectWidth = gridWidth - 2*x;
        int rectHeight;

        boolean fontFits = false;
        Font font = g.getFont();
```

```
                FontMetrics fontMetrics = g.getFontMetrics();
                while (!fontFits) {
                    if ((fontMetrics.getHeight() <= maxCharHeight)
                        && (fontMetrics.stringWidth("drawRoundRect()")
                            <= gridWidth)) {
                        fontFits = true;
                    } else {
                    //At first, accidentally left out "g.", which worked
                    //but fontMetrics never changed.
                        g.setFont(font = new Font(font.getName(),
                                                  font.getStyle(),
                                                  font.getSize() - 1));
                        fontMetrics = g.getFontMetrics();
                    }
                }

                stringY = gridHeight - 5 - fontMetrics.getDescent();
                rectHeight = stringY - fontMetrics.getMaxAscent() - y - 2;

                g.setColor(bg);
                g.draw3DRect(0, 0, d.width - 1, d.height - 1, true);
                g.draw3DRect(3, 3, d.width - 7, d.height - 7, false);
                g.setColor(fg);

                // drawLine(x1, y1, x2, y2)
                g.drawLine(x, y+rectHeight-1, x + rectWidth, y);
                g.drawString("drawLine()", x, stringY);
                x += gridWidth;

                // drawRect(x, y, width, height)
                g.drawRect(x, y, rectWidth, rectHeight);
                g.drawString("drawRect()", x, stringY);
                x += gridWidth;

                // draw3DRect(x, y, width, height, raised)
                g.setColor(bg);
                g.draw3DRect(x, y, rectWidth, rectHeight, true);
                g.setColor(fg);
                g.drawString("draw3DRect()", x, stringY);
                x += gridWidth;

                // drawRoundRect(x, y, w, h, arcw, arch)
                g.drawRoundRect(x, y, rectWidth, rectHeight, 10, 10);
                g.drawString("drawRoundRect()", x, stringY);
                x += gridWidth;

                // drawOval(x, y, w, h)
                g.drawOval(x, y, rectWidth, rectHeight);
```

```java
g.drawString("drawOval()", x, stringY);
x += gridWidth;

// drawArc(x, y, w, h)
g.drawArc(x, y, rectWidth, rectHeight, 90, 135);
g.drawString("drawArc()", x, stringY);
x += gridWidth;

// drawPolygon(polygon)
Polygon polygon = new Polygon();
polygon.addPoint(x, y);
polygon.addPoint(x+rectWidth, y+rectHeight);
polygon.addPoint(x, y + rectHeight);
polygon.addPoint(x + rectWidth, y)
g.drawPolygon(polygon);
g.drawString("drawPolygon()", x, stringY);

x = 5 + gridWidth;
y += gridHeight;
stringY += gridHeight;

// fillRect(x, y, width, height)
g.fillRect(x, y, rectWidth, rectHeight);
g.drawString("fillRect()", x, stringY);
x += gridWidth;

// fill3DRect(x, y, width, height, raised)
g.setColor(bg);
g.fill3DRect(x, y, rectWidth, rectHeight, true);
g.setColor(fg);
g.drawString("fill3DRect()", x, stringY);
x += gridWidth;

// fillRoundRect(x, y, width, height, arcw, arch)
g.fillRoundRect(x, y, rectWidth, rectHeight, 10, 10);
g.drawString("fillRoundRect()", x, stringY);
x += gridWidth;

// fillOval(x, y, w, h)
g.fillOval(x, y, rectWidth, rectHeight);
g.drawString("fillOval()", x, stringY);
x += gridWidth;

// fillArc(x, y, w, h)
g.fillArc(x, y, rectWidth, rectHeight, 90, 135);
g.drawString("fillArc()", x, stringY);
x += gridWidth;
```

```
        // fillPolygon(polygon)
        Polygon filledPolygon = new Polygon();
        filledPolygon.addPoint(x, y);
        filledPolygon.addPoint(x+rectWidth, y+rectHeight);
        filledPolygon.addPoint(x, y+rectHeight);
        filledPolygon.addPoint(x+rectWidth, y);
        g.fillPolygon(filledPolygon);
        g.drawString("fillPolygon()", x, stringY);
    }
}
```

EXAMPLE: **Image-Loading Applet**

ImageUpdater.java

SOURCE CODE: *http://java.sun.com/Series/Tutorial/ui/drawing/example/
    ImageUpdater.java*

Where explained:
*Loading
Images*
(page 450)

```
import java.applet.*;
import java.awt.*;
import java.awt.image.ImageObserver;

public class ImageUpdater extends Applet {
    /*
     * Written by Jim Graham.
     * This applet draws a big image scaled to its width
     * and height as specified in the
     * <APPLET> tag, and a small image
     * scaled by the same ratio as the
     * big image and positioned
     * in the center of it.
     */
    Image bigimg, smallimg;
    int smallx, smally, smallw, smallh;
    boolean sizeknown = false;
    boolean errored = false;

    public void init() {
        bigimg = getImage(getCodeBase(),
            "../images/bigimg.gif");
        smallimg = getImage(getCodeBase(),
            "../images/smallimg.gif");
        positionImages();
    }

    public boolean imageUpdate(Image theimg, int infoflags,
                               int x, int y, int w, int h) {
        if ((infoflags & (ERROR)) != 0) {
            errored = true;
```

```
    }
    if ((infoflags & (WIDTH | HEIGHT)) != 0) {
        positionImages();
    }
    boolean done = ((infoflags & (ERROR | FRAMEBITS |
                    ALLBITS)) != 0);
    // Repaint immediately if we are done, otherwise
    // repaint in 100 milliseconds.
    repaint(done ? 0 : 100);
    return !done;
}

public synchronized void positionImages() {
    Dimension d = size();
    int bigw = bigimg.getWidth(this);
    int bigh = bigimg.getHeight(this);
    smallw = smallimg.getWidth(this);
    smallh = smallimg.getHeight(this);
    if (bigw < 0 || bigh < 0 || smallw < 0 || smallh < 0) {
        return;
    }
    smallw = smallw * d.width / bigw;
    smallh = smallh * d.height / bigh;
    smallx = (d.width - smallw) / 2;
    smally = (d.height - smallh) / 2;
    sizeknown = true;
}

public synchronized void paint(Graphics g) {
    Dimension d = size();
    int appw = d.width;
    int apph = d.height;
    if (errored) {
        // The images had a problem - just draw a
        // big red rectangle.
        g.setColor(Color.red);
        g.fillRect(0, 0, appw, apph);
        return;
    }
    // Scale the big image to the width and height
    // of the applet.
    g.drawImage(bigimg, 0, 0, appw, apph, this);
    if (sizeknown) {
        // Scale the small image to the central
        // region calculated above.
        g.drawImage(smallimg, smallx, smally, smallw,
```

```
                              smallh, this);
        }
    }
}
```

EXAMPLE: **Image-Displaying Applet**

Where explained:
Displaying Images
(page 453)

HTML PAGES CONTAINING APPLET: *http://java.sun.com/Series/Tutorial/ui/drawing/ drawingImages.html*

ImageDisplayer.java

SOURCE CODE: *http://java.sun.com/Series/Tutorial/ui/drawing/example/ ImageDisplayer.java*

```java
import java.awt.*;
import java.applet.Applet;

/*
 * This applet displays a single image twice,
 * once at its normal size and once much wider.
 */

public class ImageDisplayer extends Applet {
    Image image;

    public void init() {
        image = getImage(getCodeBase(), "../images/" +
                                        "rocketship.gif");
    }

    public void paint(Graphics g) {
        //Draw image at its natural size first.
        g.drawImage(image, 0, 0, this); //85x62 image

        //Now draw the image scaled.
        g.drawImage(image, 90, 0, 300, 62, this);
    }
}
```

EXAMPLE: An Applet That Uses an Image Filter

HTML PAGES CONTAINING APPLET: *http://java.sun.com/Series/Tutorial/ui/drawing/ useFilter.html*

ImageRotator.java

SOURCE CODE: *http://java.sun.com/Series/Tutorial/ui/drawing/example/ ImageRotator.java*

Where explained:

How to Use an Image Filter (page 456)

```java
import java.awt.*;
import java.awt.image.*;
import java.applet.Applet;

/*
 * This applet displays an image. When the user enters
 * an angle, the image is rotated to the specified angle.
 */

public class ImageRotator extends Applet {
    TextField degreeField;
    RotatorCanvas rotator;
    double radiansPerDegree = Math.PI / 180;

    public void init() {
        // Load the image.
        Image image = getImage(getCodeBase(),
                               "../images/rocketship.gif");

        //Set up the UI.
        GridBagLayout gridBag = new GridBagLayout();
        GridBagConstraints c = new GridBagConstraints();
        setLayout(gridBag);

        Label l = new Label("Number of degrees " +
                            "to rotate the image:");
        gridBag.setConstraints(l, c);
        add(l);

        degreeField = new TextField(5);
        gridBag.setConstraints(degreeField, c);
        add(degreeField);

        Button b = new Button("Redraw image");
        c.gridwidth = GridBagConstraints.REMAINDER;
        gridBag.setConstraints(b, c);
        add(b);

        rotator = new RotatorCanvas(image);
```

```java
                c.fill = GridBagConstraints.BOTH;
                c.weightx = 1.0;
                c.weighty = 1.0;
                gridBag.setConstraints(rotator, c);
                add(rotator);

                validate();
            }

            public boolean action(Event evt, Object arg) {
                int degrees;

                try {
                    degrees = Integer.parseInt(degreeField.getText());
                } catch (NumberFormatException e) {
                    degrees = 0;
                }

                //Convert to radians.
                rotator.rotateImage((double)degrees * radiansPerDegree);

                return true;
            }
        }

        class RotatorCanvas extends Canvas {
            Image sourceImage;
            Image resultImage;

            public RotatorCanvas(Image image) {
                sourceImage = image;
                resultImage = sourceImage;
            }

            public void rotateImage(double angle) {
                ImageFilter filter = new RotateFilter(angle);
                ImageProducer producer = new FilteredImageSource(
                                            sourceImage.getSource(),
                                            filter);
                resultImage = createImage(producer);
                repaint();
            }

            public void paint(Graphics g) {
                Dimension d = size();
                int x = (d.width - resultImage.getWidth(this)) / 2;
                int y = (d.height - resultImage.getHeight(this)) / 2;
```

```
        g.drawImage(resultImage, x, y, this);
    }
}
```

EXAMPLE: A Filter that Rotates Images

HTML PAGES CONTAINING APPLET: *http://java.sun.com/Series/Tutorial/ui/drawing/
    useFilter.html*

RotateFilter.java

SOURCE CODE: *http://java.sun.com/Series/Tutorial/ui/drawing/example/
    RotateFilter.java*

**Where
explained:**
*How to Write
an Image Fil-
ter* (page 459)

```java
import java.awt.image.ColorModel;
import java.awt.image.ImageFilter;
import java.util.Hashtable;
import java.awt.Rectangle;

public class RotateFilter extends ImageFilter {

    private static ColorModel defaultRGB =
        ColorModel.getRGBdefault();

    private double angle;
    private double sin;
    private double cos;
    private double coord[] = new double[2];

    private int raster[];
    private int xoffset, yoffset;
    private int srcW, srcH;
    private int dstW, dstH;

    public RotateFilter(double angle) {
        this.angle = angle;
        sin = Math.sin(angle);
        cos = Math.cos(angle);
    }

    public void transform(double x, double y,
                          double[] retcoord) {
        // Remember that the coordinate system is
        // upside down so apply the transform
        // as if the angle were negated.
        // cos(-angle) =  cos(angle)
        // sin(-angle) = -sin(angle)
        retcoord[0] = cos * x + sin * y;
```

```
            retcoord[1] = cos * y - sin * x;
    }

    public void itransform(double x, double y, double[] retcoord) {
            // Remember that the coordinate system is upside down
            // so apply the transform as if the angle were
            // negated. Since inverting the transform is also the
            // same as negating the angle, itransform is
            // calculated the way you would expect to
            // calculate transform.
            retcoord[0] = cos * x - sin * y;
            retcoord[1] = cos * y + sin * x;
    }

    public void transformBBox(Rectangle rect) {
        double minx = Double.POSITIVE_INFINITY;
        double miny = Double.POSITIVE_INFINITY;
        double maxx = Double.NEGATIVE_INFINITY;
        double maxy = Double.NEGATIVE_INFINITY;
        for (int y = 0; y <= 1; y++) {
            for (int x = 0; x <= 1; x++) {
                transform(rect.x + x * rect.width,
                          rect.y + y * rect.height,
                          coord);
                minx = Math.min(minx, coord[0]);
                miny = Math.min(miny, coord[1]);
                maxx = Math.max(maxx, coord[0]);
                maxy = Math.max(maxy, coord[1]);
            }
        }
        rect.x = (int) Math.floor(minx);
        rect.y = (int) Math.floor(miny);
        rect.width = (int) Math.ceil(maxx) - rect.x + 1;
        rect.height = (int) Math.ceil(maxy) - rect.y + 1;
    }

    public void setDimensions(int width, int height) {
        Rectangle rect = new Rectangle(0, 0, width, height);
        transformBBox(rect);
        xoffset = -rect.x;
        yoffset = -rect.y;
        srcW = width;
        srcH = height;
        dstW = rect.width;
        dstH = rect.height;
        raster = new int[srcW * srcH];
        consumer.setDimensions(dstW, dstH);
    }
```

```java
public void setColorModel(ColorModel model) {
    consumer.setColorModel(defaultRGB);
}

public void setHints(int hintflags) {
    consumer.setHints(TOPDOWNLEFTRIGHT
                      | COMPLETESCANLINES
                      | SINGLEPASS
                      | (hintflags & SINGLEFRAME));
}

public void setPixels(int x, int y, int w, int h,
                      ColorModel model, byte pixels[],
                      int off, int scansize) {
    int srcoff = off;
    int dstoff = y * srcW + x;
    for (int yc = 0; yc < h; yc++) {
        for (int xc = 0; xc < w; xc++) {
            raster[dstoff++] = model.getRGB(
                pixels [srcoff++] & 0xff);
        }
        srcoff += (scansize - w);
        dstoff += (srcW - w);
    }
}

public void setPixels(int x, int y, int w, int h,
                      ColorModel model,
                      int pixels[], int off, int scansize) {
    int srcoff = off;
    int dstoff = y * srcW + x;
    if (model == defaultRGB) {
        for (int yc = 0; yc < h; yc++) {
            System.arraycopy(pixels, srcoff,
                             raster, dstoff, w);
            srcoff += scansize;
            dstoff += srcW;
        }
    } else {
        for (int yc = 0; yc < h; yc++) {
            for (int xc = 0; xc < w; xc++) {
                raster[dstoff++] = model.getRGB(
                                   pixels[srcoff++]);
            }
            srcoff += (scansize - w);
            dstoff += (srcW - w);
```

```
                    }
                }
            }

            public void imageComplete(int status) {
                if (status == IMAGEERROR || status == IMAGEABORTED) {
                    consumer.imageComplete(status);
                    return;
                }
                int pixels[] = new int[dstW];
                for (int dy = 0; dy < dstH; dy++) {
                    itransform(0 - xoffset, dy - yoffset, coord);
                    double x1 = coord[0];
                    double y1 = coord[1];
                    itransform(dstW - xoffset, dy - yoffset, coord);
                    double x2 = coord[0];
                    double y2 = coord[1];
                    double xinc = (x2 - x1) / dstW;
                    double yinc = (y2 - y1) / dstW;
                    for (int dx = 0; dx < dstW; dx++) {
                        int sx = (int) Math.round(x1);
                        int sy = (int) Math.round(y1);
                        if (sx < 0 || sy < 0 || sx >=
                            srcW || sy >= srcH) { pixels[dx] = 0;
                        } else {
                            pixels[dx] = raster[sy * srcW + sx];
                        }
                        x1 += xinc;
                        y1 += yinc;
                    }
                    consumer.setPixels(0, dy, dstW, 1, defaultRGB,
                                       pixels, 0, dstW);
                }
                consumer.imageComplete(status);
            }
        }
    }
```

Where explained:

Creating the Animation Loop (page 464)

EXAMPLE: Applet Animation Template

HTML PAGES CONTAINING APPLET: *http://java.sun.com/Series/Tutorial/ui/drawing/ animLoop.html*

Also see <u>AnimatorApplication.java</u> (page 739), which implements an application that does the same thing as this applet.

AnimatorApplet.java

SOURCE CODE: *http://java.sun.com/Series/Tutorial/ui/drawing/example/
AnimatorApplet.java*

```java
import java.awt.*;
import java.applet.Applet;

/*
 * Based on Arthur van Hoff's animation examples, this applet
 * can serve as a template for all animation applets.
 */

public class AnimatorApplet extends Applet implements Runnable
{
    int frameNumber = -1;
    int delay;
    Thread animatorThread;
    boolean frozen = false;

    public void init() {
        String str;
        int fps = 10;

        //How many milliseconds between frames?
        str = getParameter("fps");
        try {
            if (str != null) {
                fps = Integer.parseInt(str);
            }
        } catch (Exception e) {}
        delay = (fps > 0) ? (1000 / fps) : 100;
    }

    public void start() {
        if (frozen) {
            //Do nothing.  The user has requested that we
            //stop changing the image.
        } else {
            //Start animating!
            if (animatorThread == null) {
                animatorThread = new Thread(this);
            }
            animatorThread.start();
        }
    }

    public void stop() {
```

```java
            //Stop the animating thread.
            animatorThread = null;
    }

    public boolean mouseDown(Event e, int x, int y) {
        if (frozen) {
            frozen = false;
            start();
        } else {
            frozen = true;
            stop();
        }
        return true;
    }

    public void run() {
        //Just to be nice, lower this thread's priority so
        //it can't interfere with other processing going on.
        Thread.currentThread().setPriority(Thread.MIN_PRIORITY);

        //Remember the starting time.
        long startTime = System.currentTimeMillis();

        //This is the animation loop.
        while (Thread.currentThread() == animatorThread) {
            //Advance the animation frame.
            frameNumber++;

            //Display it.
            repaint();

            //Delay depending on how far we are behind.
            try {
                startTime += delay;
                Thread.sleep(Math.max(0, startTime -
                    System.currentTimeMillis()));
            } catch (InterruptedException e) {
                break;
            }
        }
    }

    //Draw the current frame of animation.
    public void paint(Graphics g) {
        g.drawString("Frame " + frameNumber, 0, 30);
    }
}
```

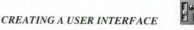

EXAMPLE: Application Animation Template
Also see <u>AnimatorApplet.java</u> (page 737), which implements an application
that does the same thing as this applet.

AnimatorApplication.java

SOURCE CODE: *http://java.sun.com/Series/Tutorial/ui/drawing/example/
AnimatorApplication.java*

**Where
explained:**
*Creating
the Anima-
tion Loop*
(page 464)

```java
import java.awt.*;

/*
 * Based on Arthur van Hoff's animation examples,
 * this application can serve as a template
 * for all animation applications.
 */
public class AnimatorApplication extends Frame implements
Runnable {
    int frameNumber = -1;
    int delay;
    Thread animatorThread;
    boolean frozen = false;

    AnimatorApplication(int fps, String windowTitle) {
        super(windowTitle);
        delay = (fps > 0) ? (1000 / fps) : 100;
    }

    public void startAnimation() {
        //Create and start the animating thread.
        if (frozen) {
            //Do nothing.  The user has requested that we
            //stop changing the image.
        } else {
            //Start animating!
            if (animatorThread == null) {
                animatorThread = new Thread(this);
            }
            animatorThread.start();
        }
    }

    public void stopAnimation() {
        //Stop the animating thread.
        animatorThread = null;
    }

    public boolean mouseDown(Event e, int x, int y) {
```

```
            if (frozen) {
                frozen = false;
                startAnimation();
            } else {
                frozen = true;
                stopAnimation();
            }
            return true;
        }


        public boolean handleEvent(Event e) {
            switch (e.id) {
              case Event.WINDOW_ICONIFY:
                stopAnimation();
                break;
              case Event.WINDOW_DEICONIFY:
                startAnimation();
                break;
              case Event.WINDOW_DESTROY:
                System.exit(0);
                break;
            }
            return super.handleEvent(e);
        }

        public void run() {
            //Just to be nice, lower this thread's priority
            //so it can't interfere with other processing going on.
            Thread.currentThread().setPriority(Thread.MIN_PRIORITY);

            //Remember the starting time
            long startTime = System.currentTimeMillis();

            //This is the animation loop.
            while (Thread.currentThread() == animatorThread) {
                //Advance the animation frame.
                frameNumber++;

                //Display it.
                repaint();

                //Delay depending on how far we are behind.
                try {
                    startTime += delay;
                    Thread.sleep(Math.max(0, startTime -
                        System.currentTimeMillis()));
```

```
        } catch (InterruptedException e) {
            break;
        }
    }
}

//Draw the current frame of animation.
public void paint(Graphics g) {
    g.drawString("Frame " + frameNumber, 5, 50);
}

public static void main(String args[]) {
    AnimatorApplication animator = null;
    int fps = 10;

    // Get frames per second from the command line argument.
    if (args.length > 0) {
        try {
            fps = Integer.parseInt(args[0]);
        } catch (Exception e) {}
    }
    animator = new AnimatorApplication(fps, "Animator");
    animator.resize(200, 60);
    animator.show();
    animator.startAnimation();
}
}
```

EXAMPLE: A First Try at Animating Graphics

HTML PAGES CONTAINING APPLET: *http://java.sun.com/Series/Tutorial/ui/drawing/ animGraphics.html*

This applet animates some primitive graphics. It's not the best example, since its display flashes. The next two examples improve on this one.

FlashingGraphics.java

SOURCE CODE: *http://java.sun.com/Series/Tutorial/ui/drawing/example/ FlashingGraphics.java*

```
import java.awt.*;
import java.applet.Applet;

/*
 * This applet animates graphics that it generates.  This
 * example isn't a good one to copy --
 * it flashes.  The next two examples
 * will show how to eliminate the flashing.
```

Where explained:
Animating Graphics (page 468)

```
*/

public class FlashingGraphics extends Applet implements
    Runnable {
    int frameNumber = -1;
    int delay;
    Thread animatorThread;
    boolean frozen = false;

    int squareSize = 20;
    boolean fillColumnTop = true;

    public void init() {
        String str;
        int fps = 10;

        //How many milliseconds between frames?
        str = getParameter("fps");
        try {
            if (str != null) {
                fps = Integer.parseInt(str);
            }
        } catch (Exception e) {}
        delay = (fps > 0) ? (1000 / fps) : 100;

        //How many pixels wide is each square?
        str = getParameter("squareWidth");
        try {
            if (str != null) {
                squareSize = Integer.parseInt(str);
            }
        } catch (Exception e) {}
    }

    public void start() {
        if (frozen) {
            //Do nothing.  The user has requested that we
            //stop changing the image.
        } else {
            //Start animating!
            if (animatorThread == null) {
                animatorThread = new Thread(this);
            }
            animatorThread.start();
        }
    }

    public void stop() {
```

```
            //Stop the animating thread.
            animatorThread = null;
        }

        public boolean mouseDown(Event e, int x, int y) {
            if (frozen) {
                frozen = false;
                start();
            } else {
                frozen = true;
                stop();
            }
            return true;
        }

        public void run() {
            //Just to be nice, lower this thread's priority so
            //it can't interfere with other processing going on.
            Thread.currentThread().setPriority(Thread.MIN_PRIORITY);

            //Remember the starting time.
            long startTime = System.currentTimeMillis();

            //This is the animation loop.
            while (Thread.currentThread() == animatorThread) {
                //Advance the animation frame.
                frameNumber++;

                //Display it.
                repaint();

                //Delay depending on how far we are behind.
                try {
                    startTime += delay;
                    Thread.sleep(Math.max(0, startTime -
                        System.currentTimeMillis()));
                } catch (InterruptedException e) {
                    break;
                }
            }
        }

        public void paint(Graphics g) {
            Dimension d = size();
            boolean fillSquare;
            boolean fillNextFrame;
            int rowWidth = 0;
```

```
int x = 0, y = 0;
int w, h;
int tmp;

//Set width of first "square". Decide whether to fill it.
fillSquare = fillColumnTop;
fillColumnTop = !fillColumnTop;
tmp = frameNumber % squareSize;
if (tmp == 0) {
    w = squareSize;
    fillNextFrame = !fillSquare;
} else {
    w = tmp;
    fillNextFrame = fillSquare;
}

//Draw from left to right.
while (x < d.width) {
    int colHeight = 0;

    //Draw the column.
    while (y < d.height) {
        colHeight += squareSize;

        //If we don't have room for a full square,
        //cut if off.
        if (colHeight > d.height) {
            h = d.height - y;
        } else {
            h = squareSize;
        }

        //Draw the rectangle if necessary.
        if (fillSquare) {
            g.fillRect(x, y, w, h);
            fillSquare = false;
        } else {
            fillSquare = true;
        }

        y += h;
    } //while y

    //Determine x, y, and w for the next go around.
    x += w;
    y = 0;
    w = squareSize;
    rowWidth += w;
```

```
                    if (rowWidth > d.width) {
                        w = d.width - x;
                    }
                    fillSquare = fillColumnTop;
                    fillColumnTop = !fillColumnTop;
                } //while x
                fillColumnTop = fillNextFrame;
            }
        }
```

EXAMPLE: **Implementing the update Method**

HTML PAGES CONTAINING APPLET: *http://java.sun.com/Series/Tutorial/ui/drawing/ update.html*

This applet animates some primitive graphics, implementing the update method
to avoid flashing.

Update.java

SOURCE CODE: *http://java.sun.com/Series/Tutorial/ui/drawing/example/ Update.java*

**Where
explained:**
Overriding the
update
Method
(page 470)

```java
import java.awt.*;
import java.applet.Applet;

/*
 * This applet animates graphics that it generates.  This
 * example eliminates flashing by overriding the update
 * method. For the graphics this example generates, overriding
 * update isn't quite good enough -- on some systems,
 * you can still see a crawling effect.
 */

public class Update extends Applet implements Runnable {
    int frameNumber = -1;
    int delay;
    Thread animatorThread;
    boolean frozen = false;

    int squareSize = 20;
    boolean fillColumnTop = true;

    public void init() {
        String str;
        int fps = 10;

        //How many milliseconds between frames?
        str = getParameter("fps");
```

```
        try {
            if (str != null) {
                fps = Integer.parseInt(str);
            }
        } catch (Exception e) {}
        delay = (fps > 0) ? (1000 / fps) : 100;

        //How many pixels wide is each square?
        str = getParameter("squareWidth");
        try {
            if (str != null) {
                squareSize = Integer.parseInt(str);
            }
        } catch (Exception e) {}
    }

    public void start() {
        if (frozen) {
            //Do nothing.  The user has requested that we
            //stop changing the image.
        } else {
            //Start animating!
            if (animatorThread == null) {
                animatorThread = new Thread(this);
            }
            animatorThread.start();
        }
    }

    public void stop() {
        //Stop the animating thread.
        animatorThread = null;
    }

    public boolean mouseDown(Event e, int x, int y) {
        if (frozen) {
            frozen = false;
            start();
        } else {
            frozen = true;
            stop();
        }
        return true;
    }

    public void run() {
        //Just to be nice, lower this thread's priority so
        //it can't interfere with other processing going on.
```

```
        Thread.currentThread().setPriority(Thread.MIN_PRIORITY);

        //Remember the starting time.
        long startTime = System.currentTimeMillis();

        //This is the animation loop.
        while (Thread.currentThread() == animatorThread) {
            //Advance the animation frame.
            frameNumber++;

            //Display it.
            repaint();

            //Delay depending on how far we are behind.
            try {
                startTime += delay;
                Thread.sleep(Math.max(0, startTime -
                    System.currentTimeMillis()));
            } catch (InterruptedException e) {
                break;
            }
        }
    }
}

public void paint(Graphics g) {
    update(g);
}

public void update(Graphics g) {
    Color bg = getBackground();
    Color fg = getForeground();
    Dimension d = size();
    boolean fillSquare;
    boolean fillNextFrame;
    int rowWidth = 0;
    int x = 0, y = 0;
    int w, h;
    int tmp;

    //Set width of first "square". Decide whether to fill it.
    fillSquare = fillColumnTop;
    fillColumnTop = !fillColumnTop;
    tmp = frameNumber % squareSize;
    if (tmp == 0) {
        w = squareSize;
        fillNextFrame = !fillSquare;
    } else {
        w = tmp;
```

```
            fillNextFrame = fillSquare;
        }

        //Draw from left to right.
        while (x < d.width) {
            int colHeight = 0;

            //Draw the column.
            while (y < d.height) {
                colHeight += squareSize;

                //If we don't have room for a full
                //square, cut if off.
                if (colHeight > d.height) {
                    h = d.height - y;
                } else {
                    h = squareSize;
                }

                //Draw the rectangle.
                if (fillSquare) {
                    g.fillRect(x, y, w, h);
                    fillSquare = false;
                } else {
                    g.setColor(bg);
                    g.fillRect(x, y, w, h);
                    g.setColor(fg);
                    fillSquare = true;
                }

                y += h;
            } //while y

            //Determine x, y, and w for the next go around.
            x += w;
            y = 0;
            w = squareSize;
            rowWidth += w;
            if (rowWidth > d.width) {
                w = d.width - x;
            }
            fillSquare = fillColumnTop;
            fillColumnTop = !fillColumnTop;
        } //while x
        fillColumnTop = fillNextFrame;
    }
}
```

EXAMPLE: Implementing Double Buffering

HTML PAGES CONTAINING APPLET: *http://java.sun.com/Series/Tutorial/ui/drawing/ doubleBuffer.html*

This applet animates some primitive graphics, implementing double buffering to avoid flashing.

DoubleBuffer.java

SOURCE CODE: *http://java.sun.com/Series/Tutorial/ui/drawing/example/ DoubleBuffer.java*

Where explained:
Implementing Double Buffering (page 471)

```java
import java.awt.*;
import java.applet.Applet;

/*
 * This applet animates graphics that it generates. This
 * example eliminates flashing by double buffering.
 */

public class DoubleBuffer extends Applet implements Runnable {
    int frameNumber = -1;
    int delay;
    Thread animatorThread;
    boolean frozen = false;

    int squareSize = 20;
    boolean fillColumnTop = true;

    Dimension offDimension;
    Image offImage;
    Graphics offGraphics;

    public void init() {
        String str;
        int fps = 10;

        //How many milliseconds between frames?
        str = getParameter("fps");
        try {
            if (str != null) {
                fps = Integer.parseInt(str);
            }
        } catch (Exception e) {}
        delay = (fps > 0) ? (1000 / fps) : 100;

        //How many pixels wide is each square?
        str = getParameter("squareWidth");
```

```java
        try {
            if (str != null) {
                squareSize = Integer.parseInt(str);
            }
        } catch (Exception e) {}
    }

    public void start() {
        if (frozen) {
            //Do nothing.  The user has requested that we
            //stop changing the image.
        } else {
            //Start animating!
            if (animatorThread == null) {
                animatorThread = new Thread(this);
            }
            animatorThread.start();
        }
    }

    public void stop() {
        //Stop the animating thread.
        animatorThread = null;

        //Get rid of the objects necessary for double buffering.
        offGraphics = null;
        offImage = null;
    }

    public boolean mouseDown(Event e, int x, int y) {
        if (frozen) {
            frozen = false;
            start();
        } else {
            frozen = true;

            //Instead of calling stop(), which destroys the
            //backbuffer, just stop the animating thread.
            animatorThread = null;
        }
        return true;
    }

    public void run() {
        //Just to be nice, lower this thread's priority so
        //it can't interfere with other processing going on.
        Thread.currentThread().setPriority(Thread.MIN_PRIORITY);
```

```java
        //Remember the starting time.
        long startTime = System.currentTimeMillis();

        //This is the animation loop.
        while (Thread.currentThread() == animatorThread) {
            //Advance the animation frame.
            frameNumber++;

            //Display it.
            repaint();

            //Delay depending on how far we are behind.
            try {
                startTime += delay;
                Thread.sleep(Math.max(0, startTime -
                        System.currentTimeMillis()));
            } catch (InterruptedException e) {
                break;
            }
        }
    }

    public void paint(Graphics g) {
        update(g);
    }

    public void update(Graphics g) {
        Dimension d = size();
        boolean fillSquare;
        boolean fillNextFrame;
        int rowWidth = 0;
        int x = 0, y = 0;
        int w, h;
        int tmp;

        //Create the offscreen graphics context,
        //if no good one exists.
        if ( (offGraphics == null)
          || (d.width != offDimension.width)
          || (d.height != offDimension.height) ) {
            offDimension = d;
            offImage = createImage(d.width, d.height);
            offGraphics = offImage.getGraphics();
        }

        //Erase the previous image.
        offGraphics.setColor(getBackground());
```

```
offGraphics.fillRect(0, 0, d.width, d.height);
offGraphics.setColor(Color.black);

//Set width of first "square". Decide whether to fill it.
fillSquare = fillColumnTop;
fillColumnTop = !fillColumnTop;
tmp = frameNumber % squareSize;
if (tmp == 0) {
    w = squareSize;
    fillNextFrame = !fillSquare;
} else {
    w = tmp;
    fillNextFrame = fillSquare;
}

//Draw from left to right.
while (x < d.width) {
    int colHeight = 0;

    //Draw the column.
    while (y < d.height) {
        colHeight += squareSize;

        //If we don't have room for a full square,
        //cut if off.
        if (colHeight > d.height) {
            h = d.height - y;
        } else {
            h = squareSize;
        }

        //Draw the rectangle if necessary.
        if (fillSquare) {
            offGraphics.fillRect(x, y, w, h);
            fillSquare = false;
        } else {
            fillSquare = true;
        }

        y += h;
    } //while y

    //Determine x, y, and w for the next go around.
    x += w;
    y = 0;
    w = squareSize;
    rowWidth += w;
    if (rowWidth > d.width) {
```

```
                    w = d.width - x;
                }
                fillSquare = fillColumnTop;
                fillColumnTop = !fillColumnTop;
        } //while x
        fillColumnTop = fillNextFrame;

        //Paint the image onto the screen.
        g.drawImage(offImage, 0, 0, this);
    }
}
```

EXAMPLE: Performing Cutout Animation

HTML PAGES CONTAINING APPLET: *http://java.sun.com/Series/Tutorial/ui/drawing/ movingImage.html*

MovingImage.java

SOURCE CODE: *http://java.sun.com/Series/Tutorial/ui/drawing/example/ MovingImage.java*

> **Where explained:**
> *Moving an Image Across the Screen* (page 473)

```java
import java.awt.*;
import java.applet.Applet;

/*
 * This applet moves one image in front of a background image.
 * It eliminates flashing by double buffering.
 */

public class MovingImage extends Applet implements Runnable {
    int frameNumber = -1;
    int delay;
    Thread animatorThread;
    boolean frozen = false;

    Dimension offDimension;
    Image offImage;
    Graphics offGraphics;

    Image stars;
    Image rocket;

    public void init() {
        String str;
        int fps = 10;

        //How many milliseconds between frames?
        str = getParameter("fps");
```

```
        try {
            if (str != null) {
                fps = Integer.parseInt(str);
            }
        } catch (Exception e) {}
        delay = (fps > 0) ? (1000 / fps) : 100;

        //Get the images.
        stars = getImage(getCodeBase(), "../images/" +
                                        "starfield.gif");
        rocket = getImage(getCodeBase(), "../images/" +
                                        "rocketship.gif");
    }

    public void start() {
        if (frozen) {
            //Do nothing.  The user has requested that we
            //stop changing the image.
        } else {
            //Start animating!
            if (animatorThread == null) {
                animatorThread = new Thread(this);
            }
            animatorThread.start();
        }
    }

    public void stop() {
        //Stop the animating thread.
        animatorThread = null;

        //Get rid of the objects necessary for double buffering.
        offGraphics = null;
        offImage = null;
    }

    public boolean mouseDown(Event e, int x, int y) {
        if (frozen) {
            frozen = false;
            start();
        } else {
            frozen = true;

            //Instead of calling stop(), which destroys the
            //backbuffer, just stop the animating thread.
            animatorThread = null;
        }
        return true;
```

```
    }

    public void run() {
        //Just to be nice, lower this thread's priority so
        //it can't interfere with other processing going on.
        Thread.currentThread().setPriority(Thread.MIN_PRIORITY);

        //Remember the starting time.
        long startTime = System.currentTimeMillis();

        //This is the animation loop.
        while (Thread.currentThread() == animatorThread) {
            //Advance the animation frame.
            frameNumber++;

            //Display it.
            repaint();

            //Delay depending on how far we are behind.
            try {
                startTime += delay;
                Thread.sleep(Math.max(0, startTime -
                    System.currentTimeMillis()));
            } catch (InterruptedException e) {
                break;
            }
        }
    }

    public void paint(Graphics g) {
        update(g);
    }

    public void update(Graphics g) {
        Dimension d = size();

        //Create the offscreen graphics context,
        //if no good one exists.
        if ( (offGraphics == null)
          || (d.width != offDimension.width)
          || (d.height != offDimension.height) ) {
            offDimension = d;
            offImage = createImage(d.width, d.height);
            offGraphics = offImage.getGraphics();
        }

        //Erase the previous image.
```

```
                    offGraphics.setColor(getBackground());
                    offGraphics.fillRect(0, 0, d.width, d.height);
                    offGraphics.setColor(Color.black);

                    //Paint the frame into the image.
                    paintFrame(offGraphics);

                    //Paint the image onto the screen.
                    g.drawImage(offImage, 0, 0, this);
                }

                void paintFrame(Graphics g) {
                    Dimension d = size();
                    int w;
                    int h;

                    //If we have a valid width and height for the
                    //background image, draw it.
                    w = stars.getWidth(this);
                    h = stars.getHeight(this);
                    if ((w > 0) && (h > 0)) {
                        g.drawImage(stars, (d.width - w)/2,
                                    (d.height - h)/2, this);
                    }

                    //If we have a valid width and height for the
                    //background image, draw it.
                    w = rocket.getWidth(this);
                    h = rocket.getHeight(this);
                    if ((w > 0) && (h > 0)) {
                        g.drawImage(rocket, ((frameNumber*5) % (w + d.width))
                                    - w, (d.height - h)/2, this);
                    }
                }
            }
```

EXAMPLE: **Performing Classic Animation**

HTML PAGES CONTAINING APPLET: *http://java.sun.com/Series/Tutorial/ui/drawing/*
imageSequence.html

ImageSequence.java

SOURCE CODE: *http://java.sun.com/Series/Tutorial/ui/drawing/example/*
ImageSequence.java

Where explained:
Displaying a Sequence of Images
(page 475)

```java
import java.awt.*;
import java.applet.Applet;

/*
 * This applet displays several images in a row.  It prevents
 * flashing by double buffering.  However, it doesn't wait until
 * the images are fully loaded before drawing them, which causes
 * the weird effect of the animation appearing from the top down.
 */

public class ImageSequence extends Applet implements Runnable {
    int frameNumber = -1;
    int delay;
    Thread animatorThread;
    boolean frozen = false;

    Dimension offDimension;
    Image offImage;
    Graphics offGraphics;

    Image[] images;

    public void init() {
        String str;
        int fps = 10;

        //How many milliseconds between frames?
        str = getParameter("fps");
        try {
            if (str != null) {
                fps = Integer.parseInt(str);
            }
        } catch (Exception e) {}
        delay = (fps > 0) ? (1000 / fps) : 100;

        //Load all the images.
        images = new Image[10];
        for (int i = 1; i <= 10; i++) {
            images[i-1] = getImage(getCodeBase(),
```

```java
                                    "../../../images/duke/T"+i+".gif");
        }
    }

    public void start() {
        if (frozen) {
            //Do nothing.  The user has requested that we
            //stop changing the image.
        } else {
            //Start animating!
            if (animatorThread == null) {
                animatorThread = new Thread(this);
            }
            animatorThread.start();
        }
    }

    public void stop() {
        //Stop the animating thread.
        animatorThread = null;

        //Get rid of the objects necessary for double buffering.
        offGraphics = null;
        offImage = null;
    }

    public boolean mouseDown(Event e, int x, int y) {
        if (frozen) {
            frozen = false;
            start();
        } else {
            frozen = true;

            //Instead of calling stop, which destroys the
            //backbuffer, just stop the animating thread.
            animatorThread = null;
        }
        return true;
    }

    public void run() {
        //Just to be nice, lower this thread's priority so
        //it can't interfere with other processing going on.
        Thread.currentThread().setPriority(Thread.MIN_PRIORITY);

        //Remember the starting time.
        long startTime = System.currentTimeMillis();
```

```java
        //This is the animation loop.
        while (Thread.currentThread() == animatorThread) {
            //Advance the animation frame.
            frameNumber++;

            //Display it.
            repaint();

            //Delay depending on how far we are behind.
            try {
                startTime += delay;
                Thread.sleep(Math.max(0, startTime -
                    System.currentTimeMillis()));
            } catch (InterruptedException e) {
                break;
            }
        }
    }

    public void paint(Graphics g) {
        update(g);
    }

    public void update(Graphics g) {
        Dimension d = size();

        //Create the offscreen graphics context,
        //if no good one exists.
        if ( (offGraphics == null)
           || (d.width != offDimension.width)
           || (d.height != offDimension.height) ) {
            offDimension = d;
            offImage = createImage(d.width, d.height);
            offGraphics = offImage.getGraphics();
        }

        //Erase the previous image.
        offGraphics.setColor(getBackground());
        offGraphics.fillRect(0, 0, d.width, d.height);
        offGraphics.setColor(Color.black);

        //Paint the frame into the image.
        offGraphics.drawImage(images[frameNumber % 10],
                        0, 0, this);
```

```
                //Paint the image onto the screen.
                g.drawImage(offImage, 0, 0, this);
        }
}
```

EXAMPLE: Using `MediaTracker` to Improve Image Animation

HTML PAGES CONTAINING APPLET: *http://java.sun.com/Series/Tutorial/ui/drawing/ improvingImageAnim.html*

MTImageSequence.java

SOURCE CODE: *http://java.sun.com/Series/Tutorial/ui/drawing/example/ MTImageSequence.java*

Where explained:

Improving the Appearance and Performance of Image Animation (page 476)

```java
import java.awt.*;
import java.applet.Applet;

/*
 * This applet displays several images in a row. It prevents
 * flashing by double buffering. MediaTracker preloads the
 * image data using multiple background threads. The program
 * doesn't draw until all the images are fully loaded.
 */

public class MTImageSequence extends Applet implements Runnable
{
    int frameNumber = -1;
    int delay;
    Thread animatorThread;
    boolean frozen = false;

    Dimension offDimension;
    Image offImage;
    Graphics offGraphics;

    Image[] images;
    MediaTracker tracker;

    public void init() {
        String str;
        int fps = 10;

        //How many milliseconds between frames?
        str = getParameter("fps");
        try {
            if (str != null) {
                fps = Integer.parseInt(str);
```

```
            }
        } catch (Exception e) {}
        delay = (fps > 0) ? (1000 / fps) : 100;

        //Load all the images.
        images = new Image[10];
        tracker = new MediaTracker(this);
        for (int i = 1; i <= 10; i++) {
            images[i-1] = getImage(getCodeBase(),
                            "../../../images/duke/T"+i+".gif");
            tracker.addImage(images[i-1], 0);
        }
    }

    public void start() {
        if (frozen) {
            //Do nothing.  The user has requested that we
            //stop changing the image.
        } else {
            //Start animating!
            if (animatorThread == null) {
                animatorThread = new Thread(this);
            }
            animatorThread.start();
        }
    }

    public void stop() {
        //Stop the animating thread.
        animatorThread = null;

        //Get rid of the objects necessary for double buffering.
        offGraphics = null;
        offImage = null;
    }

    public boolean mouseDown(Event e, int x, int y) {
        if (frozen) {
            frozen = false;
            start();
        } else {
            frozen = true;

            //Instead of calling stop(), which destroys the
            //backbuffer, just stop the animating thread.
            animatorThread = null;
        }
        return true;
```

```
        }

    public void run() {
        try {
            //Start downloading the images. Wait until
            //they're loaded
            //before requesting repaints.
            tracker.waitForAll();
        } catch (InterruptedException e) {}

        //Just to be nice, lower this thread's priority so
        //it can't interfere with other processing going on.
        Thread.currentThread().setPriority(Thread.MIN_PRIORITY);

        //Remember the starting time.
        long startTime = System.currentTimeMillis();

        //This is the animation loop.
        while (Thread.currentThread() == animatorThread) {
            //Advance the animation frame.
            frameNumber++;

            //Display it.
            repaint();

            //Delay depending on how far we are behind.
            try {
                startTime += delay;
                Thread.sleep(Math.max(0, startTime-
                                         System.current
                                         TimeMillis()));
            } catch (InterruptedException e) {
                break;
            }
        }
    }

    public void paint(Graphics g) {
        update(g);
    }

    public void update(Graphics g) {
        Dimension d = size();

        //If not all the images are loaded,
        //just clear the background
        //and display a status string.
        if (!tracker.checkAll()) {
```

```
                g.clearRect(0, 0, d.width, d.height);
                g.drawString("Please wait...", 0, d.height/2);
        }

        //If all images are loaded, draw.
        else {

                //Create the offscreen graphics context,
                //if no good one exists.
                if ( (offGraphics == null)
                   || (d.width != offDimension.width)
                   || (d.height != offDimension.height) ) {
                     offDimension = d;
                     offImage = createImage(d.width, d.height);
                     offGraphics = offImage.getGraphics();
                }

                //Erase the previous image.
                offGraphics.setColor(getBackground());
                offGraphics.fillRect(0, 0, d.width, d.height);
                offGraphics.setColor(Color.black);

                //Paint the frame into the image.
                offGraphics.drawImage(images[frameNumber % 10],
                                      0, 0, this);

                //Paint the image onto the screen.
                g.drawImage(offImage, 0, 0, this);
        }
    }
}
```

Custom Networking and Security

LESSON 22: **Working with URLs**

EXAMPLE: Parsing a URL

ParseURL.java

Where explained:
Parsing a URL
(page 498)

SOURCE CODE: *http://java.sun.com/Series/Tutorial/networking/urls/example/ ParseURL.java*

```java
import java.net.*;
import java.io.*;

class ParseURL {
    public static void main(String[] args) {
        URL aURL = null;
        try {
            aURL = new URL("http://java.sun.com:80/tutorial/"
                             + "intro.html#DOWNLOADING");
            System.out.println("protocol = "
                                    + aURL.getProtocol());
            System.out.println("host = " + aURL.getHost());
            System.out.println("filename = " + aURL.getFile());
            System.out.println("port = " + aURL.getPort());
            System.out.println("ref = " + aURL.getRef());
        } catch (MalformedURLException e) {
            System.out.println("MalformedURLException: " + e);
        }
    }
}
```

EXAMPLE: Reading from a URL

OpenStreamTest.java

Where explained:
Reading Directly from a URL
(page 500)

SOURCE CODE: *http://java.sun.com/Series/Tutorial/networking/urls/example/ OpenStreamTest.java*

```java
import java.net.*;
import java.io.*;

class OpenStreamTest {
    public static void main(String[] args) {
        try {
            URL yahoo = new URL("http://www.yahoo.com/");
            DataInputStream dis = new
                    DataInputStream(yahoo.openStream());
            String inputLine;
```

```
            while ((inputLine = dis.readLine()) != null) {
                System.out.println(inputLine);
            }
            dis.close();
        } catch (MalformedURLException me) {
            System.out.println("MalformedURLException: " + me);
        } catch (IOException ioe) {
            System.out.println("IOException: " + ioe);
        }
    }
}
```

EXAMPLE: Reading from a `URLConnection`

ConnectionTest.java

SOURCE CODE: *http://java.sun.com/Series/Tutorial/networking/urls/example/
      ConnectionTest.java*

```
import java.net.*;
import java.io.*;

class ConnectionTest {
    public static void main(String[] args) {
        try {
            URL yahoo = new URL("http://www.yahoo.com/");
            URLConnection yahooConnection =
                    yahoo.openConnection();
            DataInputStream dis = new DataInputStream(
                    yahooConnection.getInputStream());
            String inputLine;

            while ((inputLine = dis.readLine()) != null) {
                System.out.println(inputLine);
            }
            dis.close();
        } catch (MalformedURLException me) {
            System.out.println("MalformedURLException: " + me);
        } catch (IOException ioe) {
            System.out.println("IOException: " + ioe);
        }
    }
}
```

**Where
explained:**
*Reading from
and Writing to
a URLCon-
nection*
(page 503)

EXAMPLE: **Reading from and Writing to a URLConnection**

ReverseTest.java

Where explained:

Reading from and Writing to a URLConnection
(page 503)

SOURCE CODE: *http://java.sun.com/Series/Tutorial/networking/urls/example/ ReverseTest.java*

```java
import java.io.*;
import java.net.*;

public class ReverseTest {
    public static void main(String[] args) {
        try {
            if (args.length != 1) {
                System.err.println("Usage:  java ReverseTest "
                                        + "string_to_reverse");
                System.exit(1);
            }
            String stringToReverse = URLEncoder.encode(args[0]);

            URL url = new URL("http://java.sun.com/cgi-bin/"
                                + "backwards");
            URLConnection connection = url.openConnection();

            PrintStream outStream = new PrintStream(
                    connection.getOutputStream());
            outStream.println("string=" + stringToReverse);
            outStream.close();

            DataInputStream inStream = new DataInputStream(
                    connection.getInputStream());
            String inputLine;

            while ((inputLine = inStream.readLine()) != null) {
                System.out.println(inputLine);
            }
            inStream.close();
        } catch (MalformedURLException me) {
            System.err.println("MalformedURLException: " + me);
        } catch (IOException ioe) {
            System.err.println("IOException: " + ioe);
        }
    }
}
```

backwards

SOURCE CODE: *http://java.sun.com/Series/Tutorial/networking/urls/example/backwards*

```
#!/opt/internet/bin/perl
read(STDIN, , {'CONTENT_LENGTH'});
@pairs = split(/&/, );
foreach  (@pairs)
{
    (, ) = split(/=/, );
     =~ tr/+/ /;
     =~ s/%([a-fA-F0-9][a-fA-F0-9])/pack("C", hex())/eg;
    # Stop people from using subshells to execute commands
     =~ s/~!/ ~!/g;
    {} = ;
}

print "Content-type: text/plain\n\n";
print "{'string'} reversed is: ";
=reverse({'string'});
print "\n";
exit 0;
```

LESSON 23: All About Sockets

EXAMPLE: The Echo Server Client

EchoTest .java

SOURCE CODE: *http://java.sun.com/Series/Tutorial/networking/sockets/example/EchoTest.java*

```
import java.io.*;
import java.net.*;

public class EchoTest {
    public static void main(String[] args) {
        Socket echoSocket = null;
        DataOutputStream os = null;
        DataInputStream is = null;
        DataInputStream stdIn = new DataInputStream(System.in);

        try {
            echoSocket = new Socket("taranis", 7);
            os = new DataOutputStream(
                echoSocket.getOutputStream());
```

Where explained:

Reading from and Writing to a Socket (page 510)

```
            is = new DataInputStream(
                    echoSocket.getInputStream());
        } catch (UnknownHostException e) {
            System.err.println("Don't know about host: taranis");
        } catch (IOException e) {
            System.err.println("Couldn't get I/O for the " +
                                    "connection to: taranis");
        }

        if (echoSocket != null && os != null && is != null) {
            try {
                String userInput;

                while ((userInput = stdIn.readLine()) != null) {
                    os.writeBytes(userInput);
                    os.writeByte('\n');
                    System.out.println("echo: " + is.readLine());
                }
                os.close();
                is.close();
                echoSocket.close();
            } catch (IOException e) {
                System.err.println("I/O failed on the " +
                                    "connection to: taranis");
            }
        }
    }
}
```

EXAMPLE: The Knock Knock Joke Client and Server

KnockKnockServer.java

SOURCE CODE: *http://java.sun.com/Series/Tutorial/networking/sockets/example/ KnockKnockServer.java*

Where explained: *Writing the Server Side of a Socket* (page 513)

```
import java.net.*;
import java.io.*;

class KnockKnockServer {
    public static void main(String[] args) {
        ServerSocket serverSocket = null;

        try {
            serverSocket = new ServerSocket(4444);
        } catch (IOException e) {
            System.out.println("Could not listen on port: " +
                                4444 + ", " + e);
            System.exit(1);
```

```java
        }

        Socket clientSocket = null;
        try {
            clientSocket = serverSocket.accept();
        } catch (IOException e) {
            System.out.println("Accept failed: " + 4444 +
                               "," + e);
            System.exit(1);
        }

        try {
            DataInputStream is = new DataInputStream(
                    new BufferedInputStream(
                    clientSocket.getInputStream()));
            PrintStream os = new PrintStream(
                    new BufferedOutputStream(
                    clientSocket.getOutputStream(),
                    1024), false);
            KKState kks = new KKState();
            String inputLine, outputLine;

            outputLine = kks.processInput(null);
            os.println(outputLine);
            os.flush();

            while ((inputLine = is.readLine()) != null) {
                outputLine = kks.processInput(inputLine);
                os.println(outputLine);
                os.flush();
                if (outputLine.equals("Bye."))
                    break;
            }
            os.close();
            is.close();
            clientSocket.close();
            serverSocket.close();

        } catch (IOException e) {
            e.printStackTrace();
        }
    }
}
```

KKState.java

SOURCE CODE: *http://java.sun.com/Series/Tutorial/networking/sockets/example/
        KKState.java*

```java
import java.net.*;
import java.io.*;

class KKState {
    private static final int WAITING = 0;
    private static final int SENTKNOCKKNOCK = 1;
    private static final int SENTCLUE = 2;
    private static final int ANOTHER = 3;

    private static final int NUMJOKES = 5;

    private int state = WAITING;
    private int currentJoke = 0;

    private String[] clues = { "Turnip", "Little Old Lady",
                                "Atch", "Who", "Who" };
    private String[] answers = { "Turnip the heat, " +
                                "it's cold in here!",
                                "I didn't know you could yodel!",
                                "Bless you!",
                                "Is there an owl in here?",
                                "Is there an echo in here?" };

    String processInput(String theInput) {
        String theOutput = null;

        if (state == WAITING) {
            theOutput = "Knock! Knock!";
            state = SENTKNOCKKNOCK;
        } else if (state == SENTKNOCKKNOCK) {
            if (theInput.equalsIgnoreCase("Who's there?")) {
                theOutput = clues[currentJoke];
                state = SENTCLUE;
            } else {
                theOutput = "You're supposed to say \"Who's " +
                            "there?\"! Try again. " +
                            "Knock! Knock!";
            }
        } else if (state == SENTCLUE) {
            if (theInput.equalsIgnoreCase(clues[currentJoke]
                + " who?")) {
                theOutput = answers[currentJoke] +
                " Want another? (y/n)";
```

```
                        state = ANOTHER;
                } else {
                    theOutput = "You're supposed to say \"" +
                                clues[currentJoke] + " who?\"" +
                                "! Try again. Knock! Knock!";
                    state = SENTKNOCKKNOCK;
                }
            } else if (state == ANOTHER) {
                if (theInput.equalsIgnoreCase("y")) {
                    theOutput = "Knock! Knock!";
                    if (currentJoke == (NUMJOKES - 1))
                        currentJoke = 0;
                    else
                        currentJoke++;
                    state = SENTKNOCKKNOCK;
                } else {
                    theOutput = "Bye.";
                    state = WAITING;
                }
            }
            return theOutput;
        }
    }
```

KnockKnockClient.java

SOURCE CODE: *http://java.sun.com/Series/Tutorial/networking/sockets/example/ KnockKnockClient.java*

```java
import java.io.*;
import java.net.*;

public class KnockKnockClient {
    public static void main(String[] args) {
        Socket kkSocket = null;
        PrintStream os = null;
        DataInputStream is = null;

        try {
            kkSocket = new Socket("taranis", 4444);
            os = new PrintStream(kkSocket.getOutputStream());
            is = new DataInputStream(kkSocket.getInputStream());
        } catch (UnknownHostException e) {
            System.err.println("Don't know about host: taranis");
        } catch (IOException e) {
            System.err.println("Couldn't get I/O for the " +
                                "connection to: taranis");
        }
```

```
                    if (kkSocket != null && os != null && is != null) {
                        try {
                            StringBuffer buf = new StringBuffer(50);
                            int c;
                            String fromServer;

                            while ((fromServer = is.readLine()) != null) {
                                System.out.println("Server: " + fromServer);
                                if (fromServer.equals("Bye."))
                                    break;
                                while ((c = System.in.read()) != '\n') {
                                    buf.append((char)c);
                                }
                                System.out.println("Client: " + buf);
                                os.println(buf.toString());
                                os.flush();
                                buf.setLength(0);
                            }

                            os.close();
                            is.close();
                            kkSocket.close();
                        } catch (UnknownHostException e) {
                            System.err.println("Trying to connect to " +
                                                "unknown host: " + e);
                        } catch (IOException e) {
                            System.err.println("IOException:  " + e);
                        }
                    }
                }
            }
        }
```

EXAMPLE: **The Knock Knock Joke MultiClient Server**

KKMultiServer.java

SOURCE CODE: *http://java.sun.com/Series/Tutorial/networking/sockets/example/
                KKMultiServer.java*

**Where
explained:**
*Writing the
Server Side of
a Socket*
(page 513)

```
import java.net.*;
import java.io.*;

class KKMultiServer {
    public static void main(String[] args) {
        ServerSocket serverSocket = null;
        boolean listening = true;

        try {
```

```
                serverSocket = new ServerSocket(4444);
            } catch (IOException e) {
                System.err.println("Could not listen on port: " +
                                    4444 + ", " + e.getMessage());
                System.exit(1);
            }

            while (listening) {
                Socket clientSocket = null;
                try {
                    clientSocket = serverSocket.accept();
                } catch (IOException e) {
                    System.err.println("Accept failed: " + 4444 +
                                        ", " + e.getMessage());
                    continue;
                }
                new KKMultiServerThread(clientSocket).start();
            }

            try {
                serverSocket.close();
            } catch (IOException e) {
                System.err.println("Could not close server socket. "
                                    + e.getMessage());
            }
        }
    }
```

KKMultiServerThread.java

SOURCE CODE: *http://java.sun.com/Series/Tutorial/networking/sockets/example/*
KKMultiServerThread.java

```
    import java.net.*;
    import java.io.*;

    class KKMultiServerThread extends Thread {
        Socket socket = null;

        KKMultiServerThread(Socket socket) {
            super("KKMultiServerThread");
            this.socket = socket;
        }

        public void run() {
            try {
                DataInputStream is = new DataInputStream(
                                        new BufferedInputStream(
                                            socket.getInputStream()));
```

```
                        PrintStream os = new PrintStream(
                                        new BufferedOutputStream(
                                            socket.getOutputStream(),
                                            1024), false);
                        KKState kks = new KKState();
                        String inputLine, outputLine;

                        outputLine = kks.processInput(null);
                        os.println(outputLine);
                        os.flush();

                        while ((inputLine = is.readLine()) != null) {
                            outputLine = kks.processInput(inputLine);
                            os.println(outputLine);
                            os.flush();
                            if (outputLine.equals("Bye"))
                                break;
                        }
                        os.close();
                        is.close();
                        socket.close();
                    } catch (IOException e) {
                        e.printStackTrace();
                    }
                }
            }
        }
```

LESSON 24: **All About Datagrams**

EXAMPLE: The Quote-of-the-Moment Client and Server
For the applet version of this example, see <u>QuoteClientApplet.java</u> (page 605).

QuoteServer.java

SOURCE CODE: *http://java.sun.com/Series/Tutorial/networking/datagrams/example/QuoteServer.java*

```
class QuoteServer {
    public static void main(String[] args) {
        new QuoteServerThread().start();
    }
}
```

Where explained:

Writing a Datagram Client and Server
(page 522)

QuoteServerThread.java

SOURCE CODE: *http://java.sun.com/Series/Tutorial/networking/datagrams/ example/QuoteServerThread.java*

```java
import java.io.*;
import java.net.*;
import java.util.*;

class QuoteServerThread extends Thread {
    private DatagramSocket socket = null;
    private DataInputStream qfs = null;

    QuoteServerThread() {
        super("QuoteServer");
        try {
            socket = new DatagramSocket();
            System.out.println("QuoteServer listening on port: "
                                + socket.getLocalPort());
        } catch (java.net.SocketException e) {
            System.err.println("Could not create datagram " +
                                "socket.");
        }
        this.openInputFile();
    }

    public void run() {
        if (socket == null)
            return;

        while (true) {
            try {
                byte[] buf = new byte[256];
                DatagramPacket packet;
                InetAddress address;
                int port;
                String dString = null;

                    // receive request
                packet = new DatagramPacket(buf, 256);
                socket.receive(packet);
                address = packet.getAddress();
                port = packet.getPort();

                    // send response
                if (qfs == null)
                    dString = new Date().toString();
                else
```

```
                                dString = getNextQuote();
                        dString.getBytes(0, dString.length(), buf, 0);
                        packet = new DatagramPacket(buf, buf.length,
                                                    address, port);
                        socket.send(packet);
                } catch (IOException e) {
                    System.err.println("IOException:  " + e);
                    e.printStackTrace();
                }
            }
        }
        protected void finalize() {
            if (socket != null) {
                socket.close();
                socket = null;
                System.out.println("Closing datagram socket.");
            }
        }

        private void openInputFile() {
            try {
                qfs = new DataInputStream(
                        new FileInputStream(
                            "one-liners.txt"));
            } catch (java.io.FileNotFoundException e) {
                System.err.println("Could not open quote file. " +
                                    "Serving time instead.");
            }
        }
        private String getNextQuote() {
            String returnValue = null;
            try {
                if ((returnValue = qfs.readLine()) == null) {
                    qfs.close();
                    this.openInputFile();
                    returnValue = qfs.readLine(); // we know
                                                  // the file has
                                                  // at least one
                                                  // input line!

                }
            } catch (IOException e) {
                returnValue = "IOException occurred in server.";
            }
            return returnValue;
        }

    }
```

QuoteClient.java

SOURCE CODE: *http://java.sun.com/Series/Tutorial/networking/datagrams/ example/QuoteClient.java*

```java
import java.io.*;
import java.net.*;
import java.util.*;

class QuoteClient {

    public static void main(String[] args) {

        int port;
        InetAddress address;
        DatagramSocket socket = null;
        DatagramPacket packet;
        byte[] sendBuf = new byte[256];

        if (args.length != 2) {
            System.out.println("Usage: java QuoteClient "
                               + "<hostname> <port#>");
            return;
        }
        try {
                // bind to the socket
            socket = new DatagramSocket();
        } catch (java.net.SocketException e) {
            System.err.println("Could not create datagram "
                               + "socket.");
        }

        if (socket != null) {
            try {
                    // send request
                port = Integer.parseInt(args[1]);
                address = InetAddress.getByName(args[0]);
                packet = new DatagramPacket(sendBuf, 256, address,
                                            port);
                socket.send(packet);

                    // get response
                packet = new DatagramPacket(sendBuf, 256);
                socket.receive(packet);
                String received = new String(packet.getData(), 0);
                System.out.println("Quote of the Moment: "
                                   + "received");
```

```
                socket.close();
            } catch (IOException e) {
                System.err.println("IOException:  " + e);
                e.printStackTrace();
            }
        }
    }

}
```

one-liners.txt

SOURCE CODE: *http://java.sun.com/Series/Tutorial/networking/datagrams/example/one-liners.txt*

```
Life is wonderful. Without it we'd all be dead.
Daddy, why doesn't this magnet pick up this floppy disk?
Give me ambiguity or give me something else.
I.R.S.: We've got what it takes to take what you've got!
We are born naked, wet and hungry. Then things get worse.
Make it idiot proof and someone will make a better idiot.
He who laughs last thinks slowest!
Always remember you're unique, just like everyone else.
"More hay, Trigger?" "No thanks, Roy, I'm stuffed!"
A flashlight is a case for holding dead batteries.
Lottery: A tax on people who are bad at math.
Error, no keyboard - press F1 to continue.
There's too much blood in my caffeine system.
Artificial Intelligence usually beats real stupidity.
Hard work has a future payoff. Laziness pays off now.
"Very funny, Scotty. Now beam down my clothes."
Puritanism: The haunting fear that someone, somewhere may be
happy.
Consciousness: that annoying time between naps.
Don't take life too seriously, you won't get out alive.
I don't suffer from insanity. I enjoy every minute of it.
Better to understand a little than to misunderstand a lot.
The gene pool could use a little chlorine.
When there's a will, I want to be in it.
Okay, who put a "stop payment" on my reality check?
We have enough youth, how about a fountain of SMART?
Programming is an art form that fights back.
"Daddy, what does FORMATTING DRIVE C mean?"
All wiyht. Rho sritched mg kegtops awound?
My mail reader can beat up your mail reader.
```

Never forget: 2 + 2 = 5 for extremely large values of 2.
Nobody has ever, ever, EVER learned all of WordPerfect.
To define recursion, we must first define recursion.
Good programming is 99% sweat and 1% coffee.

LESSON 25: Providing Your Own Security Manager

EXAMPLE: Security Manager for File I/O

PasswordSecurityManager.java

SOURCE CODE: *http://java.sun.com/Series/Tutorial/networking/security/example/ PasswordSecurityManager.java*

Where explained:
Writing a Security Manager
(page 531)

```java
import java.io.*;

class PasswordSecurityManager extends SecurityManager {

    private String password;

    PasswordSecurityManager(String password) {
        super();
        this.password = password;
    }

    private boolean accessOK() {
        int c;
        DataInputStream dis = new DataInputStream(System.in);
        String response;

        System.out.println("What's the secret password?");
        try {
            response = dis.readLine();
            if (response.equals(password))
                return true;
            else
                return false;
        } catch (IOException e) {
            return false;
        }
    }
    public void checkRead(FileDescriptor filedescriptor) {
        if (!accessOK())
            throw new SecurityException("Not a Chance!");
    }
```

```
    public void checkRead(String filename) {
        if (!accessOK())
            throw new SecurityException("No Way!");
    }
    public void checkRead(String filename,
                            Object executionContext) {
        if (!accessOK())
            throw new SecurityException("Forget It!");
    }
    public void checkWrite(FileDescriptor filedescriptor) {
        if (!accessOK())
            throw new SecurityException("Not!");
    }
    public void checkWrite(String filename) {
        if (!accessOK())
            throw new SecurityException("Not Even!");
    }
}
```

SecurityManagerTest.java

Where explained:
Installing Your Security Manager (page 534)

SOURCE CODE: *http://java.sun.com/Series/Tutorial/networking/security/example/ SecurityManagerTest.java*

```
import java.io.*;

import java.io.*;

class SecurityManagerTest {
    public static void main(String[] args) {
        try {
            System.setSecurityManager(new
                    PasswordSecurityManager("Booga Booga"));
        } catch (SecurityException se) {
            System.err.println("SecurityManager already set!");
        }

        try {
            DataInputStream fis = new DataInputStream(
                                    new FileInputStream(
                                        "inputtext.txt"));
            DataOutputStream fos = new DataOutputStream(
                                    new FileOutputStream(
                                        "outputtext.txt"));
            String inputString;
            while ((inputString = fis.readLine()) != null) {
                fos.writeBytes(inputString);
                fos.writeByte('\n');
```

```
            }
            fis.close();
            fos.close();
        } catch (IOException ioe) {
            System.err.println("I/O failed for "
                            + "SecurityManagerTest.");
        }
    }
}
```

inputtext.txt

SOURCE CODE: *http://java.sun.com/Series/Tutorial/networking/security/example/ inputtext.txt*

```
Now is the time for all good men
to come to the aid of their country.
```

Where explained:

Installing Your Security Manager (page 534)

Integrating Native Methods into Java Programs

LESSON 26: Step By Step

**Where
explained:**

*Step 1: Write
the Java Code
(page 546)*

EXAMPLE: "Hello World" Implemented Using Native Methods

HelloWorld.java

SOURCE CODE: *http://java.sun.com/Series/Tutorial/native/stepbystep/example/
HelloWorld.java*

```
class HelloWorld {
    public native void displayHelloWorld();

    static {
        System.loadLibrary("hello");
    }
}
```

Main.java

SOURCE CODE: *http://java.sun.com/Series/Tutorial/native/stepbystep/example/
Main.java*

```
class Main {
    public static void main(String[] args) {
        new HelloWorld().displayHelloWorld();
    }
}
```

HelloWorldImp.c

**Where
explained:**

*Step 5: Write
the Native
Method Imple-
mentation
(page 550)*

SOURCE CODE: *http://java.sun.com/Series/Tutorial/native/stepbystep/example/
HelloWorldImp.c*

```
#include <StubPreamble.h>
#include "HelloWorld.h"
#include <stdio.h>

void HelloWorld_displayHelloWorld(struct HHelloWorld *this) {
    printf("Hello World!\n");
    return;
}
```

LESSON 27: **Implementing Native Methods**

EXAMPLE: The Character Replacement Program

Replace.java

SOURCE CODE: *http://java.sun.com/Series/Tutorial/native/implementing/example/ Replace.java*

Where explained:
The Charac-ter Replace-ment Program
(page 556)

```java
class Replace {

    public static void Usage() {
        System.out.println("\nUsage: java Replace char1 "
                            +"char2 inFile outFile");
    }

    public static void main(String[] args) {
        InputFile in = null;
        OutputFile out = null;
        char former = 'A';
        char latter = 'A';
        byte[] buf;

        try {
                former = args[0].charAt(0);
        } catch (ArrayIndexOutOfBoundsException e) {
            Usage();
            System.err.println("you must supply the "
                            +"character to replace\n");
            System.exit(-1);
        }

        try {
                latter = args[1].charAt(0);
        } catch (ArrayIndexOutOfBoundsException e) {
            Usage();
            System.err.println("you must supply the new "
                            +"character\n");
            System.exit(-1);
        }

        try {
            in = new InputFile(args[2]);
        } catch (ArrayIndexOutOfBoundsException e) {
            Usage();
            System.err.println("you must supply the input "
                            +"replacement file\n");
            System.exit(-1);
```

```
        }

        try {
            out = new OutputFile(args[3]);
        } catch (ArrayIndexOutOfBoundsException e) {
            Usage();
            System.err.println("you must supply the output "
                               +"replacement file\n");
            System.exit(-1);
        }

        System.out.println("Replacing "+args[0]+" with "+
                           args[1]+" from "+
                           args[2]+" to "+args[3]);

        if (in.open() == false) {
            System.out.println("Unable to open input file "+
                               in.getFileName());
        }

        if (out.open() == false) {
            System.out.println("Unable to open output file "+
                               out.getFileName());
        }

        buf = new byte[1];
        while (in.read(buf, 1) == 1) {
            if (buf[0] == former)
                buf[0] = (byte)latter;
            if (out.write(buf, 1) != 1) {
                System.out.println("Error writing to "+
                                   out.getFileName());
            }
        }
        in.close();
        out.close();
    }
}
```

File.java

SOURCE CODE: *http://java.sun.com/Series/Tutorial/native/implementing/example/ File.java*

```
public class File {

    protected String path;
```

```
    public static final char separatorChar = ':';

    public File(String path) {
        if (path == null) {
            throw new NullPointerException();
        }
        this.path = path;
    }

    public String getFileName() {
        int index = path.lastIndexOf(separatorChar);
        return (index < 0) ? path : path.substring(index + 1);
    }

    public String getPath() {
        return path;
    }
}
```

InputFile.java

SOURCE CODE: *http://java.sun.com/Series/Tutorial/native/implementing/example/ InputFile.java*

```
public class InputFile extends File {

    static {
        try {
            System.loadLibrary("file");
        } catch (UnsatisfiedLinkError e) {
            System.err.println("can't find your library");
            System.exit(-1);
        }
    }

    protected int fd;

    public InputFile(String path) {
        super(path);
    }

    public native boolean open();
    public native void close();
    public native int read(byte[] b, int len);
}
```

InputFileImpl.c

SOURCE CODE: *http://java.sun.com/Series/Tutorial/native/implementing/example/*
InputFileImpl.c

```c
#include <StubPreamble.h>
#include <javaString.h>

#include "InputFile.h"
#include "OutputFile.h"

#include <sys/types.h>
#include <sys/param.h>
#include <stdio.h>
#include <fcntl.h>
#include <errno.h>


static void
convertPath(char *path)
{
    while (*path != '\0') {
        if ((*path == InputFile_separatorChar) ||
            (*path == OutputFile_separatorChar)) {
            *path = LOCAL_PATH_SEPARATOR;
        }
        path++;
    }
    return;
}

long InputFile_open(struct HInputFile *this)
{
    int             fd;
    char            buf[MAXPATHLEN];

    javaString2CString(unhand(this)->path, buf, sizeof(buf));
    convertPath(buf);

    fd = open(buf, O_RDONLY);
    if (fd < 0)
        return(FALSE);

    unhand(this)->fd = fd;
    return(TRUE);
}

void InputFile_close(struct HInputFile *this)
```

```c
{
    close(unhand(this)->fd);
    unhand(this)->fd = -1;
    return;
}

long InputFile_read(struct HInputFile *this,
                    HArrayOfByte *b,
                    long len)
{
    char *data      = unhand(b)->body;
    int  count      = obj_length(b);
    int  actual;

    if (count < len) {
        actual = count;
    }
    else {
        actual = len;
    }
    actual = read(unhand(this)->fd, data, actual);
    if (actual == 0)
        return(-1);
    return(actual);
}
```

OutputFile.java

SOURCE CODE: *http://java.sun.com/Series/Tutorial/native/implementing/example/
OutputFile.java*

```java
public class OutputFile extends File {

    static {
        try {
            System.loadLibrary("file");
        } catch (UnsatisfiedLinkError e) {
            System.err.println("can't find your library");
            System.exit(-1);
        }

    }

    protected int fd;

    public OutputFile(String path) {
        super(path);
    }
```

```
        public native boolean open();
        public native void close();
        public native int write(byte[] b, int len);
}
```

OutputFileImpl.c

SOURCE CODE: *http://java.sun.com/Series/Tutorial/native/implementing/example/*
      OutputFileImpl.c

```c
#include <StubPreamble.h>
#include <javaString.h>

#include "OutputFile.h"
#include "InputFile.h"

#include <sys/types.h>
#include <sys/param.h>
#include <stdio.h>
#include <fcntl.h>
#include <errno.h>


static void
convertPath(char *path)
{
    while (*path != '\0') {
        if ((*path == InputFile_separatorChar) ||
            (*path == OutputFile_separatorChar)) {
            *path = LOCAL_PATH_SEPARATOR;
        }
        path++;
    }
    return;
}

long OutputFile_open(struct HOutputFile *this)
{
    int             fd;
    char        buf[MAXPATHLEN];

    javaString2CString(unhand(this)->path, buf, sizeof(buf));
    convertPath(buf);
    fd = open(buf, O_RDWR|O_CREAT|O_TRUNC, 0644);
    if (fd < 0)
        return(FALSE);
    unhand(this)->fd = fd;
    return(TRUE);
```

```
    }

    void OutputFile_close(struct HOutputFile *this)
    {
        close(unhand(this)->fd);
        unhand(this)->fd = -1;
        return;
    }

    long OutputFile_write(struct HOutputFile *this,
                          HArrayOfByte *b,
                          long len)
    {
        char *data       = unhand(b)->body;
        int   count      = obj_length(b);
        int   actual;

        if (count < len) {
            actual = count;
        }
        else {
            actual = len;
        }
        actual = write(unhand(this)->fd, data, actual);
        return(actual);
    }
```

EXAMPLE: Miscellaneous Example Native Methods

NativeExample.java

SOURCE CODE: *http://java.sun.com/Series/Tutorial/native/implementing/example/
    NativeExample.java*

```
    public class NativeExample {

        private int myValue;

        static {
            Runtime.getRuntime().loadLibrary("example");
        }

        NativeExample(int v) {
            myValue = v;
        }

        native static String quote(int index)
                                throws IllegalArgumentException;
```

Where explained:

Using C++ in Native Method Implementations (page 574), *Throwing Exceptions from Within a Native Method* (page 573), *Using a Java Object in a Native Method* (page 564)

```
        native int twoTimes();

        native NativeExample doubleUp();

        public static void main(String[] args) {
            String s = quote(2);
            System.out.println("Testing quote(): \"" + s + "\"");

            NativeExample ne = new NativeExample(13);
            System.out.println("Testing twoTimes() "
                                    + ne.twoTimes() +
                                    " (should be 26)");

            ne = new NativeExample(24);
            NativeExample ne2 = ne.doubleUp();
            System.out.println("Testing doubleUp() " + ne2 +
                                    " (should be 48)");
        }
    }
```

example.c

SOURCE CODE: *http://java.sun.com/Series/Tutorial/native/implementing/example/example.c*

```c
#include <native.h>
#include "NativeExample.h"

static char *quotes[] = {
    "The truth is out there -- X-Files",
    "I suppose it will all make sense when we grow " +
    "up -- Calvin & Hobbes",
    "Who died and made you king? -- my dad"
};

struct Hjava_lang_String *
NativeExample_quote(struct HNativeExample *unused, long index)
{
    char *quotation;

    if (index < 1 || index > 3) {
        SignalError(0, "java/lang/IllegalArgumentException", 0);
        return NULL;
    }

    quotation = quotes[index - 1];
    return makeJavaString(quotation, strlen(quotation));
}
```

```
long
NativeExample_twoTimes(struct HNativeExample *hInst)
{
    return unhand(hInst)->myValue * 2;
}

struct HNativeExample *
NativeExample_doubleUp(struct HNativeExample *hInst)
{
    HNativeExample *hNewInst;
    long twoX;

    hNewInst = (HNativeExample *)execute_java_constructor(
        0, "NativeExample", 0, "(I)", unhand(hInst)->myValue);

    twoX = (long)execute_java_dynamic_method(
        0, (HObject *)hNewInst, "twoTimes", "()I");

    unhand(hNewInst)->myValue = twoX;
    return hNewInst;
}
```

EXAMPLE: Producer/Consumer Using Native Methods

ProducerConsumerTest.java

SOURCE CODE: *http://java.sun.com/Series/Tutorial/native/implementing/example/
    ProducerConsumerTest.java*

```
class ProducerConsumerTest {
    public static void main(String[] args) {
        CubbyHole c = new CubbyHole();
        Producer p1 = new Producer(c, 1);
        Consumer c1 = new Consumer(c, 1);

        p1.start();
        c1.start();
    }
}
```

Where explained:

Native Methods and Thread Synchronization (page 571)

Producer.java

SOURCE CODE: *http://java.sun.com/Series/Tutorial/native/implementing/example/ Producer.java*

```java
class Producer extends Thread {
    private CubbyHole cubbyhole;
    private int number;

    public Producer(CubbyHole c, int number) {
        cubbyhole = c;
        this.number = number;
    }

    public void run() {
        for (int i = 0; i < 10; i++) {
            cubbyhole.put(i);
            System.out.println("Producer #" + this.number +
                            " put: " + i);
            try {
                sleep((int)(Math.random() * 100));
            } catch (InterruptedException e) {
            }
        }
    }
}
```

Consumer.java

SOURCE CODE: *http://java.sun.com/Series/Tutorial/native/implementing/example/ Consumer.java*

```java
class Consumer extends Thread {
    private CubbyHole cubbyhole;
    private int number;

    public Consumer(CubbyHole c, int number) {
        cubbyhole = c;
        this.number = number;
    }

    public void run() {
        int value = 0;
        for (int i = 0; i < 10; i++) {
            value = cubbyhole.get();
            System.out.println("Consumer #" + this.number +
                            " got: " + value);
```

```
            }
        }
    }
```

CubbyHole.java

SOURCE CODE: *http://java.sun.com/Series/Tutorial/native/implementing/example/
        CubbyHole.java*

```
class CubbyHole {
    private int seq;            // This is the condition variable.
    private boolean available = false;

    public native synchronized int get();
    public native synchronized void put(int value);

    static {
        try {
            System.loadLibrary("threadex");
        } catch (UnsatisfiedLinkError e) {
            System.err.println("can't find your library");
            System.exit(-1);
        }
    }
}
```

CubbyHoleImpl.c

SOURCE CODE: *http://java.sun.com/Series/Tutorial/native/implementing/example/
        CubbyHoleImpl.c*

```
#include <StubPreamble.h>
#include <javaString.h>

#include "CubbyHole.h"

long CubbyHole_get(struct HCubbyHole *this) {
    while (unhand(this)->available == 0) {
        monitorWait(obj_monitor(this));
    }
    unhand(this)->available = 0;
    monitorNotify(obj_monitor(this));
    return unhand(this)->seq;
}

void CubbyHole_put(struct HCubbyHole *this, long value) {
    while (unhand(this)->available > 0) {
```

> **Where explained:**
> *Native Methods and Thread Synchronization (page 571)*

```
            monitorWait(obj_monitor(this));
    }
    unhand(this)->seq = value;
    unhand(this)->available = 1;
    monitorNotify(obj_monitor(this));
}
```

Reference

THIS appendix contains the following reference information:
- Java language keywords
- Operator precedence in Java
- The `<Applet>` tag

Java Language Keywords

Here's a list of Java's keywords. These words are reserved—you cannot use any of these words as names in your Java programs.

abstract	double	int	static
boolean	else	interface	super
break	extends	long	switch
byte	final	native	synchronized
case	finally	new	this
catch	float	null	throw
char	for	package	throws
class	goto *	private	transient *
const *	if	protected	try
continue	implements	public	void
default	import	return	volatile
do	instanceof	short	while

* indicates a keyword that is not currently used

Operator Precedence in Java

The following table lists the Java operators. Operators higher in the table have higher precedence than those lower in the table. Operators on the same line have the same precedence.

postfix operators	`[]  .  (params)  expr++  expr--`
unary operators	`++expr  --expr  +expr  -expr  ~  !`
creation or cast	`new  (type)expr`
multiplicative	`*  /  %`
additive	`+  -`
shift	`<<  >>  >>>`
relational	`<  >  <=  >=  instanceof`
equality	`==  !=`
bitwise AND	`&`
bitwise exclusive OR	`^`
bitwise inclusive OR	`|`
logical AND	`&&`
logical OR	`||`
conditional	`?  :`
assignment	`=  +=  -=  *=  /=` `%=  ^=  &=  |=  <<=  >>=  >>>=`

The <APPLET> Tag

This section gives you the complete syntax for the <APPLET> tag. A gentler introduction to the <APPLET> tag is in <u>Adding an Applet to an HTML Page</u> (page 163).

When you build <APPLET> tags, keep in mind that words such as APPLET and CODEBASE can be entered either as shown or in any mixture of uppercase and lowercase. **Bold font** indicates something you should type in exactly as shown, except that letters don't need to be uppercase. *Italic font* indicates that you must substitute a value for the word in italics. Square brackets ([and]) indicate that the contents of the brackets are optional.

```
< APPLET
    [CODEBASE = codebaseURL]

    CODE = appletFile
    [ALT = alternateText]
    [NAME = appletInstanceName]
    WIDTH = pixels
    HEIGHT = pixels
    [ALIGN = alignment]
    [VSPACE = pixels]
    [HSPACE = pixels]

>

[< PARAM NAME = appletParameter1 VALUE = value >]
[< PARAM NAME = appletParameter2 VALUE = value >]

. . .

[alternateHTML]

</APPLET>
```

CODEBASE = codebaseURL

This optional attribute specifies the base URL of the applet—the directory or folder that contains the applet's code. If this attribute is not specified, then the document's URL is used.

CODE = appletFile

This required attribute gives the name of the file that contains the applet's compiled `Applet` subclass. This file is relative to the base URL of the applet. It cannot be absolute.

ALT = alternateText

This optional attribute specifies any text that should be displayed if the browser understands the <APPLET> tag but can't run Java applets.

NAME = appletInstanceName

This optional attribute specifies a name for the applet instance, which makes it possible for applets on the same page to find and communicate with each other.

WIDTH = pixels **HEIGHT** = pixels

These required attributes give the initial width and height in pixels of the applet display area, not counting any windows or dialogs that the applet brings up.

ALIGN = `alignment`

This required attribute specifies the alignment of the applet. The possible values of this attribute are the same (and have the same effects) as those for the <IMG> tag: LEFT, RIGHT, TOP, TEXTTOP, MIDDLE, ABSMIDDLE, BASELINE, BOTTOM, ABSBOTTOM.

VSPACE = `pixels` **HSPACE** = `pixels`

These optional attributes specify the number of pixels above and below the applet (VSPACE) and on each side of the applet (HSPACE). They're treated the same way as the <IMG> tag's VSPACE and HSPACE attributes.

< **PARAM NAME** = `appletParameter1` **VALUE** = `value` >

<PARAM> tags are the only way to specify applet-specific parameters. Applets read user-specified values for parameters with the `getParameter` method. See <u>Defining and Using Applet Parameters</u> (page 175) for information about `getParameter`.

`alternateHTML`

If the HTML page containing this <APPLET> tag is viewed by a browser that doesn't understand the <APPLET> tag, then the browser will ignore the <APPLET> and <PARAM> tags, and will instead interpret any other HTML code between the <APPLET> and </APPLET> tags. Java-compatible browsers ignore this extra HTML code.

In the online version of this tutorial, we use alternate HTML to show a snapshot of the applet running, with text explaining what the applet does. Other possibilities for this area are a link to a page that is more useful for the Java-ignorant browser, or text that taunts the user for not having a Java-compatible browser.

Colophon

BECAUSE this book started out as an online, hyperlinked collection of intersecting HTML files, its production consisted of three phases:
- Creating the HTML version
- Converting the HTML version into book format
- Producing the book

Creating the HTML Version

When we first started writing this tutorial, few HTML tools existed. As a result, the HTML version of this tutorial is handwritten in an intermediate format, called mem4 which allows us to define macros and variables, and to include Java source files and other HTML files into the mem4 file. Mary developed a macro processor that converts mem4 files into pure HTML files. This saves us a lot of time and energy for two reasons:
- Whenever we change the source for an example, the HTML file that includes the example is automatically updated to reflect the change. This ensures that the code examples in the text of the book are correct as the examples get compiled whenever we generate the HTML files from the mem4 files.
- We don't have to duplicate the HTML commands for all of our headers and footers. Rather, we define the headers and footers in a separate file and include them where needed. So when we change our page design, we only have to change the header and footer files—not every file in the tutorial.

To orchestrate and manage the approximately 450 mem4 files and 265 example Java source files, we created a set of Makefiles to generate the final HTML files from the `mem4` files, and to build the code examples. The Makefiles also perform HTML and link verification, and generate PostScript versions of the HTML files using Jan Kärrman's `html2ps` conversion program. Visit the following URL for information about `html2ps` and to download it:

```
http://www.tdb.uu.se/~jan/html2ps.html
```

Converting the HTML Version into Book Format

To create this book from the online tutorial, we converted the original HTML to Maker Interchange Format (MIF) using a number of scripts and filters hand-crafted by Chris Warth. These scripts and filters were comprised of:

- Nearly 1000 lines of Java code for parsing the HTML and generating the basic MIF code.
- 200 lines of Perl to automatically include Java programs in the HTML and to fix up cross references among the generated MIF files.
- Just over 100 lines of KornShell scripts to tie the other scripts together.
- Hundreds of lines of Makefiles (both Solaris Make and GNUmake) to collate, iterate, and remake the scripts, the book, and the code appendix.

These scripts and filters were custom built for this tutorial and are not suitable for general purpose filtering. If you want to try doing something like this yourself, you should start by following the links from:

```
http://www.w3.org/hypertext/WWW/Tools/html2things.html
```

After the automated conversion into MIF, a couple of weeks of hand editing followed to clean up the loose ends that the filtering process left behind and to make the tutorial work as a book. For example, the online tutorial frequently uses headings (followed by brief discussions) that link to detailed discussions. Although this seems to work well online, reviewers found it confusing when reading the tutorial in book form. We also added front and back matter.

Producing the Book

Addison-Wesley's Mike Hendrickson, Senior Acquisitions Editor, and Katie Duffy, Assistant Editor, were responsible for manuscript development and manuscript review efforts. Addison-Wesley's Pamela Yee was the production coordinator responsible for the complete production process of the book from manuscript to bound books.

The manuscript was copy edited by Sarah H. Lemaire, proofread at Joy Enterprises, and indexed by Henry McGilton at Trilithon Software.

The Java Series cover and theme were designed by Addison-Wesley's Simone R. Payment; the cover art was illustrated by Sara Ciaffaroni. The text layout was designed by Kenneth J. Wilson at Wilson Graphics & Design. Text was set in 11 point Times, headers were set in Avant Garde, and code was set in Lucida Sans.

Except for the trail map, which Nathan Walrath created in Adobe Photoshop, figures were created in Adobe Illustrator by Pamela Yee. Screen dumps were captured by the authors, mainly using the JDK and HiJaak 95 on a PC running Windows 95. The trail icons were created in Adobe Photoshop by Marsh Chamberlain.

This book was typeset by Pure Imaging Publishing, Newton, MA, in FrameMaker on a Macintosh. It was printed at Maple-Vail Book Manufacturing Group, Manchester, PA, on a mini web press on 45# Restor-cote recycled and acid-free paper. The cover was printed at Phoenix Color, Hingham, MA, on a 4-color process offset press.

CD contents were prepared and organized by Randy Nelson at JavaSoft with some assistance from Doug Stein at Addison-Wesley Interactive. The CD-ROM was premastered at Isomedia, Redmond, WA. The CD label was designed by Pamela Yee.

Examples Index

807

Index

The Java Tutorial CD

In addition to the on-line version of the tutorial on which the book is based, the Java Tutorial CD contains Java development tools and collections of HTML pages that show off Java applets. The following platforms are directly supported by this CD: MacOS, Windows 95, and Solaris, both Sparc and Intel versions. (Note that while the Windows 95 content will run unchanged on Windows NT, this CD's format cannot be read by versions of Windows NT prior to version 4.0) The resources available depend on which platform you are using to access them.

Java Tools

MacOS
>   JavaSoft JDK 1.0.2
>   Metrowerks Code Warrior Lite

Win 95
>   JavaSoft JDK 1.0.2
>   SunSoft Java Workshop (pre-release)
>   JavaSoft Hot Java Browser (pre-release)
>   Symantec Cafe Lite

Solaris Sparc
>   JavaSoft JDK 1.0.2
>   SunSoft Java Workshop (pre-release)
>   JavaSoft Hot Java Browser (pre-release)

Solaris Intel
>   JavaSoft JDK 1.0.2
>   SunSoft Java Workshop (pre-release)

HTML

All Platforms
>   Java Tutorial
>   Java API
>   Java Platform White Paper
>   Thought, Inc. Class Library Demo

Win 95 & Solaris
>   Java Cup Winners

The development tools are shipped as compressed archive files. Copy the archive file to your hard disk before attempting to uncompress and/or unarchive the tool. Disk space needed for use and installation is noted below. MacOS files are in self-extracting-archive format (which can be run from the CD). Windows 95 files are shipped as executables: some will launch a setup program; others will uncompress into separate files, which in some cases contain a setup program, which should then be launched. The Solaris files are tarred and compressed. Use the following model to uncompress and untar these files:

```
prompt% uncompress someDevTool.tar.Z
prompt% tar xvf someDevTool.tar
```

You can use the HTML files directly from the CD. Note that these files are supplied to give you examples of large-scale, complete pages that use applets. These pages are snapshots of dynamic content, taken from a dynamic medium. They have not been modified for the CD, and they are not a substitute for the real experience of the web. You should expect that in some cases the links in the disk-based pages will fail. Moreover, although these disk-based pages provide you with a terrific body of work to refer to, since the subject matter, Java, is extremely dynamic, you should consider the web as the only source for up-to-date content.

To view these pages, use the `Open File` command or its equivalent in your Java-aware browser. For most of these collections, select the `index.html` file to start at the logical top of a collection of pages. Alternatively, you can enter a file URL directly. For example, to reach the tutorial on the CD...

MacOS:
`file:///JAVA/HTML/JavaTutorial/index.html`

Solaris:
`file:///cdrom/java/HTML/JavaTutorial/index.html`

Windows 95: (assumes your CD-ROM drive is D:)
`file:///D|/HTML/JavaTutorial/index.html`

Note that the different platforms, Macintosh, Windows and UNIX, use different conventions to signal the end of a line in a text file. While this is transparent to Java-aware tools, you may want to use a text editor that can convert from one standard to another. The majority of the files on the CD were created with UNIX line endings.

See the book's web page at: `http://java.sun.com/Series/Tutorial/book.html`
for pointers to the latest versions of this content and to contact its suppliers. The content is not supported and is provided as is, with no expressed or implied warranty.

All of Java's licensees were given an opportunity to contribute to this CD. Please contact us at `tutorial@java.sun.com` if you are interested in submitting content for inclusion with future versions of the tutorial.

Getting Started

JavaSoft JDK 1.0.2

The Java Development Kit is the starting point for most programmers new to the Java platform.

PLATFORM	COMPRESSED	INSTALLER	INSTALLED	TO INSTALL
MacOS (install from CD)		2.7	7.7	7.7
Win 95		3.7	5.1	8.8
Solaris Sparc	4.7	8.2	8.4	16.6
Solaris Intel	6.8	12.3	12.2	24.5

SunSoft Java Workshop (pre-release)

Java Workshop is a complete Java development environment, written in Java. It includes a version of the JDK. This version expires on October 15, 1996. On Windows the installation creates a program group. On Solaris Sparc, use `.../JWS/sparc-S2/bin/jws`. On Solaris Intel, use `.../JWS/intel-S2/bin/jws`.

PLATFORM	COMPRESSED	INSTALLER	INSTALLED	TO INSTALL
Win95		5.6	11.7	17.3
Solaris Sparc	5.8	15.1	14.9	30.0
Solaris Intel	5.5	14.0	13.6	27.6

JavaSoft Hot Java Browser (pre-release)

Hot Java is an extensible Web Browser, written in Java.

PLATFORM	COMPRESSED	INSTALLER	INSTALLED	TO INSTALL
Win 95		2.5	3.6	6.1
Solaris Sparc	3.1	6.0	6.0	12.0

Metrowerks Code Warrior Lite

Code Warrior Lite is an unsupported, limited version of the Code Warrior development environment. This version will allow you to use existing projects, but will not allow you to create and save new ones. Projects for all of the examples in the book, save for those involving native code, can be found in the Java Tutorial Projects directory.

PLATFORM	COMPRESSED	INSTALLER	INSTALLED	TO INSTALL
MacOS (install from CD)		5.2	26.3	26.3

Symnatec Cafe Lite

Cafe Lite is an unsupported, full version of the entry-point Symantec development environment.

PLATFORM	COMPRESSED	INSTALLER	INSTALLED	TO INSTALL
Win 95		9.0	26.2	35.2

Java Tutorial

The Java Tutorial is the HTML version of this book. Start with the page .../JavaTutorial/index.html

Java API

The Java API is the application programming interface for version 1.0.2 of the Java platform. Start with the page .../API/index.html

Java Platform White Paper

The Java Platform White Paper provides an overview of the Java platform. Start with the page .../JavaPlatform/CreditsPage.doc.html

Thought, Inc. Class Library Demo

This collection of three demos from Thought Inc. gives an example of a third-party library. Start with the page .../ThoughtIncDemo/index.html

Java Cup Winners

The first annual Java Cup competition produced this collection of best-of-breed applets. Use the .../winners_circle/index.html page for an overview. Note that the links found on this page will not work from the CD. Select the applet.html page from each of the project subdirectories to experience the applets, like .../winners_circle/education/ED0Z047X/applet.html

Known Bugs

A few of the files on the CD have filenames that exceed the MacOS limit of 31 characters. These filenames are truncated on the MacOS version of the CD. Note that this is reason that the Java Cup Winners are unavailable on the MacOS version of the CD. A special version of the API was created for the MacOS to manage this issue: because of this, the filenames used on the MacOS version are not the full class names you use to select these pages on other platforms.

References in the CD version of the tutorial to the API do not refer to the CD version of the API, but rather to the on-line version.

Some Java-aware browsers, including the Hot Java browser included on the CD, do not properly interpret the HTML tags that describe alternate content intended for browsers that are not Java-aware. In these browsers, the alternate tags are interpreted along with those that run the applet, rather than instead of them. Thus, you see both the applet and the alternate content, which typically tells you you cannot see the applet.

In the Code Warrior Lite product, using certain disabled functions, like attempting to create a new project, brings up a dialog that mentions a coupon in the back of the book. There is no coupon: instead, use the information found in the Metrowerks Products & Order document in the Code Warrior Lite directory.